Sally Gore

G000150174

Drafting

Drafting

Inns of Court School of Law
Institute of Law, City University, London

OXFORD
UNIVERSITY PRESS

Great Clarendon Street, Oxford OX2 6DP

Oxford University Press is a department of the University of Oxford.
It furthers the University's objective of excellence in research, scholarship,
and education by publishing worldwide in

Oxford New York

Auckland Bangkok Buenos Aires Cape Town Chennai
Dar es Salaam Delhi Hong Kong Istanbul Karachi Kolkata
Kuala Lumpur Madrid Melbourne Mexico City Mumbai Nairobi
Sao Paulo Shanghai Taipei Tokyo Toronto

Oxford is a registered trade mark of Oxford University Press
in the UK and certain other countries

Published in the United States
by Oxford University Press Inc., New York

© Inns of Court School of Law, 2004

The moral rights of the author have been asserted
Database right Oxford University Press (maker)

All rights reserved. No part of this publication may be reproduced,
stored in a retrieval system, or transmitted, in any form or by any means,
without the prior permission in writing of Oxford University Press,
or as expressly permitted by law, or under terms agreed with the appropriate
reprographics rights organization. Enquiries concerning reproduction
outside the scope of the above should be sent to the Rights Department,
Oxford University Press, at the address above

You must not circulate this book in any other binding or cover
and you must impose the same condition on any acquirer

British Library Cataloguing in Publication Data

Data available

Library of Congress Cataloging in Publication Data

Data available

ISBN 0-19-927289-1

1 3 5 7 9 10 8 6 4 2

Typeset by Style Photosetting Limited, Mayfield, East Sussex
Printed in Great Britain
on acid-free paper by
Ashford Colour Press, Gosport, Hampshire

FOREWORD

These Manuals are designed primarily to support training on the Bar Vocational Course, though they are also intended to provide a useful resource for legal practitioners and for anyone undertaking training in legal skills.

The Bar Vocational Course was designed by staff at the Inns of Court School of Law, where it was introduced in 1989. This course is intended to equip students with the practical skills and the procedural and evidential knowledge that they will need to start their legal professional careers. These Manuals are written by staff at the Inns of Court School of Law who have helped to develop the course, and by a range of legal practitioners and others involved in legal skills training. The authors of the Manuals are very well aware of the practical and professional approach that is central to the Bar Vocational Course.

The range and coverage of the Manuals have grown steadily. This year, the major revisions of last year have been consolidated and updated to ensure currency and to reflect the changing demands of Bar students.

This updating and revision is a constant process and we very much value the comments of practitioners, staff and students. Legal vocational training is advancing rapidly, and it is important that all those concerned work together to achieve and maintain high standards. Please address any comments to the Bar Vocational Course Director at the Inns of Court School of Law.

With the validation of other providers for the Bar Vocational Course it is very much our intention that these Manuals will be of equal value to all students wherever they take the course, and we would very much value comments from tutors and students at other validated institutions.

The enthusiasm of the publishers and their efficiency in arranging production and publication of the Manuals is much appreciated.

The Hon. Mr Justice Elias
Former Chairman of the Advisory
Board of the Institute of Law
City University, London
August 2004

OUTLINE CONTENTS

Foreword		v
1	The skill of drafting	1
2	The use of precedents	9
3	Drafting in plain English	15
4	Rules and principles relating to statements of case	21
5	Headings	35
6	Claim forms	41
7	Basic particulars of claim in tort and contract	49
8	Basic defences in tort and contract	70
9	Further particulars of claim	89
10	Further defences	121
11	Misrepresentation	132
12	Additional precedent for claims	145
13	Defence and counterclaim	169
14	Reply and defence to counterclaim	180
15	Part 20 claims	187
16	Amendment of statements of case	197
17	Request for further information	202
18	Further information	215
19	Interim injunctions	222
20	Written evidence	244
21	Judgments and orders	265
22	Claims for judicial review	277
23	Skeleton arguments	296
24	Indictments	313
25	Criminal grounds of appeal	335
26	Part 8 claims	355
27	Construction claims	365
28	Claims for breach of trust and the recovery of trust property	387
29	Assessment criteria	402
Index		425

DETAILED CONTENTS

Foreword   *v*

1   The skill of drafting   1

1.1   What is drafting?   1
1.2   The aim of drafting   1
1.3   Standards   2
1.4   Learning to draft   2
1.5   The objectives of the course   3
1.6   Content of drafts   3
1.7   The use of precedents   4
1.8   Working on your draft   4
1.9   Style   6
1.10   Leaving gaps in your draft   6
1.11   The use of this Manual   7
1.12   Learning by doing   8

2   The use of precedents   9

2.1   Precedents in practice   9
2.2   The advantages of precedents   10
2.3   The drawbacks of precedents   10
2.4   The sources of precedents   11
2.5   Working with precedents   12

3   Drafting in plain English   15

3.1   Introduction   15
3.2   Should we draft in plain English?   15
3.3   The lawyer's difficulty   16
3.4   Drafting in plain English   17
3.5   How to draft in plain English   17
3.6   Modern alternatives for old-fashioned words & phrases   19

4   Rules and principles relating to statements of case   21

4.1   The Civil Procedure Rules   21
4.2   What is a statement of case?   21
4.3   The principles behind statements of case   22
4.4   Rules about statements of case   23
4.5   Contents of statements of case   27
4.6   The statement of truth   31
4.7   Further reading   32

4.8   Exercise   32

5   Headings   35

5.1   Titles of proceedings   35
5.2   Claim numbers   35
5.3   Names of parties   36
5.4   Examples   37
5.5   Exercise   40

6   Claim forms   41

6.1   The contents of a claim form   41
6.2   Rules for claiming interest   43
6.3   Abbreviated particulars of claim   46
6.4   Exercise A   48
6.5   Exercise B   48
6.6   Exercise C   48

7   Basic particulars of claim in tort and contract   49

7.1   Rules for particulars of claim   49
7.2   The essence of particulars of claim   50
7.3   Ingredients of particulars of claim   51
7.4   Tort: negligence: ingredients   51
7.5   Tort: negligence: basic formula   52
7.6   Example   56
7.7   Breach of contract: ingredients   60
7.8   Breach of contract: basic formula   62
7.9   Example   65
7.10   Exercise A   68
7.11   Exercise B   68
7.12   Exercise C   69

8   Basic defences in tort and contract   70

8.1   Rules for defences   70
8.2   The essence of a defence   72
8.3   The structure of a defence   73
8.4   Drafting the defence   75
8.5   Example defence: tort   81
8.6   Example defence: contract   85
8.7   Exercise A   87
8.8   Exercise B   88

9   Further particulars of claim   89

9.1   Tort: occupiers' liability   89
9.2   Tort: employers' liability: breach of statutory duty: provisional damages   92
9.3   Tort: fatal accidents   98
9.4   Negligent misstatement   101
9.5   Contract: debt claim   105
9.6   Contract: anticipatory breach: debt claim: damages for wasted expenditure   107
9.7   Contract: failure of consideration: recovery of money paid   110
9.8   Contract: sale of goods: implied terms   111
9.9   Contract: supply of services: implied terms   113
9.10   Professional negligence   115
9.11   Exercise A   118
9.12   Exercise B   119

10   Further defences   121

10.1   Tort: occupiers' liability: trespasser   121
10.2   Tort: *volenti non fit injuria*: pure accident   124
10.3   Contract: exclusion clause: remoteness   126
10.4   Contract: tender before claim   128
10.5   Exercise   129

11   Misrepresentation   132

11.1   Introduction   132
11.2   Basic formula for particulars of claim   133
11.3   Claim for rescission and negligent misrepresentation   135
11.4   Claim for negligent misrepresentation and breach of contract   137
11.5   Claim for fraudulent misrepresentation and breach of collateral warranty   139
11.6   Defence: reasonable belief: *restitutio in integrum* impossible   141
11.7   Exercise A   143
11.8   Exercise B   143

12   Additional precedents for claims   145

12.1   Clinical negligence   145
12.2   Nuisance   148
12.3   Nuisance, *Rylands v Fletcher*, negligence   150
12.4   Assault and false imprisonment   152
12.5   Trespass to goods: damage   153
12.6   Conversion: wrongful interference with goods   154
12.7   Simple bailment   156
12.8   Bailment, breach of contract, negligence   157
12.9   Trespass to land   159
12.10   Agency: claim for an account   160
12.11   Specific performance: sale of chattels   163
12.12   Specific performance: sale of land   164
12.13   Injunction   166
12.14   Exercise   167

13   Defence and counterclaim   169

13.1   Principles   169
13.2   Defence and counterclaim: without set-off   171
13.3   Defence and counterclaim: partial set-off   174
13.4   Defence and counterclaim: total set-off   176
13.5   Exercise   178

14   Reply and defence to counterclaim   180

14.1   Principles   180
14.2   Reply   182
14.3   Reply and defence to counterclaim   183
14.4   Defence to counterclaim   185
14.5   Exercise   186

15   Part 20 claims   187

15.1   Part 20 Procedure   187
15.2   Indemnity, contribution or damages   188
15.3   Drafting the Part 20 claim   189
15.4   Proposals for change   191
15.5   Part 20 Claim against joint tortfeasor   191
15.6   Part 20 claim in contract   194
15.7   Exercise   196

16   Amendment of statements of case   197

16.1   General   197
16.2   The original defence   198
16.3   The amended defence   199
16.4   Exercise   201

17   Request for further information   202

17.1   Introduction   202
17.2   To ask or not to ask?   203
17.3   Drafting the request for further information   206
17.4   Request for further information about a claim   207
17.5   Request for further information about a defence   210
17.6   Exercise   214

18   Further information   215

18.1   Form of further information   215
18.2   Drafting the further information   215
18.3   Example   216
18.4   Exercise   220

19   Interim injunctions   222

19.1   Procedure   222
19.2   Drafting injunction orders   223
19.3   Standard forms of injunction   224
19.4   Documents for application with notice in the High Court   233
19.5   Alternative drafts   236
19.6   A further example   240
19.7   Exercise   242

20	**Written evidence**	**244**
20.1	General	244
20.2	Rules about affidavits and witness statements	245
20.3	The General Council of the Bar's guidelines	247
20.4	Drafting written evidence	249
20.5	Witness statement for use at trial	251
20.6	Witness statement in support of application for interim injunction	255
20.7	Affidavit in support of application for interim injunction	258
20.8	Witness statement in interim procedural application	262
20.9	Exercise	264

21	**Judgments and orders**	**265**
21.1	The procedural background	265
21.2	Drafting judgments and orders	266
21.3	Consent orders	268
21.4	Judgment after trial before judge	270
21.5	Judgment in a personal injury claim	271
21.6	Judgment for provisional damages	272
21.7	Consent order	273
21.8	*Tomlin* order	274
21.9	Exercise A	276
21.10	Exercise B	276

22	**Claims for judicial review**	**277**
22.1	General matters	277
22.2	Claim for a mandatory order	280
22.3	Claim for a quashing order and mandatory order	287
22.4	Prohibiting order	294
22.5	Exercise	295

23	**Skeleton arguments**	**296**
23.1	General	296
23.2	Skeleton argument for use at a civil trial	300
23.3	Skeleton argument in support of interim application	304
23.4	Skeleton argument in a criminal case	307
23.5	Exercise A	310
23.6	Exercise B	311

24	**Indictments**	**313**
24.1	Introduction	313
24.2	What offences should be included in an indictment?	315
24.3	General form	316
24.4	Counts in particular cases	318
24.5	Exercise	333

25	**Criminal grounds of appeal**	**335**
25.1	Procedure	335
25.2	Grounds of appeal against conviction	336
25.3	Grounds of appeal against sentence	337
25.4	Drafting grounds of appeal	338
25.5	Example	340
25.6	Draft advice and grounds	343
25.7	Commentary	349
25.8	Exercise A	352
25.9	Exercise B	352

26	**Part 8 claims**	**355**
26.1	General	355
26.2	Drafting the Part 8 claim form	356
26.3	Appointment of new trustees	357
26.4	Applications under Trusts of Land and Appointment of Trustees Act 1996, section 14	360
26.5	Applications under Trustee Act 1925, section 57	363
26.6	Exercise	364

27	**Construction claims**	**365**
27.1	Introduction	365
27.2	Re Rupert Sayer	368
27.3	Re Charles Elliott	375
27.4	Re Charles Augustus Fortescue	380
27.5	Exercise A	385
27.6	Exercise B	386

28	**Claims for breach of trust and the recovery of trust property**	**387**
28.1	Introduction	387
28.2	Basic breach of trust	389
28.3	Breach of trust: liability to account: tracing	391
28.4	Constructive trustee: tracing against third party	394
28.5	Trusts of Land and Appointment of Trustees Act 1996, section 14	398
28.6	Exercise A	400
28.7	Exercise B	401

29	**Assessment criteria**	**402**
29.1	Assessment in drafting skills	402
29.2	Criteria for statements of case	403
29.3	Criteria for a request for further information	409
29.4	Criteria for an injunction order	412
29.5	Criteria for a witness statement	416
29.6	Criteria for a criminal appeal	419

Index	425

The skill of drafting

1.1 What is drafting?

By drafting, we mean the composition of legal documents: statements of case, originating processes, witness statements, affidavits, court orders, indictments, appeals, skeleton arguments, contracts, wills, settlements, deeds, legislation, or any other piece of writing with a legal content or which serves a legal purpose. A barrister's practice may involve drafting any of these. Like advocacy, drafting is something which all barristers are supposed to be good at, and in which they can offer specialist skills.

Drafting is a written word skill, but a special one. It is hoped that **Chapters 1** to **3** in the *Opinion Writing Manual* have given you a slight taste of what is involved in drafting. When you are composing legal documents, you cannot write as you would in an everyday letter or in an opinion: every word counts, every word must be chosen with care, every phrase must be apt, every sentence should be immaculately constructed. This means that there is less fluency in the writing process. Drafting involves trial and error, chopping and changing, until what you have is right.

1.2 The aim of drafting

Whatever document you are composing, it is intended to serve a purpose or fulfil a function. Your aim should always be to make sure it serves that purpose or fulfils that function to perfection. If it is to do this, it must have all the qualities of good writing (see **Chapter 2** of the *Opinion Writing Manual*). It must be clear, precise, unambiguous, comprehensible and complete. It goes without saying that it should also contain no errors of spelling, punctuation, grammar or syntax.

When you approach the task of composing, you must always know what purpose the document is to serve, exactly what you want to say in it, for whose benefit it is being written and what pitfalls you want to avoid. Your aim then is to say exactly what needs to be said, neither more nor less, as clearly as you can, with a perfect balance between completeness and conciseness, and all within a logical structure.

1.3 Standards

When you are drafting, you are writing and composing documents to a professional standard. In choosing to become a barrister, you have chosen to put yourself forward as someone who can and will, for a fee, write to such a professional standard. This means that you must be highly skilled in the English language. You must be able to write without error. You must understand the precise meaning of every word you use. You must understand the structure of sentences and how to punctuate them. You must be able to develop an argument over a series of paragraphs. You must convey your meaning and reasoning accurately in words. If you do not, you cannot honourably justify charging your professional fee.

This almost certainly means that you will have to make an adjustment to the speed at which you write. If you find that drafting is a slow and painstaking process, that is probably a very good sign — it shows that you are striving for perfection. If you find you draft quickly and easily, you either have a natural talent, or you are not setting yourself high enough standards.

1.4 Learning to draft

There is a great deal to learn and a great deal to be said about drafting. That is why there are so many examples and so many detailed explanations in this Manual. But in the end you learn to draft by experience and practice, not by being told how to do it, which is why this is a comparatively short introduction. There is only one way to develop your drafting skills: by having a go and trying it out for yourself. What at first sight seems daunting becomes relatively straightforward with experience and practice.

Basic drafting skills are transferable. That is, if you can draft well, you can draft anything. This course does not therefore aim to teach you to draft every kind of document you might have to draft in practice. Instead it concentrates very heavily on one kind of document: statements of case. Other documents are covered, but statements of case, or 'pleadings', predominate.

Drafting skills are taught initially and primarily through the drafting of statements of case for two reasons:

(a) They are such an important part of a barrister's life that even if we taught drafting skills primarily through the medium of some other type of document, there would still need to be a course on the construction and content of statements of case. It makes sense therefore to combine the two.

(b) The drafting skills involved in drafting a statement of case are wide-ranging and comprehensive: learning to draft them brings into play every aspect of good drafting.

However, the emphasis remains on developing drafting skills through the medium of statements of case, rather than on learning how to draft statements of case in all the types of case a newly-qualified barrister might encounter. You will see, therefore, that most of the statements of case we cover on the course relate to actions in tort and contract. That is not because other areas are not important, but because tort and contract are the most important areas for general practice and also the best areas in which to start developing your skills. Other areas tend to be more technical. But remember: drafting skills are transferable. So if you become adept at pleading in tort and contract, then with the use of precedents and the necessary legal research, you should also be able to cope with any other area of law.

1.5 The objectives of the course

By the end of the course you should:

(a) Understand the nature, purpose and operation of statements of case.

(b) Know how to go about drafting all the legal documents covered by the course.

(c) Be able to seek out and use precedents for drafts you are unfamiliar with.

(d) Have improved your written word skills substantially in the specialised area of drafting.

(e) Have had a considerable amount of practice at elementary drafting.

(f) Have a fair amount of practice at more complex drafting.

(g) Be able to cope with any drafting required in the practical training exercises and assessments.

1.6 Content of drafts

There are no rules of content for drafting in general, beyond the qualities of good writing. There are, however, rules of law and practice when it comes to the contents of statements of case or any other court documents, which you must learn. There are rules laid down by the Civil Procedure Rules and Practice Directions; there are guidelines set out in the Court Guides; there are also customs that are so universally followed that they are in effect rules of practice. In addition there are rules and customs for types of statement of case, and even for types of statement of case in types of case, which you also need to be aware of and should be prepared to follow. These rules and customs must be mastered before you will be able to perfect your actual drafting skill.

Do not think, however, that different types of statement of case can be learned off pat, just by following the rules. Some can be substantially composed in that way, but never entirely. There will always be some individual thought required for every draft, no matter how run-of-the-mill it may seem to be. And in practice there may be no set form: you may have to compose the entire statement of case from scratch.

Set forms, such as exist, are called precedents and can be used as guides. **Chapter 2** goes into more detail about the use of precedents. But if there are no precedents, you are on your own. This is nothing to be frightened of; all that is required is thought. If you have prepared the case properly, you know what all the issues are. If you have researched the law properly, you know what must be established to give your client a good case in law. Your statement of case is then exactly what it says it is: you set down those facts and allegations which, if established by the evidence, would give your client a good case in law. This is the guiding principle of all statements of case. If stuck, follow it.

Nor should you assume that there can only be one 'right answer' when you are drafting a document. Different barristers may approach the same draft in different ways, and their versions may all be equally good. There are many different considerations that go into producing a draft. Remember particularly that very often what you are drafting is for your own use. A statement of case should put the case the way you want to present it. A skeleton argument puts the argument in the way you wish to make it. A witness statement helps to prove the case that you are trying to win on behalf of your client. You will produce a draft that plays to the strengths and weaknesses of the case as you see them. Your drafting frequently acts as a precursor to your advocacy.

1.7   The use of precedents

Barristers do not use precedents except as a guide or as a means of checking their work. They will never slavishly copy out a precedent or use it without thought, as if it were some kind of bible or 'right' answer. If you find yourself using precedents in this way, stop yourself at once.

Over-reliance on precedents has caused confusion among some students in the past. They have followed precedents to the letter in their drafting, thinking they must therefore be drafting to a very high standard, and are then puzzled when criticised for it.

This is not puzzling if you remember that it is drafting skills that count. The very good draft will look like it has come out of the writer's head, not out of a precedent book. A barrister who has made use of a precedent will not usually allow this to be apparent in his or her drafting. The barrister who simply relies on precedents is a very plodding barrister indeed. A student who does so is trying to rely on someone else's skill rather than his or her own.

So learn to draft by working on your draft for yourself, using your own words. Sticking too closely to a precedent is one of the most common symptoms of weak drafting and one of the most common causes of errors.

1.8   Working on your draft

It has been said that there is no such thing as good writing: only good rewriting. If true, this is particularly apt in drafting. You cannot get away with your first attempt. You need trial and error.

You also need a structured approach. No matter what you are drafting, the following basic approach will almost certainly work.

1.8.1   Step 1 — analyse and research

The starting points are the facts and the law. You should know the facts of your case. You either know or can look up or research the law. The law then shows you how to organise and give legal significance to the facts. This is a process of fact management which you will learn a lot more about in Case Preparation and Opinion Writing.

1.8.2   Step 2 — determine the essential content of your draft

You must identify, maybe in your head, maybe in list form, maybe through various notes, everything which you must include in your draft. This may be dictated by law (for example the essential ingredients of a cause of action when you are drafting a claim), by the needs of your client (for example when you are drafting an injunction order), by your own logic (for example in a skeleton argument) or by what is needed to prove a case (for example in a witness statement). There may also be rules of court which require certain content, and this will need to be added to your list.

Without this content properly identified, it is impossible to go further.

1.8.3   Step 3 — create a skeleton plan

Always plan your draft first. Never begin to actually draft until you have a skeleton plan, showing how many paragraphs you are going to have, what the content of each paragraph will be, in what order the paragraphs will come, and so on.

Try to give each paragraph a 'name'. This may turn into a subheading, or it may just be for your own use. But it helps you to focus the content of each paragraph and keep to the point. It stops you mixing up in a single paragraph what really belongs in two or more. Then note in fairly fully everything that you will want to put in each paragraph. This does not mean you start to draft it, but you should ensure that every essential detail is clearly placed in its appropriate paragraph. Do not be superficial or simplistic about this process, or you are likely to miss out something important.

1.8.4   Step 4 — check the plan against your list

Go back to the list you created at step 2, and methodically check it off, ensuring that every necessary item of content has been slotted into your skeleton at an appropriate point. Then look at the plan and check that each paragraph hangs together and does not contain anything which should not really be there, or which belongs somewhere else. In other words, ensure that your content and structure are perfectly matched and organised.

1.8.5   Step 5 — draft one paragraph at a time

You can now start to draft. You should work on your draft one paragraph at a time, knowing exactly what you are trying to say in that paragraph. You no longer need to worry about whether you should be saying something else, or whether you should be saying it elsewhere, because everything is worked out. Your skeleton plan is actually very liberating in this respect. It means you can concentrate only on the language rather than the content. This makes the paragraph easier to draft.

Work on each paragraph in turn, experimenting until the words say just what you want them to say and in the right way. This means chopping and changing, rearranging words, phrases and ideas, trying different grammatical structures, altering the punctuation, varying the length of sentences, running sentences together, dividing sentences into two, adding or discarding brackets. You are composing, not dashing something off. Remember the 'name' you gave to the paragraph. You should ideally draft it in such a way as to signal early on what it is all about. This aids comprehension.

By the time you have finished with that paragraph it should be instantly comprehensible, precise, unambiguous, concise, grammatically correct, elegant and as far as possible in plain English. Once this is achieved, you can go on to the next paragraph!

1.8.6   Step 6 — look back over your draft

Never just assume you have finished your draft when you get to the end of the last paragraph. Almost certainly you will want to read it through again, maybe several times. Look particularly at the bits where as you were drafting you thought 'That'll do'. 'That'll do' almost always means 'Not quite right'. It should be rare indeed that you do not find improvements or alterations that you want to make.

1.9   Style

In the end, you should and will develop your own personal style. However, a personal style of drafting takes a lot longer to develop than a personal style of opinion writing, or writing in general, and it is probably not a good idea to try too hard to develop an individual style too early. It is vital to gain skill at the use of language in drafting first.

You will discover that there is a certain amount of formal, terse, stylised language in statements of case. This is not there for its own sake, but usually for the sake of precision and conciseness. The Woolf reforms encouraged all lawyers to write in plain English, and you should do so as far as possible. Be wary of old-fashioned language and avoid it when there is a simple modern English equivalent. But take care: it is actually harder to be absolutely unambiguous in plain English than in the kind of language used in the past. Do not sacrifice precision for modernity. You need to strike a balance. There is more about plain English in **Chapter 3**.

You will also come across numerous 'stock phrases' which occur again and again in statements of case. These are undoubtedly useful: they have become stock phrases because they are so accurate, convenient, tried and tested. But do not become a slave to them. Do not start to use them religiously where you could do better or where they are not really appropriate.

Any statement of case you draft is for the benefit of the court and your client, but it is to a degree for your own benefit as well. You have charge of the case and will wish to conduct it as you think best for the client. So it is true to say that a statement of case is *your* statement of case. You set out the case, on behalf of the client, the way you want to present it, in your words. Providing you do your duty to the court and the client, and comply with the rules, you do have the right to draft it as you wish.

1.10   Leaving gaps in your draft

Students are often worried about what to do when something needs to be included in a document they are drafting (usually a statement of case) but the information required does not appear in the instructions. You may wonder whether you should leave a gap to be filled in by the client or by the instructing solicitor.

This may be the only solution while you are training and so cannot phone someone up to discover the missing information, as you would do in practice. But as a general rule leaving gaps is unwise, because it means that something you have drafted, and which bears your name, may be finalised by someone who does not have your understanding of what is needed. It may be fairly harmless if all that is missing is, for example, a non-contentious date or name. But it would be very unwise to leave crucial figures or particulars to be filled in by someone else, even if you give precise instructions.

1.11   The use of this Manual

Beginning with **Chapter 4**, this Manual presents a structured course in drafting. It is designed to be read and studied in the order in which it is presented. Its effectiveness will be compromised if you take chapters out of order, or leave chapters out.

Nearly every chapter begins by introducing a new type of draft, with explanation, rules and procedure. These are introduced in a logical order, and by and large in ascending order of difficulty. The text is written on the assumption that the lessons of all previous chapters have been already assimilated. There is a danger that you will not understand certain things, or find yourself out of your depth, if you jump too soon to a later chapter.

Every chapter contains examples, and each example is followed by a commentary which attempts to explain fairly comprehensively what every part, and sometimes every word, of the draft is doing. These commentaries are cumulative — that is to say that things are explained when they first appear, and may be reinforced on a second appearance, but then knowledge of the point is assumed in later commentaries. So if you attempt to read the commentary on an example when you have not read every previous commentary, you are likely to find certain matters unexplained, and there is a risk that you will never absorb everything that is there to be learned.

At the end of every chapter there is an exercise, sometimes two or more. These exercises are also designed to be cumulative. Not only do they give you the opportunity to apply the lessons of the chapter in which they appear, but they also from time to time require you to make use of what you have learned from the examples and exercises in previous chapters. More than this, most exercises are designed to bring out a few learning points that were *not* covered by the text, examples or commentaries in the chapter, so they have an add-on effect. Therefore you should never consider that you have completed your work on a chapter until you have not only read it and understood it, but also completed the exercise(s) at the end of it. Only having done so will you be ready for what comes next.

This is why you should make it a rule to actually *do* all the exercises that are part of the course, and which are printed in this Manual. *Never fail to complete an exercise.* The value of simply looking at an exercise and then consulting the suggested answer is almost nil.

1.12 Learning by doing

This is because drafting, along with all other skills, is something that can only be learned by practising the skill. This may sound obvious, but it seems to be unique among the skills taught on the Bar Vocational Course in that there is a widespread attitude among students that it can be learned without actually doing the exercises.

It is a common observation that students frequently seem to believe that if they study the exercise, and then read the suggested answer, they will learn as much as if they had done the exercise themselves. They make no attempt to draft their own answer, they simply collect a suggested answer, file it away, and then assume they have learned the lesson. But this is a dangerous fallacy. By acting in this way you may perhaps gain an understanding of what is involved, and appreciate the drafting skills of someone else, but you will never gain the ability to draft for yourself. Without practice, you will never develop the thought processes that enable you to produce a draft independently. The suggested answer needs to be compared with your own draft if it is to have any value.

Here is what one body of students wrote by way of advice to the next body of students in an 'Alternative Prospectus':

Drafting. Here, unfortunately, the ICSL is right. It is very difficult to pass the drafting assessments (and to learn to draft) without practising drafting — ie doing the course work. Otherwise, you look at the exercise, and then look at the suggested answer; you understand it perfectly well and you think 'I can do this'; and then you get one without a suggested answer and you do not have a clue — until you see the suggested answer when it again looks quite easy.

Trying to learn drafting by reading suggested answers is like trying to learn advocacy by watching videos.

The use of precedents

2.1 Precedents in practice

Precedents are drafts that have been published for others to use as a guide in their own drafting. They are widely available and frequently used in practice. They have their uses, and can often be of considerable value. But they should be approached with caution if you are learning to draft, because it is easy to use them in the wrong way, and over-reliance on precedents can hinder your learning process. In essence, when you are making use of a precedent, you are relying to an extent on someone else's knowledge and skill rather than your own.

Always remember that a published precedent is almost certainly what someone else drafted in another case, or a deliberately created template designed to cover a large number of different possible cases. It is not and cannot be something created specifically for the case in which you are drafting. Almost never will a precedent apply exactly to your needs. You should never therefore assume that what appears in a precedent is appropriate for your purposes. The draft you produce must in the end be just right for the facts of *your* case, and it should be *your* draft, not someone else's. You are responsible to your client, and in litigation to the court, for getting your draft right. It must therefore be drafted as you think it should be, and you must be able to justify every word of it.

You should treat a precedent as a guide, and a source of valuable information, which can assist you in the production of your own draft. You should not treat it as a crutch that removes any need for you to think for yourself or to use your own drafting skill. It can help you perfect your draft; it cannot do your drafting for you.

Nevertheless, precedents properly used can be very valuable and can save you time. Electronic precedents can save a great deal of time, but they have their own dangers. If you are going to practise the law, you need to be able to make use of precedents. But you must always be aware of the dangers and drawbacks, as well as the advantages, if you are to use them properly.

Distinguish precedents from 'set forms'. There are many set forms published by the Court Service or specified by Practice Directions. They usually impose a fixed structure, which is convenient. They also often lay down standard drafting for formal paragraphs that are largely identical in every case, and it is to everyone's advantage to use that standard form. Set forms are indeed templates and should be followed. But they will almost never provide any guidance as to how to draft the part of the document that is specific to the facts of the case, so they are not really precedents in the usual sense.

2.2 The advantages of precedents

The chief advantages of precedents are as follows:

(a) To help you identify the legal requirements of what you are drafting. In statements of case, these are the legal ingredients that must be made out before a claim can succeed. You can study a precedent and see what facts have been stated, and thus identify any gaps in the list you have prepared. The precedent can help prevent error, particularly error by omission.

(b) To help you organise the material that you have gathered and know that you must include in your draft. By looking at a precedent you can identify a suitable structure, or a sequence of paragraphs, or a story line that will suit your draft.

(c) To show you a successful way of actually putting a thought or idea into words. Sometimes precedents are the product of many years of experience, during which the writer has worked out a particularly clear way of expressing an idea, or a particularly succinct formulation of a common statement. Precedents often contain some well tried and apt phrases. While you must still draft in your own words, a precedent may help you to draft more clearly and concisely than you would otherwise be able to do without a lot of attempts at re-writing. It can help you both in your choice of words, and in your sentence structure.

(d) To act as a check after you have produced your own draft. Even if you have drafted from first principles, without using a precedent, sometimes a look at a precedent after you have finished can confirm you have got it right and give you confidence in your own abilities. If you are lucky you will feel that your version is better than that suggested by the precedent.

(e) In these ways the use of a precedent can save you time. It can speed up the process of working out what needs to be included and drawing up a skeleton plan. It can reduce the amount of time spent wrestling with words, trying to make your draft say exactly what you want it to say.

(f) Electronic precedents can be particularly time-saving, because you can draft simply by editing rather than writing something out from scratch. But see **2.3**(e) below.

2.3 The drawbacks of precedents

However there are many drawbacks, even dangers, in using precedents. These include the following:

(a) You may rely too heavily on the precedent, and assume that what it contains can simply be lifted with minor adaptations to suit your case. This is particularly tempting if you are not confident in your own drafting ability. The result will be that your draft contains flaws and errors. It may omit vital matters because they did not appear in the precedent, and you did not think to include them. It may contain irrelevant matters because they did appear in the precedent, and you did not recognise the need to remove them. You must work out for yourself what needs to go into your draft, whether you have a precedent to guide you or not.

(b) The precedent may be based on out of date law. Precedent books are not updated with great frequency. When the law changes, alterations may need to be made to precedents based on earlier law. Sometimes these alterations may be significant, requiring the rewriting or addition of whole paragraphs. Sometimes they may be apparently small — the addition of a single word may be crucial to the success of a claim. You need to recognise the changes in the law and adapt your own draft accordingly. If the change in the law is recent, there will be no precedent to guide you. You must work it out for yourself.

(c) Some published precedents are quite simply bad. Many are poorly drafted. Occasionally you find one that seems to be unsound in law. A good barrister will recognise a bad precedent and either not rely on it, or correct it when producing his or her own draft. Your knowledge of the law and your facility with the English language must be good enough for you to avoid following bad precedents.

(d) If you do not have the confidence to draft without a precedent to guide you, you will always look for one. The one that you find, which seems to be nearest to what you need, may in fact be so far away from being appropriate that it is a positive hindrance. Either you recognise its defects and spend even longer trying to adapt it than you would have done starting from scratch; or you don't realise how inappropriate it is and your own draft ends up equally inappropriate.

(e) There is a real danger with the use of electronic precedents, which is that if you do the job of editing with less than meticulous care, there will be odd details that remain unchanged from the precedent, which then appear, incorrectly, in your draft. This is an incredibly easy mistake to make, and you need to check with real diligence, concentrating especially on things like names, dates, figures, paragraph numbers and all cross-references. The danger is at its highest in the drafting of contracts, where shoddy editing can result in paragraphs being included that do not belong and internal inconsistencies.

(f) If everyone simply copied precedents, legal language would become ossified and increasingly archaic. If we lawyers are to improve the use of language within our profession, we need to create new precedents all the time by writing new drafts, not relying on old ones. A glance at precedent books published even since the advent of the Civil Procedure Rules 1998 will show how much old-fashioned language is still being recommended.

(g) If you rely too heavily on precedents, you will never gain confidence in your own ability to draft and so never really learn the underlying skills. If your first thought is always to find a precedent, if you decide you cannot draft without one, then you are preventing your own skill developing. It is far better to think for yourself than to rely on someone else to do your thinking for you.

2.4 The sources of precedents

Precedents can be found in a very large number of different places, but here are some of the most well-known or useful:

(a) *Atkin's Court Forms* (Butterworths, 2nd edn, 1995–2003). This is a 41-volume series containing precedents, mostly for pleadings, in just about every area of law you can think of. Some of them are very old. Its most valuable feature is that each section begins with a practical potted version of the law, highlighting those matters which will affect the way you plead a case. These introductions are often more valuable than the precedents themselves. You should get to know *Atkin*, but you will probably find it most useful when you are drafting in an obscure area of law.

(b) *Bullen & Leake & Jacob's Precedents of Pleadings* (Sweet & Maxwell, 15th edn, 2004). Generally known simply as *Bullen & Leake*, this 2-volume work is recommended by many practitioners. It is all pleadings, and concentrates on areas of law particularly useful in practice. There is very little explanatory text — it is just packed full of precedents. This is another work you should get to know.

(c) *Butterworths Civil Court Precedents* (Butterworths, looseleaf, 3 volumes). There are many precedents in this work, but a good many are poorly drafted. It tends to be relied upon more by solicitors than barristers.

Many other specialist works contain precedents relating to practice in that area. One that you may find useful in early practice is:

(d) *Butterworths Personal Injury Litigation Service* (Butterworths, general editors Iain Goldrein & Margaret de Haas, looseleaf, 5 volumes). As its name suggests, this contains precedents purely for personal injury practice, which you will find in volume 2.

In addition to these, many Chambers have built up a library of precedents drafted by, and for the use of, members of Chambers, which are usually stored in electronic form.

But above all, you should start to build up your own personal library. You may use all the examples in this Manual as precedents — that will give you a good start. Every exercise in this Manual has a suggested answer, and you may keep these as precedents also. In addition, all the practical training exercises you do on the Bar Vocational Course come with suggested answers, which you can add to your collection.

Once you have qualified, do as all barristers do — keep a copy of every statement of case (or other document) you ever draft. You never know when it will come in handy for the future!

2.5 Working with precedents

Let us assume that you are going to work with an appropriate precedent, and see how you will go about using it. For the sake of this example, we will assume you are going to draft particulars of a claim.

2.5.1 Know the facts and the law

Inevitably, the first thing you need to do is get to grips with the facts of your case. You then need to decide, through your general knowledge or through legal research, what cause or causes of action you will plead and what remedy or remedies you will seek.

2.5.2   Find a suitable precedent

Armed with this knowledge, you can set about finding a precedent or precedents. Take care over this. Before you place reliance on any precedent you need to be sure what cause of action it is pleading, whether that is precisely the same cause of action that you wish to plead, and if not how it differs. For example:

(a) You wish to plead misrepresentation. Beware of a precedent for a claim for negligent misstatement. The two causes of action are significantly different, and it is unlikely that this precedent will be appropriate.

(b) You are making a claim for professional negligence. Decide first whether you will plead in negligence, contract or both. Then check carefully to see what is pleaded in the precedent, and whether it is the same as you intend. If not, you will need to make some adaptations.

(c) You are going to draft a claim for personal injury alleging breach of statutory duty under an Act or Regulations. Your precedent pleads this cause of action, but not under the same Act or Regulations. You may find the precedent useful, but you will need to be aware of the ways in which the statutory requirements differ, and make the necessary adjustments.

(d) You are making a claim for breach of contract, and the remedy you seek is specific performance. You have a precedent which involves very similar facts, but it is making a claim for damages. You need to be aware that you cannot simply copy out the precedent and change only the remedy sought at the end. More substantial alterations will be required.

Sometimes you will find more than one precedent, and you decide that what will best suit your needs is an amalgamation of them. For example, you intend to plead two causes of action, but you cannot find a precedent that does this. So you decide to use two precedents, each pleading one of those causes of action singly. Or you may find one precedent which is sound for the cause of action, but another which helps you to plead the specific remedy sought. Or possibly you have found a precedent which has a structure and clarity that you like, but it does not contain the precise cause of action that you need; this you find in another, less well-drafted, precedent. You may decide to follow the structure of the first, but use the legal content of the second.

2.5.3   Identify the essential ingredients

Having found a suitable precedent, do *not* now start to draft. You must work out the essential ingredients that need to be established before the claim can succeed. These are derived from your knowledge or research into the law. By all means look at the precedent to see what ingredients have been included, and to see if the list corresponds with your own. Sometimes the precedent will help you by reminding you of something you must plead, but which you have forgotten. But do not assume that if there are any differences you must be wrong and the precedent right. It may be that the different facts give rise to different requirements. This is where blind reliance on precedents can lead you badly astray.

2.5.4   Work out an appropriate structure

This is part of your skeleton plan. Remember that you need a skeleton plan that will enable you to draft, for *yourself*, what *you* think is right for *this* case. It is you who must decide what the content of your pleading should be, how it should be structured, what will appear in each paragraph and how each paragraph should be drafted. The precedent may well give you ideas, help you decide on a suitable story line, and put forward a suitable sequence of paragraphs. But there is nothing which requires you to follow the structure of the precedent rather than the structure you feel to be correct. This is particularly so if you are using a precedent which is not entirely similar to what you are trying to draft, or if you are amalgamating precedents.

2.5.5   Using precedents to help you draft

Once your skeleton plan is complete, you can start the actual drafting. Precedents may be helpful in this process, because they can suggest words and phrases which you find appropriate, clear and succinct. By all means borrow such words and phrases — some of them will be almost universally used as a matter of convention. But never, ever copy out words from a precedent unless you know exactly what they mean and why you are using them. If you do so, you will not be drafting for yourself and you run the risk of drafting inaccurately.

This is one of the most common faults in the drafting of student barristers. Over and over again we see phrases and sentences which have been lifted from precedents (usually examples in this Manual or suggested answers given out during the course) without proper understanding and used in contexts where they are not accurate or appropriate. It stands out a mile when this has happened, and it betrays a lack of clarity in the student's thinking and writing which can only be criticised.

At the end of the day, any draft you produce must be your work, not someone else's. It should say what *you* believe should be said, in words of *your* choosing.

Drafting in plain English

3.1 Introduction

Chapter 3 of the *Opinion Writing Manual* introduces plain English and explains its importance to lawyers. It goes on to explain what we mean by plain English, and to give you some advice as to how to go about writing in plain English. It is not intended here to repeat too much of that chapter, so you are advised to read it before continuing with this one.

But to recap briefly, writing plain English involves using language which conveys its meaning to the reader clearly, simply and directly. It is the modern alternative to 'legalese', the old-fashioned jargon language much loved by lawyers for centuries. It has the following qualities:

(a) It is very clear.

(b) It is simple to understand.

(c) It avoids obscure words when common ones will do.

(d) It avoids jargon words when everyday ones will do.

(e) It is written in short sentences.

(f) It is structurally simple.

It takes a bit of practice to write plain English easily and fluently, and it involves ditching some of the bad habits that we have all acquired when writing in a legal context. It generally takes longer to write plain English than legalese, because we have to achieve simplicity and clarity without sacrificing precision. Legalese largely came into existence because of the search for precision, but it went too far and lost its clarity and simplicity.

It is also important to remember that although the use of plain English can often produce a shorter piece of writing, there are also occasions when the plain English version will be longer. Sometimes legalese is unclear because it is unnecessarily verbose, but sometimes it is so concise that its very density renders it impenetrable.

3.2 Should we draft in plain English?

The answer to this question has to be 'yes'. The movement towards the use of plain English in all legal contexts is now unstoppable. To begin with, lawyers attempting to draft in plain English were in a minority. Then more of us became aware of the growing trend, some converting, some burying their heads in the sand and some thinking 'Good idea, but just not yet, I haven't got the time'.

But since the advent of the Civil Procedure Rules 1998, it is now generally accepted that legal documents, particularly those in the context of litigation, should be drafted in plain English. The CPR themselves are drafted in plain English, and although there is nothing to say that statements of case should also use plain English, there is a clear implication that they should. There have been practice statements by judges discouraging the use of Latin phrases, all new forms and precedents since 1999 have been in plain English, many law firms have changed their house rules to require plain English, and most students and trainees have been encouraged since 1999 to draft in plain English.

That does not mean that the use of plain English in practice is now universal. Old habits die hard and there is undoubtedly resistance in some quarters. But even those who are not drafting in plain English often feel that they would like to if only they could learn to do it; and many other lawyers think they have started to draft in plain English when they have in reality taken no more than a few token steps. It will probably be some years before the conversion is complete!

3.3 The lawyer's difficulty

Drafting in plain English is not easy, and often does not come naturally. It is in drafting, rather than in letter writing, or opinion writing, that we find the worst examples of legalese. There are some good reasons for this:

(a) If 'drafting' means the composition of legal documents, then it follows that most of those documents are intended for the eyes only of other lawyers. So the need to make a document comprehensible to a non-lawyer is less pressing.

(b) Legal documents usually need to be very precise in their meaning. Legalese, whatever its faults, is a very precise language.

(c) Legal documents usually aim to be a concise as possible. Indeed the CPR require statements of case to be as concise as possible. Legalese is also a very concise language.

(d) Legal documents are often intended to serve a formal legal purpose, and it follows that they should have an air of formality about them. Legalese is a formal language.

(e) Precedents are often not in plain English, and precedents are catching.

It is therefore very easy to drift into bad habits and unclear English. The journey that a student follows in learning to draft is usually as follows:

(1) You begin by using everyday English, because that is what you know, but in a way that is far too woolly for drafting purposes. Your drafting is full of vagueness and ambiguity, and so is not clear or precise enough.

(2) You discover precision by adopting the formal and old-fashioned phrases that you find in precedent books, using longer, more obscure words and by thinking in a more precise way. Your drafting starts to become more precise; you also find that it is becoming more concise.

(3) You think you are getting the hang of it, particularly because the unusual words and phrases are becoming more familiar to you, and you appreciate their cleverness and usefulness. You start to draft more quickly and more precisely. Hopefully, what you

draft is still clear to other lawyers, but you have moved quite a long way from everyday English.

It may be inevitable that everyone has to go through stages 1–3. The real problem comes when you get to stage 4:

(4) You have now reached the level where you can start to move towards a real expertise in drafting. If you carry on in the way that you have been going, your drafting will become even more concise, even more cleverly precise, and probably less and less simple and clear. You have mastered legalese.

But we need a new stage 4, which is:

(4) You start to look at your drafting, realise that it is no longer really in a modern style of writing, and start to work out how you can achieve the same degree of precision, and maybe conciseness, but using plain English instead.

3.4 Drafting in plain English

Our aim is to reverse the trend, and get back to plain English but without sacrificing any of the essential precision that a good draft requires. You will find that you need to work more slowly, often going through more drafts before you arrive at your finished version. You will also need to make a mental adjustment and start to recognise how stilted your language has become.

But remember that plain English does not necessarily mean everyday English. You are drafting as a lawyer and what you are drafting serves a specialised legal purpose rather than a general one. Writing plain English involves using the simplest and most straightforward language possible in the circumstances, not the simplest or most straightforward language available. A lawyer cannot sacrifice precision for simplicity, or clarity for the sake of shorter words. It is more important that what you are writing should fulfil its function than that it should make sense to someone who has no need to understand it.

There are times, therefore, when technical terms are preferable to lay terms; when uncommon words carry precisely the meaning you want while commonplace ones do not; when a long sentence gives the right emphasis while a short simple one does not. The rule is to use simple language wherever possible but not at all costs.

But that said, you should find it rare that you need to draft in a way that is not in fact entirely comprehensible to an educated non-lawyer.

3.5 How to draft in plain English

If only it were that simple! It is impossible to set out a how-to-do-it guide. There is advice on writing generally in plain English in **Chapter 3** of the *Opinion Writing Manual*. Here are some further tips specific to drafting:

(a) Break down your draft into as many paragraphs, sub-paragraphs and even sub-sub-paragraphs as it is reasonable to do. By and large, each paragraph should contain a single idea. If the idea is a complex one, different parts of the idea can be in separate sub-paragraphs. Use plenty of space on the page, and number each sub-paragraph. If you have a lot of particulars, enumerate them. If you have a lot of heads of damage, itemise them.

(b) There is no rule that every paragraph should contain only a single sentence. If you have more than one sentence, you may consider whether you ought really to have two paragraphs, or whether you should use sub-paragraphs. But if your two sentences clearly belong in the same paragraph, and are not by their nature separate sub-paragraphs, it's better to leave them where they are. Don't think you must turn them into a single sentence.

(c) If you do have a paragraph which consists of a single sentence, and it is long, give serious thought to breaking it down into several shorter sentences.

(d) Use correct legal terminology where this is necessary. Do not, for example, say 'the Defendant said that ...' when you ought to say 'the Defendant represented that ...'. But do not use unnecessary legal terminology, which then sounds like jargon.

(e) Avoid archaic language, even if you are trying to ensure precision. The chief culprit is the adjective 'said', as in 'the said contract'. Ask yourself, if you were to leave out the word 'said', would there be any possible ambiguity about which contract you were referring to? If not, you don't need it. If so, then it is far better to identify separate contracts by giving them a name and defining those names.

(f) Use definitions wherever you are going to use terms on a regular basis. It avoids ambiguity and makes for much plainer reading once the definition has been established. But make sure you are consistent in your terminology!

(g) Try to maintain simplicity at all times. Simplicity is usually the result of taking one idea at a time, expressing it accurately, and then moving on to the next idea. If a sentence looks complicated, there is almost always a simpler way of putting what you are saying.

(h) Ensure your grammar, syntax and punctuation are correct. If you make grammatical or punctuation errors, you lose clarity as well as precision. By far the most common errors observed in students' drafting are:

(i)   Two separate sentences separated by a comma rather than by a full stop or semi-colon.

(ii)   A sentence which contains no main verb, sometimes because there is a full stop where there ought to be a comma.

(iii) Verbs in the wrong tense.

(iv)   Omission of the definite or indefinite article.

(i) Remember that there will be times when a draft in plain English requires more words than the unclear but more concise draft you started with.

(j) Test your drafting by reading it out loud. Plain English comes over clearly and easily if read aloud. It is also easy to read out loud. If you find it hard to read aloud, it may not be plain English.

3.6 Modern alternatives for old-fashioned words & phrases

Here is a list of suggested alternatives to the most common archaic words and phrases. Most have been adopted in this Manual. You may find these useful when attempting to update precedents from other sources. There is no suggestion, of course, that there are not other alternatives, some of which may actually be better than those proposed here.

Old language	Equivalent modern language
'Accordingly'	'So' 'Therefore'
'Aforementioned'	'Set out above' or as for '[the] Said'
'And/or'	This phrase does have its uses, but sometimes you should simply choose 'and' or 'or'.
'Aver'	'Contend' 'Allege' 'Say'
'By reason of'	'As a result of'
'Damages and interest thereon'	'Damages and interest' 'Damages and interest on those damages'
'Foregoing'	'Above' 'This'
'Forthwith'	'Immediately'
'Herein'	'In this action' 'In this defence' 'Below'
'Hereinafter'	'Below'
'Hereinafter mentioned'	'Set out below'
'Hereinbefore'	'Above'
'Inter alia'	The literal translation is 'among other things', but this doesn't often sound right. If the phrase is 'the defendants carry on business, inter alia, as manufacturers of bricks', try 'the defendants' business includes the manufacture of bricks'.
'In the premises'	'In these circumstances' 'In the above ways'
'Per annum'	'A year'
'Pleaded'	'Set out' 'Stated' 'Alleged' 'Referred to'
'Pursuant to'	'Under' 'In accordance with' 'Duly'
'[the] Said'	(1) Try deleting 'said' altogether; if there is no possible ambiguity or confusion, leave it out. (2) Alternatively, give a definition to whatever is being referred to at its first mention. (3) Repeat whatever it was in full. (4) Otherwise try: 'this' 'that' 'the above' 'the … referred to in paragraph 2 above'.

Old language	Equivalent modern language
'Save as aforesaid'	'Otherwise'
'Save that'	'Except that'
'Servants'	'Employees'
'So to do'	'To do so'
'Such'	'The'
	'This'
	'That'
	'Those'
'The defendants aver that ...'	Simply delete these four words
'The foregoing'	'The matters set out above'
'The matters aforesaid'	'The matters set out above'
'Thereafter'	'Then'
	'After that time'
'Thereby'	'By that ...'
'Therefrom'	'From that ...'
'Therein'	'In that ...'
'Thereon'	'On that ...'
'Thereto'	'To that ...'
'Therewith'	'With that ...'
'The same'	'It'
	'Them'
	'The ...'
	'This ...'
	'The matters referred to above'
'Whatsoever'	Delete
'Whomsoever'	Delete
'Whereby'	'By which'
'Whereof'	'Of which'
	'Of whom'
'Whereto'	'To which'
'Without prejudice to the generality of the foregoing denial'	'In particular, but not exclusively'
	'Including, in particular,'
	'Without detracting from this denial'
	'Without restricting the scope of this denial'

Rules and principles relating to statements of case

4.1 The Civil Procedure Rules

The Civil Procedure Rules 1998 introduced an entire new framework for civil litigation. Previously, a civil case was founded on 'pleadings'; it is now founded on 'statements of case'. They serve very much the same function and a great many of the rules are similar or identical. The fundamental purpose of pleadings has not changed, and what was good practice in drafting a pleading has remained good practice in drafting the equivalent statement of case. There were some new rules, designed to put an end to bad practice in the drafting of pleadings, and they appear to have achieved this effect. But there is little to suggest that any more fundamental changes were expected or have come about. The new rules were also designed to make it easier for a litigant in person to draft a statement of case without falling foul of any technical rules. But that does not mean that lawyers should now start to draft like litigants in person.

As explained above, statements of case used to be called 'pleadings' and the verb 'to plead' meant to draft a pleading or to state in a pleading. These old words are much more convenient than the new ones, and are still much used in practice. In particular there is often no good alternative to 'plead' as a verb. This Manual will attempt to use the modern terminology, but be prepared to meet the old, both in teaching and in chambers.

In this chapter and then throughout this Manual the Civil Procedure Rules 1998 will be referred to as CPR, and the Practice Directions made under the CPR as PD. So, for example, PD 16 means the Practice Direction made under Part 16 of the CPR.

4.2 What is a statement of case?

The following are statements of case (CPR, r 2.3(1)):

Statement of case	Served by
Claim form	Claimant
Particulars of claim	Claimant
Defence	Defendant
Defence and counterclaim	Defendant
Reply	Claimant

Statement of case	Served by
Defence to counterclaim	Claimant
Part 20 claim form	Part 20 claimant
Particulars of Part 20 claim	Part 20 claimant
Part 20 defence	Part 20 defendant
Further information provided under CPR, Part 18	Any party.

4.3   The principles behind statements of case

4.3.1   The function of statements of case

A statement of case is a document in which one party (or group of parties) to a civil case sets out the basis of his case against another party or parties. The basis of the case is the facts relied on and the allegations made, so it largely consists of facts and allegations, not law, evidence or argument.

4.3.2   The overriding objective

Part 1 of the CPR sets out the overriding objective, which will apply to statements of case as much as anything else. The overriding objective is to enable the court to deal with cases justly. This includes, so far as is practicable, ensuring that the parties are on an even footing, saving expense, dealing with the case in ways which are proportionate to the complexity of the issues, and ensuring that the case is dealt with expeditiously and fairly.

4.3.3   The objective of statements of case

It is not difficult to see how statements of case can assist in fulfilling the overriding objective. They make civil litigation more efficient, thereby saving expense and ensuring that the case is dealt with expeditiously. They ensure that the parties are on an even footing — neither can take the other by surprise. They enable the court to deal with the case justly, because they help to ensure that a case is won or lost on its merits. Statements of case are designed to achieve these objectives by:

(a) Informing the other side of the case they have to meet.

(b) Enabling the other side to know what evidence they need to prepare.

(c) Defining the matters which are and are not in dispute.

(d) Focusing on the real issues in the case.

(e) Tying the parties to the case they have set out in advance.

4.3.4   The court's power to strike out a statement of case

Under CPR, r 3.4(2) the court may strike out a statement of case, or part of one, if:

(a) it discloses no reasonable grounds for bringing or defending the claim;

(b) it is an abuse of the court's process or is otherwise likely to obstruct the just disposal of the proceedings;

(c) there has been a failure to comply with a rule, practice direction or court order.

It seems from this that a statement of case could be struck out for failing to comply not only with a specific rule, but also with the overriding objective, because it was simply badly drafted, overlong, full of irrelevance etc.

4.3.5   The tactical function of statements of case

However, statements of case also serve a tactical function. Statements of case are primarily designed on the assumption that the case will eventually go to trial. The reality, of course, is that only a tiny percentage of civil cases end up at trial. The great majority are compromised at some stage on the way. Statements of case can be used to encourage the other side to settle or capitulate. The stronger a party can make his case seem, the more likely it is that this will happen. So statements of case are drafted not only with a view to fulfilling their function at trial, but also with a view to achieving the client's more immediate objective. This objective may be to persuade the other side to settle, to gain as much as can be gained in all the circumstances, or simply to knock the other side out with a well-aimed death blow.

It is not easy for students to pick up tactical pleading, and it is not the best place to start. You can't think in terms of tactics until you have learned the basic rules and conventions. But it is something to bear in mind as you develop your drafting skills. As you work through the course, you will gradually become more aware of the tactics in pleading, and start to learn how to use those tactics. You will find the book recommended at the end of this Chapter — *Pleadings Without Tears* by William Rose — particularly helpful in this respect.

4.4   Rules about statements of case

4.4.1   Rules as to format

There are some general rules about the format of all court documents laid down by PD 5. The important ones relevant to drafting are:

(a) By PD 5, para 2.2, every document including a statement of case prepared by a party for filing or use at the court must be divided into numbered paragraphs and have all numbers, including dates, expressed as figures.

Nevertheless, it is generally accepted in practice that numbers from one to ten (apart from dates) are better expressed as words.

(b) By PD 5, para 2.1, statements of case and other documents drafted by a legal representative should bear his signature, and if they are drafted by a legal representative as a member or employee of a firm should be signed in the name of the firm.

Contrary to this, however, both the Chancery Guide and the Commercial Court Guide require a statement of case to bear the name(s) of the individual lawyer(s) who drafted it.

4.4.2   Rules of general application as to content

Under the old system the Rules of the Supreme Court laid down some fundamental rules of pleadings. Now the Civil Procedure Rules 1998 lay down very few rules relating to statements of case generally — nearly all the rules relate to particular types of statement of case.

The only rules of general application to statements of case are in PD 16, para 13.3, which says that a party may:

(a) refer in his statement of case to a point of law;

(b) give in his statement of case the name of any witness he proposes to call;

(c) attach to his statement of case a copy of any document which he considers necessary to his case (including especially any expert's report).

Note that none of the above is obligatory.

4.4.3   Rules to be taken as being of general application

However, there are some other rules which are expressed as applying solely to particulars of claim, but which ought logically to apply to defences and other statements of case as well. This is probably an oversight.

4.4.3.1   The primary rule

Chief among these is CPR, r 16.4(1)(a):

(1)   Particulars of claim must include—

    (a)   a concise statement of the facts on which the claimant relies;...

This should be taken as applying also to defences for the following reasons:

(a) It was the rule under the old procedure and is within the spirit of the new procedure.

(b) PD 3, para 1.6(1) says that a defence is likely to be struck out if it 'sets out no coherent statement of facts'.

(c) CPR, r 16.5(2) says:

(2)   Where a defendant denies an allegation—

    (a)   he must state his reasons for doing so; and

    (b)   if he intends to put forward a different version of events from that given by the claimant he must state his own version.

(d) Paragraph 5.6.2 of the Queen's Bench Guide reads:

The particulars of claim ... should set out the claimant's claim clearly and fully. The same principle applies to the defence.

The requirement to state facts is dealt with more fully in **4.5** below.

4.4.3.2   Other rules

Other rules which should also apply to defendants where appropriate are set out in PD 16, para 8:

(a) By para 8.1 a claimant who wishes to rely on evidence that someone has been convicted of an offence must state that he intends to do so and give details of the conviction, namely the offence, the date of conviction, the court and the issue in the claim to which the conviction is relevant.

(b) By para 8.2 a claimant must specifically set out the following matters if he wishes to rely on them:

    (i)   any allegation of fraud;

    (ii)   the fact of any illegality;

    (iii) details of any misrepresentation;

    (iv) details of all breaches of trust;

    (v)   notice or knowledge of a fact;

    (vi) details of unsoundness of mind or undue influence;

    (vii) details of wilful default;

    (viii) any facts relating to mitigation of loss or damage.

This is about giving particulars. The above matters always required particularisation under the old rules by whichever party alleged them. There is more about particulars in **4.5** below.

Item (iii) in particular is often an allegation made by a defendant against a claimant. It would be most odd if he did not have to give details of it.

Item (v) is a matter often alleged by a defendant. When a party alleges that another party knew a fact he should usually give 'particulars of knowledge': that is he should say why or how that party knew that fact. If he alleges that the other party ought to have known a fact he should certainly give particulars of knowledge.

Item (viii) is far more likely to be of relevance to a defendant than a claimant. A claimant should give credit for any successful mitigation, but there is no reason why he should have to set out details of failed attempts at mitigation. A defendant must surely be required on the other hand to give details of any allegation of failure to mitigate by the claimant.

4.4.3.3 The Court Guides

Three Guides have been published for the benefit of court users which have a bearing on the drafting of statements of case. These are the Queen's Bench Guide, the Chancery Guide and the Commercial Court Guide. Paragraph 5.6.4 of the Queen's Bench Guide, Appendix 1 of the Chancery Guide and Appendix 4 of the Commercial Court Guide set out further guidelines for the drafting of statements of case. They incorporate several matters which used to be rules under the old procedure, but which do not appear in the CPR or PD. Paragraph 5.6.4 of the Queen's Bench Guide is set out below. The guidelines in the Chancery Guide and Commercial Court Guide are very similar. Paragraph 5.6.4 states:

In addition to the information contained in Part 16 and the Part 16 Practice Direction, the following guidelines on preparing a statement of case should be followed:

    (1) a statement of case must be as brief and concise as possible;

    (2) a statement of case should be set out in separate consecutively numbered paragraphs and sub-paragraphs;

    (3) so far as possible each paragraph or sub-paragraph should contain no more than one allegation;

    (4) the facts and other matters alleged should be set out as far as reasonably possible in chronological order;

    (5) the statement of case should deal with the claim on a point by point basis, to allow a point by point response;

    (6) where a party is required to give reasons, the allegation should be stated first and then the reasons listed one by one in separate numbered sub-paragraphs;

    (7) a party wishing to advance a positive claim must identify that claim in the statement of case;

    (8) any matter which if not stated might take another party by surprise should be stated;

(9) *where they will assist, headings, abbreviations and definitions should be used and a glossary annexed; contentious headings, abbreviations, paraphrasing and definitions should not be used and
every effort should be made to ensure that they are in a form acceptable to the other parties;*

(10) *particulars of primary allegations should be stated as particulars and not as primary allegations;*

(11) *schedules or appendices should be used if this would be helpful, for example, where lengthy particulars are necessary, and any response should also be stated in a schedule or appendix;*

(12) *any lengthy extracts from documents should be placed in a schedule.*

Most of these guidelines are easily followed and coincide with long-standing good drafting practice. Guidelines (5) and (6), while obviously representing good practice, probably
need some common sense applied. If taken absolutely literally, then even the most
straightforward statements of case will end up being unduly long and complex. Even a
simple matter like the description of a collision between two cars could be broken down
into ten or more 'points' if the writer so desired. But this does not coincide with established practice, neither does it make for clarity. This issue is further explored in the commentary to paragraph 1 in **7.6.3.1**.

The reasons for a denial must be given, and it must be right that the denial is made before the reasons, but if the reasons are invariably listed one by one in separate sub-paragraphs, again a very short case will end up unnecessarily lengthy. This issue is further
explored in **8.4.1.2**.

On the other hand, these guidelines are undoubtedly of considerable value and importance in long and complex statements of case. It is submitted that they should be followed
in such cases, but only followed in simple cases to the extent that they help clarity and
conciseness. Most of the examples in this Manual are of the relatively straightforward
kind.

4.4.4 Rules relating to particular statements of case only

These will be dealt with in subsequent chapters as each type of statement of case is introduced. See in particular **Chapters 7, 8, 14 and 15**.

4.4.5 Alternative facts

It used to be provided expressly in the rules that a party could raise alternative and inconsistent sets of facts or alternative and inconsistent defences. As a matter of principle it
must still be possible to do so. A party may always say that one or other of two versions of
the facts is true, but he does not at present know which (see *Clarke v Marlborough Fine Art
(London) Ltd* The Times, 4 December 2001). It should be made clear, however, that this
does not mean that a party can state alternative facts that are within his knowledge, so
that one or other must be a lie. A claimant can quite properly state 'the defendant hit me
deliberately; if he didn't he did so carelessly'. But a defendant cannot say 'I wasn't the
driver of the car, I was the passenger; but if I was the driver I hadn't been drinking'.

4.5   Contents of statements of case

4.5.1   The primary rule

The primary rule is in CPR, r 16.4(1)(a):

> *(1)   Particulars of claim must include—*
>
>   *(a)   a concise statement of the facts on which the claimant relies;...*

For the reasons explained above, this must be taken to apply to defences and other statements of case as well. It should be contrasted with the old primary rule which said:

> *... every pleading must contain, and contain only, a statement in summary form of the material facts on which the party pleading relies for his claim or defence, as the case may be, but not the evidence by which those facts are to be proved, and the statement must be as brief as the nature of the case admits.*

In spite of initial appearances, it is submitted that the new rule is in substance the same. The requirement to include a 'concise' statement of the facts comes to much the same thing as the requirement to plead in 'summary form' and to be 'as brief as the nature of the case admits'. The 'facts on which the claimant relies' are by definition what used to be called the 'material facts' (see below). The only potential difference is the removal of the requirement not to plead anything other than the material facts, especially evidence.

4.5.2   May statements of case contain evidence?

You will doubtless hear the view expressed in practice that they may, and indeed it is true that evidence is not forbidden. But you will be taught that as a general rule statements of case should not contain evidence. There is less contradiction here than appears at first sight.

4.5.2.1   Why evidence is not forbidden

It is submitted that the bar on evidence was removed for the following reasons:

(a) So as not to penalise a litigant in person who cannot easily distinguish fact from evidence. Provided he has stated the facts on which he relies, it does not matter if he has also set out his evidence.

(b) Because the new rules seek to put a stop to bad pleading practice. One of the worst habits of some pleaders in the past was to plead facts without sufficient particulars. This was justified on the basis that the particulars amounted to evidence.

(c) To streamline the documents in very simple cases and small claims. There is provision in the rules for statements of case to be used as written evidence in interim applications if desired. This is only likely to be realistic in very straightforward cases, but it would be undesirable to have different rules in different types of case. In a small claim, where the facts are often very straightforward, it may be unnecessarily pedantic to draw a rigid distinction between fact and evidence — the case can be decided quite easily in any event.

4.5.2.2   Why evidence should not be included

It is submitted that lawyers should continue to draw a distinction between fact and evidence and avoid putting evidence into statements of case for the following reasons:

(a) There is still throughout the CPR a clear distinction drawn between statements of case and written evidence. Suggestions in the first Woolf Report that some law and evidence might come into statements of case did not find their way into the final rules.

(b) A statement of case which contained both fact and evidence, or worse still muddled them up, would not fulfil its function so well and would be less likely to comply with the overriding objective.

(c) One of Woolf's objectives was to reduce the number of inordinately long pleadings, and the insertion of evidence was one of the most common reasons for pleadings being too long.

(d) If the intention had been to change decades of practice among lawyers and require evidence as well as material facts, the rules would surely have said so expressly.

(e) Appendix 4 of the Commercial Court Guide states:

> 12.   *Particular care should be taken to set out only those factual allegations which are necessary to support the case. Evidence should not be included.*

And Appendix 1 of the Chancery Guide states:

> 12.   *The names of any witness to be called may be given, and necessary documents (including an expert's report) can be attached or served contemporaneously if not bulky (PD 16; Guide paragraph 2.11). Otherwise evidence should not be included.*

4.5.2.3   Evidence and particulars

It is possible to see why evidence should be excluded, and to learn to exclude it, if you draw a distinction between particulars and evidence. Material facts which are included in a statement of case should be set out in proper detail. You do not just state that there was a contract between the claimant and the defendant, you give details of it, say when it was made, what its relevant terms were and so on. You do not just allege that the defendant was negligent, you say in what way he was negligent: what were the acts and omissions that amount to negligence. This kind of detail is called 'giving particulars'. People who ask for the evidence to be included are often asking simply for more particulars. But facts which go beyond this are likely to be background circumstances, and purely evidence. We will look at this is more detail below.

4.5.3   Stating facts

The following principles can be derived from the primary rule, and if followed will enable you to comply with it.

4.5.3.1   State facts

'Facts' includes allegations of fact, for example, 'The defendant was negligent'; 'the delay amounted to a breach of contract'; 'the defendant knew that ...'.

Facts must be distinguished from law and evidence, but it is not always easy to do so.

4.5.3.2   State the material facts

Material facts are those necessary to establish the cause(s) of action or the defence relied upon and the party's entitlement to any remedy claimed. In other words, the party must set out those facts and allegations which, if proved, would entitle him to the remedy sought, or provide him with a defence, as a matter of law.

Facts which do not strictly come within the above definition, but which are an essential part of the narrative, without which the nature of the case cannot readily be understood, should also be regarded as material facts.

So, for example, to establish a claim in negligence, a claimant must state:

(a) the relationship of proximity giving rise to a duty of care;

(b) an allegation that the defendant was in breach of that duty (with particulars);

(c) that the defendant's negligence caused the claimant loss and damage;

(d) the nature and extent of that loss and damage with sufficient explanation to show that it was reasonably foreseeable.

And to establish a claim for breach of contract, a claimant must state:

(a) the existence of a contract (so agreement, obligation and consideration);

(b) that the claimant and defendant were parties to the contract;

(c) any terms which the defendant has breached, or which entitle the claimant to his remedy;

(d) breach of the contract by the defendant;

(e) that the defendant's breach has caused the claimant loss and damage;

(f) the nature and extent of that loss and damage;

(g) the defendant's knowledge of any facts which put that loss and damage reasonably within his contemplation at the time of the contract.

But a fact is only material if it is material at the present stage. Do not anticipate a defence that has not yet been raised, or attempt to answer allegations that have not yet been made. So, for example, a claimant does *not* state in his claim that he was not contributorily negligent, or that the defendant cannot rely on an exclusion clause. A defendant does *not* in his defence attempt to refute allegations that may have been made in correspondence but do not appear in the particulars of claim.

4.5.3.3 State all material facts

If any material fact is left out, the statement of case is unsound in law, and the claim or defence cannot succeed unless it is amended.

4.5.3.4 Do not include law

This is the basic rule. Do not put propositions of law, or legal argument, in your statements of case. It is not usual to state 'the defendant is liable to compensate the claimant', or even 'the defendant owed the claimant a duty of care'.

However, under PD 16, para 13.3 points of law may be referred to in statements of case, and there are circumstances where it is a good idea to do so, because otherwise the nature of the case would not be clear. But it is never fatal to fail to include a point of law.

4.5.3.5 Do not include evidence

This is a very important rule and also a very difficult one to comply with. It is important because without it statements of case would be inordinately long, and would not serve their purpose of helping to define and clarify the issues. But it is difficult, because in practice there is almost never a clear line between what is fact and what is evidence.

Your aim is to state the material facts which you will seek to prove, but not the evidence which proves them. However, allegations must be particularised, and one fact may evidence another. So, for example, a claimant may allege that a defendant was negligent. The claimant may particularise that allegation by alleging that the defendant failed to heed a clear warning given. What that warning was, when it was given and by whom is all evidence of negligence; but these are also particulars relied upon to substantiate the allegation, and should be stated.

There are also circumstances in which a party will want to state more than the strictly material facts in order to strengthen his case. For example a claimant needs to plead that the parties agreed some term of a contract which on the face of it is very unusual and inherently unlikely to have been agreed. If he does not give a good reason why it was a term of the contract, his claim runs the risk of appearing to be made up. So he includes some particulars of how this term came to be a term. Or a defendant wants to state that the parties did not enter into the agreement alleged, but entered into some other, quite different agreement. If he merely denies the existence of the agreement without more, it looks as though his defence is a sham. So he sets out the alternative agreement, even though he does not need to show the existence of it in order to have a complete defence.

In both these instances the party is arguably including evidence, but what is set out will be called 'facts relied upon in support of an allegation', 'reasons for a denial', or simply 'particulars'. The important thing is to state these facts in such a way as to make them look like facts rather than evidence.

Sometimes the difference between stating fact and evidence is simply the way an allegation is put. Contrast:

The claimant returned home to find the defendant's car parked in his driveway. (*Evidence*)

and:

Whilst the claimant was out, the defendant parked her car in his driveway. (*Fact*).

It is often the case that matters set out look like evidence if you put the particulars before the material fact that is being particularised. Reverse them, and it looks right again. For example:

On 15th March the claimant telephoned the defendant and offered to buy 100 widgets at a price of £50 each. The defendant accepted this offer. There was therefore a binding agreement for the sale of these widgets by the defendant to the claimant at that price. The claimant asked how soon the widgets could be delivered. The defendant replied that he could deliver them on 10th April and the claimant said that this would be acceptable. This was therefore an express term of the agreement.

This can be better put as follows:

By an oral agreement made by telephone on 15th March the defendant agreed to sell to the claimant 100 widgets at a price of £50 each. It was an express term of the agreement that the defendant would deliver the widgets on 10th April.

Another common tendency is to plead in a narrative form, focusing on the evidence rather than the essential material fact. For example:

On 15th March the claimant arranged to visit the defendant at his factory in Oak Lane Barchester. This visit took place the next day. The claimant asked the defendant what the turnover of the company was. The defendant replied that the turnover in 2002 was £500,000. The claimant asked if he could see this in writing, and the defendant gave the claimant a copy of the 2002 accounts which showed this figure for turnover.

The material fact here is that the defendant made a representation, but it is not at all clear that this is the material allegation. The paragraph would be much more succinct and to the point if put like this:

On 16th March, at his factory in Oak Lane Barchester, the defendant represented to the claimant, both orally and by showing the claimant a copy of the 2002 accounts, that the turnover of the company in 2002 was £500,000.

You will learn with experience where to draw the line between fact and evidence, and how to draft one rather than the other. In the early stages of learning to draft statements of case, some students tend to go too far one way, and some too far the other. But you will eventually develop a 'feel' for it.

4.5.3.6   Be concise

Conciseness is an essential ingredient in statements of case. All the court guides say that the document must be 'as brief and concise as possible'. This means sticking to the material facts, and aiming to set them out in chronological order. Chronological order is a rule occasionally broken, but break it only with caution and for good reason.

PD 16, para 1.4 provides further encouragement to be concise by requiring that:

If exceptionally a statement of case exceeds 25 pages (excluding schedules) an appropriate short summary must also be filed and served.

4.5.3.7   Use plain English

There is nothing in the rules to say so, but as explained in **Chapter 3** it seems to be consistent with the whole spirit of Woolf and the CPR that everything should be drafted in plain English. In the past pleadings tended to contain phrases like 'the said', 'by reason of the matters aforesaid', 'inter alia', 'save as hereinafter set out', 'without prejudice to the generality of the foregoing', etc.

Such phrases were entirely accurate and comprehensible to lawyers, but often used unnecessarily. This Manual will therefore attempt to do without them. You will find, however, that the plain English equivalent is often longer. It is harder to be wholly unambiguous in plain English than in archaic language. Do not expect an overnight revolution in the profession as a whole! For some tips on modern alternatives, see **3.6**.

4.6   The statement of truth

Every statement of case must be verified by a statement of truth (CPR, r 22.1). This must be signed by the party whose statement of case it is, in person, or if a company by a person holding a senior position in the company. Alternatively it may be signed by a legal representative on the party's behalf.

The wording of the statement of truth must be:

[I believe] [the claimant/defendant believes] that the facts stated in [this claim form] [these particulars of claim] [this defence] are true.

The statement of truth is *not* part of the statement of case. It will usually be most convenient to append it at the end of the document, but it may be in a separate document which refers to the relevant statement of case.

4.7 Further reading

As a companion to this Manual and in conjunction with your work on the exercises, you are strongly advised to acquire and read another book, written by a former practising barrister, now a circuit judge, which will do much to explain why we do what we do when drafting. This is: Rose, William M., *Pleadings Without Tears*, 6th edn, Oxford: Oxford University Press, 2002.

4.8 Exercise

Using the 'blue-pencil' approach, remove the law, evidence and immaterial facts from the following 'draft statement of case', to leave a simple particulars of claim.

IN THE HIGH COURT OF JUSTICE   Claim No 2004 HC 8332
QUEEN'S BENCH DIVISION

BETWEEN

RICHARD WILLIS   Claimant

and

DENNIS UNDERWOOD   Defendant

PARTICULARS OF CLAIM

1.   On 1st May 2003 at about 9.00 p.m. there was a nasty accident on the A45 in Warwickshire. The Claimant, Richard Willis, who lives at 27 Mead Close, Stratford-upon-Avon, was driving his Jaguar motor car registration N208 RGD. He had only bought the car a few days earlier and was very proud of it, so he was driving carefully, lawfully and safely.

2.   With the Claimant in his Jaguar motor car were his wife Helen and his two children Jennifer, aged 8 and Nigel, aged 5. They were returning from a visit to the Claimant's wife's mother. The Claimant had not been drinking alcohol. As the Claimant proceeded in a westerly direction along the A45 highway he was travelling at about 45 m.p.h. when at the junction of the highway with Offchurch Lane, near Drexford, the accident occurred.

3.   Drexford is in Warwickshire and it was accordingly the Warwickshire Police who were called to the scene. PC Edwards of the Warwickshire Police will say that the position of the vehicles and the tyre marks showed that the accident was caused by the Defendant, Mr Dennis Underwood, who lives at 12 The Hawthorns, Solihull, West Midlands.

4.   According to PC Edwards, Mr Underwood drove his vehicle, which was an Austin Metro motor car registration number W283 KEN, into the Claimant's motor car by emerging from Offchurch Lane while the Claimant's car was passing.

5.   Since the Claimant and the Defendant were both using the public highway at the same time, it was reasonably foreseeable that an accident might occur if either of them failed to take reasonable care. Accordingly the Defendant owed the Claimant a duty of care and this claim is founded on his negligence (*Donoghue v Stevenson*).

6.   The Claimant had no way of knowing that the accident was about to occur and so was unable to take avoiding action. The accident was therefore caused solely and absolutely by the appalling negligence of the Defendant.

PARTICULARS OF NEGLIGENCE

The Defendant owed a duty of care and did not take proper care for the safety of other users of the highway. This means he was negligent. There were many ways in which he could have avoided the accident, but the Claimant will say that he was particularly at fault in that:

(a) He did not look where he was going. The Claimant's car had its lights on and the Defendant should have seen it, but nevertheless drove on to the A45 highway from Offchurch Lane without looking to see if the road was clear. In breach of the Highway Code he was therefore not keeping a proper or indeed any look-out.

(b) He was on a minor road and the Claimant was on a major road. The Defendant should therefore have given way to the Claimant but failed to do so. If he had been driving with due care and attention he would have been alert enough to give precedence to the Claimant's car at the junction. Although it was dusk, nevertheless it was not entirely dark, and the Claimant had his lights on: accordingly the Claimant will say *res ipsa loquitur.*

(c) He was at a stop sign, but the skid marks show that he failed to stop. He also made no attempt to steer or otherwise control his car so as to avoid the accident.

7.   The Defendant's negligence resulted in him striking the Claimant's motor car. The Defendant was injured in the accident, but the Claimant is not responsible for that.

8.   As a result of the matters set out above the Claimant suffered pain and injury, but his wife and children were unhurt. The accident also meant that the Claimant sustained loss and damage. This loss and damage was all reasonably foreseeable and the Defendant is liable to compensate the Claimant for it.

PARTICULARS OF INJURY

(a) Shock, pain, concussion.

(b) Severe fractures to both ankles.

(c) Fractures necessitating removal of both patellas.

The Claimant was taken to the Tiger Smith Memorial Hospital where X-ray examination revealed the fractures. Both kneecaps were removed and the ankle fractures reduced under general anaesthetic. The Claimant's legs were in plaster for six months and he was unable to walk. He is now able to walk only with the aid of walking sticks. The Claimant's condition is expected to deteriorate. The onset of osteo-arthritis is likely in five years' time which will restrict the Claimant's movements and mobility further.

The Claimant's occupation prior to the accident was as a scaffolder. He has not resumed work and he will never be able to do so. The Claimant was born on 20th November 1952.

Further particulars of the Claimant's injuries are set out in the medical report of Kenneth Brand served with these particulars of claim.

PARTICULARS OF SPECIAL DAMAGE

(1)	Loss of earnings from date of accident to the present date and continuing at £750 per week	£
(2)	Cost of repairs to motor car	£1,400
(3)	Cost of hire of alternative car for use by Claimant's wife in her employment	£ 600
(4)	Damage to clothing and wrist-watch	£ 100

The special damages claimed by the Claimant are more fully set out in the schedule of expenses and losses served with these particulars of claim.

9.   Further the Claimant claims interest pursuant to section 35A of the Supreme Court Act 1981 on the amount found to be due to the Claimant at such rate and for such period as the Court thinks fit.

AND the Claimant claims:

(1)   Damages.

(2)   Interest pursuant to section 35A of the Supreme Court Act 1981 to be assessed.

DAVID AMISS

STATEMENT OF TRUTH

I believe that the facts stated in these particulars of claim are true.

Richard Willis

Dated 5th May 2004

The Claimant's Solicitors, to whom documents should be sent, are:

Smith and Smith
100 Donelley Avenue
Edgbaston
Warwickshire

Headings

5.1 Titles of proceedings

In the past there was some variation in how proceedings were entitled, but there is now a form prescribed by PD 7, paras 4.1 and 4.2.

Paragraph 4.1 says that a claim form and every other statement of case must be headed with the title of the proceedings. The title should state:

(a) the claim number;

(b) the court or division in which the claim is proceeding;

(c) the full name of each party;

(d) his status in the proceedings (ie claimant/defendant).

Paragraph 4.2 says that where there is more than one claimant and/or more than one defendant the parties should be described in the title in this form:

(1)	AB	
(2)	CD	
(3)	EF	Claimants

and

(1)	AB	
(2)	CD	
(3)	EF	Defendants

When a claim form or other printed document is being filled in, the layout will be determined by the boxes that have to be filled in. When however a separate document is being drafted, the layout is, by convention, as set out in the examples below in **5.4**.

5.2 Claim numbers

Every claim is given a claim number by the court when the claim form is filed. When drafting a claim, do not invent a number. Just write 'Claim No'. When drafting any subsequent statement of case, include the claim number that appears on the claim form and/or particulars of claim.

In the High Court, the most usual format is that the claim number begins with the year, followed by the letters HC followed by the number allocated by the court.

In the county court the most common system is that numbers consist of two letters which refer to the court, followed by a single digit identifying the year, and then the number allocated by the court. This number is retained if the case is transferred to another county court.

5.3   Names of parties

(a) Give individuals their full names (if known).

(b) Companies are identified by the inclusion of the word 'limited' or 'plc'.

(c) A partnership may sue and be sued in the name of the firm, or in the names of its partners. If the firm name is used, put '(a firm)' after the name. Never use the word 'firm' to denote a limited company. This is journalists' terminology.

(d) A limited liability partnership sues or is sued in the name of the partnership, adding the letters 'LLP'.

(e) When a person uses a trading name, that name should be added after his or her name, using the formula 'trading as' (sometimes abbreviated to 't/a').

(f) A person under 18 should be identified as a 'child' and is represented in the proceedings by his or her 'litigation friend', who should also be named and described. Eg:

JANE SMITH

(a child, by her litigation friend ELIZABETH SMITH)   <u>Claimant</u>

(g) Personal representatives sue or are sued as follows:

(1) JOHN SMITH

(2) ANDREW BROWN

(executors of the Will of MARK SMITH deceased)   <u>Defendants</u>

(h) A bankrupt may only sue or be sued by the trustee in bankruptcy, who, for example, is named: The Trustee of the estate of ANTHONY MARSHALL, a bankrupt.

(i) Where the sex of a party is not clear from the name, the word 'male' or 'female' may be added in brackets.

(j) Where the claimant does not know the defendant's first name, he may use the surname only, adding the sex, eg JONES (male).

5.4 Examples

5.4.1 Queen's Bench Division

5.4.1.1 Heading

<u>IN THE HIGH COURT OF JUSTICE</u>   Claim No 2004 HC 2116
<u>QUEEN'S BENCH DIVISION</u>

[Portsmouth District Registry]

BETWEEN

ARTHUR WRIGHT   <u>Claimant</u>

and

PULLITOFF LIMITED   <u>Defendants</u>

PARTICULARS OF CLAIM

5.4.1.2 Commentary

Note carefully which words are in capitals (upper case), which are in lower case and which are underlined. Observe also the positioning on the page: left margin, right margin or centred. This formatting is conventional and should be observed.

The court is always in the top left-hand corner in capitals and underlined, and the claim number in the top right-hand corner.

The name of the relevant district registry only appears where the claim has been filed in a district registry of the High Court rather than in London.

The names of the parties are always in capitals and centred, with their description alongside against the right margin, in lower case and underlined.

Note that the word 'Limited' is spelt out in full, not abbreviated to 'Ltd'.

The defendant is a company and is described as the 'Defendants' (plural). Whether to make a company, or a statutory body, singular or plural is a matter of choice in the Queen's Bench Division or County Court, but you should be consistent. Purists rightly point out that a company is by nature a singular creature. However, it is run by its officers, and it is often easier to draft the body of the statement of case when a company is plural, because it is less confusing to use the pronoun 'they' than 'it'.

The title of the statement of case appear in capitals, centred and enclosed in 'tramlines'.

5.4.2 Chancery Division

5.4.2.1 Heading

<u>IN THE HIGH COURT OF JUSTICE</u>   Claim No 2004 HC 1467
<u>CHANCERY DIVISION</u>

BETWEEN

(1) MARY ROCKFORD
(2) SUSAN MILLETT
(trading together as ALPHA
ENGINEERING SERVICES, a firm)   <u>Claimants</u>

and

PULLITOFF LIMITED   <u>Defendant</u>

DEFENCE

5.4.2.2 Commentary

Note that there are two claimants: in such a case they must be numbered as in the example. Where they are joined in their capacity as partners in a firm, it is conventional to identify the name of the firm as well, which is why the words in brackets appear.

This example is in the Chancery Division, where companies are always referred to in the singular, so Pullitoff Limited is the defendant this time.

5.4.3 County court

5.4.3.1 Heading

<u>IN THE BRENTFORD COUNTY COURT</u>   Claim No BF4/01624

BETWEEN

JOHN GOODFELLOW
(a child, by his litigation
friend PETER GOODFELLOW)   <u>Claimant</u>

and

(1) TIMBER TRADERS PLC
(2) PAINT SUPPLIES (a firm)   <u>Defendants</u>

PARTICULARS OF CLAIM

5.4.3.2 Commentary

Here is an example of a child claimant, described as explained in **5.3**(e).

There are two defendants, so they must be numbered in the usual way. The abbreviation 'PLC' or 'plc' is acceptable: it is not usual to write out 'public limited company'. The second defendant is a firm. It would not be wrong to name the partners as defendants as in the previous example, but where the liability is purely that of the firm and no partner is being sued in any other capacity, the name of the firm alone will suffice.

5.4.4   Part 20 Proceedings

5.4.4.1   Heading

<u>IN THE HIGH COURT OF JUSTICE</u>   Claim No 2004 HC 8234
<u>QUEEN'S BENCH DIVISION</u>
<u>TECHNOLOGY AND CONSTRUCTION COURT</u>

BETWEEN

SARAH MARKS   <u>Claimant</u>

and

CRAIG MESSITER
(trading as ACE
BUILDERS)   <u>Defendant/Part 20 Claimant</u>

and

TIMBER TRADERS PLC   <u>Part 20 Defendant</u>

PARTICULARS OF PART 20 CLAIM

5.4.4.2   Commentary

Technology and construction cases in the High Court are assigned to their own subdivision of the Queen's Bench Division. In such cases the Technology and Construction Court is named in the heading.

Ace Builders has no legal status; it is neither a company nor a partnership, it is simply a trading name used by the defendant. When a party uses a trading name in this way, it should be added for the sake of clarity as in this example.

Craig Messiter has a dual capacity: he is being sued by the claimant, but has also issued a Part 20 claim against Timber Traders plc, so he is described as the 'Defendant/Part 20 Claimant' — see PD 20, para 7.1 and **15.3.2**.

See, however, **15.4** for proposed changes.

5.4.5   Additional Part 20 Parties

5.4.5.1   Heading

<u>IN THE BIRMINGHAM COUNTY COURT</u>   Claim No BM4 4816

BETWEEN

PINSTRIPES LIMITED   <u>Claimant/</u>
                                         <u>Part 20 Defendant (2nd claim)</u>

and

ARNOLD LAYNE   <u>Defendant/</u>
                                         <u>Part 20 Claimant (1st Claim)</u>

and

RUBBER FINANCE LIMITED

                                         <u>Part 20 Defendant (1st claim)/</u>
                                         <u>Part 20 Claimant (2nd claim)</u>

and

SOUTHERN BANK PLC

                                         <u>Part 20 Defendant (2nd claim)</u>

5.4.5.2   Commentary

See if you can work this one out! It is actually derived from the example specifically given in PD 20, para 7.3.

Pinstripes Limited has issued a claim against Arnold Layne, who then issued a Part 20 claim (what used to be called a third party claim) against Rubber Finance Limited. Rubber Finance Limited next issued what used to be called a fourth party claim (but is now the second Part 20 claim) naming Pinstripes Limited and Southern Bank plc as defendants. You are not alone if you think the old terminology would have been clearer!

See, however, **15.4** for proposed changes.

5.5   Exercise

You act for Mr Malcolm Jackson, of Ealing, London, whose two sons, Jason aged 16 and Fergus aged 18, were severely injured in a road accident involving four vehicles: the car driven by Fergus, in which Jason was a passenger; a motor cycle driven by Ms Lee Jones; a car driven by Mr Harry Wicks, a sales representative travelling on business for his employers Wundacola Ltd to whom the car belonged; and a van belonging to P and Q Motors, a partnership between William Peters and Deborah Quinn, and driven by William Peters. From the evidence before you it appears that the accident was caused by the negligence of Ms Jones, Mr Wicks and Mr Peters and that the value of the claim will exceed £50,000. Construct the heading for the particulars of claim.

Claim forms

6.1 The contents of a claim form

6.1.1 Rules for claim forms

By CPR, r 16.2(1) a Part 7 claim form must:

    (a) contain a concise statement of the nature of the claim;

    (b) specify the remedy which the claimant seeks;

    (c) contain a statement of value if the claim is for money;

    (d) contain such other matters as may be set out in a Practice Direction.

The only additional matters required by PD 16 are the claimant's address, and the defendant's address (if the claimant knows it).

PD 16, para 3.1 says that if practicable, the particulars of claim should be set out in the claim form. The amount of space provided in the form is such that this is only likely to be practicable where the particulars of claim are very short, or where an abbreviated form is used (see **6.3** below).

6.1.2 The nature of the claim and the remedy sought

These details will be inserted in the space on the claim form headed 'brief details of claim'. Note that they must be provided even where the particulars of claim are also set out in or attached to the claim form, even though this means there will be some repetition of information.

Stating the nature of the claim probably involves identifying the cause or causes of action, and giving enough factual information to enable the court and the other side to know what sort of case it is (eg if the cause of action is negligence, whether it is a personal injury claim, a fatal accident claim, or a claim for professional negligence; if the cause of action is breach of contract, what sort of contract is involved, whether a contract of employment, or for the sale of goods, or for the supply of services, etc). It is probably a good idea also to identify the incident involved by date and place, especially if the particulars of claim are not attached.

Stating the remedy or remedies sought should be regarded as essential, but it is not fatal if a remedy gets left out. Rule 16.2(5) says that the court may grant a remedy which is not specified in the claim form. If the claim is for damages, interest should be included (unless it is not sought). If the claim is for a debt, then the remedy is payment of the sum due, not damages. It is not necessary to specify costs, which is not strictly speaking a remedy.

6.1.3   Examples of details of claim

6.1.3.1   Tort: negligence

The claim is for damages for loss and expense arising from a fire which occurred on 3rd January 2004 at 4 Gray's Inn Place, London WC1 and which was caused by the negligence of the Defendant, together with interest under section 69 of the County Courts Act 1984.

6.1.3.2   Tort: personal injury: negligence: breach of statutory duty

The claim is for:

(1) Damages for personal injury and loss arising out of an accident which occurred on 3rd January 2004 at 216 Commercial Road, Manchester and which was caused by negligence and breach of statutory duty under the Construction (Health, Safety and Welfare) Regulations 1996 on the part of the Defendants their employees or agents.

(2) Interest on those damages under section 35A of the Supreme Court Act 1981.

6.1.3.3   Tort: fatal accident: negligence

The claim arises out of a fatal road traffic accident which occurred on 27th March 2003 on the A31 near Ringwood in Hampshire in which the deceased Joseph Poole was killed. The Claimant is the administratrix of his estate and seeks:

(1) Damages under the Fatal Accidents Act 1976 on behalf of the dependants of the deceased, whose death was caused by the negligence of the Defendant.

(2) Damages under the Law Reform (Miscellaneous Provisions) Act 1934 on behalf of the estate of the deceased for the loss caused to him by the negligence of the Defendant.

(3) Interest on those damages under section 35A of the Supreme Court Act 1981.

6.1.3.4   Contract: breach of contract

The claim is for damages for breach of a written contract for the manufacture and delivery of space hoppers dated 4th April 2003 made between the Claimants and the Defendants together with interest under section 35A of the Supreme Court Act 1981.

6.1.3.5   Contract: payment of money due

The claim is for:

(1) £25,681 being salary due from the Defendants to the Claimant for work done between March and September 2003 under a written contract of employment dated 28th February 2003 made between the Claimant and the Defendants.

(2) Interest on the sum of £25,681 under section 69 of the County Courts Act 1984.

6.1.3.6   Misrepresentation: rescission: damages

The claim is for:

(a) Rescission of a written contract dated 1st December 2003 made between the Claimant and the Defendant for the purchase by the Claimant of an ironmongery business at the Old Forge, Barchester, Barset.

(b) Alternatively, damages in lieu of rescission.

(c) Further or alternatively, damages for misrepresentation by which the Defendant induced the Claimant to enter into this contract.

(d) Further or alternatively, damages for breach of the contract.

(e) Interest under section 35A of the Supreme Court Act 1981.

6.1.4 The statement of value

6.1.4.1 Rules

CPR, r 16.3 deals with the statement of value. Broadly, the claimant must state (r 16.3(2)):

(a) the specified amount he is claiming; or

(b) that he expects to recover

    (i)   not more than £5,000

    (ii)   more than £5,000 but not more than £15,000

    (iii) more than £15,000; or

(c) that he cannot say how much he expects to recover.

If the claim is commenced in the High Court the claimant must state (r 16.3(5)) that he expects to recover more than £15,000, or that the claim can only be commenced in the High Court by virtue of a specified enactment.

Other rules apply in personal injury cases:

(a) By r 16.3(3) the claimant must state whether he expects to recover not more than £1,000 or more than £1,000 for pain, suffering and loss of amenity.

(b) By r 16.3(5)(c) if the claim is commenced in the High Court the claim form must state that the claimant expects to recover £50,000 or more.

In valuing the claim, disregard interest, costs, set-off, contributory negligence and recovery of benefits (r 16.3(6)).

6.1.4.2 Examples

The statement of value in a personal injury action commenced in the High Court might look like this:

The claimant expects to recover £50,000 or more, including a sum of more than £1,000 as general damages for pain suffering and loss of amenity.

The statement of value in a personal injury action commenced in the county court might look like this:

The claimant expects to recover more than £5,000 but not more than £15,000, including a sum of not more than £1,000 as general damages for pain suffering and loss of amenity.

6.2 Rules for claiming interest

This may seem to be an odd place to deal with interest, but the rules for claiming interest and setting out that claim need to be explained before we get on to drafting particulars of claim to be included in the claim form.

6.2.1   Power to award interest

There are various bases on which the court has a power to award interest and on which a party may claim interest:

(a) Under a contract, where the contract between the parties provides for interest to be paid and/or the basis on which it is to be calculated.

(b) Under the Bills of Exchange Act 1882, s 57, on a dishonoured cheque. The award of interest is *prima facie* mandatory, but the court has a discretion to refuse.

(c) Under the Late Payment of Commercial Debts (Interest) Act 1998. This Act inserts an implied term for the payment of interest on debts into contracts for the supply of goods or services made between two parties each acting in the course of a business.

(d) Under various other statutory provisions — do not be concerned about these at present.

(e) In the High Court, under the Supreme Court Act 1981, s 35A. The award of interest is discretionary, except (i) on a claim for a specified amount of money which is admitted by the defendant under CPR, r 14.4, where it is as good as mandatory because judgment will include interest (CPR, r 14.14); and (ii) on damages for personal injury or death, where it is *prima facie* mandatory, but there is a discretion to refuse for special reasons (s 35A(2)).

(f) In the county court, under the County Courts Act 1984, s 69. Similar provisions to the Supreme Court Act 1981, s 35A.

(g) Under the court's equitable jurisdiction. Where the court grants an equitable remedy, for example, rescission or specific performance, it may in its discretion award interest on any sum ordered to be paid. Arguably this covers interest on damages in lieu of specific performance, rescission etc but such interest is also covered by s 35A.

In ordinary circumstances, all interest is simple interest. However the court has the power to award compound interest if a claimant is able to show that this is justified.

6.2.2   Rates of interest

(a) Contractual interest: the rate will be in accordance with the contract.

(b) Interest under the Late Payment of Commercial Debts (Interest) Act 1998: the rate is 8% above the official dealing rate (Bank of England base rate) in force on the last 30 June or 31 December before interest starts to run. The official dealing rate is changed from time to time, but at the time of writing has been 4% since 5 February 2004. The current rate, and the historical rates, can be found on the Bank of England website – www.bankofengland.co.uk.

So if interest starts to run on 1 May 2004, since the official dealing rate on 31 December 2003 was 3.75%, the rate of interest will be 11.75%, even though the official dealing rate has since altered.

In addition to statutory interest, the creditor is entitled to a fixed 'compensation payment' by virtue of s 5A of the Act. This is £40 on debts less than £1,000, £70 on debts of £1,000 or more but less than £10,000, and £100 on debts of £10,000 or more.

(c) Damages for personal injury and death. Special rules: see the *Remedies Manual*, **Chapters 11** and **12**.

(d) Otherwise the rate is within the court's discretion. Generally, two rates are used:

   (i)   the Special Investment Account rate (at the time of writing 6%);

   (ii) the rate applied to judgment debts under the Judgments Act 1838 ('the Judgments Act rate') (at the time of writing 8%).

   Both these rates are set from time to time by the Lord Chancellor.

(e) It is usual to claim the Judgments Act rate, where a rate needs to be specified. Providing the rate claimed does not exceed the Judgments Act rate, then interest on a specified amount will automatically be ordered if the defendant admits the claim (CPR, r 14.14).

6.2.3   Period of interest

This is within the court's discretion, but the following is normal practice:

(a) Contractual interest — in accordance with the contract.

(b) Interest under the Late Payment of Commercial Debts (Interest) Act 1998 — from the relevant day defined by s 4, which is the date agreed for payment or 30 days after the date on which the goods or services are supplied or the date on which the purchaser has notice of the amount of the debt.

(c) Damages for personal injury and death — special rules: see the *Remedies Manual*, **Chapters 11** and **12**.

(d) Damage to property — from the date of repair, or the decision to write off.

(e) Debts — from the date money was due. For the purposes of calculation, 'day 1' is the first day that payment was overdue.

(f) Other economic loss (eg, loss of profit) — from the date of the loss, if this can be identified, otherwise any other suitable date in the court's discretion.

(g) Other non-economic loss — from the date of service of the claim form.

(h) In each case — until date of judgment or sooner payment.

6.2.4   Setting out an interest claim

The claim for interest should be set out in the particulars of claim (CPR, r 16.4(1)(b)). It is necessary to state the statutory or other basis on which interest is claimed (r 16.4(2)(a)).

If the claim is for an unspecified amount, it is sufficient to claim interest under the Supreme Court Act 1981, s 35A or the County Courts Act 1984, s 69, to be assessed.

If the claim is for a specified amount, it is necessary to state (r 16.4(2)(b)):

(a) the rate of interest claimed,

(b) the starting date,

(c) the date to which interest so far has been calculated,

(d) the amount of interest claimed to that date,

(e) the equivalent daily rate thereafter.

The purpose of this rule is to make it possible for a defendant wishing to settle a claim to know exactly how much he needs to pay on any given date.

6.3 Abbreviated particulars of claim

6.3.1 When will abbreviated particulars of claim be used?

If practicable, the particulars of claim should be set out in the claim form (PD 16, para 3.1). The amount of space provided in the form is such that this is only likely to be practicable where the particulars of claim are very short, or where an abbreviated form is used.

An abbreviated form should only be used in certain types of case. It should not be used in any case where it is expected that the defendant will put in a valid defence. Its real use is in debt recovery cases where the claimant believes that the defendant has no defence and will either pay up on receipt of proceedings, or admit the claim, or that the claimant will seek judgment in default or summary judgment.

Although the particulars of claim are drafted in shorthand, if you study them closely you will see that all the essential elements necessary to establish the claimant's cause of action and right to recover the sum due are expressly or obliquely referred to. The words 'at [the defendant's] request' (or something equivalent) are particularly crucial in this regard.

6.3.2 Example 1: goods sold and delivered

6.3.2.1 Particulars of claim

IN THE RUGBY COUNTY COURT   Claim No RU4 68194

BETWEEN

TIM TOTTERIDGE & CO LIMITED   <u>Claimant</u>

and

(1) ELOISE PALMER
(2) T. PALMER (Male)   <u>Defendants</u>

PARTICULARS OF CLAIM

1.   The Claimant's claim is for £30,613.62, the balance of the price of goods sold and delivered to the Defendants at their request.

PARTICULARS

15th February 2003 Invoice No AB 123	£30,475.25
28th February 2003 Invoice No AB 147	<u>£5,138.37</u>
	£35,613.62
Less paid 5th May 2003	<u>£5,000.00</u>
	£30,613.62

2.   The Claimant further claims interest under section 69 of the County Courts Act 1984 on the sum of £30,613.62 from 6th May 2003 at the rate of 8% a year, amounting to £3,180.46 at 23rd August 2004 and then continuing until judgment or sooner payment at the rate of £6.71 per day.

JOSEPH BLOGGS

6.3.2.2 Commentary

The claimant does not know the full name of the second defendant (who is presumably the first defendant's husband), so he uses the style explained in **5.3**(j).

Paragraph 1 is in standard form. The claimant needs to show and therefore to allege that there was a contract between the claimant and the defendants for the sale of goods, what those goods were, what the price of the goods was to be, that the claimant delivered those goods, but that the defendants have failed to pay the full contractual price, despite the time for payment having arrived, and that the sum outstanding has been specified. In an oblique way, all these ingredients are included in paragraph 1. The words 'sold' and 'at their request' implicitly allege a contract of sale. The allegations that it is the claimant who claims the price and that the goods were sold to the defendants establish that the contract was between the claimant and the defendants. It must be presumed that the goods are specified in the invoices (if they are not, they should be specified here). The price of the goods is stated in the particulars. Delivery is alleged expressly. The failure to pay is implicit in the demand. The sending of invoices establishes that payment is now due. Credit is given for the deposit paid, so that the sum outstanding is clearly specified. What might take five paragraphs of a more complete statement of case is condensed into 41 words.

Paragraph 2 is also in standard form. The claim is for interest on a specified amount, so all the details required by CPR, r 16.4(2) (see **6.2.4** above) are included. Decimals are rounded to the nearest penny.

This is a statement of case drafted by a legal representative, so his signature appears at the bottom. See PD 5, para 2.1 and **4.4.1** above.

6.3.3 Example 2: work done and materials supplied

6.3.3.1 Particulars of claim

IN THE HIGH COURT OF JUSTICE   Claim No 2004 HC 1234
QUEEN'S BENCH DIVISION
TECHNOLOGY AND CONSTRUCTION COURT

BETWEEN

B. LEAKE AND SONS (a firm)   <u>Claimants</u>

and

BELINDA JARROW   <u>Defendant</u>

PARTICULARS OF CLAIM

1.   The Claimants' claim is for £57,489.50, the price of work done and materials supplied to the Defendant at her request. Full particulars are set out in the attached estimate and invoice.

2.   The Claimants further claim interest under section 35A of the Supreme Court Act 1981 on the sum of £57,489.50 from 6th April 2004 at the rate of 8% a year, amounting to £1,965.67 at 10th September 2004 and then continuing until judgment or sooner payment at the rate of £12.60 per day.

JOSEPH BLOGGS

6.3.3.2 Commentary

The formula is very similar to that in the previous example, but the particulars of the work done, materials supplied and the amount due are provided by reference to attached documents rather than incorporated into the particulars of claim. This is the convenient way to do it if the particulars are lengthy. The invoice must of course specify the sum of £57,489.50.

6.4   Exercise A

A has sued B for a debt of £9,187.50 due on 10 May 2003 and has claimed interest at 8% per annum and £520.25 costs. B wishes to settle A's claim in full today. How much should B pay?

6.5   Exercise B

On 6 May 2002 Edward Moss, age 45, went to Greenbridge Town Hall to pay his council tax. As he was walking up a stone staircase, which was being washed, he slipped on a wet step, tried to steady himself on an iron banister which was rusty and gave way, and fell a distance of some 12 feet to the floor, sustaining injuries to his back. He was in hospital for seven weeks and it was about a year before he was able to walk properly. He is a self-employed consultant engineer earning about £40,000 a year net. He was off work for six months, but has now been able to resume. He wishes to sue the London Borough of Greenbridge and the cleaning contractors, Big Blue Cleaning Services Ltd. Draft the brief details of the claim to be inserted on the claim form.

6.6   Exercise C

On 10 February 2004 Hot Air plc agreed orally with Snoozey Ltd to deliver and install air-conditioning equipment at Snoozey's offices in Finchley. The prices agreed were £9,420 for the air-conditioning units and £3,500 for the installation, less 10% if the installation was not complete by 30 March 2004. Terms agreed included payment in full within 28 days of completion of installation. Snoozey paid a deposit of £1,000 on 10 February 2004; Hot Air delivered the air-conditioning units on 11 March 2004 and invoiced Snoozey for £8,420 on 14 March; installation was completed on 5 April 2004 and Hot Air sent a further invoice for £3,150 on 7 April 2004. No payment on either invoice has been received despite frequent reminders. Hot Air plc wishes to start an action to recover the sum due. Draft abbreviated particulars of claim for the claim form.

Basic particulars of claim in tort and contract

7.1 Rules for particulars of claim

7.1.1 General

Rules that are of general application to all statements of case, or which should be so treated, have been dealt with in **4.4**. The rules relating to the claim for interest appeared in **6.2.4**. Here are some more rules which apply specifically to particulars of claim. They are to be found in CPR, r 16.4 and PD 16:

(a) If the claimant is seeking aggravated or exemplary damages, the particulars of claim must make a statement to that effect and his grounds for claiming them (r 16.4(1)(c)).

(b) If the claim is for an injunction in respect of land, the particulars of claim must state whether it relates to residential premises and identify the land (PD 16, para 7.1).

(c) If the claim is to enforce a right to recover possession of goods, the particulars of claim must state the value of the goods (PD 16, para 7.2).

(d) If the claim is based on a written agreement, a copy of the contract or documents constituting the agreement should be attached or served with the particulars of claim (PD 16, para 7.3). This means that the attached document should also be referred to in the particulars of claim.

(e) If the claim is based on an oral agreement, the particulars of claim should set out the contractual words used and state by whom, to whom, when and where they were spoken (PD 16, para 7.4).

(f) If the claim is based on an agreement by conduct, the particulars of claim should specify the conduct relied on and state by whom, when and where the acts constituting the conduct were done (PD 16, para 7.5).

7.1.2 Personal injury claims

(a) A personal injury claim is defined by CPR, r 2.3(1), to include a fatal accident claim.

(b) In personal injury claims the particulars of claim must contain the claimant's date of birth and brief details of the claimant's personal injuries (PD 16, para 4.1).

(c) The particulars of claim must be accompanied by a schedule of details of any past and future expenses and losses (PD 16, para 4.2).

(d) The particulars of claim must be accompanied by a medical report about the claimant's injuries (PD 16, para 4.3).

(e) If the claimant is seeking provisional damages the particulars of claim must make a statement to that effect and grounds for claiming them (r 16.4.(1)(d)). PD 16, para 4.4, gives more details of what is required:

    (i)   state that there is a chance that at some future time the claimant will develop some serious disease or suffer some serious deterioration in his physical or mental condition;

    (ii)   specify the disease or type of deterioration in respect of which an application may be made at a future date.

(f) In fatal accident claims the claimant must state that the claim is brought under the Fatal Accidents Act 1976, name the dependants on whose behalf the claim is made, give the date of birth of each dependant, and include details of the nature of the dependency claim (PD 16, para 5.1).

7.1.3 Other types of case

Particulars required in other types of case are also specified in PD 16:

(a) Hire purchase claims have particulars prescribed in para 6.

(b) Claims which raise Human Rights Act issues have particulars prescribed in para 15.

7.2 The essence of particulars of claim

The essence of particulars of claim is that they tell a story. Your fundamental guiding principle when drafting particulars of claim is quite simply:

7.2.1 Tell the story

The story is from the claimant's point of view, and it is essentially a very simple story. It goes like this:

To the defendant:

1.   This is who we are ...

2.   This is what has happened ...

3.   The result was ...

4.   And so this is what I want from you ...

As you learn in more detail (and from a more legal point of view!) what goes into particulars of claim, and start to get into the niceties of actual drafting, it is very easy to lose sight of this basic idea. Try to hold on to it, at all times. Never forget the need to tell the story.

7.3 Ingredients of particulars of claim

However, the story is based on the essential ingredients of the claim, not on an evidential narrative. Remember that the particulars of claim must set out those facts and allegations which, if proved, would give the claimant the right to the remedy sought as a matter of law. So if you are drafting a claim you need to be aware of all the ingredients that must be established in order to achieve this result, and ensure that your draft covers these. For most causes of action the law is so well established and clear that there can be no doubt what these ingredients are: you learned them early on in your study of law at the academic stage.

The most common causes of action in practice, upon which the great majority of civil claims are founded, are the tort of negligence and breach of contract. It is not surprising therefore that not only is the law relating to each of these causes of action clear, but that there has grown up a basic formula by which the cause of action can be established. This formula is of course founded on the essential ingredients, and if followed will ensure that all the ingredients are included, and in the correct chronological order.

There are of course variations on the formula, to meet different types of case, and many additional formulae for other less common causes of action. We cannot in this Manual spell them all out. Indeed, once you have grasped the basic concepts, they are largely self-explanatory. So we will confine ourselves in this chapter to setting out the ingredients and formulae for negligence and breach of contract. Once you have seen how the ingredients, the formulae and the sample drafts relate to each other, you will understand how to go about drafting any particulars of claim.

7.4 Tort: negligence: ingredients

7.4.1 Identify the ingredients

The essential ingredients of a successful claim for damages in negligence, leading to full recovery, are:

(a) Defendant (D) owes Claimant (C) a duty of care. Such a duty will be owed if:
   (i)   there is a relationship of proximity between them;
   (ii)   it is reasonably foreseeable that negligence by D might cause harm to C;
   (iii) it is fair, just and reasonable to impose a duty on D.

(b) D has breached that duty, ie he has been negligent.

(c) C has suffered injury, loss and damage.

(d) That loss and damage was caused by D's negligence.

(e) The loss is of a recoverable kind (eg not pure economic loss).

(f) The loss is not too remote, ie it is reasonably foreseeable, both in its nature and its causation.

(g) The claim is not statute-barred. (The limitation period is prima facie six years, but three years in a case of personal injury.)

(h) C has not been contributorily negligent.

(i) C has not failed reasonably to mitigate his loss.

7.4.2 What needs to be stated

From this list of ingredients, you can work out what needs to be stated, namely:

(a) Who the parties are, their relationship to each other and/or their proximity, sufficient to give rise to a duty of care.

(b) What has happened, the events which gave rise to a duty of care, the context within which it was reasonably foreseeable that negligence by D might cause damage to C.

(c) The duty of care owed, where this is specific to the facts of the case.

(d) An allegation that D was negligent and the acts or omissions constituting that negligence.

(e) An allegation that C has suffered injury, loss and damage. The nature of the injury, loss and damage. If damage to property is involved, that the property belonged to C.

(f) When the damage occurred.

(g) That the loss was caused by D's negligence, and how this happened.

(h) What C is seeking to recover by way of damages.

(i) Anything else that should be stated to make the story clear (see **7.2** above).

7.4.3 What does not need to be stated

You can also work out what does not need to be stated:

(a) That D owed C a duty of care, where this is a legal inference drawn from the facts you have set out.

(b) That the loss is not too remote. It is enough to state what the loss is and how it has been caused. It is for the defence to allege that it is too remote.

(c) That the action is not statute-barred. This is a point for the defence to take.

(d) That C was not contributorily negligent. This is a point for the defence to take.

(e) That C has not failed reasonably to mitigate. This is a point for the defence to take.

7.5 Tort: negligence: basic formula

From the above you can see how practitioners have arrived at the basic formula for a claim for damages for personal injury and/or damage to property in negligence (and related causes of action such as occupier's liability and breach of statutory duty). The formula is:

Stage 1:   the parties and the facts which give rise to the duty

Stage 2:   the accident, the events, or the cause of complaint

Stage 3:   the cause or causes of action

Stage 4:   causation, loss and damage

Stage 5:   the claim for interest

Stage 6:   the remedies sought.

Note that these six stages do *not* necessarily coincide with paragraphs. Sometimes more than one stage can be combined in a single paragraph. Very often several paragraphs may be required to complete one stage.

We shall now look at the content of each stage in a little more detail.

7.5.1   Stage 1: the parties and the facts which give rise to the duty

This may involve stating essential ingredients or it may just be background for the purpose of story-telling. Think in terms of stating who the parties are as individuals and in relationship to each other, what their occupation or status is, and what property they own. Also identify any relevant people, places and things. Be alert to what it is that gives rise to the duty. For example:

(a) If relying on occupier's liability, you will need to state that the defendant was an occupier and the claimant was his visitor.

(b) If relying on a statutory or common law duty owed by an employer to his employees you will need to state that the claimant was employed by the defendant.

(c) If a regulation imposes a duty on building contractors you will need to state that the defendant was a building contractor.

(d) If a regulation applies to anyone doing demolition work you will need to state that the defendant was doing demolition work.

Surprising as it may seem, it is not usually necessary to state that the defendant owed the claimant a duty of care. This can be inferred where the duty arises as a matter of law. There are occasions where it is necessary to do so however, which you will come across in due course, in particular where the duty arises as a matter of fact in the individual case.

If you are going to allege damage to the claimant's property, you must state that he owned that property. Note the significant difference between saying 'the claimant was driving *a* car' and 'the claimant was driving *his* car'. If the claimant's house has been damaged, you will need to state not only that he was the occupier of it (which might be sufficient to establish a duty of care) but that he was the *owner* of it.

Sometimes, where there is nothing of significance to say about the parties or the background, stage 1 can be combined with stage 2. For example, in the case of a collision between two cars on a highway, the only relevant fact about the parties is that they were driving their cars on the same road and collided — that is what gives rise to the duty of care. Deal with the parties and the collision in the same paragraph.

7.5.2   Stage 2: the accident or events

Describe the accident, or whatever it is that has led to the loss and damage, accurately and concisely. Give the date of it. If the accident occurred in a complicated way, or was the culmination of a series of events, it may take several paragraphs to describe it. Do not at this stage make any allegation of negligence, breach of duty, injury, loss or damage. The aim is to draft a paragraph which simply describes events, so that with luck the defendant will admit it.

7.5.3   Stage 3: the cause or causes of action

State that the accident, or the matters complained of, were *caused* by the defendant's negligence or breach of duty. If the duty is statutory, identify the relevant section or regulation. Then give particulars.

Particulars of negligence should be drafted with care; they form the basis of your case and how you frame them may determine whether you win or lose the case. You must set out all the ways in which you allege the defendant was negligent. This can only be done by listing specific acts and omissions, that is all the things which the defendant did which he shouldn't have done or failed to do which he should have done. Your allegations must be reasonable and based on the evidence. You do not have to be sure that every one of your particulars will be established; it is enough that they all have a reasonable prospect of being established on the evidence as it may turn out. Make sure you cover all eventualities. For example, the phrase 'failed to take any *or any adequate* steps' is a common one. It alleges that the defendant either took no steps at all, or if he did, that the steps taken were inadequate.

Your particulars must be as particular as you can make them. Generalised allegations will not do. For example, 'failing to take safety precautions' immediately gives rise to the question 'what safety precautions should have been taken?'. The only exception is that it is not uncommon, as a final particular, to make a generalised allegation summing up the nature of the complaint. But this should only be done by reference to the previous particulars. For example, 'failing, in the ways set out above, to make reasonable provision for the claimant's safety'.

Particulars of any breach of statutory duty must be drafted by reference to the precise words of the statute or regulation. The case can only be established if the defendant has done *exactly* what he is forbidden to do. Conversely, where you are alleging an omission, the defendant will be liable unless he has done *exactly* what he is required to do.

If you are relying on more than one cause of action, the best rule is to use a separate paragraph, and a separate set of particulars, for each new cause of action. The only good exception is where you have two causes of action which can be particularised in the same way, the most common example being negligence and occupier's liability. In some precedent books you will see examples of two causes of action alleged in a single paragraph, with two separate sets of particulars. Provided the particulars are kept separate, this is acceptable, but in the author's view less good, and you will not see it done that way in this Manual. Sometimes you will see precedents where two causes of action are pleaded with only one set of particulars, some of which seem to relate to the allegation of negligence, and others of which relate to a statutory duty, without clear distinction. In the author's view this is bad pleading, and should not be followed.

If you are suing more than one defendant, you should allege the negligence of each defendant in a separate paragraph, with a separate set of particulars. The only exception is where each defendant is alleged to be liable in exactly the same way, but this is rare.

If you are relying on a conviction under s 11 of the Civil Evidence Act 1968, this must be expressly stated by virtue of PD 16, para 8.1. This will be a part of stage 3. For an example, see the particulars of claim in **9.3**.

7.5.4   Stage 4: causation, loss and damage

State that the claimant has suffered injury and/or loss and damage (as the case may be) *as a result of* the accident or the matters complained of. You must then particularise the injury (if any) and the special damage.

Remember PD 16, paras 4.2 and 4.3. The claimant must attach a schedule of past and future expenses and losses, and a copy of any medical report on which he relies.

The particulars of injury should make reference to the medical report. The particulars and the medical report should not contradict each other. It *may* be sufficient to draft particulars of injury simply by reference to the medical report, but this is unusual and may be unwise, since the report may not contain all the facts that need to appear under the particulars of injury. What is required is all the facts to which you would wish the court to have regard in the quantification of the award for pain, suffering and loss of amenity, and facts giving rise to the recovery of other heads of general damage. So it is usual to include at least the following in the body of the claim, in a concise form:

(a) a list of the injuries themselves;

(b) the claimant's date of birth (this is compulsory) and age;

(c) the treatment for the injuries;

(d) the present situation — the degree of recovery, the lasting losses of amenity;

(e) the prognosis;

(f) other relevant facts, eg the claimant's occupation, way of life, promotion prospects, handicap on the labour market, whether the claimant is right- or left-handed.

Particulars of special damages are usually identified simply by reference to the schedule of expense and loss, to avoid repetition. This schedule is a separate document which may nevertheless be drafted at the same time as the particulars of claim. It should set out each item of financial loss, as an itemised list, giving figures as precise as possible. Note that it must contain an estimate of future financial loss as well as loss and expense already incurred. It does not have to produce a fixed total figure for special damages — where loss is continuing this would be impossible. But it should give the figures which would enable a total figure to be calculated on the day of assessment.

If you are making a claim for provisional damages, this must be expressly stated by virtue of CPR, r 16.4(1)(d) and details given in accordance with PD 16, para 4.4. So include a paragraph to this effect at this stage. For an example, see the particulars of claim in **9.2**.

7.5.5 Stage 5: the claim for interest

This must be set out in the body of the claim. In tort it is rare for a claim to be for a specified amount, so there is no need to calculate daily interest. The usual form is simply to claim interest at such rate and for such period as the court thinks fit. State the statutory or other basis for the claim.

7.5.6 Stage 6: the remedies sought

At the end of the particulars of claim it is usual to identify once again the remedy or remedies sought, as an itemised list. This used to be called 'the prayer' and this term is still widely used in practice, though it does not appear anywhere in the CPR. It is arguable that since the remedies sought now appear on the claim form, the prayer is no longer necessary. It is submitted however that it is good practice to include it. It is the final ingredient in the 'story', and it can also be a helpful way of linking a particular remedy to the cause of action which entitles the claimant to it.

7.6 Example

7.6.1 Particulars of claim

IN THE HIGH COURT OF JUSTICE   Claim No 2004 HC 6003
QUEEN'S BENCH DIVISION

BETWEEN

MARJORIE TIMMS   Claimant

and

CATHERINE HOBBS   Defendant

PARTICULARS OF CLAIM

1.   On 6th May 2003 at about 12.15 p.m. the Claimant was crossing the northbound carriageway of Regent Street, London W1 just north of Oxford Circus at the traffic lights. She was walking from west to east on the marked crossing controlled by the pedestrian aspect of the automatic traffic signals which were showing green in her favour when she was struck and thrown to the ground by a Rover 200 motor car registration number JB01 FNB being driven by the Defendant northwards up Regent Street and over Oxford Circus.

2.   This accident was caused by the negligence of the Defendant.

PARTICULARS OF NEGLIGENCE

The Defendant was negligent in that she:

(a) drove too fast in all the circumstances,

(b) failed to stop at the traffic lights although the lights were at red,

(c) failed to give precedence to the Claimant at the crossing,

(d) failed to give any or any sufficient warning of her approach,

(e) failed to keep any or any proper look-out,

(f) failed to stop, slow down, steer or otherwise control her motor car so as to avoid hitting the Claimant.

3.   As a result of the accident the Claimant suffered pain and injury and sustained loss and damage.

PARTICULARS OF INJURY

(a) Shock and severe pain.

(b) Fracture to head of right femur.

(c) Fracture to mid shaft of right tibia and fibula.

(d) Bruising and operation scars to right hip.

The Claimant was born on 10th April 1978 and was 25 years of age at the date of the accident. She was taken by ambulance to the Accident and Emergency Department of the

Middlesex Hospital where she was admitted for treatment. Her fractures were manipulated under general anaesthetic and fixed with wire. The Claimant was able to leave the hospital on 11th May 2003 in a non-weight-bearing plaster. Healing was complicated and the Claimant was admitted on 17th June 2003 to St Thomas's Hospital, London SE1 for treatment of an infection in the hip joint and for physiotherapy. The tibia and fibula fractures have united well. The injury to the femur has not healed satisfactorily and the Claimant is unable to walk distances exceeding half a mile and then only with the use of a walking stick. She is severely limited in her daily activities and had to resign from her job as an environmental health inspector for the Bluebridge Borough Council on 30th April 2004. The Claimant is restricted to sedentary employment. The Claimant's disabilities are permanent. The Claimant is handicapped on the labour market.

Further particulars of the Claimant's injuries are set out in the medical report of Dr Jane Philby served with these Particulars of Claim.

PARTICULARS OF SPECIAL DAMAGE

The special damages claimed by the Claimant are set out in the schedule of past and future expenses and losses served with these Particulars of Claim.

4.   Further the Claimant claims interest under section 35A of the Supreme Court Act 1981 on the amount found to be due to the Claimant at such rate and for such period as the Court thinks fit.

AND the Claimant claims:

(1) Damages.

(2) Interest under section 35A of the Supreme Court Act 1981 to be assessed.

JOSEPH BLOGGS

STATEMENT OF TRUTH

Dated etc.

7.6.2   Schedule of expenses and losses

IN THE HIGH COURT OF JUSTICE   Claim No 2004 HC 6003
QUEEN'S BENCH DIVISION

BETWEEN

MARJORIE TIMMS Claimant

and

CATHERINE HOBBS Defendant

SCHEDULE OF PAST AND FUTURE EXPENSES AND LOSSES

Special damages

(1) Damage to clothing   £165.00

(2) Cost of travel for physiotherapy treatment   £140.00

(3) Cost of holiday booked for August 2003 and cancelled as a result of the Claimant's injuries	£1,400.00
(4) Net loss of earnings as environmental health inspector 6th May 2003 to 30th April 2004 @ £15,000 per annum	£14,794.52
(5) Net loss of earnings as temporary liaison officer for Bluebridge Borough Council from 1st May 2004 to 11th June 2004 @ £4,000 per annum	£460.27
(6) Cost of home help to assist the Claimant in the care of her family and children commencing 1st November 2003 to 11th June 2004 at £50 per week	£1,600.00
	£18,559.54

Future loss

(1) Net loss of earnings as temporary liaison officer from 12th June 2004 until 31st October 2005, when this post will cease	£5,539.73
(2) Continuing loss of earnings from 1st November 2005 at £15,000 a year to age 60; multiplier 22.28	£334,200.00
(3) Continuing cost of home help from 12th June 2004 for 10 years; multiplier 8.86	£23,099.28
	£362,839.01

7.6.3 Commentary

7.6.3.1 Commentary on particulars of claim

Paragraph 1. Stages 1 and 2 are combined. There is nothing of significance to say about either party except that she was involved in the accident, so the parties and the accident can be taken together. The date of the accident is essential: it establishes that the claim has been brought within the limitation period. The time of the accident is not essential, but helpful. The accident is described accurately and concisely. Note that there is no allegation that the defendant was negligent or that the claimant was injured. The line is drawn at the moment of collision. Cars are always identified by make, model and registration number.

This paragraph provides a good illustration of the point made in **4.4.3.5**. If you count them, there are 18 separate allegations in this paragraph, even more if you are pedantic. It would be absurd to put them in a list; it would not even help the defendant to respond to this paragraph, since most of it is almost certain to be admitted. What one might do is make some concession to the guideline, by drafting paragraph 1 like this:

1.1 On 6th May 2003 at about 12.15 p.m. the Claimant was crossing the northbound carriageway of Regent Street, London W1 just north of Oxford Circus at the traffic lights.

1.2 She was walking from west to east on the marked crossing controlled by the pedestrian aspect of the automatic traffic signals.

1.3 The traffic signals were showing green in her favour.

1.4 As the Claimant was crossing Regent Street as described above she was struck and thrown to the ground by a Rover 200 motor car registration mark JB01 FNB being driven by the Defendant northwards up Regent Street and over Oxford Circus.

But it is hard to see that even this slight separation into sub-paragraphs does much to help either side state its case.

Paragraph 2. Stage 3, the cause of the accident. The first short sentence is conventional; it is clear and concise. Use it. There then follow the particulars of negligence. These are invariably set out under a heading, in capital letters, underlined and centred.

There are two common ways of setting out the particulars: one as here, with an introductory phrase 'the defendant was negligent in that she', followed by a series of verbs in the past tense; the other has no introductory phrase, and instead uses present participles — 'driving too fast', 'failing to stop' etc. Each particular should be itemised, using numbers or letters.

How to draft the particulars is explained in **7.5.3**. Remember that every particular must allege an act or omission by the defendant and be justified by the evidence. Nevertheless, some particulars are fairly standard in road accident cases: particulars (a), (e) and (f) here will be found in most claims. Particulars (b), (c) and (d) are tailored to the specific facts of this case.

Note in particular (d) the use of the phrase 'any or any sufficient'. This is very common and is good drafting. It covers more than one eventuality. It is saying that the defendant failed to sound her horn, or if she did, she did not sound it long or loud enough. Without the words 'or any sufficient', if the defendant established that she did sound her horn, the claimant would be unable, without amending the particulars of claim, to argue that the defendant was negligent because she gave only a brief toot, whereas a long blast would have been appropriate.

The same reasoning lies behind the phrase 'any or any proper' in particular (e). Either the defendant did not have her eyes on the road at all (unlikely), or assuming she did, she was not paying proper attention.

You might think that particular (f) is rather generalised, and amounts to little more than an allegation that the defendant was negligent in that she failed to avoid the accident. This criticism is probably justified, but this particular is almost universally used in practice, so you would be wise to follow tradition.

Paragraph 3. Stage 4, injury loss and damage. Again, this paragraph is introduced with a short conventional sentence, which you should use. There then follow two sets of particulars, each headed in the same conventional way as the particulars of negligence. The particulars of injury always come first.

The drafting of particulars of injury is explained in **7.5.4**. This is often the longest part of a personal injury claim, because you need to include every fact you wish the court to take into account in quantifying the general damages. Begin with the list of injuries, taken from the medical report. Shock and pain almost always appear. The claimant's date of birth is required by PD 16, para 4.1. There then follows a lengthy paragraph which covers the treatment given to the claimant ('She was taken by ambulance ... for physiotherapy.'), the present situation and the losses of amenity ('The tibia and fibula fractures ... sedentary employment.'), the prognosis ('These disabilities are permanent.') and other relevant matters ('The Claimant is handicapped on the labour market.'). This last is essential if a claim is to be made under this head. A medical report must accompany the particulars of claim (PD 16, para 4.3), so it makes sense to refer to it at this point.

Particulars of special damage must be set out and proved, but these days it is the almost invariable practice simply to refer to the schedule of expenses and losses which must accompany the particulars of claim (PD 16, para 4.2).

Note that all these particulars are contained within paragraph 3 of the particulars of claim, and are not separate numbered paragraphs.

Paragraph 4. Stage 5, the claim for interest. This is an example of a standard form where interest is claimed on damages of an unspecified amount.

Prayer. By convention the list of remedies sought is introduced by the words 'AND the claimant claims', with word 'AND' in capitals. The remedies are then itemised, even though in a case of this kind there are only ever two.

Joseph Bloggs is the name of the barrister who drafted the statement of case. The original you should sign. Thereafter your signature is represented by your name in capital letters, against the right margin.

The Statement of Truth usually follows at this point, though it may appear in a separate document. For the purposes of drafting, there is no need to set it out in full. The convention is that you simply remind instructing solicitors of the need to add it, and the other formalities, by inserting the words 'Statement of Truth' and 'Dated etc' at the foot of your draft.

7.6.3.2 Commentary on schedule of expenses and losses

This is a separate document, but treat the drafting of it as part of the drafting of the particulars of claim. Every item of loss and expense should be identified and numbered. Set out what the claimant claims (possibly in a best case scenario). Do not mix past and future items of loss together. It is to be hoped that the past losses (the special damages) can be agreed, even if the amount for future loss is not.

The special damages naturally come first. Items (1), (2) and (3) are simply fixed amounts of past loss. Items (4) and (5) are the claimant's past loss of earnings. She was unemployed until 30 April 2004 and so suffered full loss of earnings. From 1 May 2004 she has obtained a temporary 18-month contract at £11,000 net per annum, so her loss is reduced to £4,000 per annum. But this loss lies partly in the future, so it must be split into two items — the amount to date, item (5) under special damages, and the future loss, item (1) under future loss. The cost of the home help similarly has to be divided into two — the amount so far is item (6) under special damages.

The future losses come second. Item (1) is the continuing loss from the temporary post. Item (2) is the claimant's full loss once that post comes to an end. Doubtless the sum claimed will have to be reduced to take account of her earning capacity, but in prospect at the moment is full unemployment until retirement age. Item (3) is the future cost of the home help. Note that where items of loss will be calculated using a multiplier, an appropriate multiplier is suggested. This is not strictly necessary, but since the aim is to estimate future losses, it is good practice. The defendant may of course dispute the multiplier.

7.7 Breach of contract: ingredients

7.7.1 Identify the ingredients

The essential ingredients of a successful claim for damages for breach of contract, leading to full recovery, are:

(a) There was a contract. This involves:
  (i) agreement;
  (ii) a promise;
  (iii) consideration;
  (iv) an intention to create legal relations.
(b) The contract was between the claimant (C) and the defendant (D).
(c) The contract contained the obligation which D is alleged to have breached.
(d) C has performed any obligation which was a precondition to the performance of D's obligation.
(e) The contract subsisted, ie it had not been brought to an end by C's conduct or some other event.
(f) D was in breach of his obligation.
(g) C has suffered loss and damage.
(h) That loss and damage was caused by D's breach of contract.

(i) The loss is of a recoverable kind (eg damages for distress are in most cases not recoverable).

(j) The loss is not too remote, ie it was reasonably within the contemplation of the parties at the time they entered into the contract as a likely consequence of the breach, in the light of their knowledge at the time.

(k) There is no term in the contract which prevents or restricts liability or the recoverability of damages.

(l) The claim is not statute-barred. (The limitation period is six years, or three years if a claim for personal injury is included.)

(m) C has not failed reasonably to mitigate his loss.

7.7.2 What needs to be stated

From this list of ingredients, you can work out what needs to be stated, namely:

(a) Who the parties are, their pre-contractual and contractual relationship.

(b) The contract, including the promise, the consideration, the parties to it and the date of it.

(c) Any term of the contract which D is alleged to have breached, or which entitles C to the relief sought.

(d) That C has performed any obligations required of him under the contract. This *may* be taken as read, but it is a good idea to say what C has done (eg paid the price). It is essential to cover this where the relief sought is specific performance rather than damages.

(e) An allegation that D was in breach of contract.

(f) The date of the breach.

(g) An allegation that C has suffered loss and damage. The nature of the loss and damage. If loss of or damage to property is involved, that the property belonged to C.

(h) That the loss was caused by D's breach.

(i) D's knowledge of any fact by virtue of which the loss was reasonably within his contemplation as a likely result of his breach.

(j) What C is seeking to recover by way of damages.

(k) Anything else that should be set out to make the story clear (see **7.2** above).

7.7.3 What does not need to be stated

You can also work out what does not need to be stated:

(a) That the parties intended to create legal relations. This is an inference to be drawn from the facts you have set out.

(b) That C is not himself in breach of contract and that the contract subsists. This will be an issue for the defence to raise.

(c) That the loss was reasonably within the contemplation of the parties. Providing any prerequisite knowledge has been alleged, this can be inferred from the facts. It is for the defence to allege that any loss is too remote.

(d) That there is no exclusion clause or limitation clause preventing or restricting liability. This is a point for the defence to take.

(e) That the action is not statute-barred. This is a point for the defence to take.

(f) That C has not failed reasonably to mitigate. This is a point for the defence to take.

7.8   Breach of contract: basic formula

From the above you can see how practitioners have arrived at the basic formula for a claim for damages for breach of contract. The formula is:

Stage 1:   the parties and background

Stage 2:   the contract

Stage 3:   the terms

Stage 4:   the defendant's knowledge

Stage 5:   performance of the contract

Stage 6:   the breach

Stage 7:   causation, loss and damage

Stage 8:   the claim for interest

Stage 9:   the remedies sought.

As with tort claims, the stages do not necessarily correspond with paragraphs. Stages 4 and 5 are not invariably necessary and should be omitted if they are not.

We shall now look at the content of each stage in a little more detail.

7.8.1   Stage 1: the parties and background

As in tort claims, this stage is partly a matter of setting out essential ingredients to do with the parties, and partly a matter of story-telling. If either party has a business, or is a company, then you will almost always state what that party's business is. This may be an essential ingredient if you have to establish any of the following, for example:

(a) that a party entered into the contract in the course of his business;

(b) that a party was dealing as a consumer;

(c) that a term should be implied because it is customary;

(d) that a party held himself out as having a particular skill or expertise.

If the terms of a contract are to be inferred from the previous course of dealing between the parties, then you will need to set out concisely the previous dealings. If there have been significant pre-contractual negotiations, then you may need to set these out in order to make the story clear. If the claimant is making a claim for the loss of or damage to his property, then he needs to state his ownership of the property.

It is comparatively rare in breach of contract claims that you will have nothing to say about the parties before going on to stage 2.

7.8.2 Stage 2: the contract

To set out the contract properly, you must state the following:

(a) That there was a contract. *Always* use the word 'contract' or 'agreement'.

(b) The date of the contract, if this can be precisely determined. If not give an approximate date, or give the date of the offer and acceptance.

(c) The parties to the contract, ie that it was made between the claimant and the defendant (if there were other parties too, name them).

(d) If the parties acted through employees or agents in agreeing the contract, say so, and identify the agents. For example, two companies cannot make an oral agreement, so the individuals concerned need to be identified. But make sure you do not allege that the contract was made between the agents, as opposed to the parties!

(e) The form of the contract, ie whether it was written, oral, part written and part oral, or to be implied from a number of circumstances or a series of letters and/or conversations.

(f) If the contract is wholly or partly written, identify the document(s) in which it is contained and state that a copy is attached.

(g) If the contract is wholly oral, state the contractual words used (the gist rather than the actual words will usually do). However this is not invariably done, and is probably unnecessary when there is no dispute as to what was actually agreed. Also state where the contract was made.

(h) The subject matter of the contract, ie what the contract was for, what was promised. You should only copy out the precise *words* of the contract if they are material. Normally you should give a concise description of the *effect* of the contract, which will be quite sufficient if a copy is attached.

(i) The consideration. If this was money, state the amount, if it was determined. If not, state, eg, 'at a price to be determined', or 'for a fee', or 'it was implied that the claimant would pay a reasonable price for the goods'.

(j) Any document which evidences the contract. Even if the contract was not made in writing it may well have been later set down in writing, or there may be documents (eg letters, invoices, delivery notes) which evidence its terms. If so, identify all the documents which you allege must be looked at in order to ascertain the terms of the contract, and state that copies are attached.

7.8.3 Stage 3: the terms

At this stage you should set out any other material terms which have not been covered at stage 2. It is a matter of judgment whether a term is really part of the basic subject matter of the contract (in which case it belongs in stage 2) or whether it is a separate term. A term is material if it is one which you are going to allege the defendant has breached, or if it is a term which entitles you to the remedy you seek. State whether the term is an express or implied term, and then set out its effect. If the term is long or complicated, do not copy it out word for word, but state the effect of it. Do not set out any terms which are not material.

If you are alleging an implied term you should state the basis on which it is to be implied, unless either it is obvious, or it is implied by statute. To state the basis, say that it is to be implied by custom, or to give business efficacy to the agreement and/or 'to be implied from the following facts and matters' and then set them out.

Where you are relying on both express terms and implied terms, the convention is that express terms always come first.

7.8.4   Stage 4: the defendant's knowledge

Where you are relying on the defendant's knowledge of certain facts to show that the loss and damage you are seeking to recover was within his contemplation and so is not too remote, you need to state those facts and allege that he had that knowledge. The material time is at the time of the contract, so it is usual to insert a paragraph at this stage. Actually, applying the strict chronological order rule, it ought perhaps to come before stage 2, and it would not be wrong to put it there, but it may make the story a bit confusing. It is easier to regard stages 2, 3 and 4 as all being chronologically simultaneous.

7.8.5   Stage 5: performance of the contract

It may be that the defendant was only obliged to carry out his obligations under the contract if the claimant had first performed his part of the bargain. For example, the claimant may be obliged first to perform certain work, or give the defendant some required notification, or pay the contract price. Such performance by the claimant may be presumed but it is better to set it out at this stage. You may also want to do some story-telling at this stage, if there have been several events between the contract and the breach of it.

7.8.6   Stage 6: the breach

Breach of contract must be expressly alleged and particularised. Start by alleging that the defendant was in breach of contract and then set out in full what it is that constitutes the breach. It may be an act, or an omission, or a state of affairs, or the fact that some representation was untrue. If you want to allege that the defendant's breach brought the contract to an end, then say so expressly, by using the word 'repudiate'. If the defendant has repudiated the contract, thereby giving the claimant the right to treat the contract as at an end, and the claimant has done so, state that the claimant accepted the repudiation.

Where the breach consists of an act, omission or event, give the date of it.

It may also at this stage be necessary to include any additional facts which entitle the claimant to the relief sought, for example that certain circumstances provided for in the contract have arisen.

7.8.7   Stage 7: causation, loss and damage

As in tort, it is essential to allege causation as well as damage. This may take a considerable amount of explanation. It is by no means always obvious why the breach alleged should have led to the loss claimed. A failure to give this explanation is a very common fault in students' drafts. A typical example might look like this:

6. In breach of the contract the defendant delivered to the claimant the wrong size of widget.

7. As a result of this breach the claimant was forced to cease trading.

The causal connection between the size of the widget and the cessation of trading is not obvious. Even if it is obvious to the *parties*, it is not obvious to the court. Explain it.

You must also give particulars of loss and damage. State the nature of the loss and the basis on which the claimant wants damages to be assessed, set out the financial losses in an itemised list, and quantify each item as far as possible. If a precise figure is claimed, show how that figure is calculated.

7.8.8 Stage 8: the claim for interest

As in tort, this must be set out in the body of the claim. If the claim is for a specified amount, set out the claim for interest on a daily basis (see **6.2.4**).

7.8.9 Stage 9: the remedies sought

As in tort. Where one remedy is alternative to another, make this clear.

7.9 Example

7.9.1 Particulars of claim

IN THE HIGH COURT OF JUSTICE   Claim No 2004 HC 1427
QUEEN'S BENCH DIVISION

BETWEEN

BETTAPRINTA LIMITED	Claimants
and	
MASTERGRAPH MACHINES PLC	Defendants

PARTICULARS OF CLAIM

1.   The Claimants are and were at all material times a company carrying on business as printers and binders. The Defendants at all material times carried on business as manufacturers and sellers of printing machines.

2.   By a contract contained in facsimile transmissions passing between the Claimants and the Defendants on 2nd and 3rd February 2004, the Defendants in the course of their business agreed to manufacture and sell to the Claimants and the Claimants agreed to buy from the Defendants 3 Mastergraph Series 2 printing machines at a price of £20,500 each. The faxes referred to, copies of which are attached, are:

(1) Fax from Claimants to Defendants on 2nd February 2004, time 10.15 a.m.

(2) Fax from Defendants to Claimants on 3rd February 2004, time 11.30 a.m.

(3) Fax from Claimants to Defendants on 3rd February 2004, time 4.25 p.m.

3.   The contract included an express term that the printing machines should be capable of printing at a rate of 250 sheets per minute using A4 size 80 g/m^2 paper.

4.   The contract included an implied term that the printing machines should be of satis-factory quality.

5.   In due performance of the contract, in March 2004 the Defendants delivered to the Claimants 3 printing machines, serial numbers 100785–7 ('the New Machines'), and the Claimants installed the New Machines in replacement of 3 of their existing printing ma-chines, which they scrapped.

6.   In breach of the express and/or the implied term set out above, none of the New Ma-chines was capable of printing at a rate exceeding 120 sheets per minute.

7.   As a result of the matters set out above, the Claimants have suffered loss and damage.

PARTICULARS OF LOSS

Loss of profit

   (a) From March 2004 until 31st August 2004:

(i)	estimated receipts from warranted output		48,173.58
(ii)	actual receipts		23,456.22
			24,717.36

   (b) Continuing from 1st September 2004 at the following annual rate:

(i)	estimated receipts from warranted output		673,592.00
(ii)	estimated actual receipts		274,456.00
			399,136.00

8.   Further the Claimants claim interest under section 35A of the Supreme Court Act 1981 on the amount found to be due to the Claimants at such rate and for such period as the Court thinks fit.

AND the Claimants claim:

   (1) Damages.

   (2) Interest under section 35A of the Supreme Court Act 1981 to be assessed.

JOSEPH BLOGGS

STATEMENT OF TRUTH

Dated etc.

7.9.2 Commentary

Both parties are companies — the claimant has chosen to make them plural. Note that this decision must be carried consistently through the whole statement of case. It is a common fault to find a company made singular in the heading and then becoming plural in the body, or vice versa.

Paragraph 1. Stage 1, the parties. They are introduced briefly by reference to their respective busi-nesses. Note the phrase 'are and were at all material times'. This is widely used for absolute accuracy. To say what the claimants *are* (ie today) is not strictly relevant; it is what they were at the time of the contract and/or breach that is important. On the other hand, to say only that the claimants *were* printers is misleading because it could suggest that they are no longer. So 'are and were at all material times' is the usual phrase, though in simple cases 'are' alone will do. The claimants only allege what the defendants were at all material times — if their business has since changed this is outside the claimants' knowledge and irrelevant.

Paragraph 2. Stage 2, the contract. All the requirements set out in **7.8.2** must be incorporated. It is often thought that this must lead to an inordinately long paragraph, but as you can see, it can be done quite concisely and elegantly. The date of the contract is left open, though by implication it must be either 2 or 3 February 2004. This is probably because the claimants are not sure what exactly as a matter of law was an offer, counter-offer or acceptance, and it does not actually much matter. The contract is alleged to be written, so the documents in which it is contained are identified with absolute precision and attached. The subject matter and the consideration are straightforward and obvious. The words 'sell' (the defendants' promise) and 'buy' (the claimants' promise) both appear, for the sake of precision.

The words 'in the course of their business' are important. As you will have seen, the claimants are relying on breach of an implied term that the machines should be of satisfactory quality. Such a term is implied by s 14(2) of the Sale of Goods Act 1979, but only if the goods were sold in the course of a business. This is therefore an essential ingredient which must be stated.

Paragraphs 3 and 4. Stage 3, the material terms. These are separate issues, so they are set out in two paragraphs. By saying the contract 'included' an express/implied term, you are alleging incorporation, while at the same time making it clear that you do not allege this to be the only express or implied term of the contract.

There is no stage 4 in this statement of case. The recoverability of the losses does not depend on the claimants showing any special knowledge on the part of the defendants.

Paragraph 5. Stage 5, performance of the contract. This is not an essential ingredient in this case, but the story simply does not make sense without it. The claimants can only have suffered loss if the machines print too slowly, which they can only have discovered if they have been delivered and installed. The words 'in due performance of the contract' are important — without them you would not be establishing that the machines that were delivered were those promised by the contract as opposed to some others, and you would have no link between the contract and the alleged breach. An alternative phrase would be 'the Defendants duly delivered'. The serial numbers of the machines is not a crucial piece of information, but it helps to identify the machines in case, for example, they have to be examined by an expert. It is an easy way to show that the machines examined are those in dispute.

The words in brackets ('the New Machines') are very useful. A concise definition has now been provided so that the term 'the New Machines' has a precise meaning. Without it, any future reference to the new machines would have to be along the lines of 'the said printing machines, serial numbers 100785-7'. Even the term 'the said machines' would be ambiguous, because paragraph 5 refers to two sets of printing machines. Always look out for situations where a definition of this kind can help your drafting. It is very common and very good practice. It is the convention that terms defined in this way are given initial capital letters.

Paragraph 6. Stage 6, breach. This paragraph consists of two parts: the allegation of breach and the particulars of breach. The allegation of breach comes first, and the keyword 'breach' must be used. It is generally good practice to identify the actual term or terms which have been breached, though it is sufficient to say merely 'in breach of the contract'. The allegation is then particularised: you must state the facts which, if established, will amount to a breach. Here, it is not some act or omission on the defendant's part, simply a state of affairs that constitutes the breach.

Note that it would be erroneous to state what at first thought might be the simplest thing to say, namely that 'the New Machines were not capable of printing at a rate exceeding 120 sheets per minute'. This would create an ambiguity as to whether each machine had the same problem or the three machines together were too slow. The words 'none of' are essential and it would be sloppy drafting to omit them. This is a good example of the mental discipline required in drafting. Would you have thought of this? If not, you need to train your mind to think to such a level of detail that you would have thought of it.

The compression 'and/or' may seem bad English, but it is widely used in drafting statements of case, because the most concise alternative is 'and further or alternatively' and the plainest alternative is 'in breach of the express and the implied terms, or in breach of either of them'.

Paragraph 7. Stage 7, loss and damage. The first sentence is another concise and simple standard form. It is essential to allege not only that the claimant has suffered loss, but also that this loss is the result of the breach(es). The capitalised, underlined and centred heading appears as usual. The particulars that follow are divided into past and future loss, in each case set out so as to explain by means of a sum, in broad terms, how the loss claimed is calculated. The past loss is specified precisely, and the future loss is claimed as an annual sum. Of course the claimants will not recover this annual loss for an indefinite period, but the claim maximises the amount they seek to recover.

Paragraph 8, Prayer, Formalities. See **7.6.3.1**. There is nothing new in these parts of the statement of case.

7.10   Exercise A

Brian Flanaghan will say:

I was born on 27th March 1931. I was a keen driver and I used to drive everywhere until I had my accident on 18th February 2004. It was in King's Drive, Chester at 10.20 a.m. I was driving along the main road when a car drove out from Brookside Avenue on my left and ran straight into me. It was indicating that it was turning right. I braked when I saw it coming but it was too late. In the accident I twisted my left ankle and had cuts scratches and bruises to my knees, shoulder, face, chest and arms. I was in a terrible state of shock. I had to stay indoors for a fortnight until my daughter managed to coax me out. I don't think I could ever drive again. I get scared as soon as I sit behind the wheel. My car, an Austin Metro reg no D147 PTC was written off after the accident.

Instructing solicitors would add that the driver of the other car (a Peugeot 306 reg no N200 RLF) was Mrs Brenda Dingle who was injured rather more seriously than Mr Flanaghan. Liability is very much in issue: Mrs Dingle alleges that Mr Flanaghan was signalling that he was going to turn left into Brookside Avenue.

Counsel is asked to draft particulars of claim to be filed in the Chester County Court. A medical report is being prepared, as is a schedule of expense and loss.

7.11   Exercise B

Eleanor Moore will say:

I and my partner Steven Phillips run a cleaning firm, 'Dapper Cleaners'. In March 2004 we got the contract to clean the Sunshine Hotel, Reading, Berkshire, an establishment owned by Small Time Hotels Ltd. The contract was arranged at the Hotel on 27 March 2004 between myself and Mr Peter Williams for the company and set out in a letter from the company to us dated 28 March 2004, which I accept is an accurate record of the contract. We agreed that Dapper Cleaners would clean the halls and corridors and public rooms and bedrooms seven days a week at a price of £700 per week. It was a one-year contract, commencing Monday 5 April 2004. We carried out, and were paid for, cleaning for 12 weeks, but on Sunday 27 June 2004 Mr Williams told me that our services were no longer required as he had engaged other cleaners to start on Monday 28 June 2004, and gave me two weeks' money 'in lieu of notice' as he put it. We have been unable to find another contract to replace the Sunshine Hotel contract and are unlikely to be able to do so. We had to lay off two employees, paying them £300 each. We anticipated net profit of £150 per week (£7,800 per annum) on this contract.

Instructing solicitors have been in contact with solicitors acting on behalf of Small Time Hotels Ltd. The company allege that there was a term to the effect that there would be a 12-week trial period and that either side could terminate the contract with notice after that time. They rely on the words in the letter 'all other terms as agreed between the parties'.

That phrase does appear, but Eleanor Moore is adamant that no such term was agreed. This is the first she has heard of it.

Counsel is asked to draft particulars of claim to be filed in the Reading County Court.

7.12   Exercise C

Charles Prendergast will say:

I am the owner and occupier of Mill Cottage, Mill Lane, Bogmarsh, Herefordshire. During most of this year construction has been under way on the M52 motorway which is being built at the top of Bog Peak, a nearby hill, by George Harding (Construction) plc. Mill Cottage is at the end of Mill Lane and right opposite Mill Cottage the lane turns sharp right into an access road which runs straight up the hill to the construction site. The contractors regularly park their lorries overnight on a steep slope at the top of the hill, facing downhill. On 25 June 2004 at 6.00 p.m. my wife and I went out for the evening in my wife's car. When we returned at 11.30 p.m. we found one of the constructors' lorries, registration number T876 BPJ in our front garden. It appeared to have smashed through the front garden wall and collided with my Rover car, registration number CDP 100, which was parked in the driveway. A large double-glazed window of the house had also been smashed by a flying brick from the wall. My neighbour Mr Oliver was in his garden all evening having a barbecue. He says he saw nobody walk past on the way up the hill and when he heard the lorry smash into my wall he and several of his guests went to investigate and saw no signs of anyone running away.

Instructing solicitors would add that according to the police, the tyre marks showed that the lorry had rolled unattended down the access road. They concluded that it had been unsafely parked at the top of the hill and that no crime had been committed. The constructors not surprisingly allege that it was the act of vandals, but have not produced any convincing evidence to this effect. In any event this conflicts with the view of the police investigator and it must therefore be assumed that the lorry ran away of its own accord and that only the constructors are to blame for this damage.

Mr Prendergast's repair costs were: wall £587.85; car £3,026.70 and window £430.50.

Counsel is asked to draft particulars of claim to be filed in the Hereford County Court.

Basic defences in tort and contract

8.1 Rules for defences

In addition to the rules referred to in **4.4**, there are some very important rules relating to defences, which effectively define what should be included in every defence.

8.1.1 The fundamental rule

The fundamental rule is in CPR, r 16.5:

> *(1) In his defence, the defendant must state—*
>
> > *(a) which of the allegations in the particulars of claim he denies;*
> > *(b) which of the allegations he is unable to admit or deny, but which he requires the claimant to prove; and*
> > *(c) which allegations he admits.*
>
> *(2) Where the defendant denies an allegation—*
>
> > *(a) he must state his reasons for doing so; and*
> > *(b) if he intends to put forward a different version of events from that given by the claimant, he must state his own version.*
>
> *(3) A defendant who—*
>
> > *(a) fails to deal with an allegation; but*
> > *(b) has set out in his defence the nature of his case in relation to the issue to which that allegation is relevant, shall be taken to require that allegation to be proved.*
>
> *(4) Where the claim includes a money claim, a defendant shall be taken to require that any allegation relating to the amount of money claimed be proved unless he expressly admits the allegation.*
>
> *(5) Subject to paragraphs (3) and (4), a defendant who fails to deal with an allegation shall be taken to admit that allegation.*

8.1.2 The effect of the fundamental rule

8.1.2.1 Admitting, denying and requiring proof

By CPR, r 16.5(1) every allegation in the particulars of claim must be dealt with individually. There are only three responses a defendant can give: to admit, deny or require the claimant to prove.

You should admit an allegation when your instructions are to the effect that the allegation is true, or the evidence in front of you shows it to be true and there is no evidence to the contrary. You may also admit an allegation when, although you do not know it to be true, you have no desire to make an issue of it.

You should deny an allegation when the matter is within the defendant's knowledge and your instructions are that it is not true and you intend to put forward a positive case to the contrary. When the defendant denies a fact he is saying 'that is not so, and I will produce evidence and/or arguments to show that it is not so'.

The third alternative is to say 'the defendant is unable to admit or deny but requires the claimant to prove'. You should do this in relation to allegations and facts which are outside the defendant's knowledge and against which you have no evidence, but for which you also have no evidence in support. When the defendant requires proof of a fact he is saying 'I cannot show that that is not so, and will not attempt to do so, but I do not admit it and so you must prove it if you wish to rely on it; and I reserve the right to argue that you have failed to prove it'.

Under the old rules, this third alternative was to 'not admit' a fact. The result of this was to require the claimant to prove it, so the new wording has no difference in effect. However, the wording was changed because in the past there was a tendency to not admit a fact not only when the defendant was unable to admit or deny it, but also when he preferred to reserve his position. This was strictly contrary to the rules, but was nevertheless commonly done. The new formula requires the defendant to say expressly that he is 'unable to admit or deny' and sign a statement of truth to this effect. Nevertheless, the phrase 'not admit' is still being used in practice, though it is not recommended in this Manual.

8.1.2.2   Guidance of the Professional Standards Committee

The Professional Standards Committee of the General Council of the Bar has given some guidance as to how counsel should deal with the situation where he is instructed to reserve the client's position by requiring the claimant to prove a fact, even though there is evidence on the issue. The guidance is to the effect that it might well be unethical to require the claimant to prove something when it is possible to admit or deny. Requiring proof is likely to give rise to the inference that the defendant does not have any evidence on the matter. If this turns out not to be the case he is likely to be criticised and incur a costs penalty, and if counsel was aware that there was evidence which undermined the statement that the defendant was unable to admit or deny, he might well be in breach of the Code of Conduct by not stating the case in accordance with the evidence. This guidance reinforces the interpretation of CPR, r 16.5 put forward above.

8.1.2.3   Giving reasons for a denial

CPR, r 16.5(2)(a) was a new rule, and it has had quite a profound effect on defences. It is the alternative to what is known as a 'bare denial'. Actually the bare denial was forbidden under the old rules too, but was still frequently encountered. Good pleading always involved giving reasons for denials (and setting out a different version of events is just one way of doing this). This is now be compulsory in every case. The effect is that defences are now little longer than they were in the past. There is more about giving reasons for denials below in **8.4.1.2**.

8.1.2.4   The consequence of failing to deal with an allegation

The basic rule is strict: if the claimant makes an allegation and the defendant does not respond to it, he will be taken to have admitted it. It follows that allegations must be gone through one by one, and each admitted, denied or required to be proved. There are, however, two exceptions.

The first is that a claimant will always be required to prove an allegation as to the amount of any loss and damage claimed unless the defendant expressly admits it. This makes it possible for the defendant to admit that the claimant has suffered loss without being taken to have admitted the quantum of the claim.

The second is that a defendant who sets out the nature of his case in relation to an issue in such a way as to suggest that he does not admit it, without expressly denying it, will be taken to require the claimant to prove it. This was effectively the position under the old procedure as well, though there was no rule to that effect. The purpose of this is probably twofold: first, to protect the litigant in person who does not know how to draft like a lawyer, and secondly to discourage the use of the 'general traverse'.

In the past it was very common for a defence to end with what was known as a general traverse, which went like this: 'Save as hereinbefore specifically admitted or not admitted the Defendant denies each and every allegation contained in the particulars of claim as if the same were herein set out and traversed seriatim'. Opinions differed as to whether it actually added anything. The purpose was an attempt to protect the defendant's position in case any essential allegation had been left unanswered, but many believed it did not achieve that result. The new rule is effectively trying to say: 'If in doubt, protect your position by setting the defendant's version of events out fully rather than by relying on a technical formula of dubious validity'.

8.1.3 Other rules

CPR, r 16.6 specifically permits a defendant to assert a defence of set-off. See **Chapter 13** for an explanation of this defence.

The defence of tender before claim is governed by CPR, r 37.3, which requires payment into court of the amount tendered, or the defence will not be available. It is therefore necessary to state that the payment-in has been made. For an example of this defence see **10.4**.

Further requirements of defences appear in PD 16:

(a) The defendant must give details of the expiry of any relevant limitation period (para 13.1).

(b) In a personal injury claim the defendant must state in his defence whether he agrees, disputes, or neither agrees nor disputes, but has no knowledge of the matters contained in the claimant's medical report served with the particulars of claim. Where he disputes any part of the medical report, he must give in his defence his reasons for doing so and attach his own medical report if he has one (para 12.1).

(c) In a personal injury claim the defendant must include in or attach to his defence a counter-schedule of expenses and losses, stating which of the claimant's items he agrees, disputes or neither agrees nor disputes, but has no knowledge of. Where he disputes any item, he must supply alternative figures (para 12.2).

8.2 The essence of a defence

The essence of a defence is that it responds to the claimant's story and tells an alternative one. Your fundamental guiding principle when drafting a defence is: **respond to the claimant's story by telling the defendant's story**.

You do this by telling the claimant what you think of his story, and where appropriate telling the same story from the defendant's point of view. The defendant's response goes something like this:

I have read your story and:

1. To A I say 'Yes; but you omit to say that ...'

2. To B I say 'Not exactly; rather ...'

3. To C I say 'No; on the contrary ...'

4. To D I say 'Maybe so; so what?'

5. And anyway what also happened was ...

6. So you are not entitled to what you want.

Or even, on occasions, like this:

I have read your story and:

1. It's a load of rubbish.

2. What really happened was this ...

3. So get lost.

The defendant's story, or the story from the defendant's point of view, must emerge clearly from your response to the claimant's story. It is even easier to lose sight of the story you are trying to tell when drafting a defence than it is when drafting particulars of claim.
   This is because the defence serves two functions:

- to respond to the claim;
- to state the defendant's case.

It is the first of these that can make you lose sight of the story and it is the second of these that students often overlook.

8.3 The structure of a defence

Surprising as it may seem at first, the two functions mentioned above are *not* taken separately when drafting a defence. You do not work through the particulars of claim responding to every allegation with an admission, denial or requirement or proof and only then set out the facts and matters on which the defendant relies. The two functions are in fact inseparable and are performed more or less simultaneously.

8.3.1 Step 1: analyse the particulars of claim

What you have to do first of all in planning your defence is to analyse the particulars of claim into its component stages and issues. Identify which paragraphs belong to each stage of the formula set out in **7.5** or **7.8** (or in a less standard case work out the formula that has been applied) and identify what issue is being dealt with in each paragraph. It may help to give each paragraph a label. You can then understand the structure of the particulars of claim. Your aim is to draft your defence using the same basic structure, taking each issue in the same order.

So, if for example, the basic structure of the particulars of claim is (a) the accident, (b) the cause of action and (c) the damage, an appropriate structure for the defence might be:

(a) Deal with the claimant's description of the accident.

(b) Raise further facts about the accident.

    (c) Deny the cause of action.

    (d) Allege what the defendant says caused the accident.

    (e) Require the claimant to prove the alleged loss and damage.

    (f) Allege remoteness and/or failure to mitigate.

Or, if the basic structure of the particulars of claim is (a) the contract and its terms, (b) the breach and (c) the loss, an appropriate structure for the defence might be:

    (a) Deal with the claimant's description of the contract and its terms.

    (b) Allege any further terms on which the defendant relies.

    (c) Deny breach.

    (d) Raise a specific defence (eg reliance on an exclusion clause).

    (e) Deal with the claimant's allegations of loss.

    (f) Deny causation in any event.

8.3.2 Step 2: structure your defence

Think next of what you need to say in your defence. Everything that constitutes a total or partial defence is something which in effect 'knocks out' one or more of the essential ingredients of the claimant's claim (see **7.4.1** and **7.7.1**). The defendant only has to knock out one of them and the claimant's claim cannot as a matter of law fully succeed. You must be aware which of these ingredients each point you are making in the defence is aiming to knock out. You then look for the paragraph in the particulars of claim which seeks to establish that ingredient, and note the point of the defence that must be set out in relation to it. If what you want to say relates to something that is not mentioned in the particulars of claim, then look through the stages to find where that issue would have come if it had been included, and slot your point in at the appropriate stage.

The result of this process will be that you have a list of stages and issues in the sequence in which they appear in the particulars of claim, together with a list of points that need to be made in the defence in the same sequence, each related to a stage or paragraph in the particulars of claim. If it helps, you can tabulate this on paper.

Here is an example for the defence in **8.5**, which is a response to the claim in **7.6**.

Stage	Particulars of claim		Defence	
1. Parties	Paragraph 1	Parties and accident	Paragraph 1	Admit accident, deny green light
2. Accident				
3. Cause	Paragraph 2	Negligence	Paragraph 2	Deny negligence and causation Give reasons
			Paragraph 3	Brake failure
			Paragraph 4	Garage's negligence
			Paragraph 5	Contributory negligence
4. Damage	Paragraph 3	Injury, loss and damage	Paragraph 6	Require proof of injury, loss and damage
			Paragraph 7	Response to medical report
5. Interest	Paragraph 4	Interest		—
6. Remedies		Remedies		—

Here is another example, this time in a contract case: the particulars of claim are in **9.7** and the defence in **10.3**.

Stage	Particulars of claim		Defence	
1. Parties	Paragraph 1	Parties	Paragraph 1	Admit parties and contract
2. Contract	Paragraph 2	Contract and performance		
3. Terms	Paragraph 3	Implied term	Paragraph 2	Express term — limitation clause
			Paragraph 3	Admit implied term
4. Story	Paragraph 4	Accident	Paragraph 4	Require proof of accident
5. Breach	Paragraph 5	Negligence	Paragraph 5	Deny breach and negligence Give reasons
6. Damage	Paragraph 6	Loss and damage	Paragraph 6	Deal with loss and damage and causation
			Paragraph 7	Remoteness
			Paragraph 8	Rely on limitation clause
7. Interest	Paragraph 7	Interest		—
8. Remedies		Remedies		—

You will see that in each of these examples the defence follows the same basic formula as the claim, and deals with the issues in the same order. Every paragraph in the claim has a paragraph in the defence which corresponds to it, but their numbers do not necessarily coincide. Nevertheless, it would be possible to place the claim and the defence side by side in two columns and with suitable spacing ensure that every point raised in the defence appeared opposite its corresponding point in the claim. No rearrangement of paragraphs would be needed. This is in essence what a judge needs to be able to do when reading the statements of case for the first time, and that is why it is so important that they both follow the same structure.

8.4 Drafting the defence

Once you have worked out the correct structure for your defence, you can think more closely about what exactly you want to say. You need to take each stage and each paragraph of the particulars of claim in turn, and decide what exactly you are going to say in response to the claimant's case, and what new facts and matters relating to that issue you are going to set out.

8.4.1 Responding to the claim

8.4.1.1 Unpacking allegations

Every allegation made in the particulars of claim must be admitted or denied or the claimant must be required to prove it. You are presumed to admit anything you do not deal with, so you must do this with care. Exactly what is to be admitted or denied is of course derived from your instructions. You cannot decide what would be most helpful to your client and draft accordingly. You cannot concoct a defence. You must admit any facts that appear from your instructions to be correct, even if this weakens your case. You should not deny a fact when you can produce no evidence to counter it.

It is important to break down even the most simple allegations into their component parts if you are to be sure you do not miss anything. Suppose, for example, the claimant has alleged that 'the defendant threw a lump of concrete through the sun-roof of the claimant's car'. The defendant's defence is that he accidentally dislodged a tile from the roof of his house, which fell through the open sun-roof of the car. The allegation must be denied, but not in its entirety. There are eight separate allegations contained within it, namely that:

(a) the *defendant* (as opposed to anyone else) did it;

(b) the defendant *threw* the lump of concrete;

(c) it was a *lump* of concrete that was thrown;

(d) the lump was made of *concrete*;

(e) the lump of concrete went *through* the sun-roof (ie it ended up inside the car);

(f) it entered through the *sun-roof* (as opposed to a window);

(g) what it entered was a *car*;

(h) the car belonged to the *claimant*.

There is also an ambiguity as to whether the sun-roof was open or shut at the time.

If you simply deny the allegation, you will have denied all of the above, which it is not appropriate to do. You must target your denial at the allegations 'threw' and 'lump of concrete'. You also want to avoid perpetuating the ambiguity. So you would say something like this: 'The defendant accidentally dislodged a roof-tile, which fell through the open sun-roof of the claimant's car. Otherwise, [the allegation] is denied.'

8.4.1.2   The problem with bare denials

Here is another example. The claimant and defendant are neighbouring house-owners, who share a common driveway, with an invisible boundary running down the middle of it. The claimant alleges that the defendant frequently parks her car on his side of the drive-way, and makes a claim for trespass. The particulars of claim contains the following paragraph:

'3.   On 1st May 2004 the defendant parked her car on the claimant's driveway.'

There are seven (or even eight) allegations here:

(a) the trespass occurred on *that date;*

(b) it was the *defendant* (as opposed to anyone else) who parked;

(c) what she did was to *park* her car (as opposed to drive it);

(d) the thing she parked was a *car;*

(e) the car belonged to the *defendant;*

(f) it was parked on a *driveway* (as opposed to the road);

(g) that driveway belonged to the *claimant.*

A purist or a philosopher might even add an eighth:

(h) it was *on* (as opposed to over, under or beside) the driveway.

Let us consider various possible defences:

(1)   The defendant took her car to the garage for service, but was too busy to collect it. The garage therefore agreed to deliver it back to her. They mistakenly parked it on the wrong side of the driveway. In this case the allegation denied is (b) and the defence would perhaps read:

'Except that the car was parked by Moonlight Motors Ltd and not by the defendant, paragraph 3 is admitted.'

(2)   The defendant was reversing out of her side of the driveway, which involved briefly crossing onto the claimant's side (over which she has a right of way), when her engine seized and she was unable to move the car. In this case the allegation denied is (c) and the defence would perhaps read:

'Paragraph 3 is denied. The engine of the defendant's car unexpectedly seized and she had no alternative but to abandon it temporarily on the claimant's driveway.

(3)   The real dispute here is not actually about trespass at all — it is a boundary dispute, and both parties claim that the part of the driveway where the defendant parked her car is on their property. In this case the allegation denied is (g) and the defence would perhaps read:

'Paragraph 3 is denied. The car was parked on the defendant's driveway. The position of the car is marked on the plan attached.'

(4)   The defendant had a lot of visitors and her side of the driveway was full of cars, so she had no room to park her own. She therefore knocked on the claimant's door and asked the claimant's wife for permission to park on the claimant's side of the driveway just for one afternoon. The claimant's wife gave her that permission. In this case, no part of paragraph 3 is denied at all (or rather, it is the implicit allegation that the defendant parked 'wrongfully' which is denied). So the defendant needs to plead a new fact, and the defence might perhaps read:

'Paragraph 3 is admitted. The defendant parked her car with the express permission of the claimant's wife.'

In all cases a bare denial would be far too broad, and would not state the defendant's case accurately.

But sometimes the bare denial is wrong not because it denies too much, but because it denies too little. Let us take two classic examples:

(a)   Allegation: 'The claimant paid the defendant £500 on 27th July'. Bare denial: 'It is denied that the claimant paid the defendant £500 on 27th July'. This is wrong because it only denies that the claimant paid the defendant £500 (as opposed to any other sum of money) on 27th July (as opposed to any other date). The correct response is: 'It is denied that the claimant paid the defendant £500 or any sum on the date alleged or at all'.

(b)   Allegation: 'The accident was caused by the negligence of the defendant'. Bare denial: 'It is denied that the accident was caused by the negligence of the defendant'. This is absolutely disastrous — all that has been denied is causation, not negligence, which is thereby deemed to be admitted. The correct response is: 'It is denied that the defendant was negligent or that the accident was caused by any negligence on his part'.

Always look at the allegations in the claim with care, and make sure you have dealt with every part of them. Where it is alleged that something has been caused, you need to deal both with the causation and the outcome. Where an allegation of loss has been quantified, you need to deal not only with the fact of loss, but the amount or extent of it also (though if you do not, you will be taken to require the claimant to prove it, rather than to admit it).

8.4.1.3   Giving reasons for denials

Good statements of case have always been inclined to give reasons for denials and put forward the facts on which the defendant relies, even under the old rules, so to many practitioners the need to give reasons for denials was neither new nor strange. However, to comply with the rule we need to go a bit further than we did in the past. Denials of simple factual allegations as to events, statements, actions etc can readily be explained: it is largely a matter of setting out the defendant's alternative version. This is part of the defendant's positive case. But denials of allegations like negligence cause more problems.

It is not sufficient simply to respond with the standard formula: 'It is denied that the defendant was negligent as alleged or at all'. One may still start with that formula, but it is necessary to go on to look at the particulars of negligence, and decide what more detailed reasons for the overall denial can be given. It may be that a lot of the reasons will in fact have already been stated in earlier paragraphs, in which case it will probably be unnecessary to repeat them. For example, by setting out an alternative version of how the accident occurred, the claimant will have done a lot already to say why he was not negligent. But it is likely that some further explanation for the denial will need to be given, and what you draft will need to cover all the particulars of negligence.

This probably does not mean that you must deal with each particular of negligence in an individual sub-paragraph, though of course you may do it that way. It will normally be perfectly possible to explain why the defendant was not negligent by setting out positive facts and conflating the answer to several different particulars into one.

What the rule might seem to do is to require some rather pointless reasons to be given. If the allegation is 'the defendant was negligent in that he did not keep a proper lookout', is it really necessary to add, after denying the allegation, that it is denied because the defendant *did* keep a proper lookout? Or if you write 'it is denied that the defendant was drunk', do you really have to add 'the defendant was sober'? The solution to this potential absurdity is actually to leave out the specific denial and then simply set out the positive allegation. For example: 'It is denied that the defendant was negligent as alleged or at all. At the time of the accident he was sober and was keeping a careful lookout.'

If the particular allegation of negligence contains a fact which the defendant disputes, it must be denied in such a way as to make it clear that that fact is disputed. For example, a particular of negligence to the effect that the defendant failed to heed a warning given by the claimant may be denied for three different reasons: because no warning was given; because the defendant did not fail to heed it; or because the circumstances were such that there was no reason to heed it. A defence that does not make it clear which of these three is alleged has failed to give reasons for the denial.

All three Court Guides contain a guideline to the effect that the denial should be stated first and then the reasons listed one by one in separate numbered sub-paragraphs. It is submitted that this guideline should not be taken as being of universal application. Although it makes sense to deny first and then give reasons, it is by no means always easy to list the reasons in an itemised way. In many cases the reasons are inherent in facts stated elsewhere in the defence. Often the reasons are inextricably linked to each other and cannot be separated like this. A pedantic list of reasons could easily make the defence unnecessarily wordy and clumsy. It is suggested that this guideline should only be followed where it is helpful to do so.

8.4.1.4 Requiring the claimant to prove an allegation

In the past the formula was 'not admitted'. This was rather shorter and more convenient than the new formula 'the claimant is unable to admit or deny but requires the claimant to prove', which if adopted religiously leads to some very clumsy and wordy drafting. Some practitioners seek to continue with the old phrase and state that allegations are not admitted, and some judges allow this. But they will not do so if they feel it is an excuse for not putting the defendant's cards on the table. The suggestion adopted in this Manual is to use the phrase 'require the claimant to prove' as the norm, only adding 'unable to admit or deny' where the circumstances seem to demand it. The old phrase 'the claimant is put to strict proof' ought logically to disappear in time.

8.4.1.5 Responding to allegations of injury and loss

In the past the usual formula was simply to make no admission that the claimant had suffered loss as alleged or at all. This was often ridiculous. The defendant was well aware that the claimant had been injured and/or had suffered loss. What was really in issue was the extent of the injury and the loss, and maybe the causation of the loss.

Under the CPR the defendant is required to state which matters in the claimant's medical report are agreed and which are disputed. In parallel with this he should be similarly precise with regard to the particulars of injury. So the defence cannot simply require the claimant to prove the nature and extent of his injury. Only those matters about which there is a genuine dispute will remain in issue. But this is likely to lengthen the defence in many instances, especially where there are conflicting medical reports. The rule says that the areas of agreement and dispute must be set out in the *defence*, not just in another medical report. But if the areas of dispute are numerous, it would be wise to use a schedule.

Under the new regime the claimant is encouraged to provide the defendant with full particulars of his loss and the evidence to substantiate it before bringing a claim, so it is likely to be much more common for a defendant to admit loss, and maybe even the amount of it, subject to liability. In personal injury cases, the schedule and counter-schedule of loss and expense will clarify the precise areas of dispute.

8.4.1.6 Parts of the claim requiring no response

Two stages of the particulars of claim do *not* need to be answered: the claim for interest and the statement of remedies sought. You may dispute the claimant's right to recover interest, but you cannot deny that he is claiming it. Similarly, what appears in the list of remedies is simply the claimant's claim. You should make no mention of it in the defence.

8.4.1.7 Reference to paragraph numbers

Sometimes you will see that allegations are dealt with simply by reference to a paragraph number, for example: 'paragraph 1 of the particulars of claim is admitted', or 'otherwise, paragraph 2 is denied'. This is fine where the facts dealt with in this way are relatively straightforward or have been largely dealt with in another part of the defence. But it is not a good idea to deal with significant or complex facts, or fundamental allegations in this way. For example, always deny negligence or breach of contract expressly: do not just say 'paragraph 6 is denied'.

It is, however, a good idea to draft each paragraph of the defence in such a way that it is clear which paragraph of the claim is being responded to, so frequent reference to paragraphs of the claim is helpful.

8.4.2 Setting out the defendant's case

As we have seen, in parallel with responding to the claimant's claim, you are also putting the defendant's case. This involves stating new facts, either as an alternative or as an addition to the facts set out in the claim. There is no particular way in which you do this. Remember to take only one issue at a time.

Where you are setting out facts which are alternative to those alleged by the claimant, you have a choice to make whether to deal first with the claimant's case and then state the defendant's alternative, or whether to set out the defendant's case first and then deal with the claimant's version. Either may be appropriate. It depends which would be clearer or easier to draft. If you take the first approach, you will probably say something like: 'Paragraph 3 is denied. The defendant, on 1st June ...' etc. If you take the second approach, you will set out the facts as the defendant would have them and then conclude: 'Otherwise paragraph 3 is denied'.

Where you are stating facts which are only partly alternative to the claimant's case, so that you want to admit some and deny some of what the claimant has alleged, there are two possible approaches. You can either adopt the second approach above, or use the very common formula: 'Except that it is denied that ..., paragraph 3 is admitted'; or: 'Except that it is admitted that ..., and the claimant is required to prove that ..., paragraph 3 is denied'. If using this formula, take care not to fall into a very common trap, which is to leave out 'it is denied that' after 'Except that'. For example: 'Except that the defendant was drunk, paragraph 3 is admitted'. The writer presumably meant to deny that the defendant was drunk, but has managed to allege that he was. The correct approach is either: 'Except that it is denied that the defendant was drunk, paragraph 3 is admitted' or 'Except for the allegation that the defendant was drunk, which is denied, paragraph 3 is admitted'.

When you are stating new facts which are simply additional to what has gone before, then you set them out in much the same way as you would in the particulars of claim. If they constitute a new line of defence, you should make it clear whether this new line of defence is consistent with a previous line either by introducing it with the word 'Further' (to show that it is) or 'Alternatively' (to show that it is not). If, as is most usual, the new line of defence is consistent with your previous line, but you want it to stand as an alternative if the first line fails, you begin with the words 'Further or alternatively'.

Sometimes you find yourself seeking to establish a defence which you will only need to rely on if the claimant succeeds in establishing something you have denied. To raise it may therefore seem inconsistent with your previous defence. It looks contradictory, for example, to say in one paragraph that the defendant was not in breach of contract, and in the next that the defendant's breach did not cause the loss. The way around this difficulty is to use the common and useful phrase 'If, which is denied, ...' etc.

8.5   Example defence: tort

8.5.1   Defence

(See particulars of claim in **7.5**.)

IN THE HIGH COURT OF JUSTICE   Claim No 2004 HC 6003
QUEEN'S BENCH DIVISION

BETWEEN

	MARJORIE TIMMS	Claimant
	and	
	CATHERINE HOBBS	Defendant/Part 20 Claimant
	and	
	DALY'S AUTOS LIMITED	Part 20 Defendant

DEFENCE

1.   Except that it is denied that the pedestrian aspect of the automatic traffic signals was showing in the Claimant's favour when she was walking on the crossing, paragraph 1 of the Particulars of Claim is admitted.

2.   It is denied that the Defendant was negligent as alleged in paragraph 2 of the Particulars of Claim or at all. It is further denied that the accident was caused by any negligence on the part of the Defendant. The Defendant was driving at a safe speed and keeping a proper lookout. Since the traffic lights were in her favour, she had no obligation to give precedence to the Claimant or warn her of her approach.

3.   The accident was caused or contributed to by the failure of the brakes on the Defendant's car. The brakes did not respond properly or at all when the Defendant applied them and she was unable to stop her car and avoid striking the Claimant.

4.   The failure of the brakes, and accordingly the accident, were caused by the negligence of the Part 20 Defendant, which operates a garage where the Defendant's car was serviced on 3rd May 2003.

PARTICULARS OF NEGLIGENCE

(a) Failing properly to tighten a joint in the brake hydraulic system which they fitted to the Defendant's car, so allowing brake fluid to leak from the system.

(b) Failing to carry out repairs and service to the Defendant's car in a safe and workman-like manner.

(c) Allowing the Defendant to drive her car away when it was not safe or roadworthy.

(d) Failing to warn the Defendant that the brakes on her car were or might be or might become defective.

5.   Further or alternatively the accident was caused or contributed to by the negligence of the Claimant.

<u>PARTICULARS OF NEGLIGENCE</u>

(a) Crossing the road when the pedestrian aspect of the traffic signal showed red.

(b) Failing to look to see if it was safe to step on to the crossing before doing so.

(c) Failing to observe or heed the Defendant's car.

(d) Failing to stop, step aside or take any other action to avoid being struck by the Defendant's car.

6.   Except as set out in paragraph 7 below, and in the counter-schedule of loss and expense served with this Defence, the Claimant is required to prove the extent of her injuries and of any loss and damage claimed.

7.   *[Deal with matters set out in Claimant's medical report, stating which are agreed, which are disputed, and which are matters the Defendant has no knowledge of.]*

BESS TOFFER

<u>STATEMENT OF TRUTH</u>

Dated etc.

See also the Part 20 claim in **15.5**.

8.5.2   Counter-schedule

<u>IN THE HIGH COURT OF JUSTICE</u>   Claim No 2004 HC 6003
<u>QUEEN'S BENCH DIVISION</u>

BETWEEN

MARJORIE TIMMS   <u>Claimant</u>

and

CATHERINE HOBBS   <u>Defendant/Part 20 Claimant</u>

and

DALY'S AUTOS LIMITED   <u>Part 20 Defendant</u>

DEFENDANT'S COUNTER-SCHEDULE OF
PAST AND FUTURE EXPENSES AND LOSSES

<u>Special damages</u>

Items (1), (2) and (3): agreed, subject to the Claimant proving the amounts claimed.

Items (4) and (5): agreed, both as to loss and amount.

Item (6): the Claimant is required to prove her need for home help and the amount claimed.

<u>Future loss</u>

Item (1): agreed, both as to loss and amount.

Item (2): disputed. The claim is based on the assumption that the Claimant will gain no further employment after 31st October 2005 which is denied. The Claimant's earning capacity must be taken into account.

The Defendant contends that the Claimant's earning capacity has been reduced by no more than £1,000 per annum and that an appropriate multiplier would be 15.78: total £15,780.

Item (3): the Claimant is required to prove her need for home help, the likely duration of that need, and the amount claimed.

8.5.3   Commentary

8.5.3.1   Commentary on defence

Heading. Note the addition of Daly's Autos Limited as Part 20 defendant. A Part 20 claim should be filed before or at the same time as the defence is filed, or else permission is required. So by the time this defence is filed, Daly's Autos Limited has become a party, and so they appear in the heading of all statements of case from now on. But see **15.4**.

Paragraph 1. Deals with stages 1 and 2 and paragraph 1 of the claim. Basically the defendant admits the accident, except that she disputes one matter: she says the traffic lights were green in her favour, so the pedestrian light cannot have been in the claimant's favour. Note the importance of the words 'it is denied that'. A common error made by students is to omit these words, so that the paragraph begins 'Except that the pedestrian aspect ... was showing in the claimant's favour' thus asserting the opposite of what is meant.

Paragraph 2. Deals with stage 3 and paragraph 2 of the claim. The first two sentences are in standard form, and deny negligence and causation. Both negligence and causation are alleged in paragraph 2 of the claim and *both* must be denied. Note the phrase 'as alleged or at all'. This is the usual way of denying negligence. If you simply said 'it is denied that the defendant was negligent' you would be denying the basic allegation, but not the more detailed particulars of negligence. If you added just 'as alleged', there would be a clear suggestion that you were *only* denying negligence in the particulars alleged, and were tacitly conceding that you might have been negligent in some other way. The additional words 'or at all' prevent this construction.

Then reasons for the denial must be given. These reasons must directly or obliquely respond to all the particulars of negligence, and can only be drafted by reference to those particulars. However, it is not necessary to have sub-paragraphs (a) to (f), corresponding to particulars (a) to (f). This would be unnecessarily clumsy and lengthy. 'The Defendant was driving at a safe speed and keeping a proper look out' gives reasons for the denial of particulars (a) and (e); 'Since the traffic lights were in her favour' gives a reason for denying particular (b); 'she had no obligation to give precedence to the Claimant' gives a reason for denying particular (c); and 'or warn her of her approach' gives a reason for denying particular (d). Particular (f) is itself generalised and so its denial is effectively explained by the reasons already given.

The claim now goes on to stage 4, loss and damage, but the defendant has a great deal more to say in relation to stage 3: paragraphs 3, 4 and 5 of the defence are all still part of stage 3.

Paragraph 3. Having denied that the accident was caused by her negligence, the defendant must now go on to say what else *did* cause it. There are two allegations to make: the first is the negligence of the garage, but before that can be alleged, it is necessary to state the more immediate cause of the accident, namely the failure of the brakes. This is done in paragraph 4, not just baldly stated (the first sentence), but with some explanation added (the second sentence) so as to state the defendant's case fully. Note the words 'caused or contributed to'. These are very common and cover two eventualities: that the failure of the brakes was either the sole cause or a partial cause of the accident.

Paragraph 4. Once the failure of the brakes has been alleged, the fact that this was the result of the garage's negligence can be alleged. This is the first mention of the Part 20 defendant, so it is necessary to introduce them by saying how they are involved: 'which operates a garage where the Defendant's car was serviced'. The date of the service is included because it is significant: it was only three days before the accident. (Had it been three weeks before, it would be a lot harder to pin the blame on the garage.)

Once the allegation has been made, it must be particularised. This is so, even though it is not an allegation made against the claimant. These particulars could only be drafted by reference to an expert report, and it must be assumed that the expert will justify all these allegations. Note the three eventualities incorporated into particular (d). You should be getting used to this technique by now.

Paragraph 5. The second alternative cause of the accident is that it was the claimant's own fault. This would provide a complete defence. Alternatively there was some contributory negligence, which will go to reduce the damages payable. These two lines of defence can be merged with that useful phrase 'caused or contributed to'. The words 'Further or alternatively' which introduce the paragraph are another very common phrase. They make it clear that the defence case is that the accident was caused either by the garage's negligence, or by the claimant's negligence, or by the negligence of both of them.

The allegation of negligence must of course be particularised, and suitable particulars are not difficult to come up with on the facts of this case. Yet again, note the two eventualities covered by 'observe or heed' in particular (c). Either the claimant did not see the defendant's car, or if she did, she didn't pay attention to it. One or other is probably the case, but we do not know which. Particular (d) is generalised, but makes the useful point that maybe the claimant could have got out of the way.

Paragraphs 6 and 7. Only now, once the defendant has completed stage 3, can she come on to stage 4, the injury loss and damage. There are four allegations made by the claimant to be dealt with: the fact of injury, the extent of the injury, the fact of loss and the extent of the loss. It would be daft not to admit the fact of injury, and it is probable that the defendant admits at least some loss, but it is unlikely that the extent of the injury and loss can be admitted in full. The defendant is required by PD 16, para 12.1 to say which matters in the medical report she agrees, disputes and has no knowledge of, and this is covered in paragraph 7 (which is not set out here). She is also required by PD 16, para 12.2 to serve a counter-schedule of expense and loss, saying which items of loss she agrees, disputes and has no knowledge of. This is referred to in paragraph 6 (but not set out here). The effect of paragraph 6 is then to say that except for the matters which are agreed and disputed, the claimant is required to prove the extent of her injury and loss.

Stages 5 and 6. Note that no response is required to paragraph 4 of the claim or the prayer — see **8.4.1.5.**

The defence is rounded off in the same way as the particulars of claim: with counsel's name, the statement of truth and the formalities.

8.5.3.2   Commentary on counter-schedule

It is necessary to make clear which items are agreed, which are disputed, and which the claimant must prove. It is important also to distinguish whether dispute or agreement is related to the nature of the loss claimed, or merely the quantum of it.

Structure the counter-schedule so that it can be read item by item in conjunction with the claimant's schedule. So make sure you maintain the division into special damages and future loss, and take each item in the same order.

Special damages. The Defendant does not dispute the claimant's right to recover damages for clothing, travel for physiotherapy or the lost holiday, but requires proof of the amounts. The claim for past loss of earnings is fully agreed — doubtless evidence of the relevant figures has already been supplied. The defendant does not take it for granted that the claimant is in need of home help: she requires her to prove this need, and the amount claimed.

Future loss. The current continuing loss of earnings is agreed, for the same reason as above. The bulk of the future loss of earnings obviously cannot be agreed, however — the claim assumes almost 35 years of total unemployment, which is obviously most unlikely. The defendant establishes that there is a dispute, gives the reason for it, and puts forward an alternative quantum. The claim for future home help is challenged on the same ground as the special damages claim.

8.6   Example defence: contract

8.6.1   Defence

(See particulars of claim in **7.9**.)

<u>IN THE HIGH COURT OF JUSTICE</u>   Claim No 2004 HC 1427
<u>QUEEN'S BENCH DIVISION</u>

BETWEEN

BETTAPRINTA LIMITED   <u>Claimants</u>

and

MASTERGRAPH MACHINES PLC   <u>Defendants</u>

DEFENCE

1.   Paragraph 1 of the Particulars of Claim is admitted.

2.   Except that the contract was made orally in a telephone conversation between Alan Watkins on behalf of the Claimants and Geraldine Patterson on behalf of the Defendants on 3rd February 2004 and was partly evidenced by but not wholly contained in the faxes referred to, paragraph 2 of the Particulars of Claim is admitted.

3.   Paragraph 3 of the Particulars of Claim is denied. It was expressly stated by Geraldine Patterson to Alan Watkins during that telephone conversation that there was a typographical error in a fax sent by the Defendants to the Claimants on 2nd February 2004 (by which the figure 250 appeared instead of the correct figure 150) and that the printing machines were capable of printing at a rate of 150 but not 250 sheets per minute when using Mastergraph Superspeed Ink.

4.   Paragraph 4 of the Particulars of Claim is admitted.

5.   It is admitted that the Defendants delivered the New Machines to the Claimants between 16th and 20th March 2004 in due performance of the contract. Otherwise the Claimant is required to prove the matters stated in paragraph 5 of the Particulars of Claim.

6.   It is denied that the Defendants are in breach of the alleged or any terms of the contract. It is further denied that none of the New Machines is capable of printing at a rate exceeding 120 sheets per minute. Each of the New Machines is capable of printing at a rate of 150 sheets per minute using Mastergraph Superspeed Ink.

7.   The Claimants are required to prove that they have suffered the alleged or any loss and damage, and it is denied that any loss and damage suffered by the Claimants was caused by the matters complained of. If, which the Claimants are required to prove, none of the New Machines is printing at a rate above 120 sheets per minute, this is the result of the Claimants' failure to use Mastergraph Superspeed Ink.

8.   Further or alternatively, if, which is denied, the Claimants have suffered loss as a result of the matters complained of, they failed to take reasonable steps to mitigate such loss by:

   (a) using Mastergraph Superspeed Ink; and/or

(b) purchasing or leasing and installing printing machines which were capable of printing at the rate desired by the Claimants.

BESS TOFFER

STATEMENT OF TRUTH

Dated etc.

8.6.2 Commentary

The heading matches that of the particulars of claim precisely, except for the title of the statement of case. Thereafter the structure follows that of the claim very closely: paragraphs 1–7 correspond to paragraphs 1–7 of the claim. This is simply the nature of the case; as we have seen, it is not always that way.

Paragraph 1. There is no dispute as to who the parties are. There rarely is, unless the claimant has said something controversial.

Paragraph 2. The contract. The defendants cannot admit that the contract was written, because one of the faxes alleged to contain it incorporates the misprint that has embarrassed the defendants. On the other hand, they do not deny the existence of the contract or most of its terms, nor do they deny that the faxes set most of them out, so they need to assert a slightly different case on the form of the contract and when it was made. The simple way of dealing with this is to begin with the words 'except that', then state the contrary facts and finish with an assertion that otherwise paragraph 2 is admitted.

Paragraph 3. The alleged express term. The claimants are apparently relying on a misprint to assert the existence of their term. So we must deny the term (in the short first sentence) and then give reasons for this denial (the rest of the paragraph). This is largely a matter of explaining what happened in a convincing but concise way. At the end of the paragraph the defendants touch on another aspect of their defence — that the claimants are using the wrong make of ink. This is necessary because the claimants allege that they are not even getting 150 but only 120 sheets per minute out of the machines.

This paragraph is a good example of the grey area between material fact and evidence. What is set out here is arguably evidence; but it is also the reasons for the denial and the factual basis for the defendants' case, so it must be included.

Paragraph 4 admits the existence of the implied term. Since the term is implied by statute, there is no choice but to admit it. Admitting its existence does not of course amount to admitting breach of it.

Paragraph 5 gives a mixed response to the matters set out in paragraph 5 of the claim. The defendants obviously admit that they delivered the new machines and that they did so in accordance with the contract. They add the date(s) of delivery. Some purists assert that the defendants cannot *admit* that they delivered the new machines between 16th and 20th March, when those dates have not been alleged by the claimants; one should admit delivery and then add in a separate sentence that delivery was between those dates. Well, maybe. But this way of adding uncontroversial facts is often used, and it does make the paragraph shorter and simpler.

Note the use of the phrase 'the New Machines'. Once a term has been defined in one statement of case, the same term can be adopted in subsequent statements of case without further definition. The capital initials indicate that this is a defined term.

The second sentence of the paragraph is what might be called a 'mop-up'. Apart from the admission, proof is required of everything else. Sometimes the mop-up is a denial, sometimes it is an admission: structure your paragraph in the most concise and convenient way. Here, in effect, the claimants are required to prove that they installed the new machines and scrapped the old ones — these are matters outside the defendants' knowledge, but which they certainly do not wish to admit.

Paragraph 6. This is the denial of breach. There are three stages to this denial. The first sentence simply denies breach. The phrase 'the alleged or any' serves the same function as the phrase 'as alleged or at all' (see the commentary on paragraph 2 in **8.5.2**). Without it the denial is either incomplete, or suggests the defendant has something to hide. The second sentence denies the particulars of breach.

Without this sentence it would be unclear whether the defendant was saying 'the machines can print faster than 120 sheets per minute' or 'they cannot print faster than 120 sheets per minute, but that is not a breach of the contract'. The third sentence gives the reason for the denial and states what the defendants allege to be the true fact, again looking forward to their point about the type of ink, which will be alleged properly in paragraphs 7 and 8. The defendants use the phrase '*each* of the New Machines' for exactly the same reason as the claimants used the phrase '*none* of the New Machines' in paragraph 6 of the claim.

Paragraph 7. Responds to the allegation of loss and damage. Paragraph 7 of the claim alleges loss, the amount of the loss and the causation of the loss, so all three must be dealt with. The claimants are required to prove the fact of loss in the first part of the first sentence. The words 'alleged or any' appear for exactly the same reason as they appeared in paragraph 6. The amount of loss is not dealt with expressly. Remember that by CPR, r 16.5(4), the claimants are automatically required to prove this unless it is admitted. One could, however, add some words expressly requiring proof of the amount, and this is not uncommonly done.

The causation of loss is here denied. Even if the claimants have suffered loss, the defendants say it was not caused by any breach of contract on their part. The reason for the denial must be given, and this appears in the second sentence of paragraph 7. In effect the defendants are saying what *did* cause the loss. But there is an apparent contradiction if they do not admit the loss actually exists. So the allegation is made conditional: the sentence begins with an 'if' and the claimants are required to prove that none of the new machines is printing at a rate above 120 sheets per minute, because that is a matter outside the defendants' knowledge.

Paragraph 8. The defendants have more to say before they complete stage 7. Even if the claimants establish liability and the full extent of their loss, the defendants say the claim is still massively overstated. If the claimants are really suffering losses at the rate of nearly £400,000 per annum, they should have mitigated their loss by using the right kind of ink and by acquiring faster printing machines. These presumably can be purchased or leased for a far lesser sum than the loss claimed. So the allegation of failure to mitigate must be made, and particularised. Particulars of failure to mitigate require you to state what steps the claimants ought to have taken but did not.

8.7 Exercise A

Peter Williams will say:

I am employed by Small Time Hotels Ltd as manager of the Sunshine Hotel. When after many years our former cleaners did not renew their contract, I invited several firms to tender for the cleaning contract at the Sunshine Hotel. I engaged Dapper Cleaners, a local firm, who gave much the lowest quote. The contract was negotiated orally, at a meeting on 27 March 2004 between myself and Eleanor Moore. The terms as stated by the Claimants are correct as far as they go, but an important term has been omitted. Although the contract was for one year, I made it clear to Eleanor Moore that there was to be a 12-week trial period and that either side could cancel the contract after that time with reasonable notice. Due to an oversight this term does not appear expressly in the letter, but it is covered by the phrase which does appear: 'All other terms as agreed between the parties'. It was clear from the start that Dapper Cleaners were hopeless. The standard of cleaning was appalling. I spoke to Eleanor Moore several times, but nothing improved. The problem was that they were trying to use only two cleaners whereas the old contractors used four. The job is simply too big for two people. Dapper Cleaners said they could not afford any more. I therefore decided to terminate the contract after the trial period. Since I had already contracted with another firm of cleaners to start on Monday 28 June 2004 I gave Dapper Cleaners two weeks' pay in lieu of notice.

Counsel is asked to settle a defence to the particulars of claim (see **7.11**).

8.8   Exercise B

Counsel is instructed on behalf of George Harding (Construction) plc, defendants in this claim brought by Charles Prendergast (see **7.12**), and is referred to the enclosed witness statements of Percy Crampton (the site manager), Harry Shockett (the driver of the lorry) and Roland Andrews (the construction engineer).

It is conceded that the lorry was parked at the top of the hill facing downhill, but only on a slight slope, not so steep that the driver considered it necessary to take any particular precautions. Mr Shockett says that the parking brake was functioning correctly both before and after the lorry came down the hill, and he had left the lorry with the brake fully on and the doors locked. After the accident he found two cigarette ends on the floor of the driver's cab. No other driver had been using the lorry apart from him, and he is a non-smoker.

Mr Crampton says that the access road is not straight, but windy, so the lorry could not have reached Mill Cottage without running off the road unless it was steered. He is further able to produce documents to show that the lorry has been properly and regularly maintained.

Mr Andrews investigated the scene of the collision on the morning of Saturday 26 June 2004. He says that the wall had been flattened to a width of about 10 feet, and calculates that the lorry would have impacted with the wall at a speed of about 25 mph. The window was at an angle of about 45 to the wall and some 40 feet from the point of impact. From this he calculates that a brick could only have flown from the wall through the window if it had left the wall at a speed vastly greater than 25 mph, and that therefore the window must have been broken by some other means.

Our conclusion is that, in spite of a police view to the contrary, the lorry did not roll down the hill unattended, but was driven or steered by vandals. The site was properly protected and nothing more could have been done to prevent them gaining access to the lorry. Our clients cannot be held responsible for the acts of total strangers.

The loss and damage claim is accepted, subject to liability.

Counsel is asked to settle a defence to the particulars of claim.

Further particulars of claim

9.1 Tort: occupiers' liability

9.1.1 Particulars of claim

IN THE WEST LONDON COUNTY COURT   Claim No WL4/10114

BETWEEN

EDWARD MOSS   Claimant

and

(1) LONDON BOROUGH OF GREENBRIDGE
(2) BIG BLUE CLEANING SERVICES LIMITED   Defendants

PARTICULARS OF CLAIM

1. On 6th May 2003 the Claimant, who is a Greenbridge resident, entered Greenbridge Town Hall, which is owned and occupied by the First Defendants, in order to pay to the First Defendants an instalment of his council tax. The Claimant was therefore a visitor of the First Defendants.

2. As the Claimant was climbing a stone staircase in Greenbridge Town Hall during this visit he slipped on a step which was wet because the staircase was being washed by the employees or agents of the Second Defendants, under their contract with the First Defendants. The Claimant attempted to steady himself by grasping an iron banister which was rusty and gave way, so that the Claimant fell a distance of about 12 feet to the floor.

3. This accident was caused by negligence and/or breach of statutory duty under section 2 of the Occupiers' Liability Act 1957 on the part of the First Defendants, their employees or agents.

PARTICULARS OF NEGLIGENCE AND/OR BREACH OF STATUTORY DUTY

The First Defendants, their employees or agents were negligent and/or in breach of statutory duty in that they:

(a) Allowed the Claimant to walk up the staircase when it was wet and unsafe.

(b) Failed to direct the Claimant to make use of an alternative staircase.

(c) Allowed the staircase to be washed in such a manner that all parts of it were wet at the same time, which was unsafe.

(d) Failed to supervise the Second Defendants, their employees or agents, adequately or at all.

(e) Failed to keep the Claimant or other visitors away from the staircase while it was being washed, by putting a rope barrier across the foot of it or by some other means.

(f) Failed to give the Claimant any or any adequate warning that the staircase was wet and unsafe.

(g) Allowed the iron banister to become and/or to remain rusty, unsafe and liable to collapse.

(h) Failed in all the circumstances to take reasonable care for the Claimant's safety.

4.   Further or alternatively the accident was caused by the negligence of the Second Defendants, their employees or agents.

PARTICULARS OF NEGLIGENCE

The Second Defendants their employees or agents were negligent in that they:

(a) Allowed the Claimant to walk up the staircase when it was wet and unsafe.

(b) Failed to direct the Claimant to make use of an alternative staircase.

(c) Washed the staircase in such a manner that all parts of it were wet at the same time, which was unsafe.

(d) Failed to keep the Claimant or other persons away from the staircase while it was being washed, by putting a rope barrier across the foot of it or by some other means.

(e) Failed to give the Claimant any or any adequate warning that the staircase was wet and unsafe.

5.   As a result of the matters set out above the Claimant suffered pain and injury and sustained loss and damage.

PARTICULARS OF INJURY

(a) Fractures to lumbar vertebrae 3, 4 and 5.

(b) Damage to spinal canal.

(c) Bruising, pain and shock.

The Claimant, who was born on 28th November 1957, was taken to Royal Northampton Hospital where he was required to lie flat and motionless for a week. An operation was then performed to rebuild the affected vertebrae. He remained in hospital for 7 weeks, with severely limited mobility. He was able to walk with the aid of a frame after about 3 months and with a stick after about 6 months. He was able to walk unaided after about a year. The Claimant has made a good recovery and is able to live life almost as normal, though he has to avoid strenuous activities. The Claimant is a self-employed consultant engineer. He was off work for 6 months, but has been able to resume his work since then.

Further details of the Claimant's injuries are set out in the medical report of Mr Thomas Butler served with these Particulars of Claim.

<u>PARTICULARS OF SPECIAL DAMAGE</u>

The Claimant's losses are set out in the schedule of expenses and losses served with these Particulars of Claim.

6.   Further the Claimant claims interest under section 69 of the County Courts Act 1984 on the amount found to be due to the Claimant at such rate and for such period as the court thinks fit.

AND the Claimant claims:

(1) Damages.

(2) Interest under section 69 of the County Courts Act 1984 to be assessed.

JOSEPH BLOGGS

<u>STATEMENT OF TRUTH</u>

Dated etc.

9.1.2   Commentary

This example is based on the same facts as the exercise in **6.5**. It is our first example of a claim against two defendants.

Paragraph 1. The parties, or in this case the claimant and first defendants. Since this claim is based on occupier's liability, it is essential to state the facts which will give rise to the duty of care, namely that the defendant is an occupier and the claimant was his visitor. Hence these statements appear and these actual words are used. Sometimes the words 'within the meaning of the Occupier's Liability Act 1957' are added. That the claimant is a Greenbridge resident and that he was paying his council tax are necessary facts, because they are what effectively gave him implied permission to enter the town hall, so making him a lawful visitor. The fact that the town hall is owned as well as occupied by the first defendants is not essential.

Paragraph 2. The accident, but also more about the parties — it introduces the second defendants. The second defendants could have been introduced separately first, but it is convenient and perfectly clear to do it like this. The description of the accident is simple. Note that the paragraph stops with the fall, and does not go on to the consequent injury.

Paragraph 3. The cause of action against the first defendants. Note that it is generally unacceptable to allege two causes of action simultaneously. The normal rule is to put each new cause of action in a new paragraph. The only exception is where the particulars of each allegation are in effect identical, and the only situation in which that really happens in practice is where you are alleging occupier's liability and negligence. So in this case (and *only* in this case) the two causes of action can be stated simultaneously. The paragraph is set out in the usual form of a negligence paragraph, but with the words 'and/or breach of statutory duty' added where appropriate. The defendants are a statutory body, so they cannot act except through individuals acting on their behalf. This problem is solved by the use of the standard formula 'the defendants, their employees or agents'. Always remember to include the employees and agents where appropriate.

The particulars of negligence are based on common sense, though maybe on evidence from a cleaning contractor, and are largely self-explanatory. Particular (c) is based on the idea that the proper way to wash a staircase (or corridor) which is in use, is to wash first one side, allowing people to walk on the other side, then when it is dry to wash the second side, allowing people to walk on the side washed first. The phrases 'adequately or at all' in particular (d) and 'any or any adequate' in particular (f) are further examples of the good drafting technique explained in **Chapter 7**. Note the words in particular (e) 'by putting a rope barrier across the foot of it or by some other means'. If the allegation is simply 'failing to keep people away from the staircase' this gives rise to the question 'what should they have done to achieve this?', which might come by way of a request for further information. So good drafting requires us to specify the steps that should have been taken as far as possible. There is another example of two eventualities being covered in particular (g): 'to become and/or to remain'. There are two quite distinct omissions alleged here: make sure you do not muddle them up, or omit one of them.

The final particular is a kind of summing up. It actually adds nothing to particulars (a)–(g) and cannot possibly stand on its own, since it would be far too generalised. It is completely unnecessary, but very common in practice, so it is included here by way of example.

Paragraph 4. The cause of action against the second defendants. This is introduced in the usual way. The words 'further or alternatively' are correct, because the court could find either defendant or both of them liable. The particulars of negligence are identical to those in paragraph 3, omitting (d), (g) and (h).

Paragraph 5. Injury loss and damage. The content and style are similar to those of the example in **7.6.1**. See therefore the commentary to that example in **7.6.3**.

9.2   Tort: employers' liability: breach of statutory duty: provisional damages

In order to draft a claim for breach of statutory duty it is essential to consult the relevant statute or regulations and to have the appropriate sections or regulations in front of you while drafting. You must check that the conditions which have to be satisfied before a duty can arise are present and state the facts which show that those conditions are satisfied. This involves considering and (usually) setting out the exact wording of the statute or statutory instrument. The conditions that have to be satisfied are:

(a) That the statute or regulations apply to this business, operation, place or person.

(b) That the duty is imposed on the defendant.

(c) That the duty is owed to the claimant.

(d) That breach of the statute or regulation gives rise to civil liability.

(e) That the defendant's act or omission amounts to a breach.

(f) That the claimant has suffered injury or damage.

(g) That the injury/damage was caused by the breach.

(h) That the damage was of the kind that the statute/regulations were intended to prevent.

For further explanation see the *Remedies Manual*, **Chapter 4**.

9.2.1   Example: relevant regulations

Construction (Health, Safety and Welfare) Regulations 1996

2.—(1)   In these Regulations, unless the context otherwise requires—
'construction work' means the carrying out of any building, civil engineering or engineering construction work
...

3.—(1)   Subject to the following paragraphs of this regulation, these Regulations apply to and in relation to construction work carried out by a person at work.

4.—(1)   ... it shall be the duty of every employer whose employees are carrying out construction work ... to comply with the provisions of these Regulations insofar as they affect him or any person at work under his control or relate to matters which are within his control.

...

(3) ... it shall be the duty of every employee carrying out construction work to comply with the requirements of these Regulations insofar as they relate to the performance of or the refraining from an act by him.

(4) It shall be the duty of every person at work—

(a)   as regards any duty or requirement imposed on any other person under these Regulations, to co-operate with that person so far as is necessary to enable that duty or requirement to be performed or complied with.

6.—(1)   Suitable and sufficient steps shall be taken to prevent, so far as is reasonably practicable, any person falling.

Lifting Operations and Lifting Equipment Regulations 1998

2.—(1)   In these Regulations, unless the context otherwise requires—
'lifting equipment' means work equipment for lifting or lowering loads and includes its attachments used for anchoring, fixing or supporting it.

3.—(2)   The requirements imposed by these Regulations on an employer in respect of lifting equipment shall apply in relation to lifting equipment provided for use or used by an employee of his at work.

4.   Every employer shall ensure that—
(a)   lifting equipment is of adequate strength and stability for each load, having regard in particular to the stress induced at its mounting or fixing point;

6.—(1)   Every employer shall ensure that lifting equipment is positioned or installed in such a way as to reduce to as low as is reasonably practicable the risk—
(a)   of the lifting equipment or a load striking a person; or
(b)   from a load—
(i)   drifting;
(ii)   falling freely; or
(iii)   being released unintentionally;
and it is otherwise safe.

8.—(1)   Every employer shall ensure that every lifting operation involving lifting equipment is—
(a)   properly planned by a competent person;
(b)   appropriately supervised; and
(c)   carried out in a safe manner.
(2)   In this regulation 'lifting operation' means an operation concerned with the lifting or lowering of a load.

9.2.2   Example: particulars of claim

IN THE HIGH COURT OF JUSTICE   Claim No 2004 HC 6151
QUEEN'S BENCH DIVISION

BETWEEN

RICHARD ALLEN   Claimant

and

H. A. JOHNS (CONSTRUCTION) LIMITED   Defendants

PARTICULARS OF CLAIM

1.   At all material times the Defendants were building contractors and the Claimant was an employee of the Defendants.

2.   On 29th September 2003 the Claimant was engaged in the course of his employment with other employees of the Defendants in pile-driving at a site at Porterfield, London

E17, which was construction work within the meaning of the Construction (Health, Safety and Welfare) Regulations 1996 ('the Construction Regulations'). The pile-driving was being carried out with the assistance of a mobile crane operated by Patrick Connelly, a foreman employed by the Defendants, which was lifting equipment within the meaning of the Lifting Operations and Lifting Equipment Regulations 1998 ('the Lifting Regulations').

3.   At about 2 p.m. on 29th September 2003 the Claimant was instructed by Patrick Connelly to climb onto the lead for driving the piles, and did so. The lead was then hoisted into the air. While the Claimant was on the lead the crane suddenly collapsed and fell, causing the Claimant to be thrown to the ground.

4.   This accident was caused by a breach on the part of the Defendants, their employees or agents of their statutory duties under the Construction Regulations and the Lifting Regulations.

PARTICULARS OF BREACH OF STATUTORY DUTY

(a) Unnecessarily requiring the Claimant to climb onto the lead and so failing to take suitable and sufficient steps to prevent the Claimant falling from it, contrary to regulation 6(1) of the Construction Regulations.

(b) Failing to ensure that the crane was of adequate stability for the load being carried, contrary to regulation 4 of the Lifting Regulations.

(c) Failing to ensure that the crane was positioned and installed in such a way that it was safe, contrary to regulation 6(1) of the Lifting Regulations.

(d) Failing to ensure that the lifting operation described in paragraph 3 above was carried out in a safe manner, contrary to regulation 8(1) of the Lifting Regulations.

5.   Further or alternatively, the accident was caused by the negligence of the Defendants, their employees or agents.

PARTICULARS OF NEGLIGENCE

(a) Requiring the Claimant to climb onto the lead.

(b) Causing or permitting the lead to be hoisted into the air while the Claimant was on it.

(c) Failing to ensure the stability of the crane having regard to the nature of the work carried out and of the condition of the ground.

(d) Failing to ascertain the degree to which the jib (or boom) of the crane could be safely extended having regard to the weight carried.

(e) Causing or permitting the jib (or boom) to be extended excessively.

(f) Causing or permitting the crane to be operated when they knew or ought to have known that it was not safe to do so.

(g) Starting to lift the lead too quickly and/or in a jerky manner.

(h) Failing in all the circumstances to provide a safe system of work at the site.

(i) The Claimant will further contend that the fact that the crane fell over in itself gives rise to a presumption of negligence on the part of the Defendants.

6.   As a result of the accident the Claimant suffered pain and injury and sustained loss and damage.

PARTICULARS OF INJURY

(a) Pain and shock.

(b) Fracture of the head of the right femur.

(c) Bruising to right side of body.

(d) Operation scars to right hip.

The Claimant was taken to the Stuckley Hospital and admitted for the fracture to be fixed under general anaesthetic and traction treatment. The Claimant was discharged after 2 weeks in a full leg plaster and needing crutches to walk. Unfortunately an infection set in and the Claimant was readmitted for a further 3 months. He then underwent physiotherapy treatment. The fracture has not healed satisfactorily, and the Claimant is not able to walk without the aid of a stick, and then not more than about half a mile. He is severely limited in his daily activities and was unable to return to his pre-accident employment. He is currently unemployed as a result of his injury and is unlikely to be able to find suitable employment in the future. There is a severe risk of osteo-arthritis in the hip joint in 10 to 15 years' time. There is a further risk that the infection may recur in the future and if it does so that the Claimant's right leg will have to be amputated. The Claimant was born on 16th October 1966. These disabilities are permanent.

The Claimant will further rely on the medical report of Dr Barry Green served with these Particulars of Claim.

PARTICULARS OF SPECIAL DAMAGE

The Claimant's losses are set out in the schedule of expenses and losses served with these Particulars of Claim.

7.   The Claimant will ask the Court to award him provisional damages under section 32A of the Supreme Court Act 1981 assessed on the assumption that the infection will not recur and that his right leg will not need to be amputated and to permit him to make a further application for damages if the infection recurs and his leg requires amputation in the future.

8.   Further the Claimant claims interest under section 35A of the Supreme Court Act 1981 on the amount found to be due to the Claimant at such rate and for such period as the Court thinks fit.

AND the Claimant claims:

(1) Provisional damages; alternatively damages.

(2) Interest under section 35A of the Supreme Court Act 1981 to be assessed.

JOSEPH BLOGGS

STATEMENT OF TRUTH

Dated etc.

9.2.3 Commentary

9.2.3.1 The Regulations

The claim must be drafted not only to establish the claim in negligence, but also to establish the claim for breaches of statutory duty under the Regulations. Having found relevant regulations through legal research, it becomes necessary then to examine the Regulations to see what exactly will need to be stated in order to incorporate all the essential ingredients.

Construction (Health, Safety and Welfare) Regulations 1996

Regulation 3(1) says that the Regulations apply to 'construction work carried out by a person at work'. So make a note that you will need to state that what the defendants were doing was construction work, and that the claimant was at work.

Regulation 4(1) imposes a duty on an employer whose employees are carrying out construction work. So make a note that you will need to state that the defendants were the claimant's employers.

Regulations 4(3) and (4) also impose duties on employees. From this we can conclude that the foreman Patrick Connelly was also in breach of statutory duty under reg 6, and that the defendants will be vicariously liable for his breach; but further that the claimant himself was probably in breach of reg 6 as well, which may in due course give rise to a finding of contributory negligence.

Regulation 6(1) imposes a very broad duty to take steps to prevent a person falling. Since the allegation is that it was dangerous to allow the claimant to be hoisted into the air at all, it is easily arguable that the required steps were to refrain from lifting him at all and that therefore the duty has been breached.

Lifting Operations and Lifting Equipment Regulations 1998

Regulation 2(1) defines lifting equipment in such a way as to include the mobile crane. So make a note that it will be necessary to state that the crane was lifting equipment.

Regulation 3(2) says that the Regulations apply when lifting equipment is provided for use by an employee at work. So make a note that it will be necessary to state that the crane was being used by the relevant employees in the course of their work.

Regulation 4 imposes what is probably a strict duty with regard to strength and stability, which has clearly been breached. It is stability that we are concerned with here — there does not appear to be any basis on which to allege that the crane was not strong enough for the job.

Regulation 6(1) imposes a strict duty to ensure that the crane was positioned or installed so that it was safe. If strict, there can be no doubt about breach. Arguably there is also breach of a duty to install it so as to reduce to as low as is reasonably practicable the risk of the load drifting, but that is not alleged.

Regulation 8(1) imposes another strict and very broad duty to ensure that the lifting operation is carried out in a safe manner. This too has obviously been breached.

9.2.3.2 The particulars of claim

Paragraph 1. Introduces the parties. By stating that the defendants were building contractors, we have started to show that they were doing construction work (so helping to establish that the Construction Regulations apply — see reg 3(1)) and that the relevant duties are imposed on them (see reg 4(1)). By stating that the claimant was an employee of the defendants we have further established that the relevant statutory duties are imposed on the defendants (see reg 4(1)), that they also owe a common law duty (arising by virtue of the employer/employee relationship), and that all these duties were potentially owed to the claimant (assuming he was acting in the course of his employment).

Paragraph 2. More about the parties and necessary background. That the claimant was in the course of his employment is essential to establish that the statutory and common law duties were owed to him. The pile-driving is the construction work which makes the Construction Regulations apply, so needs to be stated. The crane is introduced and is stated to be 'lifting equipment', which is what makes the Lifting Regulations apply. This is a convenient place to introduce Patrick Connelly, who needs to be identified individually, both to tell the story clearly and to establish the defendants' vicarious liability for his acts — note the importance of adding that he was employed by the defendants. The fact that the two sets of Regulations apply does not *have* to be expressly stated if the facts that make them apply have been set out, but it is good practice for the sake of clarity. It also gives us the opportunity to give them a definition ('the Construction Regulations', 'the Lifting Regulations'), so avoiding the need to use their full name from here on.

Paragraph 3. The accident can now be set out straightforwardly. That the foreman instructed the claimant to climb onto the lead is likely to be disputed, but it is part of the claimant's case, so must be included.

Paragraph 4. There are two causes of action, which do not have the same particulars, so they must be set out in separate paragraphs. By convention statutory duty comes first. The formula is a simple adaptation of the formula you have already seen. Remember to add the 'employees or agents'. The particulars must be drafted strictly in accordance with the words of the relevant regulations. The defendants will be in breach only if they have done *exactly* what is forbidden or unless they have complied *exactly* with their statutory obligations. In each case you should specify the precise paragraph(s) alleged to have been breached. Note how closely each particular matches the regulation that gives rise to it. Where possible, give further factual particularisation — only really possible in particular (a) in this case.

Paragraph 5. The second cause of action is negligence, set out in the usual way. A new cause of action is almost always introduced with the words 'further or alternatively' because it is possible for the defendants to be found liable under either or both heads. The particulars of course do not have to follow any precise wording; they can be tailored to the facts of the case and your evidence. The words 'causing or permitting' in particulars (b), (e) and (f) are very common and useful. The defendants are vicariously liable for the acts of their employees, so they can be in breach because they did something (causing it to happen) or less directly because they did nothing to prevent the forbidden act (permitting it to happen). The words 'knew or ought to have known' in particular (f) are another very common phrase. We do not know whether the defendants knew the crane was unstable or not — but if they did not, they should have done, so it does not matter much: we say they were negligent either way. Particular (h) is another 'summing up' particular, but this time it does serve a valid purpose: it identifies the particular branch of the employer's duty (to provide a safe system of work) which is alleged to have been breached.

The claimant also alleges *res ipsa loquitur*. This is the meaning of particular (i). Reliance on *res ipsa loquitur* is very much a last resort, but here it is arguable that the mere fact of the crane's falling over indicates that the person in control of it must have been negligent. Before the CPR, the convention was simply to add those three words of Latin; but nowadays one probably ought to spell out their meaning in plain English.

Paragraph 6. Injury, loss and damage set out in standard form. Note the pre-penultimate sentence of the particulars of injury. There is a claim for provisional damages in this case, so the claim must set out the facts relating to the risk of deterioration or the onset of disease in the future, in this case the risk of a recurring infection, leading to amputation of the right leg (PD 16, para 4.4). The severe risk of osteo-arthritis does not give rise to a claim for provisional damages — this is a normal risk inherent in the claimant's condition and will be taken into account in the initial award.

Paragraph 7. The fact that the claimant seeks provisional damages must be expressly stated — see CPR, r 16.4(1)(d) and **7.1.2**(e).

Prayer. Note the claim for provisional damages or damages in the alternative. The court does not have to award provisional damages just because the claimant asks for them.

9.3 Tort: fatal accidents

9.3.1 Particulars of claim

IN THE HIGH COURT OF JUSTICE   Claim No 2004 HC 2048
QUEEN'S BENCH DIVISION

BETWEEN

AMANDA BRIDGES
(widow and executrix of the
Will of COLIN BRIDGES deceased)   Claimant

and

MAMMOTH TRANSPORT PLC   Defendants

PARTICULARS OF CLAIM

1. The Claimant is the widow and executrix of the will of Colin Bridges deceased ('the Deceased') and brings this action on behalf of the Deceased's estate under the Law Reform (Miscellaneous Provisions) Act 1934 and for the benefit of the dependants of the Deceased under the Fatal Accidents Act 1976. Probate was granted on 12th February 2004.

2. On 17th November 2003 the deceased was driving his Peugeot 405 motor car registration no X421 ALC on the A354 Salisbury to Blandford road in Dorset when a lorry registration no S866 DPR owned by the Defendants and driven by their employee Clive Yardley, which was travelling in the opposite direction to the Deceased, crossed on to the wrong side of the road and collided head-on with the Deceased's car.

3. The collision was caused by the negligence of Clive Yardley, acting in the course of his employment.

PARTICULARS OF NEGLIGENCE

(a) Driving on the wrong side of the road when it was not safe to do so.

(b) Failing to heed the presence of the deceased's car on the road.

(c) Failing to keep any or any proper look-out.

(d) Failing to stop, slow down, swerve, or otherwise steer or control the lorry so as to avoid colliding with the deceased's car.

4. Further the Claimant intends under section 11 of the Civil Evidence Act 1968 to adduce evidence at trial that Clive Yardley was on 8th January 2004 at Salisbury Magistrates' Court convicted of careless driving contrary to section 3 of the Road Traffic Act 1988 in respect of his driving on the occasion of the accident, as evidence of his negligence.

5. As a result of the accident the Deceased suffered injuries from which he died on 19th November 2003. As a result of his death the Deceased's estate and dependants have suffered loss and damage and the Claimant has suffered bereavement.

PARTICULARS OF INJURY

Severe multiple injuries including fractured skull. The Deceased was rendered unconscious by the collision. He was taken by ambulance to Queen Elizabeth Hospital in Blandford and transferred on 18th November 2003 to St Mary's Hospital, Bournemouth where on 19th November 2003 he died without regaining consciousness. Further particulars are set out in the medical report of Dr John Cluett, a copy of which is attached.

PARTICULARS OF DEPENDENCY

The claim under the Fatal Accidents Act 1976 is brought on behalf of the following dependants:

(1) The Claimant, who was born on 30th April 1962, widow of the Deceased.

(2) Maria Bridges, who was born on 18th July 1987, daughter of the Deceased.

(3) Anthony Bridges, who was born on 5th May 1990, son of the Deceased.

The Deceased, who was born on 19th December 1960, was a self-employed IT consultant who earned £40,658 net in the last full year of his life and whose income would have increased substantially had he lived. A substantial part of his income was spent for the benefit of his dependants and this would have continued had he not died. In addition the Deceased carried out household repairs, decorations and improvements to the family home to a value of no less than £1,000 per year.

PARTICULARS OF SPECIAL DAMAGE

	£
(1) Value of Peugeot 405 car damaged beyond repair	8,300.00
(2) Damage to clothing	220.00
(3) Loss of earnings, 17th November 2003 to 19th November 2003	334.18
(4) 4 theatre tickets not used on 18th November 2003	110.00
(5) Funeral expenses	879.75
	9,823.93

Further particulars are set out in the attached schedule of expenses and losses.

6.   Further the Claimant claims interest under section 35A of the Supreme Court Act 1981 on the amount found to be due to the Claimant at such rate and for such period as the Court thinks fit.

AND the Claimant claims:

(1) Damages on behalf of the deceased's estate under the Law Reform (Miscellaneous Provisions) Act 1934.

(2) Damages on behalf of the deceased's dependants under the Fatal Accidents Act 1976.

(3) Damages for bereavement under section 1A of the Fatal Accidents Act 1976.

(4) Interest under section 35A of the Supreme Court Act 1981 to be assessed.

JOSEPH BLOGGS

STATEMENT OF TRUTH

Dated etc.

9.3.2 Commentary

Heading. Note the description of the claimant. An action under the Fatal Accidents Act 1976 must normally be brought by the personal representative(s): the executor(s) of the will or administrator of the estate of the deceased. It is necessary to identify the claimant's capacity in this way. The fact that she is the deceased's widow (and so also a dependant) is not actually necessary, but usually added where it is the case.

Paragraph 1. This is very much a standard form paragraph introducing the claimant. The fact that the claim is brought under the 1976 Act must be stated (PD 16, para 5.1 — see **7.1.2**(e)). If the claim is also under the Law Reform (Miscellaneous Provisions) Act 1934 — as it usually is — this should be stated too. The grant of probate (or letters of administration) must be stated — it is what entitles the claimant to act on behalf of the estate and dependants.

Paragraph 2. Once the formalities of paragraph 1 are out of the way, a fatal accident claim can proceed in much the same way as a personal injury claim. But make sure you refer to the 'deceased' as opposed to the claimant — an easy mistake to make. This paragraph sets out the parties and the accident. The defendants' liability is purely vicarious, for the negligence of Clive Yardley, so he should be named, and the fact that he was their employee stated.

Paragraph 3. It would be absurd to use the usual formula 'caused by the negligence of the defendants, their employees or agents' when the negligence relied upon can only be that of one particular individual, so make the allegation as it appears here. Remember to add that Clive Yardley was acting in the course of his employment, the other ingredient required to establish vicarious liability. The particulars are standard or obvious.

Paragraph 4. This is part of stage 3 — the causes of action. The claimant wishes to rely in evidence on Clive Yardley's conviction, as permitted by s 11 of the Civil Evidence Act 1968. The intention to do so, and other particulars must be included in the claim by virtue of PD 16, para 8.1 — see **4.4.3.2**(a). The other particulars required are the offence (careless driving), the date of the conviction (8 January 2004), the court (Salisbury Magistrates' Court) and the issue in this claim to which the conviction is relevant ('as evidence of his negligence'). Note the importance of the words 'in respect of his driving on the occasion of accident'. Without them the conviction would not have any relevance to the facts of the case.

Paragraph 5. Injury, death, loss and damage. There are several differences between this paragraph and a standard injury loss and damage paragraph in a personal injury claim. In this case there is an injury claim, because death was not immediate, so it must be stated that the deceased was injured and died as a result of his injuries. The date of death is essential for the calculation of damages. Note that it is the estate and dependants, not the deceased, who have suffered loss and damage. Only the claimant (as the widow) has a claim for bereavement under the 1976 Act, so only she is alleged to have suffered it.

There are then three sets of particulars, all within paragraph 5. The first, particulars of injury, only needs to appear where there is a claim for pain suffering and loss of amenity which survives for the benefit of the estate under the Law Reform (Miscellaneous Provisions) Act 1934. Include any facts relevant to quantification.

The particulars of dependency are required by PD 16, para 5.1 — see **7.1.2**(f). It is necessary to set out who the dependants are, giving their date of birth and relationship to the deceased. Then give details of the value of the dependency, so far as it is possible to do. This will necessarily include the deceased's date of birth, the nature and amount of his earnings, the extent of his financial contribution and any contributions in money's worth (eg the household repairs, decorations and improvements). The fact that the deceased's income would have increased is obviously relevant: the dependants are entitled to recover the financial support he would have provided had he not died. For the same reason the words 'this would have continued had he not died' are essential to establish the claim.

The particulars of special damage are set out in full. This is not necessary if reference is made to the schedule of expenses and losses, but it may be done, particularly where they are straightforward.

Prayer. In fatal accident claims the prayer is quite complicated. Note that there are three separate claims for damages to be made.

9.4 Negligent misstatement

9.4.1 Introduction

A claim for negligent misstatement, or for negligent professional advice, is a claim for negligence and involves stating the same essential ingredients as are required for any claim in negligence (see **7.4**), but with certain modifications and additions:

(a) Care must be taken when stating the facts which give rise to the duty of care.

    (i)   One way in which the duty may come into existence is that there has been an assumption of responsibility by the defendant with regard to the accuracy of his statements and advice to the claimant.

    (ii)   There is an additional element of reasonable foreseeability required: it must be reasonably foreseeable that the claimant will rely on the statements or advice of the defendant. In many cases it can safely be alleged that the defendant actually knew that the claimant would rely on his statements or advice, and this is then usually pleaded. In cases where the statement is made not to the claimant specifically but to the world at large, an actual intention that it should be relied on must be pleaded and proved.

    (iii)   In some cases no duty of care is owed unless or until the defendant makes the statement. In these cases the making of the statement is itself one of the facts which give rise to the duty.

(b) The duty of care in these cases does not arise by operation of law, but on the basis of the unique facts of the case. So it will always be necessary to allege that the defendant owed the claimant a duty of care and to define its scope.

(c) The 'event' in the context of which the defendant has been negligent will always be the making of the statement.

(d) There is an additional element of causation required, namely that the claimant did actually rely on the statement or advice.

(e) Another essential ingredient, which is not the same as negligence, is the allegation that the statement or advice was in fact wrong.

The formula (see **7.5** for the basic version) for a claim in negligent misstatement will therefore be as follows:

Stage 1:   The parties.

Stage 2:   The facts giving rise to the duty. These must include any assumption of responsibility, an allegation that it was reasonably foreseeable, or that the defendant knew or ought to have known, or that the defendant intended, that the claimant would rely on his statements or advice. Where appropriate the making of the statement must also be pleaded at this stage.

Stage 3:   The duty of care; its existence, its nature and scope.

Stage 4:   The making of the statement or the giving of the advice (unless pleaded at Stage 2).

Stage 5:   What the claimant did in reliance on the statement or advice.

Stage 6:   The statement or advice was in fact wrong.

Stage 7:   Negligence. This is more than just repetition of the fact that the statement was wrong. It involves identifying the acts or omissions which caused the defendant to be wrong.

Stage 8:   Causation and loss.

Stage 9:   Interest.

Stage 10: The remedies sought.

9.4.2   Particulars of claim

IN THE HIGH COURT OF JUSTICE   Claim No 2004 HC 6411
QUEEN'S BENCH DIVISION

BETWEEN

BEET AND CANE LIMITED   Claimants

and

EASTERN BANK PLC   Defendants

PARTICULARS OF CLAIM

1.   The Claimants are and were at all material times a company carrying on business as wholesale sugar dealers.

2.   The Defendants are bankers, carrying on business at their branch at 200 Pell Mell, London WC1 ('the Branch') and elsewhere. At all material times, Sugarex Holdings Limited ('Sugarex') was a customer of the Defendants at the Branch.

3.   By letter dated 24th March 2004 sent to the Branch, the Claimants' bankers on behalf of the Claimants enquired of the Defendants concerning the creditworthiness of Sugarex and of the suitability of Sugarex for the grant of credit to the extent of £300,000 per month.

4.   By a letter dated 7th April 2004 ('the Credit Reference') sent to the Claimants' bankers, the Defendants replied that Sugarex were: 'respectable and trustworthy. A long-established private company that should prove good for your purpose — trade credit of £300,000 per month.' A copy of the Credit Reference is attached.

5.   The Defendants knew or ought to have known that the Claimants, as the customer on whose behalf the Credit Reference had been sought, would or would be likely to rely upon the statements it contained. The Defendants therefore owed a duty to the Claimants to take reasonable care to ensure that the matters stated in the Credit Reference were true.

6.   Induced by and in reliance upon the matters stated in the Credit Reference, the Claimants supplied goods to the value of £277,516 to Sugarex upon credit terms.

7.   In fact, at the time the Credit Reference was given by the Defendants, Sugarex was not a sound or creditworthy company but was insolvent and unable to pay its creditors.

8.   In stating in the Credit Reference that Sugarex should prove good for trade credit of up to £300,000 per month, the Defendants acted negligently.

PARTICULARS OF NEGLIGENCE

The Defendants were negligent in that they:

(a) Failed to make any or any adequate enquiries as to the financial position of Sugarex before giving the Credit Reference.

(b) Failed to state in the Credit Reference that the Defendants had returned cheques to the value of £150,386 drawn by Sugarex in March 2004 unpaid because there were insufficient funds in Sugarex's accounts.

(c) Stated that Sugarex was good for substantial trade credit at a time when the Defendants knew that cheques issued by Sugarex to trade creditors had been dishonoured.

(d) Stated that Sugarex was good for trade credit at a time when they ought to have known (from the information available to them as bankers to Sugarex) that Sugarex was or was likely to become insolvent.

9.   On 22nd May 2004, when Sugarex still owed the Claimants the full price of the goods supplied to it by the Claimants, Sugarex was ordered to be compulsorily wound up. The assets of Sugarex are insufficient for any dividend to be payable in the liquidation to unsecured creditors such as the Claimants.

10.   As a result of the matters set out above, the Claimants have suffered loss and damage.

PARTICULARS

Loss of the sum of £277,516 due from Sugarex to the Claimants.

11.   Further the Claimants claim interest under section 35A of the Supreme Court Act 1981 on the sum of £277,516 at the rate of 8% per year from 22nd May 2004, amounting to £11,678.48 at 30th November 2004 and then continuing until judgment or sooner payment at the rate of £60.83 per day.

AND the Claimants claim:

(1) Damages.

(2) Interest under section 35A of the Supreme Court Act 1981, amounting to £11,678.48 at 30th November 2004 and continuing at the daily rate of £60.83.

JOSEPH BLOGGS

STATEMENT OF TRUTH

Dated etc.

9.4.3   Commentary

Paragraphs 1 and 2. These identify the parties, and also a relevant third person, Sugarex.

Paragraphs 3 and 4. Stage 2. Once the parties are introduced, the next stage is to set out the facts which give rise to the duty of care. This is one of those cases where the duty comes into existence only when the statement is made: there is no relationship between the parties prior to that event. So the making of the statement is pleaded at this stage. Paragraph 3 sets out the claimants' request for a credit reference. That in itself gives rise to no duty — the defendants had no obligation to the claimants to provide a reference. So paragraph 4 sets out the statement, or representation. By agreeing to provide the reference, the defendants took on the obligation, or assumed responsibility, to provide an accurate one. The representation was in writing, so the exact words are known. The quotation marks show that precise words are being pleaded.

Paragraph 5. Stage 3 — the duty of care. The final ingredient required to establish the duty of care is that it was reasonably foreseeable that the claimants would rely on the representation. As explained in **9.4.1** this is often expressed in the form 'knew or ought to have known'. When an allegation is made that someone knew something, it is good practice to add 'particulars of knowledge', that is how or why did they know, unless it is obvious. The particulars here are obvious, but are included: 'as the customer on whose behalf the credit reference had been sought'.

The paragraph concludes by stating the duty owed. This is important. Although in negligence cases generally the norm is simply to plead the facts giving rise to the duty, leaving the existence of the duty to be inferred, in a case of negligent misstatement, the duty of care should be expressly stated. There are two reasons for this. First, because it helps to make it clear that the claim is in negligence rather in misrepresentation. Secondly, and more importantly, because the alleged duty needs to be defined. In cases where a duty arises by operation of law, the duty will always be the same. But where it arises by the special relationship between the parties, it will be unique to that relationship. If we were simply to allege that the defendants owed the claimants *a* duty, the claim would be incomplete, because there is no general duty owed by a bank to a non-customer. So the duty which the claimants contend exists must be spelt out: 'to take reasonable care to ensure that the matters stated in the Credit Reference were true'.

Paragraph 6. Stage 5. The next requirement is to state expressly that the claimants did rely on the statement, and then what they did in reliance on it. The addition of 'induced by' is not really necessary, but is common, borrowing from the standard formula in misrepresentation cases (see **Chapter 11**).

Paragraph 7. Stage 6 — the falsity of the representation, with particulars. The words 'in fact' are simple and widely used to differentiate the falsehood from the truth of a statement.

Paragraph 8. Stage 7 — negligence. The particulars are full, but fairly clear. Note that each particular of negligence, as always, consists of an act or omission. A common failing in claims of this kind is to draft particulars of negligence which merely repeat the facts stated in paragraph 7. You then end up with a claim which says, in effect: 'The statement was wrong. In making the statement the defendant was negligent, in that it was wrong.' Note in particular (d) the particulars of knowledge attached to the allegation that the defendants ought to have known something. Never forget your particulars of knowledge.

Paragraphs 9 and 10. Stage 8. Before the loss can be established as simply stated in paragraph 10, the causation of it needs to be explained. This causation is set out in paragraph 9.

9.5 Contract: debt claim

9.5.1 Particulars of claim

IN THE HIGH COURT OF JUSTICE   Claim No 2004 HC 98744
QUEEN'S BENCH DIVISION
MANCHESTER DISTRICT REGISTRY

BETWEEN

SHILTON MACHINE TOOLS LIMITED   Claimant

and

BANKS PLASTIC MOULDINGS LIMITED   Defendant

PARTICULARS OF CLAIM

1.   By a contract contained in or evidenced by the Defendant's Order dated the 13th March 2004, a copy of which is attached, the Claimant agreed to sell and deliver four plastic moulding machines ('the Machines') to the Defendant for the sum of £60,000 plus VAT, namely £70,500.

2.   The Claimant and the Defendant were each acting in the course of their respective businesses and it was an implied term of the contract, under section 1(1) of the Late Payment of Commercial Debts (Interest) Act 1998, that any qualifying debt created by the contract would carry statutory interest under that Act.

3.   The Claimant duly delivered the machines to the Defendant on 3rd May 2004 and rendered an invoice number ST9922 dated 8th May 2004.

4.   Payment was due 30 days after invoice, but in breach of the contract the Defendant has failed to pay all or any part of the price of the machines and the Defendant therefore owes the Claimant the sum of £70,500, a qualifying debt.

5.   The Claimant claims statutory interest at the rate of 11.75% per year on the sum of £70,500 from the 7th June 2004 to the 22nd September 2004 amounting to £2,428.39 and continuing from the 23rd September 2004 to judgment or earlier payment at the daily rate of £22.70.

6.   The Claimant further claims the sum of £100 by way of compensation under section 5A of the Late Payment of Commercial Debts (Interest) Act 1998.

AND the Claimant claims:

(1) The sum of £70,500.00.

(2) Statutory interest on the sum of £70,500 amounting to £2,428.39 to the 22nd September 2004, and continuing at the daily rate of £22.70.

(3) Compensation of £100.

JOSEPH BLOGGS

STATEMENT OF TRUTH

9.5.2 Commentary

We have seen that simple debt claims in contract are often drafted in short form (see **6.3**). However this is not wise where any contest is anticipated. In this case, the claimant knows that there is a dispute over the quality of the goods and anticipates a defence and counterclaim, so the claim is set out in full. But as you can see, it is still relatively short. The essential ingredients for a debt claim are: the contract; the price; performance by the claimant; date payment was due; failure to pay by the defendant; the sum due; and interest.

It is usually clumsy and longwinded to insist on giving each of these ingredients a paragraph to itself; they can often be merged, as they are in this example.

Paragraph 1. The contract, and obviously also the agreed price, are stated in the usual way.

Paragraph 2. This paragraph is probably needed where the claimant will seek to claim statutory interest under the Late Payment of Commercial Debts (Interest) Act 1998. Under the Act there is some confusion of terminology. The Act inserts an implied term providing for interest into contracts to which the Act applies, but then refers to that interest as 'statutory' rather than contractual interest. It is possible that this paragraph could be omitted, and a simple claim made for interest under the Act in paragraph 5.

Paragraph 3. Performance by the claimant. The invoice helps to establish the date payment was due. If there were an express term as to when payment was due, this would have been pleaded as paragraph 3, and the delivery of the machines would have been in paragraph 4. But in the absence of any express term, there is an implied term that payment is due within a reasonable time. If no demand for payment is made, a reasonable time may be rather a long and indeterminate period, but the normal commercial practice is to send an invoice specifying a period within which payment should be made. This is therefore expressly stated.

Paragraph 4. Date payment was due, breach by non-payment, and statement of the sum due. Thirty days is universally regarded as a reasonable time within which to demand payment. This is therefore probably what the invoice said. If it didn't, then 30 days is probably what is implied by normal commercial custom, and it is the default period laid down by the Late Payment of Commercial Debts (Interest) Act 1998. This period is therefore specified, followed by the failure of the defendant to pay the sum due. The allegation 'in breach of contract' is included for the sake of correctness, but you will often find in practice that these words are omitted in debt claims. The words 'or any part of the price' are vital. If the claimant only alleges that the defendant has failed to pay the price, this is ambiguous: he has alleged a failure to pay £70,500, but has left open the possibility that the defendant may have paid £70,499. So the words 'or any part' are invariably added in these circumstances. The statement that the defendant owes the sum of money due is usual, since it alleges the debt. It is the equivalent of pleading particulars of loss and damage. The words 'a qualifying debt' are added to satisfy the 1998 Act.

Paragraph 5. The claim is for a specified amount, and therefore interest needs to be stated in full in accordance with CPR, r 16.4(2)(b) — see **6.2.4**. In this case statutory interest under the late payment of Commercial Debts (Interest) Act 1998 is claimed, hence the rate of 11.75%, because base rate was 3.75% on 31st December 2003 (see **6.2.2(b)**).

Paragraph 6. Compensation can also be claimed under s 5A of the 1998 Act.

Prayer. The claim is not for damages, but for a specified sum of money. The interest is also set out in some detail, although this is repetitive. The aim is to make it as simple as possible for the defendant to pay or admit the claim, or for the claimant to obtain summary judgment for the sum due and interest.

9.6 Contract: anticipatory breach: debt claim: damages for wasted expenditure

9.6.1 Particulars of claim

IN THE NORTHAMPTON COUNTY COURT   Claim No NN4/1079

BETWEEN

HURLINGHAM IRONWORKS LIMITED   <u>Claimants</u>

and

FLIC PLC   <u>Defendants</u>

PARTICULARS OF CLAIM

1.   The Claimants are and were at all material times a company carrying on business as manufacturers, among other things, of cigarette-lighter parts.

2.   By a written agreement dated 20th October 2003 ('the Contract') the Claimants agreed to manufacture 500,000 base plugs for cigarette-lighters to a specification set out in the Contract and the Defendants agreed to buy those base plugs at a price of 25 pence each. A copy of the Contract is attached.

3.   It was an express term of the Contract:

   (a) that the Claimants would deliver the base plugs to the Defendants at the rate of 2,000 per week, beginning on or about 1st February 2004; and

   (b) that the Defendants would make payment in cash within seven days of delivery of each instalment.

4.   The Claimants and the Defendants were each acting in the course of their respective businesses and it was an implied term of the Contract, under section 1(1) of the Late Payment of Commercial Debts (Interest) Act 1998, that any qualifying debt created by the contract would carry statutory interest under that Act.

5.   At the time of entering into the Contract the Defendants knew that:

   (a) the base plugs manufactured to the Defendants' specification would be of no use to anyone other than the Defendants; and

   (b) that the Claimants would need to install special equipment in order to manufacture the base plugs.

6.   The Claimants duly manufactured and delivered to the Defendants two instalments each of 2,000 of the base plugs on 2nd February 2004 and on 9th February 2004 respectively.

7.   In breach of the Contract, the Defendants have failed to pay the £500 price of either instalment or any part of that sum within 7 days of delivery or at all. The Defendants are therefore indebted to the Claimants in the sum of £1,000, the total price of the 2 deliveries, which is a qualifying debt.

8.   Further or alternatively, in repudiatory breach of the Contract by letter dated 12th February 2004 sent to the Claimants the Defendants refused to accept delivery of further

instalments of the base plugs. The Claimants accepted this repudiation by their letter dated 17th February 2004 sent to the Defendants.

9. As a result of the matters set out above, the Claimants have suffered loss and damage.

PARTICULARS

(a) In order to manufacture the base plugs the Claimants installed special machinery and cut special dies at a cost in excess of £15,000.

(b) In addition to those delivered, the Claimants manufactured 6,000 base plugs, now unsaleable because made to a special design and therefore of no value, at a cost of £750.

10. The Claimants further claim:

(a) statutory interest on the sum of £1,000:

(i) amounting to £83.54 being interest on £500 from 9th February 2004 and on £500 from 16th February 2004 until 29th October 2004 at the rate of 11.75% per annum;

(ii) from 29th October 2004 until judgment or sooner payment at the same rate, equivalent to a daily rate of £0.32;

(b) interest under section 69 of the County Courts Act 1984 on the amount of the damages found due to the Claimants at such rate and for such period as the Court thinks fit.

11. The Claimants further claim the sum of £70 by way of compensation under section 5A of the Late Payment of Commercial Debts (Interest) Act 1998.

AND the Claimants claim:

(1) Under paragraph 7 above, £1,000.

(2) Under paragraph 10(a)(i) above, statutory interest of £83.54.

(3) Under paragraph 10(a)(ii), further statutory interest from 29th October 2004 until judgment or sooner payment.

(4) Under paragraph 9 above, damages.

(5) Under paragraph 10(b) above, interest under section 69 of the County Courts Act 1984 to be assessed.

(6) Under paragraph 11 above, £70 compensation.

JOSEPH BLOGGS

STATEMENT OF TRUTH

Dated etc.

9.6.2 Commentary

This is our first example of particulars of claim setting out two separate claims: in this case one for payment of a debt, and another for damages. They both arise out of the same contract, but the actual facts required to establish each cause of action are not the same, so the claims are distinct. Your initial thought might be that in those circumstances one would set out all the facts required to establish the first cause of action, incorporating stages 1 to 9, and then go back to the beginning and set out the second cause of action. But that is not the way it is done. It would be clumsy and repetitious. Instead, you tell the story chronologically, incorporating the facts required to establish each cause of action as and when they arise, but taking care to draft the claim in such a way that the two causes of action could be separated if necessary. In the above example, the debt claim alone would be established by paragraphs 1, 2, 4, 6, 7, 10(a) and 11, and the damages claim alone by paragraphs 1, 2, 5, 8, 9 and 10(b).

Paragraph 1. The claimants' business. The defendants' business is immaterial to the claim and is not dealt with. The words 'among other things' avoid giving the misleading impression that cigarette lighter parts are the only things manufactured by the claimants.

Paragraph 2. Simple setting out of the contract. The phrase 'to a specification set out in the contract' is a useful way of stating the material fact that these were not any old base plugs for cigarette lighters, but made to the defendants' specification, while at the same time avoiding the need to set out the precise specification which is not in issue in this case. The contract is written, so a copy must be attached to the particulars of claim under PD 16, para 7.3(1). In this example, unlike in previous examples, 'the Contract' is given a definition. This is probably not strictly necessary where there is only one contract, and no possible ambiguity, but it is frequently done in practice.

Paragraph 3. The material terms. These terms are material to the debt claim. The defendants have failed to pay for two instalments by the due date, so it is necessary to state what the due date was. Since that date is defined by reference to delivery dates, it becomes material to set out the term relating to delivery.

Paragraph 4. This is here for the reasons explained in the previous example.

Paragraph 5. This is stage 4 — defendants' knowledge. The damages claim is for wasted expenditure incurred in order to fulfil this abortive contract. In order for it to be within the defendants' reasonable contemplation at the time of the contract that this expenditure might be wasted in the event of breach, it is necessary to allege and prove that they had the knowledge from which that outcome could be inferred. So this paragraph becomes a necessary part of the statement of case, to show that the loss is not too remote.

Paragraph 6. Performance. No payment was due from the defendants until after delivery, so the delivery must be stated. The word 'duly' establishes the connection to the contract. Without it, the defendants would not necessarily be obliged to pay for the base plugs, because they would not necessarily be the ones they had promised to pay for.

Paragraph 7. The first breach — non-payment of the price of two instalments. Note the essential words 'or any part of that sum' and 'or at all'. Without these words you are not alleging that the defendants have not paid, only that they have not paid the full amount, or have not paid on the due date. The second sentence of this paragraph does not actually do much more than say that 500 + 500 = 1000, but it is not uncommon in debt claims to allege not only failure to pay but also that the sum is still owed. This is arguably tautologous, but perhaps helps to signal that this is a claim for a debt not damages. Add 'qualifying debt' for statutory interest purposes.

Paragraph 8. The second breach. Where the breach is alleged to amount to a repudiation of the contract, you must use the word 'repudiate' and also state the fact that, and when and how, the claimants accepted the repudiation. The particulars of the breach are the refusal to accept further deliveries. Doubtless the claimants know why the defendants repudiated the contract, and it may be that the defendants will in their defence allege some breach of contract by the claimants, but that is not part of the claimants' case and does not appear.

Paragraph 9. The loss and damage claimed for the second breach. The claimants have chosen to claim their wasted expenditure rather than their lost profit, as they have the right to do. Note the need to give some explanation of the causation of the loss, without which the claim is incomplete.

Paragraph 10. The claim for interest is divided into two. The debt claim is a claim for a specified amount, which requires interest to be set out with all the particulars prescribed by CPR, r 16.4(2) (paragraph 9(a)). This is a debt which qualifies for statutory interest under the 1998 Act. The rate claimed is 11.75%, because base rate on 31 December 2003 was 3.75%. Interest on damages can be left to be assessed in the usual way (paragraph 9(b)). This can only be under s 69 of the County Courts Act 1984.

Paragraph 11. Compensation, as in the previous example.

Prayer. Note the itemisation by reference to paragraphs in the body of the statement of case. This is not compulsory, but particularly clear and helpful in a case like this.

9.7   Contract: failure of consideration: recovery of money paid

9.7.1   Particulars of claim

IN THE MIDDLESBROUGH COUNTY COURT   Claim No MB4/21074

BETWEEN

JOSEPHINE DRURY   Claimant

and

SIDNEY KETTLE (trading as
SID'S AUTOS)   Defendant

PARTICULARS OF CLAIM

1.   By an oral agreement made on or about 17th May 2004 between the Claimant and the Defendant at the Defendant's premises in Lower Dock Street, Middlesbrough, and evidenced in writing by a handwritten invoice dated 17th May 2004 signed by the Defendant (a copy of which is attached), the Defendant agreed to sell and the Claimant agreed to buy a Volkswagen motor caravan registration No P27 ONF ('the Vehicle') for the price of £7,500.

2.   It was an implied condition of the agreement that the Defendant would have the right to sell the Vehicle at the time when the property was to pass.

3.   On 19th May 2004 the Claimant paid the Defendant the price of £7,500 and took delivery of the Vehicle.

4.   The Defendant was not at any material time the owner of the Vehicle nor had he at any material time the right to sell it, and was therefore in breach of the implied condition.

5.   On 30th June 2004, the Claimant was obliged to deliver the Vehicle to Rubber Finance Limited, who were its lawful owners.

6.   Because of the matters set out above the consideration for the payment of the sum of £7,500 has wholly failed. In the alternative the Claimant has suffered loss and damage of £7,500 because of the Defendant's breach of the implied condition.

7.   Further, the Claimant claims interest under section 69 of the County Courts Act 1984 on the sum of £7,500 at the rate of 8% per year from 19th May 2004, amounting to £269.59 at 30th October 2004 and then continuing until judgment or sooner payment at the rate of £1.64 per day.

AND the Claimant claims:

(1) £7,500; alternatively damages of £7,500.

(2) Interest under section 69 of the County Courts Act 1984, amounting to £271.23 at 30th October 2004 and continuing at the daily rate of £1.64.

JOSEPH BLOGGS

STATEMENT OF TRUTH

Dated etc.

9.7.2 Commentary

This is another claim setting out two causes of action, but in this case they arise out of the same facts and are strictly alternative to each other, as the drafting makes clear.

Paragraph 1. The only thing that is relevant about the parties is that the defendant sold the vehicle to the claimant, so stages 1 and 2 (parties and contract) can be combined. This is an oral agreement, so note the need to say *where* the agreement was made, but it is evidenced in writing, so the evidencing document can be attached. The date is given using the formula 'on or about'. This is a very common phrase, useful where the date is not absolutely certain. But do not use it when the date *is* certain.

Paragraph 2. The material term. This condition is implied by s 12 of the Sale of Goods Act 1979, so it is unnecessary to say why it is implied.

Paragraph 3. Performance.

Paragraph 4. Breach and the particulars of breach. In this example, unusually, the particulars of breach come first and the allegation of breach second. There is nothing wrong with setting it out like this in a straightforward case, if it seems convenient. But do not put the particulars of breach first if they are lengthy or complex.

Paragraph 5. This is the causation of the loss, which obviously needs to be set out.

Paragraph 6. Sets out two alternative claims for loss. The first, stated in the first sentence, is total failure of consideration, which gives rise to a claim for restitution of the contract price. Such a claim is established simply by making the short simple statement that the consideration has wholly failed. The second claim is for damages, for breach of the implied condition. The damages are quantified as the purchase price, so the value of the two claims is identical, but they are obviously alternative: the court can grant a remedy for either one but not both.

Paragraph 7. Both claims are for a specified amount, so in either case, interest needs to be set out in detail.

Prayer. Note the alternative claim in item (1): either restitution of £7,500 or damages of that amount.

9.8 Contract: sale of goods: implied terms

9.8.1 Particulars of claim

IN THE WOLVERHAMPTON COUNTY COURT   Claim No WV4/12680

BETWEEN

AGATHA PARTINGTON   Claimant

and

ACE DETERGENTS LIMITED   Defendants

PARTICULARS OF CLAIM

1. The Claimant is the proprietor of the Morning Sunshine guest-house in Newby Gardens, Wolverhampton. The Defendants are and were at all material times in the business of selling cleaning products.

2. On 14th June 2004 the Defendants in the course of their business sold to the Claimant 5 litres of Ace liquid detergent at a price of £36.00.

3.   At the time of the sale the Claimant made it known to the Defendants that the detergent was required for the purpose of cleaning the carpets in the guest-house.

4.   It was therefore an implied term of the contract of sale that the detergent should be:

(a) reasonably fit for that purpose; and

(b) of satisfactory quality.

5.   On 15th June 2004 the Claimant used the detergent to clean the carpets in the guest-house.

6.   In breach of the above implied terms the detergent was not fit for the required purpose and not of satisfactory quality in that:

(a) It contained a chemical substance or substances which damaged the Claimant's carpets beyond repair.

(b) It gave off toxic and irritant fumes which made the guest-house uninhabitable for three days.

7.   As a result of the matters set out above the Claimant has suffered loss and damage.

PARTICULARS OF DAMAGE

	£
(1) Value of carpets ruined	4,300.00
(2) Cost of removing carpets and relaying new carpets	750.00
(3) Loss of profit over 3 days	290.00
	5,340.00

8.   Further the Claimant claims interest under section 69 of the County Courts Act 1984 on the sum of £5,340 at the rate of 8% per year from 15th June 2004, amounting to £160.35 at 30th October 2004 and then continuing until judgment or sooner payment at the rate of £1.17 per day.

AND the Claimant claims:

(1) Damages of £5,340.

(2) Interest pursuant to section 69 of the County Courts Act 1984, amounting to £160.35 at 30th October 2004 and continuing at the daily rate of £1.17.

JOSEPH BLOGGS

STATEMENT OF TRUTH

Dated etc.

9.8.2 Commentary

More implied terms in this example — this time the terms implied into contracts for the sale of goods under s 14 of the Sale of Goods Act 1979, that the goods will be of satisfactory quality and fit for any purpose made known to the seller at the time of the purchase.

Paragraph 1. The parties. Straightforwardly setting the scene.

Paragraph 2. The contract, and also the performance of it. Where the contract simply involves the sale of goods, and there will be no dispute as to the sale, it is unnecessarily cumbersome to have one paragraph alleging that the defendant agreed to sell the goods to the claimant at a certain price, and then another alleging that pursuant to that contract the defendant handed over the goods and the claimant handed over the price. The simple word 'sold' covers it all. The words 'in the course of their business' are essential — see **7.9.2**.

Paragraph 3. Before the implied term as to fitness for purpose can arise, that purpose must have been made known to the seller. So it is an essential part of stage 3 — the terms — to state this. The material time is at or before the time of sale, so this time must also be stated.

Paragraph 4. After the pre-requisite is stated, the implied terms can then be set out.

Paragraph 5. Simple story telling, without which the causation of loss cannot be explained.

Paragraph 6. Breach. The particulars of breach are not ideal. One would prefer to be able to state what the offending substance(s) were, and what chemical process caused the damage. But this would involve expert evidence, and maybe there is nothing left for an expert to examine. So we do the best we can and particularise the breach by reference to the *result* of the breach rather than the breach itself because no more is known. This should be sufficient, because the court should not find it difficult to infer that if this was the result of using the detergent then it was not of satisfactory quality or fit for its purpose, even if no one knows why.

Paragraph 7. The loss and damage is straightforward and needs no explanation. The claimant cannot of course recover the cost of the new carpets, only the value of the old ones, which she will have to prove.

Paragraph 8. This is a claim for damages, which in principle can be assessed by the court. However, the claimant has chosen to specify an exact figure for damages, and so made this a claim for a specified amount. This therefore requires interest to be set out in full, in accordance with CPR, r 16.4(2)(b).

9.9   Contract: supply of services: implied terms

9.9.1   Particulars of claim

IN THE SHREWSBURY COUNTY COURT   Claim No SY4/74001

BETWEEN

DENNIS LISTER   <u>Claimant</u>

and

HOMEWOOD GARDEN CENTRE LIMITED   <u>Defendants</u>

PARTICULARS OF CLAIM

1.   The Defendants operate a garden centre business, in the course of which they repair and service motor mowers. The Claimant is a long-standing customer of the Defendants.

2.   On 15th May 2004 the Claimant took his motor mower to the Defendants' premises to be repaired and serviced by them, which they agreed to do. This agreement is partly evidenced by the Defendants' service invoice No 0251 dated 19th May 2004, a copy of which is attached. The Defendants carried out the repairs and service and the Claimant paid them their charge of £102.70 when he collected his motor mower on 19th May 2004.

3.   It was an implied term of the agreement that the Defendants would repair and service the Claimant's motor mower with reasonable care and skill.

4.   On 20th May 2004 the Claimant was using his motor mower in the garden at his home, when the throttle return spring on the mower came adrift, so that the mower was stuck at full throttle, ran out of control and smashed into the Claimant's greenhouse.

5.   The matters complained of were caused by a breach of the above implied term and/or negligence by the Defendants, their employees or agents, who failed to attach the throttle return spring properly to the frame of the motor mower and so did not use reasonable care and skill in carrying out the repairs and service.

6.   As a result of the matters set out above the Claimant has suffered loss and damage.

PARTICULARS OF DAMAGE

£

(1)	Cost of repairs to greenhouse	635.00
(2)	Value of plants in greenhouse damaged. Some plants were damaged by the mower and/or falling glass. Other tropical plants were killed by the sudden loss of temperature.	5,250.00
(3)	Loss of prize money. The Claimant was rearing marrows in his greenhouse in the certain expectation of winning a prize by displaying them at the Midland Garden Show in August 2004. The Claimant will rely on the fact that his marrows have won a prize at the Midland Garden Show in each of the last five years.	
	Estimated at	200.00

7.   Further the Claimant claims interest under section 69 of the County Courts Act 1984 on the amount found to be due to the Claimant at such rate and for such period as the Court thinks fit.

AND the Claimant claims:

(1) Damages.

(2) Interest under section 69 of the County Courts Act 1984 to be assessed.

JOSEPH BLOGGS

STATEMENT OF TRUTH

Dated etc.

9.9.2 Commentary

This is another claim for breach of an implied term — this time the term implied into contracts for services by s 13 of the Supply of Goods and Services Act 1982.

Paragraph 1. Note the words 'in the course of which'. The implied term which the claimant relies on is a term which is only implied into a contract for services where the supplier is acting in the course of a business, so this fact is a material fact which must be included. As we saw in **7.9** and **9.7**, the best way of doing this is to say that the supplier agreed to provide the services in this particular case in the course of its business, incorporating this phrase into paragraph 2. However it is not uncommonly done as here, by stating at the outset that the defendants provide services generally in the course of their business. It is less specific, but it will do.

The fact that the claimant is a long-standing customer of the defendants looks irrelevant at first, but is stated because the claimant anticipates a potential defence that the damages claimed for loss of prize money are too remote. It is not appropriate to anticipate this defence before it is alleged, but we can do a little to head it off by stating this fact which helps to show that such loss might reasonably have been within the defendants' contemplation.

Paragraph 2. Deals with both the contract and its performance. As in the previous example, where there is unlikely to be any dispute in these areas, they can conveniently be taken together, even if this strictly breaks the rule about chronological order.

Paragraph 3. Sets out the term to be implied under s 13.

Paragraph 4. Simple story telling — the causation of the loss.

Paragraph 5. Breach of an implied term under s 13 is contractual negligence. It follows that if there is a duty of care at common law as well, there is a concurrent claim in tort. It does not actually matter too much whether the common law duty exists or not, because it is almost impossible to draft a claim for contractual negligence without alleging common law negligence at the same time, since the material facts required to establish both claims are the same. Therefore it is usual, and it is good practice, to recognise this potential concurrent liability by alleging not only that the defendants were in breach of the implied term, but also that they were negligent.

The particulars of breach and negligence are the same: failing to attach the throttle return spring properly.

Paragraph 6. Three items of loss are claimed. The first needs no explanation, but the next two do. Failure to explain the causation of loss is a very common fault in students' drafts. Note particularly the claim for loss of prize money, which the claimant clearly anticipates will be contentious. He needs to show that he would probably have won a prize, so he states the fact that he has won regularly in the past.

9.10 Professional negligence

9.10.1 Particulars of claim

IN THE HIGH COURT OF JUSTICE   Claim No 2004 HC 7401
QUEEN'S BENCH DIVISION

BETWEEN

ALISTAIR GREATBATCH   Claimant

and

(1) HENRY WILLIAMS
(2) SCOTT WILLIAMS (a firm)   Defendants

PARTICULARS OF CLAIM

1.   The First Defendant is a chartered surveyor and valuer and is a partner in the Second Defendants who are a firm of surveyors, estate agents and valuers who carry on business from their offices at 21 Dean Street, London W1. At all material times the Defendants held themselves out as experienced, skilled and competent surveyors and valuers.

2.   In about February 2004 the Claimant was contemplating the purchase of a freehold house at 10 Elm Avenue, London SW1 ('the House') and on 21st February 2004 at the De-

fendants' offices orally instructed the First Defendant for a fee to survey and value the House and to advise him about its structure and condition, which the First Defendant on his own behalf or on behalf of the Second Defendants agreed to do. The agreement is evidenced in writing by the Defendants' invoice No 0287 dated 14th March 2004, a copy of which is attached.

3.   The First Defendant knew at the time of the agreement that the Claimant would rely on his survey, advice and valuation in deciding whether to purchase the House and if so at what price.

4.   It was an implied term of the agreement that the First Defendant in surveying and valuing the House and in advising the Claimant would exercise all reasonable care and skill to be expected of an experienced, skilled and competent surveyor and valuer. Further or alternatively the Defendants owed the Claimant a duty to exercise such care and skill.

5.   The First Defendant in performance of the contract surveyed or purported to survey the House and by a written report ('the Report') to the Claimant dated 14th March 2004 advised the Claimant that (apart from certain minor defects set out in the Report) the House was of substantial construction, was structurally sound and in good condition, and valued it at £175,000. A copy of the Report is attached.

6.   In reliance on the Report and valuation, by exchange of contracts on 14th April 2004 the Claimant bought the House for £175,000.

7.   In fact the House was at all material times structurally unsound and in a defective condition in the respects set out in the schedule attached to these particulars of claim.

8.   In giving the Report and valuation referred to above the Defendants were in breach of the implied term of the agreement and/or the First Defendant was negligent in that:

PARTICULARS OF NEGLIGENCE

   (a) He failed to inspect the House properly or at all.

   (b) He failed to observe the defects in the House set out in the schedule or any of them.

   (c) He failed to advise the Claimant of those defects fully or at all.

   (d) He gave a value for the House which did not take account of all its defects.

   (e) He failed in all the circumstances to exercise the care and skill to be expected of a competent surveyor and valuer.

9.   As a result of the matters set out above of the Claimant has suffered loss and damage.

PARTICULARS OF DAMAGE

The actual value of the House at the date of the Report was no greater than £125,000. The Claimant has accordingly suffered loss of at least £50,000.

10.   Further the Claimant claims interest under section 35A of the Supreme Court Act 1981 on the amount found to be due to the Claimant at such rate and for such period as the Court thinks fit.

AND the Claimant claims:

   (1) Damages.

   (2) Interest pursuant to section 35A of the Supreme Court Act 1981 to be assessed.

JOSEPH BLOGGS

STATEMENT OF TRUTH

Dated etc.

9.10.2   Commentary

Professional negligence claims can arise both in contract and in tort. In the typical case, there is a contract between the claimant and the professional defendant, and so the claim is primarily contractual, but there is concurrent liability in tort. But there are other cases, particularly clinical negligence claims where the patient was treated under the NHS, which arise solely in the tort of negligence. There is an example of such a claim in **12.1**. This is a claim against a negligent surveyor, and so there is concurrent liability. As in the previous example, the claim is drafted primarily in contract, but there is no doubt about the concurrent tortious liability here, and so it is expressly stated. The negligence claim is of course a claim for negligent advice, and so the structure and content of this claim closely follows that of the example in **9.4**.

Heading. Both the individual surveyor and his firm are named as defendants. The claimant is unsure whether Henry Williams was acting on his own behalf or on behalf of the firm.

Paragraph 1. Introduces the defendants. The second sentence is a crucial part of the claim. For the claim in contract, the material term is that implied under s 13 of the Supply of Goods and Services Act 1982, that the surveyor would act with reasonable care and skill. However, the standard of care expected varies according to the level of expertise professed by the defendant. If the defendant is a professional, or a specialist, or an expert, then the standard of care is that reasonably to be expected of such a professional, specialist or expert. It is necessary therefore to state what expertise the defendant professed to have. For the claim in negligence, the duty of care arises if the defendant had a special skill, upon which the claimant relied, and it was reasonably foreseeable that the claimant would rely on that skill. So again it is essential to state what special skill the defendant had.

The usual formula for setting out this material fact, which is an essential part of both the contractual and negligence claims, is that which appears here: 'held themselves out as experienced skilled and competent' in whatever the specialist field is.

Paragraph 2. Introduces the claimant and the house, and states the contract. In contracts of this kind it is often understood that a fee will be payable, but the instructions to act are accepted without a fixed fee being agreed. One simple way of dealing with the impossibility of specifying the consideration precisely is to use the words 'for a fee'. It is important in cases of this kind to specify what exactly the defendant agreed to do. It was not merely to survey and value, but also to *advise* the claimant. The claim is for negligent advice. 'On his own behalf or on behalf of the Second Defendants' — because the claimant is unsure which.

Paragraph 3. These are the facts that give rise to the duty of care at common law, and so must be stated. It is sufficient in law that it was reasonably foreseeable that the claimant would rely on the defendant's advice, but if actual knowledge can be shown, which it obviously can in this case, it is usual to allege that the defendant *knew* the claimant would rely on his advice. It is important to add for what purposes it was foreseeable that the claimant would rely on the advice. There will be no duty of care if the advice is relied upon for an unforeseeable purpose. Note that the giving of the advice is *not* one of the facts giving rise to the duty, as it is in the example in **9.4**. In this case the duty of care came into existence before the negligent advice was given.

Paragraph 4. Alleges the implied term and the duty of care. The implied term is of course that the defendant would exercise reasonable care and skill, but in a case of professional services, the heightened standard of care explained above under paragraph 1 can be implied. So this paragraph should specify not just the existence of the duty but the standard of care expected as well. This must by definition match whatever you have said the defendant held himself out as capable of in paragraph 1, so there must be a correlation between the words used in these two paragraphs. The duty of care owed at common law will be identical. The existence of the duty is stated expressly, thereby leaving no room for doubt that the claim is brought in negligence as well as in contract.

Paragraph 5. Performance of the agreement — what the defendant did, and the advice he gave. Do not at this stage allege it to be wrong advice. The words 'or purported to survey' are perhaps a bit cheeky, but are intended to cover the possibility that the defendant never really had a close look at the house at all. The date of the report is essential. In contract, time for limitation purposes runs from the date of breach, and the giving of the advice in the report is the breach. It is not necessary to attach a copy of the report, but it is probably helpful and good practice.

Paragraph 6. Reliance. That the claimant relied on the advice is an essential ingredient of liability in negligence in its own right. In contract it is material in that it is what caused the loss. State what the claimant did in reliance on the advice. The date of exchange of contracts is essential. In tort, time for limitation purposes runs from the date of damage, and the date of damage is the date at which the claimant was committed to the purchase at an overvalue.

Paragraph 7. The fact that the house was defective and the advice unsound comes next, before the allegation of breach and negligence. It is a separate fact: the fact that the house was defective is not in itself a particular of negligence. This paragraph is of course strictly out of chronological order: the house was always defective, and the advice was unsound at the time it was given, so you might think this paragraph should have come before paragraph 6. But it looks distinctly odd to allege that the house was defective and then that the claimant bought it. So this paragraph is usually placed here, corresponding to the moment in time at which the claimant discovered that the house was defective. Note the use of a schedule to set out detailed particulars. If they are numerous and lengthy, this is a good way to do it. Your aim is to keep the particulars of claim concise.

Paragraph 8. Remember to allege both breach of the implied term and negligence. The breach is that of both defendants; the negligence is that of the first defendant alone. The particulars are fairly obvious. Note the use of the words 'or at all' and 'or any of them'. We have had several examples of this type of phrase now, and hopefully you are starting to find it comes naturally in your own drafting. Particular (e) is another general summing up particular — entirely unnecessary, but conventional.

Paragraph 9. The loss recoverable in a case of negligent survey or valuation of domestic property is always assessed on a diminution in value basis — the difference between the purchase price and the true value.

9.11   Exercise A

Counsel is instructed on behalf of Mrs Geraldine Mackintosh, the administratrix of the estate of her husband Sean who was killed in the factory where he worked as a welder on 25 September 2003. Letters of administration were granted on 5 January 2004. She wishes to bring an action against his employer, Hogarth Engineering Ltd.

The evidence of Mr Ben Jones, a fellow employee of Mr Mackintosh, is that Mr Mackintosh was working on a steel gallery 12 feet above the factory floor when he slipped on a patch of oil on the gallery floor, fell through the open hatchway which provided access to the gallery, and died instantaneously as he hit the ground. Mr Jones will say that the hatchway had a guard rail on one side only and that he had often complained about oil on the platform. The hatchway should have been closed, but someone had left it open. The words 'close me' were written on the underside of the hatch, but there was no other warning notice or indication of danger.

The employers contend that if the hatchway was open it was Mr Mackintosh who left it open, that the single guard rail is sufficient if the hatchway is closed, and that they had no knowledge of oil being on the floor either on this occasion or generally. It must have been a one-off event that they could not have done anything about other than expect any employee who saw it to clean it up.

Mr Mackintosh earned £300 per week net and kept £100.00 per week for himself, giving his wife the rest for housekeeping and family expenses. There is one child of the family,

Louise, born 27th January 1998. Other dates of birth: Sean Mackintosh, 29th October 1976, Mrs Mackintosh 1st May 1980. Special damages are broken wrist-watch £30.00 and funeral expenses £921.85. For Counsel's convenience some extracts from the Workplace (Health, Safety and Welfare) Regulations 1992 are reproduced below.

Counsel is asked to draft particulars of claim.

2.—(1)   In these Regulations, unless the context otherwise requires—
'workplace' means … any premises or part of premises which are not domestic premises and are made available to any person as a place of work, and includes
(a)   any place within the premises to which such person has access while at work; …

4.—(1)   Every employer shall ensure that every workplace … which is under his control and where any of his employees works complies with any requirement of these Regulations which—
(a)   applies to that workplace ….; and
(b)   is in force in respect of the workplace …

12.—(1)   Every floor in a workplace and the surface of every traffic route in a workplace shall be of a construction such that the floor or surface of the traffic route is suitable for the purpose for which it is used.
(2)   Without prejudice to the generality of paragraph (1), the requirements in that paragraph shall include requirements that—
(a)   the floor, or surface of the traffic route, shall have no hole or slope, or be uneven or slippery so as, in each case, to expose any person to a risk to his health or safety; …
(3)   So far as is reasonably practicable, every floor in a workplace and the surface of every traffic route in a workplace shall be kept free from obstructions and from any article or substance which may cause a person to slip, trip or fall.
(4)   In considering whether for the purposes of paragraph (2)(a) a hole or slope exposes any person to a risk to his health or safety—
(a)   no account shall be taken of a hole where adequate measures have been taken to prevent a person falling; …

13.—(1)   So far as is reasonably practicable, suitable and effective measures shall be taken to prevent any event specified in paragraph (3).
(2)   So far as is reasonably practicable, the measures required by paragraph (1) shall be measures other than the provision of personal protective equipment, information, instruction, training or supervision.
(3)   The events specified in this paragraph are—
(a)   any person falling a distance likely to cause personal injury;
(b)   any person being struck by a falling object likely to cause personal injury.
(4)   Any area where there is a risk to health and safety from any event mentioned in paragraph (3) shall be clearly indicated where appropriate.

9.12   Exercise B

Sophie Harrington will say:

I own an oil painting, *Portrait of a Pauper with Tulips*, by the 19th-century artist William Biggs, valued in January 2003 at £24,000. On 3 March 2004 I took it to Bond Galleries Ltd with a view to having it cleaned and restored. They told me that they could carry out this work, that it would take about three weeks and that it would cost about £3,000. I agreed, and left the painting with them. On 21 March 2004 I received a telephone call from Bond Galleries to say that the painting was ready and that the charge was £2,800 plus VAT. I was too busy to call in for a few days so I asked my secretary to go to collect it and wrote out and gave him a cheque for £3,290 payable to Bond Galleries. When he returned with the painting later that day I found that it was badly damaged. There were several patches of paint which had flaked off, some of the colours had dulled badly and the overall life of the painting was seriously diminished. I have had it revalued at only £8,000. I am advised by the valuers that cleaning and restoration would not have made a great difference to its value before it was damaged: it might have gained about £1,000 in value at most. I wish to bring an action for damages against the restorers, who have also refused to refund my money.

Counsel is asked to draft particulars of claim to be filed in the Central London County Court.

Further defences

10.1 Tort: occupiers' liability: trespasser

10.1.1 Defence

(See particulars of claim in **9.1**.)

<u>IN THE WEST LONDON COUNTY COURT</u>   Claim No WL4/10114

BETWEEN

EDWARD MOSS   <u>Claimant</u>

and

(1) LONDON BOROUGH OF GREENBRIDGE
(2) BIG BLUE CLEANING SERVICES LIMITED . <u>Defendants</u>

DEFENCE OF THE FIRST DEFENDANTS

---

1.   The First Defendants are unable to admit or deny the purpose of the Claimant's visit to Greenbridge Town Hall or the manner and cause of his fall to the floor, and require the Claimant to prove these matters. It is denied that the Claimant was a lawful visitor of the First Defendants on the staircase or at the material time. Otherwise, paragraphs 1 and 2 of the Particulars of Claim are admitted.

2.   The staircase referred to is in the western section of Greenbridge Town Hall which was closed to members of the public at the material time. The Claimant entered the Town Hall by the west door on which a notice was prominently displayed informing members of the public that the western section was closed, that the west door was not to be used and directing them to use the east door. The Claimant was therefore a trespasser on the staircase at the time of his accident.

3.   It is denied that the First Defendants, their employees or agents were negligent or in breach of statutory duty as alleged or at all. It is further denied that the accident was caused by the alleged or any negligence or breach of statutory duty on the part of the First Defendants, their employees or agents.

PARTICULARS

(1) Because the western section of the Town Hall was closed to members of the public, and the First Defendants took reasonable steps to keep the Claimant out of that

area, and direct him to an alternative staircase, they had no obligation to take any further steps to keep the Claimant off the staircase, or to warn him that it was wet.

(2) The manner in which the staircase was washed was solely the responsibility of the Second Defendants and did not require supervision. The First Defendants rely on the matters set out in paragraph 4 below.

(3) It is admitted that the iron banister was rusty and unsafe. This was part of the reason why the western section of the Town Hall was closed, as it was in the process of being repaired and refurbished.

4.   If, which the Claimant is required to prove, a duty of care was owed by the Second Defendants to the Claimant, the accident was caused by the negligence of the Second Defendants, their employees or agents.

PARTICULARS OF NEGLIGENCE

The Second Defendants, their employees or agents were negligent in that they:

(a) Allowed the Claimant to walk up the staircase when it was wet and unsafe.

(b) Failed to direct the Claimant to make use of an alternative staircase.

(c) Washed the staircase in such a manner that all parts of it were wet at the same time, which was unsafe.

(d) Failed to keep the Claimant or other persons away from the staircase while it was being washed by putting a rope barrier across the foot of it or otherwise.

(e) Failed to give the Claimant any or any adequate warning that the staircase was wet and unsafe.

5.   Further or alternatively the accident was caused or contributed to by the negligence of the Claimant.

PARTICULARS OF NEGLIGENCE

(a) Failing to observe or heed the notice on the west door.

(b) Entering the western section of the Town Hall and climbing the staircase when he knew or ought to have known he was not permitted to do so.

(c) Failing to take care when walking on a wet staircase.

(d) Failing in the above respects to take any or any proper care for his own safety.

6.   Except as set out in paragraph 7 below, and in the counter-schedule of expenses and losses served with this Defence, the Claimant is required to prove the extent of his injuries and of any loss and damage claimed.

7.   *[Deal with matters set out in Claimant's medical report, stating which are agreed, which are disputed, and which are matters the Defendant has no knowledge of.]*

BESS TOFFER

STATEMENT OF TRUTH

Dated etc.

10.1.2 Commentary

Note that this is the defence of the first defendants only, and is entitled as such. The defence is that the claimant went into a part of the town hall from which he was expressly excluded, and so was a trespasser. The first defendants also deny that they were in breach of their duty as occupiers under the Occupiers' Liability Act 1957, and *a fortiori* in breach of any duty they would owe to the claimant as a trespasser under the Occupiers' Liability Act 1984. They also, somewhat as a last resort, blame the second defendants and allege contributory negligence by the claimant.

Paragraph 1. Deals with the first two paragraphs of the claim — the parties and the accident. Obviously the first defendants are unable to admit or deny the purpose of the claimant's visit; they admit that he fell from the staircase, but not what caused him to fall. Note the careful drafting by which the claimant is required to prove the manner and cause of the fall, but not the fall itself. That the claimant was a lawful visitor has to be denied if the trespasser defence is to be established. The paragraph is structured so that apart from the matters just mentioned, the rest of paragraphs 1 and 2 can be dealt with in a 'mop-up' admission.

Paragraph 2. The reasons for the denial made in paragraph 1 must now be given. This involves stating the facts relied upon by the first defendants to show that the claimant was a trespasser. This is arguably evidence, but it is evidence of the kind that must be stated, as it is the basis of the defence. Finish by stating the conclusion to be drawn, namely that the claimant was a trespasser: not, of course a trespasser in the town hall as a whole — only in one particular part of it.

Paragraph 3. Starts with the standard denials of negligence (adding breach of statutory duty) and causation. Under the heading 'PARTICULARS' are then set out the reasons for these denials. Remember that you must cover all the particulars of negligence alleged by the claimant, but not necessarily in the same order. Particular (1) effectively relies on the facts stated in paragraph 2 to justify the denial of the claimant's particulars (a), (b), (e) and (f), all four of which are expressly but concisely covered. The first defendants say they did take reasonable steps to keep the claimant away from the staircase. They do not deny that they gave no warning that the staircase was wet; they argue that there was no need to do so. Particular (2) deals with the claimant's particulars (c) and (d), and bases the denial on the second defendants' negligence, to which forward reference is made. Particular (3) deals with the claimant's particular (g). The first defendants can only admit that the banister was rusty, but are able to give a reason why this does not amount to negligence. The claimant's particular (h) adds nothing and needs no separate reason for its denial.

Paragraph 4. We are still on stage 3. If the accident was not caused by the first defendants' negligence, they must say what did cause it, and their next argument is that it was all the fault of the second defendants. However, there is a potential contradiction: if the second defendants were at fault, they must have been negligent, and if they were negligent they must be in breach of a duty owed to the claimant, a duty which probably only exists if he was not a trespasser, which is contrary to the defence already set out. So the first defendants want to allege it is the fault of the second defendants without admitting that the second defendants are liable. To do this, they make the allegation conditional on the claimant's establishing the existence of a duty, which they require him to prove. The particulars of negligence are lifted from those alleged by the claimant himself.

Paragraph 5. Alleges the negligence of the claimant, alternatively contributory negligence. See the commentary in **8.5.2**. As always the particulars cover several eventualities. The claimant may or may not have seen the notice. If he did, he was negligent in not heeding it and he knew he was not permitted to use the staircase; if he did not, he was negligent in failing to observe it, and he ought to have known he was not permitted to use the staircase. The phrase 'knew or ought to have known' is very common and useful.

Paragraphs 6 and 7. These are identical to those in **8.5.1** — see the commentary to that example.

10.2   Tort: *volenti non fit injuria:* pure accident

10.2.1   Defence

(See particulars of claim in **9.2.2**.)

<u>IN THE HIGH COURT OF JUSTICE</u>   Claim No 2004 HC 6151
<u>QUEEN'S BENCH DIVISION</u>

BETWEEN

RICHARD ALLEN   <u>Claimant</u>

and

H. A. JOHNS (CONSTRUCTION) LIMITED   <u>Defendants</u>

<u>DEFENCE</u>

1.   Except that it is denied that Patrick Connelly or any other person instructed the Claimant to climb onto the lead, paragraphs 1, 2 and 3 of the Particulars of Claim are admitted.

2.   It is denied that the Defendants, their employees or agents were in breach of the alleged or any statutory duties. It is further denied that the accident was caused by any breach of statutory duty by the Defendants, their employees or agents.

PARTICULARS

(1) The Claimant was not required to climb onto the lead, but did so of his own volition, without the knowledge or consent of the Defendants.

(2) The crane was of adequate stability for the load being carried. At about 11 a.m. on 29th September 2003 Patrick Connelly carried out a test ('the Test') by which he established the stability of the crane under loading conditions greater than those required for pile driving.

(3) The crane was therefore safely installed and positioned.

(4) The lifting operation was carried out in a manner which would have been safe but for the claimant's own act in climbing onto the lead.

3.   It is denied that the Defendants, their employees or agents were negligent as alleged in paragraph 5 of the Particulars of Claim or at all or that the accident was caused by any negligence on the part of the Defendants, their employees or agents.

PARTICULARS

(1) The Defendants rely on the matters set out in paragraph 2 above.

(2) Patrick Connelly ascertained the degree to which the jib could be safely extended in the Test.

(3) At the time of the accident the jib was extended to a radius of about 8 feet, compared to its limit in the Test of 15 feet with the load being carried.

(4) The crane was not operated too quickly or in a jerky manner.

(5) The Defendants further rely on the matters set out in paragraphs 4 and 5 below.

4.   The collapse of the crane was caused by the ground upon which it was standing suddenly giving way under the right front leg of the crane, causing the crane to become unbalanced and fall over. The ground below the surface gave way because the site had previously been filled with rubble, a fact unknown to the Defendants at the material time and which they could not reasonably have discovered.

5.   Further, the Claimant knew or ought to have known, having been so instructed by Patrick Connelly on at least two occasions prior to the accident, that it was dangerous to climb on the lead whilst it was in the air. In the circumstances the Claimant impliedly consented to run the risk of injury arising from his actions.

6.   Further or in the alternative the accident was caused or contributed to by the negligence of the Claimant and/or his own breach of statutory duty under regulation 6(1) of the Construction Regulations.

PARTICULARS

(a) Climbing onto the lead when he knew or ought to have known it was dangerous to do so.

(b) Ignoring the instructions of Patrick Connelly.

(c) In all the circumstances failing to have any or any sufficient regard for his own safety.

7.   The Defendants admit that the Claimant was injured in the accident but deny that the Claimant is unable to walk without the aid of a stick and will contend that he is able to walk further than alleged and is less limited in his daily activities than alleged. He has a good chance of finding suitable employment if he seeks it. Otherwise the Defendants agree the matters set out in the medical report of Dr Barry Green but require the Claimant to prove the extent of his injury and its consequences and to prove his loss and damage. The Defendants will rely on the medical report of Dr Martin Birts, a copy of which is attached. A counter-schedule of loss and expense is also attached.

BESS TOFFER

STATEMENT OF TRUTH

Dated etc.

10.2.2   Commentary

Paragraph 1. Except for one important denial, everything to do with the parties, background and accident is admitted. Strictly speaking a reason should be given for this denial, but it is hard to see how you can give a reason for a denial when you are simply saying that something never happened. The reason would simply repeat the denial. But actually, one could argue that the reason is given in paragraph 2: 'The Claimant climbed onto the lead of his own volition and without the knowledge, consent or instruction of the Defendants'.

Paragraph 2. A standard denial of breach of statutory duty and causation, followed by the reasons for the denial, set out as particulars. This introduces a new fact relied upon by the Defendants, namely the test, which supports their case, so it is expressly stated. The only possible defence to particular (d) in the claim, which alleges a breach of an absolute duty, is that it was only the claimant's own act that rendered the lifting operation unsafe in the circumstances.

Paragraph 3. Negligence and causation are denied in a similar way, using particulars to answer all the particulars of negligence. Particular (1) effectively deals with the claimant's particulars (a), (b), (c), and (f). Particulars (2), (3) and (4) provide specific responses to particulars (d), (e) and (g) respectively. Particular (g), being general, requires no specific response. Particular (5), looking ahead to paragraph 4, states the defendants' case on *res ipsa loquitur* (particular (g)).

Paragraph 4. Essentially alleges the defence of 'pure accident', ie that although the accident happened, it was unavoidable and involved no breach of duty by anyone. The full facts relied upon by the defendants must be set out. It is obviously necessary to add that these facts were unknown to the defendants and that they could not reasonably have discovered them. (This is weak, and as we shall see, the weakness can be exposed by a good request for further information (see **17.5**), but it is the defendants' case and must be stated.)

Paragraph 5. This is the defence of *volenti non fit injuria*, occasionally raised but very rarely successful. As a matter of law, it is only a defence to the claim in negligence, not to the claim for breach of statutory duty. The essence of the allegation, in English, is that the claimant impliedly consented to run the risk of injury arising from his actions, but one must add the facts in support of this, here the fact that he knew it was dangerous to climb on the lead. The words 'knew or ought to have known' appear once again. Whenever you allege that somebody knew something, you must give consideration to adding what is called 'particulars of knowledge', that is saying *why* or *how* they knew, giving the facts from which that knowledge was gained or can be inferred. If you allege that somebody ought to have known something, you should always add particulars of knowledge. Here the particulars of knowledge are 'having been so instructed by Patrick Connelly on at least two occasions prior to the accident'.

Paragraph 6. An allegation of contributory negligence, coupled with an allegation of contributory breach of statutory duty. As we observed when considering the particulars of claim, the claimant himself is in breach of reg 6(1) — see **9.2.3.1**. The particulars are straightforward and obvious. The particulars of the knowledge alleged in particular (a) have already been given and do not need to be repeated.

Paragraph 7. The injury, loss and damage is dealt with at greater length than usual, because in this case the defendants actually deny some aspects of the injury. They accuse the claimant of exaggerating the extent and consequences of his injuries. Of course they must have some evidence before making these allegations, so they attach a copy of an alternative medical report.

10.3   Contract: exclusion clause: remoteness

10.3.1   Defence

(See particulars of claim in **9.9**.)

IN THE SHREWSBURY COUNTY COURT   Claim No SY4/74001

BETWEEN

DENNIS LISTER   Claimant

and

HOMEWOOD GARDEN CENTRE LIMITED   Defendants

DEFENCE

1.   Paragraphs 1 and 2 of the Particulars of Claim are admitted.

2.   It was an express term of the agreement, set out in writing on the service invoice referred to, that the Defendants should not be liable for any loss arising out of the repairs and service to the mower except insofar as such loss consisted of and arose from damage to the mower caused by faulty and negligent execution of the repairs and service.

3.   Paragraph 3 of the Particulars of Claim is admitted.

4.   The Defendants are unable to admit or deny the matters set out in Paragraph 4 of the Particulars of Claim and the Claimant is required to prove them.

5.   It is denied that the Defendants are in breach of any implied term, or were negligent in carrying out the repairs and service, as alleged or at all. If, which the Claimant is required to prove, the throttle return spring was not properly attached to the frame of the motor mower, it was either in that condition when the mower was brought to the Defendants for service and repair, or it came about after the mower was returned to the Claimant. The repairs and service did not involve any adjustment to or interference with the throttle return spring.

6.   The Defendants admit the cost of repairs to the greenhouse and the value of the plants damaged, but require the Claimant to prove the alleged loss of prize money and the causation of all loss and damage claimed.

7.   Further or alternatively the alleged loss of opportunity to win prize money at The Midland Garden Show, which the Claimant is required to prove, was not reasonably foreseeable and/or was not reasonably within the parties' contemplation at the time of the agreement and is too remote for the Claimant to recover damages in respect of it.

8.   Further or alternatively the Defendants rely on the express term referred to in paragraph 2 above.

BESS TOFFER

STATEMENT OF TRUTH

Dated etc.

10.3.2 Commentary

Paragraph 1. As the claimant anticipated, there is no dispute as to the parties, the contract or the performance of it.

Paragraph 2. Stage 3 — terms. To rely on an exclusion clause in a defence, two matters need to be established: first that the term was incorporated into the contract, and secondly that it is effective to exclude or limit liability. This means it must be dealt with at two stages: first at stage 3 (the material terms) then later at stage 6 (breach) if the clause excludes liability altogether, or at stage 7 (loss and damage) if the clause limits the loss recoverable as the result of a breach. So the defendants must at this stage set out the express term on which they rely. Since the convention is that express terms come before implied terms, this comes first, before paragraph 3. A copy of the term has already been attached to the particulars of claim, so there is no need to copy it out in full — merely state the effect of it.

Paragraph 3. The existence of the implied term obviously has to be admitted.

Paragraph 4. What happened when the claimant used the mower is obviously entirely outside the defendants' knowledge.

Paragraph 5. Denial of breach and/or negligence. Since both are alleged, deny both, and of course add reasons for the denial. The phrase 'If, which the claimant is required to prove' is very useful. The defendants do not know whether the throttle return spring was properly attached or not, but the reasons they give for denying negligence are based on the assumption that it was not, so the allegation is made conditional on the claimant establishing the facts alleged by him.

Paragraph 6. The claimant has presumably provided the defendants with satisfactory evidence of the cost of repairs and the value of the plants. By admitting the loss, the defendants are not admitting liability, only the amount of damages under these heads if liability is established. The prize money, as the claimant expected, is contentious and the defendants require proof of causation under all heads, because they still do not know what actually happened.

Paragraph 7. Still dealing with loss and damage, the defendants now say that even if the claim for lost prize money is made out in terms of its existence and causation, they are still not liable for it because it is too remote. Since the claim is framed both in contract and in negligence, the defendants need to state the basis on which the loss would be too remote both in tort ('not reasonably foreseeable') and in contract ('not reasonably within the parties' contemplation at the time of the agreement').

Paragraph 8. Finally, the defendants rely on their exclusion clause, simply by stating that they do so. If effective, it limits damages to the cost of repairing the mower, a loss for which the claimant has surprisingly not claimed, so it would provide a complete defence. This paragraph comes last, because the clause only bites if the defendants would otherwise be liable for loss.

10.4 Contract: tender before claim

10.4.1 Defence

(See particulars of claim in **6.3.3**.)

IN THE HIGH COURT OF JUSTICE   Claim No 2004 HC 1234
QUEEN'S BENCH DIVISION
TECHNOLOGY AND CONSTRUCTION COURT

BETWEEN

B. LEAKE AND SONS (a firm)   Claimants

and

BELINDA JARROW   Defendant

DEFENCE

1.   By an oral agreement made by telephone on or about 17th January 2004 between the Defendant and Mr Leake on behalf of the Claimants, the Claimants agreed to construct an extension to the Defendant's house, Mon Repos, Acacia Avenue, London SE27, in accordance with an estimate previously supplied by the Claimants to the Defendant, but at a price of £51,280 and not £57,489.50 as specified in the estimate. Mr Leake agreed to this reduction in the price when the Defendant agreed to lengthen the hours which the Claimants could work.

2.   The Claimants constructed the extension between June and July 2004 in accordance with the oral agreement and the Defendant on 10th October 2004, before the issue of the claim form, tendered the sum of £51,280 by cheque to the Claimants in respect of the sum due under the agreement. The Claimants rejected the tender, without objecting that it was made by cheque.

3.   The Defendant has paid the sum of £51,280 into Court.

4.   The Defendant denies that the Claimants have done work or supplied materials other than in accordance with the oral agreement, and denies that the Claimants are entitled to the sum claimed or any sum in excess of £51,280.

BESS TOFFER

STATEMENT OF TRUTH

Dated etc.

10.4.2 Commentary

The particulars of claim in this case were in short form, because the claimants did not anticipate a valid defence. This hands the advantage to the defendant, who now gets the opportunity to be the first to set the full facts out for the benefit of the court. So the defendant states a lot of facts that might have been expected to appear in the particulars of claim if it had been drafted in full.

The defence is simple: tender before claim. This means that before the claim was commenced, the defendant offered unconditionally to pay the full amount due. In fact the dispute in this case is not over whether any sum is due, but over how much. There is a disagreement over what price was agreed for the work done. So the issue to be resolved is a simple one, and the defence will succeed if the sum due is held to be that which the defendant says she tendered. The tender shows her good faith.

Paragraph 1. Sets out the contract as it might have been stated in the particulars of claim, but in the form the defendant would have it. The draft makes it clear that the dispute is over the agreed price. The defendant has a problem, because the written evidence of the contract, the estimate, supports the claimants' case, so she states the basis on which she says the agreed price was arrived at.

Paragraph 2. Performance of the contract, and the defence of tender before claim. There are four ingredients to this defence for the defendant to establish: that (i) before the claim was commenced; (ii) she unconditionally tendered the sum due; (iii) the claimants rejected that tender; and (iv) the sum due has now been paid into court. Elements (i), (ii) and (iii) are dealt with in this paragraph. The fact that the tender was by cheque shows it to be unconditional. 'Without objecting that it was made by cheque' is important. No one is obliged to accept a cheque in settlement of a debt. They can insist on cash. So it needs to be established that it was not the cheque, but the tender itself which the claimants rejected.

Paragraph 3. This is the only occasion on which one states that money has been paid into court, because it is an essential ingredient of the defence.

Paragraph 4. You may wonder why this paragraph denies allegations that have not been made. This is because the defendant is anticipating a possible reply along the lines of '£51,280 was the sum agreed, but extras were later agreed as well, and the claim includes the extras'. We have seen that a claim should not anticipate a defence, but sometimes a defence needs to anticipate a reply, because there is no statement of case after a reply, so if the defendant does not say it now, she will not be able to say it later. Note that the defendant does not deny the claimants' claim, only that they are entitled to more than the agreed sum.

10.5 Exercise

Instructing solicitors act for Mr Ian Stein and Ms Farrah Day, who in early 2001 invented what is now called the 'Steinday Perpetual Magnetic Motor'. They were anxious to secure sufficient finance to be able to further develop and then promote and market this motor. They were approached by a Mr John Potter Gold, who insisted on coming to see them. A meeting was arranged at Mr Stein's house on 24th September 2001 at which all three were present. Mr Potter Gold offered to invest £30,000 in the project and to use his business connections to attempt to promote and find industrial and commercial developers or backers for the motor. In return he wanted to become a partner in the enterprise with them, receiving one-third of any proceeds of sale of the motor, including one-third of any royalties received. Mr Stein and Ms Day were reluctant, but felt compelled to agree to all this as it seemed to be the only way their project would ever get off the ground. The only written evidence of the agreement is a short document which Mr Potter Gold got Mr Stein and Ms Day to sign on 8th October 2001 which reads: 'We, being the owners and inventors of the Steinday Perpetual Magnetic Motor, hereby agree that John Potter Gold shall be entitled to a one-third share from the sale of the motor, to include any royalties received'. It is countersigned by John Potter Gold.

On 6th October 2001 the Defendants received a cheque dated 2nd October 2001 for £30,000 drawn on the account of John Potter Gold Limited.

They are adamant that their agreement was with Mr Potter Gold personally however. Mr Stein and Ms Day have now spent all this money on the as yet still unsuccessful development of the motor. Mr Potter Gold has not, as far as they are aware, done anything to find backers for the motor.

On 4th March 2004 each of the Defendants received a letter dated 2nd March from John Potter Gold Limited demanding repayment within a week of the 'loan' of £30,000. They say that this is the first time anyone has referred to the money as a loan, and they are unable to repay it, even if they are liable to. They have used up all the money invested by Mr Potter Gold and have not yet received a penny by way of sales and royalties.

Counsel is asked to draft the Defence.

IN THE ABERYSTWYTH COUNTY COURT   Claim No AB4/61609

BETWEEN

JOHN POTTER GOLD LIMITED   Claimants

and

(1) IAN STEIN
(2) FARRAH DAY   Defendants

PARTICULARS OF CLAIM

-----

1.   The Claimants' claim is for the sum of £30,000 which was sent to the Defendants by the Claimants by way of loan, in accordance with an agreement between the Claimants and the Defendants.

2.   It was a term of the agreement that the Defendants' liability in respect of the repayment of the sum would be joint and several, and that the loan would be repaid by the Defendants when the Claimants made a written request for repayment, which they have done.

3.   Notwithstanding this request, the Defendants have failed and/or refused to repay the sum of £30,000 or any part of it, and that sum still remains owing to the Claimants.

4.   The Claimants further claim interest under section 69 of the County Courts Act 1984 on the sum of £30,000 at the rate of 8% per year from 11th March 2004, amounting to £1,479.45 at 22nd October 2004 and continuing until judgment or sooner payment at the rate of £6.58 per day.

AND the Claimants claim:

    (1) £30,000.

    (2) Interest as claimed in paragraph 4 above.

Titus Oates & Co.

STATEMENT OF TRUTH

I believe that the facts stated in these particulars of claim are true.

John Potter Gold, Managing Director of Claimants

Dated 22nd October 2004

11

Misrepresentation

11.1 Introduction

Misrepresentation is not a single cause of action, but rather a cause of complaint that may give rise to various causes of action, some tortious and some contractual. These causes of action all have different ingredients and give rise to different remedies. The only thing they have in common is that the defendant has made a representation to the claimant, who has acted upon it, and has thereafter discovered it to be false. There is fuller consideration of these causes of action and the remedies available in the *Remedies Manual*, **Chapter 7**. Which cause or causes of action a claimant relies on will depend on which is appropriate on the facts of the case. The main differences are in the nature of the representation, the state of mind of the defendant and the remedy sought.

The causes of action that come under the umbrella of 'misrepresentation' are:

(a) *Innocent misrepresentation*. 'Innocent' in this context means anything less than fraudulent. It is an action simply for rescission, though the court may award damages in lieu of rescission under the Misrepresentation Act 1967, s 2(2).

(b) *Deceit*. This is a claim in tort where it can be established that the representation was made fraudulently. The claimant is entitled to damages and may also be granted rescission. Fraud must not be alleged unless you are instructed to do so and have before you reasonably credible material which as it stands establishes a *prima facie* case of fraud.

(c) *Negligent misrepresentation*. This is a claim for damages under the Misrepresentation Act 1967, s 2(1). It is often called 'negligent' misrepresentation, but negligence is not actually an essential ingredient; the claimant need only show that he entered into a contract in reliance on a false representation and suffered loss as a result. But there is a defence if the defendant can show that he reasonably believed the representation to be true, which he will only be able to do if he was *not* negligent. Damages are assessed on a tortious basis, as if the claim had been brought in deceit.

(d) *Breach of contract*. This claim can only arise if the representation has become a term of the contract. It is a question of fact whether it has done so. The remedy is damages for breach of contract in the usual way.

(e) *Breach of collateral warranty*. If the representation has not become a term of the contract, it may nevertheless be possible to establish that there was a collateral contract. In consideration of the collateral warranty made by the defendant, the claimant agreed to enter into the main contract. The remedy is again contractual damages.

(f) *Negligence*. This is not a claim for misrepresentation at all, but a claim for damages for negligent misstatement under *Hedley Byrne & Co v Heller & Partners Ltd* [1964] AC 465. Claims under this head have been dealt with in **Chapter 9**. We will give it no further consideration here. It is only mentioned because it is sometimes referred to as misrepresentation.

It is quite rare for only one cause of action to be relied upon. Usually more than one is arguable and it is in your client's interests to include any arguable cause of action. Negligent misstatement is the only one that is more likely to be alleged on its own — it usually only arises where the parties are *not* in a contractual relationship with each other.

11.2 Basic formula for particulars of claim

As in ordinary contract and tort claims, we can identify a basic formula, which is as follows:

Stage 1:   the parties

Stage 2:   the representations

Stage 3:   the contract

Stage 4:   the terms or warranties

Stage 5:   the falsity of the representations or the breach of contract

Stage 6:   fraud (where appropriate)

Stage 7:   the loss and damage

Stage 8:   the claim for interest

Stage 9:   the remedies sought.

Not all these stages are required in every case. You need to make a selection appropriate to the causes of action you are relying on. You will also find that they do not always appear in this order. In particular, stages 2 and 3 may be reversed, especially where the claim is primarily contractual.

Let us look at the stages a bit more closely.

(a) *Stage 1.* As usual this stage includes any relevant background. This may be for the purpose of story-telling or it may be material, for example if the representation was not made expressly but is to be implied from the defendant's conduct.

(b) *Stage 2.* Set out the representations as accurately as possible. This is one of the occasions where the precise words *are* material, so use precise words where known. If so, put them in inverted commas to indicate this fact. Say whether each representation was made orally or in writing, and if in writing identify the document. Do *not* at this stage allege that the representations were false; you are simply alleging that the defendant made them. It is usual to state that the defendant made the representations with the intention that the claimant should rely on them or with the intention of inducing a contract. Arguably this is only an essential ingredient in fraud, but the advice of the editors of both *Atkin's Court Forms* and *Bullen & Leake's Precedents of Pleading* is to allege it in every case.

(c) *Stage 3.* The only cause of action that does not require a contract is deceit (though in cases of deceit there usually is one). Set out the contract in the usual way (see **7.8.2**) adding only that the claimant entered into it induced by and/or in reliance on the representations. Reliance is an essential ingredient. In cases of deceit state instead what action the claimant took in reliance on the representations.

(d) *Stage 4.* If you are making a claim for breach of contract, you must allege at this stage that the representations were or became terms of the agreement. Use the word 'term' or 'warranty'. If it is clear, say whether they were express or implied terms, but it is not unusual to leave this unstated. If you are relying on breach of a collateral contract, state that the representation was a collateral warranty in consideration of which the claimant agreed to enter into the agreement. You can allege that the representations were terms or collateral warranties in the alternative.

(e) *Stage 5.* This is one stage that is essential in every case. Allege that the representations were in fact false, and give particulars. Alternatively, allege breach of contract or warranty, with particulars. The breach consists of the falsity of the representations, so if you are alleging both misrepresentation and breach of contract you only need one set of particulars. If you feel this stage comes out of chronological order, because the representations must have been false at the time they were made, remember that the claimant only discovered them to be false after the event, so this is the correct chronology from his point of view.

(f) *Stage 6.* If you are alleging fraud, allege at this stage that the representations were made fraudulently. This stage may also appear to come out of chronological order, since the defendant must have been fraudulent before the representation was made. But it is hardly logical to allege fraud before alleging that the representation was false. Note that you do *not* allege negligence if relying on negligent misrepresentation under s 2(1) of the Misrepresentation Act 1967 — once the claimant has established that he entered into a contract in reliance on the defendant's representation and has suffered loss, the burden of proof shifts onto the defendant to show that he reasonably believed the representation to be true, both at the time it was made and at the date of the contract. This will be for the defendant to set out in his defence: see **11.6**.

(g) *Stage 7.* Set out loss and damage in the usual way. Remember that the quantum may be different using the tortious measure and the contractual measure, so make sure that you set out the particulars of loss in such a way that you can arrive at the correct quantum both in tort and in contract. If you are seeking rescission then you also need at this stage to state that the claimant rescinded the contract.

(h) *Stage 8.* The claim is usually for an unspecified amount, even where it is for repayment by way of rescission, since such a payment has to be assessed by the court, so interest will usually be 'to be assessed'. Interest may be under the equitable jurisdiction of the court where rescission is ordered, though it can also be awarded under the Supreme Court Act 1981, s 35A or County Courts Act 1984, s 69.

(i) *Stage 9.* List all the remedies sought in the usual way, making alternatives clear where appropriate.

11.3   Claim for rescission and negligent misrepresentation

11.3.1   Particulars of claim

IN THE HIGH COURT OF JUSTICE   Claim No 2004 HC 4062
QUEEN'S BENCH DIVISION

BETWEEN

ARTHUR DENT   Claimant

and

HITCHHIKER MOTOR COMPANY LIMITED   Defendants

PARTICULARS OF CLAIM

1.   The Defendants are and were at all material times motor dealers, carrying on business at their showrooms at Acacia Avenue, Mill Hill, London NW7.

2.   On 18th August 2004 at the Defendants' showrooms, in order to induce the Claimant to enter into a contract with the Defendants to buy a Lamborghini motor car, registration number S421 END ('the Motor Car') the Defendants' employee or agent Joseph Soap, acting on behalf of the Defendants, orally represented to the Claimant that the Motor Car had been driven no more than 15,000 miles from new.

3.   In reliance upon and induced by this representation, the Claimant entered into a written contract dated 18th August 2004 with the Defendants to buy the Motor Car and, on 20th August 2004 paid to the Defendants the sum of £80,000 as the purchase price and took delivery of the Motor Car. A copy of the contract is attached.

4.   In fact, the Defendants' representation was false, in that the Motor Car had been driven a true mileage of approximately 80,000 from new.

5.   As soon as he discovered the true facts, the Claimant by letter to the Defendants dated 29th August 2004 rescinded the contract.

6.   As result of the matters set out above, the Claimant has suffered loss and damage.

PARTICULARS

Difference between the price paid for the Motor Car (£80,000) and the value of the Motor Car as sold and delivered to the Claimant (£15,000): £65,000.

7.   Further the Claimant is entitled to and claims interest under the equitable jurisdiction of the Court alternatively under section 35A of the Supreme Court Act 1981 on the sum of £80,000 from 20th August 2004 at the rate of 8% per year, amounting to £1,928.77 at 8th December 2004 and then continuing until judgment or sooner payment at the rate of £17.53 a day; alternatively at such rate and for such period as the Court thinks fit.

AND the Claimant claims:

(1) Rescission of the contract; and

(2) Return of the sum of £80,000; and

(3) Interest under the equitable jurisdiction of the Court alternatively under section 35A of the Supreme Court Act 1981, amounting to £1,928.77 at 8th December 2004 and continuing at the daily rate of £17.53.

Alternatively:

(4) Damages for misrepresentation; and

(5) Interest under section 35A of the Supreme Court Act 1991 to be assessed.

JOSEPH BLOGGS

STATEMENT OF TRUTH

Dated etc.

11.3.2 Commentary

This is a claim for rescission on the basis of 'innocent' misrepresentation in equity, with an alternative claim for damages under s 2(1) of the Misrepresentation Act 1967.

Paragraph 1. Stage 1 — the parties. Only the defendants need any introduction.

Paragraph 2. Stage 2 — the representation. You need to say who (Joseph Soap), when (18 August 2004), represented what (the mileage of the car), how (orally), to whom (the claimant). If the representation was oral, add where (at the defendants' showrooms). The indention to induce a contract is also an essential ingredient. Remember to add that Joseph Soap was the defendants' employee or agent, or there is no reason why they should be liable for his representations.

Paragraph 3. Stage 3 — the contract. Include all the usual particulars of the contract, but add at the outset that it was entered into in reliance on and/or induced by the representation. There is unlikely to be any dispute about the sale, so performance of the contract (payment and delivery) are also included.

There are no other terms of the contract relied upon, so there is no stage 4.

Paragraph 4. Stage 5 — misrepresentation. This is usually stated simply by saying 'in fact the representation was false', and then setting out the true facts, which are the particulars of misrepresentation.

There is no fraud to be alleged, so there is no stage 6.

Paragraph 5. By the end of paragraph 4 you have set out all you need for the claim under s 2(1) (except the loss and damage). But for the remedy of rescission, it is necessary to show that the claimant sought to rescind the contract without undue delay, so the claimant's letter to that effect must be referred to.

Paragraph 6. Stage 7 — loss and damage. The measure of damages is such as will restore the claimant to the position he would have been in had the misrepresentation not been made, which he says in this case would have meant that he would not have bought the car.

Paragraph 7. Stage 8 — interest. Note that interest is claimed not only under s 35A of the Supreme Court Act 1981, but also under the court's equitable jurisdiction. See **6.2.1**(g). Rescission is an equitable remedy, which if granted will result in the return of the purchase price. Interest can be awarded on that payment in equity. This is a claim for a specified amount, and so the interest claim needs to be set out in full. However the claim is in the alternative for damages, which is not a claim for specified amount, since the true value of the car will need to be assessed by the court. So interest on damages is also to be assessed by the court, and therefore this is stated in the alternative.

Prayer. Note how the alternative and complementary remedies sought are set out clearly. This is not entirely a claim for a specified amount, since the value of the car and the amount to be refunded has to be assessed by the court. There is the added complication (see the defence in **11.7**) that the car is now in fact a write-off.

11.4 Claim for negligent misrepresentation and breach of contract

11.4.1 Particulars of claim

IN THE BRIGHTON COUNTY COURT   Claim No BN4/16380

BETWEEN

EDWARD GRANBY   Claimant

and

LEISURE BREAKS LIMITED   Defendants

PARTICULARS OF CLAIM

1.   The Defendants are holiday and tour operators, who published a brochure entitled 'Fishermen's Holidays 2004' a copy of which they sent to the Claimant at his request in January 2004, with the intention of inducing the Claimant to enter into a contract with them for the provision of holiday accommodation and services as advertised in the brochure.

2.   This brochure advertised, among others, holidays at the Lakeside Hotel, Redburn, Cumbria ('the Hotel') and represented that:

(a) The Hotel was on the shores of Lake Pikewater ('the Lake').

(b) Visitors to the Hotel would have the right to fish in the Lake.

(c) These holidays were suitable for fishermen.

3.   In reliance on and induced by these representations the Claimant on 1st February 2004 entered into a written contract with the Defendants by which the Defendants agreed to provide accommodation and a fishing holiday at the Hotel from 16th to 30th July 2004 for the Claimant and 11 of his friends ('the Holiday') at a price of £4,500.

4.   The representations set out in paragraph 2 above were express, alternatively implied terms of the contract.

5.   The Claimant paid the Defendants the price of £4,500 on 30th May 2004 and he and his friends took up the Holiday.

6.   In fact the representations were false and the Defendants were in breach of contract in that:

(a) The Hotel is two miles from the Lake.

(b) The Lake is private and guests at the Hotel were not permitted to fish in it.

(c) The nearest place available for fishing is Lake Minnowpool which is 20 miles from the Hotel and accordingly the Holiday was not suitable for fishermen.

7.   As a result of the matters set out above the Claimant and his friends were unable to fish every day of the Holiday as they intended and they suffered disappointment and distress. In order to be able to fish in Lake Minnowpool they had to hire a minibus for 10 days. In

all the circumstances the Holiday was spoiled and as a result the Claimant has lost the value of the Holiday and has further suffered loss and damage.

PARTICULARS OF SPECIAL DAMAGE

(1) Cost of hire of minibus	£1,468.75
(2) Value of Holiday	£4,500.00
	£5,968.75

8.   Further the Claimant claims interest under section 69 of the County Courts Act 1984 on the amount found to be due to the Claimant at such rate and for such period as the Court thinks fit.

AND the Claimant claims:

(1) Damages.

(2) Interest under section 69 of the County Courts Act 1984 to be assessed.

JOSEPH BLOGGS

STATEMENT OF TRUTH

Dated etc.

11.4.2   Commentary

Paragraph 1. The parties are introduced. This case involves representations in a holiday brochure, so the brochure is identified. In this example, some of the required elements of the representations are incorporated into paragraph 1, while the representations themselves are set out in paragraph 2. This seems a more natural way of doing it in this case.

Paragraph 2. There are three separate representations which the claimant relies on, and for the sake of clarity they are itemised (a), (b) and (c). Useful definitions of the hotel and the lake are included.

Paragraph 3. The contract is set out with the additional element of reliance. The holiday is particularised and defined as 'accommodation and a fishing holiday at the Hotel from 16th to 30th July 2004 for the claimant and 11 of his friends'.

Paragraph 4. If the claim is to be in contract as well as under the Misrepresentation Act, then the material terms must be stated. In cases of misrepresentation, it is the representations which must be alleged to have become terms or warranties. They are probably express terms, having been set out in the brochure; but if they are not, representation 2(c) at least must arguably be an implied term of a contract to provide a fishermen's holiday.

Paragraph 5. This is simply story telling — there can be no loss and damage unless the claimant actually went on holiday!

Paragraph 6. Misrepresentation and breach. Make sure you allege both. Since the breach of contract consists of the falsity of the terms set out in paragraph 4, which are in turn the representations alleged in paragraph 2, particulars of misrepresentation and breach are the same. Note how the particulars (a), (b) and (c) correspond to the representations in paragraph 2.

Paragraph 7. Loss and damage. In spoilt holiday cases there is often a claim not only for financial loss but also for general damages for distress and disappointment, so this must be alleged and particularised (unable to fish every day). The causation of the cost of hire of the minibus is explained. The key words 'holiday was spoiled' and 'lost the value of the holiday' should be included.

11.5 Claim for fraudulent misrepresentation and breach of collateral warranty

11.5.1 Particulars of claim

IN THE HIGH COURT OF JUSTICE   Claim No 2004 HC 4742
QUEEN'S BENCH DIVISION

BETWEEN

WALTER POSTLETHWAITE   <u>Claimant</u>

and

DAISY ARTHURS   <u>Defendant</u>

PARTICULARS OF CLAIM

1.   In or about March 2003 the Defendant advertised for sale freehold premises at Timber Cottage, Timber Lane, Broadhill, Gloucestershire together with the goodwill of the grocery and general provisions business she conducted at that address, the fixtures and fittings and the stock in hand at the date of sale ('the Shop'). In March 2003 the Claimant entered into negotiations with the Defendant with a view to purchasing the Shop.

2.   During the negotiations, on or about 11th April 2003, in order to induce the Claimant to enter into a contract to purchase the Shop, the Defendant orally represented to the Claimant at the shop premises that the Shop had made a net profit of £20,000 in the year ending 31st December 2002 ('the Representation').

3.   Induced by and in reliance upon the Representation the Claimant entered into a written contract dated 13th May 2003 with the Defendant (a copy of which is attached) by which the Claimant agreed to purchase the Shop from the Defendant for the sum of £140,000. Completion of the purchase was on 21st June 2003.

4.   The Representation amounted to a collateral warranty, in consideration of which the Claimant entered into the contract.

5.   The Representation was in fact false and the Defendant was in breach of the collateral warranty in that the Shop had not made a profit of £20,000 or any profit in the year ending 31st December 2002 but had made a loss of £5,000 in that period.

6.   The Defendant made the Representation fraudulently in that she knew it was false, or did not believe it to be true, or was reckless, not caring whether it was true or false.

PARTICULARS OF FRAUD

The Defendant had in her possession no later than 31st March 2003 accounts relating to the Shop prepared by Googhan & Googhan, Chartered Accountants, in respect of the year ended 31st December 2002 which showed the loss of £5,000. Further the Claimant knew or ought to have known that she had derived no income from the Shop since October 2001.

7.   As a result of the matters set out above the Claimant has suffered loss and damage.

PARTICULARS OF DAMAGE

	£
(1) Value of Shop as represented and/or warranted, and price paid	140,000
(2) Value of Shop as purchased by Claimant	40,000
(3) Difference in value	100,000

8.   Further the Claimant claims interest under section 35A of the Supreme Court Act 1981 on the amount found to be due to the Claimant at such rate and for such period as the Court thinks fit.

AND the Claimant claims:

(1) Damages for fraudulent misrepresentation or breach of warranty.

(2) Interest under section 35A of the Supreme Court Act 1981 to be assessed.

JOSEPH BLOGGS

STATEMENT OF TRUTH

Dated etc.

11.5.2 Commentary

Paragraph 1. Parties and background. It is obviously necessary to define the shop, which is quite a complex collection of land, chattels and goodwill: 'freehold premises ... stock in hand at the date of sale'. The advertisement and the negotiations are not strictly material, but it is very common to find this background included.

Paragraph 2. The oral representation, with all necessary particulars.

Paragraph 3. Reliance, contract and performance of the contract by completion.

Paragraph 4. As an alternative to the claim in deceit, there is also a contractual claim. It is not arguable that an oral representation can be a term of a formal written contract for the sale of land, so it is alleged to be a collateral warranty. Simply state this fact, adding the consideration, namely the claimant's agreement to purchase the shop.

Paragraph 5. Misrepresentation and breach of warranty with particulars. Note that there is no allegation of fraud at this stage.

Paragraph 6. Stage 6 — the allegation of fraud. There are three mental states that amount to deceit, and so all three are usually identified in the alternative, as here: knowing the representation to be false, not believing it to be true, or reckless as to its truth. An allegation of fraud must only be made if you have clear evidence to support it, so the allegation must be particularised in such a way as to show that you have that evidence. The fact that the defendant was in possession of accounts showing the contrary to her representation must be strong evidence. The accounts presumably also show no directors' drawings from the business since October 2001, a fact of which she must have been aware, so 'knew or ought to have known'.

Paragraph 7. Loss and damage. The measure of damages in the contract is the difference between what was promised and what she received. The measure of damages in deceit is arguably the difference in value between what was represented and what was purchased, or more probably the difference between purchase price and true value. As set out, it all comes to the same amount.

11.6   Defence: reasonable belief: *restitutio in integrum* impossible

(See particulars of claim at **11.3**.)

11.6.1   Defence

<u>IN THE HIGH COURT OF JUSTICE</u>   Claim No 2004 HC 4062
<u>QUEEN'S BENCH DIVISION</u>

BETWEEN

ARTHUR DENT   <u>Claimant</u>

and

HITCHHIKER MOTOR COMPANY LIMITED   <u>Defendants</u>

DEFENCE

1.   Paragraph 1 of the Particulars of Claim is admitted.

2.   Except that it is denied that Joseph Soap made the alleged or any oral representation in order to induce the Claimant to enter into any contract, paragraph 2 of the Particulars of Claim is admitted. The representation was not a material representation, since it was simply made as an answer to a direct question by the Claimant. Half way through the conversation between the Claimant and Joseph Soap on 18th August 2004 the Claimant asked 'What's the mileage?' and Joseph Soap replied 'Fifteen thou'. The remainder of the conversation was on other matters about the Motor Car.

3.   Except that the Claimant is required to prove that he relied upon or was induced by any representation made by the Defendants, paragraph 3 of the Particulars of Claim is admitted.

4.   Paragraph 4 of the Particulars of Claim is admitted to the extent that the true mileage was greater than 15,000. The Claimant is required to prove the true mileage alleged.

5.   The Defendants and Joseph Soap had reasonable grounds to believe and did believe up to the time that the contract was made that the representation was true.

PARTICULARS

(a) The Defendants sold the Motor Car to Percy Grubb in January 2003, when the true mileage was 11,782.

(b) The Defendants serviced the Motor Car on behalf of Percy Grubb in December 2003 when the mileometer reading was 13,980.

(c) The Defendants repurchased the Motor Car from Percy Grubb in May 2004 when the mileometer reading was 14,999, which reading remained unaltered until the Claimant purchased the Motor Car.

6.   It is admitted that by a letter dated 29th August 2004 to the Defendants the Claimant purported to rescind the contract. Otherwise the Claimant is required to prove the matters stated in paragraph 5 of the Particulars of Claim.

7. On or about 27th August 2004 the Motor Car was damaged beyond repair in an accident and accordingly the Claimant is unable to return it to the Defendants in the same condition as he received it and for that reason was not on 29th August 2004 and is not entitled to rescind the contract.

8. It is admitted that the value of the Motor Car would have been £80,000 if the mileage had been 15,000 and £15,000 if (which the Claimant is required to prove) the true mileage is 80,000. Otherwise the Claimant is required to prove that he has suffered loss and damage as alleged or at all.

BESS TOFFER

STATEMENT OF TRUTH

Dated etc.

11.6.2 Commentary

There are two defences raised here. To the claim for rescission the defendants say that *restitutio in integrum* is no longer possible; ie that it is no longer possible to restore the parties to their pre-contractual position because the car cannot be returned in its original condition. To the claim for damages, they rely on the statutory defence in s 2(1) of the Misrepresentation Act 1967, that they reasonably believed the representation to be true.

Paragraph 2. It is admitted that Joseph Soap made the representation, but the defendants seek to avoid liability by saying it was not made in order to induce a sale, so that it was not a material representation. So the response to the claimant's paragraph 2 is a general admission except for one denial. The reasons for that denial then have to be given, so they are spelt out in some detail, incorporating what might seem to be a certain amount of evidence, but which is probably necessary.

Paragraph 3. The sale is obviously admitted, but the claimant is required to prove reliance on the representation. Take care not to deny reliance, unless you mean to do so. You should only deny reliance if you have a positive case, that is you can show or argue that the claimant relied on something else.

Paragraph 4. In the light of facts they are now aware of, the defendants are forced to admit that the representation was false, though not to the extent alleged by the claimant, which he is required to prove. This does not damage their defence significantly, in view of the other lines of defence raised.

Paragraph 5. This is the defence of reasonable belief. Start with the words of s 2(1): 'had reasonable grounds to believe and did believe up to the time of the contract that the representation was true'. This belief must then be particularised by setting out the reasonable grounds on which it was based. Those stated here seem to lend weight to the defence case, and suggest that it may be difficult for the claimant to prove that the true mileage was 80,000. Note the distinction between 'mileage' and 'mileometer reading'.

Paragraph 6. The defendants do not admit rescission, but must admit receipt of the letter, so they admit that the claimant *purported* to rescind. The other matters which the claimant is required to prove are simply that he acted 'as soon as he discovered the true facts'.

Paragraph 7. These are the facts on which the defendants rely to show that *restitutio in integrum* is no longer possible. The paragraph concludes with the proposition to be drawn from these facts, namely that the claimant cannot rescind.

Paragraph 8. The claimant is required to prove that he has suffered loss and damage, because there is a dispute over the true mileage of the car. However the claimant's valuations are accepted, subject to liability.

11.7   Exercise A

Pamela O'Grady will say:

I am the owner of The Manor, Old Market Street, Sudbury, Suffolk, which is my home, and where I also run a retirement home for the elderly. In the summer of 2002 Sudbury became a smokeless zone and I had to install solid-fuel burners in The Manor instead of the open grates in which I had previously burned coal and logs. In August 2003 a company called Winter Warmers Ltd supplied and installed ten new Hotray burners and recommended that I should use Winterlite solid fuel, which they could supply. Their salesman, Oliver Smart, told me that this fuel was particularly suitable as it was slow burning, produced more heat than any other solid fuels and was recommended by Hotray Ltd for use in their burners. He told me that twenty tonnes would '... see me through the winter'. I therefore ordered twenty tonnes of Winterlite from Winter Warmers Ltd on 2 September 2003, for which I paid £8,400 on delivery (16 September 2003). We had problems throughout last winter. We found that Winterlite was too fast-burning to keep the fires alight all night as it was supposed to. Only if we piled the fires high last thing at night would they ever still be alight in the morning, but even so they frequently went out. When the weather was cold, the fires could not keep the rooms warm and we had to use additional electric heaters. The twenty tonnes in the bunker ran out in mid-February 2004, after only five months. I consulted Hotray Ltd, who told me that Winterlite was not recommended by them, was unsuitable for their burners as it was too fast-burning and did not give off much heat and recommended I should use Glowworm fuel. They supplied me with four tonnes of Glowworm at a cost of £1,440, which kept the fires alight and the house warm for the remaining two months of the winter. I estimate I have used £9,200 worth of additional electricity as a result of using the wrong fuel.

Counsel is asked to draft particulars of claim to be filed in the Ipswich County Court.

11.8   Exercise B

Counsel is instructed on behalf of Leisure Breaks Ltd (the company), who are being sued by a Mr Edward Granby for damages for a spoilt holiday. A copy of the particulars of claim is enclosed (see **11.4**).

The company are holiday and tour operators with a high reputation and are embarrassed by Mr Granby's claim, which appears to be justified. They did indeed make the representations alleged in the claim, but they did so in good faith, relying on representations made to them by Cumbrian Hotels Ltd, the owners of the Lakeside Hotel, in a letter dated 20 September 2003. Cumbrian Hotels stated expressly that the hotel was on the shores of Lake Pikewater, and that visitors to the hotel could fish in it. It is not surprising in the circumstances that the company described holidays at the hotel as suitable for fishermen.

Relying on this letter, the company booked accommodation at the hotel from 1 April to 30 October 2004 at a total price of £50,650, and sold holidays to their customers, including Mr Granby, through their brochure. The cost of the holidays included accommodation and board only. No charge was made for fishing facilities.

It turns out that the hotel is indeed two miles from the lake, but the company only have the claimant's word for it that visitors are not entitled to fish in the lake. They also have no knowledge of alternative places to fish.

Amazingly the claimant is the only customer to have complained so far, but others may follow. It seems to instructing solicitors that the company must defend the claim while seeking to recover any damages they may have to pay from Cumbrian Hotels Ltd.

Counsel is asked to settle the defence, and Part 20 claim.

(**Note:** The Part 20 claim will be found in **15.6.**)

Additional precedents for claims

12.1 Clinical negligence

12.1.1 Particulars of claim

CLINICAL NEGLIGENCE

IN THE HIGH COURT OF JUSTICE   Claim No 2004 HC 5497
QUEEN'S BENCH DIVISION

BETWEEN

MERVYN GRADE   Claimant

and

(1) MIDLANDS HOPSITALS TRUST
(2) DENZIL GRACE   Defendants

PARTICULARS OF CLAIM

1.   The First Defendant at all material times managed and administered the Rutland Hospital, Exton Park, Oakham, Rutland ('the Hospital'), where it provided specialist medical and orthopaedic services under the National Health Service. The Second Defendant was at all material times employed by the First Defendant as a registrar orthopaedic surgeon.

2.   On 14th June 2002 the Claimant attended the hospital complaining of a lump on the dorsum of his right wrist and pain in his right wrist radiating up the right forearm. On examination and diagnosis he was found to have an asymptomatic ganglion, and right carpal tunnel syndrome (compression of the right median nerve) with tenosynovitis. It was decided that the Claimant should attend the hospital for day surgery to excise the ganglion and decompress the right carpal tunnel ('the Operation').

3.   The Defendants and each of them owed the Claimant a duty to exercise all due skill and care reasonably to be expected of a skilled experienced and competent orthopaedic surgeon in carrying out the Operation.

4.   The Operation was performed at the hospital on 12th July 2002 by the Second Defendant acting in the course of his employment by the First Defendant. During the Operation the median nerve branches to the ulna and residual side of the thumb and the radial side of the index finger were damaged and/or divided. This damage was not noticed by the Second Defendant during the Operation.

5.   After the Operation the Claimant suffered from pain in the right hand and a loss of sensation in his right thumb and index and middle fingers, which did not correct itself. Therefore the Claimant underwent a second operation ('the Second Operation') at the Rutland Hospital on 13th September 2002.

6.   At the Second Operation the damage caused to the median nerve during the Operation was discovered. Repair to the median nerve was no longer possible. Therefore a sural nerve was grafted from the outer aspect of the Claimant's left ankle to bridge the gaps in the median nerve.

7.   If the damage to the median nerve had been noticed at the Operation, it would have been possible to carry out an immediate repair and the Second Operation would not have been necessary.

8.   The Second Defendant was negligent during the Operation.

PARTICULARS OF NEGLIGENCE

(1) Causing or permitting damage to the branches of the right median nerve.

(2) Failing to take any or any adequate precautions to avoid damage to the median nerve.

(3) Failing to notice the damage to the median nerve.

(4) Failing to take any or any appropriate steps, whether by way of examination, test or otherwise, to discover whether any damage to the median nerve had occurred.

(5) Failing to carry out an immediate repair to the median nerve.

9.   As a result of the negligence of the Second Defendant the Claimant has suffered pain, injury, loss and damage.

PARTICULARS OF INJURY

(1) Damage to the right median nerve.

(2) Sensory deficit in the right hand.

(3) Partial loss of function in the right hand.

(4) Operation scar to the left ankle.

(5) Loss of sensation in the left little toe.

The Claimant, who is right handed, and was born on 26th May 1957, regained some sensation and use of his right hand after the Second Operation, but is handicapped in his day-to-day activities and social life. He is dependent on his wife's assistance for domestic chores. Full details of the Claimant's injuries, current situation and prognosis are set out in the medical report of Mr Ivor Hope served with these Particulars of Claim. If the median nerve had not been damaged, he would not have suffered any lasting or significant injury to his right hand. If the damage had been discovered and repaired during the Operation, the outcome and prognosis would have been significantly better.

The Claimant was self-employed running a dry cleaning franchise, but has had to give up this work and is currently unemployed. He is handicapped on the labour market.

<u>PARTICULARS OF SPECIAL DAMAGE</u>

Full details of the special damages claimed are set out in the schedule of expenses and losses served with these Particulars of Claim.

10.   Further the Claimant claims interest under section 35A of the Supreme Court Act 1981 on the amount found to be due to the Claimant at such rate and for such period as the Court thinks fit.

AND the Claimant claims:

(1) Damages.

(2) Interest under section 35A of the Supreme Court Act 1981 to be assessed.

JOSEPH BLOGGS

<u>STATEMENT OF TRUTH</u>

Dated etc.

12.1.2 **Commentary**

Clinical negligence claims can give rise to particular difficulties and can be quite lengthy and complicated. The example above is comparatively short and straightforward. A particular matter that you must ensure is drafted correctly is causation. Generally speaking, the claim arises out of the treatment given to the claimant for some condition. The claimant was not entirely healthy before the treatment, nor quite likely would he have been entirely cured after proper treatment. The claim is based on the difference between what the outcome would have been if there had been no negligence, and what it now is. This difference must be made clear.

It is not unusual in clinical negligence claims to see the full history of the treatment, the outcome and the resulting injury loss and damage set out before any allegation of negligence is made. This is often the easiest way to draft, because the detailed outcome is the 'event' that has been caused by the defendant's negligence. But it is also possible to draft the claim with a more conventional structure, and the above example attempts to do this.

It is based simply on negligence, since the claimant's treatment was under the National Health Service. If the treatment were private, then the claim would be brought concurrently in contract (see **9.10**).

Heading. PD 16, para 9.3 requires the words 'clinical negligence' to be inserted at the top of all statements of case in clinical negligence cases. There are two defendants. Although the first defendant is vicariously liable for the acts of the second, it is usual in clinical negligence cases to join the doctor or surgeon who was negligent, even when he or she was employed by an NHS trust.

Paragraph 1. A simple introduction of the defendants.

Paragraph 2. Introduces the claimant and starts to tell the story of the condition for which the claimant required treatment and the treatment given. The story needs to begin with the facts which give rise to the duty of care — here the decision to carry out the operation.

Paragraph 3. The duty of care. It is good practice to state the duty alleged, though in simple cases like this it is so obvious that it is sometimes left to be inferred. But in more complex cases it may need to be defined with some precision, in which case it should certainly be stated.

Paragraph 4. The operation. State when it was carried out, who did it, and what happened, so far as it is material. Here the damage done to the nerve is the crucial fact, which will inevitably have to be admitted by the defendants. The failure to notice the damage during the operation is included because in due course this will also give rise to an allegation of negligence.

Paragraphs 5 and 6. You might have expected the allegation of negligence to come next, but it would be difficult to draft without completing the story of the treatment received by the claimant (see commentary on paragraph 7 below). So we go on to the second operation, which was an attempt to correct the damage done at the first operation.

Paragraph 7. This is an essential part of the causation relied upon by the claimant. This fact needs to be stated before the allegation of negligence can be made; and for this reason the second operation also needs to come before the negligence.

Paragraph 8. The allegation of negligence, with particulars. This is straightforward. The allegations must of course be based on expert evidence available to you.

Paragraph 9. Sets out the remaining consequences of the negligent treatment. At this point the claim becomes a claim for personal injury and must be drafted in accordance with the rules for personal injury claims. Note the careful clarification of the claimant's case on causation set out in the particulars of injury.

Paragraphs 8 and 9 might have been placed the other way around by many barristers.

12.2 Nuisance

12.2.1 Particulars of claim

IN THE OLDHAM COUNTY COURT   Claim No OL4/2745

BETWEEN

(1) ERNEST PETTY

(2) MAUREEN PETTY   Claimants

and

GOODLIFE CHEMICALS PLC   Defendants

PARTICULARS OF CLAIM

1.   The Claimants are the owners and occupiers of a house and land at 27 Rosemary Lane, Waycroft Green, Berkshire. The Defendants are the owners and occupiers of a factory at Sunshine Estate, Waycroft, Berkshire where they carry on the business of manufacturing chemical products. The Defendants' factory is situated approximately 250 yards from the Claimants' house.

2.   Since about August 2001 the Defendants in the course of their business have wrongfully caused or permitted noxious and offensive fumes, vapours and smoke to be discharged from their factory and into the atmosphere. These fumes, vapours and smoke have on numerous occasions spread over and onto the Claimants' house and property and so constituted a nuisance to the Claimants.

3.   These vapours, fumes and smoke are dangerous to the health of the Claimants, their family and visitors to their house and they have caused the Claimants annoyance and discomfort and loss and damage.

PARTICULARS OF SPECIAL DAMAGE

	£
(1) Damage to exterior paintwork on house	450.00
(2) Damage to First Claimant's car	625.00
(3) Damage to trees, plants and flowers growing in the Claimants' garden	320.00

(4) Damage to clothing put out to dry on washing line	540.00
(5) Loss in value of Claimants' house	10,000.00
	11,935.00

4.   The Defendants threaten and intend, unless restrained by the Court, to continue to discharge the fumes, vapours and smoke and thus to continue to commit a nuisance and cause further loss and damage to the Claimants.

5.   Further the Claimants claim interest under section 69 of the County Courts Act 1984 on the amount found to be due to the Claimants at such rate and for such period as the Court thinks fit.

AND the Claimants claim:

(1) An injunction to forbid the Defendants whether by their employees, agents, officers or otherwise from carrying on or permitting to be carried on their business of manufacturing chemicals at their factory premises in such a manner as to cause the discharge of noxious and offensive fumes, vapours and smoke onto the Claimants' land.

(2) Damages.

(3) Interest under section 69 of the County Courts Act 1984 to be assessed.

JOSEPH BLOGGS

STATEMENT OF TRUTH

Dated etc.

12.2.2   Commentary

Paragraph 1. States the material facts about the parties. These are that the claimants are owners and occupiers of their land — without this there is no liability in nuisance, and no claim for damages — and that the defendants are in control of an adjacent or nearby piece of land.

Paragraph 2. States the nuisance. Simply describe the nuisance in such a way as to make it clear that the defendants are responsible for it, and that it is affecting the claimants' enjoyment of their land. Use the words 'wrongfully' and 'nuisance'.

Paragraph 3. The claim for damages. There is a claim for general damages (annoyance and discomfort) as well as for the financial losses.

Paragraph 4. The damages claim by itself is not enough — the claimants seek an injunction to prevent repetition. The key ingredient for this claim is that the defendants 'threaten and intend, unless restrained by the court' to continue committing the nuisance and, if appropriate, cause further loss and damage.

Prayer. Note that the claimants cannot claim 'an injunction'. They must spell out the terms of the injunction they seek. The drafting of injunctions is covered in **Chapter 19**.

12.3 Nuisance, *Rylands v Fletcher*, negligence

12.3.1 Particulars of claim

IN THE PENZANCE COUNTY COURT   Case No PZ4/01668

BETWEEN

ARTHUR PENHALIGON   Claimant

and

TOURIST ENTERPRISES LIMITED   Defendants

PARTICULARS OF CLAIM

1.   The Claimant is and was at all material times the owner and occupier of a house and land known as Clay Cottage, Didgett's Cross, Cornwall. The Defendants are and have been since January 2003 the owners and occupiers of a site adjacent to the Claimant's house previously known as Burnt Field but renamed by the Defendants as Atlantic Leisurama.

2.   The boundary between the Claimant's and the Defendants' land runs half-way up a steep slope, at the top of which lies the Defendants' land and at the bottom of which lies the Claimant's land.

3.   During the month of April 2004 the Defendants, their employees or agents brought on to their land a large quantity of gravel and earth ('the Gravel and Earth') and deposited it on the upper part of the slope, above the boundary, so as to level off the upper part of the slope.

4.   On or about 3rd May 2004 the Gravel and Earth rolled down the slope in a landslide and onto the Claimant's land, causing damage to the Claimant's house and land.

5.   The matters complained of in paragraph 3 constituted a non-natural use of the Defendants' land and the Defendants failed to prevent the escape of the Gravel and Earth from their land to the Claimant's land.

6.   Further or alternatively the matters complained of constituted a nuisance caused or permitted by the Defendants, their employees or agents.

7.   Further or alternatively the matters complained of were caused by the negligence of the Defendants, their employees or agents.

PARTICULARS OF NEGLIGENCE

(a) Depositing the Gravel and Earth in a position from which they knew or ought to have known it was liable to slip onto the Claimant's land.

(b) Failing to take any or any sufficient precautions to prevent the Gravel and Earth descending the slope, by building a barricade or otherwise.

(c) Failing to observe the instability of the Gravel and Earth deposited on the slope.

(d) Depositing further Gravel and Earth on the slope after they knew or ought to have known that the Gravel and Earth already deposited was unstable and liable to fall in a landslide.

(e) The Claimant will further contend that the facts set out in paragraph 4 above are sufficient in themselves to establish that the Defendants were negligent.

8. As a result of the matters set out above the Claimant lost the use of his garden for three weeks while the Defendants removed the Gravel and Earth and has further suffered loss and damage.

PARTICULARS OF SPECIAL DAMAGE

		£
(1)	Value of demolished garden shed	1,250.00
(2)	Cost of repainting back wall of house stained by earth	1,125.00
(3)	Cost of landscaping, replanting lawn, flowers, shrubs etc	3,250.00
		5,625.00

9. Further the Claimant claims interest under section 69 of the County Courts Act 1984 on the amount found to be due to the Claimant at such rate and for such period as the Court thinks fit.

AND the Claimant claims:

(1) Damages.

(2) Interest under section 69 of the County Courts Act 1984 to be assessed.

JOSEPH BLOGGS

STATEMENT OF TRUTH

Dated etc.

12.3.2 Commentary

Three causes of action are alleged in the alternative here, because all three are arguable, but the chief purpose of this example is to demonstrate the drafting of a claim under *Rylands v Fletcher*.

Paragraph 1. Once again, it is essential to establish that the parties are owners and occupiers of adjacent pieces of land.

Paragraph 2. The lie of the land needs to be described, or the events will not make sense. Treat this as part of the material facts about the parties. A bit of geography is not uncommonly required.

Paragraph 3. The next ingredient of the *Rylands v Fletcher* claim is that the defendants brought something onto their land that was not naturally there. What they did with the gravel and earth is stated for story-telling purposes.

Paragraph 4. The central ingredient of the *Rylands v Fletcher* claim is that the gravel and earth escaped from the defendants' land onto the claimant's land.

Paragraph 5. Finally, to establish the *Rylands v Fletcher* claim, it must be stated that the bringing of the gravel and earth onto the land was a 'non-natural use' of the land. Liability is then strict, so it needs to be alleged only that the defendants failed to prevent the escape, not that they did so negligently.

Paragraph 6 and 7. The *Rylands v Fletcher* claim is now complete, but two further causes of action are alleged: nuisance in paragraph 6 and negligence in paragraph 7. Note the inclusion of an allegation of *res ipsa loquitur*.

Paragraph 8. The damages claim in paragraph 8 applies to all three causes of action. Note that it incorporates an element of general damages (loss of use of garden, which is loss of enjoyment of land) as well as the financial losses.

12.3.3 Damage by escaping fire

Claims for damage by escaping fire may be framed in negligence, nuisance or under *Rylands v Fletcher*, depending on the facts of the case. If the fire starts purely accidentally, that is neither deliberately nor as a result of negligence, on an occupier's premises, then the Fire Prevention (Metropolis) Act 1774 removes strict liability. In the case of a fire which starts on someone's land, therefore, the most likely cause of action is negligence because there can be no liability without negligence

---

12.4 Assault and false imprisonment

12.4.1 Particulars of claim

IN THE SOUTHEND COUNTY COURT   Case No SS4/20099

BETWEEN

TIMOTHY KNOWLES
(A child, by his litigation friend
SANDRA KNOWLES)   Claimant

and

BASIL HOOKHAM   Defendant

PARTICULARS OF CLAIM

1.   On 20th July 2004 the Claimant was in the Marina Amusement Arcade in Southend, Essex, when at about 10.00 p.m. the Defendant, who is the owner and operator of the Arcade, wrongfully and without lawful justification arrested the Claimant and imprisoned him in a room at the Arcade.

2.   Then at about 10.15 p.m. the Defendant assaulted and beat the Claimant with his fists and compelled him to remove his outer garments.

3.   The Defendant wrongfully accused the Claimant of theft, but did not call the police or conduct him to a police station. The Defendant wrongfully detained the Claimant in the room until about 2.00 a.m. on 21st July 2004 when he released him.

4.   As a result of the matters set out above the Claimant lost his liberty and suffered pain and injury and sustained loss and damage.

PARTICULARS OF INJURY

(a) Bruising to the face and upper chest, which subsided after about three weeks.

(b) Cut lip which healed in about four days.

(c) Pain.

(d) Shock.

The Claimant was born on 28th September 1988.

Further details are set out in the medical report served with these Particulars of Claim.

PARTICULARS OF SPECIAL DAMAGE

Torn jacket damaged beyond repair   £50.00

5.   Further the Claimant claims interest under section 69 of the County Courts Act 1984 on the amount found to be due to the Claimant at such rate and for such period as the Court thinks fit.

AND the Claimant claims:

(1) Damages.

(2) Interest under section 69 of the County Courts Act 1984 to be assessed.

JOSEPH BLOGGS

STATEMENT OF TRUTH

Dated etc.

12.4.2   Commentary

Paragraph 1. False imprisonment. The key words are 'wrongfully and without lawful justification arrested and/or imprisoned'.
   Paragraph 2. Assault and battery. The key words are the obvious ones: 'assaulted and beat'.
   Paragraph 3. Further false imprisonment. The ingredient 'without lawful justification' is covered by particularisation in the first sentence.
   Paragraph 4. The damages for false imprisonment are for loss of liberty, so this allegation is made. For assault, the damages are simply for personal injury in the usual form.

12.5   Trespass to goods: damage

12.5.1   Particulars of claim

IN THE WANDSWORTH COUNTY COURT   Case No WT4/48636

BETWEEN

JAMES KIRBY   Claimant

and

JULIET STEVENS   Defendant

PARTICULARS OF CLAIM

1.   The Claimant is and was at all material times the owner and in possession of a BMW 323i motor car registration number V564 RGT.

2.   On 15th August 2004 in the street outside the Claimant's home at 23 Arcadia Mansions, Battersea, London SW11, the Defendant wrongfully and repeatedly struck that car with a sledgehammer, causing it to be damaged.

3.   As a result of the matters set out above, the Claimant has suffered loss and damage.

PARTICULARS OF DAMAGE

	£
(1) Cost of repairs to car	6,462.50
(2) Cost of hiring car: 2 weeks @ £288.46 per week	576.92
	7,039.42

4.   Further the Claimant claims interest under section 69 of the County Courts Act 1984 on the sum of £7,039.42 at the rate of 8% per year from 15th August 2004, amounting to £166.63 at 1st December 2004 and then continuing until judgment or sooner payment at the rate of £1.54 per day.

AND the Claimant claims:

(1) Damages.

(2) Interest under section 69 of the County Courts Act 1984, amounting to £166.63 at 1st December 2004 and continuing at the daily rate of £1.54.

JOSEPH BLOGGS

STATEMENT OF TRUTH

Dated etc.

12.5.2   Commentary

This example is so straightforward as to be self-explanatory. All that needs to be established is that the claimant is the owner of the property and that the defendant wrongfully and deliberately damaged it.

12.6   Conversion: wrongful interference with goods

12.6.1   Particulars of claim

IN THE LANCASTER COUNTY COURT   Claim No LA4/40197

BETWEEN

HODGE AND DAUGHTER LIMITED   Claimants

and

(1) SAMUEL VINCENT
(2) MATHESON & CO LIMITED   Defendants

PARTICULARS OF CLAIM

1.   The Claimants are and were at all material times the owners of and entitled to possession of a Ford Mondeo motor car registration number PR51 YPG ('the Car'), of the value of £9,500.

2.   The First Defendant was until 30th April 2004 employed by the Claimants and in the course of his employment was permitted by the Claimants to have the custody and use of the Car.

3.   On or about 1st May 2004 the First Defendant wrongfully pledged and delivered the Car to the Second Defendants and so converted it to his own use.

4.   By a letter dated 28th May 2004 the Claimants demanded the return of the Car from the Second Defendants but the Second Defendants have not returned the Car and wrongfully detain it from the Claimants.

5.   As a result of the matters set out above the Claimants have been deprived of the Car and have suffered loss and damage.

PARTICULARS OF DAMAGE

	£
(1) Value of Car	9,500.00
(2) Loss of use of Car from 29th May 2004 to 7th June 2004 and continuing at £50 per day	950.00
	10,450.00

6.   Further the Claimants claim interest under section 69 of the County Courts Act 1984 on the amount of damages found to be due to the Claimants at such rate and for such period as the Court thinks fit.

AND the Claimants claim:

(1) Against the First Defendant, damages for conversion.

(2) Against the Second Defendants, an order for the delivery up of the Car or its value, namely £9,500, and damages for its detention; alternatively damages.

(3) Against both Defendants, interest under section 69 of the County Courts Act 1984 to be assessed.

JOSEPH BLOGGS

STATEMENT OF TRUTH

Dated etc.

12.6.2   Commentary

Paragraph 1. Because the claim is not just for the value of the car but for the return of it, you need to state that the claimants are not just the owners but also entitled to possession of it.

Paragraph 2. Explain how the first defendant came into possession of the car.

Paragraph 3. The conversion by the first defendant. The key words are 'wrongfully' and 'converted it to his own use'. What he has done, in layman's language, is sell the car. But you must not use the word 'sold', because it suggests that he passed good title, so use the words 'pledged and delivered' instead.

Paragraph 4. The conversion by the second defendants, which is simply wrongful detention. State that the claimants have demanded it back, but that the second defendants have not given it back, ie they 'wrongfully detain' it.

Paragraph 5. The loss and damage claimed is not just the value of the car, but also ongoing damages for loss of its use. A statement of the value of the car is required by PD 16, para 7.2.

Prayer. Note that when different remedies are sought against each defendant, the prayer must specify what is sought against whom. Since the first defendant is no longer in possession of the car, the only possible remedy against him is damages. As against the second defendant, the remedies sought are strictly in accordance with s 3(2) of the Torts (Interference with Goods) Act 1977.

12.7   Simple bailment

12.7.1   Particulars of claim

IN THE BURNLEY COUNTY COURT   Claim No ZP4/37119

BETWEEN

MYRTLE HAWKINS   Claimant

and

JEREMY WIDGETT
(trading as CLOCK WORKS)   Defendant

PARTICULARS OF CLAIM

1.   The Defendant conducts a business at his shop at 13A Station Approach, Burnley, Lancashire, in the course of which he carries out repairs to clocks.

2.   On 23rd March 2004 the Claimant delivered to the Defendant at his shop her antique clock for repair, to be re-delivered to the Claimant at her request.

3.   On 28th April 2004 and on numerous dates after that the Claimant requested the Defendant to re-deliver the clock to her, but he has failed to do so.

4.   As a result of the matters set out above, the Claimant has suffered loss and damage.

PARTICULARS OF DAMAGE

Value of clock   £6,500

5.   Further the Claimant claims interest under section 69 of the County Courts Act 1984 on the amount found to be due to the Claimant at such rate and for such period as the Court thinks fit.

AND the Claimant claims:

(1) The return of the clock or £6,500 its value.

(2) Alternatively damages.

(3) Interest under section 69 of the County Courts Act 1984 to be assessed.

JOSEPH BLOGGS

STATEMENT OF TRUTH

Dated etc.

12.7.2 Commentary

This is a claim for breach of a bailee's duty in tort. Liability is strict. All that the claimant needs to establish is that she delivered the clock to the defendant (paragraph 2), that he had the obligation to return it to her on demand (paragraph 2) and that he has failed to do so (paragraph 3). The obligation to return the clock on request is to be implied from the circumstances of the bailment.

The background to this claim is likely to be one of two things: either the defendant has lost the clock, in which case he has no defence, or he is exercising a lien on it because the claimant has refused to pay for the repairs, in which case this defence will be alleged in due course, but does not form part of the claimant's claim. The claimant's reasons for refusing to pay will appear in her reply.

12.8 Bailment, breach of contract, negligence

12.8.1 Particulars of claim

IN THE OSWESTRY COUNTY COURT   Claim No OS4/25598

BETWEEN

PETER BOGGIS   Claimant

and

RURAL MOTORS LIMITED   Defendants

PARTICULARS OF CLAIM

1.   The Defendants are and were at all material times a company carrying on business as a vehicle service station, in the course of which they service and store motor cars.

2.   By an oral agreement made by telephone on or about 7th July 2004 between the Claimant and a Mr Wort for the Defendants, it was agreed that the Defendants would in the course of their business carry out a 12,000 mile service on the Claimant's Volvo motor car X400 BOG ('the Car') on 14th July 2004 at the prevailing price, and then store it for about two weeks at an additional daily cost.

3.   It was an express, alternatively an implied term of the agreement that the Defendants would take proper care of the Car and its contents while servicing and/or storing them.

4.   The Claimant duly delivered the car to the Defendants on 14th July 2004 at which time the Defendants became aware that it contained a laptop computer ('the Computer') belonging to the Claimant, which they agreed, through Mr Wort, would remain in the Car during the servicing and storage of the Car.

5.   Further or alternatively, in the circumstances the Defendants owed a duty to the Claimant to take reasonable care for the safety and security of the Car and its contents, including the Computer.

6.   In breach of the agreement and/or negligently, on a date unknown to the Claimant, but between 14th July and 28th July 2004, the Defendants failed to take proper care of the Car and its contents, as a result of which the Computer has been lost or stolen.

7.   On 28th July 2004 the Claimant orally requested the Defendants to return the Computer, but the Defendants have at all times since that date failed to do so.

8.   As a result of the matters set out above the Claimant has suffered loss and damage.

PARTICULARS OF DAMAGE

	£
(1) Replacement cost of the Computer	3,199.00
(2) Loss of use of Computer for 86 days and continuing @ £25 per day	2,150.00
	5,349.00

9.   Further the Claimant claims interest under section 69 of the County Courts Act 1984 on the amount found to be due to the Claimant at such rate and for such period as the Court thinks fit.

AND the Claimant claims:

(1) The return of the Computer or £3,199 its value and damages.

(2) Alternatively, damages.

(3) Interest under section 69 of the County Courts Act 1984 to be assessed.

JOSEPH BLOGGS

STATEMENT OF TRUTH

Dated etc.

12.8.2 Commentary

There are three alternative causes of action alleged here: the main two are breach of contract, since the bailment was for reward, and negligence, but it is impossible to avoid alleging breach of the bailee's strict duty as well.

Paragraph 1. The defendants' business: the fact that they service and store cars in the course of their business is there to support the implied term stated in paragraph 3.

Paragraph 2. The contract in usual form.

Paragraph 3. This could be an express term if there was an express oral undertaking to care for the car and its contents. Otherwise it is a term to be implied as a matter of common sense or under s 13 of the Supply of Goods and Services Act 1982.

Paragraph 4. The delivery of the car and the computer to the defendants. This acts as performance of the agreement for the contract claim, and as the facts giving rise to the duty of care in negligence. It is also sufficient to give rise to the bailee's strict duty. For this reason, it is important to state that the defendants were aware that the computer was in the car.

Paragraph 5. The duty of care owed. The facts that give rise to it have already been stated.

Paragraph 6. Breach of contract and/or negligence, with particulars.

Paragraph 7. The request for return of the computer and the failure to do so is part of the claim in strict bailment. It is not strictly necessary in contract and negligence.

The rest of the claim is explained by the commentaries on the previous examples.

12.9 Trespass to land

12.9.1 Particulars of claim

<u>IN THE HIGH COURT OF JUSTICE</u>   Claim No 2004 HC 6469
<u>CHANCERY DIVISION</u>

BETWEEN

GILBERT SOPWITH   <u>Claimant</u>

and

ARNOLD BRITAIN   <u>Defendant</u>

PARTICULARS OF CLAIM

1. The Claimant is and was at all material times the owner and entitled to possession of a plot of land known as Pink Orchard near Little Bredy in Dorset.

2. Some time between January 1999 and 13th July 2002 the Defendant wrongfully entered and took possession of Pink Orchard and has since remained in possession of it.

3. In or about April 2003 the Defendant his servants or agents wrongfully erected a stone wall ('the Wall') on Pink Orchard so as to block access to Pink Orchard from the public highway.

4. As a result of the matters set out above the Claimant has been deprived of the use and enjoyment of Pink Orchard and has therefore suffered damage. A reasonable sum for the use and enjoyment of Pink Orchard is £200 per month.

5. By the letter from the Claimant's solicitors dated 21st June 2003 the Claimant requested the Defendant to remove the Wall but the Defendant has failed to do so.

6. No part of Pink Orchard consists of residential premises.

AND the Claimant claims:

(1) Possession of Pink Orchard.

(2) Mesne profits at the rate of £200 per month until possession is delivered up.

(3) An order that the Defendant do within 7 days pull down and remove the Wall.

(4) Alternatively, damages and interest on those damages under section 35A of the Supreme Court Act 1981.

(5) Further or other remedies.

(6) Costs.

JOSEPH BLOGGS

STATEMENT OF TRUTH

Dated etc.

12.9.2 Commentary

Paragraph 1. This is a claim for the recovery of land, so the claimant is stated to be not just the owner but also entitled to possession of the land, which is also identified as required by CPR, PD 16, para 7.1(2).

Paragraph 2. The trespass. The key word is 'wrongfully'.

Paragraph 3. The claim seeks an injunction for the removal of the wall, so it is necessary to state that the defendant built it.

Paragraph 4. The damage suffered is that the claimant has been 'deprived of the use and enjoyment' of the land. The loss is measured by reference to what would have been a reasonable sum for the use and enjoyment of it (ie what a fair rent would have been).

Paragraph 5. To get an order for the removal of the wall, it is good to establish that the defendant has refused to remove it voluntarily, so as to establish that this can only be achieved by court order.

Paragraph 6. PD 16, para 7.1(1) requires that in an action for the recovery of land the particulars of claim must state whether the order sought relates to residential premises.

Prayer. The claimant seeks possession and 'mesne profits'. This is an ancient legal term, which means the equivalent of rent; but you must not use the term 'rent', because it refers to a payment made by a tenant to his landlord, and so would implicitly acknowledge the defendant's right to be in possession of the land. These are equitable remedies. In the alternative the claimant seeks the common law remedy of damages.

The last two remedies sought are traditionally added in the Chancery Division. This is the first example of a claim in the Chancery Division, so the first occasion on which you have seen this. Neither is necessary. The court is not limited to the remedies claimed, and is not precluded from making an order for costs because the claimant has not mentioned it in the claim form or particulars of claim. But the Chancery Division has a few quirks of its own, which you had better follow.

12.10 Agency: claim for an account

12.10.1 Particulars of claim

IN THE HIGH COURT OF JUSTICE   Claim No 2004 HC 2379
CHANCERY DIVISION

BETWEEN:

QUINNLATE LIMITED Claimant

and

DIVECARS LIMITED Defendant

PARTICULARS OF CLAIM

1.   At all material times the Claimant was in business providing car hire services to tourists at seaside resorts around the United Kingdom.

2.   At all material times the Defendant acted as the Claimant's agent and arranged the supply of additional car hire services for customers of the Claimant in resorts in north Wales.

3.   A written agency arrangement was made between the Claimant and the Defendant on or about 1st January 1999 which contained the following express terms, among others:

(1) The Defendant would act as seller of car hire services for the Claimant and would hold money received for the Claimant's account.

(2) The Defendant would keep all money received separate from other funds in its possession or control pending remittance to the Claimant of that money (less agreed commission) and transfer of its commission to any other account.

(3) The Defendant would remit to the Claimant money due by the last working day of each calendar month.

(4) Each remittance would be of all the sums paid or due to the Defendant since the last remittance, less a retention of commission due to the Defendant of 40% of the sums paid for additional car hire services.

4.   Further or alternatively it was an implied term of the agency agreement that the Defendant would preserve and be constantly ready with correct accounts of all its dealings and transactions in the course of its agency.

5.   In breach of the agreement the Defendant has:

(1) failed to account to the Claimant in respect of all sums received and/or due to the Claimant;

(2) failed to keep money received on behalf of the Claimant separate from other funds in its possession; and

(3) failed to provide the Claimant with proper accounts of all its dealings during the course of its agency and/or to produce to the Claimant correct accounts of all its dealings and transactions in the course of its agency.

6.   Further, the Claimant claims interest under section 35A Supreme Court Act 1981 on the amount found to be due to the Claimant at such rate and for such period as the Court shall think fit.

AND the Claimant claims:

(1) An account of all sums received by the Defendant as agent for the Claimant in respect of car hire services.

(2) A declaration that the Defendant is not entitled to retain any sum in respect of commission which might otherwise have been due upon all sums found to have been received on the taking of the account.

(3) An order for all necessary and proper inquiries and directions for the taking of the account.

(4) An order for the payment by the Defendant to the Claimant of the amount found due on the taking of the account.

(5) An order for the payment of such interest on the sums found due to the Claimant as the Court thinks fit, under section 35A of the Supreme Court Act 1981.

(6) Further or other remedies.

(7) Costs.

JOSEPH BLOGGS

STATEMENT OF TRUTH

12.10.2 Commentary

This is a claim for an account. It is a very useful remedy where the defendant is in possession of money or other property rightfully due to the claimant, but the claimant does not know its whereabouts, or how much is owing. This may be due to the dishonesty (as in this example) or negligence of the defendant. A common situation arises where an agent receives money on behalf of his principal, and fails to account for it. His obligations may arise expressly, or by implication in equity or in contract. Here, only express contractual obligations are relied on. In essence the claimant trusted the defendant to provide accurate accounts of all money received though hiring cars on the claimant's behalf, but it has not produced proper accounts and the claimant believes the defendant has kept for itself money due to the claimant.

Paragraphs 1 & 2. The parties are introduced. The benefit of the contract from the defendant's point of view was that it had the right to provide additional services to the claimant's customers, and retain 40% of the cost of these additional services.

Paragraph 3. The contract and its express material terms are set out in a single paragraph. This is acceptable where you would otherwise have a very short paragraph to say there was a contract, before starting a new paragraph for the terms. The term in paragraph 3(2) would be implied by law if it were not expressly incorporated.

Paragraph 4. This term is implied into the contract by law. An agent must be ready to account at any time.

Paragraph 5. Breach. Essentially the defendant has been under-declaring to the claimant the money it has received, and transferring the stolen amounts to other accounts. So paragraph 5(1) alleges a breach of the terms set out in paragraph 3(3) and (4); paragraph 5(2) alleges a breach of the term set out in paragraph 3(2); and paragraph 5(3) alleges a breach of the implied term in paragraph 4.

At this point in a claim for damages you would expect to see an allegation that the claimant has suffered loss, and the particulars of it. But the claimant is unable to do this: only the defendant knows how much it has stolen. This does not matter, because the claim is for an account. So the claim goes straight on to:

Paragraph 6. The claim for interest. Although illogical in this case, since there has not yet been an allegation that any sum of money is due on which interest could be charged, it is a requirement of CPR, r 16.4(1) that the claim for interest be stated in the particulars of claim.

Prayer. The meat of the claim is actually in the prayer. If these remedies are ordered by the court, the defendant will be required to produce an account (item 1), if necessary under the supervision of a court-appointed accountant, showing all the sums received. Item 2 arises because a defaulting agent loses his right to benefit under the contract, so the defendant forfeits its commission. Item 3 may be useful in case, for example, the court needs to make an order for the appointment of a supervisor, or conduct a factual inquiry into where the money has gone. Item 4 is the end result — once the account has been produced, the amount due must be paid, plus (item 5) interest. Items 6 and 7 are there because we are in the Chancery Division — see the commentary in **12.9.2**.

12.11 Specific performance: sale of chattels

12.11.1 Particulars of claim

IN THE HIGH COURT OF JUSTICE   Claim No 2004 HC 1142
CHANCERY DIVISION

BETWEEN

MICHAEL EDWINS   Claimant

and

BONNINGTON ANTIQUES LIMITED   Defendant

PARTICULARS OF CLAIM

1.   The Claimant is a descendant of the 1st Duke of Dartmoor. The Defendant carries on business as an antique dealer at 216 Portobello Road, London W10.

2.   By an oral agreement made between the Claimant and Camilla Buxton on behalf of the Defendant on 1st June 2004 the Defendant agreed to sell to the Claimant and the Claimant agreed to buy an ornamental snuff-box engraved in the name of the first Duke of Dartmoor ('the Snuff-Box') for a price of £12,000, one half of which was to be payable before, and one half upon delivery of the Snuff-Box to the Claimant.

3.   On 2nd June 2004 the Claimant paid to the Defendant £6,000 under the agreement.

4.   In breach of the agreement the Defendant has refused and still refuses to deliver the Snuff-Box to the Claimant despite repeated requests, oral and written, by the Claimant to the Defendant to do so.

5.   The Claimant remains willing and able to pay to the Defendant £6,000, the balance of the purchase price.

AND the Claimant claims:

(1) Specific performance of the agreement.

(2) Further or alternatively, damages for breach of the agreement.

(3) Interest on those damages under section 35A of the Supreme Court Act 1981 to be assessed.

(4) Further or other remedies.

(5) Costs.

JOSEPH BLOGGS

STATEMENT OF TRUTH

Dated etc.

12.11.2   Commentary

The claim for specific performance is still a claim for breach of contract: only the remedy sought is different. So you will notice that paragraphs 1–4 are exactly as they would be if the claim were for damages.

Paragraph 1. The claimant is described as a descendant of the 1st Duke of Dartmoor in an attempt to get over one of the hurdles to a claim for specific performance of a sale of goods contract, namely to show that the goods are unique in some way. Strictly speaking the uniqueness should be to do with the goods themselves, not any special worth they have to an individual, but the claimant here is trying to say all he can to show that he should be granted his remedy.

Paragraph 5. This paragraph is important. In order to be granted specific performance the claimant must show that he has fulfilled all his obligations under the contract and/or remains willing and able to fulfil his remaining obligations.

Prayer. Damages are claimed as an alternative to specific performance. Since specific performance is a discretionary remedy, this is wise. The body of the claim does not allege that the claimant has suffered loss and damage because he has not done so yet: he will only suffer loss if he does not get the snuff box. So this aspect of the claim is mentioned in the prayer only. Since the claim is in the Chancery Division, further or other remedies and costs are included in the prayer (see **12.9.2**).

12.12   Specific performance: sale of land

12.12.1   Particulars of claim

IN THE HIGH COURT OF JUSTICE   Claim No 2004 HC 6788
CHANCERY DIVISION

BETWEEN

JASMINE FENOUGHTY   Claimant

and

ZENA CHALMERS   Defendant

PARTICULARS OF CLAIM

---

1.   By a contract in writing dated 10th April 2004 and made between the Defendant and the Claimant the Defendant agreed to sell and the Claimant agreed to buy the freehold interest with vacant possession in the house and premises situated at and known as 10 Prospect Place, London W12 ('the Property') for the sum of £196,500. Title to the Property is registered at HM Land Registry under Title Number NGL 392224. A copy of the contract is attached.

2.   The contract incorporated the Standard Conditions of Sale 2nd Edition (a copy of which is attached) except insofar as the standard conditions were inconsistent with the special conditions. By general condition 6.6 it was provided that if the sale was not completed by the completion date provided for in the special conditions either party being ready, willing and able to complete their own obligations should be entitled to serve upon the other notice to complete within a fixed number of days and that time would then become of the essence of the period for completion.

3.   It was further provided by the special conditions of the contract (a copy of which is attached) that the contract should be completed on 17th April 2004 and that the period for completion to be specified in a notice to complete served under general condition 6.6 should be 7 days.

4.   The Claimant has complied with or alternatively is now and has at all material times been ready, willing and able to comply with all her obligations under the contract.

5.   The Defendant failed to complete the contract on 17th April 2004. By notice in writing pursuant to general condition 6.6 (amended as set out above) served on the Defendant on 20th April 2004 the Claimant required the Defendant to complete the contract on or before 27th April 2004. The Defendant has, however, failed to comply with the notice to complete.

AND the Claimant claims:

(1) Specific performance of the contract for sale.

(2) Further or alternatively, damages for breach of contract.

(3) Alternatively:

   (a)   A declaration that because of the repudiation of the contract by the Defendant the Claimant is relieved of all liability for the further performance of her obligations under it.

   (b)   Repayment to the Claimant of the deposit of £19,650 paid under the contract.

   (c)   A declaration that the Claimant is entitled to a lien on the Property for her deposit and any damages and costs awarded in this claim.

(4) Further or other remedies.

(5) Costs.

JOSEPH BLOGGS

STATEMENT OF TRUTH

Dated etc.

12.12.2 Commentary

Claims for specific performance of contracts for the sale of land are very common — land is always considered unique, and so the remedy is routinely granted. The precedent here is basically part of conveyancing practice, but it is a claim for breach of contract and you might have to draft one like this. Fortunately it is pretty much in standard form.

Paragraph 1. The parties and the contract, and particularly the land, which must be precisely identified. If the land is registered land, the title number should be given.

Paragraph 2. The material terms. Contracts for the sale of land almost always contain standard conditions in a published edition. Refer to and attach the relevant conditions, but then state the particular condition(s) on which you rely.

Paragraph 3. More material terms. As well as general conditions which do not vary from case to case, contracts contain special conditions, which are specific to that sale. Paragraphs 2 and 3 obviously need to be read together.

Paragraph 4. The essential statement of performance by the claimant.

Paragraph 5. Breaches by the defendant. Once these are set out, nothing more is required but the prayer.

Prayer. This is in standard form, and in normal circumstances all of these remedies should be sought.

12.13 Injunction

12.13.1 Particulars of claim

IN THE HIGH COURT OF JUSTICE   Claim No 2004 HC 4243
QUEEN'S BENCH DIVISION

BETWEEN

WUNDACOLA PLC   <u>Claimants</u>

and

HEINZ BERNSTEIN   <u>Defendant</u>

PARTICULARS OF CLAIM

1.   The Claimants are and were at all material times manufacturers of soft drinks. The Defendant is a food scientist.

2.   By a written contract of employment dated 1st August 1998 (a copy of which is attached) the Claimants agreed to and did employ the Defendant as a research and development scientist at an annual salary of (initially) £42,000.

3.   It was an express term of the contract that during the continuance of the contract and for a period of three years after its termination the Defendant would not be employed by or enter into any contract of personal service with Supacola Limited, a competitor of the Claimants.

4.   It was further an express term of the contract that the Defendant would not at any time reveal to anyone any secret recipes or manufacturing processes of the Claimants.

5.   During the course of his employment in about 2001 the Defendant was involved in creating for the Claimants a soft drink known as Apricola, the recipe for which is a secret of the Claimants known only to a very few people including the Defendant.

6.   The Defendant ceased to be employed by the Claimants on 1st October 2004.

7.   The Defendant threatens and intends, unless restrained by the Court, to enter into the employment of Supacola Limited and to reveal to them the recipe of Apricola, in breach of the express terms set out above.

AND the Claimants claim:

(1) An injunction ordering the Defendant not to enter into or continue in the employment of Supacola Limited before 1st October 2007.

(2) An injunction ordering the Defendant not to divulge or cause or permit to be divulged to Supacola Limited, their officers, employees or agents or to any other

person the recipe or manufacturing process of Apricola or any other secret recipes or manufacturing processes of the Claimants.

(3) Further or alternatively, damages, together with interest on those damages under section 35A of the Supreme Court Act 1981.

JOSEPH BLOGGS

STATEMENT OF TRUTH

Dated etc.

12.13.2   Commentary

We saw a claim for an injunction in tort (to prevent a nuisance) in **12.2**. This is a claim seeking injunctions to enforce restrictive covenants in a contract of employment. Remember this example — it returns in **Chapters 19** and **20**.

Paragraphs 1 and 2. The parties are identified in paragraph 1 and the contract and its performance are dealt with in paragraph 2. There will obviously be no dispute here, so these issues can be taken together.

Paragraphs 3 and 4. The restrictive covenants are of course express terms, and so they are set out properly here. Many practitioners would in this case choose to copy the terms out word for word, but the actual words are not strictly speaking material.

Paragraphs 5 and 6. Story telling. These are not strictly speaking material facts (without which the claim cannot succeed), but the rest of the claim makes no sense without them.

Paragraph 7. The threatened breaches. As in **12.2** the standard formula 'threatens and intends, unless restrained by the court' is used.

Prayer. The injunctions must of course be drafted in full. How and why these orders are drafted as they are will be explained in **Chapter 19**. The alternative damages claim needs to be included in case the injunctions are not granted, but appears only in the prayer because no loss will have been suffered if they are.

12.14   Exercise

Counsel is instructed on behalf of Norman Gorbutt and the Markup Insurance Company Ltd, his home and contents insurers. The claim arises out of a fire which appears to have been caused by Mr Harry Hastings, his next-door neighbour. Counsel will see that Mrs Thelma Stirling, the fire investigation expert, says in her report that there was a gas leak in the kitchen of No 33 due to some gas connections being left overnight in an unfinished state which was ignited by an electrical spark caused by unfinished wiring which had been left live. The fire spread so quickly because of a large quantity of petrol stored by Mr Hastings in the room above the kitchen. Mr Gorbutt will say as follows:

I live at 35 Baker's Lane, Tadcaster, Yorkshire, which I also own. It is a semi-detached house, and my neighbour at No 33, the other side of the building, was until January 2004 Mr Harry Hastings. I am an interior designer, and Mr Hastings is a general builder and carpenter. In October 2003 Harry and I were discussing home improvements over a drink in the Black Swan pub, our local. We discovered that we were both thinking of putting a new kitchen and bathroom into our respective houses. In order to save ourselves a bit of money we came to an arrangement by which I would design his kitchen and bathroom for him, and he would put my kitchen and bathroom in for me: making the units, doing the tiling, flooring, plumbing, gas-fitting and electrics. We would each pay for our own materials and furnishings. Our tastes were very different, so I did a separate design for each kitchen and bathroom, and showed him these designs at the beginning of December. He was quite happy with them, and we agreed that he would build his own kitchen and bathroom first and would start work in my house in February 2004. Because I wanted to take advantage of the low prices, I bought a new oven, hob, cooker hood, microwave, fridge/freezer, washing machine, dishwasher, sink, bath, basin, lavatory, shower and bidet in the January sales at a total cost of £4,000 VAT. There was nowhere for me to store them, since we have a large family of four children, so Harry, who is single and lives alone, allowed me to put all these purchases in a spare room in his house until he could install them.

On 18 January 2004 at about 3 am there was a big explosion in Harry's house and it went up in flames. The fire was so severe that it spread through the roof spaces into my house, causing substantial damage to my building, furniture, carpets and personal property on the 1st and 2nd floors. Further damage was caused by water from the fire brigade's hoses. Harry's house was completely gutted and nothing within it was saved. It is now an empty shell, and my house has had to be shored up until No 33 can be rebuilt. My house took four months to repair, during which we had to live in a hotel. Everything was covered by my insurance, and my total claim, which the insurance company settled, was for £100,580. I wish to make a claim for this amount, for the value of my kitchen and bathroom units destroyed, and for my design services. I would ordinarily have charged £2,000 VAT for designing Harry's kitchen and bathroom. Harry was not insured in respect of liability to me, but has received over £200,000 in insurance money for the loss of his house, and so can afford to satisfy my claim.

Defence and counterclaim

13.1 Principles

13.1.1 What is a counterclaim?

A counterclaim is a claim made by a defendant against a claimant in the same case. It exists by virtue of CPR, r 20.4. If a defendant has a claim against the claimant, he could in theory commence a separate claim, but it is more convenient to combine the counterclaim with the claim in the same case under Part 20.

There does not need to be any factual, causal or legal connection between the claimant's claim and the defendant's counterclaim (though there usually is). He does not need permission to make a counterclaim provided he files it with his defence. The defendant may make other persons, apart from the claimant, defendants to his counterclaim, but he will then need the court's permission (r 20.5).

PD 20, para 6.1 says that where a defendant to a claim serves a counterclaim, the defence and counterclaim should normally form one document, with the counterclaim following on from the defence. This is useful, because it avoids the need to file a Part 20 claim form.

It follows that a counterclaim does not stand alone, but will always be part of a statement of case entitled 'defence and counterclaim'. This is subdivided into two parts. The defence always comes first, and will be drafted exactly as it would have been had there been no counterclaim, except that a defence of set-off may be added (see below). The defence is followed by the counterclaim, which is exactly as particulars of claim based on the same cause of action would have been in terms of its *content*. It may, however, be abbreviated in its *form*.

This abbreviation is possible because where some or all of the facts necessary to found the counterclaim have already been set out, either in the defence, or in the particulars of claim and admitted in the defence, they do not need to be stated again, but can be incorporated into the counterclaim by simply stating, for example, 'Paragraphs 1 to 6 above are repeated'. However, do not do this without thinking carefully of all the ingredients necessary to establish the cause of action in the counterclaim, because you must still repeat the right paragraphs, and incorporate any essential ingredients not already set out.

13.1.2 The defence of set-off

The defence of set-off arises where the fact that the defendant has a claim for money against the claimant provides a total or partial defence to the claimant's claim for money against the defendant. It can arise in the following circumstances:

(a) By way of mutual debt. If the claimant and defendant both owe each other specified amounts of money, even if unconnected, the defendant's debt should be set off against the debt to the claimant.

(b) Under the Sale of Goods Act 1979, s 53(1). Where the seller sues for the price of goods sold and delivered, the buyer can set off a claim for damages for breach of the statutory implied terms as to satisfactory quality, fitness for purpose, or correspondence to description.

(c) Defective workmanship. On a claim for the price of services, the defendant can set off a claim for damages for poor workmanship.

(d) Equitable set-off. A set-off can arise in other circumstances in equity. The scope of this set-off is not defined, but it is quite common. However it does not arise whenever there is a counterclaim for money. The claims must be very closely connected and it must be inequitable to allow the claimant to enforce payment without taking into account the defendant's cross-claim.

13.1.3 Pleading set-off

The pleading of the defence of set-off is covered by CPR, r 16.6:

Where a defendant—

(a) contends he is entitled to money from the claimant; and

(b) relies on this a defence to the whole or part of the claim,

the contention may be included in the defence and set off against the claim, whether or not it is also a Part 20 claim.

The defence exists not only where the defendant is counterclaiming the sum he is owed, but in any case where the fact that it is owed will provide a complete or partial defence. However, in this chapter we are concerned with counterclaims. In such a case you should state in the defence that the defendant seeks to set off the sum due or the sum claimed in the counterclaim against any sum the claimant may be entitled to recover in his claim. The counterclaim can be proceeded with whether or not the claimant wins his case, but if he does, and the counterclaim is also successful, then the amount the defendant has to pay will be set off against the amount the claimant has to pay him. The set-off may be stated to be a partial set-off, which will go to reduce the claimant's claim (if successful), or a total set-off, which will extinguish the claimant's claim altogether; or both in the alternative, if it is not certain which of the two claims is for the larger amount.

Remember that the set-off is part of the *defence*, not the counterclaim. By convention and logic it always comes last.

13.1.4 Title

It is not entirely clear whether in the case of a straightforward counterclaim by a defendant against a claimant the parties can simply be described as claimant and defendant, or whether (as is usually required under Part 20) as 'Claimant/Part 20 Defendant' and 'Defendant/Part 20 Claimant'. It is probably safer to use the latter form in the heading, to indicate that there is a counterclaim. However, it is submitted that there is no need in the body of the statement of case to call the parties anything other than Claimant and Defendant: there can be no possible confusion, and it's a lot simpler.

However, see **15.4**: there are proposals for change.

13.2 Defence and counterclaim: without set-off

13.2.1 Defence and counterclaim

(For particulars of claim see **7.10**.)

IN THE CHESTER COUNTY COURT   Claim No CH4/28011

BETWEEN

BRIAN FLANAGHAN   <u>Claimant/Part 20 Defendant</u>

and

BRENDA DINGLE   <u>Defendant/Part 20 Claimant</u>

DEFENCE AND COUNTERCLAIM

<u>DEFENCE</u>

1.   Except that the Defendant denies that she drove into a collision with the Claimant's car, and except as set out in paragraph 2 below, paragraph 1 of the Particulars of Claim is admitted.

2.   The Defendant stopped at the junction of Brookside Avenue and King's Drive, intending to turn right into King's Drive, and waited for the Claimant's car to pass. The Claimant then switched on his indicator to show that he intended to turn left into Brookside Avenue, whereupon the Defendant drove forward, but stopped again when she realised that the Claimant was not slowing down in preparation for his left turn, and her car was stationary when it was struck by the Claimant's car.

3.   The Defendant denies that she was negligent as alleged or at all or that the collision was caused by any negligence on her part. She relies on the facts set out in paragraph 2 above.

4.   The collision was caused solely by or contributed to by the negligence of the Claimant.

<u>PARTICULARS OF NEGLIGENCE</u>

(a) Indicating that he was turning left when he did not intend to do so.

(b) Driving straight ahead when he had indicated that he was turning left.

(c) Driving too fast in all the circumstances.

(d) Failing to keep any or any proper look-out.

(e) Causing his car to collide with the Defendant's car.

(f) Failing to stop, steer or otherwise control his car so as to avoid striking the Defendant's car.

5.   The Claimant is required to prove that he is too afraid to drive and is unlikely ever to drive again. Otherwise the Claimant's injury, loss and damage are admitted. The contents of the medical report served by the Claimant are agreed.

<u>COUNTERCLAIM</u>

6.   The Defendant repeats paragraphs 1, 2 and 4 above. The Defendant was the owner of the Peugeot 306 car.

7.   As a result of the matters set out above the Defendant has suffered pain, injury, loss and damage.

<u>PARTICULARS OF INJURY</u>

The Defendant, who was born on 9th May 1976 and was aged 27 years at the date of the accident, suffered:

(a) Scalp laceration.

(b) Vomiting.

(c) Soft tissue injury to neck.

The Defendant was taken to hospital and given 5 sutures to close the laceration to the scalp. She went home at her own request but was readmitted the next day (19th February 2004) after a night of persistent headache and vomiting. She was kept under observation and discharged on 23rd February 2004. There was still pain in the neck and she required analgesics. The scalp wound healed after about 3 weeks, but the neck injury has been slower to heal. There has been some improvement but she still has a limited range of movement. She is in continuous pain and continues to take analgesics, though is less dependent on them than she was. She suffers from loss of sleep. The situation is likely to improve over the next 18 months but it is unlikely that her symptoms will disappear entirely. The Defendant was off work for 6 months as a result of her injury.

Further particulars of the Defendant's injuries are set out in the medical report served with this Defence and Counterclaim.

<u>PARTICULARS OF SPECIAL DAMAGE</u>

The Defendant's losses are set out in the schedule of expenses and losses served with this Defence and Counterclaim.

8.   Further the Defendant claims interest under section 69 of the County Courts Act 1984 on the amount found to be due to the Defendant at such rate and for such period as the Court thinks fit.

AND the Defendant counterclaims:

(1) Damages.

(2) Interest under section 69 of the County Courts Act 1984 to be assessed.

BESS TOFFER

<u>STATEMENT OF TRUTH</u>

Dated etc.

13.2.2   Commentary

This is the defence to the claim you drafted as an exercise, so the particulars of claim cannot be printed in this Manual. However, it should be perfectly clear by now what is in those particulars of claim, and this defence can be related easily to the imagined statement of case if necessary.

Heading. The reason for the description of the parties is explained in **13.1.3**. The title of the statement of case is 'defence and counterclaim' and that is what appears in tramlines. However, there are two subtitles, first 'defence', and later on 'counterclaim'. The two parts of the statement of case must be kept distinct from each other.

Defence. You will notice that the defence is drafted exactly as it would have been had there been no counterclaim attached.

Paragraph 1. The defendant obviously admits that the accident occurred, but not how. In particular she says the claimant's car struck hers, whereas the claimant alleged that the defendant's car ran into his.

Paragraph 2. The alternative version of events is set out. The allegation about the left indicator is arguably evidence, but the defendant relies on it to show negligence, so it should be included.

Paragraph 3. The standard denial of negligence must of course be given reasons. Here there is nothing that needs to be said except that reference is made to paragraph 2. The reasons are simply the different version of events, a version which plainly suggests that the accident was the fault of the claimant, not the defendant.

Paragraph 4. The allegation here is 'caused solely by or contributed to by'. The defendant seeks to establish if possible that all the blame attaches to the claimant, but wishes to rely on contributory negligence as an alternative.

Paragraph 5. Apart from one contentious matter which the defendant requires the claimant to prove, the injury loss and damage are all admitted. This is not unrealistic in a straightforward case where there is an agreed medical report and the pecuniary losses are all special damages.

If there were to be a set-off relied on, this is where it would come. But there is none. In the event of both parties being held partly to blame, neither party wants the damages awarded to cancel each other out. Each wishes to recover some compensation from the insurers of the other. So it would not be equitable to allow a set-off, in spite of the close connection between the claims.

Counterclaim. This is a claim for personal injury by the defendant arising from the same accident, and based on the negligence of the claimant, and what appears is exactly that, drafted in accordance with usual practice, but *abbreviated* to avoid unnecessary repetition.

Paragraph 6. The defendant must first of all state the accident. By repeating paragraphs 1 and 2, she has restated the accident in her version of events. Then the defendant must allege that the accident was caused by the negligence of the claimant. But this has already been alleged in the defence, so all that is necessary is to repeat paragraph 4. A final fact is alleged: that the defendant owns her car. The claimant only alleged that she was driving it. She must add this if she wants to recover damages for the repairs to her car.

Paragraphs 7 and 8. These are drafted in full, and in exactly the same way as they would have been if the claim had been commenced first by the defendant, though care must be taken to refer to the defendant rather than the claimant (a careless mistake easily made).

Prayer. Note 'the defendant counterclaims' instead of 'the claimant claims'.

13.3 Defence and counterclaim: partial set-off

13.3.1 Defence and counterclaim

(See particulars of claim in **9.10**.)

IN THE HIGH COURT OF JUSTICE   Claim No 2004 HC 7401
QUEEN'S BENCH DIVISION

BETWEEN

ALASTAIR GREATBATCH   Claimant/Part 20 Defendant

and

(1) HENRY WILLIAMS   First Defendant
(2) SCOTT WILLIAMS (a firm)

Second Defendants/Part 20 Claimants

DEFENCE OF FIRST AND SECOND DEFENDANTS
AND COUNTERCLAIM OF SECOND DEFENDANTS

DEFENCE

1.   Paragraphs 1 and 2 of the Particulars of Claim are admitted. The First Defendant was at all material times acting on behalf of the Second Defendants. It was expressly agreed between the First Defendant and the Claimant on 21st February 2003 that the consideration for the survey, valuation and advice would be 1% of the value placed upon the House by the First Defendant.

2.   Paragraphs 3 and 4 of the Particulars of Claim are admitted.

3.   The First Defendant did survey the House on 24th February 2004. Some of the defects set out in the Report were more than minor. Otherwise paragraph 5 of the Particulars of Claim is admitted.

4.   The Claimant is required to prove the facts alleged in paragraph 6 of the Particulars of Claim.

5.   It is denied that the House was structurally unsound or in a defective condition. If, which the Claimant is required to prove, there were any defects other than those identified in the Report they were not material to the value of the House. The Defendants rely on the survey report of Angelina Howard, a copy of which is attached.

6.   Alternatively, if, which is denied, the House was structurally unsound or in a defective condition, any material defects other than those identified in the Report were latent and could not reasonably have been discovered by the First Defendant exercising all reasonable care and skill.

7.   It is therefore denied that the Defendants are in breach of the agreement or that the First Defendant was negligent as alleged in paragraph 8 of the Particulars of Claim or at all.

8.   The Claimant is required to prove the alleged loss and damage, in particular the actual value alleged.

9.   Further or alternatively, if contrary to this Defence the Second Defendants are held liable to the Claimant, they will seek to reduce the Claimant's claim by setting off the sum counterclaimed below.

COUNTERCLAIM

10.   Paragraphs 1 to 9 above are repeated. *— Why all of them ??? (See over)*

11.   On 14th March 2004 the Second Defendants by invoice demanded from the Claimant their fee of £1,750 under the agreement. Despite frequent requests for payment, oral and written, the Claimant has not paid the Second Defendants their fee or any part of it.

12.   Further the Second Defendants claim interest under section 35A of the Supreme Court Act 1981 on the sum of £1,750 at the rate of 8% per annum from 1st April 2004, amounting to £85.53 at 16th November 2004 and then continuing until judgment or sooner payment at the rate of £0.38 per day.

AND the Second Defendants counterclaim:

(1) £1,750.

(2) Interest under section 35A of the Supreme Court Act 1981, amounting to £85.53 at 16th November 2004, and then continuing at the daily rate of £0.38.

BESS TOFFER

STATEMENT OF TRUTH

Dated etc.

13.3.2 Commentary

The defendants are denying liability and counterclaiming their unpaid fee.

Heading. The title of the statement of case is complicated, because this is the defence of both defendants but the counterclaim only of one of them. For this reason it probably *is* necessary in this case to give the parties their full description.

Paragraph 1. The defendants admit the parties and the contract. The claimant was unsure whether the first defendant was acting on his own behalf or on behalf of the firm, so the defendants take this opportunity to clarify this. The consideration is spelt out in full. The claimant simply said 'for a fee', but the second defendants want to counterclaim a specified amount, so they need to justify that amount. A purist would argue that this point should be saved for the counterclaim: it is not strictly a matter which helps to establish the defence. But it is usually dealt with at this point: otherwise one would not find all the matters relating to the terms of the contract in one place, which is potentially unhelpful.

Paragraph 2. The defendants do not deny their contractual and tortious obligations: their defence is based on a denial that they failed to fulfil them.

Paragraph 3. Admitting the report and the advice within it, though there is a small quibble of the seriousness of the defects found by the first defendant. 'Did' survey because the claimant suggests that he may only have 'purported' to survey it. The date of the survey is added for completeness.

Paragraph 4. There is no reason why the defendants should admit actual reliance by the claimant, however likely it may seem. They probably have no knowledge of the date of purchase or the price, so the claimant must prove these matters too.

Paragraph 5. The defendants deny that there is anything substantially wrong with the house at all. They maintain that they found all the material defects. This denial is somewhat surprising, and suggests that there will be contradictory expert evidence. So it is rather important to indicate immediately that the defendants have an expert to substantiate this denial, and her report is referred to and attached. The reasons for the denial will obviously be found in this report.

Paragraph 6. Puts forward the alternative line of defence. There is an apparent contradiction here, so the phrase 'if, which is denied' is important. It must be presumed that this defence is also substantiated by the report of Angelina Howard.

Paragraph 7. Breach and negligence need to be denied, and reasons given. The reasons have all been stated or referred to in paragraphs 5 and 6, and these paragraphs are referred to by adding the word 'therefore'.

Paragraph 8. Obvious.

Paragraph 9. The set-off. This comes last, because it looks forward to the counterclaim and only comes into play if the defence fails. But remember that it is part of the defence, not the counterclaim. The drafting is basically just a standard formula. You can copy this, or redraft it in your own words if you prefer. There is no chance of the counterclaim being for a greater amount than the claim, so it is alleged that it only goes to *reduce* the claimant's claim, not wipe it out altogether.

Counterclaim. The counterclaim is for payment of a sum due under a contract, so the defendants need to state the parties, the contract, the consideration agreed, performance, the fee falling due and failure to pay.

Paragraph 10. The parties, contract, consideration and performance have all been stated already, so can be incorporated by repetition. You might more correctly repeat simply paragraphs 1 and 3, which would cover the necessary, but it is very common in practice to repeat the whole defence, just in case!

Paragraph 11. The payment falls due either on an agreed date, or after a reasonable time, or on demand. Here the defendants rely on a demand, so this must be stated and the relevant document identified. The frequent requests are to head off a potential defence that the claimant has been given insufficient time to pay. You must also state that the claimant has not paid, and do not forget the important words 'or any part of it'.

Paragraph 12. This is a claim for a debt, so interest needs to be set out in full.

Prayer. The claim is for the sum of money due, not for damages. See **9.4**.

13.4   Defence and counterclaim: total set-off

13.4.1   Defence and counterclaim

(See particulars of claim in **12.6**.)

IN THE LANCASTER COUNTY COURT   Claim No LA4/40197

BETWEEN

HODGE AND DAUGHTER LIMITED

Claimants/Part 20 Defendants

and

(1) SAMUEL VINCENT

First Defendant/Part 20 Claimant

(2) MATHESON & CO LIMITED   Second Defendants

DEFENCE AND COUNTERCLAIM OF
THE FIRST DEFENDANT

DEFENCE

1.   Subject to the set-off and counterclaim set out below, the First Defendant admits the Claimants' claim.

2.   The First Defendant will seek to extinguish his liability to the Claimants by setting off as much of the sum counterclaimed below as necessary.

COUNTERCLAIM

3.   By a written contract dated 19th November 2002 (a copy of which is attached) made between the Claimants and the First Defendant the Claimants agreed to employ the First Defendant as a sales manager at a basic salary of £12,000 per year.

4.   It was an express term of the contract that the Claimants would pay to the First Defendant by way of commission 0.5% of the retail value of all sales of electronic goods achieved by the area sales department managed by the First Defendant.

5.   On 5th October 2003, in breach of this express term, the Claimants gave the First Defendant notice in writing that they were delaying payment of commission, and have not paid the First Defendant any sum by way of commission since that date.

6.   On 30th April 2004 the First Defendant left his employment.

7.   As a result of the matters set out above the First Defendant has suffered loss and damage.

PARTICULARS

The First Defendant estimates the commission on sales due to him for the period 30th September 2003 to 30th April 2004 at not less than £20,000.

8.   Further the First Defendant claims interest under section 69 of the County Courts Act 1984 on the amount found to be due to him at such rate and for such period as the Court thinks fit.

AND the First Defendant counterclaims:

(1) Damages.

(2) Interest under section 69 of the County Courts Act 1984 to be assessed.

BESS TOFFER

STATEMENT OF TRUTH

Dated etc.

13.4.2   Commentary

This is the defence and counterclaim only of the first defendant. The second defendants will serve their own separate statement of case. In fact the first defendant does not deny liability at all: his defence is simply that he has a counterclaim for an even larger sum which he will set off against his liability to the claimants.

Heading. In the circumstances, the full description of the parties is probably again required in the heading.

Paragraph 1. Admits liability. There is therefore nothing more to be said by way of defence.

Paragraph 2. A standard form for the drafting of a set-off where the counterclaim will extinguish the claim.

Counterclaim. There is nothing that can be incorporated by repetition, so the first defendant needs to state his claim in full, just as he would if he were the claimant. It is a straightforward claim for damages for breach of contract. So we get the parties and contract in paragraph 3, the material express term in paragraph 4, the breach in paragraph 5, an obvious bit of story-telling in paragraph 6 and the loss and damage in paragraph 7. None of these paragraphs needs any commentary.

13.5 Exercise

Percy Hopcroft, managing director of the defendants, will say:

In September 2003 we received an order from an old customer, Miss Rebecca Peters, to supply and install four greenhouses, complete with heating systems, for the hothouse plants at her garden centre. Our company supplied the greenhouses and we arranged for our usual electrical contractor, Harold Todd, to wire up and connect the heating systems at a charge of £658. The greenhouses were delivered and fully installed on 15th October 2003. Miss Peters paid a deposit of £1,000 and we invoiced her for £9,698 on 24th October 2003 When I wrote to her in March 2004 to ask her why we had not received the balance (payable within six weeks of installation) she told me for the first time that the glass was cracked and the heating systems had broken down and that she had lost all her hothouse plants. It is the first I had heard of anything being wrong. She could not explain why she had not contacted us immediately, so I do not know what if anything was the problem. Mr Todd told me that this installation went ahead perfectly normally and he could not understand Miss Peters saying that the heating had since failed. Nor do my men remember any of the window-panes being cracked. I therefore denied liability and the next thing I knew we were served with the claim.

Counsel is asked to settle a defence and counterclaim.

IN THE SHREWSBURY COUNTY COURT   Claim No SY4/12996

BETWEEN

REBECCA PETERS   Claimant

and

HOMEWOOD GARDEN CENTRE LIMITED   Defendants

PARTICULARS OF CLAIM

---

1.   The Claimant owns and runs a garden centre at Merry Orchard, Downside, Shropshire. The Defendants carry on business as a garden centre and garden supplies merchants at 36 Acre Lane, Shrewsbury, Shropshire.

2.   By letters dated 9th September 2003 and 11th September 2003 passing between the Claimant and the Defendants, the Defendants in the course of their business agreed to supply to and install for the Claimant at her garden centre four greenhouses model K245 together with heating systems at a price of £10,698.

3.   In her letter dated 9th September 2003 the Claimant made it known to the Defendants that she required the greenhouses and heating systems for the purpose of keeping and heating hothouse plants.

4.   In the circumstances it was an implied term of the agreement that the greenhouses and heating systems should be:

(a) of satisfactory quality; and

(b) reasonably fit for the purpose of keeping and heating hothouse plants.

5.   In purported performance of the agreement the Defendants delivered and installed the greenhouses and heating systems at the Claimant's garden centre on 15th October 2003.

6.   In breach of the implied terms the greenhouses and heating systems were not of satisfactory quality and not reasonably fit for their purpose in that:

(a) Four glass panels on the greenhouses were cracked.

(b) The heating systems were defective and incorrectly wired and completely ceased to function after a few days causing many valuable plants to be killed or damaged by exposure to frost.

7.   As a result of the matters set out above the Claimant has suffered loss and damage.

PARTICULARS OF DAMAGE

	£
(1) Cost of repairing glass panels	278.00
(2) Cost of repairing heating systems	312.00
(3) Loss of profit on plants killed or damaged	11,000.00
	11,590.00

8.   Further the Claimant claims interest under section 69 of the County Courts Act 1984 on the amount found to be due to the Claimant at such rate and for such period as the Court thinks fit.

AND the Claimant claims:

(1) Damages.

(2) Interest under section 69 of the County Courts Act 1984 to be assessed.

JOHN SMITH

STATEMENT OF TRUTH

Dated etc.

Reply and defence to counterclaim

14.1 Principles

14.1.1 Reply

14.1.1.1 When is a reply needed?

The central rule relating to replies is in CPR, r 16.7:

> *(1) A claimant who does not file a reply to the defence shall not be taken to admit the matters raised in the defence.*
>
> *(2) A claimant who—*
> > *(a) files a reply to a defence; but*
> > *(b) fails to deal with a matter raised in the defence,*
> > *shall be taken to require that matter to be proved.*

This rule is the opposite to that for defences. A claimant who does not serve a reply is not at risk of compromising his position. He is not taken to admit anything, so he is free to say at trial either that he denies an allegation in the defence, or that he requires the claimant to prove it. However, by not serving a reply, he does not make it clear which matters he denies, which he admits and which he requires the defendant to prove.

A reply is therefore not a necessary statement of case, and there will not be a reply in every case. However, a reply may be required or desirable in the following circumstances:

(a) Where the claimant wishes to admit facts alleged in the defence to save costs.

(b) Where the claimant wishes actively to contest some matter raised in the defence; to do so he should deny it, rather than merely require the defendant to prove it.

(c) Where the claimant wishes to confess and avoid an allegation made in the defence; without a reply the claimant's case would not be fully stated.

(d) Where merely remaining silent would not sufficiently define the issues between the parties, because it needs to be clear whether something is denied or requires proof.

(e) Where the defence has misconstrued or misstated the claimant's cause of action.

A claimant who does serve a reply does not need to deal with every issue in the defence. Any issue on which he is silent, he will be taken to require to be proved. So once he decides to file a reply, the claimant needs expressly to admit every fact which ought to be admitted, and to deny every allegation which is in fact denied.

It is arguable that as a matter of good practice, when in doubt a reply should be served. The 'cards on the table' approach to civil litigation under the CPR requires that where possible a defendant should not be left in the dark as to whether something he has alleged in his defence will merely require proof, whether it will meet with active resistance in the form of a denial, or indeed whether it will be admitted. For example an allegation of contributory negligence by the claimant, not replied to, may well leave the defendant and the court unsure of what facts in that allegation are actually in issue. A reply can help to clarify those issues.

14.1.1.2 To reply or to amend?

A reply is *not* an alternative to amending the particulars of claim. A party must say nothing in the reply which is inconsistent with any previous statement of case. If, as a result of seeing the defence, you think you need to try a different or additional mode of attack, or you realise you have made a mistake in the particulars of claim, then you should seek to amend your claim rather than serve a reply. A reply is only appropriate where you are seeking to respond to a point made in the defence. It may be an issue you were aware of before you drafted the particulars of claim, but which you correctly did not anticipate at that stage, because you needed to wait for the defendant to raise it. Except where you are making admissions, a reply is essentially a 'defence to the defence'. If what you want to say is really part of your case against the defendant, then you should amend your claim.

14.1.1.3 Drafting the reply

A reply can usually be kept quite short, because it does not need to deal with every issue in the defence. If any issue is simply ignored, the defendant is still required to prove it, so if that is the claimant's position, nothing needs to be said.

As the reply will only refer to certain paragraphs of the defence, it is helpful to refer to them as you go along, for example, 'As to paragraph 6 of the defence the claimant's case is that ...' etc.

Stylistically it is generally not a good idea to be too defensive in a reply. It is better to assert facts than to deny facts alleged by the defendant if at all possible. As with the defence, it is to the claimant's advantage to set out a positive case.

14.1.2 Defence to counterclaim

A counterclaim is a Part 20 claim, and most of the rules that apply to claims apply also to counterclaims, including Part 12 (default judgment) (CPR, r 20.3(1) and (3)). A defence to counterclaim is therefore a necessary statement of case. A defence to counterclaim is also subject to CPR, r 16.5, so failure to require the claimant to prove, or to deny and set out a contrary case on any issue raised in the counterclaim will result in a deemed admission. It must therefore be drafted in exactly the same way as any other defence, giving reasons for denials. It may either be drafted separately, or be incorporated into a 'Reply and Defence to Counterclaim'. The latter is much more usual, even if the reply does no more than expressly require the defendant to prove matters raised in the defence.

14.2 Reply

14.2.1 Reply

(See particulars of claim in **9.9** and defence in **10.3**.)

<u>IN THE SHREWSBURY COUNTY COURT</u>   Claim No SY4/74001

BETWEEN

DENNIS LISTER   <u>Claimant</u>

and

HOMEWOOD GARDEN CENTRE LIMITED   <u>Defendants</u>

<u>REPLY</u>

1.   Paragraph 2 of the Defence is admitted.

2.   As to paragraph 7 of the Defence, the Claimant contends that the loss of opportunity to win prize money at the Midland Garden Show is not too remote. The Claimant will rely on the following facts and matters:

   (a) The Defendants knew that the Claimant was rearing vegetables with a view to winning a prize at a garden show.

   (b) The Claimant has been a customer of the Defendants for over 10 years, during which time they regularly serviced, maintained and repaired the Claimant's garden machinery and fully appreciated the consequences that might ensue for the Claimant if such machinery was not in good working order.

3.   As to paragraph 8 of the Defence, the Claimant contends that the express term referred to is of no effect in that it does not satisfy the test that it was fair and reasonable and the Claimant relies on the provisions of section 3 of the Unfair Contract Terms Act 1977.

4.   Except as stated above, and except where it contains admissions, the Claimant requires the Defendant to prove the matters set out in the Defence.

JOSEPH BLOGGS

<u>STATEMENT OF TRUTH</u>

Dated etc.

14.2.2 Commentary

The reply does not deal with all the issues covered in the defence. It picks out two issues only: those raised for the first time in the defence and which need a response which goes beyond merely requiring the defendant to prove something. These are the exclusion clause, and the issue of remoteness of damage. Note that each paragraph makes clear reference to the relevant paragraph of the defence, usually beginning with the words 'as to paragraph x of the defence'. This is very important, because without this reference it would be very difficult to relate what is said in the reply to the allegation in the defence to which it relates.

Paragraph 1. An admission. There is no dispute that the exclusion clause was a term of the contract. This paragraph saves the expense of the defendants having to prove that it was.

Paragraph 2. On the issue of remoteness, the claimant has a positive case to put forward to show why the claim for prize money is recoverable. He contends that it is, and then sets out the facts on which he relies, which can be seen as particulars. It is arguable that these facts should have appeared in the particulars of claim, and that they should now be stated by amending the particulars of claim, but that would require permission, and since a reply is required anyway, it is much more convenient to set them out here.

Paragraph 3. Back to the exclusion clause. Although the claimant admits its existence, he denies the effect of it. He alleges it is unreasonable under the Unfair Contract Terms Act 1977. He is here raising a point of law, as he is entitled to do (see **4.5.3.4**). You might expect to see further particulars here: the facts relied upon to show that the clause is unreasonable. But the burden of proof is now on the defendant (who seeks to rely on it) to show that it *is* reasonable (s 11(5) of the 1977 Act), so the claimant needs to say no more.

Paragraph 4. This is a mop-up paragraph. It does no more that state the effect of CPR, r 16.7, and so is entirely unnecessary. However it is invariably included, so respect tradition in this instance!

14.3 Reply and defence to counterclaim

14.3.1 Reply and defence to counterclaim

(See defence and counterclaim in **13.2**.)

IN THE CHESTER COUNTY COURT   Claim No CH4/28011

BETWEEN

BRIAN FLANAGHAN   Claimant/Part 20 Defendant

and

BRENDA DINGLE   Defendant/Part 20 Claimant

REPLY AND DEFENCE TO COUNTERCLAIM

REPLY

1.   Except as set out below, and except where it contains admissions, the Claimant requires the Defendant to prove the matters set out in the Defence.

2.   As to paragraph 2 of the Defence, the Claimant admits that he briefly switched on his left indicator by mistake, but he turned it off again and it was off when the collision occurred.

3.   The Claimant denies that he was negligent as alleged in paragraph 4 of the Defence or at all or that the accident was caused or contributed to by his negligence. The Claimant was driving at about 30 mph, keeping a good look-out and relies on the matters set out in paragraph 2 above.

DEFENCE TO COUNTERCLAIM

4.   Paragraphs 1 to 3 above are repeated.

5.   The Claimant admits that the Peugeot 306 motor car was owned by the Defendant.

6.   The Defendant's injury is admitted and the contents of the medical report served by the Defendant are agreed. Except as admitted in the attached counter-schedule of expenses and losses, the defendant is required to prove her loss and damage.

JOSEPH BLOGGS

STATEMENT OF TRUTH

Dated etc.

14.3.2 Commentary

This is another two-part statement of case, so the overall title of it appears in tramlines, and then there are two sub-headings, 'reply' and 'defence to counterclaim'. As with the defence and counterclaim, make sure you keep these two parts separate, and deal with issues in the right part.

Paragraph 1. The standard paragraph, the equivalent of paragraph 4 in the previous example, except that it comes first.

Paragraph 2. The claimant deals with the issue of the left indicator by 'confession and avoidance'. The claimant's case on this issue would not be clearly stated if there were no reply, so it needs to be dealt with.

Paragraph 3. Denies the defendant's allegation of negligence by the claimant, adding some fairly straightforward reasons for the denial. It is arguable that this denial should appear in the counterclaim rather than in the reply. The defence and counterclaim alleges negligence by the claimant twice: first in paragraph 4 of the defence, and second (by repetition) in paragraph 6 of the counterclaim. When the allegation is made in the defence, the claimant can if he wishes ignore it, because he will not be taken to have admitted it (CPR, r 16.7). But when the same allegation is made in the counterclaim, the claimant cannot ignore it, or he *will* be taken to have admitted it (CPR, r 16.5). So it is the allegation of negligence in the counterclaim that most needs to be countered. However, as explained above (**14.1.1.1**) by not responding to the allegation of negligence in the defence, the claimant is only requiring the defendant to prove it, not denying it. So if the claimant does wish to show that he was not negligent, then arguably the issue ought to be dealt with in the reply.

Paragraph 4. As in a counterclaim, it usual in a defence to counterclaim to begin by repeating some or all of the reply. The repetition of paragraphs 1 and 2 restates the claimant's case on how the accident occurred. More crucially, the repetition of paragraph 3 denies negligence, so preventing any deemed admission of liability.

Paragraph 5. The claimant unsurprisingly chooses not to make an issue of this.

Paragraph 6. There is probably an agreed medical report on behalf of the defendant, so an admission of the injuries. The special damages are probably also agreed, and this will be made clear in the schedule of expenses and losses. More contentious items of loss the defendant is required to prove.

14.4 Defence to counterclaim

14.4.1 Defence to counterclaim

(See particulars of claim in **12.6** and defence and counterclaim in **13.4**.)

IN THE LANCASTER COUNTY COURT   Claim No LA4/40197

BETWEEN

HODGE AND DAUGHTER LIMITED

<u>Claimants/Part 20 Defendants</u>

and

(1) SAMUEL VINCENT

<u>First Defendant/Part 20 Claimant</u>

(2) MATHESON & CO LIMITED

<u>Second Defendants</u>

DEFENCE TO COUNTERCLAIM
OF FIRST DEFENDANT

---

1.   Paragraphs 3 and 4 of the Defence and Counterclaim are admitted.

2.   The Claimants contend that on a true construction of the express term referred to they agreed and were obliged to pay the First Defendant commission only so long as he was in fact managing the area sales office. Alternatively there was an implied term to that effect in the contract.

3.   On 1st October 2003 the Claimants relieved the First Defendant of his responsibilities as area sales manager on the ground of his incapacity through ill health. They continued to employ him, though with reduced responsibilities, at his salary of £12,000. Therefore, the First Defendant was not from that date managing the area sales department and ceased to be entitled to receive any commission.

4.   Except that the Claimants deny that they acted in breach of contract as alleged or at all, paragraphs 5 and 6 of the Defence and Counterclaim are admitted.

5.   In the circumstances it is denied that the First Defendant has suffered the alleged or any loss and damage.

JOSEPH BLOGGS

STATEMENT OF TRUTH

Dated etc.

14.4.2 Commentary

This is just a defence to counterclaim. The defendant has admitted liability on the claimants' claim, so no purpose whatever is served by a reply. However, the claimants dispute the counterclaim, and therefore by implication the right to a set-off.

Paragraph 1. Admits the employment contract and the material express term concerning the payment of commission.

Paragraph 2. The basis of the defence is that the claimants admit non-payment of the commission, but contend that as a matter of construction of the contract it was not in the events which happened due. This is our first example where a point of construction is taken. The construction contended for must be set out; sometimes, particularly if the construction is a peculiar one, with further particulars in support of that construction. It is usual to add as an alternative that the same result can be achieved by implying a term to that effect.

Paragraph 3. The claimants deny breach in paragraph 4, but here are set out the reasons for the denial. These reasons follow on naturally from the facts alleged in paragraph 2, so precede the denial of breach. They also come before the alleged breach chronologically.

Paragraph 4. The claimants admit the particulars of breach, but deny the allegation of breach itself. You could add 'for the reasons set out in paragraph 3 above', but that is probably stating the obvious.

Paragraph 5. In this context a denial of loss is appropriate: if the defence succeeds the defendant has suffered no loss.

14.5   Exercise

Counsel is instructed on behalf of John Potter Gold Limited, who are seeking repayment of a loan of £30,000 from Ian Stein and Farrah Day (see **10.5**). What seemed to be a straightforward claim has resulted in a defence denying the existence of the loan or indeed any contract with John Potter Gold Limited. Mr John Potter Gold admits that the company is in reality just a 'one man band', but insists that he acted at all times on behalf of the company, not personally. The written memorandum referred to by the defendants does refer to an agreement with John Potter Gold, but Mr Potter Gold says that his secretary typed it out in a hurry and he did not notice that she had omitted the word 'Limited'. It was, however, on company notepaper. It also seems to be admitted that the £30,000 cheque came from the company, not Mr Potter Gold personally.

The rest of the contract was indeed oral. There was an agreement for the £30,000 loan, which was for an indeterminate period, so as to allow the defendants every opportunity to develop their motor. There was certainly no partnership entered into. Mr Potter Gold did agree to use his best endeavours to promote and find potential industrial and commercial developers and backers for the motor. The royalties were to be paid to the company, not John Potter Gold personally.

Mr Potter Gold demanded repayment of the £30,000 when it became clear to him that the motor was little more than a pipe dream. Doubtless the defendants have spent it all, but their work was futile. The 'invention' was no more than a bright idea, the motor never had the slightest chance of working, and it was money down the drain. Mr Potter Gold never made any efforts to find backers and developers because the defendants at no stage after the date of the contract ever gave him any papers, specifications, drawings, models, research results or anything else he could tout around. He says he could not ask anyone to put money into the project when he could not prove that the motor really existed, let alone worked. It is significant that although the defendants appear in their defence to be alleging breach of contract by Mr Potter Gold, they have not made any claim against him, doubtless because they would be unable to prove any loss.

The defence to this claim is believed to be sham, and counsel is asked to draft a reply.

Part 20 claims

15.1 Part 20 Procedure

15.1.1 What is a Part 20 claim?

A Part 20 claim is defined by CPR, r 20.2(1) as 'any claim other than a claim by a claimant against a defendant' and it includes:

(a) a counterclaim by a defendant against the claimant or against the claimant and some other person;

(b) a claim by a defendant against any person (whether or not already a party) for a contribution, indemnity or some other remedy;

(c) where a Part 20 claim has already been made against a person who is not already a party, any claim made by that person against any other person (whether or not already a party).

Counterclaims (category (a) above) have already be dealt with in **Chapter 13**. This chapter will concentrate on claims by a defendant against some other person (category (b) above). Such claims used to be called 'third party notices', and the Part 20 defendant was the 'third party'. Claims by the third party against some other person (category (c) above) used to be called 'fourth party notices'. Now that the procedure all comes within Part 20, there is nothing different to say about category (c) claims. So all the examples in this chapter will be of category (b) claims.

15.1.2 Issuing a Part 20 claim

A defendant may join a person as Part 20 defendant in two main circumstances:

First, the defendant has a right to seek an indemnity or contribution from the Part 20 defendant in respect of the claimant's claim against the defendant. This will be done under CPR, r 20.6 or r 20.7.

An indemnity is an obligation to reimburse someone for expenditure or loss. It is a claim for fulfilment of an obligation, not a claim for damages for breach of one. A contribution is a partial indemnity.

A right to an indemnity may arise by contract, by statute or by operation of law. The most common situations in which a right to an indemnity arises, are:

(a) By contractual obligation, where one party has agreed to indemnify the other in the circumstances which have arisen.

(b) Under the Civil Liability (Contribution) Act 1978, where if two persons are held jointly liable to the same claimant for the same damage, each may claim a contribution against the joint liability from the others.

Second, the defendant has a claim for relief or a remedy which is substantially the same as that which is claimed by the claimant, and which arises out of the same facts. This will more often than not be a claim for damages against the Part 20 defendant. It may be a claim which arises in any event, or it may be a claim which will only arise if the defendant is found liable to the claimant. This will be done under CPR, r 20.7.

A defendant who wishes to make a claim for contribution or indemnity against another defendant may do so simply by filing and serving a notice containing a statement of the nature and grounds of his claim (CPR, r 20.6). This is called a contribution notice. A contribution notice requires the court's permission unless it is filed with the defence.

A defendant (including a Part 20 defendant) who wishes to make any other Part 20 claim (eg a claim for damages against a third party) must issue a Part 20 claim form, for which no permission is required provided it is done before or at the same time as he files his defence (CPR, r 20.7).

15.2   Indemnity, contribution or damages

A Part 20 claim for money may seek an indemnity, a contribution or damages, or some combination of these. Deciding which to claim can be difficult, particularly since the terminology is not always accurate in practice.

There are four possible situations:

(a) The defendant is claiming a contractual indemnity from the Part 20 defendant, who agreed to indemnify the defendant against any liability to the claimant in the circumstances which have arisen.

   The most obvious example is a claim under an insurance policy.

   This can only be a claim for an indemnity.

(b) The defendant alleges that the Part 20 defendant is liable to the claimant in contract or tort, irrespective of whether the defendant is also liable.

   The typical situation is where the claimant has been injured in an accident and alleges that the defendant was negligent, while the defendant alleges that the Part 20 defendant was also negligent and is wholly or partly to blame for the claimant's injuries.

   In this case the claim should be for an indemnity or a contribution. Under the Civil Liability (Contribution) Act 1978, strictly speaking 'contribution amounting to an indemnity' is more accurate terminology than 'indemnity'. In the case of joint tortfeasors, a 100% indemnity is in any event normally an impossibility, since apportionment of liability wholly to the Part 20 defendant would remove any liability from the defendant who has therefore nothing to be indemnified for. The only exception is where the Part 20 defendant is the defendant's employee or agent.

(c) The defendant does not allege that the Part 20 defendant is liable to the claimant, but alleges that the Part 20 defendant is in breach of a contractual or tortious duty owed to the defendant, which breach may have caused the defendant to be liable to the claimant. The defendant's loss is his liability to the claimant, so the Part 20 claim only comes into operation if the defendant is found liable to the claimant.

The typical situation is where the defendant has agreed to supply goods to the claimant and has agreed to purchase those goods from the Part 20 defendant. The Part 20 defendant lets the defendant down, for example by supplying defective goods, or by missing the delivery date, and so the defendant is in breach of his contract with the claimant. The defendant's liability to the claimant is strict, and the Part 20 defendant has no liability to the claimant, so the defendant's remedy can only be against the Part 20 defendant.

In this case the Part 20 claim is strictly for damages, but is frequently stated in practice to be a claim for an indemnity or contribution. It should be stated to be conditional on the defendant being found liable to the claimant.

It does not follow that if the Part 20 claim succeeds, the Part 20 defendant will be liable to the defendant to the same extent that the defendant is liable to the claimant: the Part 20 defendant's breach of duty may have caused only some of the defendant's liability to the claimant. Hence the tendency to claim indemnity or contribution.

(d) The defendant has a claim in tort or contract against the Part 20 defendant irrespective of whether the defendant is found liable to the claimant. The loss is the defendant's own loss, caused by the Part 20 defendant.

The typical situation is where there has been an accident involving three vehicles, and both the claimant and the defendant have been injured. The claimant alleges his injuries were caused by the defendant, but the defendant alleges that his own injuries (and doubtless the claimant's also) were caused by the Part 20 defendant. To the extent that the Part 20 claim is to recover the defendant's own loss, it is independent of the claimant's claim against the defendant.

This can only be a claim for damages.

More than one of these situations can arise at the same time.

15.3   Drafting the Part 20 claim

15.3.1   General

The Part 20 Claim form, like a Part 7 claim form, must include brief details of the Part 20 claimant's claim and the remedy sought, and also contain the particulars of claim if practicable. If not the particulars of claim will be attached or served separately.

The Part 20 particulars of claim are setting out a claim by a (Part 20) claimant for a remedy and therefore the Part 20 particulars of claim fundamentally resemble the particulars of claim by a claimant against a defendant. The defendant must set out those facts and matters which, if proved, would entitle him to whatever remedy he seeks from the Part 20 defendant.

15.3.2 Heading

This is where things can get complicated! PD 20, paras 7.1 and 7.5 say that the full combined description of each party must be given in the heading. So you can end up with something that looks like the example in **5.4.5**, which is almost indecipherable at first glance. However, para 7.5 goes on to say that once the combined status has been identified, thereafter the parties can be identified by name, so you don't have to refer to the 'Claimant/Part 20 Defendant (2nd Claim)' throughout.

15.3.3 The body

Although a Part 20 claim is basically just particulars of claim in a standard form, nevertheless you need to take account of the fact that it is not where the case starts. There has already been a claim by the claimant and a defence from the defendant. If the Part 20 claim was drafted without reference to these previous pleadings it would seem unconnected and the overall picture in the case would be unclear. It would also be very difficult to draft with any precision. The Part 20 defendant needs to understand what has gone before.

So for the sake of clarity, and to put the Part 20 claim into context, the convention is that the first two or three paragraphs of the Part 20 claim explain the context, and introduce the existing parties and the previous pleadings.

The first paragraph typically introduces the claimant and defendant and sets out the broad nature of the claimant's claim. There is no need to set out the detailed allegations, unless they are material to the Part 20 claim. How the claim arises and what remedies are claimed will probably be sufficient.

The second paragraph then typically states that the defendant denies the claim, and sometimes states the broad nature of his defence. Again, the detailed case need not be set out. It then goes on to state why the Part 20 claim is being brought.

If there is more than one Part 20 claim, you may also need a paragraph introducing the other Part 20 claims and differentiating them from this one. Indicate which is the first and which is the second (or third) Part 20 claim.

If the defendant is making more than one Part 20 claim (eg a counterclaim as well as a third party claim), it will also be important to differentiate them.

All of this can be done in a few short paragraphs. Details of the other statements of case are not required because in any event copies of them must be served with the Part 20 claim (CPR, r 20.12).

In some precedents you will see this information provided in an introductory, unnumbered paragraph. This is because it was typically done this way in the old third party notice, but the style adopted in this Manual is recommended when drafting under the CPR.

If you are going to take advantage of PD 20, para 7.5 and use names rather than descriptions for the parties, you will also need to define the names in the early paragraphs. Abbreviated names, even initials, are acceptable (PD 20, para 7.4).

Another quirk of the old third party notice was that it was conventionally drafted using the second person singular or plural ('you') to address the third party, rather than the third person ('he', 'she', 'it' or 'they'). Since the Part 20 claim is now almost identical to the Part 7 claim, you are advised to draft in the same style. However you will still see the old style in some precedents.

The old third party notice did not always have a prayer, since the remedies sought were traditionally set out at the beginning. But it is submitted that good practice now involves listing the remedies sought at the end, just as in any other particulars of claim.

15.4 Proposals for change

In October 2003 the Department for Constitutional Affairs (DCA) issued a consultation paper, proposing that the term 'Part 20 claim' should be abolished and replaced with the term 'additional claim'. The terms 'Part 20 claimant' and 'Part 20 defendant' would also go. Instead, the original claimant(s) and defendant(s) would be known simply by that description, no matter what additional status they might gain, and all additional parties would be known as 'third party', 'fourth party', etc, in the order in which they are joined to the proceedings, no matter by whom or in what way.

This is a change more in form than substance, but it would simplify both the description of the parties and the headings in Part 20 claims.

The DCA invited responses to the consultation by mid-January 2004, and suggested that the Rules and Practice Direction might be changed quite soon after that. However, it might be some time before they could come into effect because of the need to alter standard forms and guidance leaflets.

At the time of writing, the outcome of this proposal is still awaited, and so no alterations have been made in this chapter in anticipation of the changes.

15.5 Part 20 Claim against joint tortfeasor

15.5.1 Particulars of Part 20 claim

(See particulars of claim in **7.6** and defence in **8.5**.)

IN THE HIGH COURT OF JUSTICE   Claim No 2004 HC 6003
QUEEN'S BENCH DIVISION

BETWEEN

MARJORIE TIMMS   Claimant

and

CATHERINE HOBBS   Defendant/Part 20 Claimant

and

DALY'S AUTOS LIMITED   Part 20 Defendant

PARTICULARS OF PART 20 CLAIM

1.   This claim has been brought by the Claimant ('Mrs Timms') against the Defendant/ Part 20 Claimant ('Mrs Hobbs'). In it Mrs Timms claims against Mrs Hobbs damages with interest for personal injury arising out of an accident which occurred on 6th May 2003 at Oxford Circus, London W1 and which Mrs Timms alleges was caused by the negligence of Mrs Hobbs, as appears from the Particulars of Claim, a copy of which is served with this Part 20 claim.

2.   Mrs Hobbs denies that she is liable to Mrs Timms, on the grounds set out in her Defence, a copy of which is also served with this Part 20 claim. These Particulars of Claim set out Mrs Hobbs's claim against the Part 20 Defendant ('Daly's Autos').

3.   On 29th April 2003 by telephone Daly's Autos agreed with Mrs Hobbs in the course of their business that they would on 3rd May 2003 carry out repairs and service to her Rover 200 motor car registration No JB01 FNB and it was implied that Mrs Hobbs would pay a reasonable charge for these repairs and service.

4.   It was an implied term of the agreement that Daly's Autos would carry out the repairs and service with reasonable care and skill.

5.   On 3rd May 2003 Daly's Autos carried out the repairs and service and Mrs Hobbs paid them £209.32 in consideration for this work. In the course of the repairs they supplied and fitted to Mrs Hobbs's car a new joint in the brake hydraulic system.

6.   Mrs Timms's accident was caused or contributed to by the failure of the brakes on Mrs Hobbs's car. The brakes did not respond properly or at all when she applied them because Daly's Autos had not tightened the new joint fully or at all and brake fluid had leaked out of the hydraulic system, so that she was unable to stop her car and avoid striking Mrs Timms.

7.   In the circumstances Daly's Autos did not carry out the repairs and service with reasonable care and skill and are in breach of the implied term referred to in paragraph 4 above.

8.   Further or alternatively the failure of the brakes, and accordingly the accident, were caused by the negligence of Daly's Autos.

PARTICULARS OF NEGLIGENCE

(a) Failing to tighten the new joint fully or at all.

(b) Failing to carry out repairs and service to Mrs Hobbs's car in a safe and workmanlike manner.

(c) Allowing Mrs Hobbs to drive her car away when it was not safe or roadworthy.

(d) Failing to warn Mrs Hobbs that the brakes on her car were or might be or might become defective.

9.   After striking Mrs Timms, the Defendant's car ran on about 10 yards and struck a lamp-post.

10.   As a result of the matters set out above Mrs Hobbs suffered shock and has sustained loss and damage.

PARTICULARS OF SPECIAL DAMAGE

(1) Cost of repairs to Defendant's car	£1,225.80
(2) Cost of repairs to lamp-post	£520.00
	£1,745.80

11.   Further Mrs Hobbs claims interest under section 35A of the Supreme Court Act 1981 on the damages found to be due to the Defendant at such rate and for such period as the Court thinks fit.

AND Mrs Hobbs claims:

(1) An indemnity or contribution in respect of:

(a)   Mrs Timms's claim

(b)   any costs which Mrs Hobbs may be ordered to pay to Mrs Timms

(c)   any costs incurred by Mrs Hobbs in defending Mrs Timms's claim.

(2) Damages.

(3) Interest under section 35A of the Supreme Court Act 1981 to be assessed.

BESS TOFFER

STATEMENT OF TRUTH

Dated etc.

15.5.2 Commentary

This Part 20 claim arises out of situations (b) and (d) as described in **15.2**. It is a situation (b) claim because the defendant alleges that the Part 20 defendant owed a duty of care to the claimant, so that it would also be liable to the claimant for her losses if sued. The defendant therefore seeks a contribution or indemnity under the Civil Liability (Contribution) Act 1978. It is also a situation (d) claim because the defendant is claiming damages for loss and damage caused to her by the Part 20 defendant's breach of implied term and/or negligence. This claim exists quite independently of the outcome of the claimant's claim.

Situation (c) does not arise. The defendant can only be liable to the claimant if she was negligent, and nothing the Part 20 defendant has done can have caused the defendant to be negligent.

Heading. This will be the same as that for the defence. The title of the statement of case could be either 'Particulars of Part 20 Claim' or 'Part 20 Particulars of Claim'.

Paragraph 1. This is the conventional introduction, setting the scene and explaining the nature of the claimant's claim against the defendant/Part 20 claimant. Think of it as setting out 'what the claimant is doing'. The opportunity is also taken to give these parties names, so that there is no need to refer to them by their full descriptions (see **15.3.2**).

Paragraph 2. This is also conventional, stating that the defendant has a defence (not bothering to state the basis of the defence since this should be clear from the defence itself), introducing the Part 20 claim and naming the Part 20 defendant. Think of it as setting out 'what the defendant is doing'. The remedies claimed from the Part 20 defendant are not stated, since they appear in the prayer.

From this point onwards the Part 20 claim is barely distinguishable from any ordinary particulars of claim.

Paragraph 3. The parties and contract. Mrs Hobbs's claim for damages is based on breach of an implied term that Daly's Autos would service her car with reasonable care and skill, so the contract needs to be fully stated, and also the fact that it was made in the course of Daly's Autos' business. The consideration in such cases is rarely agreed in advance, but a reasonable charge is implied by statute.

Paragraph 4. The implied term obviously comes next.

Paragraph 5. This paragraph can be seen as story-telling, but both parts of it are actually material. The first sentence states the performance of the contract, and the second sentence goes on to start explaining the causation of the accident.

Paragraph 6. This paragraph further sets out the causation of the accident and in effect also particularises the breach of implied term which is about to be alleged in the next paragraph ('because Daly's Autos had not tightened the new joint fully or at all'). Note that 'Mrs Timms's accident' can be referred to simply as such. It does not need to be stated all over again, because it has been fully stated in the other statements of case. There is no need to state again facts which have been stated in the defence, or stated in the particulars of claim and admitted in the defence, except for direct allegations against the Part 20 defendant, which must be stated again.

Paragraph 7. Alleges breach of the contractual duty owed to the defendant. This is purely part of the claim for damages. The essential particular has been stated in paragraph 6 and incorporated by the use of the words 'in the circumstances'. Further particulars are set out in paragraph 8.

Paragraph 8. The allegation of negligence against Daly's Autos is part of the contribution claim and the damages claim. Although this allegation has been made in the defence, it needs to be repeated here, because it is a direct allegation against the Part 20 defendant. The particulars are virtually identical to those alleged in the defence. To draft anything different would be most unwise, as it would tend to suggest inconsistency in the defendant's case.

Paragraph 9. The contribution claim is now complete, but more is needed for the damages claim. This paragraph states a new fact for the first time — a secondary accident.

Paragraph 10. The defendant must particularise her damages claim. Note that she does *not* claim her liability (if any) to the claimant as an item of loss and damage. Such loss cannot have been caused by the negligence of Daly's Autos.

Prayer. The claim for an indemnity or contribution is the remedy in the type (b) claim. Although in reality it can only be a claim for a contribution, as explained in **15.2** 'indemnity' is frequently added. The contribution claimed is not only towards damages, but also claimant's costs and defendant's costs. The claims for damages and interest are the remedies in the type (d) claim.

15.6   Part 20 claim in contract

15.6.1   Particulars of Part 20 claim

(See particulars of claim in **11.4** and defence in **11.9**.)

IN THE BRIGHTON COUNTY COURT   Claim No BN4/16380

BETWEEN

EDWARD GRANBY   Claimant

and

LEISURE BREAKS LIMITED

Defendants/Part 20 Claimants

and

CUMBRIAN HOTELS LIMITED   Part 20 Defendants

PARTICULARS OF PART 20 CLAIM

1.   This action has been brought by the Claimant ('Mr Granby') against the Defendants/ Part 20 Claimants ('L.B. Ltd'). In it Mr Granby claims damages and interest for breach of contract and/or misrepresentation as appears from the Particulars of Claim a copy of which is served with this Part 20 claim.

2.   L.B. Ltd deny that they are liable to Mr Granby, on the grounds set out in their Defence, a copy of which is also served with this Part 20 claim. These Particulars of Claim set out L.B. Ltd's claim against the Part 20 Defendant ('Cumbrian Hotels').

3.   Cumbrian Hotels are the owners of the Lakeside Hotel, Redburn, Cumbria ('the Hotel') and by a letter dated 20th September 2003, with the intention of inducing L.B. Ltd to enter into a contract with them for the provision of accommodation at the Hotel, they represented to L.B. Ltd that:

(a) the Hotel was on the shores of Lake Pikewater ('the Lake'); and

(b) visitors to the Hotel had the right to fish in the Lake.

4.   By letters dated 22nd and 24th September 2003 Cumbrian Hotels and L.B. Ltd agreed that Cumbrian Hotels would provide accommodation at the Hotel between 1st April and 30th October 2004 for clients of L.B. Ltd at a total price of £50,650. This accommodation included that which was taken up by Mr Granby. L.B. Ltd entered into the contract induced by and in reliance upon the above representations.

5.   Further or alternatively, those representations were express terms of the contract.

6.   In fact the representation set out in paragraph 3(a) above is false and Cumbrian Hotels are in breach of contract in that the Hotel is two miles from the Lake.

7.   Mr Granby alleges that visitors to the Hotel were not permitted to fish in the Lake. L.B. Ltd are unable to admit or deny this allegation and have required him to prove it, but if it is established, the representation set out in paragraph 3(b) above is false and Cumbrian Hotels are in breach of contract in the manner alleged by Mr Granby.

8.   Any representations which L.B. Ltd made to Mr Granby with regard to the Hotel and the Lake were made in reasonable reliance upon the representations made by Cumbrian Hotels to L.B. Ltd.

9.   If L.B. Ltd are found liable to Mr Granby they will contend that this liability arose because of Cumbrian Hotels' breach of contract and/or misrepresentation as set out above, as a result of which L.B. Ltd have suffered loss and damage as follows:

(a) their liability (if any) to Mr Granby;

(b) any costs which they might be ordered to pay to Mr Granby;

(c) any costs incurred in defending Mr Granby's claim.

AND L.B. Ltd claim damages.

BESS TOFFER

STATEMENT OF TRUTH

Dated etc.

15.6.2   Commentary

This Part 20 claim arises only out of situation (c) as described in **15.2**. The liability of the Part 20 defendants will arise only if the defendants are found liable to the claimant, because the defendants' liability will have been caused by the Part 20 defendants.

The defence is not printed in the Manual, since you drafted it as an exercise, but it can easily be imagined.

Paragraphs 1 and 2. The standard introductory paragraphs. The Part 20 claim is based on misrepresentation by Cumbrian Hotels, so the shape of the claim that follows is according to the pattern described for misrepresentation claims in **Chapter 11**.

Paragraph 3. Introduces the Part 20 defendants and states the representations made. These are the same as two of the representations made in turn by the defendants to the claimant.

Paragraph 4. The contract stated in the usual way with the allegation of reliance and inducement. Note the importance of adding that the accommodation included that which was taken up by Mr Granby. Without this the defendants will be unable to establish the causation of their alleged loss, which is their liability to the claimant.

Paragraph 5. The defendants claim for breach of contract as well as misrepresentation, so the terms must be stated.

Paragraph 6. The misrepresentations are taken separately, because the defendants have a slightly different case on each. Here the first representation is alleged to be false in the usual way, with breach and particulars added.

Paragraph 7. The second representation cannot however be said to be false, because in their defence the defendants did not admit that it was; they required the claimant to prove it. So the allegation has to be made conditional on the claimant's proving it.

Paragraph 8. This is the causation. The defendants' liability comes about because they reasonably relied on Cumbrian Hotels' misrepresentations. Note that the claim says '*any* representations'. This is to cover the third representation which the defendants themselves added, namely that the holidays were suitable for fishermen.

Paragraph 9. The loss and damage. Again, this has to be stated to be conditional. It only exists if the defendants are found liable to the claimant, but if they are, then the loss is the amounts they are ordered to pay to him by way of damages and costs and their own costs.

Prayer. The remedy sought is damages, which is strictly correct, though it might be expressed as an indemnity or contribution (see **15.2**(c)). There is no claim for interest, because the defendants are not yet out of pocket.

15.7 Exercise

See **13.5**.

Percy Hopcroft will say:

Further to my previous statement I have now consulted Ben Dodds & Co who carried out the repairs to the heating systems in Miss Rebecca Peters' greenhouses. They tell me that the heating units which we supplied were obviously old stock and there was an accumulation of dust and particles on the elements. This had after a while caused a short circuit which caused the heaters to cut out because the wiring used had a maximum load rating of 15 amps whereas 30 amp wire should have been used. I am also satisfied that if there were any cracked panes of glass, these must have been broken by the electrical contractors. In the circumstances I wish to bring a claim against Harold Todd.

Counsel is asked to draft particulars of claim, so that permission to make a Part 20 claim may be sought. It would also appear that the Defence and Counterclaim will need amendment.

Amendment of statements of case

16.1 General

Statements of case are quite often amended after they have been served. A party may find that he has not stated his case as accurately as he would like, or he may be forced into amendment by an amendment by the other side. There are various rules relating to when and how a statement of case may be amended.

A statement of case can be only be amended without permission before it has been served. Once served, a party who wishes to amend requires the permission of every other party, or the court (CPR, r 17.1).

An amended statement of case will need to be re-verified by a new statement of truth.

An amended statement of case may just be a new draft substituted for the old. However, the court may order that the amended version should show both the original version and the amendments (PD 17, para 2.2). This is in any event the usual practice. Amendments should be shown in colour, with deletions struck through in colour, and insertions either in coloured text or underlined in colour. The sequence of colours for successive amendments is (1) red, (2) green, (3) violet, (4) yellow. If colour is not possible a numerical code should be used. However, whatever the rules say, for a first amendment striking through and underlining in black, as in the example that follows, has been widely accepted in practice.

Apart from these technicalities, there is no special technique or skill in amending a statement of case. You just redraft it as you now want it to appear, and then work out what needs to be struck through and what needs to be underlined. By way of example, there follows an original defence of a first defendant, which has been amended after seeing the defence of the second defendant. No commentary is attached, since it is hoped and believed that the example is self-explanatory.

16.2 The original defence

IN THE COLCHESTER COUNTY COURT   Claim No CO4/01908

BETWEEN

(1) TASKER & HOLT LIMITED
(2) ISABEL ESMOND
(3) GEORGE ESMOND   Claimants

and

(1) MICHAEL LUMLEY
(2) THOMAS TUCKER   Defendants

DEFENCE OF THE FIRST DEFENDANT

1.   Except that no admissions are made as to the ownership of the BMW motor vehicle, paragraph 1 of the Particulars of Claim is admitted.

2.   The First Defendant alleges that there were three collisions at the date, time and place referred to in paragraph 1 of the Particulars of Claim. Those collisions were:

(a) an initial collision between the Ford Capri motor vehicle driven by the Second Defendant and the rear of the First Defendant's stationary Vauxhall Astra motor vehicle, which collision propelled the First Defendant forward causing the second collision;

(b) a second collision between the front of the First Defendant's vehicle and the rear of the BMW motor vehicle which collision propelled the BMW motor vehicle forward causing the third collision;

(c) a third collision between the BMW motor vehicle and a Porsche motor vehicle driven by Beatrix Harper.

3.   Otherwise the Claimant is required to prove the matters set out in paragraph 2 of the Particulars of Claim.

4.   It is denied that the First Defendant was negligent as alleged in paragraph 3 of the Particulars of Claim or at all, or that any of the collisions was caused by his negligence. The First Defendant relies on the facts stated in paragraph 2 above.

5.   The collisions referred to in paragraph 2 above were caused by the negligence of the Second Defendant.

PARTICULARS OF NEGLIGENCE

The Second Defendant was negligent in that he:

(1) drove too fast or at a speed which was excessive in all the circumstances, in particular at such speed that he could not stop within the distance which he could see to be clear as required by the Highway Code or in such circumstances as ought reasonably to have been foreseen; and/or

(2) failed to keep any or any adequate look-out and/or observe or heed the presence of the First Defendant's vehicle ahead; and/or

(3) failed to apply his brakes in time, adequately or at all or otherwise to steer manage or control his vehicle so as to avoid colliding with the First Defendant's stationary motor vehicle; and/or

(4) the First Defendant will further say that the circumstances set out above give rise to an inference of negligence upon the part of the Second Defendant.

6.   Further, the First Defendant will rely upon the conviction of the Second Defendant by the Colchester Magistrates' Court on 24th February 2002 for driving without due care and attention which conviction is relevant to the issues in these proceedings since it was founded upon the driving referred to in paragraph 2 above.

7.   Except as set out in the attached schedules the First Defendant requires the Second and Third Claimants to prove the extent of their injuries and their loss and damage.

STATEMENT OF TRUTH

Dated 6th September 2004

16.3 The amended defence

IN THE COLCHESTER COUNTY COURT   Case No CO4/01908

BETWEEN

(1) TASKER & HOLT LIMITED
(2) ISABEL ESMOND
(3) GEORGE ESMOND   Claimants

and

(1) MICHAEL LUMLEY
(2) THOMAS TUCKER   Defendants

AMENDED DEFENCE OF THE FIRST DEFENDANT
Amended by Order of District Judge Oakes on 22nd October 2004

1.   Except that no admissions are made as to the ownership of the BMW motor vehicle, paragraph 1 of the Particulars of Claim is admitted.

2.   The First Defendant alleges that there were three collisions at the date, time and place referred to in paragraph 1 of the Particulars of Claim. Those collisions were:

(a) an initial collision between the Ford Capri motor vehicle driven by the Second Defendant and the rear of the First Defendant's stationary Vauxhall Astra motor vehicle, which collision propelled the First Defendant forward causing the second collision;

(b) a second collision between the front of the First Defendant's vehicle and the rear of the BMW motor vehicle ~~which collision propelled the BMW motor vehicle forward causing the third collision~~;

(c) a third collision between the BMW motor vehicle and a Porsche motor vehicle driven by Beatrix Harper.

3.   Further, or in the alternative, at the time of the third collision the BMW was already partly on the opposite carriageway of the road and in the path of the Porsche motor vehicle and was commencing an overtaking manoeuvre.

~~3.~~ 4.   Otherwise ~~the Claimant is required to prove~~ the matters set out in paragraph 2 of the Particulars of Claim are denied.

~~4.~~ 5.   It is denied that the First Defendant was negligent as alleged in paragraph 3 of the Particulars of Claim or at all, or that any of the collisions was caused by his negligence. The First Defendant relies on the facts stated in paragraph 2 above.

6.   The First Defendant alleges that the collision between the BMW and the Porsche motor vehicle was caused by the negligence of the Second Claimant.

PARTICULARS OF NEGLIGENCE

(1) Driving too fast.

(2) Attempting to overtake slow moving and/or stationary traffic when it was unsafe to do so.

(3) Moving the BMW to the opposite carriageway when it was unsafe to do so.

(4) Failing to heed the presence of the oncoming Porsche motor vehicle.

~~5.~~ 7.   Further or in the alternative, ~~T~~the collisions referred to in paragraph 2 above were caused by the negligence of the Second Defendant.

PARTICULARS OF NEGLIGENCE

The Second Defendant was negligent in that he:

(1) drove too fast or at a speed which was excessive in all the circumstances, in particular at such speed that he could not stop within the distance which he could see to be clear as required by the Highway Code or in such circumstances as ought reasonably to have been foreseen; and/or

(2) failed to keep any or any adequate look-out and/or observe or heed the presence of the First Defendant's vehicle ahead; and/or

(3) failed to apply his brakes in time, adequately or at all or otherwise to steer manage or control his vehicle so as to avoid colliding with the First Defendant's stationary motor vehicle; and/or

(4) the First Defendant will further say that the circumstances set out above give rise to an inference of negligence upon the part of the Second Defendant.

~~6.~~ 8.   Further, the First Defendant will rely upon the conviction of the Second Defendant by the Colchester Magistrates' Court on 24th February 2002 for driving without due care and attention which conviction is relevant to the issues in these proceedings since it was founded upon the driving referred to in paragraph 2 above.

7. 9.   Except as set out in the attached schedules the First Defendant requires the Second and Third Claimants to prove the extent of their injuries and their loss and damage.

10.   The Third Claimant's personal injury was caused or contributed to by his own negligence.

PARTICULARS OF NEGLIGENCE OF THE THIRD CLAIMANT

The Third Claimant was negligent in that he failed to wear the seat belt installed in the BMW motor vehicle for use of front seat passengers.

STATEMENT OF TRUTH

Note: A new Statement of Truth is required, referring to the amended defence.

Dated 6th day of September 2004

Re-dated 29th day of October 2004

16.4 Exercise

Draft the amended defence in the case of *Rebecca Peters v Homewood Garden Centre Ltd* (see **13.5** and **15.7**).

Request for further information

17.1 Introduction

17.1.1 The old procedures

There has always been a procedure by which one party can ask another party to provide further information about his case. Before the Civil Procedure Rules 1998, there were two methods: the Request for Further and Better Particulars (RFBP) and Interrogatories.

RFBPs asked the other side to give further particulars of a pleading. You could only ask for particulars of an allegation which appeared in the other side's pleading. You were asking for a fuller statement of what had already been alleged. You could not therefore use the request to raise issues that had not already been raised. You could only ask for facts, not evidence. RFBPs were very common.

Interrogatories were less restrictive: they asked questions of the other side about their case in general. The questions did not have to relate to matters pleaded, but they still had to be requests for facts, not evidence. Interrogatories were not so common.

Both procedures were a way of narrowing the issues between the parties, enabling the party making the request to have a better idea of the case he had to meet and to prepare better for trial. The purpose was to leave less in issue at the trial itself.

17.1.2 The new procedure

Both these procedures were abolished by the Civil Procedure Rules 1998. Instead there is now a single procedure: the Request for Further Information under Part 18. The basic rule is r 18.1 which says:

> (1) The court may at any time order a party to—
>
>   (a) clarify any matter which is in dispute in the proceedings; or
>   (b) give additional information in relation to any such matter,
>   whether or not the matter is contained or referred to in a statement of case.

However, PD 18, para 1 says that before making an application to the court, a party must first of all ask the other side to provide the desired information voluntarily, by serving a written request for clarification or information. There is no point in seeking an order if the information can be obtained less formally. The request may be made by letter (if it and the likely answer are both brief) or in a more formal document, the Request for Further Information (RFI). The RFI must have a full case heading, state that it is made under Part 18, say which party is making the request of which other party and set out each request in a separate numbered paragraph. If the RFI relates to a document (eg it is for clarification of a statement of case), then it must identify the document and the relevant paragraph or words to which it relates. It must also state the date by which the party making the request expects a response. These requirements are contained in PD 16, para 1.6. Most of this is very similar to the old RFBP.

17.2 To ask or not to ask?

There is never a case in which there is not some further information or clarification which you could ask for. The question is whether you should ask for it. This is a much more difficult issue under the Civil Procedure Rules 1998 than it was under the old rules. It is still not clear what the overall trend in practice is. Some reports suggest that RFIs are being used to the same extent as RFBPs used to be, and in the same way. Other reports suggest that requests of all kinds are fading out of use.

17.2.1 What information may be asked for?

CPR, r 18.1(1)(a) (clarification of any matter which is in dispute) is more or less the equivalent of the old RFBP, and r 18.1(1)(b) (further information in relation to any such matter) is more or less the equivalent of an interrogatory. In neither case does the matter have to be referred to in a statement of case. At first sight, therefore, it looks as if one can ask for anything one could previously ask for, maybe even more, because nothing is expressly forbidden.

However, sub-paragraph (a) refers to 'a matter which is in dispute' and sub-paragraph (b) refers to 'any such matter', so in both paragraphs the limitation is the same: the request must relate to a matter which is in dispute. If a matter is in dispute, one would expect it to be referred to in the statements of case; if it isn't, then it probably ought to be. So RFIs are still based very heavily on the statements of case. They may resemble RFBPs or interrogatories or both, but they can still only ask for factual matters, not evidence, law or argument.

17.2.2 Whether a request should be made

There is a very clear guiding principle here — PD 18, para 1.2 which says:

A Request should be concise and strictly confined to matters which are reasonably necessary and proportionate to enable the first party to prepare his own case or to understand the case he has to meet.

This ties in with the overriding objective, and is clearly designed to put a stop to unnecessary requests. But it is difficult to say how rigidly it is to be interpreted.

On a very strict interpretation, you should only make an RFI if you are simply paralysed without the information requested. If you cannot take the next step in the action without knowing more about the other side's case, then of course you must have the right to ask.

On a slightly more liberal interpretation, you can ask for more information where it will genuinely help you to prepare your case or understand the case you have to meet, even if you could probably manage without it. The test might be to ask yourself: 'If the information is not provided, will I seek an order for it, in the expectation that the information will be ordered by the court?' If you think you would not bother to seek an order, or that the court might not make the order, it is arguable that you should not be making the request in the first place.

On the most liberal interpretation, you can make a request even where you would not seek an order if the information is not forthcoming, because there is a tactical advantage in so doing. Under the old rules, most RFBPs were made for purely tactical reasons, and in many quarters there is a continuing desire among practitioners to use RFIs in the same way. So we can only consider whether an RFI of this kind should be made by looking at the tactical advantages and disadvantages.

17.2.3   The tactical request for further information

There will always be some tactics behind an RFI. What the tactic is, depends on the objective with which each request is made. The following objectives are doubtless well within PD 18, para 1.2 and can be easily justified:

(a) to narrow the issues between the parties;

(b) to remove genuine ambiguities and uncertainties from a statement of case;

(c) to pin the other side down to specific allegations;

(d) to obtain full particulars of an allegation which ought to have been included in a statement of case but has been omitted;

(e) to enable your side to prepare its case better by knowing what case it has to meet.

It must be assumed that all of these objectives are permissible.

But the following objectives can also be achieved by a good RFI:

(a) to expose weaknesses in the other side's case;

(b) to make the other side tone down exaggerated allegations;

(c) to extract an admission;

(d) to make the other side withdraw allegations for which they have no evidence;

(e) to persuade the other side to reach a settlement;

(f) even, rarely, to persuade the other side to capitulate.

These objectives may or may not be permissible. They are all potentially legitimate, and could in the end result in a cost saving. If the RFI achieves this, then it might well be allowed. However, if the likely result is to increase confrontation or protract proceedings unnecessarily, or hinder settlement, then the request will almost certainly not be considered permissible. The test might well be 'Will it work?'. If the request achieves one of the above objectives, it was probably worthwhile; but if it fails to do so, it was probably a waste of time and money. There is a risk of a costs penalty if you do not get the desired result.

On the other hand, there is reason to suppose that many practitioners still feel the risk to be worth taking. It is arguable that any request that has a reasonable prospect of persuading the other side to offer a settlement, or to alter its case, was properly made; and these can be the results of a good RFI. At the very least, even if nothing else is achieved, there is a tactical advantage in having made the request, which is that you have inserted into the papers which the judge will read a document pointing out some of the weaknesses in the other side's case. If there is no answer to it, this may make your own case seem stronger.

There was, however, one objective that was pursued in the past which cannot be justified under the CPR, which is:

(1) to increase the other side's costs just for the mischief of it.

This is of course the side effect of an RFI. The moment you send one, the other side has to deal with it. Even considering whether to answer it takes a bit of time. Answering it in full may involve a lot of time, trouble and expense, so increasing costs. They may need to do a lot of work, prepare schedules, employ inquiry agents, employ accountants, consult experts and then instruct counsel to draft the answers to the requests. If this was the only objective, then the request was almost certainly not within the spirit of the Civil Procedure Rules. But yet again, the end result may be to put pressure on the other side to negotiate a settlement, so as to save costs, in which case arguably it was justified.

So it is not surprising that many practitioners continue to use RFIs in much the same way as they used RFBPs and interrogatories in the past. But whatever practice develops, remember the overriding objective and PD 18, para 1.2. You will always have to justify any request on the basis that it is reasonably necessary and proportionate. In all the circumstances therefore, it may be wise for practitioners to feel their way cautiously until the courts pronounce on how much we can get away with!

17.2.4   The disadvantages of a request for further information

Whenever you decide to make an RFI, you need to balance the hoped for benefit against the potential disadvantages.

The first disadvantage, already touched on above, is that you may suffer a penalty in costs. If you make an RFI which is answered at great expense by the other side, and it then turns out that the information you obtained had no real relevance to the issues between the parties, it is open to the other side to argue that you should bear the costs of answering the request in any event. If you make an RFI which is not answered, you then have to consider whether to seek an order. If you seek an order which is not granted, it is quite likely that you will have to bear the costs of that application in any event. If you do not seek an order, the other side could argue that you should never have made the request in the first place, and might claim their costs (admittedly, probably not great) of considering the request, deciding not to provide the information requested, and replying to this effect.

The second disadvantage is that you may get an answer that you do not want. As William Rose puts it in *Pleadings Without Tears*:

Above all things remember the golden rule:

THERE IS A SERIOUS RISK THAT IF YOU ASK THE OTHER SIDE A QUESTION THEY MIGHT ANSWER IT!

Every time you send the other side an RFI, you have given them the opportunity to consider how to strengthen their own case. If they do so, then this is clearly to your disadvantage. Do not make a request unless you are reasonably confident:

(a) that they do not actually have the information asked for, the point of the request being to expose this weakness in their case; or

(b) that the answer you expect to receive will strengthen your case or weaken theirs; or

(c) that you simply have to have the information, good or bad, in order to prepare your own case properly.

17.3   Drafting the request for further information

Most RFIs can be drafted in the same way as RFBPs were in the past. Interrogatories were comparatively less common, and as explained above, most requests are in reality for clarification of a statement of case. A great many of the objectives explained above can be achieved, even with this limitation, by seeking further information relating to a statement of case.

Remember that what you are asking for is facts and particulars, not evidence. If the matter you are asking about is raised in the other side's statement of case, then you are really asking for further particulars. If it is not, then whatever you ask must be based on information available to you. You cannot go 'fishing', which is to ask for information the only purpose of which is to discover whether there is some further allegation you can make against the other side, which you do not have the evidence to support at the moment. You must ensure you are asking the other side to clarify *their* case; you cannot ask them for information which merely invites them to respond to *your* case, unless you know it is a matter in issue.

If you are seeking clarification of a statement of case or other document, then you must 'pin' each request onto the word, phrase, sentence or paragraph that contains the matter you want further particulars of.

It is proper to ask 'what?', 'when?', 'where?', 'who?', 'whether' and 'how?'. If you are asking for further information about a matter not included in a statement of case, then you might ask 'did you?', or 'is it true that?'. But it is rarely if ever appropriate to ask 'why?'. If you do so, you are probably fishing for evidence, or asking for particulars of something not pleaded. But you can often get over this difficulty by asking for 'the precise causation' or for 'the full facts and matters relied upon in support of the allegation that ...'.

It is wrong to ask for further information about something which you have admitted. This is no longer in dispute and so it is a waste of time and money. You may ask for further information about something you have required the other side to prove, but there may not be much point, since you have stated that you will not contest the issue, so you may well just be asking for the evidence by which the other side will prove the matter. You can most certainly ask for further information about a matter which you have denied.

You cannot ask why a matter has been admitted or why you have been required to prove something. But you may well ask for the reasons for any denial if they have not been properly set out. For example, the claimant may allege that the defendant was negligent in that he 'failed to give any warning'. The defendant denies that he was negligent 'as alleged or at all'. Within this denial is a denial that he failed to give a warning, which contains an implicit allegation that he did give a warning. So the claimant may ask for further particulars of the warning which the defendant apparently alleges he gave. The hope, of course, is that the defendant will be forced to admit that no warning was given.

A well-drafted RFI consists of a series of questions designed to drive the other side into a bit of a corner. It is a bit like cross-examination: do not ask the question unless you know what answer you are hoping to get, and frame the question in such a way that the other side will have no option but to give you the answer you want. Very often it is a series of questions which will achieve the desired result, and you need to ask every one of those questions to get it. Remember that you are very probably trying to damage the other side's case or force them to damage their own, so they will want to get out of their difficulties if at all possible. The better you draft the questions, the harder it will be. It is a very precise form of drafting that is required.

17.4 Request for further information about a claim

17.4.1 Request for further information

(See particulars of claim in **7.9** and defence in **8.6**.)

IN THE HIGH COURT OF JUSTICE   Claim No 2004 HC 1427
QUEEN'S BENCH DIVISION

BETWEEN

BETTAPRINTA LIMITED   <u>Claimants</u>

and

MASTERGRAPH MACHINES PLC   <u>Defendants</u>

REQUEST FOR FURTHER INFORMATION
UNDER CPR PART 18

This is a request made on 1st October 2004 by the Defendants of the Claimants for further information and clarification of their Particulars of Claim. The Defendants expect a response by 25th October 2004.

<u>In relation to paragraph 3 of the Particulars of Claim</u>

Of the whole paragraph

1. (a) Please state whether the alleged term was written or agreed orally.

   (b) If written, please identify the document or documents in which it was set out and provide a copy of any such document.

   (c) If oral, please state when, where and by whom the term was agreed, and state as precisely as possible the words used.

<u>In relation to paragraph 5 of the Particulars of Claim</u>

Of 'installed the New Machines'

2. Please state:

   (a) When precisely the New Machines were installed.

   (b) When the Claimants started using each of them.

<u>In relation to paragraph 6 of the Particulars of Claim</u>

Of 'none of the New Machines was capable of printing at a rate exceeding 120 sheets per minute'

3. (a) Please state whether it is alleged that none of the New Machines was capable of printing at a rate exceeding 120 sheets per minute:

   (i) when using Mastergraph Superspeed Ink, or

   (ii) when using another ink, or

(iii)   in either case.

(b) If the answer to 3(a) above is (ii) or (iii), please identify the other ink or inks used.

<u>In relation to paragraph 7 of the Particulars of Claim</u>

Of '(a) ... (i) estimated receipts from warranted output £48,173.58'

4. Please state with full particularity:

(a) how the estimated receipts are calculated;

(b) on what basis they are estimated; and

(c) how the figure of £48,173.58 is arrived at.

And of '(b) ... (i) estimated receipts from warranted output £673,592.00'

5. Please give the equivalent particulars as are asked for in request 4 above.

And of '(b) ... (ii) estimated actual receipts £274,456.00'

6. Please give the equivalent particulars as are asked for in requests 4 and 5 above.

<u>In relation to the Claimant's case generally</u>

7. Did not a telephone conversation take place between Alan Watkins on behalf of the Claimants and Geraldine Patterson on behalf of the Defendants on 3rd February 2004?

8. Did not Geraldine Patterson in that telephone conversation:

(a) Point out to Alan Watkins that there was a typographical error in a fax sent by the Defendants to the Claimants on 2nd February 2004 (by which the figure 250 appeared instead of the correct figure 150)?

(b) Expressly state that the printing machines were capable of printing at a rate of 150 but not 250 sheets per minute when using Mastergraph Superspeed Ink?

9. Have the Claimants used any of the New Machines with Mastergraph Superspeed Ink?

10. (a) If so, at what speed did the New Machines print?

(b) If not, what steps have the Claimants taken to obtain and use Mastergraph Superspeed Ink?

11.   Have the Claimants continued to use the New Machines notwithstanding that they are allegedly incapable of printing at the rate desired by the Claimants?

12.   If the answer to question 11 is 'yes':

(a) What prevented the Claimants from using other machines instead?

(b) What efforts did the Claimants make to obtain by purchase, lease or otherwise machines which would print at the desired rate of 250 sheets per minute?

BESS TOFFER

17.4.2 Commentary

Heading. Remember the requirements of PD 18, para 1.6. The request must have a full case heading, and in its heading state that it is made under Part 18, identify the party making the request and the party to whom the request is made, and state the date of the request. The example gives a suggestion as to how these requirements might be complied with. The date by which a response is expected has to be given, though not necessarily in the heading. However this seems to be a sensible place to put it. If the request relates to a document, the document must be identified. So here the particulars of claim is identified as the relevant document.

Layout. Each request must be made in a separate numbered paragraph, and must identify the paragraph or words in the particulars of claim to which it relates. The conventional way of doing this is that which you see here. Identify the paragraph number first, then cite the relevant words, then set out the request in a numbered (and if appropriate sub-numbered) paragraph. The use of the word 'please' is not compulsory, but there is no good reason not to be polite!

Request 1. This is a very common and typical form of request. Whenever the other side allege the existence of anything in the form of words (a term, information, a statement, a representation etc) without further particulars you can ask for the information requested here: oral/written — if written, what document — if oral, when, where, words used. You can also ask for a copy of any relevant document. It is generally unreasonable to ask for the precise words used if oral, but it is acceptable to ask for them 'as precisely as possible' or 'so far as someone is able to remember them' or for the 'gist' of the words used.

The defendants' objective in making this request is to narrow down the scope of the claimants' allegation that there was a term that the machines would print at the rate of 250 sheets per minute, which the defendants deny. They hope that the claimants will respond by saying the term is to be found in the fax of 2 February 2004, because they will then be able to rely on their contention that this was a known misprint, and if there is no other basis for the term then the claimants' case is weakened.

Request 2. This is a fairly innocuous request, aimed at obtaining clarification of the claim for lost profits. The claimants can only calculate their claim if these dates are known, and so should be willing to state them. The defendants also hope to obtain ammunition in support of their contention that the claimants have failed to take reasonable steps in mitigation. The longer they have been running the machines at a loss, the sooner they should have done something about it.

Request 3. The aim here is to extract an admission that the claimants have been using the wrong make of ink. However a direct question asking what kind of ink the claimants have been using cannot really be said to be seeking clarification of the particulars of claim, because there is nothing about ink in the particulars of claim. That would be asking about the defendants' case rather than the claimants'. So the question is asked in a way which clearly pins the issue onto something alleged by the claimants. Note how the question is formulated so that it will be difficult for the claimants to avoid making the admission the defendants are hoping for if it is in fact true. Of course this would be a dangerous question to ask if the defendants are not pretty sure that the claimants have *not* been using Mastergraph Superspeed Ink.

Requests 4, 5 and 6. There is no trickery here, simply a valid request for the claimants to particularise their alleged losses with more care than they have done in the particulars of claim. Since the defendants are saying the claim is wildly exaggerated, they want to see how the claimants have arrived at their inflated figures. Note in requests 5 and 6 how you can make similar requests without having to copy out the same words all over again.

Requests 7 to 12. The first six requests are all in a form similar to the old requests for further and better particulars. But the remaining requests are set out in a form similar to that which was used in the old interrogatories. These requests are about the claimants' case in general and go beyond the particulars of claim. They may be harder to justify if the claimants refuse to answer them, but the defendants can argue that they all address live issues between the parties, and if answered could help to narrow the issues and reduce the amount of evidence required. They are all in effect asking the claimants to make admissions, and are founded on the defendants' case. They are all closed questions, drafted rather in the style of a cross-examination. This gives the defendants greater control over the information they get, and helps to prevent the claimants giving them information they do not want.

Requests 7 and 8. These requests are designed to try and resolve the issue of the misprint. The defendants hope to find out whether the phone call is admitted, and whether there will be any dispute over what was said in it. Even if the answers are not favourable to the defendants, they will at least have a better idea of the case they have to meet. They may however be going too far: they seem to be asking the claimants about the defendants' case, not their own.

Requests 9 and 10. These requests further address the issue of whether the claimants are using the wrong make of ink. As with request 3, requests 9 and 10(a) are dangerous unless the defendants are pretty sure of the answers. Request 10(b), which they expect to be the case, will hopefully produce the answer 'none'.

Requests 11 and 12. These requests are designed to support the defendants' case on failure to mitigate. They could be said to be fishing for evidence, but the defendants will argue that since the claimants say their loss of profit from the use of these machines is continuing at nearly £400,000 per annum, they must by implication be alleging that they have no option but to continue to use the new machines, so these requests really are seeking clarification of the claimants' case.

Signature. The request for further information is not a statement of case, but it is a document drafted by the party's legal representative, so should be signed by counsel if drafted by counsel (PD 5, para 2.1).

17.5 Request for further information about a defence

17.5.1 Request for further information

(See particulars of claim in **9.2.2** and defence in **10.2**.)

IN THE HIGH COURT OF JUSTICE   Claim No 2004 HC 6151
QUEEN'S BENCH DIVISION

BETWEEN

RICHARD ALLEN   Claimant

and

H. A. JOHNS (CONSTRUCTION) LIMITED   Defendants

REQUEST FOR FURTHER INFORMATION
UNDER CPR PART 18

This is a request made on 1st October 2004 by the Claimants of the Defendants for further information and clarification of their Defence. The Claimants expect a response by 25th October 2004.

In relation to paragraph 2(2) of the Defence

Of 'The crane was of adequate stability for the load being carried'

1.   Please state whether the alleged test was the only step taken to ensure the stability of the crane, and if not please give full particulars of all other steps taken.

And of '... Patrick Connelly carried out a test ('the Test') ...'

2.   Please give full and precise particulars of the nature of the Test, the procedure(s) adopted and the result(s) of the Test, and without narrowing the scope of this request, please state in particular:

(a) Whether the Test was carried out using the crane which fell over, or another crane.

(b) If another crane, whether that crane was identical to the crane which fell over.

(c) If not identical, giving full particulars of all material differences between the two cranes.

(d) Whether the crane was tested in the precise position in which it was standing when it fell over.

(e) If in a different position, precisely where the Test was carried out.

(f) What was the weight of the load lifted during the Test?

(g) To what radius the jib or boom was extended whilst carrying the load during the Test.

(h) For how long a time the load was carried at that radius.

And of '... by which he established the stability of the crane'.

3.   Please state:

(a) Whether it is here alleged that Patrick Connelly by the Test established that the crane could not fall over under the loading conditions used in the Test.

(b) If not, what precisely was established by the Test.

And of 'loading conditions greater than those required for the pile driving'.

4. (a) Please give full particulars, so far as not already provided in response to the above requests, of the loading conditions under which the crane was tested.

(b) Please state what are the loading conditions required for pile driving.

(c) Please state whether the loading conditions 'required' are the same as those prevailing at the moment the crane fell over.

(d) If not, please state what load was being carried at the time the crane fell over.

In relation to paragraph 2(3) of the Defence

Of ' The crane was therefore safely installed and positioned'

5.   Please give full particulars of all the steps taken to ensure that the crane was (a) safely installed and (b) safely positioned.

In relation to paragraph 4 of the Defence

Of 'a fact unknown to the Defendants at the material time and which they could not reasonably have discovered'

6. (a) Please say when and by what means the Defendants became aware that the site had previously been filled with rubble.

(b) Please give full facts and matters relied upon in support of the allegation that they could not reasonably have discovered this alleged fact before the accident.

In relation to paragraph 5 of the Defence

Of '... having been so instructed by Patrick Connelly on at least two occasions prior to the accident'

7.   Please state precisely how many occasions are relied upon and in relation to each occasion, please state:

(a) The date, time and place at which any instruction was given.

(b) Whether the instruction was given orally or in writing.

(c) If orally, the actual words used, so far as Mr Connelly remembers them, otherwise please state as precisely as possible the gist of the instruction.

(d) If in writing, please identify the document in which the instruction was given, provide a copy, and state how that document was communicated to the Claimant.

(e) Whether it is alleged that the instruction was given to the Claimant individually or to a group of employees of which he was one.

(f) The circumstances in which the instruction was given.

In relation to paragraph 7 of the Defence

Of 'he is able to walk further than alleged'

8.   Please state how far it is alleged that the Claimant is able to walk and whether this is with or without the aid of a stick.

And of '... is less limited in his daily activities than alleged'

9.   Please list:

(a) Each daily activity which the Claimant contends he is unable to undertake but which the Defendants allege he can.

(b) Each daily activity in which the Defendants allege the Claimant is less limited than he contends, stating for each activity the manner in which and the extent to which the limitation alleged by the Defendants is less than that alleged by the Claimant.

And of 'He has a good chance of finding suitable employment'

10. (a) Please identify each and every employment or type of employment which is being referred to.

(b) Please state more precisely what chance it is alleged the Claimant has of finding such employment.

(c) Please give full facts and matters relied upon in support of the allegation that he has such a chance.

JOSEPH BLOGGS

17.5.2 Commentary

This request for further information is more tactical than the previous example, and is designed to expose weaknesses in the defence case. The requests are all in the form of the old request for further and better particulars, and are to a considerable extent a cross-examination of the defendants on their defence.

Request 1. This request simply picks up a lack of particularisation in the defence. The defendants had a statutory obligation to ensure the stability of the crane. If they allege that they did so they must be prepared to say what steps they took. The test alone may not be enough, especially if the ground was unstable.

Requests 2 and 3. The allegation that 'Patrick Connelly carried out a test by which he established the stability of the crane' is highly dubious. How can it have done so if the crane in fact fell over? The allegation is exaggerated, and the aim of these requests is to expose the uselessness of the test and the defendants' reliance on it, forcing them to admit that the test established no such thing. The request needs to be made in two stages. Ask first about the test itself, then about the relevance of the test.

Request 2. The test itself. There must be a high degree of probability that the test did not reproduce the identical conditions under which the crane eventually fell over, so the objective is to tease out some significant differences which will render the test meaningless. So a great deal of information is requested here. The request begins by asking in general for full particulars, but that would be too open-ended by itself, allowing the defendants to provide whatever information they chose to provide. So more particular requests follow. But these are expressly stated to be asked 'without narrowing the scope of this request', so requiring the defendants to go beyond merely answering points (a) to (h). Sub-paragraphs (a) to (c) are looking for differences in the crane, (d) and (e) are looking for differences in the position of the crane, and (f) to (h) are looking for differences in the loading conditions.

Request 3. The relevance of the test. This is framed as penetratingly as possible. If the defendants answer 'yes', they are obviously making the absurd allegation that they established that the crane could not fall over when in fact it did. So they will hopefully be forced to answer 'no', in which case they have in effect retracted the allegation made in the defence. To make things even more awkward, request 3(b) is designed to make them concede that the test is in all the circumstances irrelevant to their defence.

Request 4. This request will probably not take the claimant much further than request 2. It does however invite the defendants to concede that the loading conditions at the time of the collapse of the crane were normal, so precluding any possibility of a defence that conditions were unexpected or unforeseeable.

Request 5. This request again picks up a lack of particularisation. The statutory obligation is absolute. If the defendants contend that the crane was safe, even though it fell over, they must be prepared to say what steps they took. The question, in essence is 'why was the crane safe?', but as explained above, 'why?' is a bad question because it gives too much scope for a generalised answer. 'What steps were taken?' is much more precise and effective.

Request 6. There is something pretty unimpressive about the defence that they could not reasonably have discovered the ground conditions before they used the crane, when they have apparently discovered them since. So the aim of this request is to test the strength of the defence case by getting the defendants to provide an explanation. The request is obviously made in the belief that the explanation will be unconvincing. One would not make it if the result would simply be to give the defendants the opportunity to reinforce their case. The phrase 'please give full facts and matters relied upon in support of the allegation that' is a common one when asking for particulars, but use it with care. It is an open question which invites the other side to say whatever they want, which is always dangerous if you think they might have a good case.

Request 7. The claimant obviously says that he was never given any such instructions by Patrick Connelly, or if he was they were so vague as to be meaningless. The aim here is therefore to make a request that the defendants may not be able to answer, but which they ought to be able to answer if their allegation is correct. Again, this is dangerous if it is the claimant whose evidence is suspect. But on the assumption that the claimant is correct, the more details you ask for about these (apparently non-existent) occasions the better. When an allegation is vague or generalised ('at least two occasions') it is always reasonable to ask for proper particularisation. The defendants may be unable to say exactly how many there were (or why would they have said 'at least'?), but they can be made to say how many they *rely* on. Then do not just ask for more particulars; say what particulars are required in relation to each occasion. The hope is, of course, that the defendants will be unable to be much more particular than they have already been, in which case it will appear that Mr Connelly's evidence on this allegation is unlikely to be reliable.

Requests 8, 9 and 10. The defendants have claimed to know more about the claimant's injury and losses of amenity than he does. They seem to be suggesting he is malingering, or exaggerating the effect of his injuries. The claimant has every right to know what case he has to meet on this issue. Yet again it is dangerous to make these requests if the claimant's evidence is indeed suspect. Each of these requests puts the defendants on the spot somewhat, but is justified because of the vagueness of the allegation made: 'further' than alleged; 'less limited' than alleged; 'good' chance; 'suitable' employment.

Overall, provided you are confident about the claimant's case and his evidence, this request for further information should punch a few holes in the defence.

17.6 Exercise

Draft a request for further information about the particulars of claim in the case of *Rebecca Peters v Homewood Garden Centre Ltd* (see **13.5**, **15.7** and **16.4**). Take it that this request will be served with the amended defence and counterclaim.

Further information

18.1 Form of further information

The response to a Request for Further Information is called, not surprisingly, Further Information. The relevant rules are in PD 18, para 2. The Further Information must be provided in writing, fully headed and identify the request to which it is a response. It must set out each request in full and then set out the response immediately after each request. Any documents referred to which are not already in the other side's possession must be attached. Finally, it must be verified by a statement of truth, because the Further Information counts as a statement of case.

18.2 Drafting the further information

To some extent this is just a matter of answering the questions asked according to your instructions. However, the first decision you need to make is whether to answer at all. Remember it is only a request, and you are not obliged to answer. You certainly have a right not to answer if you feel the request is not reasonably necessary and proportionate, or 'oppressive'; that is that the cost of answering the request is out of proportion to the importance of the issue or the value of the claim. There is also no need to answer if you think the request is for something the other side are not entitled to, or for evidence, or that the particulars requested have already been set out sufficiently fully or are premature. In such a case you will simply answer, for example:

'Full information will be provided upon disclosure.'

'The Defendants are not entitled to the information requested.'

'The Request is for evidence and the Claimant is not obliged to answer this Request.'

'The matters requested have already been sufficiently set out.'

'The Request is oppressive.'

But otherwise, assuming you are going to provide an answer, your objective will be to answer in such a way as to avoid falling into any of the traps set by the other side. Try to damage your own case as little as possible. This will often mean providing exactly what has been asked for and no more. Do not add more information if the more you say, the more you weaken your case.

However, sometimes the request will have been unwise. The other side may have thought you would not have a good answer to it, but in fact you do. In such circumstances you can obviously answer very fully, and it may be that the more information you provide, the more you can strengthen your case. Do not hold back, if it is to your advantage; take the opportunity provided.

18.3 Example

18.3.1 Further information

(See particulars of claim in **7.9**, defence in **8.6** and Request for Further Information in **17.4**.)

IN THE HIGH COURT OF JUSTICE   Claim No 2004 HC 1427
QUEEN'S BENCH DIVISION

BETWEEN

BETTAPRINTA LIMITED   <u>Claimants</u>

and

MASTERGRAPH MACHINES PLC   <u>Defendants</u>

FURTHER INFORMATION

This further information and clarification of the Particulars of Claim is provided by the Claimants pursuant to the Request for Further Information dated 1st October 2004 made by the Defendants.

<u>In relation to paragraph 3 of the Particulars of Claim</u>

Of the whole paragraph

REQUEST

1. (a) Please state whether the alleged term was written or agreed orally.

    (b) If written, please identify the document or documents in which it was set out and provide a copy of any such document.

    (c) If oral, please state when, where and by whom the term was agreed, and state as precisely as possible the words used.

ANSWER

The term was set out in the Defendant's fax to the Claimants on 3rd February 2004. Further in the Claimants' fax of 2nd February 2004, the Claimants stipulated that they required any new printing machine purchased by them to be capable of printing at the rate of 250 sheets per minute. Copies of these faxes were attached to the Particulars of Claim.

<u>In relation to paragraph 5 of the Particulars of Claim</u>

REQUEST

Of 'installed the New Machines'

2. Please state:

   (a) When precisely the New Machines were installed.

   (b) When the Claimants started using each of them.

ANSWER

The New Machines were installed on 28th March 2004. The Claimants started to operate all 3 on 31st March 2004.

In relation to paragraph 6 of the Particulars of Claim

REQUEST

Of 'none of the New Machines was capable of printing at a rate exceeding 120 sheets per minute'

3. (a) Please state whether it is alleged that none of the New Machines was capable of printing at a rate exceeding 120 sheets per minute:

   (i)   when using Mastergraph Superspeed Ink, or

   (ii) when using another ink, or

   (iii) in either case.

   (b) If the answer to 3(a) above is (ii) or (iii), please identify the other ink or inks used.

ANSWER

None of the New Machines was capable of printing at a rate exceeding 120 sheets per minute when using Groover's Ink, an ink listed by the Defendants in their literature as suitable for use with their machines.

In relation to paragraph 7 of the Particulars of Claim

REQUEST

Of '(a) ... (i) estimated receipts from warranted output £48,173.58'

4. Please state with full particularity:

   (a) how the estimated receipts are calculated;

   (b) on what basis they are estimated; and

   (c) how the figure of £48,173.58 is arrived at.

ANSWER

The estimated receipts are estimated on the basis of comparison with receipts from the use of three Groover's A28 machines owned and operated by the Claimants, which are capable of printing at a rate of 250 sheets per minute. The calculations which arrive at the figure claimed are set out in the attached schedule.

REQUEST

And of '(b) ... (i) estimated receipts from warranted output £673,592.00'

5. Please give the equivalent particulars as are asked for in request 4 above.

ANSWER

The Claimants repeat the answer to request 4.

REQUEST

And of '(b) ... (ii) estimated actual receipts £274,456.00'

6. Please give the equivalent particulars as are asked for in requests 4 and 5 above.

ANSWER

The estimated actual receipts are estimated on the basis of comparison with receipts from the new machines between 31st March and 12th September 2004. The calculations which arrive at the figure claimed are set out in the attached schedule.

In relation to the Claimant's case generally

REQUEST

7. Did not a telephone conversation take place between Alan Watkins on behalf of the Claimants and Geraldine Patterson on behalf of the Defendants on 3rd February 2004?

ANSWER

Yes.

REQUEST

8. Did not Geraldine Patterson in that telephone conversation:

   (a) Point out to Alan Watkins that there was a typographical error in a fax sent by the Defendants to the Claimants on 2nd February 2004 (by which the figure 250 appeared instead of the correct figure 150)?

   (b) Expressly state that the printing machines were capable of printing at a rate of 150 but not 250 sheets per minute when using Mastergraph Superspeed Ink?

ANSWER

The answer to both parts of this question is 'no'. The gist of the conversation was to the effect that the new machines would print at the rate of 250 sheets per minute if used with an approved ink, of which Mastergraph Superspeed Ink was but one.

REQUEST

9. Have the Claimants used any of the New Machines with Mastergraph Superspeed Ink?

ANSWER

No. The Claimants have at all times used Groover's Ink, an ink listed by the Defendants in their literature as approved for use with their machines.

REQUEST

10. (a) If so, at what speed did the new machines print?

    (b) If not, what steps have the Claimants taken to obtain and use Mastergraph Superspeed Ink?

ANSWER

10(a) is not applicable. The Claimants have not used any ink other than Groover's Ink, because they would be in breach of their contract with Groover plc if they were to do so. The

Claimants at all time relied on the Defendants' warranty that Groover's Ink was an approved ink for use with their machines.

REQUEST

11. Have the Claimants continued to use the New Machines notwithstanding that they are allegedly incapable of printing at the rate desired by the Claimants?

ANSWER

Yes. Not to have done so would have resulted in increased loss to the Claimants.

REQUEST

12. If the answer to question 11 is 'yes':

(a) What prevented the Claimants from using other machines instead?

(b) What efforts did the Claimants make to obtain by purchase, lease or otherwise machines which would print at the desired rate of 250 sheets per minute?

ANSWER

The Defendants are not entitled to this information.

JOSEPH BLOGGS

STATEMENT OF TRUTH

Dated etc.

18.3.2 Commentary

Heading. Note that the heading must be full and that you must start by identifying the request to which this is a response.

Layout. Each request must be set out in full, and followed immediately by the response. The sub-headings 'REQUEST' and 'ANSWER' are helpful in this regard.

Answer 1. The request needs only a short straight answer. However the claimants are aware of the misprint issue, and the term they rely on is contained in the fax with the misprint. So they take the opportunity to bolster their case by adding that the requirement was made known in a previous fax. There is no need to provide a further copy of a document which has already been served.

Answer 2. There is no trap here, so a straight answer can easily be provided.

Answer 3. The claimants are obviously aware of what the defendants are trying to get at, but they have a good answer: they were not using Mastergraph Superspeed Ink, but the ink they were using is approved by the defendants. So if the defendants want to allege that the claimants should not be using Groover's Ink, they will have to explain their literature.

Answers 4, 5 and 6. These can all be given straight answers if the claimants have the relevant information to hand. A schedule is probably a better place to set out complicated information such as mathematical calculations.

Answer 7. There is nothing wrong with a one word answer if it does your case no damage.

Answer 8. The claimants put their case. This answer helps to clarify for both parties that the dispute will be over what was said on the phone rather than what was in the faxes. The claimants take a further opportunity to state their case on the ink issue.

Answer 9. Here the one word answer without more does not do full justice to the claimants' case, so they expand on the answer by reiterating their point about Groover's Ink.

Answer 10. The claimants are not asked why they are using Groover's Ink, but they say why anyway. This answer makes it clear that a central issue in the case is likely to be whether the claimants could use any approved ink or only Mastergraph Superspeed Ink to obtain the printing speed they wanted.

Answer 11. The straight answer is unavoidable here. Some explanation is obviously needed or the answer looks like a concession. The explanation is obviously incomplete, and the claimants may have a rather weak case on the issue of mitigation, but it is for the defendants to prove a failure to mitigate, not for the claimants to prove that they have reasonably mitigated.

Answer 12. The claimants refuse to answer, because (they will contend) the defendants are asking for evidence to help them prove their allegation of failure to mitigate, not information about the claimants' case. The defendants' probable contention as to why they should be entitled to this information is explained in **17.4.2**.

18.4 Exercise

(See **13.5**, **15.7**, **16.4** and **17.6**.)

Counsel is asked to draft Further Information on behalf of the claimant Rebecca Peters in response to the Request for Further Information served by Homewood Garden Centre Ltd. With this request was served an amended defence and counterclaim and a copy of a Part 20 claim against the sub-contractor Harold Todd, to which Counsel is referred.

Instructing Solicitors have shown these documents to Miss Peters and her further instructions are as follows:

I had no idea that Homewood used a sub-contractor when installing my greenhouses. I was working in my offices and left them to get on with it. It took one whole day. At the end of the day someone came and knocked on my door and invited me to inspect the greenhouses. I did not notice any cracked glass at that point. I was told that the heaters were all on. The next day I started to stock the greenhouses with plants. They were nice and warm, but it was a very mild, almost summery October day. It was only a couple of days later, when the weather turned frosty, that I found the temperature had dropped in three of the greenhouses, which I will call Nos 1, 2 and 4. No 2 was colder than Nos 1 and 4. I found that there was a cracked wall panel in No 1, a cracked door panel in No 4 and a cracked roof and a wall panel in No 2. I think they must have been cracked when I first inspected them, even though I did not notice this, because no one went into them after that without my being present, so I would have been aware if any of my employees had done the damage. I called Percy Hopcroft but he was not available and I was told nothing could be done till next Monday, so I called in an emergency glass service to replace the cracked glass.

I do not know precisely when each heater broke down, but I remember being surprised at how quickly in succession it occurred. I do know that the heater in No 2 blew up first, I think two days after the glass panels were replaced. It happened overnight. The next morning I moved all the plants from No 2 into the other three greenhouses, but within a few hours No 3 went. We were able to save some of the plants, but there was simply no room for all of them in Nos 1 and 4, so some had to be moved to unheated greenhouses. Sometime the next night the last two heaters broke down, so I no longer had any heated greenhouses. The plants started to die immediately, because it was a frosty night. By next morning it was too late to save them.

I do not keep an inventory of every single plant I have in stock. It is not possible to count precisely. When a plant is divided do you call it one or two? When cuttings are taken, do you treat each cutting as a new plant? What if more than one plant is in the same pot? I can say that most of the plants in the greenhouses died, though a small number (perhaps 10%) survived in a damaged state and could be propagated. I spent £10,000 on the purchase of tropical plants to stock the greenhouses. The profit would have been made over up to seven years, depending on how large I allowed plants to grow before selling them. The bigger the plant, the more it costs to grow it, but the higher the price you can get for it. The costs are in heat, light, food, space and staff hours. I cannot provide figures for each plant. The figure of £11,000 is the best estimate I can give of my loss. After repairs, I restocked the greenhouses at a cost of £10,500, but will probably be able to recoup £2,500 net after costs over three years from the few plants that survived.

I did not want to be messed around any more by Homewood, so I got Ben Dodds & Co to repair the heating systems. They told me that the heating systems had failed because of (a) an accumulation of dust and particles on the elements which had caused a short circuit and (b) the wiring was defective in that 15 amp wire had been used instead of 30 amp. The same faults were present on all four heating systems, though either fault would have been enough alone to cause a breakdown. They did not tell me what precisely had caused the breakdown in each case.

Interim injunctions

19.1 Procedure

Injunctions are almost always sought with some urgency. It follows that most injunctions in practice are interim injunctions. In cases of extreme urgency, or where there is a need for secrecy, they may be sought and made without notice to the other side.

The documents needed to seek an interim injunction are:

(a) A claim form to commence the claim. If possible particulars of claim should be attached.

(b) An application notice. This must be on Form N244, or in the county court, Form N16A.

(c) A draft of the order sought. This must be in one of the prescribed forms. Surprisingly the Civil Procedure Rules 1998 have not yet prescribed a standard form for general use under the new procedure. This means that there is still a different form prescribed in the High Court and county court. The draft should if possible be provided on disc as well as on paper.

(d) Written evidence, setting out the evidence upon which the applicant relies. This may be in the form of a witness statement, a statement of case or evidence inserted onto the application notice, unless the court, a rule or a practice direction requires the evidence to be given by affidavit. A witness statement will be the most usual form. However, PD 25, para 3.1 requires evidence in support of an application for a search order or a freezing injunction to be given by affidavit. If the application notice is to be relied on as evidence, it must be verified by a statement of truth.

In applications without notice the same documents will be needed, but they will probably not have been served on the other side. The applicant must undertake to serve them as soon as practicable after the order has been made, together with the order itself. If the application is exceptionally urgent, the application can be made without issuing a claim form or filing an application notice. In this case the applicant must additionally undertake to issue a claim form and file an application notice on the same or the next working day and serve them with the order. It may even be necessary to make the application without written evidence, in which case the applicant must inform the judge of the evidence that will in due course be forthcoming, and undertake to produce such evidence. The respondent to an injunction made without notice has the right to apply to the court to vary it or set it aside.

An interim injunction will usually last until trial or further order. An injunction without notice will usually only be made to last until the return day, when another hearing will be held at which the respondent can be present. The order must give notice of the return day.

The order must contain all necessary undertakings, including the claimant's undertaking as to damages, the injunction itself and an order concerning costs. An order without notice will need to contain the further undertakings mentioned above. It will also give the respondent notice of his right to apply to vary or set aside the order. It may also give the applicant permission to apply to extend the duration of the order.

In the order it appears that the Claimant and Defendant should be referred to as the Applicant and Respondent. There is no rule to this effect, but this is the terminology used in CPR, Parts 23 and 25, and in the standard forms for search orders and freezing injunctions prescribed by PD 25.

We are concerned in this chapter with the drafting of claim forms, application notices, orders and undertakings. Written evidence is dealt with in **Chapter 20**.

19.2 Drafting injunction orders

19.2.1 The essential requirements

The terms of the order, and to a lesser extent any special undertakings, require real drafting skill. Once you have drafted these, the documents required can be completed without difficulty. An injunction order needs to fulfil certain criteria:

(a) It must enable the defendant to know exactly what he may, must and must not do. If this is in any way uncertain in the draft order the judge will not grant the order in the terms sought. It must therefore be drafted with clarity and precision, and ideally in plain English.

(b) It can only be granted in support of a legal right. It must therefore be drafted so that it does not go one inch beyond the claimant's legal entitlement, or again the judge will be unable to make the order sought.

(c) It must enable the claimant to achieve his objectives. It must be drafted in such a way that it does actually cure the mischief aimed at. If the action is in any way contentious, the defendant will be looking for loopholes. So the order must not fall one inch short of giving the claimant his legal entitlement, and it must be absolutely watertight, so that the defendant is compelled to comply in precisely the way intended by the claimant.

To achieve these objectives great care and thought is required. In particular you need to develop the ability to perceive loopholes, and to recognise when provisos and savings are required to make the order enforceable. You need to be very particular. A woolly or generalised order would be impossible to comply with. It often helps to look at the draft order from the defendant's point of view and see how you would respond to it if you were in his shoes.

It is in this area that the use of precedents is most dangerous and inappropriate. An order that may have met the facts of one case may be quite inaccurate on the facts of another case, even if it is superficially very similar. In the end every order is unique, and tailored to the precise circumstances of each individual case. Never copy a precedent blindly unless you know exactly what the circumstances were in which that order was made, and why they are indistinguishable from the circumstances of this case. Much the best rule is to draft injunctions without reference to precedents at all.

19.2.2   Mandatory and prohibitory orders

Injunctions may be mandatory or prohibitory. A mandatory order is one which requires a defendant to do something. A prohibitory order is one which forbids him to do something. You have to decide in drafting whether to seek mandatory and/or prohibitory orders.

Whether an injunction is mandatory or prohibitory is strictly speaking a matter of substance, not of the form of words used. So, an order telling the defendant that he must not refrain from doing something is mandatory, and an order requiring the defendant to stop doing something is prohibitory. A claimant is supposed to couch what is in substance a mandatory order in positive terms and what is in substance a prohibitory order in negative terms.

However, strictly speaking mandatory orders are harder to obtain. An interim mandatory order is particularly hard to obtain, because there may be no going back once the defendant has been ordered to do something. An interim mandatory order without notice is the most difficult of all to obtain. There is therefore a widespread tendency in practice to seek to draft mandatory orders in prohibitory terms. This can always be done. Rather than ordering a defendant to remove something, you order him not to leave it where it is. Instead of ordering him to give you something, you order him not to withhold it from you. You can even try ordering a defendant to stop refusing to do something.

The more modern practice is to draft an order which contains both prohibitory and mandatory terms designed to achieve the same result, and leave it to the judge to decide in what terms he or she will grant the injunction.

19.2.3   Plain English

It was in the drafting of orders that lawyers in the past were particularly guilty of using legal jargon and archaic legal language. This was often unfair, because the person on whom the order was to be served would quite often not be a lawyer, and if it was an injunction order that ordered him not to do something, and he did not understand it, he could find himself in contempt of court through no real fault of his own. Freezing injunctions and search orders were exceptionally difficult to fathom for a layman. So the courts started to prescribe new forms, drafted in plain English, and as far as possible comprehensible by a layman without legal advice. But of course only the formal parts of the order could be prescribed. However there is a clear understanding these days that since the forms are in plain English, the actual orders drafted by lawyers should be in plain English too. You should take this as your objective, remembering that it is even harder to be absolutely precise in plain English than it is in legalese.

19.3   Standard forms of injunction

There are five forms prescribed for general use in the High Court by *Practice Direction* [1996] 1 WLR 1551. However, they are not set out — there is merely an invitation to obtain copies of them from the Royal Courts of Justice. We therefore set out the main two, *Order for Injunction* and *Order for an Injunction Before the Issue of a Claim Form*, below in **19.3.1** and **19.3.2**. The other three are: *Order Containing Undertaking Instead of an Injunction*, *Adjournment of Application for an Injunction* and *Application for an Injunction Treated as Trial of the Action*. These are most unlikely to be required by Bar students and are not included in this Manual.

There are further specialised forms prescribed for freezing injunctions (*Mareva* orders) and search orders (*Anton Piller* orders) by PD 25. Since reference can readily be made to these forms, they are also not included in this Manual.

Note the use of plain English in all the above forms.

The standard form prescribed in the county court is Form N16. It has been around a few years longer than the High Court forms, so is a little more old fashioned, though still in plain English. It is set out below in **19.3.4**, followed by the General Form of Undertaking (Form N117) in **19.3.5**. A new standard form for use both in the High Court and the county court was promised in 1999, but has not yet appeared. When published, it is likely to resemble the High Court version.

All the standard forms printed below have been altered slightly to comply with the new terminology and procedure.

19.3.1 Order for injunction: High Court

IN THE HIGH COURT OF JUSTICE   Claim No
[CHANCERY] [QUEEN'S BENCH] DIVISION

MR JUSTICE [   ]

[*Date*]

BETWEEN

                                                              Claimant/Applicant

                                    and

                                                              Defendant/Respondent
                    _____

                        ORDER FOR AN INJUNCTION
                    _____

IMPORTANT

NOTICE TO THE RESPONDENT

(1) **This Order [prohibits you from doing] [obliges you to do] the acts set out in this Order. [You should read it carefully. You are advised to consult a Solicitor as soon as possible.] You have a right to ask the Court to vary or set aside this Order.**

(2) **If you disobey this Order you may be found guilty of Contempt of Court and [any of your directors] may be sent to prison or fined [and you may be fined] or your assets may be seized.**

   (Include the words in square brackets in the case of a corporate Defendant. This notice is not a substitute for the indorsement of a penal notice.)

An Application was made on the [*date*] by Counsel for the Applicant to the Judge [and was attended by Counsel for the Respondent]. The Judge heard the Application and read the written evidence listed in Schedule 1 and accepted the undertakings in Schedule 2 at the end of this Order.

IT IS ORDERED that:

THE INJUNCTION

(1) Until after [*date*] [final judgment in this claim] the Respondent must/must not [*Body of injunction to go here*]

COSTS OF THE APPLICATION

(2) [The Respondent shall pay the Applicant's costs of this Application.] [The costs of this Application are reserved to be dealt with by the Judge who tries this Action.] [The costs of this Application are to be costs in the case.] [The costs of this Application are the Applicant's costs in the case.]

VARIATION OR SETTING ASIDE OF THIS ORDER

The Respondent may apply to the Court at any time to vary or set aside this Order but if he wishes to do so he must first inform the Applicant's Solicitors in writing at least 48 hours beforehand.

NAME AND ADDRESS OF APPLICANT'S SOLICITORS

The Applicant's Solicitors are:

[*Name, address and telephone numbers both in and out of office hours.*]

INTERPRETATION OF THIS ORDER

(1) In this Order the words 'he' 'him' or 'his' include 'she' or 'her' and 'it' or 'its'.

(2) Where there are two or more Respondents then (unless the contrary appears):

(a) references to 'the Respondent' mean to both or all of them;

(b) an Order requiring 'the Respondent' to do or not to do anything requires each Respondent to do or not to do it.

THE EFFECT OF THIS ORDER

(1) A Respondent who is an individual who is ordered not to do something must not do it himself or in any other way. He must not do it through others acting on his behalf or on his instructions or with his encouragement.

(2) A Respondent which is a corporation and which is ordered not to do something must not do it itself or by its directors, officers, employees or agents or in any other way.

SCHEDULE 1

Written Evidence

The Judge read the following written evidence before making this Order:

[*Insert list*]

SCHEDULE 2

Undertaking given to the Court by the Applicant

If the Court later finds that this Order has caused loss to the Respondent, and decides that the Respondent should be compensated for that loss, the Applicant will comply with any Order the Court may make.

All communications to the Court about this Order should be sent to [Room 307] [Room E15] Royal Courts of Justice, Strand, London WC2A 2LL quoting the case number. The office is open between 10am and 4.30 pm Monday to Friday. The telephone number is 020 7936 [6148] [6336].

19.3.2 Injunction before the issue of a claim form: High Court

IN THE HIGH COURT OF JUSTICE   Claim No
[CHANCERY] [QUEEN'S BENCH] DIVISION

MR JUSTICE [   ]

[*Date*]

BETWEEN

Applicant

and

Respondent

the Claimant and Defendant in an Intended Claim

ORDER FOR AN INJUNCTION BEFORE THE
ISSUE OF A CLAIM FORM

IMPORTANT

NOTICE TO THE RESPONDENT

(1) This Order [prohibits you from doing] [obliges you to do] the acts set out in this Order. [You should read it carefully. You are advised to consult a Solicitor as soon as possible.] You have a right to ask the Court to vary or set aside this Order.

(2) If you disobey this Order you may be found guilty of Contempt of Court and [any of your directors] may be sent to prison or fined [and you may be fined] or your assets may be seized.

(Include the words in square brackets in the case of a corporate Respondent. This notice is not a substitute for the indorsement of a penal notice.)

An Application was made on the [*date*] by Counsel for [*Applicant's name*] (who is to be the Claimant in a Claim against [*Respondent's name*]) to the Judge who heard the Application supported by the written evidence listed in Schedule 1 and accepted the undertakings in Schedule 2 at the end of this Order.

IT IS ORDERED that up to and including [*date* ('the Return Date')] [trial of the intended Action]:

The Respondent must/must not [*Body of injunction to go here*]

VARIATION OR SETTING ASIDE OF THIS ORDER

The Respondent may apply to the Court within 7 days of this Order to vary it or set it aside but if he wishes to do so he must first inform the Applicant's Solicitors [in writing].

NAME AND ADDRESS OF APPLICANT'S SOLICITORS

The Applicant's Solicitors are:

[*Name, address and telephone numbers both in and out of office hours.*]

INTERPRETATION OF THIS ORDER

(1) In this Order the words 'he' 'him' or 'his' include 'she' or 'her' and 'it' or 'its'.

(2) Where there are two or more Respondents then (unless the contrary appears):

   (a) references to 'the Respondent' mean to both or all of them;

   (b) an Order requiring 'the Respondent' to do or not to do anything requires each Respondent to do or not to do it;

   (c) a requirement relating to service of this Order or of any legal proceedings on 'the Respondent' means on each of them.

THE EFFECT OF THIS ORDER

(1) A Respondent who is an individual who is ordered not to do something must not do it himself or in any other way. He must not do it through others acting on his behalf or on his instructions or with his encouragement.

(2) A Respondent which is a corporation and which is ordered not to do something must not do it itself or by its directors, officers, employees or agents or in any other way.

SCHEDULE 1

Written Evidence

The Judge read the following written evidence before making this Order:

[*Insert list*]

SCHEDULE 2

Undertakings given to the Court by the Applicant

(1) If the Court later finds that this Order has caused loss to the Respondent, and decides that the Respondent should be compensated for that loss, the Applicant will comply with any Order the Court may make.

(2) As soon as practicable the Applicant will issue and serve on the Respondent a Claim Form [in the form of the draft produced to the Court and initialled by the Judge] claiming appropriate remedies together with this Order.

[(3) The Applicant will cause written evidence to be filed confirming the substance of what was said to the Court by the Applicant's Counsel/Solicitors.]

[(4) As soon as practicable the Applicant will serve on the Respondent an Application Notice for the Return Date together with a copy of the written evidence and exhibits containing the evidence relied on by the Applicant.]

All communications to the Court about this Order should be sent to [Room 307] [Room E15] Royal Courts of Justice, Strand, London WC2A 2LL quoting the case number. The office is open between 10 am and 4.30 pm Monday to Friday. The telephone number is 020 7936 [6148] [6336].

19.3.3 Commentary

19.3.3.1 Standard order for injunction

Heading. Note that on orders, after the court, the name of the judge who makes the order appears, followed by the date of the order. The parties are described as applicant and respondent as well as claimant and defendant.

Introduction. After the notice to the respondent is a brief paragraph which needs to be adapted to state who appeared and who made the application etc.

Injunction. In the High Court the words used to give the order are that the respondent 'must' (in a mandatory order) or 'must not' (in a prohibitory order) do something. The judge will either make the interim order until a specified date or until final judgment — which depends on the circumstances of the case.

Costs. Various options are set out in the form. Delete all but the order you are applying for.

Variation or setting aside. The judge will almost certainly require this part of the order. The amount of notice required depends on the nature of the case.

Interpretation. This makes it possible simply to refer to a single (male) respondent throughout the order, without worrying about whether the order will be rendered unenforceable simply because the gender of the respondent is inaccurately stated. Without (2)(b) (and until this form was published) it was often necessary to use the phrase 'the respondents and each of them' repeatedly.

Effect of the order. This is very important and you need to understand why this is here and the value of it. A respondent who objects to an injunction being made against him will often be looking for loopholes to exploit. One of the most obvious is that if the respondent is ordered not to do something and no more, he will seek to get someone else to do it on his behalf. So in the past the practice was always to insert two safeguards into every order. The first was to order the 'respondent, whether by himself, his servants or agents or otherwise' not to do something. The second was to order the respondent not to do or 'cause or permit' (or sometimes 'cause, permit or suffer') to be done whatever act was forbidden. Causing something to be done involves deliberately making it happen (without actually doing it oneself); permitting it means giving permission for it to be done, or not doing anything to prevent it; suffering it to be done means being aware that it is being done and turning a blind eye.

The formula here enables these extra words to be dispensed with, though you will still find 'cause or permit' widely used and occasionally serving some purpose. You will also need to draft in the old form when setting out the terms of an injunction in a context where this formula cannot be incorporated (for example in the list of remedies at the end of particulars of claim).

Schedule 2. The undertaking printed is the standard undertaking as to damages. If the judge requires any further undertakings, they will be inserted after this one.

19.3.3.2 Injunction before claim form

Heading. There is no claim in existence, so there can be no claimant and defendant. The parties are therefore simply applicant and respondent, but there is an additional line indicating that a claim is about to be brought by the applicant against the respondent.

Order. An interim injunction without notice is not likely to be made to last for anything but a short period until the respondent can be heard. This date is known as the return date.

You will notice that this form makes no apparent provision for an order as to costs. This is presumably an oversight. By analogy with the previous form, the costs order will appear after the terms of the injunction.

Variation or setting aside. The time given for the respondent to apply is likely to be closely related to the return date.

Schedule 2. There are several additional undertakings that will or may be required when the application is without notice and before the issue of a claim form. See **19.1**.

19.3.4   Form N16 (General form of injunction): county court

IN THE [   ] COUNTY COURT   Claim No

ISSUED ON [*date*]

BETWEEN

Claimant/Applicant

and

Defendant/Respondent

_____

INJUNCTION ORDER

_____

If you do not obey this order you will be guilty of contempt of court and you may be sent to prison

On the   of   20   the court considered an application for an injunction

The Court ordered that [The name of the person the order is directed to]
be forbidden (whether by himself or by instructing or encouraging any other person) [*The terms of the restraining order. If the respondent is a limited company, delete the words in brackets and insert 'whether by its servants, agents, officers or otherwise'*]

This order shall remain in force until (the   of
20   at   o'clock
unless before then it is revoked by a further order of the court

And it is ordered that [*The name of the person the order is directed to*]

shall [*The terms of any orders requiring acts to be done*]

on or before [*Enter time (and place) as ordered*]

It is further ordered that [*The terms of any other orders costs etc*]

Notice of further hearing [*Use when the order is temporary or without notice otherwise delete*]

The court will re-consider the application and whether the order should continue at a further hearing at

on   the   day of   20   at   o'clock

If you do not attend at the time shown the court may make an injunction order in your absence.

You are entitled to apply to the court to re-consider the order before that day [*Delete if order made on notice*]

If you do not fully understand this application you should go to a Solicitor, Legal Advice Centre or a Citizens' Advice Bureau.

The Court office at
is open from 10am to 4pm. When corresponding with the court, address all forms and letters to the Court Manager and quote the claim number.

Injunction Order — Record of hearing   **Claim No** ....

On .... the .... day of .... 20 ....
Before H   Honour (District) Judge ....
The court was sitting at ....

The ☐ **Claimant** ☐ **Applicant** ☐ **Petitioner**   **(Name)** ....
was ☐ represented by Counsel
        ☐ represented by a Solicitor
        ☐ in person

The ☐ **Defendant** ☐ **Respondent**   **(Name)** ....
was ☐ represented by Counsel
        ☐ represented by a Solicitor
        ☐ in person
        ☐ did not appear having been given notice of this hearing
        ☐ not given notice of this hearing

The court read the written evidence in the witness statement/application notice of
☐ the Claimant/Applicant/Petitioner   dated
☐ the Defendant/Respondent   dated
And of .... dated ....
The court heard spoken evidence on oath from

....
....

The Claimant/Applicant/Petitioner gave an undertaking (through his counsel or solicitor) promising to pay any damages ordered by the court if it later decides that the Defendant/Respondent has suffered loss or damage as a result of this order.*

* Delete this paragraph if the court does not require the undertaking.

19.3.5   Form N117 (General form of undertaking): county court

IN THE [   ]COUNTY COURT   Claim No

BETWEEN

Claimant/Applicant

and

Defendant/Respondent

This form is to be used only for an undertaking not for an injunction.

On the   day of   20   ,

[Name of the person giving the undertaking]

[appeared in person] [was represented by Solicitor/Counsel]

and gave an undertaking to the Court promising [Set out terms of undertaking]

And to be bound by these promises until [*Give the date and time or event when the undertaking will expire*]

The Court explained to [*Name of the person giving undertaking*]
the meaning of his undertaking and the consequences of failing to keep his promises,

And the Court accepted his undertaking [*The judge may direct that the party who gives the undertaking shall personally sign the statement overleaf*] [and [*if so ordered*] directed that [*Name of the person giving undertaking*] should sign the statement overleaf].

And the Court ordered that [*set out any other directions given by the court*]

Dated

Important Notice

To [*Name of the person giving undertaking*]

of [*Address of the person giving undertaking*]

- You may be sent to prison for contempt of court if you break the promises that you have given to the Court.

- If you do not understand anything in this document you should go to a Solicitor, Legal Advice Centre or a Citizens' Advice Bureau.

The Court office at
is open from 10 am to 4 pm. Monday to Friday. When corresponding with the court, address all forms and letters to the Court Manager and quote the claim number.

The Court may direct that the party who gives the undertaking shall personally sign the statement below.

Statement

I understand the undertaking that I have given, and that if I break any of my promises to the Court I may be sent to prison for contempt of Court.

Signed

19.3.6 Commentary

19.3.6.1 The injunction order (form N16)

You can see that very much the same ground is covered by the county court form, but in a different way.

In the county court a prohibitory order is made in terms that the respondent 'is forbidden' to do something, and a mandatory order in terms that the respondent 'shall' do something.

The problems of 'servants or agents' and 'causing or permitting' are dealt with in brackets at the start of the order itself. For individuals the phrase is 'whether by himself or by instructing or encouraging any other person'; for companies the phrase is 'whether by its servants, agents, officers or otherwise'.

The duration of the order is dealt with in a separate paragraph, and notice of the return date is also given a paragraph to itself.

The section headed 'Injunction Order — Record of Hearing' is on the back of the form and enables a lot of formalities to be dealt with by form-filling and box-ticking.

At the end of the form appears the undertaking as to damages, in slightly different terms to the High Court version.

19.3.6.2 The form of undertaking (form N117)

You will see that form N16 includes only the standard undertaking as to damages. If the court requires any further undertakings to be given, or if it accepts undertakings from the respondent rather than make an injunction order, such undertakings must be given in form N117. This includes any procedural undertakings given when the application is made before the issue of a claim form and/or without notice.

Form N117 itself is self-explanatory and needs no further commentary.

19.4 Documents for application with notice in the High Court

19.4.1 Details on claim form

The following would be appropriate for the section of the claim form requiring brief details of the claim and the remedies sought. The particulars of claim will be found in **12.13**.

IN THE HIGH COURT OF JUSTICE   Claim No 2004 HC 4243
QUEEN'S BENCH DIVISION

BETWEEN

WUNDACOLA PLC   Claimants

and

HEINZ BERNSTEIN   Defendant

The claim is for:

(1) An order that the Defendant must not enter into or continue in the employment of Supacola Limited before 1st October 2007.

(2) An order that the Defendant must not divulge to Supacola Limited, their officers, employees or agents or to any other person the recipe or manufacturing process of a

soft drink known as Apricola or any other secret recipe or manufacturing process of the Claimants.

(3) Further or alternatively damages for breach of contract.

(4) Interest on those damages under section 35A of the Supreme Court Act 1981.

19.4.2 Application notice (Form N244)

IN THE HIGH COURT OF JUSTICE   Claim No 2004 HC 4243
QUEEN'S BENCH DIVISION

BETWEEN

WUNDACOLA PLC   Claimants/Applicants

and

HEINZ BERNSTEIN   Defendant/Respondent

APPLICATION NOTICE

We, Randall & Randall, on behalf of the Claimants

intend to apply for an order (a draft of which is attached) that

the Defendant must not breach the restrictive covenants in his contract of employment with the Claimants

because

the Defendant has threatened to do so, or is already doing so.

We wish to rely on:

the attached witness statement of Ernest Bellingham Coke.

Dated etc.

19.4.3 Draft injunction order

IN THE HIGH COURT OF JUSTICE   Claim No 2004 HC 4243
QUEEN'S BENCH DIVISION

MR JUSTICE [   ]

[*Date*]

BETWEEN

WUNDACOLA PLC   Claimants/Applicants

and

HEINZ BERNSTEIN   Defendant/Respondent

DRAFT ORDER FOR AN INJUNCTION

IMPORTANT

NOTICE TO THE RESPONDENT ... etc

An Application was made on 15th October 2004 by Counsel for the Applicants to the Judge and was attended by Counsel for the Respondent. The Judge heard the Application and read the Witness Statement listed in Schedule 1 and accepted the undertaking in Schedule 2 at the end of this Order.

IT IS ORDERED that:

THE INJUNCTION

1.   Until after final judgment in this Claim the Respondent must not:

(1) Enter into or continue in the employment of Supacola Limited before 1st October 2007.

(2) Divulge to Supacola Limited, their officers, employees or agents or to any other person the recipe or manufacturing process of a soft drink known as Apricola or any other secret recipe or manufacturing processes of the Applicants.

COSTS OF THE APPLICATION

2.   The Respondent shall pay the Applicants the costs of this Application.

VARIATION OR DISCHARGE OF THIS ORDER ... etc

NAME AND ADDRESS OF APPLICANTS' SOLICITORS ... etc

INTERPRETATION OF THIS ORDER ... etc

THE EFFECT OF THIS ORDER ... etc

SCHEDULE 1

Witness statements

The Judge read the following witness statement before making this Order:

Statement of Ernest Bellingham Coke dated 9th October 2004.

SCHEDULE 2

Undertaking given to the Court by the Applicants

If the Court later finds that this Order has caused loss to the Respondent, and decides that the Respondent should be compensated for that loss, the Applicants will comply with any Order the Court may make.

19.4.4 Commentary

19.4.4.1   Details on claim form

The remedies sought must appear on the claim form. If one or more of the remedies is an injunction then the injunction(s) sought must appear. The nature of the injunction must therefore be stated. It may not be strictly necessary to set out the full terms of the injunction as you have drafted them, but once you have drafted them, why set them out any differently? Here the remedies sought are two injunctions, damages and interest.

The actual drafting of the injunctions is dealt with below, in relation to the order itself.

19.4.4.2   Application notice

Note that the claimants have now also become the applicants and the defendant the respondent. This application notice follows the form of N244. Since the draft order is attached, and referred to, it is suggested that there is no need in the application notice to set out the full terms of the order sought. Therefore the order is described broadly but not drafted. This document is very straightforward to draft.

19.4.4.3   Injunction order

See also the commentary in **19.3.3**.

For learning and assessment purposes, if drafting the relevant bits to be inserted into the approved form, the standard parts of the order can be abbreviated as they are in this example.

This is an order on an application with notice, so the introduction makes it clear that both sides were represented by counsel.

The injunction itself must be drafted with all the precision and clarity you can achieve. This is the High Court, so the prohibitory order is drafted in terms that the respondent 'must not'. It is only an interim injunction, so it must be limited in time: 'until after final judgment'.

Injunction (1). The applicants are unsure whether the respondent actually has started employment with Supacola. If he has, an order saying that he must not 'enter into the employment' of Supacola would be useless — it would not prevent him continuing in it. On the other hand, if he has not yet commenced this employment, an order that he must not continue in it would not necessarily prevent him signing a contract of employment. So we need 'enter into or continue in' if the order is to be effective. But the order must be limited in time. The covenant is only for three years after the termination of the respondent's employment with Wundacola. If the draft order went beyond that period, the claimants would be asking for more than their legal entitlement. So without the words 'before 1st October 2007' the judge could not make the order.

Injunction (2). The act that must be prevented can be specified by a single verb 'divulge'. Here it is 'what' and 'to whom' that needs careful thought. Supacola is a company. If the respondent was only prevented from divulging secrets to the company he would arguably still be free to divulge them to individual representatives of the company. So the addition of 'their officers, employees or agents' is essential. But that still does not give the claimants their full entitlement. The respondent agreed not to divulge secrets to *anyone*. So for complete protection add 'or to any other person'. Why not simply order the respondent not to divulge the secret 'to anyone', making no reference to Supacola? Because the immediate threat is in respect of Supacola, so you want to name them to be sure that the respondent will understand what he must not do.

Similar reasoning applies to the definition of *what* the respondent must not divulge. The recipe of Apricola is what the applicants fear he will divulge imminently, so should be specified. But he also promised not to divulge any other secret recipe, so include 'any other' as well. 'Recipe or manufacturing process' is what appears in the contract (see **12.13**) so use these words. But note that he never agreed not to divulge *any* recipe or manufacturing process, only a *secret* recipe *of the applicants*, so these words must appear, or the draft goes beyond the applicants' legal entitlement.

The costs order is what the applicants are asking for, though they may well not get a final costs order.

The witness statement referred to appears in the next chapter at **20.6**.

19.5   Alternative drafts

19.5.1   Application without notice

If the order in the above case were sought without notice, and before the issue of the claim form, it would read as follows:

IN THE HIGH COURT OF JUSTICE   Claim No 2004 HC 4243
QUEEN'S BENCH DIVISION

MR JUSTICE [   ]

[*Date*]

BETWEEN

WUNDACOLA PLC   <u>Applicants</u>

and

HEINZ BERNSTEIN   <u>Respondent</u>

<u>the Claimant and Defendant in an Intended Claim</u>

DRAFT ORDER FOR AN INJUNCTION

IMPORTANT

NOTICE TO THE RESPONDENT ... etc

An Application was made on the 15th October 2004 by Counsel for Wundacola PLC (who are to be the Claimants in a Claim against Heinz Bernstein) to the Judge who heard the Application supported by the witness statement listed in Schedule 1 and accepted the undertakings in Schedule 2 at the end of this Order.

IT IS ORDERED that:

<u>THE INJUNCTION</u>

1.   Up to and including [*date*] ('the Return Date') the Respondent must not:

(1) Enter into or continue in the employment of Supacola Limited before 1st October 2007.

(2) Divulge to Supacola Limited, their officers, employees or agents or to any other person the recipe or manufacturing process of a soft drink known as Apricola or any other secret recipe or manufacturing processes of the Applicants.

<u>COSTS OF APPLICATION</u>

2.   The costs of this application are reserved.

VARIATION OR DISCHARGE OF THIS ORDER ... etc

NAME AND ADDRESS OF APPLICANTS' SOLICITORS ... etc

INTERPRETATION OF THIS ORDER ... etc

THE EFFECT OF THIS ORDER ... etc

SCHEDULE 1

Witness statements

The Judge read the following witness statement before making this Order:

Statement of Ernest Bellingham Coke made on 9th October 2004.

SCHEDULE 2

Undertakings given to the Court by the Applicants

(1) If the Court later finds that this Order has caused loss to the Respondent, and decides that the Respondent should be compensated for that loss, the Applicants will comply with any Order the Court may make.

(2) As soon as practicable the Applicants will issue and serve on the Respondent a Claim Form in the form of the draft produced to the Court and initialled by the Judge claiming appropriate remedies together with this Order.

(3) As soon as practicable the Applicants will serve on the Respondent an Application Notice for the Return Date together with a copy of the written evidence and exhibits containing the evidence relied on by the Applicants.

19.5.2   Draft application for Form N16A

If the order in the above case were sought in the county court, the applicants would apply using Form N16A (General form of application for injunction) instead of Form N244. It would look like this:

IN THE MAYOR'S AND CITY OF LONDON COUNTY COURT   Case No MY4/42430

BETWEEN

WUNDACOLA PLC   Claimants/Applicants

and

HEINZ BERNSTEIN   Defendant/Respondent

By application in pending proceedings.

This application raises no issues under the Human Rights Act 1998.

The Applicants Wundacola plc apply to the court for an injunction in the following terms:

That the Respondent Heinz Bernstein be forbidden (whether by himself or by instructing or encouraging any other person) to:

(1) enter into or continue in the employment of Supacola Limited before 1st October 2007; and

(2) divulge to Supacola Limited, their officers, employees or agents or to anyone else the recipe or manufacturing process of a soft drink known as Apricola or any other secret recipes or manufacturing processes of the Applicants.

And that the Respondent pay the Applicants' costs of today.

The grounds of this application are set out in the written evidence of Ernest Bellingham Coke signed on 9th October 2004. This written evidence is served with this application.

This application etc ...

19.5.3   Draft order in the County Court

If the order in the above case were sought in the county court, the draft order would look like this:

IN THE MAYOR'S AND CITY OF LONDON COUNTY COURT   Claim No MY4/42430

ISSUED ON ...

BETWEEN

WUNDACOLA PLC   <u>Claimants/Applicants</u>

and

HEINZ BERNSTEIN   <u>Defendant/Respondent</u>

DRAFT INJUNCTION ORDER

If you do not obey ... etc.

On 15th October 2004 the court considered an application for an injunction.

The court ordered that Heinz Bernstein is forbidden (whether by himself or by instructing or encouraging any other person) to:

(1) enter into or continue in the employment of Supacola Limited before 1st October 2007; and

(2) divulge to Supacola Limited, their officers, employees or agents or to anyone else the recipe or manufacturing process of a soft drink known as Apricola or any other secret recipes or manufacturing processes of the Applicants.

This order shall remain in force until further order of the court.

It is further ordered that Heinz Bernstein pay the Applicants' costs of today.

etc.

19.5.4   Commentary

19.5.4.1   High Court application without notice

By following the commentaries in **19.3.3.2** and **19.4.4.3** you can see how this example has been drafted. The form contains no paragraph relating to costs, so the costs order is inserted at the end of the injunction order. On a without notice application 'costs reserved' is the only likely order. The terms of the order are unchanged except for the duration of it. The expected additional undertakings are included.

19.5.4.2   Form N16A

Before Woolf, N16A was the standard form of injunction application in the county court. Although N244 has now been introduced, PD 4 says that N16A will continue to be used. It is unclear whether this means it *must* be used or only *may* be used. This Manual assumes the former. County court terminology is used in accordance with **19.3.4**. For learning and assessment purposes, the abbreviation 'this application etc' is acceptable.

19.5.4.3   County court order

In the light of all the previous examples this example should be self-explanatory. For learning and assessment purposes, the abbreviations are acceptable.

19.6 A further example

19.6.1 Draft injunction order

<u>IN THE LLANELLI COUNTY COURT</u>   Claim No LI4/29661

ISSUED ON ...

BETWEEN

PETER POE   <u>Claimant/Applicant</u>

and

(1) SANDRA ELKINGTON
(2) PAUL HOUNSELL   <u>Defendants/Respondents</u>

DRAFT INJUNCTION ORDER

If you do not obey ... etc.

On 28th June 2004 the court considered an application for an injunction.

The court ordered that the Respondents Sandra Elkington and Paul Hounsell and each of them be forbidden (whether by themselves or by instructing or encouraging any other person) from:

(1) using any violence against the Applicant or his son Edgar;

(2) harassing, threatening or pestering the Applicant or his son Edgar;

(3) entering or loitering on the Applicant's land known as The Otters, Ruddocks Road, Llanelli, ('The Otters'), except when exercising their right of way on foot only along the pathway through The Otters known as Otters Lane ('their Right of Way');

(4) leaving the gate between Otters Lane and Ruddocks Road ('the Gate') open, or touching or interfering with it, except when opening and closing it in order to exercise their Right of Way;

(5) attaching any padlock, chain or other form of restraint to the Gate, or leaving it so attached;

(6) causing or permitting any dog under their control to enter any part of The Otters except in the exercise of their Right of Way, and then under full control and restraint;

(7) driving or wheeling any motorcycle or other vehicle across any part of The Otters, including Otters Lane;

(8) causing or permitting any dog under their control to bark continually on their premises at Crewe House, Ruddocks Road, Llanelli ('Crewe House') or on Otters Lane;

(9) starting or running any motorcycle or other engine in or at Crewe House;

(10) placing or leaving any skip or other obstruction on Otters Lane or any other part of The Otters.

This order shall remain in force until further order of the court.

And it is ordered that Sandra Elkington and Paul Hounsell shall:

(11) immediately remove the padlock and chain from the Gate;

(12) remove the skip from Otters Lane within 48 hours.

It is further ordered that Sandra Elkington and Paul Hounsell pay the Applicant's costs of today.

etc.

19.6.2   Commentary

This case is new. To understand the order you need to know the facts, which you will find in the written evidence in support of this injunction application (see **20.7**).

The abbreviations in the formal parts of this order are acceptable for drafting purposes.

Note the words 'and each of them' in the first sentence of the order. The standard High Court order makes these words unnecessary, but not the county court form. Without these words it is arguable that the order only applies to the respondents acting jointly, not individually.

There are a lot of parts to this order, designed to put a stop to all the various kinds of anti-social behaviour detailed in the affidavit. It is clearer drafting to enumerate this in a list like this, rather than to try and run it all together in longer sentences. There are ten prohibitory orders and two mandatory orders.

Order (1). There is evidence of assault, but 'assault' is not the best word to use in the order — it has a technical legal meaning, and will not be so readily understood by the defendants as 'violence'. Only the applicant and Edgar are protected, because only they have been assaulted so far. If you think you could persuade the judge that by inference Mrs Poe is at risk as well, then you could add her.

Order (2). The old word used to be 'molesting', but again it is not readily understood. The modern formulation is 'harassing, threatening or pestering' which covers both molestation and some forms of assault.

Order (3). This order is to prevent trespass. This has largely taken the form of loitering, but the applicant is entitled to prevent any trespass, so 'entering or loitering' is the most complete formulation. This is the first mention of the applicant's land, so its address must be given, and to save repetition a definition ('The Otters') is added. The exception is important. The respondents have a right of way, so this order could not be made without the exception, because it would go beyond the applicant's legal entitlement. The exception should however not be any broader than it needs to be, so the limitation 'on foot only' is included.

Order (4). The order needs to prevent the respondents doing anything untoward to the gate, which first of all needs to be identified and defined. The padlock is dealt with separately in the next order; this order deals with leaving it open, or doing anything else to it. The only lawful reason the respondent could have for ever touching the gate is the exercise of their right of way, so it is not unreasonable to forbid 'touching or interfering' with it, provided the exception is included. Again the exception prevents the injunction being too wide and so unorderable.

Order (5). The respondents have used a padlock and chain to fix the gate shut, but obviously 'any other form of restraint' should be added or the order would be ineffective. We need both 'attaching' and 'leaving it so attached'. If the chain is on at the moment the order is served, then forbidding them only to attach it would be useless. If it is not attached at that moment, then 'leaving it attached' would not prevent them re-attaching it.

Order (6). Care needs to be taken not to make this order too wide. Clearly the respondents cannot reasonably be ordered to keep any dog off The Otters, only their dog. But 'their dog' would be too narrow — they might borrow another one. So 'any dog under their control' is what is required. They also cannot be made responsible for any unpreventable behaviour of their dog. So they are forbidden from 'causing or permitting' it to enter The Otters — then only deliberate acts on their part are forbidden. Again an exception has to be made for the right of way, which must include a right to walk a dog along Otters Lane. But it is reasonable to insist that in such circumstances the dog should be under 'full control and restraint'.

Order (7). We now come on to the motorcycle. They have no right of way other than on foot, so the applicant is entitled to an order that forbids any method of moving a motorcycle across his land, and 'driving or wheeling' are the only obvious methods. You could add 'carrying' if the motorcycle is light enough! The applicant is entitled to expand the order to include any other form of vehicle as well. Since there is no right of way to preserve, 'any part of The Otters' is appropriate, and to make the point absolutely clear 'including Otters Lane' is added.

Order (8). Back to the dog, so 'causing or permitting' and 'any dog under their control' are needed for the same reasons as in order (6). Forbidding barking altogether is probably unfair, so 'continually' is added. Although the evidence is that the barking has been only in the garden, the nuisance could quite easily be committed at a window or in Otters Lane as well, so broaden the scope of the order.

Order (9). The noise of the motorcycle is what Mr Poe calls 'revving' or 'testing'. Maybe these words would do, but 'starting or running' is probably more accurate. For obvious reasons the type of engine forbidden is not limited to motorcycle engines.

Order (10). The skip is in Otters Lane at the moment, so we want to prevent the respondents leaving it there, but if we do not add 'placing' it there as well, they could put it back after removing it. Broaden the order also to include not only a skip but any other form of obstruction, and not only Otters Lane but any other part of The Otters. The reasons behind this will be obvious from the earlier commentary.

The duration of the order must be specified, so 'until further order' is added at the end, to include all the prohibitory orders.

Orders (11) and (12). Then come the two mandatory orders. These are simpler to draft, since they need to specify only what the respondents must do, and by when. The time is essential: suggest whatever is reasonable in all the circumstances. There is no good reason why they should not remove the padlock and chain immediately, but it would be too much to demand the immediate removal of the skip, so a reasonable period is given.

The application is for costs in any event. If the injunctions are granted and obeyed, it is unlikely that the applicant will return to court for a final injunction or a damages claim.

19.7 Exercise

For the purpose of this exercise it is 2.00 pm on Wednesday 1 December 2004. Your instructing solicitor was able to jot down some notes from an interview with the client, which you have received by fax with instructions to draft the terms of an order to be sought this afternoon without notice and before the issue of a claim form.

Notes of interview with Ronnie Rowland (RR):

Need to get into Victoria Sports Centre, West Molesworth by 6.00 pm this evening at the latest or boxing match cannot go ahead.

Fight due to take place next Monday. All sold out. To be televised by Western TV Limited on cable.

Stage and seating contractors turned up at 9.00 am this morning but were unable to get in. Lighting contractors also unable to get in at 11.00 am.

Period of hire 1 to 7 December inclusive. Contract dated and signed 11 September 2004 with West Molesworth Borough Council. Council own hall. Contract in very short form, £10,000, one week's hire, RR sole users of hall during that period, though council employees allowed to use their offices, caretaker and technical advice available, council provide electricity. Made copy of contract.

RR's council contact is Will Isaacs (WI), i/c premises letting. First hint of trouble came yesterday when WI telephoned RR to warn him that Council were meeting last night and on the agenda was a proposal to ban the fight. Council policy is not to permit 'blood sports' in the borough, and many members think of boxing as a blood sport. Council notorious for maladministration and loony policies. Criticised severely in administrative court last week over housing policy.

RR cannot understand why it's come so late. Negotiated with WI in August/September. Told him the hire was for a boxing match. Council have known all along — no recent change in council.

Now locked into contracts with everyone else involved in the fight. Welsh flyweight champ Jonnie Pugg v Bonzo Jacks of Australia, £10,000 each. Contractors for stage and seating, lighting contractors, WTV exclusive TV rights £50,000. Audience all advance credit card bookings. Terrible administrative nightmare if had to refund all ticket money. Total loss if fight cancelled impossible to say but could be £100k, dubious if company (Ronnie Rowland Enterprises Ltd, RR is Chairman and MD) could survive.

Unable to gain further information yesterday. First news this morning when contractor rang to say hall locked and caretaker at hall refusing admission. Said the hall was closed until further notice for safety reasons, and he had instructions to allow no one into hall. He then left to go and turn off electricity and water. Same message two hours later from lighting contractor.

Telephoned WI. WI said council did vote to ban fight. Also voted to ban WTV in sympathy with employees on strike. Did not know anything about safety issue. Thought militant council staff quite likely to put up physical obstacles and difficulties should any attempt be made to enter or use hall.

Too late to organise fight anywhere else. If it doesn't go ahead on Monday, it'll be weeks before it can be re-organised, if at all.

RR very angry. Pays council council tax personally (£2,000 p.a.) and business rates (£10,000 p.a.) which are both very high.

6.00 pm is really a deadline. By working through the night it may be possible to catch up the lost hours but any later than that and the fight will not go ahead.

Written evidence

20.1 General

20.1.1 The barrister's involvement

The standard procedure in civil proceedings these days is for evidence to be presented first in written form. Witness statements must be served before trial and will stand as the witnesses' evidence in chief unless the judge orders otherwise. All interim applications must be supported by written evidence. It is very likely that the barrister in the case will be instructed to draft the key evidence, or may even advise that he or she should be instructed to do so.

20.1.2 Forms of written evidence

Written evidence, other than documentary exhibits, comes in four main forms: witness statements, affidavits, statements of case and application notices. A party can only rely on a statement of case or application notice as written evidence in proceedings other than at trial (eg in interim applications) and if it is verified by a statement of truth. However, it will be rare that a party will rely on a statement of case alone, or evidence on an application notice alone, because a statement of case does not generally contain enough evidence, and there is not enough room on the standard form of application notice except in the most straightforward of cases. So for the purposes of this chapter, written evidence means witness statements and affidavits.

20.1.3 When to use which form

Written evidence for use at trial will take the form of a witness statement, which will stand as the witness's evidence in chief unless the court orders otherwise (CPR, r 32.5(2)).

At proceedings other than at trial evidence should generally be in the form of a witness statement (CPR, r 32.6(1)). However, an affidavit must be used instead in certain circumstances (PD 32, para 1.4):

(a) Where required by an enactment, statutory instrument, rule, order or practice direction. The footnote to para 1.4 gives s 3(5)(a) of the Protection from Harassment Act 1997 as an example of where an affidavit is required by statute.

(b) In support of an application for a search order, freezing injunction, or an order requiring an occupier to permit another to enter his land.

(c) In any application for an order against anyone for alleged contempt of court.

However, there is nothing to stop a party using an affidavit if he so chooses, though he may not recover the additional cost of doing so (CPR, r 32.15). An affidavit is slightly more expensive than a witness statement because payment needs to be made to someone to administer the oath.

There is no essential difference between a witness statement and an affidavit. A witness statement must be verified by a statement of truth (PD 32, para 20); an affidavit must be sworn (and is sometimes known as a 'sworn statement'). The consequences of making a false statement in an affidavit and a witness statement are equally serious — proceedings may be brought against the person making the false statement for contempt of court (witness statement) or perjury (affidavit).

The person who swears an affidavit is called the 'deponent'. A deponent who is unable to swear an affidavit through lack of religious belief may instead make an affirmation. The differences are minimal, the status is the same.

The rules that relate to the form of witness statements and affidavits are separate, but so similar that we will take them together.

20.2 Rules about affidavits and witness statements

There are quite a lot of rules about the content and presentation of affidavits, witness statements and exhibits, found in PD 32. If some of the rules about presentation seem pernickety, bear in mind that in cases where there is a lot of documentation, the court must be able to identify each document clearly, easily and quickly.

(a) The witness statement/affidavit should have a full case heading: court, claim number and parties.

(b) In the top right-hand corner of the first page (and on the backsheet) of the witness statement/affidavit must appear:

    (i)   the party on whose behalf it is made;

    (ii)   the initials and surname of the witness/deponent;

    (iii) the number of the statement/affidavit in relation to that witness/deponent;

    (iv) the identifying initials and number of each exhibit referred to;

    (v)   the date the affidavit was sworn or the witness statement was made.

(c) The witness statement/affidavit must be expressed in the first person and should be as far as practicable in the witness's/deponent's own words.

(d) A witness statement must give the full name of the witness and his address. An affidavit must begin with the words: 'I (*full name*) of (*address*) state on oath ...'. For example, 'I, EDWARD WILLIAM JONES, of 27 Old Street, Barchester, Barset, STATE ON OATH:'.

An affirmation should use the words 'do solemnly and sincerely affirm' instead of 'state on oath'.

The address in each case should be the residential address, unless the witness/deponent is giving evidence in a professional, business or occupational capacity (eg, as an expert, or as the solicitor to one of the parties, or as a representative of a company) in which case the work address should be used, and the witness/deponent should also state the position he holds and the name of his firm or employer.

(e) A witness/deponent must give his occupation, or if he has none, his description.

(f) If the witness/deponent is a party to the proceedings, or an employee of a party to the proceedings, he must say so.

(g) It is usual and appropriate to deal with the requirements in (d), (e) and (f) above at the outset, in the first numbered paragraph. It would be usual to add at this stage (though this is not a rule) the purpose for which the evidence is being presented, eg, 'in connection with the events of 3rd March 2002' or 'in support of my application for an interim injunction'.

(h) The witness statement/affidavit should be divided into numbered paragraphs.

(i) All numbers, including dates, should be expressed in figures.

(j) The reference to any document mentioned should be given in the margin or in bold text.

(k) A witness statement/affidavit must indicate which of the statements in it are made from the witness's/deponent's own knowledge, and which are matters of information or belief (ie hearsay evidence), and give the source for any matters of information or belief. The usual way of doing this is for the witness/deponent to say in the first paragraph something like this: 'The matters set out below are within my own knowledge, except where I indicate to the contrary.'

Wherever the witness/deponent states facts not within his personal knowledge this must be made clear, by the use of some phrase such as 'I have been told by Mr Smith and believe that ...' or 'I have been advised by my solicitors and believe that ...'.

(l) It is usually convenient for the witness statement/affidavit to follow the chronological sequence of events or matters dealt with; each paragraph should as far as possible be confined to a distinct portion of the subject. 'It is usually convenient' are the words of the rule, which presumably means that you should do so unless there is good reason not to. Actually, it is not uncommon for there to be good reason to break chronological order (see **20.4.2.2** below).

(m) Exhibits should be introduced in witness statements in this form: 'I refer to the (*description of exhibit*) marked "EWJ1"'. Exhibits in affidavits should be introduced in this form: 'There is now shown to me marked "EWJ1" the (*description of exhibit*)'.

The reference to the exhibit is composed of the initials of the witness/deponent and the exhibit number. If the witness/deponent has made more than one statement/affidavit with exhibits, the numbering should not start again with the second statement/affidavit, but run on consecutively.

(n) Exhibits may consist of more than one document, bundled together, in which case they must be in chronological order and the front page must be a list of the documents in the exhibit, giving dates. Correspondence *must* be bundled into a single exhibit in this way. In the case of exhibits to an affidavit, it saves costs to bundle documents together — when the oath is administered there is a small extra charge for each exhibit. When referring to an item in a bundled exhibit, the witness should say: 'I refer to the letter dated 15th July 2004 at pages 10–11 of exhibit "EWJ1".'

(o) An affidavit must finish with the 'jurat' (possibly the only Latin word to have found its way into the CPR?!). The jurat is the statement which authenticates the affidavit — the equivalent of the statement of truth. It must be signed by the deponent and the person before whom the affidavit is sworn, whose address must be given and whose name and qualification must be set out under his signature. An affirmation is 'affirmed' rather than 'sworn'. The jurat must not be on a separate page, it must follow on from the text of the affidavit. So if your computer tries to put a page break just before the jurat, you must break the page at an earlier point.

There are actually even more rules of an even more pernickety nature about the typing, labelling, bundling, page numbering and filing of witness statements, affidavits and exhibits. See PD 32.

20.3 The General Council of the Bar's guidelines

The following guidelines are extracted from a document published by the Bar Council 'Guidance on Preparation of Witness Statements — Preparing Witness Statements for Use in Civil Proceedings — Dealings with Witnesses — Guidance for Members of the Bar'. It is written primarily to concern witness statements for use at trial, so needs to be understood in that context.

Witness statements

3.   The cardinal principle that needs to be kept in mind when drafting or settling a witness statement is that, when the maker enters the witness box, he or she will swear or affirm that the evidence to be given will be the truth, the *whole truth* and nothing but the truth. In most civil trials almost the first question in chief (and not infrequently the last) will be to ask the witness to confirm, to the best of his belief, the accuracy of the witness statement. It is therefore critical that the statement is one that accurately reflects, to the best of Counsel's ability, the witness's evidence.

4.   Witnesses often misunderstand the function of those drafting and settling witness statements. The function of Counsel is to understand the relevant evidence that a witness can give and to assist the witness to express that evidence in the witness's own words. It is important it is made clear to the witness (by reminder to the professional client or the witness, if seen by Counsel) that the statement once approved is the witness's statement. Ultimately it is the witness's responsibility to ensure that the evidence he gives is truthful. It is good practice to remind witnesses expressly of this from time to time, especially where Counsel is assisting the witness to formulate in his own words a particular aspect of the evidence or putting forward a particular piece of drafting for the witness's consideration (which is expressly permitted by the proviso to Rule 704 of the Code of Conduct).

5.   It is not Counsel's duty to vet the accuracy of a witness's evidence. We all may doubt the veracity of our clients and witnesses occasionally. Counsel is, of course, entitled and it may often be appropriate to draw to the witness's attention other evidence which appears to conflict with what the witness is saying and is entitled to indicate that a Court may find a particular piece of evidence difficult to accept. But if the witness maintains the evidence, it should be recorded in the witness statement. If it is decided to call the witness, it will be for the Court to judge the correctness of the witness's evidence.

6.   It follows that the statement:

(i)   Must accurately reflect the witness's evidence. Rule 704 of the Code of Conduct states:

A barrister must not devise facts which will assist in advancing the lay client's case and must not draft any ... witness statement [or] affidavit ... containing:

(d)   in the case of a witness statement or affidavit any statement of fact other than the evidence which in substance according to his instructions the barrister reasonably believes the witness would give if the evidence contained in the affidavit or witness statement were being given in oral evidence;

provided that nothing in this paragraph shall prevent a barrister drafting a document containing specific factual statements or contentions included by the barrister subject to confirmation of their accuracy by the lay client or witness.

(ii)   Must not contain any statement which Counsel knows the witness does not believe to be true. Nor should the witness be placed under any pressure to provide other than a truthful account of his evidence.

(iii) Must contain all the evidence which a witness could reasonably be expected to give in answer to those questions which would be asked of him in examination in chief. The witness statement should not be drafted or edited so that it no longer fairly reflects the answers which the witness would be expected to give in response to oral examination in chief in accordance with the witness's oath or affirmation. Although it is not the function of a witness statement to answer such questions as might be put in cross-examination, great care should be exercised when excluding any material which is thought to be unhelpful to the party calling the witness and no material should be excluded which might render the statement anything other than the truth, the whole truth and nothing but the truth. While it is permissible to confine the scope of examination in chief to part only of the evidence which a witness could give, that is always subject to Counsel's overriding duty to assist the Court in the administration of justice and not to deceive or knowingly or recklessly to mislead the Court (Rule 302 of the Code of Conduct). Consequently, it would be improper to exclude material whose omission would render untrue or misleading anything which remains in the statement. It would also be improper to include fact A while excluding fact B, if evidence-in-chief containing fact A but excluding fact B could not have been given consistently with the witness's promise to tell the truth, the whole truth and nothing but the truth. Whether it is wise and in the client's interest in any given case to exclude unfavourable material which can properly be excluded is a matter of judgment.

(iv)   Save for formal matters and uncontroversial facts, should be expressed if practicable in the witness's own words. This is especially important when the statement is dealing with the critical factual issues in the case — eg the accident or the disputed conversation. Thus the statement should reflect the witness's own description of events. It should not be drafted or edited so as to massage or obscure the witness's real evidence.

(v)   Must be confined to admissible evidence that the witness can give, including permissible hearsay. Inadmissible hearsay, comment and argument should be excluded.

(vi)   Should be succinct and exclude irrelevant material. Unnecessary elaboration is to be avoided. It is not the function of witness statements to serve as a commentary on the documents in the trial bundles. Nor are they intended to serve as another form of written argument.

7.   Sometimes it becomes apparent, after a witness statement has been served, that the witness's recollection has altered. This may happen if the witness sees or hears how another witness puts the facts in a witness statement served by another party. Where Counsel learns that the witness has materially changed his evidence—

(i)   He should consider with, and if necessary advise, his professional or BarDirect client whether, in the circumstances, a correction to the original statement needs to be made in order to avoid another party being unfairly misled.

(ii)   Where a correction to the original statement is appropriate, this should be done by recording the changed evidence in an additional witness statement and serving it on the other parties (and if appropriate filing it at court). If this is impracticable, eg because it occurs very shortly before the hearing, the other parties should be informed of the change immediately and the statement should be corrected at an early stage in court.

(iii) The underlying principle is that it is improper for a litigant to mislead the court or another party to the litigation.

(iv)   If a lay or BarDirect client refuses to accept Counsel's advice that disclosure of a correction should be made, Counsel's duty is to withdraw from further acting for the client.

20.4 Drafting written evidence

20.4.1 General principles

Witness statements and affidavits contain evidence. Each witness statement/affidavit (with a few exceptions) is the written testimony of a single witness. There are accordingly no constraints on what may be said or how it should be expressed, except the obvious ones that the evidence should be (a) admissible, (b) relevant, (c) clearly expressed, (d) complete, and (e) set out in a logical way.

Written evidence will normally therefore coincide with what a witness could or would say in oral testimony.

Barristers repeatedly say that a witness statement or affidavit is one of the things that requires the most care in the drafting of it. This is not surprising, because you are drafting the evidence in support of your case or application, and the case or application is won or lost in most cases on the evidence. You need to ensure that you have got your evidence just right to maximise the chances of winning the case or being granted the remedy you seek.

But remember the ethical issue: you are strictly limited in what you include in a witness statement or affidavit to what the witness/deponent can actually say he believes to be true. There must be no element of embellishment, or helping the evidence along inserted by the person drafting the statement, which must coincide in terms of content with what the witness himself would have drafted. Only in terms of presentation do you have any leeway.

However, there is a distinction between witness statements intended for use at trial and witness statements or affidavits intended for use other than at trial, eg to support an interim application. At trial the judge will make his decision based on the evidence and nothing else. If the claimant proves his case, the judge has no alternative but to find in his favour and grant the remedy sought. It follows that the evidence should be presented in a factual, dispassionate, objective way. It may need to contain a lot more precise detail than would be necessary in a witness statement in support of an interim application. However, on an interim application a judge has a discretion. He needs to be *persuaded* to grant the remedy sought. It follows that the written evidence may need to contain an element of persuasion, of argument, of inference, of advocacy.

20.4.2 An approach to drafting written evidence

The rules and conventions set out above will get you through the heading, the introduction and the first paragraph or two of the witness statement/affidavit. But thereafter you are absolutely on your own. There are no formalities, conventions or requirements to take you any further. The draft must come out of your head. Only in very formal situations is there a precedent which you can adapt.

But all written evidence can be drafted by taking the same basic approach. Ask yourself four questions:

(1) What needs to be proved to get my client what he wants or enable him to win the case?

(2) From the instructions I have, what can this witness say that will go to prove what needs to be proved?

(3) How shall I organise that material and set it out?

(4) How can what needs to be said be best expressed?

Then you can draft the evidence, remembering at all times that your objective at trial is to establish a case clearly and thoroughly and in the case of an interim application is to persuade a tribunal why a remedy should be granted or refused. It follows that you must seek to be as clear and complete and/or as persuasive as you can be.

20.4.2.1   Steps (1) and (2)

Steps (1) and (2) are to do with analysis — working out what the necessary material is. This can only be done by reference to your knowledge of the case, the issues in it and your client's instructions. You will be clear and persuasive if you get in everything that needs to go in, and leave out nothing of importance. You will not be clear or persuasive if you put in a lot of irrelevant material that clouds rather than clarifies the true nature of the case.

20.4.2.2   Step (3)

Step (3) is to do with structure and story-telling. It is most unlikely that your witness statement or affidavit will be persuasive if the evidence is all jumbled up, or if the reader is given too much information at one time, or in the wrong order. There is almost certainly a story to be told: this story should be told clearly and coherently, one step at a time.

It is likely that a well-told story will put events in their chronological order, at least to a considerable extent. This is almost always true in the case of a witness statement for use at trial. But beware of sticking rigidly to chronological order in written evidence for use other than at trial. There will be many occasions when this results in a story that is hard to follow. There may for example be several parallel strands to the case, which need to be clearly separated if they are to be properly identified. Chronological order might weave them all together in a most confusing way. There are also many instances where you want to begin with the central events, those which are the foundation of the application, and then go back to the background that sheds light on these events. If you begin with the background events, chronologically, it may be many paragraphs before the reader will have any idea what the application is actually all about!

20.4.2.3   Step (4)

What you are drafting is supposedly the words of the witness/deponent, saying what he would say in a witness box, and doing so in his own way. Giving oral evidence, a witness would describe events from his own point of view, putting his perspective and interpretation on them. In the witness statement or affidavit, you should try to achieve the same result. Do not have your witness/deponent using technical legal language or argument which he would not personally understand or use.

If your witness/deponent has in his instructions used a particularly telling or vivid phrase, you may wish to adopt that phrase. It is generally good to use the deponent's own words where it is appropriate to do so. But do not carry this to extremes. It does not look good if you attempt to 'characterise' the witness/deponent, as a novelist or playwright would do! If your witness/deponent comes over as somewhat inarticulate, do not draft the witness statement in an inarticulate way! If they use a lot of exaggerated and angry words, do not make them sound cantankerous. More often than not you are using your words and phrases to say what the witness/deponent wishes to say.

Apart from this, in the case of a witness statement for use at trial, the only vital thing is clarity. But in the case of a witness statement or affidavit for use in an interim application, it is in your choice of words that persuasiveness really comes into play. Remember that you are not simply trying to present the evidence in a cold detached way.

Because the witness statement/affidavit is seeking to persuade a tribunal to grant or refuse relief, it follows that there is an element of argument and advocacy in the drafting as well. Do not just say what happened — you can make the witness/deponent describe the effect of what happened as well. The witness statement/affidavit can draw inferences from the evidence; it can set out the events and then go on to say what view of those events the witness/deponent takes, thereby inviting the court to make the same inferences and take the same view.

But a word of caution is necessary. It is of course possible to go too far. Your witness statement/affidavit will cease to be persuasive in any way if what comes over is seen to be an exaggeration, or if unreasonable inferences are drawn, or if the language used is too colourful or emotive. You must maintain your lawyer's restraint and objectivity at all times. A very strong case always looks stronger if it is couched in moderate and dispassionate terms.

20.4.2.4   Other requirements

When a witness statement/affidavit is to be used in an application without notice, it must contain 'adverse facts', that is pieces of factual evidence which do not support, or even undermine the applicant's case, but which must be put before the court if it is to be apprised of all the relevant facts. It must also contain evidence to show why the matter is so urgent that formal notice cannot be given to the respondent.

A witness statement/affidavit in support of an application for an interim injunction should seek to show why damages would not be an adequate remedy (unless the court is unlikely to be concerned about this, eg in cases of nuisance). It should also express the applicant's willingness to give any necessary undertakings, and if there is likely to be any doubt about it, should show that he has the means to comply with his undertaking as to damages if necessary.

20.5   Witness statement for use at trial

20.5.1   Witness statement

(See amended defence in **16.3**.)

Made on behalf of the Applicant
Witness: G. Esmond
1st Statement of Witness
Exhibits: None
Dated: 23 May 2004

IN THE COLCHESTER COUNTY COURT   Claim No CO4/01908

BETWEEN

(1) TASKER & HOLT LIMITED
(2) ISABEL ESMOND
(3) GEORGE ESMOND   Claimants

and

(1) MICHAEL LUMLEY
(2) THOMAS TUCKER   Defendants

WITNESS STATEMENT OF GEORGE ESMOND

1.   I live at 'Braeside', Stone Street, Mayfair and 'The Larches', Castlewood, and make this statement in connection with the accident which I was involved in on Saturday 8th July 2001. The contents are within my own knowledge.

2.   I am the Third Claimant in this action. I was born on the 19th August 1942. I was at the date of the accident and am now a director of a large number of advertising companies, but I have no connection with the First Claimant of which my wife is a director. I am married to the Second Claimant who was driving the First Claimant's car at the time of the accident.

3.   I have held a full driving licence for more than 30 years. When my wife and I go out in a car she normally drives as she is an extremely competent driver and is a more experienced driver than I am. So far as I am aware my wife had never had an accident before this occasion and has not had one since. Prior to the accident my wife had a series of powerful BMW motor vehicles. They all had the registration number TH 276 so I cannot recall exactly how long she had been using the red coupe which was involved in the accident but it was more than 2 years. At that time I had a company car which was a limited edition Jaguar motor vehicle which was considerably faster than the BMW. We also owned a Ferrari Testarossa which we tended to use only for driving abroad. My wife drove both those cars on occasions, but most of the time she drove the BMW coupe. She was therefore extremely familiar with the BMW car at the time of the accident.

4.   On the weekend of the accident we had travelled to our cottage near Castlewood. On the Saturday morning we went out shopping. We were returning to the cottage when the accident happened. My wife was driving and I was sitting in the front passenger seat.

5.   I note that it is alleged that I was not wearing my seat belt. That is not correct. I always wear a seat belt. My wife has always insisted that I wear a seat belt and would not have driven off if I had not been wearing it. I have known her refuse to start the car until a passenger puts on his or her seat belt. She would have noticed whether I was wearing the belt as there is a warning light on the dashboard of the car which is lit if anyone sits on the front seat but doesn't use the belt.

6.   I have a very clear recollection of the accident even though I was injured. As we were travelling towards Castlewood we used the A1006. We both know the road extremely well. We were the last car in a line of traffic travelling in the same direction. We were not in a hurry. The traffic slowed down. The car immediately in front of us was a Maestro, although I cannot now recall the colour of that car. I thought the Maestro stopped rather sharply. My wife slowed and stopped but did not have to brake sharply. I could see there were cars in front of the Maestro but I could not see why the cars stopped. Suddenly my wife allowed the BMW to creep forward slightly, turned the wheel to the off side and exclaimed 'Oh my God'. There was the most tremendous jolt from the rear and we shot forward onto the other side of the road. I saw a car on top of us which hit my door and spun us round. I then heard another loud crash.

7.   I am absolutely certain that there were three separate crashes in quick succession although everything happened very quickly. The BMW came to rest exactly across the road and we had been pushed through slightly more than 90 degrees. When the car stopped I undid my seat belt but I could not open my door. I tried to open the sunroof to climb out

but the electric motor would not work. Although the windows in the car were broken I couldn't get out. My wife was still strapped into her seat and seemed to be unconscious. I couldn't get past her to use the driver's door. The car is a two door coupe and so I had to wait until help arrived.

8.   After some time the fire brigade helped me out through the windscreen of the car. I refused to go to hospital until my wife was freed so the ambulance waited. The fire brigade cut the entire roof off the car and then lifted my wife out. I remember one of the other drivers making a fuss about the roof being cut off. I am not sure whether it was the First or Second Defendant. I told the fire brigade to do whatever they wanted as the last thing I cared about was the car. When my wife was free we both went to Castlewood Hospital.

9.   I did not talk to the police or to the other drivers. At the hospital I was able to give the police some details so that they would not disturb my wife who was in a very bad state. I recall that the car which ran into us looked like an Astra, but I cannot be absolutely certain of the make. I saw other damaged cars but did not really note the makes or colours.

10.   I have been shown the medical report about me prepared by Mr Peter James Knox dated 16th February 2003. I can confirm that the factual contents of that report are correct.

11.   I have also seen the medical report prepared on my wife and wish to say that she is in considerable pain quite often in the evenings after a long day. I do not think the report on my wife takes sufficient notice of her continuing pain.

12.   I have been shown the schedule of expenses and losses prepared in this claim. I can confirm that the costs set out in that statement which relate to me were incurred as a direct result of the accident. Receipts for all those costs have been disclosed to the Defendants.

13.   I have been shown the statements of case which have been filed in this claim. I note that the Defendants allege that my wife was driving too fast. I reject that assertion completely as the car was stationary or merely creeping forward. I note it is alleged that she was attempting to overtake the stationary or slow moving traffic and pulled onto the opposite carriageway. That is nonsense. The car was propelled across the road by the very violent impact from the rear. Finally it is alleged that she failed to heed the presence of an oncoming Porsche motor vehicle. The first time that I saw the Porsche was immediately before it hit the passenger door of our car. I did not realise it was a Porsche until after the accident.

14.   The Defendants also alleged that I was partly to blame for my own injuries by not wearing a seat belt. I have already explained that I was wearing a seat belt before the accident but took it off afterwards to try to get out of the car.

15.   I blame the Defendants for this accident. If they had been paying attention they would have seen our car slowing down at the back of a queue of traffic and would both have stopped. There would then have been no accident.

STATEMENT OF TRUTH

20.5.2 Commentary

Note the five lines of information in the top right-hand corner. The requirement is explained in **20.2**(b). Include these lines in your drafts. There is also a full heading, as required by the rules.

Paragraphs 1 and 2. The witness statement begins with the formal requirements: the witness's name (in tramlines) and address (paragraph 1), his occupation (paragraph 2), the fact that he is a party to the claim and his relationship to the other parties (paragraph 2), the purpose of the witness statement (paragraph 1). Also in paragraph 1 the witness indicates which matters are within his own knowledge (in this case all of them).

Paragraph 3. Once these formalities are out of the way, the witness can give his evidence in chronological order, beginning in paragraph 3, where relevant matters pre-dating the accident are set out. Note the phrase 'So far as I am aware', which is useful when a witness cannot state something to be categorically true. Avoid in all circumstances the common but ambiguous phrase 'to my knowledge', which can mean both 'I know for a fact that' or 'As far as I know'.

Paragraphs 4 and 5. The events leading up to the accident are in paragraph 4 and paragraph 5 deals with the specific issue of whether the witness was wearing a seat belt which, it emerges from the statements of case, it is alleged that he was not. Chronologically this also comes before the accident itself.

Paragraphs 6 to 9. The accident is described in paragraphs 6 and 7, and its aftermath in paragraphs 8 and 9. Note that the witness does not describe what happened in an objective way, or try to give an overall picture, as would be proper in a statement of case. Instead he says what he heard, saw, felt and did. There is no objection at all to the witness indicating how clear or strong his recollection is, or how confident he feels about the correctness of his evidence. So phrases like 'I have a very clear recollection' (in paragraph 6) and 'I am absolutely certain that' (in paragraph 7) should be used where appropriate. There is also no harm in the witness saying what he is less certain about, what he did not see, or does not remember: this can help protect him against fruitless cross-examination. See for example 'I am not sure whether it was the First or Second Defendant' (paragraph 8), 'I cannot now recall the colour of that car' (paragraph 6), and 'I ... did not really note the makes and colours' (paragraph 9).

Paragraphs 10, 11 and 12. These are important: the witness needs where possible to adopt any matters set out in the medical reports and schedules of loss as part of his evidence, in order to establish the truth and accuracy of them. He can also take the opportunity to add what a medical report does not say (as in paragraph 11).

Paragraphs 13 and 14. It is obviously important for the witness to address the specific issues in the case, so in paragraphs 13 and 14 he responds to allegations made in the defences, dealing with any particulars of negligence alleged on which he is in a position to give evidence.

Paragraph 15. The witness simply states his overall perception of who was to blame for the accident.

Note that the witness statement as a whole is drafted in a very matter-of-fact way. There is no element of persuasion, and no attempt to put any colour into the evidence. This is a witness statement for use at trial, and the witness will possibly be asked to give oral evidence to supplement it, and will certainly be cross-examined on it. The judge will therefore make his mind up on the evidence as a whole, not just the witness statement.

20.6 Witness statement in support of application for interim injunction

20.6.1 Witness statement

(See **19.4** for the injunction.)

Made on behalf of Applicants
Witness: E.B. Coke
1st Statement of Witness
Exhibits: EBC1–3
Dated: 9th October 2004

IN THE HIGH COURT OF JUSTICE
QUEEN'S BENCH DIVISION

Claim No 2004 HC 4243

BETWEEN

WUNDACOLA PLC Applicants

and

HEINZ BERNSTEIN Respondent

WITNESS STATEMENT OF ERNEST BELLINGHAM COKE

1.   I am a director and the company secretary of the Applicants, whose address is Cola Tower, Capital Street, London W1. I make this statement in support of the Applicants' application for an interim injunction against the Respondent. The matters set out below are within my own knowledge, except where I indicate to the contrary.

2.   The Applicants are an international company with an annual turnover of more than £500 million. We manufacture and market soft drinks, in particular Wundacola, which has been the brand leader in the European cola market since 1971. Our closest competitors are Supacola Limited, who manufacture and market Supacola. Competition between the two companies is intense and it is vital to the Applicants' commercial interests that their recipes and manufacturing processes are kept secret from all competitors, but in particular from Supacola Limited.

3.   The Respondent was employed by the Applicants as a research and development scientist from 1st August 1998 to 30th September 2004. I refer to a copy of the Respondent's written contract of employment signed by himself and by me on behalf of the Applicants, marked **EBC1**.

4.   The contract contains two express terms which are incorporated into the contracts of all Wundacola's senior employees: by clause 17(a) the Respondent agreed that he would not during the continuance of the contract and for a period of three years thereafter be employed by or enter into any contract of personal service with Supacola Limited (the three-year period expires on 30th September 2007); and by clause 17(b) the Respondent agreed that he would not at any time reveal to anyone any secret recipes or manufacturing processes of the Applicants.

5.   During 2000 and 2001 the Applicants were attempting to develop a new soft drink which would combine the taste of cola with that of a fruit drink. The Respondent by a paper dated 18th March 2001 set out the results of his research into a recipe involving

apricot juice. I refer to a copy of this paper marked **EBC2**. The paper shows that the Respondent had discovered a manufacturing process that would make the production of an apricot-flavoured cola feasible, although it does not contain either the details of the process or the recipe for the drink. Following the receipt of this paper, in April 2001 the Applicants gave the Respondent the resources to develop and perfect the recipe and manufacturing process for the new drink which was marketed under the name of Apricola from January 2002.

6.   Only the Respondent and three other employees of the Applicants know the recipe for Apricola and only about 20 employees of the Applicants, including the Respondent, know all the details of the manufacturing process. Both the recipe and the process are therefore secret. I myself do not know the secret.

7.   Apricola has been a highly successful product on the European soft drinks market. We are about to launch it onto the American market. Profits from sales of Apricola in Europe during the financial year 2003/2004 were £10,276,450. Profits on the American market are anticipated to amount to up to three times that sum per year. If any competitor were to launch a similar product at the same time our potential losses would be incalculable. To the best of my knowledge, information and belief no competitor has as yet perfected any similar product.

8.   On 30th June 2004 the Respondent gave written notice terminating his employment. I refer to a bundle of correspondence marked **EBC3** which contains copies of two letters written by the Respondent. At page 1 of exhibit **EBC3** is the Respondent's letter of resignation. The Respondent did not tell me, and to the best of my knowledge did not tell any other employee of the Applicants what he would do or where he would go after working out his notice.

9.   On 6th October 2004 Gerard McKinley, who is an employee of the Applicants and was the Respondent's assistant at Wundacola from 1998 received a letter dated 5th October 2004 from the Respondent. A copy of this letter appears at page 2 of exhibit **EBC3**. In the letter, which was passed to me by Gerard McKinley, the Respondent asks Gerard McKinley if he would like to join him at Supacola Limited to produce a peach-flavoured cola for launch onto the European and American market within three months.

10.   I am informed by Celia Worthington, the Applicants' director in charge of research and development, and I believe, that the recipe and manufacturing process of Apricola are such that they could be simply adapted to make use of peaches rather than apricots and that it would be impossible for Supacola to research, develop and market a peach cola within three months unless they were to make use of the Applicants' secret recipe and process for the manufacture of Apricola.

11.   Accordingly, I believe that the Respondent threatens and intends unless restrained by this Court to enter the employment of Supacola Limited, or to enter into a contract of personal service with them and/or to reveal to them the secret recipe and manufacturing process of Apricola, and I respectfully ask the Court to make the order asked for by the Applicants.

STATEMENT OF TRUTH

20.6.2 Commentary

This witness statement is in support of an application for an interim injunction. It is possibly the only written evidence that will be before the court, and there will be no oral evidence, so the outcome of this application rides to a considerable extent on this witness statement. It needs to persuade the court that the injunction should be ordered, so it must contain all the necessary evidence, set out in as persuasive a way as possible. The starting point in drafting it must therefore be to remind yourself of the order you are seeking, namely to prevent the respondent (a) being employed by Supacola and (b) revealing trade secrets.

To be granted the first order, you will need to show:

(a) That he has an obligation not to work for Supacola. So you will need to give evidence of the contractual term to this effect.

(b) That he is, or is threatening to work for Supacola. So you will need to give evidence of his resignation and the letter soliciting Gerard McKinley.

To be granted the second order, you will need to show:

(a) That he has an obligation not to reveal trade secrets. So you will need to give evidence of the contractual term to this effect.

(b) That he has secret knowledge that he could divulge. So you will need to give evidence of what he knows about Apricola, and the fact that it is secret.

(c) That he is threatening to divulge the secret. This will involve giving evidence that he is in a position to do so (the imminent employment with Supacola, evidenced by the letter to Gerard McKinley) and that he is likely to do so, which can only be evidenced by inviting the judge to draw inferences from that letter. This will involve setting out the inferences that the witness draws and inviting the judge to agree with them.

Further, to be granted either order, you will need to show that damages would not be an adequate remedy.

With this analysis in mind, you can go on to the next step, which is to work out the structure of the witness statement. In this case, there is no reason to depart from chronological order. The heading and the first paragraph comply with all the rules and formalities explained earlier in this chapter, and the story begins in paragraph 2. Not surprisingly, the sequence of issues closely corresponds to the sequence in which they appear in the particulars of claim (see **12.13**).

Paragraph 2. This sets the scene by giving the background facts about the applicants, Supacola Limited and their competitive relationship. The annual turnover is included, because it is relevant to show the applicants' ability to satisfy any compensation order made against them.

Paragraph 3. This introduces the respondent and his contract of employment. The contract obviously needs to be exhibited. The way in which this is done is explained in **20.2**(m). Note that the exhibit number is in bold type.

Paragraph 4. The contractual obligations on which the applicants rely are the restrictive covenants, so evidence needs to be given about these. This is not done simply by referring the judge to the relevant clauses in the contract — the effect of them is described in the witness statement as well. This is simply for the sake of clear story-telling — it disrupts the flow of the narrative if the reader has to stop and look elsewhere before picking up the thread again.

Paragraph 5. This describes what happened during the respondent's employment, and tells how he came to be in possession of the secret of Apricola. Another exhibit helps to establish this fact.

Paragraph 6. This seeks to establish that the recipe and manufacturing process of Apricola are secret, and so covered by clause 17(b) of the contract.

Paragraph 7. This is where the witness addresses the issue of why damages would not be an adequate remedy. The reason is closely linked to the profits made from Apricola, and so this is the natural place to put this information chronologically. This paragraph also leads nicely into what comes next, by referring to competitors' inability at present to produce a similar product.

Paragraph 8. The respondent's resignation. His letter needs to be exhibited. It is not the only letter to be exhibited, so a bundle of correspondence needs to be prepared and treated as a single exhibit (see **20.2**(n)).

Paragraph 9. The crucial evidence of the threatened breaches of covenant. This is enough evidence to show an intention to be employed by Supacola.

Paragraph 10. However, more is needed to show the intention to reveal trade secrets. It is the inferences that can be drawn from the above evidence that need to be explained. This is a matter outside the witness's personal knowledge, so he has to give hearsay evidence. This must be made clear, and he must give the source of his information.

Paragraph 11. It is usual to have a final paragraph stating that the witness believes that the respondent threatens and intends to do whatever it is the injunction is intended to prevent: this sums up the effect of all the evidence given. It is also usual to conclude by respectfully asking the court to grant the orders sought. It the past witnesses were inclined to 'humbly crave', but these days 'respectfully ask' will do!

Do not forget that there must be a statement of truth attached to the witness statement. As with statements of case, the convenient place to put this is immediately after the last paragraph.

20.7 Affidavit in support of application for interim injunction

20.7.1 Affidavit

See **19.6** for the injunction.

> Made on behalf of the Applicant
> Deponent: P. Poe
> 1st Affidavit of Deponent
> Exhibits: PP1–4
> Date Sworn: 21st June 2004

IN THE LLANELLI COUNTY COURT   Claim No LI4/29661

BETWEEN

PETER POE   Applicant

and

(1) SANDRA ELKINGTON
(2) PAUL HOUNSELL   Respondents

AFFIDAVIT OF PETER POE

I, PETER POE, of The Otters, Ruddocks Road, Llanelli, Clwyd, STATE ON OATH:

1.   I am a teacher and I am the Claimant in this case. I make this affidavit in support of my application for an interim injunction against the Respondents, who are my neighbours. The matters set out below are within my own knowledge, except where I indicate to the contrary.

2.   The property known as The Otters was purchased in June 2002 in my sole name. I reside there with my wife and five year old son Edgar. The neighbouring property, known as Crewe House, was at that time occupied by the First Respondent, Miss Elkington. The properties are somewhat unusual in that, in order to obtain access to Crewe House, it is necessary to use a path through our front gate. There is now shown to me marked **PP1** a sketch plan of the area, although this is not to scale. The path (which is not wide enough to take a car) is actually named Otters Lane, and forms part of my property. There is now shown to me marked **PP2** a copy of Land Registry Title Number BJ2206001, which shows this to be so.

3. Therefore, in order to gain access to Crewe House, the occupiers have the benefit of an easement across our land. It can be seen from exhibit **PP2** that there is, in favour of the adjoining premises Crewe House, a full and free right of way and passage at all times and for all purposes, but on foot only, over and along the pathway known as Otters Lane. I have indicated Otters Lane in yellow on exhibit **PP1**. I am advised by my solicitor and believe that this easement does not give the adjoining occupiers any rights over our property other than to pass and repass along the path for lawful purposes.

4. Relations between myself and Miss Elkington were initially friendly, but matters began to deteriorate when she formed a relationship with the Second Respondent, Mr Hounsell, in about January 2004. The present situation appears to be that the two Respondents occupy Crewe House together with Mr Hounsell's son, Ivor, who I believe is now aged about 12.

5. In about January 2004, I became aware that the gate to Otters Lane was being left open by the Respondents, and I was concerned that this might cause danger, because it would allow our son to walk out of Otters Lane, which leads directly onto a busy main road. I therefore approached Mr Hounsell and politely asked him if he and his family would ensure that the gate was kept shut, as I did not want my young son to get out of the garden. To my surprise Mr Hounsell became offensive, and told me that my son shouldn't be playing in the garden in any event. He then went to the gate about 20 minutes later, opened it, and went back indoors. The next day, when he was out, I asked Miss Elkington if she could ask Mr Hounsell to shut the gate, and again explained the reasons. She started screaming and shouting at me, and said that they were the co-owners of the gate with us, and could leave it open if they liked. Not only is that untrue, but there was no common-sense reason why the gate should not have been kept shut in any event. However, from that day onwards, the Respondents seemed to go out of their way to be offensive and difficult. On several occasions in April and May 2004 one of the Respondents seemed to materialise at the gate whenever we were going out, obstruct our exit, and then deliberately open the gate after we had gone through and closed it. They also enter our back garden, over which there is no right of way, without asking permission, or loiter in pointless conversation on our property, presumably in a deliberate attempt to aggravate us.

6. This unnecessary and offensive behaviour continued throughout early 2004, and we were particularly upset when it appeared that the Respondents were encouraging Ivor to sit on an upper window sill of their premises, and make loud and personally offensive remarks to my wife and myself, when we were both in and outside our house. I am quite certain that the unpleasant and anti-social behaviour of Ivor has been actively encouraged by the Respondents, and do not believe that he would have behaved in this manner unless he had been led to believe that he would not get into trouble by doing so.

7. In April 2004 a large and ferocious Alsatian dog appeared next door, although I do not know which of the Respondents actually owns it. On frequent occasions since then it has been allowed to roam freely, and frequently gets into our front garden. Any requests that the dog be kept under control are either totally ignored, or provoke abuse from the First and Second Respondents. I am quite certain that the dog is being used in order to terrify our son, and generally to exacerbate the unpleasantness emanating from next door.

8. On Saturday 18th April 2004 I was in the house when I heard the sound of barking from the garden next door. It continued for some time, so I went out and saw Ivor with the dog, deliberately provoking and encouraging the noise. All attempts to persuade him to desist failed, and Edgar now flatly refuses to go into the garden and is terrified. Thus the use and enjoyment of our premises has been curtailed as a result of this spiteful and unnecessary behaviour.

9.   Notwithstanding their previous refusal to shut the gate, on 20th April 2004 the Respondents took it upon themselves to affix a lock to the gate. There is now shown to me marked **PP3** a bundle of correspondence, on page 1 of which is a note from the First Respondent to this effect. Notwithstanding their sudden concern for security, the Respondents had no right to interfere with the gate, which would have been perfectly secure had it been kept shut in the past.

10.   In May 2004 a motorcycle was parked for some time in the front garden of Crewe House, and could only have got there by being wheeled down Otters Lane. On various sunny afternoons in May and June it appeared to be on constant 'test', whenever it was most inconvenient to ourselves. I am certain that the constant revving of the engine was designed simply to annoy and offend us when we wished to use our garden.

11.   As a result of the above behaviour, I asked my solicitors to write to the Respondents, which they did on 18th May 2004. A copy of their letter appears at page 2 of exhibit **PP3**. No answer was ever received. A second letter dated 12th June 2004 appears at page 3 of exhibit **PP3**. Again, no reply was ever received.

12.   On 8th June 2004 I returned home at about 5.00 p.m. Ivor was at the front gate and tried physically to prevent me from closing it. I regret that I then lost my temper and called him a brat, whereupon both Respondents rushed into our garden. The Second Respondent told me to 'piss off' and physically barred my way up my garden path. He called me a 'snotty bastard', and invited me to hit him when I made no response. He then pushed me and my son into a flower bed, crushing some dahlias. I was extremely distressed and frightened. On my solicitor's advice, I went to see my doctor, and there is now shown to me marked **PP4** a copy of his report.

13.   Yesterday, 20th June 2004, a skip was delivered and placed on Otters Lane. The width of it is such that the only way of getting past it is to walk over our flower beds, risking damage to our flowers. At the same time the gate was locked again, this time with a heavy duty chain and large padlock. I saw Miss Elkington filling the skip with rubbish and approached her and asked her to have the skip removed and unlock the gate. She said there was no way she could do either, because they had lost the key to the padlock. So long as the Respondents do nothing, my wife and Edgar and I will have to squeeze round the skip and climb over the gate in order to get in and out of our home.

14.   I believe that unless restrained by this honourable court, the Respondents will continue to ride roughshod over our rights, to abuse their right of way, and to continue the acts of trespass, harassment and nuisance which have been described above. I therefore respectfully ask this honourable court to grant the remedy asked for in this application.

PETER POE

SWORN on 21st June 2004
Before me
DANIELLE CARDEW
of 27 Old Garden Lane
Llanelli
Clwyd
Solicitor and Commissioner for Oaths

20.7.2   Commentary

There is no reason why the evidence in this case needs to be given by affidavit rather than witness statement, but the applicant may do so if he wishes, and this is intended as an example.

Once again, before you can draft the affidavit you need to consider what has to be established, and what evidence will be required to persuade the judge to grant the orders sought. The draft order contains 12 injunctions, 10 prohibitory and 2 mandatory. Every one of these orders needs to be justified.

In respect of the prohibitory orders, the evidence needs to show that the applicant has a legal right to protect, that the acts of the respondents are in contravention of those rights, and that there is a real threat that the respondents will do or continue to do the acts complained of unless forbidden. The torts complained of are trespass, nuisance, assault, harassment (and possibly, if this is distinct from trespass and harassment, interference with the applicant's property). The evidence must therefore cover the following ground:

(a) The applicant's property rights (and of course the fact that they are subject to the respondents' right of way). This is essential for the torts of trespass and nuisance.

(b) No legal rights need to be established for assault and harassment other than the applicant's inherent right to prevent a tort or legal wrong being committed against him, so the tortious acts are sufficient in themselves.

(c) The acts of the respondents, making sure you cover everything in the draft order.

(d) The solicitors' letter asking the respondents to desist and their refusal to do so, to show that the wrongful behaviour is likely to continue.

(e) The general behaviour of the respondents, their attitude and the circumstances that prevail, from which a court might further draw the inference that the acts are likely to continue unless an order is made.

There is no need specifically to give evidence as to why damages would not be an adequate remedy. This is largely taken for granted in the case of injunctions to restrain a tort (see the *Remedies Manual*, **Chapter 9**).

In respect of the mandatory orders all that needs to be shown further is that there is a skip on Otters Lane and a padlock and chain on the gate, which it is within the respondents' power to remove.

Formalities. The top right-hand corner contains all the required information, this time in the form for an affidavit as opposed to a witness statement. After the title in tramlines appears the introductory line required in affidavits, which also includes the deponent's address. Paragraph 1 contains all the remaining formal requirements. Note the different words used in affidavits for the introduction of exhibits, where they appear.

Paragraph 2. Deals with ownership of The Otters and in particular Otters Lane, evidenced by the Land Registry Title document. This paragraph also introduces the respondents as the next door neighbours (obviously necessary to explain the problems) and further describes the lie of the land. Such a description is often necessary in nuisance and trespass cases, and is best reinforced by a sketch plan, which is exhibited. Do not rely solely on a sketch plan, without adding some description in the affidavit.

Paragraph 3. The respondents' right of way must be dealt with. This is a fact without which the applicant would clearly be misleading the court by exaggerating the extent of his property rights. Make it clear that the right of way is limited to 'on foot only'. Colouring in parts of a plan is the standard way of drawing attention to certain areas and is helpful to the court and the parties. The applicant does not personally understand the legal affect of the easement, but he has been advised by his solicitors. So he must make it clear in the usual way that this is evidence not within his own knowledge.

Paragraph 4. Now the story begins. Since Miss Elkington has lived at Crewe House for some years, but the applicant's complaints only go back a few months, some explanation is needed in case the court might wonder why the applicant has taken no action before.

Paragraphs 5 to 10 and 12 to 13. Over these paragraphs the various acts of the respondents are set out in chronological order. This is the correct order. Do not be tempted to follow the sequence of the injunctions in the draft order; that seems logical, but it does not tell the whole story clearly. Evidence relevant to each of the orders sought appears as follows:

Order (1)	Violence	Paragraph 12
Order (2)	Harassment	Obstruction in paragraphs 5 and 12
		Offensive remarks in paragraph 6
	Threats	Paragraphs 7 and 8
Order (3)	Trespass	Paragraph 3

Order (4)	Gate open	Paragraph 5
	Interference with gate	Paragraph 9
Order (5)	Gate locked	Paragraph 9
Order (6)	Trespass by dog	Paragraph 7
Order (7)	Trespass by motorcycle	Paragraph 10
Order (8)	Dog barking	Paragraph 8
Order (9)	Engine noise	Paragraph 10
Order (10)	Skip	Paragraph 13
Order (11)	Padlock and chain	Paragraph 13
Order (12)	Skip	Paragraph 13

But all this evidence has a cumulative effect and is referred to in many other parts of the affidavit than those tabled above. You can easily see how limiting and how much less effective it would be to draft the evidence in this way.

Paragraph 11. The solicitor's letter is set out where it happened chronologically. The fact that there has been further obnoxious behaviour since helps to reinforce the point that the respondents will not cease unless ordered to do so. The respondents' final refusal to remove the skip and padlock is dealt with in paragraph 13.

Paragraph 14. Finishes off in the usual way. Note the phrase 'ride roughshod over our rights'. These are almost certainly the claimant's own words, and so should be used. They are not the sort of words you should put into your client's mouth.

Note that the style of language throughout is objectively accurate and contains no exaggeration or embellishment, but nevertheless paints a picture as vividly as possible with the aim that the judge should not underestimate how awful the situation is from the applicant's point of view. This is entirely justifiable and is part of the persuasive aim of the affidavit. The words are all those that the applicant himself might use, and indeed seem quite restrained in the circumstances, but the tone is quite different from the tone that would be used in a witness statement for use at trial.

At the end of the affidavit is the jurat (see **20.2**(o)).

20.8   Witness statement in interim procedural application

20.8.1   Witness statement

(See particulars of claim in **9.5.1**.)

Made on behalf of the Defendant
Witness: B. Parkes
1st statement of witness
Exhibits: BP 1 to BP 3
Dated: 15th November 2004

IN THE HIGH COURT OF JUSTICE
QUEEN'S BENCH DIVISION
MANCHESTER DISTRICT REGISTRY

Claim No 2004 HC 98744

BETWEEN

SHILTON MACHINE TOOLS LIMITED   Claimant

and

BANKS PLASTIC MOULDINGS LIMITED   Defendant

WITNESS STATEMENT OF BRIAN PARKES

1.   I am Brian Parkes, of Unit 6, Elland Trading Estate, Leeds LS8 3AN. I am a director of the Defendant company. I have full knowledge of the facts of this case and I am duly authorised to make this statement on behalf of the Defendant in support of its application to set aside a default judgment entered on 6th November 2004. The matters set out below are within my own knowledge, except where I indicate to the contrary.

2.   The Defendant has a trading account with the Claimant, and it is true that it ordered 4 moulding machines from the Claimant on 13th March 2004 at a price of £60,000 plus VAT. Although the machines were delivered, they have been the subject of repeated breakdowns and have suffered a number of faults. The main problem with 2 of the machines is that despite a number of site attendances by the Claimant's engineers they have proved incapable of producing mouldings to industry standards. I have been advised by Mr Edward Knight, a consulting engineer of 36 Harrogate Road, Leeds LS3 8DQ, that these 2 machines are so badly designed that it will be impossible to put them right.

3.   As a result of the problems with all 4 machines the Defendant has suffered a substantial loss of business. In particular, it has lost a contract with United Plastic Containers Plc, under which the Defendant was producing goods valued at between £10,000 and £20,000 per month. I refer to a bundle marked **BP1** containing true copies of the Defendant's contractual documentation with United Plastic Containers Plc, monthly invoices, and recent correspondence in which the termination of the contract is explained. I have been advised by the Defendant's solicitors and believe that it has a substantial counterclaim with a value significantly above the value of the claim.

4.   As soon as I received the court papers in this action I raised the matter with Mrs Elaine Stepney, the finance director of the Claimant. I refer to a bundle of correspondence marked **BP2**. A true copy of my letter to Elaine Stepney is at page 1 of the bundle. Her reply, at page 2, says she will look into the matter. Nevertheless, judgment was entered on 6th November 2003.

5.   For the reasons set out above, I ask that this judgment be set aside on the merits. I refer to a draft defence and counterclaim marked **BP3** which the Defendant intends to file if judgment is set aside, and I confirm the truth of the contents of the draft defence and counterclaim.

6.   If judgment is set aside and the case allowed to continue, I respectfully ask that the action be transferred to the Leeds County Court, the local court of the Defendant.

STATEMENT OF TRUTH

I believe that the facts stated in this witness statement are true.

Signed: Brian Parkes

Dated: 15th November 2004

20.8.2 Commentary

This is a short witness statement to support an interim application on a procedural matter. The evidence does not need to go into great detail, but it does need to help establish what the defendant must show to be successful in its application. This is governed by CPR, r 13.3. The defendant needs to show that:

(a)   it has a real prospect of successfully defending the claim; or

(b)   there is some other good reason why the judgment should be set aside; or

(c)   there is some other good reason why the defendant should be allowed to defend the claim.

The court must also have regard to whether the defendant has made the application promptly, so the witness statement should show that he has done so.

There is a good defence, not based on a denial of liability as such, but on the basis of set-off: the defendant has a counterclaim which exceeds the value of the claim. So the witness does not make any attempt to show that the defendant does not owe the sum claimed. Instead he shows that there is a claim against the claimant for a much larger sum, based on breach of implied terms as to satisfactory quality and fitness for purpose, with significant consequential losses. This is covered in paragraphs 2 and 3 of the witness statement.

He must also explain why no defence was served in time. This is covered in paragraph 4 of the witness statement. The defendant had reason to believe that the claimant would not at present be pursuing its claim.

The draft defence and counterclaim is attached. It has not yet officially been served, so it is not verified by a statement of truth. Therefore in paragraph 5 of the witness statement the witness confirms the truth of its contents.

There is also another application before the court, to transfer to the defendant's local county court. This is purely a matter of legal argument, not of evidence, so no specific evidence is required in support of this application. The witness merely states in paragraph 6 the defendant's wish for transfer.

20.9 Exercise

Draft the written evidence of Ronnie Rowland in support of his company's application for an interim injunction without notice against West Molesworth Borough Council (see **19.7**).

Judgments and orders

21.1 The procedural background

21.1.1 Introduction

Once a judgment or order has been obtained by a party to litigation, it is necessary for the decision of the court to be drafted into a written record, incorporating that decision and any orders made by the court as a part of it. The main rules relating to judgments and orders are contained in CPR, Part 40, and apply unless other rules make different provision. Part 40 is supplemented by PD 40B. This chapter deals with the drafting of final judgments or orders. Note that the CPR also deal with other circumstances where judgments or orders will need to be drafted, eg summary judgment (Part 24 and PD 24) and interim remedies (Part 25, PD 25 and PD 25B). The drafting of injunction orders was covered in **Chapter 19**.

21.1.2 Drawing up judgments and orders

CPR, r 40.3(1) provides that every judgment or order will be drawn up by the court, unless:

(a) a party is ordered by the court to draw it up;

(b) a party, with the permission of the court, agrees to draw it up;

(c) the court dispenses with the need to draw it up; or

(d) it is a consent order under r 40.6.

There are further provisions in r 40.3(2) and (3) and PD 40B, para 1:

(a) If the judgment or order is to be drawn up by the court, the court may direct that the parties must file an agreed statement of its terms before this is done.

(b) If the judgment or order is to be drawn up by a party, the court can direct that it must be checked by the court before it is sealed.

(c) If a judgment or order is to be drawn up by a party, he must file it no later than seven days after he was ordered or permitted to draw it up. If he fails to do so, any other party may draw it up and file it.

(d) If the court requires the terms of an order which is being drawn up by the court to be agreed by the parties, it may direct that a copy of the draft order is sent to the parties for their agreement to be endorsed on it, or give notice of an appointment to attend before the court to agree the terms of the order.

It is clear from these rules that, even where the order is to be drawn up by the court, the actual drafting of it is quite likely to be done by a party's legal advisers. A barrister must therefore be able to draft a formal judgment or order.

21.2 Drafting judgments and orders

21.2.1 Form of trial judgments

When drafting a judgment following trial, PD 40B, para 14.1 provides for the use of a number of general forms in common situations. These forms were ones that were used prior to the CPR being introduced, and have been retained. The relevant forms are:

(a) for judgment after trial before a judge without a jury — form number 45;

(b) for judgment after trial before a judge with a jury — form number 46;

(c) for judgment after trial before a master or district judge — form number 47; and

(d) for judgment after trial before a judge of the Technology and Construction Court — form number 47 (with any necessary modifications).

Although the use of these forms is not compulsory, you should use them in any standard case. You will find them in the Folder of Forms supplement to *Civil Procedure* (the *White Book*).

21.2.2 General requirements for judgments and orders

The general requirements are as follows:

(a) Every judgment or order must bear the date on which it is given or was made and must be sealed by the court (CPR, r 40.2(2)).

(b) Most judgments and orders must state the name and judicial title of the person who made it (r 40.2(1)). The main exceptions are default judgments entered under Part 12, judgments entered by a court officer following an admission of liability by the defendant under Part 14, and consent orders made under r 40.6.

(c) If a judgment or order directs any deed or document to be prepared, executed or signed, the order must state who is to prepare it and, if appropriate, who is to approve it. If the parties are unable to agree the form of it, any party may apply to the court for the form to be settled, and the judge may then either settle it himself, or refer it to a master, district judge or conveyancing counsel to settle (PD 40B, para 2).

(d) If a judgment or order requires a party to pay a sum of money, the normal period allowed for payment is within 14 days of the judgment or order. This period will be deemed by r 40.11 unless the court specifies a different period, stays proceedings, or unless other rules (eg Parts 12 and 14) specify different dates.

(e) Where a judgment is for a sum of money to be paid in instalments, the order must set out (PD 40B, para 12):

   (i)   the total amount,

   (ii) the amount of each instalment,

   (iii) the number of instalments and the date on which each is to be paid, and

    (iv) to whom the instalments should be paid.

(f) Any other order which requires an act to be done must specify the time within which the act should be done (PD 40B, para 8.1).

(g) An order may specify the consequences of failing to do an act specified in the order (PD 40B, para 8.2). If so, the wording must be in the following form, eg:

> Unless the claimant serves his list of documents [*preferably*] [by 4.00 pm on Friday 23 January 2005] [*alternatively*] [within 14 days of service of this order], his claim will be struck out and judgment entered for the defendant.

(h) Where the court gives judgment for specified amounts both for the claimant on his claim and against the claimant on a counterclaim, and there is a balance in favour of one of the parties, it may order the party whose judgment is for the lesser amount to pay the balance (r 40.13). But it may still make a separate costs order against each party.

(i) If costs are to be payable, the order must include an order for costs. If there is no mention of costs, none are payable (r 44.13(1)).

21.2.3 Preambles

In certain circumstances judgments or orders must set out particular points in a preamble. These include the following:

(a) The questions put to a jury and their answers to those questions (PD 40B, para 14.2(1)).

(b) The findings of a jury and whether unanimous or by a majority (PD 40B, para 14.2.(2)).

(c) Any order made during the course of the trial concerning the use of evidence (PD 40B, para 14.2.(3)).

(d) Any matters that were agreed between the parties prior to or during the course of the trial in respect of liability, contribution or the amount of damages or part of the damages (PD 40B, para 14.2.(4)).

(e) The findings of the judge under each head of damage in a personal injury case (PD 40B, para 14.2.(5)).

(f) A statement as to where and by what means the claim form was issued, if a party requires this to be included in the judgment and the judge so orders (PD 40B, para 7).

(g) In cases where benefits will be recovered under the Social Security (Recovery of Benefits) Act 1997, or there has been an interim payment (see below).

21.2.4 Specific requirements in certain cases

21.2.4.1 Provisional damages

Where provisional damages have been obtained, an order:

(a) must specify the disease or type of deterioration in respect of which an application may be made at a future date;

(b) must specify the period within which such an application may be made; and

(c) may be made in respect of more than one disease or type of deterioration and may, in respect of each disease or type of deterioration, specify a different period within which a subsequent application may be made (CPR, r 41.2(2)).

21.2.4.2 Recoverable benefits

In a final judgment, where some or all the damages awarded fall under the heads of damage from which recoverable benefits can be deducted under the Social Security (Recovery of Benefits) Act 1997 (see the *Remedies Manual*), and the defendant has paid the recoverable benefits in accordance with the certificate, there are two requirements in PD 40B, para 5:

(a) There should be a preamble which states the amount awarded under each head of damage and the amount by which it has been reduced in accordance with the Act.

(b) The judgment or order should then provide for entry of judgment and payment of the balance.

21.2.4.3 Interim payments

In a final judgment where an interim payment has previously been made, there are requirements in PD 40B, para 6:

(a) There should be a preamble which sets out the total amount awarded by the judge and the amount and date of the interim payment(s).

(b) Where the final amount exceeds that of the interim award, the total award should be reduced to reflect this and the judgment or order should then provide for entry of judgment and payment of the balance.

(c) Where the interim payment exceeds that of the total amount awarded, an order should be made for repayment, reimbursement, variation or discharge and for interest on an overpayment.

21.2.5 Correction of errors

Under CPR, r 40.12 the court can correct an accidental slip or omission in a judgment or order at any time, and a party can apply (formally or by an informal document such as a letter) without notice for a correction. This is known in practice as the 'slip rule'.

21.3 Consent orders

21.3.1 Rules and principles for consent orders

A consent order is a judgment or order made by the court, but the terms of it have been agreed in advance by the parties, because they have compromised the claim. It therefore incorporates both the terms of an order, and the terms of a contractual agreement between the parties.

If a claim is settled after it has been commenced, it is important that the agreement should state what is to become of the claim in court. It is usually essential that the agreement should provide in some way for the settlement to be embodied in an order of the court. If this is not done, the original cause of action is entirely superseded, and if any disagreement arises over putting the settlement into effect, a new action on the contract will have to be commenced. On the other hand, if the agreement is embodied in the court order, with power to apply to the court to enforce its terms, then the settlement can be carried into effect by order of the court in the original action.

A vital term of any agreement in settlement of an action, or order, is a provision with regard to costs. If there is to be no order as to costs, this must be stated. If there is no mention of costs, there is no implied term for or against the payment of costs and the issue remains live.

CPR, r 40.6 and PD 40B, para 3 make provision for consent orders and judgments. If a claim is compromised before it reaches trial, in many cases (set out in r 40.6(3)) the consent order may be entered and sealed by a court officer without the approval of a judge. If it appears unclear or incorrect, the court officer may refer it to a judge for consideration. When a consent order is drafted:

(a) It must be drawn up in the terms agreed by the parties (ie there must be no paraphrasing).

(b) It must be expressed as being 'By Consent'.

(c) It must be signed by the legal representatives of each of the parties to whom the order relates, or by a litigant in person.

(d) It bears the name and judicial title of the judge only if it is made by a judge, not if it is entered by a court officer.

Where the consent order is in the form of a stay of proceedings on agreed terms disposing of the proceedings, and where the terms are recorded in a schedule to the order, directions relating to payment of money out of court or the payment and assessment of costs should be contained in the body of the order and not in the schedule (PD 40B, para 3.5).

Consent orders providing for provisional damages must comply with PD 41, para 4.1–4.3.

21.3.2 *Tomlin* orders

This kind of consent order is used where the terms of settlement are more complex. The terms of the settlement will be set out in a schedule to the order. It takes its name from a *Practice Note* [1927] WN 290, in which Tomlin J said that where a compromise had been agreed and it was proposed to stay the action on the terms set out in a schedule to a consent order, then it should be drawn to include the following words (slightly modernised):

And the Claimant and the Defendant having agreed to the terms set out in the schedule below, it is ordered that all further proceedings in this claim be stayed except for the purpose of carrying those terms into effect. Liberty to apply as to carrying those terms into effect.

21.4   Judgment after trial before judge

21.4.1   Order

IN THE HIGH COURT OF JUSTICE   Claim No 2004 HC 4782
QUEEN'S BENCH DIVISION

Before The Honourable Mrs Justice Blunt

BETWEEN

READYCHOC LIMITED   Claimant

and

DAILY CREAM (MILK SUPPLIES) PLC   Defendant

ORDER

This claim having been tried before the Honourable Mrs Justice Blunt without a jury at the Royal Courts of Justice;

And the Judge having ordered on 2nd November 2004 that judgment be entered for the Claimant against the Defendant as set out below:

IT IS ORDERED that:

1.   The Defendant pay the Claimant the sum of £282,219.18 (being £250,000 principal sum and £32,219.18 interest at the rate of 8% per year from 28th March 2003 to the date of this order).

2.   The Defendant pay the Claimant's costs, summarily assessed in the sum of £10,000.

Dated 2nd November 2004

21.4.2   Commentary

This example is based on Form 45. Note the insertion of the judge's name between the court and the parties. The first two paragraphs constitute what is referred to as the preamble. The two numbered paragraphs contain the actual order. Note that the order covers not just the amount of the claim, but also interest and costs. The order concludes with the date on which it was entered, which is usually the date on which judgment was given, but will be later if the court orders a party to draw up the order.

21.5 Judgment in a personal injury claim

21.5.1 Order

<u>IN THE DEWSBURY COUNTY COURT</u>   Claim No DW4/27003

Before His Honour Judge Capstick

BETWEEN

MARGARET VILLIERS   <u>Claimant</u>

and

STUDLEY BOLTS PLC   <u>Defendants</u>

ORDER

This claim having been tried before His Honour Judge Capstick at Dewsbury County Court;

And the parties having agreed the amount of special damages to be awarded to the Claimant in the event of the Defendants being held liable to her;

And the Judge having assessed damages as follows:

(1) Agreed special damages of £6,867, including damages for lost earnings of £4,943, plus agreed interest of £1,648, making a total of £8,515, which is to be reduced by £2,756 to £5,759 to take account of recoverable benefits to be paid by the Defendants under the Social Security (Recovery of Benefits) Act 1997;

(2) Damages for pain, suffering and loss of amenity of £10,000 plus agreed interest of £750, making a total of £10,750;

(3) Damages for future financial loss and expense of £26,490;

(4) Total £42,999;

And the Defendants having made an interim payment to the claimant of £5,000 on 27th February 2004;

And the Judge having ordered on 18th December 2004 that judgment be entered for the Claimant against the Defendant as set out below:

IT IS ORDERED that:

1. The Defendants pay the Claimant £37,499 inclusive of interest.

2. The Defendants pay the Claimant's costs to be the subject of detailed assessment.

Dated 23rd December 2004.

Hardwicke Meech & Co

Solicitors for the Claimant

21.5.2 Commentary

What distinguishes this example from the previous one is the lengthy preamble, which incorporates many of the requirements of PD 40B, explained in **21.2.3** and **21.2.4**: special damages were agreed; damages under each head must be set out separately; the amount of recoverable benefits paid by the defendant must be deducted; account must be taken of the interim payment that has been made. There is no set way of setting out these matters — the above is merely an example. Where the heads of damage are more numerous, and/or there are more recoverable benefits, it may well be that it would be better to set the damages and deductions out in a table. Once the preamble is complete, the order itself is straightforward. The signature at the bottom is that of the solicitors for the party ordered to draw up the order. It did not appear in the previous example, because in that case the order was drawn up by the court.

21.6 Judgment for provisional damages

21.6.1 Order

IN THE HIGH COURT OF JUSTICE   Claim No 2004 HC 1905
QUEEN'S BENCH DIVISION

Before The Honourable Mr Justice Derrington

BETWEEN

TRISTAN TELFER   Claimant

and

MAURICE WINKS   Defendant

———————

ORDER

———————

This claim having been tried before Mr Justice Derrington without a jury at the Royal Courts of Justice;

And the Judge having ordered on 4th June 2004 that judgment be entered for the Claimant against the Defendant as set out below;

IT IS ORDERED that:

1.   The Defendant pay the Claimant by way of immediate damages the sum of £195,000 (being (i) £39,500 for special damages and £4,500 agreed interest (ii) £35,000 for pain, suffering and loss of amenity and £1,000 agreed interest and (iii) £115,000 for loss of future earnings and/or earning capacity) on the assumption that the Claimant will not at a future date as a result of the act or omission giving rise to the claim develop the following disease/type of deterioration, namely epilepsy.

2.   If the Claimant at a further date does develop epilepsy he should be entitled to apply for further damages provided that the application is made on or before 1st June 2009.

3.   The documents set out in the schedule to this order be filed on the court file and preserved as the case file until the expiry of the period set out in paragraph (2) above or of any extension of that period which has been ordered.

4.   The Defendant pay the Claimant's costs to be the subject of detailed assessment.

Dated 4th June 2004

SCHEDULE

This judgment as entered

The statements of case

A transcript of the judge's oral judgment dated 4th June 2004

The medical report of Mr Percy Rawlings dated 3rd May 2004

21.6.2   Commentary

This example is based squarely on the precedent in the Annex to PD 41. In spite of what is said in PD 40B, that precedent puts the breakdown of the heads of damages in the order, rather than the preamble, so this apparent contradiction has been maintained in this example. It must be assumed for the purposes of this example that (somewhat unusually) there are no recoverable benefits to be taken into account. In all other respects the example complies with CPR, r 41.2.

21.7   Consent order

21.7.1   Order

IN THE MERTHYR TYDFIL COUNTY COURT   Claim No MT4/54631

BETWEEN

IAN MICHAEL SPEIGHT   Claimant

and

UNA RACHAEL GOWER

Defendant

CONSENT ORDER

The parties having agreed the terms of settlement of this claim;

BY CONSENT IT IS ORDERED that:

1.   The Defendant pay the Claimant the sum of £7,500 by 2 pm on Wednesday 17th December 2004.

2.   The Claimant deliver to the Defendant the golf balls described in the Particulars of Claim as '42 Findahole Excel golf balls' by 3 pm on Wednesday 17th December 2004.

3.   There be no order as to costs.

4.   Each party have liberty to apply.

Dated 10th December 2004

Smart and Able,

Solicitors for the Claimant

Messrs Capable and Sly,

Solicitors for the Defendant

21.7.2 Commentary

The judge's name does not appear where the consent order is entered by a court official, as might be the case in this example, if the parties have agreed the order and the court's approval is not required. If the order were made once the trial was in progress, it would be made by the judge, and the judge's name would appear. The fact that the order is a consent order appears in the title of the document.

The terms of the order will obviously be whatever the parties have agreed. There is usually no need for the order to state by when a payment of money should be made, but it may do so, and clearly in this case the agreement is that the payment should be made before the golf balls are delivered up. The time by when any other act is to be done must be stipulated.

Note the costs order. It is essential in a consent order to deal with the costs issue. If the order is, as here, 'that there be no order as to costs', the issue has been disposed of, and each party will bear their own costs. If there is simply no mention of costs at all, the issue is unresolved, and either party could apply for a costs order in the future, or they could argue about it.

It is usual for the consent order to give each party 'liberty to apply'. This is to enable either party to come back to the court for an enforcement order if the other party fails to perform the agreement. It is important if the order is a final order, or enforcement could involve the commencement of a new claim.

The consent order is signed by the solicitors for *both* parties.

21.8 *Tomlin* order

21.8.1 Order

IN THE HIGH COURT OF JUSTICE   Claim No 2004 HC 2786
QUEEN'S BENCH DIVISION

Mr Justice Wellbeloved

BETWEEN

COMPUTER PRODUCTS PLC   Claimant

and

UNITED DISCS PLC   Defendant

CONSENT ORDER

The parties having agreed to the terms set out in the schedule below.

BY CONSENT IT IS ORDERED that:

1.   All further proceedings in this claim be stayed, except for the purpose of carrying those terms into effect.

2.   Each party have liberty to apply as to carrying those terms into effect.

3.   There be no order as to costs.

Dated 18th December 2004

Philbeach & Youngman

Solicitors for the Claimant

J. Hastie & Co

Solicitors for the Defendant

SCHEDULE

1.   The warehouse at Lot 9, Molesworth Industrial Estate, Polehurst, Hampshire ('the Warehouse') is to be sold within 6 months of the date of this order for the best price obtainable, and the net proceeds are to be divided 60% to the Claimant and 40% to the Defendant.

2.   A valuation of the computer software remaining in the Warehouse is to be obtained by each party within 14 days of the date of this order.

3.   The Defendant is to pay to the Claimant a sum half way between these two valuations within 3 months of the date of this order.

4.   If that sum is not paid by the Defendant by the due date, it is to carry interest at the rate of 10% per year from the due date.

5.   The Defendant will within 72 hours of the making of this order destroy all copies of the 'Drawpro' programme remaining in its possession.

21.8.2 Commentary

This is just like any consent order, except that the order itself contains nothing except orders that the proceedings be stayed, for liberty to apply and for costs. The actual terms are all in the schedule. The terms in the schedule are whatever the parties have agreed, and may of course be terms which it would not have been within the court's power to order. They should be drafted with care and accuracy. The last thing either party wants is to find that there is any further dispute about what has been agreed. For further guidance on the drafting of agreed terms of settlement, see the *Negotiation Manual*, **Chapter 11**.

21.9 Exercise A

You appeared for the claimant, Mears Soaps Ltd, which was successful in a claim for breach of contract against Doom Chemicals Plc. The case was heard in the High Court before Mr Brian Beowulf QC (sitting as a High Court judge), and judgment in the claimant's favour was given last Thursday. The claimant was awarded damages of £737,416 for breach of contract, together with interest at 8% from 3rd April 2002 and costs to be assessed. The judge ordered that the claimant draw up the judgment, and you are instructed to do so.

21.10 Exercise B

You were instructed by a firm of solicitors, Hopvine & Co, to appear for the defendant, Oliver Whitbread, at Winchester County Court, where your case was listed before Her Honour Judge Fining. Mr Whitbread is being sued by Megabrewery plc for £7,500 in damages for trespass to goods. Mr Whitbread is counterclaiming for £10,000 for breach of contract.

The case was called on yesterday morning. During the short adjournment you agreed terms of settlement with the solicitors for Megabrewery plc, Messrs Grape and Porter. You agreed that both sides will discontinue their claims against the other in return for Megabrewery plc paying to Mr Whitbread the sum of £5,000 within the next 21 days. Neither party is legally aided, and both agreed to bear their own costs. You are required to draw up the appropriate consent order.

Claims for judicial review

22.1 General matters

22.1.1 Procedure

Applications for judicial review are made under CPR Part 54, supplemented by PD 54. By r 54.1 'judicial review' means a claim to review the lawfulness of an enactment, or a decision, action or failure to act in relation to the exercise of a public function. The orders available on a claim for judicial review are a mandatory order (previously known as 'mandamus'), a prohibiting order (previously known as 'prohibition'), a quashing order (previously known as 'certiorari'), a declaration, an injunction and damages. The procedure *must* be used if the remedies sought include a mandatory, prohibiting or quashing order (r 54.2). The procedure may *not* be used if the only remedy sought is damages (r 54.3).

A claim for judicial review is essentially a Part 8 claim, but with several procedural modifications. The claim is made in the Administrative Court of the High Court using Form N461. Time limits are tight. The claim form must be filed promptly, and in any event not later than three months after the grounds to make the claim first arose (r 54.5), though the court may extend this time limit under CPR, r 3.1(2)(a). Any application to extend time must be included in the claim form, or accompany it (PD 54, para 5.6(3)). Where the application is extremely urgent, or must be determined within a certain timescale, a separate form (N463: application for urgent consideration) must be filed with the claim form.

There is now a pre-action protocol for judicial review claims, which basically requires a letter before claim and a response, or a failure to respond within the time allowed, before the claim is filed. However it is recognised that the protocol will not be appropriate in every case, for example where the defendant does not have the legal power to change the decision being challenged, or where the matter is urgent. In such cases there will be no sanction for failing to comply with the protocol. The claim form must state that the protocol has been complied with, or give reasons for non-compliance.

The Administrative Court was created by *Practice Note* [2000] 4 All ER 1071. This note says that the claimant should be named as 'The Queen on the application of [name of applicant]'. However, in CPR Part 54, PD 54, the pre-action protocol, Form N461 and the guidance notes published with it, the term 'claimant' is invariably used to refer to the applicant, not the Queen. It would seem therefore that after naming the claimant in the prescribed form in the heading, the applicant becomes the claimant for all purposes thereafter, and should be described as the claimant rather than as the applicant.

A claim for judicial review once commenced can only be proceeded with by permission of the court (r 54.4). The first hurdle is therefore to obtain permission. Only if permission is granted will the claim itself be heard.

The claim form must be in Form N461 and must state or include the following (see r 54.6 and PD 54, para 5.6):

(a) the matters required by r 8.2;

(b) the name and address of any person whom the claimant considers to be an interested party;

(c) that the claimant is requesting permission to proceed with a claim for judicial review;

(d) the remedy or remedies sought;

(e) a detailed statement of the grounds for judicial review;

(f) a statement of the facts relied on;

(g) any application to extend the time limit for filing the claim form; and

(h) any application for directions.

The claim form must further be accompanied (PD 54, para 5.7) by:

(a) any written evidence in support of the claim;

(b) a copy of any order that the claimant seeks to have quashed;

(c) where the claim relates to the decision of a court or tribunal, an approved copy of the reasons for reaching the decision;

(d) copies of any documents on which the claimant relies;

(e) copies of any relevant statutory material; and

(f) a list of essential documents for advance reading by the court.

The procedure following the filing of the claim form is beyond the scope of this Manual, but is set out in Part 54 and PD 54. A procedure for urgent applications is set out in a *Practice Statement* [2002] 1 All ER 633.

22.1.2 Drafting

The claim form (Form N461) has nine sections to be filled in:

(1) *Details of the claimant(s) and defendant(s)*. Insert name, address, telephone no, fax no and e-mail address of claimant(s), claimant's solicitors to who documents should be sent, claimant's counsel, defendant(s) and defendant's solicitors to whom documents should be sent.

(2) *Details of other interested parties*. Insert name, address, telephone number, fax number and e-mail address of each such party.

(3) *Details of the decision to be judicially reviewed*. There are three boxes to be filled in: decision; date of decision; and name and address of the court, tribunal, person or body who made the decision.

(4) *Permission to proceed with a claim for judicial review*. This section contains the words 'I am seeking permission to proceed with my claim for judicial review' and then sets out five questions to be answered 'yes' or 'no' by ticking a box, with boxes for details after the last two of them:

(a)   Are you making any other applications? If Yes, complete section 7.

(b)   Is the claimant in receipt of a CLSF certificate?

(c)   Are you claiming exceptional urgency, or do you need this application to be determined within a certain timescale? If Yes, complete form N463 and file this with your application.

(d)   Have you complied with the pre-action protocol? If No, give reasons for non-compliance in the space below.

(e)   Does the claim include any issues arising from the Human Rights Act 1998? If Yes, state the articles which you contend have been breached in the space below.

(5) *Detailed statement of grounds.* The grounds may be stated here or attached.

(6) *Details of remedy (including any interim remedy) being sought.* Here the remedy or remedies must be stated.

(7) *Other applications.* Here must be set out details of any other applications being made, for example an application to extend the time limit for filing a claim.

(8) *Statement of facts relied on.* The facts relied on must be stated here or attached.

Between sections (8) and (9) is a Statement of Truth box, which must obviously be filled in and signed.

(9) *Supporting documents.* There are a large number of boxes to tick, indicating what documents are attached. There is also space to explain why a supporting document is not attached and when the claimant expects it to be available.

It can be seen from the above that for drafting purposes, it is the contents of sections 5, 6, 8 and (if appropriate) 7 that may need to be drafted by counsel.

The statement of the grounds should set out the legal basis on which the claim is made, for example, that the defendant has acted in excess of its jurisdiction, or in breach of natural justice, or has made a decision that no reasonable body properly understanding the law could make.

The remedy or remedies sought will be, for example, a mandatory order, and/or a quashing order, but should be drafted in the terms of the order asked for, not simply in general terms.

The statement of facts relied upon will be the basic outline of the story, set out much like facts in particulars of claim. Do not do this at great length — save the detail for the witness statements.

It will also be necessary to draft at least one witness statement (or affidavit). This must contain the full evidence and facts on which the claimant relies. It must be clear and complete, not concealing adverse facts. It must justify permission being granted, and should attempt to justify the judicial review remedy being granted as well. It must therefore show that the claimant has a sufficient interest, that the matter is susceptible to judicial review and that the defendant is someone against whom the remedy lies.

The claim form and written evidence must be drafted with care. The judge will normally decide whether to give permission for the claim to proceed without hearing oral argument, so the grounds, facts and evidence taken together must be persuasive. Two examples follow.

22.2 Claim for a mandatory order

22.2.1 Claim form

<u>IN THE HIGH COURT OF JUSTICE</u>
<u>ADMINISTRATIVE COURT</u>

Administrative Court Reference No:

Date filed:

Section 1   Details of the claimant(s) and defendant(s)

Claimant's name and address:
> London Borough of Greenbridge
> (add address, phone no, fax no, e-mail address)

Claimant's solicitor's address to which documents should be sent:
> (Insert name, address, phone no, fax no, e-mail address)

Claimant's Counsel's details:
> (Insert name, address, phone no, fax no, e-mail address)

First Defendant:
> James Turner

Defendant's or Defendant's solicitors' address to which documents should be sent:
> (Insert name, address, phone no, fax no, e-mail address)

Second Defendant:
> Amelia Brandt

Defendant's or Defendant's solicitors' address to which documents should be sent:
> (Insert name, address, phone no, fax no, e-mail address)

Section 2   Details of other interested parties

Hubert Lepper
> (add address, phone no, fax no, e-mail address)

Section 3   Details of the decision to be judicially reviewed

Decision:
> Decision to refuse to state a case for the consideration of the High Court in the case of *London Borough of Greenbridge v Hubert Lepper*

Date of decision:
> 15th December 2004

Name and address of the court, tribunal, person or body who made the decision to be reviewed:
> The Defendants, two Justices of the Peace for the South West London Commission Area, sitting at Greenbridge Magistrates' Court

Section 4   Permission to proceed with a claim for Judicial Review

I am seeking permission to proceed with my claim for Judicial Review.

Are you making any other applications? If Yes, complete section 7   NO

Is the claimant in receipt of a Community Legal Service Fund (CLSF) certificate?   NO

Are you claiming exceptional urgency, or do you need this application to be determined within a certain time scale? If Yes, complete Form N463 and file this with your application   NO

Have you complied with the pre-action protocol? If No, give reasons for non-compliance in the space below.   NO

> Because the Defendants do not have the legal power to reverse the decision being challenged.

Does the claim include any issues arising from the Human Rights Act 1998? If Yes, state the articles which you contend have been breached in the space below.   NO

Section 5   Detailed statement of grounds

1.   The Defendants misdirected themselves in law in deciding to refuse to state a case for the opinion of the High Court.

2.   Further or alternatively the Defendants' refusal to state a case was a decision no reasonable Justices could make.

Section 6   Details of any remedy (including any interim remedy) being sought

A mandatory order, requiring the Defendants to state a case for the opinion of the High Court of Justice following the determination by them sitting as a Magistrates' Court in Greenbridge on 17th November 2004 of a case brought by way of informations laid by the Claimant against Hubert Lepper, by which they acquitted Hubert Lepper of selling food to the prejudice of the purchaser contrary to section 14(1) of the Food Safety Act 1990, and falsely describing food, contrary to section 15(1) of the Food Safety Act 1990.

Section 7   Other applications

None

Section 8   Statement of facts relied on

1.   On 20th August 2004 the Claimant laid informations in the Greenbridge Magistrates' Court against Hubert Lepper that:

(a) he did on 9th August 2004 at 3a Old Market, Greenbridge SW22 1GG sell to the prejudice of the purchaser food, namely a burger, which was not of the substance demanded by the purchaser, namely that it should be a vegetable burger, in that it contained 40% meat or animal matter, contrary to section 14(1) of the Food Safety Act 1990; and

(b) he did on 9th August 2004 at 3a Old Market, Greenbridge SW22 1GG display with food exposed by him for sale, namely a burger, a label stating 'vegetable burgers' which falsely described the food in that the burger contained 40% meat or animal matter, contrary to section 15(1) of the Food Safety Act 1990.

2.   On 17th November 2004 the Defendants heard the informations. The Defendants found the following facts:

(a) that Hubert Lepper exposed the burger for sale with a label stating 'vegetable burgers';

(b) that the purchaser demanded a vegetable burger; and

(c) that Hubert Lepper sold to the purchaser a burger which contained 40% meat or animal matter.

3.   The Defendants dismissed the informations on the ground that neither charge was made out.

4.   On 24th November 2004 the Claimant applied to the Justices under section 111(1) of the Magistrates' Court Act 1980 to state a case for the opinion of the High Court on the following questions of law, namely:

(a) whether a person commits an offence under section 14(1) of the Food Safety Act 1990 if he sells to a purchaser who has demanded a vegetable burger a burger which contains meat and/or animal matter;

(b) whether a label describing food as a vegetable burger when that food contains 40% meat and/or animal matter describes the food falsely within the meaning of section 15(1) of the Food Safety Act 1990;

(c) whether on the facts as found by the Defendants they ought to have convicted Hubert Lepper of the offence under section 14(1) of the Food Safety Act 1990;

(d) whether on the facts as found by the Defendants they ought to have convicted Hubert Lepper of the offence under section 15(1) of the Food Safety Act 1990.

5.   By a certificate dated 15th December 2004 the Justices refused to state a case for the opinion of the High Court on the ground that the application was frivolous, pursuant to section 111(5) of the Magistrates' Court Act 1980.

Statement of Truth

I believe that the facts stated in this claim form are true.

John Francis Burnley

Borough Solicitor, London Borough of Greenbridge

Section 9   Supporting documents

[Tick boxes as appropriate]

22.2.2 Witness statement

Made on behalf of Claimant
Witness: J. Featherstone
1st Statement of Witness
Exhibits: JF1–5
Dated: 8th February 2005

IN THE HIGH COURT OF JUSTICE   No.
ADMINISTRATIVE COURT

BETWEEN

THE QUEEN, on the application of
LONDON BOROUGH OF GREENBRIDGE   Claimant

and

(1) JAMES TURNER
(2) AMELIA BRANDT   Defendants

(Justices of the Peace for the
South West London Commission
Area sitting at Greenbridge)

WITNESS STATEMENT OF JANE FEATHERSTONE

---

1.   I am employed by the Claimant at Town Hall, Greenbridge, SW22 1GG as an officer in
the environmental health department and am authorised in writing by the Claimant to
act on its behalf in all matters concerned with its statutory duties as a food authority under
the Food Safety Act 1990. I refer to a copy of my certificate of authorisation marked **JF1**. I
make this statement in support of the Claimant's claim for judicial review in the form of a
mandatory order requiring the Defendants to state a case for the opinion of this Court.
The content of this statement is within my own personal knowledge except where otherwise stated.

2.   On 9th August 2004, following a complaint made to my department by a member of
the public, I went to a butcher's shop owned and operated by Hubert Lepper at 3a Old Market, Greenbridge SW22 2FP. There I saw in the window a tray of burgers offered for sale
with a label placed on the tray which read 'Vegetable Burgers £1'. I went into the shop and
asked for a vegetable burger, without indicating the particular item I wanted. The shop assistant took a burger from the tray, placed it in a plastic bag and sold it to me for £1, which
I paid.

3.   I then informed the shop assistant that I was taking the burger as a sample for analysis.
I broke the burger into three parts and placed each part in a separate container. I sealed all
three containers and labelled them. I gave one container to the shop assistant, and the
other two I took away with me.

4.   I placed the second container in a refrigerator at Greenbridge Town Hall, where it still
is. The third container I took directly to the public analyst, Mr James Broughton BSc, and
requested him to analyse the burger in order to ascertain whether it contained 100% vegetable matter and if not what percentage of vegetable matter, animal matter or other matter it contained. In a report dated 18th August 2004 Mr Broughton stated and I believe,

that the burgers comprised approximately 60% vegetable matter and 40% meat or animal matter. I refer to a copy of this report marked **JF2**.

5.   On 20th August 2004 I laid informations in the Greenbridge Magistrates' Court in the name of the Claimant against Hubert Lepper that:

   (a) he did on 9th August 2004 at 3a Old Market, Greenbridge SW22 1GG sell to the prejudice of myself the purchaser some food, namely a burger, which was not of the substance demanded by the purchaser, namely that it should be a vegetable burger, in that it contained 40% meat or animal matter, contrary to section 14(1) of the Food Safety Act 1990; and

   (b) he did on 9th August 2004 at 3a Old Market, Greenbridge SW22 1GG display with food exposed by him for sale, namely a burger, a label stating 'vegetable burgers' which falsely described the food in that the burger contained 40% meat or animal matter, contrary to section 15(1) of the Food Safety Act 1990.

I refer to copies of these informations marked **JF3**.

6.   The hearing of the informations was on 17th November 2004 in the Greenbridge Magistrates' Court before the Defendants. Oral evidence was given by myself, and James Broughton on behalf of the food authority and by Hubert Lepper. Both informations were dismissed by the Defendants who acquitted Hubert Lepper. In giving their reasons they stated that they found the following facts:

   (a) that the burger was exposed for sale by Hubert Lepper and that he displayed with it a label stating 'vegetable burgers';

   (b) that I demanded a vegetable burger;

   (c) that a shop assistant acting on behalf of Hubert Lepper sold the burger to me; and

   (d) that the burger contained approximately 60% vegetable matter and 40% meat or animal matter.

7.   Nevertheless the Defendants held that neither charge was made out because:

   (a) the description 'vegetable burger' meant no more than that the burger contained vegetables, which was true; alternatively that it contained more vegetable than meat, which was also true;

   (b) in demanding 'a vegetable burger' I had not demanded a burger which was free of meat, but only a burger which contained vegetables; alternatively I had demanded one of the burgers displayed in the window, and labelled 'vegetable burgers', whatever it might contain.

8.   By a letter dated 24th November 2004, a copy of which I refer to marked **JF4**, the Borough Solicitor of the Claimant applied to the Defendants under section 111(1) of the Magistrates' Courts Act 1980 to state a case for the opinion of the High Court on the following questions of law, namely:

   (a) whether a person commits an offence under section 14(1) of the Food Safety Act 1990 if he sells to a purchaser who has demanded a vegetable burger a burger which contains meat and/or animal matter;

   (b) whether a label describing food as a vegetable burger when that food contains 40% meat and/or animal matter describes the food falsely within the meaning of section 15(1) of the Food Safety Act 1990;

(c) whether on the facts as found by the Defendants they ought to have convicted Hubert Lepper of the offence under section 14(1) of the Food Safety Act 1990;

(d) whether on the facts as found by the Defendants they ought to have convicted Hubert Lepper of the offence under section 15(1) of the Food Safety Act 1990.

9.   By a certificate dated 15th December 2004 from the Clerk to the Greenbridge Justices to the Borough Solicitor, a copy of which I refer to marked **JF5**, the Defendants communicated their decision to refuse to state a case on the grounds that the application was frivolous, pursuant to section 111(5) of the Magistrates' Courts Act 1980.

10.   I am advised by the Borough Solicitor and I believe that the case raises genuine questions of law for the opinion of the High Court and that there are no good grounds for the Defendants to refuse to state a case. In the circumstances I ask this court to give the Claimant permission to proceed with its claim for judicial review and to make the mandatory order sought.

STATEMENT OF TRUTH

22.2.3 Commentary

This claim is made in not uncommon circumstances. A prosecution in the magistrates' court has ended in an acquittal. The prosecution wish to appeal by way of case stated, so they apply to the magistrates to state a case, but the magistrates refuse to do so. In these circumstances the only way forward for the prosecution is to apply by way of judicial review for a mandatory order, requiring the magistrates to state a case.

22.2.3.1 Commentary on claim form

Sections 1 to 4 of the claim form simply need to be filled in. The statement of case effectively begins at section 5. The aim is to draft in a way which will make the case as persuasively as possible. There is no single correct way to do this; different barristers used to do it in different ways, and anyway this is a new procedure and a new form, so lawyers will discover by trial and error what works best. The approach illustrated in this Manual is simply a suggestion.

Section 5. In some ways it is odd that the claim form requires the grounds to be stated before the facts, since without the facts the grounds do not make much sense. However, that is what we are required to do, and the court can easily refer forward to the statement of facts if it needs to do so. There are two grounds for judicial review:

(1) The allegation is basically that the magistrates made a wrong decision. The application for judicial review can only be made if they have erred in law, rather than on the facts, so the ground is expressed as 'misdirected themselves in law'. Essentially it will be argued that the questions of law were genuine, and if there are genuine questions of law, by definition the application cannot be frivolous.

(2) This is an allegation of Wednesbury unreasonableness. This ground almost always appears in judicial review claims, no matter what the context. The argument will be that it was irrational to refuse to state a case when there were such clear questions of law arising.

Section 6. In this section set out the remedies you are seeking. These can only be some combination of mandatory order, quashing order, prohibiting order, declaration, injunction and damages. In this case it is simply a mandatory order, but it is not enough simply to state that fact — the terms of the order should be drafted and included as well. Take the opportunity to add a bit of description and explanation, as an aid to clarity. Here the nature of the prosecution, the charges and the outcome are all included.

Section 8. It is in the statement of facts relied upon that your real drafting skills come into play. You will have observed that there is some overlap between facts set out in the claim form and the evidence set out in the witness statement. This is inevitable, but it does no harm. We are well used to there being overlap between the content of a statement of case and a witness statement. The formal document will never be as full as the written evidence.

The facts that you choose to set out are not determined by any principle other than clarity. It is not like a statement of case, where you have to fulfil certain essential criteria. As a guide, select those facts which will enable the reader (the judge) to understand quickly what the case is all about and how it arises. If you can give some indication as to how the legal grounds on which you rely are to be made out, all the better, though this may only be possible once you have added the necessary evidence.

Here the facts are set out in fairly obvious stages:

(1)   The informations and the charges they contained.

(2)   The hearing; but the main point of this paragraph is the facts as found by the magistrates. These facts are necessary for an understanding of the questions of law which arise in this case.

(3)   The magistrates' decision.

(4)   The application to the magistrates to state a case and the questions of law that needed answering.

(5)   The magistrates' refusal to state a case. That the application is frivolous is the only ground on which they can refuse to state a case.

2.2.3.2   Commentary on witness statement

Heading. The usual formalities in the top right-hand corner appear as required. Note the court: the Administrative Court is a new division of the High Court. The parties are claimant and defendant.

Paragraph 1. The usual introductory paragraph. Jane Featherstone is giving evidence for her employer, so she gives the Town Hall as her address. She is a food officer and acted as such in this case. Food officers are creatures of statute and have statutory powers and duties under the Food Safety Act 1990, so she needs to show that she is a food officer, which is why she exhibits her certificate of authorisation.

Paragraphs 1 to 4. Then the story begins, and it is a straightforward chronological story. Several elements of the story have already been included in the statement of facts in the claim form, but are repeated in the witness statement, because otherwise the complete story could only be read by jumping between two documents. The starting point is the witness's test purchase (paragraphs 2 and 3), and the statement then moves on to the analysis and its results (paragraph 4), with the analyst's report exhibited. The procedure described in paragraphs 3 and 4 is a statutory requirement.

Paragraphs 5 to 9. Paragraph 5 more or less reproduces paragraph 1 of the statement of facts and exhibits the informations. Paragraph 6 covers the same ground as paragraphs 2 and 3 of the statement of facts, with a little more detail added. Paragraph 7 is new, and sets out the reasons given by the defendants for dismissing the case. Paragraphs 8 and 9 are almost identical to paragraphs 4 and 5 of the statement of facts, except that the letter and certificate are exhibited.

Paragraph 10. This rounds the witness statement off. It begins with the legal advice received by the witness. This is hearsay, so that must be made clear in the usual way. It finishes as always with the witness stating what she is asking the court to do.

22.3 Claim for a quashing order and mandatory order

22.3.1 Claim form

<u>IN THE HIGH COURT OF JUSTICE</u>
<u>ADMINISTRATIVE COURT</u>

Administrative Court Reference No:

Date filed:

Section 1   Details of the claimant(s) and defendant(s)

Claimant's name and address:
> Robert McTavish
> (add address, phone no, fax no, e-mail address)

Claimant's solicitor's address to which documents should be sent:
> (Insert name, address, phone no, fax no, e-mail address)

Claimant's Counsel's details:
> (Insert name, address, phone no, fax no, e-mail address)

First Defendant:
> London Borough of Greenbridge

Defendant's or Defendant's solicitors' address to which documents should be sent:
> (Insert name, address, phone no, fax no, e-mail address)

Section 2   Details of other interested parties

> None

Section 3   Details of the decision to be judicially reviewed

Decision:
> Decision to treat the Claimant as intentionally homeless within the meaning of section 191 of the Housing Act 1996.

Date of decision:
22nd October 2004

Name and address of the court, tribunal, person or body who made the decision to be reviewed:
> The Defendant *(add address)*

Section 4   Permission to proceed with a claim for Judicial Review

I am seeking permission to proceed with my claim for Judicial Review.

Are you making any other applications? If Yes, complete section 7   YES

Is the claimant in receipt of a Community Legal Service Fund (CLSF) certificate?   YES

Are you claiming exceptional urgency, or do you need this application to be determined within a certain time scale? If Yes, complete Form N463 and file this with your application.   NO

Have you complied with the pre-action protocol? If No, give reasons for non-compliance in the space below.   YES

Does the claim include any issues arising from the Human Rights Act 1998? If Yes, state the articles which you contend have been breached in the space below.   NO

Section 5   Detailed statement of grounds

1.   The Defendant failed to make any or any adequate enquiries in order to be satisfied that the Claimant was intentionally homeless within the meaning of section 191 of the Housing Act 1996 ('the Act').

2.   In the alternative, in the event that the Defendant did make adequate enquiries, there were no facts upon which it could reach the conclusion that the Claimant was intentionally homeless.

3.   Further or alternatively the Defendant misdirected itself in law in deciding that the Claimant had deliberately left temporary accommodation at 4 Springhill Drive, Hampstead, London NW6.

4.   Further or alternatively the Defendant misdirected itself in law in deciding that the accommodation at 4 Springhill Drive was available to the Claimant.

5.   Further or alternatively the Defendant misdirected itself in law in deciding that it was reasonable for the Claimant to continue to occupy the accommodation at 4 Springhill Drive.

6.   For the reasons set out above the decision of the Defendant was not a decision a reasonable Housing Authority could make.

Section 6   Details of any remedy (including any interim remedy) being sought

1.   A quashing order to quash a decision of the London Borough of Greenbridge to treat the Claimant as intentionally homeless within the meaning of section 191 of the Act.

2.   A mandatory order to require the London Borough of Greenbridge to secure that accommodation is made available for the Claimant's occupation in accordance with its duty under section 193 of the Act.

Section 7   Other applications

I wish to make application to extend the time limit for filing this claim form.

Section 8   Statement of facts relied on

1.   On 20th October 2003 the Claimant, having nowhere to live on being released from prison, went to stay temporarily with a friend at 4 Springhill Drive, Hampstead, London NW6.

2.   On 26th October 2003 the Claimant made an application to the Defendant, his local authority, for special housing assistance on the grounds that he was homeless and had a disability.

3.   In January 2004 the Claimant was required to leave his temporary accommodation at 4 Springhill Drive and was temporarily housed by the Defendant in bed-and-breakfast accommodation.

4. By a letter dated 22nd October 2004 the Defendant informed the Claimant of its decision to treat him as intentionally homeless within the meaning of section 191 of the Act on the ground that he had left the temporary accommodation at 4 Springhill Drive.

5. The Defendant accordingly refused to secure that accommodation was made available for the Claimant's occupation under section 193 of the Act.

6. As the Claimant has a priority need within the meaning of section 189 of the Act and has not become homeless intentionally, the Defendant has a duty under section 193 of the Act to secure that accommodation is made available for the Claimant's occupation, but the Defendant refuses to do so.

7. This claim has been delayed because:

(1) The Claimant did not receive the Defendant's letter of 22nd October 2004 until 28th November 2004.

(2) The Claimant was not granted Community Legal Service funding until 7th January 2005, the application having been made on 18th December 2004.

(3) Funding granted on 7th January 2005 was limited to obtaining counsel's opinion.

(4) Counsel was instructed on 21st January 2005 and advised on 22nd January 2005.

(5) Funding was granted to the Claimant to make a claim for Judicial Review on 11th February 2005, the renewed application having been made on 23rd January 2005.

Statement of Truth

I believe that the facts stated in this claim form are true.

Robert McTavish

Claimant

Section 9   Supporting documents

[Tick boxes as appropriate]

22.3.2   Witness statement

Made on behalf of Claimant
Witness: R. McTavish
1st Statement of Witness
Exhibits: RM1–2
Dated: 12 February 2005

IN THE HIGH COURT OF JUSTICE   No.
ADMINISTRATIVE COURT

BETWEEN

THE QUEEN, on the application of ROBERT McTAVISH   Claimant

and

LONDON BOROUGH OF GREENBRIDGE   Defendant

WITNESS STATEMENT OF ROBERT McTAVISH

1.   I am unemployed and I live at 18D Empire Road, London SE17. I am the Claimant and make this statement in support of my application for judicial review in respect of a decision by the Defendant ('the Authority') to treat me as being intentionally homeless within the meaning of the Housing Act 1996 and in support of my application for an order that the authority provide me with accommodation, as it is obliged to do under the provisions of the 1996 Act. Except where it appears otherwise, the matters set out below are within my own personal knowledge.

2.   This matter concerns the failure of the Authority to provide me with accommodation notwithstanding that I am homeless and became homeless through no fault of my own. I am informed by my solicitors and believe the Authority has a duty under the provisions of the 1996 Act to provide the homeless with accommodation. Despite my requests, the Authority has failed to provide me with accommodation. The circumstances in which I became homeless are as follows.

3.   I am a single man aged 37. I suffer from chronic arthritis in my hands and I have been unable to work since 1994. I receive a disability allowance from the DSS of £50 per week. I refer to a copy of a medical report dated 10th January 2005 marked **RM1** which contains brief details of my medical condition. Before May 2003 I lived in an unfurnished flat at 26A Park Street, Greenbridge, London SW22 with my girlfriend Mary Wishart. Mary was the protected tenant of the flat and paid the rent of £50 per week.

4.   In June 2003 I was convicted at Isleworth Crown Court of handling stolen goods and sentenced to six months' imprisonment, which I served in Wandsworth prison. I was released on 20th October 2003.

5.   On 20th October 2003 I returned to the flat at 26A Park Street and discovered that Mary was no longer living there. I contacted the landlord's agents, Bilton and Son of 84 Denman Street, London SW16, and they informed me, and I believe, that Mary served them notice to quit and left the flat during September 2003, whereupon it was relet. Mary did not inform me that she was leaving and I have not heard from her since August 2003 when she last visited me in prison.

6.   In view of the fact that I had nowhere to live, a friend of mine, Eddy Brown, told me I could stay temporarily in his house at 4 Springhill Drive, Hampstead NW6. This is a two-bedroom house. Eddy informed me that his sister was shortly coming to London to live, and that when she came I would have to leave. I accepted his offer and agreed a rent of £60 per week, which was paid by housing benefits.

7.   On 26th October 2003 I went to the housing office of the Authority. I told them I was homeless and the circumstances in which I came to be so. I also told them of my disability. I was told by the housing office that the Authority would try to find me accommodation.

8.   I remained in quite frequent contact with the Authority's housing office. I was assured that every effort was being made to find accommodation for me. In January 2004, Eddy Brown informed me his sister was arriving to live with him in the house. He accordingly asked me to leave as we had agreed. I thought I had no right to remain in the house and I am informed by my solicitors and believe that I had no right to stay. In any event, I did not wish to cause Eddy any difficulty after he had been so helpful to me.

9.   I had been in occupation of Eddy Brown's house for seven weeks when I was asked to leave. Once I left, I went again to the Authority's housing office, explained my circumstances and I was put up in bed-and-breakfast accommodation at the Park Court Hotel, 18–30 Prince of Wales Drive, Greenbridge, SW22. I was told this was to be temporary

accommodation until the Authority found suitable accommodation for me. I telephoned the Authority every couple of days or so but I was told there had been no developments as the medical authorities were still considering my case. Every two or three weeks or so, the Authority informed me it would shortly be in a position to offer me accommodation, but none was forthcoming. In May 2004 I was moved to alternative bed-and-breakfast accommodation at the Bayswater Hotel, Pole Street, London W14. I remained in this accommodation until January 2005.

10.   It was not until November 2004 that there was any development. On 28th November 2004 I received a letter from the Authority dated 22nd October 2004. This did not reach me until 28th November 2004 because it was addressed to me at the Park Court Hotel. I refer to a bundle of correspondence marked **RM2**. Page 1 of the bundle is a copy of the Authority's letter of 22nd October 2004. Although the Authority accepts I am homeless and have a priority need, it took the view I was intentionally homeless because I had left the temporary accommodation provided by Mr Brown.

11.   The Authority's decision, as recorded in this letter, reveals a misunderstanding of the nature of the accommodation provided by Mr Brown and despite the Authority's claim that it has investigated my case, this cannot be correct having regard to the content of its letter of 22nd October 2004. I did not have exclusive use of a room in Eddy Brown's house. I accept I was the only person sleeping in the room, but Eddy had access to it at all times. I was only a lodger, who had been invited to stay for a couple of weeks. I could not exclude Eddy from the bedroom. It would appear the Authority took the view I was the tenant of this room. I am informed by my solicitors and believe this is not the case. As I have said, I was a lodger. It was not reasonable for me to remain in Mr Brown's house. Mr Brown permitted me to remain until his sister arrived. I knew when I took up the offer of the room that I would be required to leave once she came. This was the basis upon which the room was offered to me in the first instance. As I have said above, I am informed by my solicitors and believe that I had no right to remain in Mr Brown's house. Accordingly, once I was asked to leave, it was pointless remaining. In these circumstances I am informed by my solicitors and believe I am not intentionally homeless within the meaning of the 1996 Act and accordingly the Authority has a duty to provide me with accommodation.

12.   I am informed by my solicitors and believe, my claim for judicial review is out of time. I therefore set out the timetable of events since I received notification of the Authority's decision on 28th November 2004. On receipt of the letter I at once went to a Citizens' Advice Bureau in Hammersmith. They sent me to my present solicitors. I went to see my solicitors on 3rd December 2004. I am informed by my solicitors and believe they wrote to the Authority on that date setting out my case. A true copy of this letter is on pages 2–3 of the bundle **RM2**. As a result of this letter, the Authority continued to pay for the bed-and-breakfast accommodation until 11th December 2004 but it indicated in a letter to my solicitors dated 10th December 2004 that the decision recorded in the letter of 22nd October 2004 would not be reversed. A copy of the letter dated 10th December 2004 is at page 4 of the bundle **RM2**.

13.   My solicitors replied to the letter of 10th December 2004 by a letter dated 12th December 2004. The Authority continued to pay for the bed-and-breakfast accommodation until 25th December 2004, but again, by letter dated 17th December 2004, the authority informed my solicitors that the original decision concerning my homelessness remained effective. Copies of the letters dated 12th and 17th December 2004 are on pages 5–7 of the bundle **RM2**.

14.   It was clear from this correspondence that the Authority was not going to reverse its decision to treat me as being intentionally homeless. I was therefore advised by my solicitors to apply for judicial review of the Authority's decision as I was advised by my solicitors and believe the Authority's decision was wrong in fact and in law. On 18th December 2004, my solicitors applied for Community Legal Service funding on my behalf. A copy of my application dated 18th December 2004 and my solicitors' letter to the Community Legal Service Fund dated 18th December 2004 are at pages 8–10 of the bundle **RM2**.

15.   I am informed by my solicitors and believe that they were informed by the Community Legal Service Fund by telephone on 7th January 2005 that emergency funding had been granted, limited to obtaining counsel's opinion. I saw my solicitors again on 17th January 2005 when I gave further instructions. I am informed by my solicitors and believe papers were received in counsel's chambers on 21st January 2005. I am informed by my solicitors and believe that counsel's opinion was received by my solicitors on 22nd January 2005.

16.   As a result of receiving counsel's advice, I am informed by my solicitors and believe an application was made to the Community Legal Service Fund to have my funding extended. I am informed by my solicitors and believe the application and a copy of counsel's opinion were sent to the Community Legal Service Fund by hand on 23rd January 2005. I am informed by my solicitors and believe there was no response from the Community Legal Service Fund, and accordingly another letter was sent to the Community Legal Service Fund by hand on 4th February 2005 requesting that they deal with my application as a matter of urgency. I am informed by my solicitors and believe they received a further certificate on 11th February 2005. Funding has been extended to cover my claim for judicial review. I am informed by my solicitors and believe instructions were sent to counsel to settle a claim for judicial review on 11th February 2005. These instructions were received by counsel on 11th February 2005. I am further informed by my solicitor and believe the papers were returned by counsel on 12th February 2005.

17.   The bulk of the delay since I learned of the Authority's decisions has been caused by my solicitors having to obtain legal funding on my behalf. The applications for funding have been made promptly and action taken promptly once funding has been obtained. I am informed by my solicitors and believe that the Authority will not be prejudiced by my late application.

18.   Since January 2005 I have been living in a squat at 18D Empire Road, London SE17. There is no telephone at the squat, and it has been difficult for me to contact my solicitors, which accounts for the apparent delay between 7th and 17th January 2005.

19.   The Authority's sole objection to providing me with accommodation is that I made myself homeless deliberately by leaving Eddy Brown's house. I had no right to remain in this house once asked to leave. Mr Brown was a friend who assisted me for a short while. To suggest I deliberately made myself homeless is incorrect. To suggest I could have reasonably stayed in Mr Brown's house is incorrect. I have not had settled accommodation since I left the 26A Park Street flat in 2003. I lost the use of that flat through no fault of my own; there was nothing I could do to prevent it. It is clear from its letter of 22nd October 2004, the Authority did not consider my previous settled accommodation and the circumstances under which I lost the use of that accommodation.

20.   In the circumstances I ask this court to give me permission to proceed with my claim for judicial review, and to make the orders sought.

STATEMENT OF TRUTH

22.3.3 Commentary

This is another case involving a local authority, this time as the defendant. The relevant area is housing law. This is in fact a real case, with only names, places and dates altered.

22.3.3.1 Commentary on claim form

The formal parts of the claim form are much the same as in the previous example, but in this case there is no other interested party, and the claimant is in receipt of CLS funding. The claimant is also applying outside the normal three-month limit, and so is also making an application for time to be extended.

Section 5. There are six legal grounds on which the defendant's decision is being challenged. There is some overlap between them, but they are all attacking the decision in a slightly different way.

(1) The allegation is of a breach of natural justice: the defendant reached a decision without obtaining the evidence on which it could base that decision.

(2) Alternatively, if the defendant did obtain the necessary evidence, it reached a decision which flew in the face of that evidence. This would either be a breach of natural justice, or perverse in the *Wednesbury* sense.

(3) The defendant has apparently come to a wrong decision on the facts, but only a legal error can be challenged by judicial review. The way round this problem is to state that the defendant 'misdirected itself in law'. This is not wholly artificial. A factual error must logically derive from a legal misunderstanding or error. Here the argument would be that the only way the defendant could come to the conclusion that the claimant had deliberately left the accommodation at 4 Springhill Drive was by misunderstanding the meaning of the word 'deliberately'.

(4) The same point again. The only way the defendant could come to the conclusion that the accommodation was available to the claimant was by misinterpreting the word 'available'.

(5) And again. The defendant has a misguided understanding of what is reasonable.

(6) As usual, an allegation of Wednesbury unreasonableness is included. Note that this is not put forward as an alternative, but as the conclusion that can be drawn from the above grounds.

Section 6. Under 'remedies sought' there are two remedies listed. Quashing orders and mandatory orders often go together. If there has been a wrong decision, you may need first to get that decision quashed, and then get an order requiring the respondent to make a different decision, or do something else instead. The slightly odd phrase 'secure that accommodation is made available' is what you will find in section 193 of the Housing Act 1996, so must obviously be adopted.

Section 7. The claimant is making a further application — for the extension of time. So this must be stated.

Section 8. The facts in full appear in the witness statement. All you need here are such facts as will make the context of the claim clear to the judge. So just state what happened in outline: the claimant went to stay with a friend (paragraph 1) and applied for special housing assistance (paragraph 2), but had to leave his friend's house and was put into temporary accommodation (paragraph 3). The defendant then decided that he was intentionally homeless (paragraph 4) and so refused to house him (paragraph 5). All very straightforward. The conclusion to be drawn from these circumstances is that the authority is refusing to perform its statutory duty (paragraph 6). If the claimant's case is made out, then this is the correct legal position.

It is then necessary to give reasons as to why time should be extended. The claimant does this in paragraph 7 by seeking to show that the bulk of the delay was for reasons outside his control: an administrative error by the defendant, followed by the time taken to apply for legal funding. These matters are dealt with in full in the witness statement; here just a list of key dates and events will probably do.

22.3.3.2 Commentary on witness statement

This is a long witness statement, but the evidence in it is all necessary. You will see it falls into two distinct main parts. After the heading and first standard paragraph, paragraphs 2 to 11 give the reasons why the claimant should be housed, and paragraphs 12 to 18 set out the detailed explanation for the delay in bringing the application to the Administrative Court. Paragraphs 19 and 20 then form the conclusion.

Paragraph 2. This is a good strong paragraph which states the claimant's case in a hard-hitting and persuasive way. The solicitors' advice is clearly stated to be such. If this were left out, then the claimant would appear to be advancing legal argument on his own behalf, which he would obviously be unable to do.

Paragraph 3. The claimant's case for housing is based not only on his homelessness, but also on his disability. So this paragraph gives the necessary evidence of his disability.

Paragraphs 4 and 5. These explain how the claimant came to be homeless in the first place. It is important to establish that the last home was in Greenbridge, which is why the defendant is the authority responsible.

Paragraphs 6 and 8. These explain how the claimant obtained and then had to leave temporary accommodation at Eddy Brown's house.

Paragraphs 7, 8 and 9. Set out all the claimant's dealings with the authority. Note that everything possible is done to show up the poor administration and contradictory messages he received from the authority. This obviously helps to make the evidence more persuasive.

Paragraph 10. Deals with the actual decision reached by the authority and the communication of it. The fact that it was sent to the wrong address is stressed: this is relevant both to the authority's incompetence and to help explain the delay.

Paragraph 11. At this point the witness statement stops telling the story and instead concentrates on persuasion. The claimant explains what is wrong with the authority's decision. Most of these arguments can properly be put into the claimant's own mouth, because they are his personal view of the situation. Where there is any element of legal argument (on three occasions), this is expressed to be the advice of the solicitors. The paragraph concludes by making the point that the authority has a duty to house the claimant.

Paragraphs 12 to 18. The reasons for the delay in full. It is largely a matter of setting out every step taken towards trying to resolve the matter together with the date of it. It is a long and complicated story. No one reason for the delay emerges: there were simply a large number of steps which had to be taken, which all added up. The slowest wheel in the system appears to have been the Community Legal Service; you will note that counsel on the other hand was always very fast!

Paragraph 19. A résumé of the whole of the evidence, just to add a nice persuasive punch at the end of the witness statement.

Paragraph 20. Sets out the remedies sought.

22.4 Prohibiting order

No full example is included of an application for a prohibiting order. It is comparatively rare. It operates in much the same circumstances as a quashing order: whereas a quashing order quashes a decision made without jurisdiction, a prohibiting order prevents a tribunal acting, or continuing to act without jurisdiction.

The statement of relief sought might read:

A prohibiting order directed to Augustus Herrington, Magistrate sitting at Inner London Magistrates' Court prohibiting him from further proceeding with the trial of the Applicant on a charge brought against him under section 1 of the Theft Act 1968.

And that all proceedings on the charge be stayed until further order.

The grounds would be similar to the grounds on which a quashing order might be sought (eg, in this example, bias).

22.5 Exercise

Fiona Lubkowska will say:

I am 22 years old and live at 16 St Andrew's Road, Greenbridge, London SW22. My father was a Polish citizen who came to this country as a child after the Second World War. My mother was an American citizen. I am a British citizen and have lived most of my life in the UK, though I have spent substantial periods of time in America. I was born in London and lived here with my parents until they were divorced in 1992. My mother then returned to America, where I lived with her for three years. In 1995 I returned to London in order to go to public school in England, and lived with my father at 16 St Andrew's Road, returning to my mother in Connecticut during the school holidays. In 2000 I left school with three A-levels and won a place at Yale University in America. By this time I had decided I wished to settle in England, but I did wish to have the opportunity to study at Yale. Accordingly, from 2000 to 2004 I lived in America during university term time, returning to England during the vacations, a total of about four months a year. I graduated in June 2004 and went to India for six months. I have now returned and am living in England permanently. My mother died in January 2003, so I no longer have much reason to live in America.

I am currently working as a waitress but I wish to become an actress. I auditioned for several drama schools this January and I have won a place at the World Academy of Dramatic Art (WADA) to start in September 2005. Since my mother's death, my family is not wealthy, so on 1 February I applied to Greenbridge Education Authority for financial support to enable me to train at WADA. It is not a degree course, but some of the students are receiving government or local authority support. I did not keep a copy of my application form.

On 11 February 2005 I received a letter dated 10 February 2005 from Greenbridge informing me that it could not consider my application for financial support because (a) I was not ordinarily resident in the United Kingdom and (b) its policy was not to regard courses at drama schools as educational courses and so no financial support was available for such courses. I rang up and asked how I could appeal against this decision, but I was informed that there is no appeals procedure and that the decision was final. I am most upset because I will not be able to go to WADA if I do not get financial support.

Counsel is asked to consider whether an order for judicial review might be obtained to compel Greenbridge to consider Miss Lubkowska's application and to draft a claim form and witness statement.

Counsel may find it helpful to know that:

(a) Under the Teaching and Higher Education Act 1998, s 22, Regulations shall make provision requiring the Secretary of State to make grants or loans to eligible students in connection with their undertaking designated courses of higher or further education.

(b) By s 23, the Secretary of State may delegate his functions under s 22 to a local education authority. Counsel may assume he has done so, and that the London Borough of Greenbridge has power to make such grants and loans.

(c) The relevant Regulations are the Education (Student Support) (No 2) Regulations 2002.

(d) By r 4 and Sch 1 to the Regulations Ms Lubkowska is an eligible student if she is settled in the UK, is ordinarily resident in the UK at the commencement of her course, and has been ordinarily resident in the UK throughout the three-year period preceding the first day of her course.

(e) By reg 5 and Sch 2 to the Regulations the course at WADA will be a designated course if WADA is an educational institution assisted by grants out of public funds (which it is) and if the course is a course providing education the standard of which is above A-level but not above first degree level (which counsel may assume to be the case).

Skeleton arguments

23.1 General

23.1.1 The importance of skeleton arguments

The ability to draft a strong, persuasive and yet precise skeleton argument in support of the case you are putting forward is now a fundamental skill required of an advocate. Owing to the importance increasingly placed by judges on skeleton arguments, the skill of preparing them should be seen by the junior barrister as one which is every bit as important as the skill involved in undertaking other forms of written work, such as drafting the statements of case at the start of the claim, or advising in writing during the lifetime of the claim.

A skeleton argument is designed to assist the court with a written outline of the main points to be put forward by a party at a subsequent oral hearing. It is produced by that party's advocate, and given to the judge, before the oral hearing. At the hearing, the judge will expect the advocate to follow it. The use of the word 'skeleton' is significant and its meaning in this context should be understood at the outset and never forgotten. The purpose of a written skeleton argument is to provide you with a structured framework on which you can hang your oral submissions to the court. It is, quite literally, the bones upon which you later build the flesh of your argument. It follows that all of the main issues which you will seek to deal with at the hearing should be covered.

It is now common practice for advocates to draft skeleton arguments, whether for use at interim applications or to form the basis of final submissions at trial after the evidence has been heard. The strict timetables imposed by the CPR have led to the ever more widespread use of written argument.

In criminal proceedings skeleton arguments are frequently used to form the basis of pre-trial argument, such as applications to exclude evidence or to sever an indictment. They are also used at the conclusion of the prosecution case if a submission of no case is to be made.

From time to time in practice advocates are asked to provide the judge with written submissions. These should be distinguished from skeleton arguments. A written submission is intended to be an *alternative* to oral argument (see *Sleeman v Highway Care Ltd* The Times, 3 November 1999). A skeleton argument is an *aid* to oral argument.

23.1.2 Practice Directions and guidelines

On 24 January 1995, Lord Chief Justice Taylor issued a *Practice Direction (Civil Litigation: Case Management)* [1995] 1 All ER 385, which applied to all lists in the Queen's Bench and Chancery Divisions, except where other directions specifically applied. The purpose of the *Practice Direction* was to improve case management, and to reduce the costs and delay of civil litigation. It required, not less than three clear days before the hearing of a claim or application, each party to lodge with the court (with copies being provided to the other parties) a skeleton argument concisely summarising that party's submissions in relation to each of the issues, and citing the main authorities relied upon, which may be attached.

Now that judicial case management takes place under the CPR, you will find in practice that for all multi-track cases in which a case management conference takes place, the court will give detailed directions for the steps to be taken up to the trial and for the trial itself. Those directions will inevitably include a provision requiring the parties to file skeleton arguments a certain number of days prior to trial or before any application of substance to a judge.

In addition, under PD 28 (the fast track) and PD 29 (the multi-track), the parties will be required to file a case summary prior to trial in the fast track and prior to a case management conference in the multi-track.

Skeleton arguments are also required when filing a notice of appeal (PD 52, para 5.9).

There is guidance on the drafting of skeleton arguments in Appendix 3 to the Chancery Guide, paragraph 7.11.12 of the Queen's Bench Guide, Appendix 9 to the Commercial Court Guide, and PD 52, paras 5.10–5.11. No matter what court you are appearing in, and for whatever type of hearing you are preparing your skeleton argument, it would be wise to follow the advice in the Chancery Guide, which is as follows.

Appendix 3   Guidelines on Skeleton Arguments and Chronologies

1.   *A skeleton argument is intended to identify both for the parties and the court those points which are, and those that are not, in issue, and the nature of the argument in relation to those points which are in issue. It is not a substitute for oral argument.*

2.   *Every skeleton argument should therefore:*

  (1)   *identify concisely*

    (a)   *the nature of the case generally, and the background facts insofar as they are relevant to the matter before the court;*

    (b)   *the propositions of law relied on with references to the relevant authorities;*

    (c)   *the submissions of fact to be made with reference to the evidence;*

  (2)   *be as brief as the nature of the issues allows — it should not normally exceed 20 pages of double-spaced A4 paper and in many cases it should be much shorter than this;*

  (3)   *be in numbered paragraphs and state the name (and contact details) of the advocate(s) who prepared it;*

  (4)   *avoid arguing the case at length;*

  (5)   *avoid formality and make use of abbreviations, eg C for Claimant, A/345 for bundle A page 345, 1.1.95 for 1st January 1995 etc.*

But take heed also of the Queen's Bench Guide which says:

7.11.12   *A skeleton argument should:*

  (1)   *concisely summarise the party's submissions in relation to each of the issues,*

  (2)   *cite the main authorities relied on, which may be attached,*

  (3)   *contain a reading list and an estimate of the time it will take the Judge to read,*

  (4)   *be as brief as the issues allow and not normally be longer than 20 pages of double-spaced A4 paper,*

  (5)   *be divided into numbered paragraphs and paged consecutively,*

  (6)   *avoid formality and use understandable abbreviations, and*

  (7)   *identify any core documents which it would be helpful to read beforehand.*

23.1.3　The length of a skeleton argument

The guidance set out above suggests a normal maximum of 20 pages of double spaced A4 paper, but in many cases skeleton arguments can and should be much shorter than this. It is wrong to assume that longer cases justify proportionately longer skeleton arguments. In the case of interim and shorter final appeals in the Court of Appeal, it should normally be possible to do justice to the relevant points in a skeleton argument of considerably less than ten pages. For short hearings before the district judge in the county court, of the type often undertaken by junior counsel in the early years of practice, and which might, for example, involve applications on disclosure issues, or seeking permission to call a particular expert witness, it is suggested that the skeleton argument should rarely exceed five pages.

In the unreported case of *Gerber Garment Technology Inc v Lectra Systems Ltd*, 18 December 1996, Staughton LJ was critical of the parties' failure to comply with the *Practice Direction* for skeleton arguments in the Court of Appeal, particularly when it came to restricting their length. In the case, the claimants had been successful for the infringement of their patents of a machine or process for cutting fabrics. The defendants had only appealed against the amount of damages awarded by the trial judge. Despite the appeal being concerned only with damages, the combined length of the written arguments was 132 pages, containing lengthy quotations from the judgment below, the evidence, and other cases. Staughton LJ commented that the cost of producing such written arguments must have been enormous, and then added:

If we are to retain oral argument in a significant degree, and not just as a cosmetic appendix to written briefs (as in the United States), wasteful duplication may result if we have so-called skeletons of such elaboration as well.

This criticism by Staughton LJ should be remembered by all counsel when determining the amount of detail to be advanced in a skeleton argument.

Accordingly, the first and foremost rule for the preparation of any skeleton argument must be to: 'keep it concise'. As Hobhouse LJ observed in the *Gerber* decision, it was unfortunately the case that in a number of appeals heard by the Court of Appeal, the written arguments were of poor quality and excessively diffuse or lengthy. He thought it might well be necessary to remind counsel that concise succinct submissions are both more helpful and more effective than diffuse ones.

23.1.4　The content and structure of a skeleton argument

There is no strict formula, but a good skeleton argument will usually:

(a) Set out the nature of the application/submission.

(b) State briefly what the case is about (if necessary).

(c) Summarise the issues between the parties (if necessary).

(d) Set out the argument in the form of a series of legal propositions and submissions supported by authority and by evidence (with page/paragraph references as necessary).

(e) Assist the court to assimilate your argument with ease.

(f) Assist you to persuade the court to grant the order you seek.

(g) Identify precisely what the court is being asked to do.

The content of the skeleton argument will inevitably vary according to the complexity of the issues and the stage in the proceedings at which the submissions are made. You should bear in mind that your skeleton argument will be read in advance by the judge and your opponent. It is therefore your first opportunity to influence the outcome of the hearing. The structure should be logical with clear paragraph numbers and sub-headings. Although your skeleton argument should be informative, it should also be concise and easily absorbed. Above all a *skeleton* argument should be just that: the argument should not be fully fleshed out. It is for the advocate to develop the submissions orally. Finally, it is good practice, particularly in civil proceedings, to assist the court by handing up a chronology in a separate document.

In the same way as you develop a style for drafting statements of case, similarly you will develop a style for the preparation of skeleton arguments. The precise form for a skeleton argument will be very much a question of personal choice, which you will develop in your own good time. Nevertheless, one can provide some very basic 'do's' and 'don'ts', which must always be adhered to.

In the case of points of law, there should be a list of the propositions of law which are going to be advanced. The skeleton argument should clearly state the point being contended for and cite the principal authority or authorities in support, with reference to the particular page(s) where the principle concerned is enunciated.

Thus in a medical negligence claim, for instance, one might see early on in the skeleton argument the proposition: 'a doctor cannot be guilty of negligence if he acts in accordance with a responsible body of medical opinion (see *Bolam v Friern Hospital Management Committee* [1957] 1 WLR 582 at 587)'.

Imagine you are acting for a claimant in a trial involving an epidural injection of anaesthetic into the client's spine which it was alleged by the claimant (and supporting medical expert opinion evidence) had been negligently administered by a young and inexperienced doctor, in the wrong place, and not by a senior consultant as contended for by the defendant health authority. The local anaesthetic has escaped into surrounding tissues where it should not have been allowed to go, causing severe long-term injury.

In dealing with breach of duty, a skeleton argument might well have a sub-heading 'Breach of Duty' and then choose to list the central factual issues to be determined by the judge at trial as follows:

(1) Who performed the injection?

(2) Where was the needle sited?

(3) Where was the anaesthetic's intended target?

(4) Was the needle site appropriate?

(5) Was the local anaesthetic released at the target site in the spine?

(6) If the answer to question (5) is 'Yes', how did the local anaesthetic escape to the site of injury?

(7) If the answer to question (5) is 'No', where was the local anaesthetic released?

If such a list of questions were to feature in a skeleton argument being handed in at the start of the trial in this imaginary claim, clearly it would be of immense assistance to the judge when it came to understanding the case in opening, and also when deciding the case later on. If a skeleton is being prepared for a trial at first instance, obviously there would be no transcripts of evidence to be referred to. Reference would, however, have to be made within the skeleton argument to the evidence within the trial bundle (both lay witness statements and reports from the medical experts), which would assist the trial judge in answering the questions you have posed.

23.1.5   Other requirements

The Court of Appeal's *Practice Direction* specifically states that in the case of an appeal on a question(s) of fact, the skeleton argument should state briefly the basis on which it is contended that the Court of Appeal can interfere with the finding of fact concerned, with cross-references to the passages in the transcript or notes of evidence which bear on the point.

In the Court of Appeal, it is mandatory for the appellant's advocate's skeleton argument to be accompanied by a written chronology of events relevant to the appeal, cross-referenced to the core bundle or appeal bundle. Chronologies are also strongly recommended by the Queen's Bench Guide and Chancery Guide. The point to note here particularly is that the chronology is a separate document, and is not to be found within the skeleton argument. It is important that the chronology is kept as a separate document from the skeleton argument, in order that it may easily be consulted in conjunction with other papers.

23.2   Skeleton argument for use at a civil trial

23.2.1   Introduction

Given the very nature and purpose of a skeleton argument, in that it seeks to present an overview of a whole claim and the party's fundamental case to be presented, it is very difficult, if not impossible, within the space available here, to provide any really useful 'model' skeleton argument.

However, there is an example of a skeleton argument provided below. It involves an imaginary case in which a hospital cleaner is alleging she fractured her wrist whilst at work following a fall down some stairs. The defendant NHS Trust's case is that there was no accident suffered at work at all! There is no real issue as to the law and the trial will turn on the resolution of the factual dispute. You should note the basic structure of the skeleton argument, namely an introduction, a list of the issues contended for, how the defendant puts its case with regard to the accident, and also what the defendant says about the injury sustained.

23.2.2   Skeleton argument

IN THE HIGH COURT OF JUSTICE   Claim No 2002 HC 6312
QUEEN'S BENCH DIVISION

BETWEEN

SANDRA LOCKWOOD   Claimant

and

HARLEY NHS TRUST   Defendant

DEFENDANT'S SKELETON ARGUMENT

INTRODUCTION

1.   The Claimant claims damages arising out of an accidental fall at work with the Defendant on 5th October 1999 ('the Material Accident') when she allegedly suffered a fracture of the scaphoid of the left wrist. The Claimant was working as a cleaner at the time of the alleged accident. Her case is that she fell down some stairs having tripped up on a defect at the top of the staircase.

2.   A default judgment for damages to be assessed has been entered and, accordingly, the hearing on 26th June 2004 is an assessment of damages. The question is what damages, that is for personal injuries and consequential financial losses, can the Claimant prove she has suffered, if any, as a result of the material accident.

THE ISSUES

3.   The Defendant contends that the principal issues are as follows:

(1) Did the Claimant in fact suffer a fracture to her left scaphoid or indeed any injury to her left wrist in the Material Accident on 5th October 1999?

(2) If the Claimant injured her left wrist in the Material Accident, what was the nature of the injury, did she have a pre-existing degenerative condition of the wrist and, if so, did the injury merely bring to light and/or exacerbate a condition that would in any event have caused the Claimant the troubles complained of and, if so, to what extent?

(3) Which absences from work (if any) have been attributable to the Material Accident and was the Claimant's medical retirement from the Defendant's employment in July 2003 (on the grounds of 'scaphoid bone cyst') attributable to the Material Accident and, if so, to what extent has the Claimant's employability thereafter been restricted as a result of matters properly attributable to the Material Accident?

THE ACCIDENT

4.   The Defendant's case is that in the Material Accident the Claimant suffered no injury to her left wrist (which is the *only* injury in respect of which she claims: see Particulars of Claim, para 7, Particulars of Injury, at Trial Bundle, page 8, 'TB 8').

5.   Trial Bundle, pages 191 to 199 ('TB 191–199') to which reference is made below are annexed to this Skeleton.

6.   On the day of the Material Accident, Tuesday 5th October 1999, at 14.00 hours first aid was given to the Claimant when she was found to be suffering from a 'badly bruised right upper arm and back of shoulder resulting from an accident at rear staircase'. The Claimant returned to duty at 14.15 hours. See First Aid Report at TB 191.

7.   On Friday 8th October 1999, the Claimant herself completed an Accident on Duty Report recording that on 5th October 1999 at 14.00 hours on the rear staircase 'I slipped on top stair' and described her injury as 'bruised right upper shoulder': see TB 192.

8.   The same day, 8th October 1999, a supervising officer's Accident on Duty Report and an entry in the Accident Book were completed (see TB 193–194 and TB 195 Entry No 935 respectively). The contemporaneous description of the Claimant's injury in both cases was 'bruised right shoulder'. The words 'plus wrist fracture' at paragraph 10 of the supervising officer's Accident on Duty Report, TB 193, were added at a later date, after, the Defendant will contend, the Claimant had attended hospital on 18th and 19th October

1999. The same contention is made in relation to the words 'fractured left wrist' which were added to and then deleted from the Accident Book entry at TB 195.

9.   The Claimant did not cease work until 18th October 1999: see her computerised sick absence record at TB 199.

10.   The Claimant did not attend her general practitioner in respect of the Material Accident or any injury to her left wrist: see the clinical record cards at TB 125.

11.   The Claimant attended the Accident and Emergency Department of the Burton General Hospital on Monday 18th October 1999 when she complained of 'Injury left wrist fell down stairs at work on Friday. Painful ever since'. (Friday would have been 15th October 1999.) She gave the history 'Friday: fell down stairs at work and hurt left wrist? mech (mechanism) of injury unable to recall how landed'. See the Casualty Officer's contemporaneous A & E Department records at TB 66–67.

12.   The following day, Tuesday 19th October 1999, the Claimant returned to the Burton General Hospital as an out-patient where she gave the history 'Had a fall 4/7 (ie 4 days ago) landed on left outstretched hand. Seen at A/E Department 1/7 (ie 1 day ago). On clinical and radiological examination, she was found to have a left scaphoid fracture. Scaphoid type POP (plaster of paris) was applied. Today POP is satisfactory circulation is okay x-ray cyst in left scaphoid (fracture) through it.': see the clinical notes at TB 68.

13.   The Claimant has never reported or complained to the Defendant of an accident at work on Friday 15th October 1999: see the Accident Book at TB 195 which records accidents up to 16th November 1999.

14.   In the circumstances, the Defendant will contend that the Claimant suffered no injury to her left wrist in the Material Accident on 5th October 1999 and, therefore, her claim fails in its entirety, as the whole of her claim for both general and special damages is based upon an alleged injury to her left wrist.

15.   In the event of this Court finding that she did injure her left wrist in the Material Accident, the Defendant's alternative arguments are outlined below.

THE NATURE OF THE INJURY

16.   The contemporaneous clinical notes at the Burton General Hospital quoted above record that when x-rays were first taken they showed a cyst in the left scaphoid with a possible fracture running through it (TB 67 foot and TB 68). A further entry on 2nd December 1999 noted, inter alia, 'X-ray no definite (fracture)': TB 69.

17.   In the circumstances, if there was in fact a fracture to the left scaphoid the most it can be blamed for is bringing to light and exacerbating an existing degenerative condition in the wrist which would, in any event, have caused such problems in due course.

18.   The Claimant was off work initially from 18th October 1999 to 4th December 1999 and then from 25th December 1999 to 1st May 2000 with problems related to her left wrist injury. Thereafter, she returned to work and had no further absences attributable to her left wrist for nearly 9 months until 29th January 2001: see the computerised sick absence record at TB 199. During those 9 months her only substantial absences were in August and November 2000, 34 days with back pain, and January 2001, a total of 19 days absence, again related to back pain.

19.   When in 2001 the Claimant again complained of problems relating to her left wrist these were said to have arisen from an injury to her wrist in February 2001 when she was

'pulling a bucket': see the memorandum from Dr Sheridan, the Defendant's Area Medical Adviser, dated 25th April 2001 at TB 108, the middle of the page. In the circumstances, the Defendant will contend that the Claimant's eventual medical retirement in July 2001 on grounds of 'scaphoid bone cyst' (see the Medical Retirement Certificate at TB 116) and her subsequent restricted working ability is not attributable to the Material Accident but to the pre-existing degenerative condition and/or a further accident, in February 2001.

20.   If necessary, the Defendant will contend that in the light of the Claimant's full sick absence record (TB 196–199), irrespective of the material accident, the Claimant's employment with the Defendant would not have continued beyond her actual retirement date in July 2001 in any event.

21.   In so far as may be necessary, in relation to the calculation of damages claimed the Defendant will rely upon its Counter Schedule dated 1st June 2004 (TB 175–181).

BESS TOFFER

23.2.3 Commentary

The above skeleton argument, when set out in the conventional way, double-spaced on A4 paper, with generous margins, is seven pages long. This is well within the guidelines on length.

It is not easy to read and understand quickly, since you cannot follow up the references to the trial bundle, and the chronology needs to be clear in your mind. But read it again carefully in conjunction with this commentary and you will find it has a compelling clarity and logic. It is a good skeleton argument.

Note above all that it does not attempt to duplicate any other documents: it is not in any way setting out what would be found in the statements of case, the witness statements, the exhibits, the medical reports or the schedules of loss, but it draws on all of these to construct the argument.

It is fully headed, and the title of the document identifies whose skeleton argument it is ('Defendant's').

Introduction. Paragraph 1 is a very brief statement of what the case is about, setting the facts out far more briefly than they would be in the particulars of claim. The chief function of this paragraph is to identify and define the material accident, which is an essential point of departure for the argument that follows. Paragraph 2 simply states the broad issue before the court.

Issues. It is essential to summarise the issues at the outset, so that the judge can know what point the argument is addressing. It is more accurate to say 'the Defendant contends that the issues are' than 'the issues are', since the claimant may well have a different set of issues in her argument. Paragraph 3 then sub-divides into the three main issues. Issue (1) is the most important and comes first: it is very clear. Issue (2) is arguably several sub-issues rolled into one, but it becomes clear when they are argued (in paragraphs 16 and 17) that they are inseparable. Issue (3) also raises several sub-issues, but they are closely connected and interdependent, so they can be identified as one.

The structure of the remainder of the skeleton argument is based on these three issues. Paragraphs 4–14 contain the argument on issue (1); paragraphs 16 and 17 contain the argument on issue (2); and paragraphs 18 to 21 contain the argument on issue (3).

Paragraphs 4 to 14. The argument on issue (1). This section begins by making a clear statement (in paragraph 4) of the proposition the argument is intended to prove, namely that there is no causal link between the accident complained of and the injury complained of. Paragraph 5 is then a formal statement of the pages annexed for the judge's convenience.

From paragraph 6 onwards the argument is built up step by step in a logical way. Note how every step in the argument is supported by evidence. The defendant is not saying what it would like to prove, but what it contends it actually can prove. Obviously the argument is based on evidence that has not yet been accepted by the court or tested by cross-examination, and it may be that when it comes to oral argument counsel for the defendant will need to make adjustments and recognise different strengths and weaknesses. But at this stage, the skeleton argument can only be based on the evidence that will go in as evidence in chief, and so it is.

In essence the argument is that:

(1) The accident on 5 October 1999 did not cause any injury to the claimant's left wrist. Evidence in support of this:

    (a) first aid report says right shoulder (paragraph 6);

    (b) claimant's accident on duty report says right shoulder (paragraph 7);

    (c) supervisor's accident on duty report says right shoulder (left wrist added later) (paragraph 8);

    (d) accident book says right shoulder (left wrist added and then deleted later) (paragraph 8);

    (e) claimant did not cease work after accident (paragraph 9);

    (f) claimant did not consult GP regarding accident (paragraph 10).

(2) If her left wrist was injured at all, it was injured in a separate accident on 15 October 1999. Evidence in support of this:

    (a) casualty notes from hospital including claimant's own complaint (paragraph 11);

    (b) further casualty notes including same complaint by C (paragraph 12).

(3) Any accident on 15 October is not alleged to be the fault of the defendant. Evidence — no entry in accident book (paragraph 13).

Paragraph 14. Sums up the argument by repeating the defendant's contention and stating the consequence that flows from it, namely that the claimant's claim fails in its entirety.

Paragraph 15. Acknowledges the fact that if the defendant succeeds on issue (1), issues (2) and (3) will not need to be argued or decided.

Paragraphs 16 to 17. The argument on issue (2). The argument here will depend on favourable medical opinion, but if the medical opinion is favourable, the argument is straightforward. The X-ray results showed a cyst (see paragraph 12) and no definite fracture (paragraph 16), so even if there was a fracture to the left wrist, and even if it was caused by the material accident, it only produced a condition which the claimant would have suffered from in due course in any event.

Paragraphs 18 to 21. The argument on issue (3). This argument addresses the quantum of damages for lost earnings and seeks to show that even if the wrist was injured in the material accident, and even if the defendant is liable for that injury, most losses of earnings claimed stem from other causes. The only concession, made at the start of paragraph 18, is that two periods of loss were due to the wrist injury. Thereafter she had periods off work due to back pain (paragraph 18), which the defendants will contend are irrelevant (it is not clear whether the claimant has claimed in respect of this loss anyway).

The main loss of earnings results from the claimant's retirement from work which the defendant contends was due either to the pre-existing condition or to yet another accident (paragraph 19). As a last resort the defendant says the claimant's sickness record taken as a whole was such that she would probably have retired when she did in any event for one reason or another (paragraph 20). The figures which flow from these contentions are to be found in the counter-schedule of loss (paragraph 21).

The skeleton argument should be signed by counsel.

23.3   Skeleton argument in support of interim application

The following is an example of a skeleton argument which might be used in an application to set aside judgment in default. The particulars of claim in this case were in **9.5**, and the witness statement in support of the application can be found at **20.8**.

23.3.1 Skeleton argument

IN THE HIGH COURT OF JUSTICE   Claim No 2004 HC 98744
QUEEN'S BENCH DIVISION
MANCHESTER DISTRICT REGISTRY

BETWEEN

SHILTON MACHINE TOOLS LIMITED   Claimant

and

BANKS PLASTIC MOULDINGS LIMITED   Defendant

SKELETON ARGUMENT OF THE DEFENDANT

---

1. Introduction

1.1 This is an application on behalf of the Defendant for judgment entered in default, under CPR, Part 12, to be set aside under CPR, r 13.3 and for transfer of the proceedings to Leeds County Court.

1.2 In support of the application the Defendant will refer to the witness statement of Brian Parkes (and the exhibits referred to in it) dated 15th November 2004.

2. Background

2.1 The claim is for the sum of £70,500, being the price of goods sold and delivered by the Claimant to the Defendant.

2.2 Claim form/particulars of claim issued: 22.9.04
Date of Service: 3.10.04
Expiry of time for filing acknowledgement of service/defence: 17.10.04
Judgment in default entered: 24.10.04

3. Application to set aside default judgment

3.1 The court's discretion

3.1.1 CPR, r 13.3(1)(a) — 'a real prospect of success'

(a) The 4 machines delivered to the Defendant by the Claimant were defective in that they were the subject of frequent breakdowns. A consulting engineer has advised the Defendant that 2 of the machines are so badly designed that they are incapable of meeting industry standards and cannot be repaired. Consequently, the Defendant has lost a lucrative supply contract with United Plastic Containers Plc. Statement of Brian Parkes, paras 2 and 3; exhibits BP1 and BP3.

(b) It is submitted that the defence has a real prospect of success.

3.1.2 CPR, r 13.3(1)(b) — 'some other good reason'

(a) The Claimant's engineers had notice of the defects in the machines after delivery: Statement of Brian Parkes, para 2.

(b) The Defendant sought the opinion of an expert in respect of the defects: Statement of Brian Parkes, para 2.

(c) The Defendant responded promptly upon receipt of the Particulars of Claim: <u>Statement of Brian Parkes, para 4; exhibit BP2</u>.

(d) It is submitted that these are matters which the court *may* take into account in the exercise of its discretion and that they amount to good reasons why the judgment should be set aside or the Defendant should be allowed to defend the claim.

3.2   <u>Matters to which the court must have regard</u>

3.2.1   In considering whether to set aside or vary judgment entered under CPR, Part 12 the matters to which the court must have regard include whether the application to set aside is made promptly: <u>CPR, r 13.3(2)</u>.

(a) Judgment entered 24.10.04.

(b) Application dated 3.11.04.

(c) It is submitted that the Defendant has acted promptly in making this application.

3.2.2   It is further submitted that in the interests of justice judgment should be set aside.

4.   <u>Application to transfer</u>

4.1   Power to transfer from High Court to county court: s 40(2), County Courts Act 1984.

4.2   <u>Matters to which the court must have regard</u>

4.2.1   These are set out in <u>CPR, r 30.3(2)</u>.

The Defendant relies upon the following factors:

(a) the financial value of the claim;

(b) whether it would be more convenient or fair for hearings (including trial) to be held in some other court; and

(c) whether the facts, legal issues, remedies or procedures involved are simple or complex.

4.2.2   Relevant matters:

(a)   Although the value of the claim exceeds the usual jurisdiction of the county court of £50,000, the facts, legal issues, remedies and procedures involved are not complex.

(b) The machines which are the subject of the dispute between the parties are located on site at the Defendant's address in Leeds.

(c) The Defendant's expert is based in Leeds.

4.3   It is submitted therefore that, if the court is minded to grant the Defendant's application to set aside judgment, the case should be transferred from the Manchester District Registry to the Defendant's local court, namely Leeds County Court.

BESS TOFFER

4th November 2004
4 Gray's Inn Place

23.3.2 Commentary

This is shorter than the previous example (not surprisingly, since this is for an interim application, whereas that one was for a trial). It is much more the sort of thing that students on a Bar Vocational Course will need to draft.

Introduction. As previously suggested, the skeleton begins by stating what the application is for. There are two applications to be made, and they need to be identified and in due course dealt with separately. Paragraph 1.2 draws the judge's attention to the relevant evidence to be looked at in conjunction with the skeleton argument.

Background. Paragraph 2 states the nature of the case and gives a brief chronology. The chronology is too short to be worth setting out in a separate document.

Paragraph 3. Sets out the argument in support of the first application. Since the order sought is a discretionary one, regulated by the CPR, Part 13, the argument must be based on the powers of the court and the circumstances in which the court may exercise its discretion in the defendant's favour. There are only two such circumstances, set out in r 13.3(1). So in paragraph 3.1 the skeleton argument seeks to show that each of these circumstances exists. The precise sub-rule is identified in each case.

First the skeleton argument tries to show (in paragraph 3.1.1) that the defendant has a real prospect of successfully defending the claim. This contention must of course be justified by the evidence, so the argument refers in outline to the relevant evidence and cites the sources of it. It concludes by stating the inference that the court will be invited to draw.

Secondly, the skeleton argument tries to show (in paragraph 3.1.2) that there is some other good reason why judgment should be set aside or the defendant should be allowed to defend the claim. It again begins by referring to the evidence upon which the argument will rely, picking out three specific points which the defendant contends are good reasons. It then submits that in the light of these three points the 'good reasons' requirement is satisfied.

But as well as showing that the court has power to set aside judgment, the argument must also show why it should do so, and this is dealt with in paragraph 3.2. There are two submissions. One matter that the court *must* have regard to is stipulated by r 13.3(2), so the argument must address this issue (paragraph 3.2.1). The fact that the application was made promptly can be shown simply by referring to the relevant dates, so these are stated, followed by the obvious submission. The second submission (paragraph 3.2.2) is not separately argued, but will obviously be supported by the matters set out in paragraph 3.1.

Paragraph 4. Sets out the argument in support of the second application. It must of course begin by identifying the court's power to make the order sought (paragraph 4.1). Then it needs to address the criteria to which the court *must* have regard (paragraph 4.2). Rule 30.3(2) sets out seven such matters, of which the defendant relies on three. If an argument is to be based on rules, it is clearly essential to refer to the rules first.

The defendant then puts forward three arguments in favour of transfer, relying on the factors already stated (paragraph 4.2.2). The precise relationship between the facts and the rules will doubtless be elaborated on orally, but for the purposes of the skeleton there is enough apparent connection for the judge to understand the outline submission.

Finally, the skeleton restates the conclusion that the court is to be invited to reach (paragraph 4.3).

23.4 Skeleton argument in a criminal case

23.4.1 Introduction

The following is an example of a skeleton argument which might be used in a criminal case. It forms the basis of an application to exclude evidence of pre-arrest questions and answers and of two police-station tape-recorded interviews. The defendant, Julia Smith, was charged with robbery jointly with Jason Barnes and Brian Lewis. The prosecution case was that on 30 April 2004 the three defendants met at an address and agreed that Smith would telephone a friend of hers, Rose Dean. The two females then arranged to meet at Dean's address. The three defendants then took a taxi to the address. Barnes remained in the car and the other two went to the front door. Smith rang the bell, spoke to Dean via the entryphone and when the door latch was released Lewis burst in with Smith, who then pretended to be a victim. Lewis then terrorised Dean, threatening her with a handgun and stole about £100 in cash from her. He then ran off and escaped with Barnes in the taxi, leaving both the females behind. Smith surrendered voluntarily to the police on 1 May 2004.

DC Jones gave evidence of the following:

(a) A conversation with Smith preceding her arrest on 1 May 2004 in which she denied all knowledge of Lewis and stated that she went to Dean's address by bus.

(b) An interview with Smith on 1 May 2004 in which Smith admitted knowledge of the plan to commit a robbery, that she assisted Lewis to gain entry and that she was present throughout. She stated that she knew Lewis and that she went along with the plan because she was frightened.

(c) A second interview on 3 June 2004 in which Smith still maintained she was frightened but made a number of inconsistent and incriminating remarks.

23.4.2 Skeleton argument

IN THE CROWN COURT AT WOOLWICH   Indictment No T041234

THE QUEEN

v

JULIA SMITH

DEFENDANT'S SKELETON ARGUMENT

Application to exclude evidence under s 78, Police and Criminal Evidence Act 1984 [Arch. 15–359].

Submissions

1. Conversation preceding arrest/caution 1st May 2004 — Failure to caution

Statement of DC Jones [Statement Bundle p 65]:

Smith:	It was terrible, as I got to her flat a masked man put a gun to my head and pushed me into Rose's flat.
DC Jones:	Do you know this man?
Smith:	No, I have never seen him before.
DC Jones:	How did you get to Rose's?
Smith:	The 35 bus.

DC Jones then went on to say that he had grounds to believe that Smith was involved in the offence and arrested and cautioned her.

It is conceded that the first remark made by the Defendant is an unsolicited comment. It is submitted, however, that the subsequent questions and answers (underlined) should be excluded because DC Jones failed to caution the Defendant before putting the questions.

Code of Practice C:10.1 [Arch. Appendix A–69 (supplement); 15–484]

R v Sparks [1991] Crim LR 128, CA

R v Pall [1992] Crim LR 126, CA

2.   Interview 1st May 2004 — 2nd tape: failure to caution after break in questioning

Interview bundle p 44:

DC Jones: I must remind you that you are still under caution. Do you understand?

Smith: mm.

It is submitted that, after the break in the interview, DC Jones should have cautioned the Defendant in full and should have ensured that she was aware that she remained under caution.

Code C:10.1, C:10.8 [Arch. Appendix A–69, 70]

3.   Interview 3rd June 2004

DC Jones: [*Caution given in full*] Do you understand the caution?

Smith: Yes.

DC Jones: Can you give me a brief explanation of what you understand by the caution, say how it affects you.

Smith: Well, if I don't say nothing now and I need to say something when I get to court I won't be able to say it because I should have said it now.

DC Jones: Right.

It is submitted that:

(1) The Defendant did not understand the caution.

(2) DC Jones did not explain it in his own words.

(3) DC Jones allowed the Defendant to continue to misunderstand the caution, thereby appearing to endorse her understanding of it.

Code C: 10D [Arch. Appendix A–72]

4.   Sufficient evidence for prosecution to succeed before interview 3rd June 2004

(1) Interview 1st May 2004: Defendant admitted knowledge of plan to commit robbery, that she assisted Lewis to gain entry and that she was present throughout.

(2) Statement of Rose Dean (victim) 1st May 2004: stated that it was a 'set up' (p. 3).

(3) Statement of Mel Stokes (taxi-driver) 18th May 2004: stated that all 3 passengers were relaxed and happy (p. 12); female not unhappy or afraid (p. 13); she had plenty of opportunities to escape or alert him (p. 13).

It is submitted that by 18th May 2004 there was sufficient evidence for this prosecution to succeed and therefore on 3rd June 2004 there should have been no further questioning of the Defendant.

Code C:11.6; C16.1 [Arch. Appendix A–73, A–89]

ELIZABETH BLAKE

1st February 2005

4 Gray's Inn Place

23.4.3 Commentary

You have now seen three different ways of laying out skeleton arguments. Do not assume that there is only one right way, or even that a barrister will always adopt the same format in every case. Choose a format that suits the structure of your argument.

As always the skeleton argument begins by stating clearly what submission is being made.

You must identify for the judge the power under which you are inviting him to act, so there follows a reference to the paragraph in *Archbold* where s 78 of the Police and Criminal Evidence Act 1984 is printed. You will have noticed there are numerous such references in this skeleton argument. *Archbold* is the bible in criminal courts, and whatever you may say the judge will want to look it up, so be helpful by giving the references. You could alternatively give references to *Blackstone's Criminal Practice*.

There are then four numbered submissions, each of which, you will argue, should lead the judge to the conclusion that some part of the evidence should be excluded.

Submission 1. The headline tells the judge the nature of the submission — failure to caution. The argument must of course be based on the evidence, so the skeleton sets out the relevant part of the evidence (after identifying where it comes from). There is no easy way to refer to the precise words in question other than by copying them out, so it is helpful to do so. This is followed by the submission itself and the authorities that will be cited in argument. PACE Code C, para 10.1 says that 'A person whom there are grounds to suspect of an offence ... must be cautioned before any questions about an offence ... are put to them, if either the suspect's answers or silence ... may be given in evidence ...'. The cases of *R v Sparks* and *R v Pall* hold that a failure to caution should be regarded as a 'significant and substantial breach' of the Code.

Submission 2. The structure of this submission is exactly the same as that of the first. There is a headline, reference to the source of the evidence, quotation from the evidence, the submission itself and legal citation. Code C, para 10.8 contains the main point: 'After any break in questioning under caution, the person being questioned must be made aware that they remain under caution. If there is any doubt the relevant caution should be given again in full when the interview resumes.' This is not perhaps your strongest point.

Submission 3. This is the first of two submissions to the effect that the whole of the interview of 3 June should be excluded. The exchange between the officer and defendant is again quoted and it is self-evident that the defendant did not correctly understand the caution, and that the officer endorsed her misunderstanding. This not surprisingly justifies the first and third submissions. The second submission is based on Code C, note 10D: 'If it appears a person does not understand the caution, the person giving it should explain it in their own words.'

Submission 4. The interview of 3 June is also challenged on the basis that the police had sufficient evidence to charge the defendant before the interview took place and so should not have proceeded with it. The argument begins by identifying the evidence available to the police after 18 May (together with its sources) and then states the conclusion to be drawn and the relevant legal sources. Code C, para 11.6 says 'The interview ... of a person about an offence with which that person has not been charged ... must cease when the officer ... (c) ... reasonably believes there is sufficient evidence to provide a realistic prospect of conviction for that offence ...'. By Code C, para 16.1, when similar conditions are satisfied, the defendant should be brought before the custody officer with a view to his being charged.

23.5 Exercise A

You are instructed to appear on behalf of the claimant, Baildon Garages Ltd, on the claimant's application for summary judgment at Bromley County Court on 17 January 2005. The brief facts are that on 15 November 2004 the defendant, Harold Spencer, purchased a Ford Mondeo from the claimant for the sum of £8,500. Mr Spencer paid by cheque and took the car away the same day. On 19 November the garage presented the cheque for payment but it was dishonoured, payment having been countermanded by Mr Spencer. The garage commenced proceedings in respect of the cheque on 3 December 2004. In his defence (filed 17 December 2004) Mr Spencer stated that he stopped the cheque because: (1) the following day the car broke down; (2) he took it to a different garage and was told that (a) the repairs would cost £1,500, (b) the car was unsafe to drive, and (c) it appeared to have previously been involved in a collision; and (3) when he tried to return the car to Baildon Garages the salesman, Robert Miller, refused to take it back. Mr Spencer is alleging breach of implied terms in the contract and total failure of consideration. Your instructions are that: (1) Mr Miller has no knowledge of any previous collision or any defects in the vehicle; (2) the car had a full service history; (3) before he bought the car Mr Spencer had a full AA inspection carried out. Copies of the relevant documents are exhibited to Mr Miller's statement. You advise that Baildon Garages are entitled to summary judgment because a mere right of set-off can never constitute a defence to a claim on a dishonoured cheque: *Jackson v Murphy* (1887) 4 TLR 92; *Esso Petroleum Co Ltd v Milton* [1997] 1 WLR 938. You are of the opinion that, although the defence relied upon (total failure of consideration) might, in principle, be recognised by the court, on these facts it would have no real prospect of success: CPR, r 24.2(a)(ii). You further advise that, in your opinion, there is no other reason why the case should be disposed of at trial: CPR, r 24.2(b).

Draft a skeleton argument which will form the basis of your application for summary judgment.

23.6 Exercise B

You represent a defendant, Joseph Palmer, who is charged with an offence under s 17(2) of the Firearms Act 1968, which provides as follows:

If a person, at the time of his committing or being arrested for an offence specified in Schedule 1 of this Act has in his possession a firearm or imitation firearm, he shall be guilty of an offence under this subsection unless he shows that he had it in his possession for a lawful object.

The relevant offence in Sch 1 in this case is assaulting a constable in the execution of his duty, contrary to s 89(1) of the Police Act 1996. The indictment alleges that Palmer had the firearm in his possession at the time of committing the assault.

At his trial at Maidstone Crown Court on 1 February 2005, the evidence of the police officer (PC Anderson) is as follows:

(1) He stopped Palmer because he was running from the direction of a burglary.
(2) He wanted to search him for stolen property.
(3) During the course of the search Palmer punched PC Anderson in the face.
(4) PC Anderson then arrested Palmer for assaulting a constable in the execution of his duty.
(5) Palmer tried to escape and was seen to drop an object in a dustbin.
(6) He was caught and a firearm was recovered from the dustbin.

In cross-examination PC Anderson admitted:

(7) Although he identified himself as PC Anderson from Croydon Police Station, he did not state the object of the search or the grounds for the search.

(8) Although he was not in uniform (because he was off duty) he did not produce his warrant card.

Having researched the law, you decide to make a submission of no case to answer at the conclusion of the prosecution case. Your researches indicate as follows:

A submission of no case should be allowed when there is no evidence upon which a reasonable jury, properly directed, could convict (*Archbold* 4-293). The judge will stop the case if there is no evidence that the crime alleged has been committed by the defendant: *R v Galbraith* (1981) 73 Cr App R 124 (see *Archbold* 4-294).

It was held by the Court of Appeal in *R v Nelson* [2000] 2 Cr App R 160 that it is not necessary to show that an offence in the schedule has been committed; see *Archbold* 19–265 and 24–50. But it seems to you that *R v Nelson* is distinguishable.

Furthermore you take the view that the offence under s 89(1) has not been committed. PC Anderson acted in breach of s 2 of the Police and Criminal Evidence Act 1984 (*Archbold* 15–52, 53) and PACE Code A, paras 3.8–3.9 (*Archbold* Appendix A-10), which set out what a police officer must do before carrying out a search. You conclude that the search was unlawful and that the prosecution have therefore not proved an essential ingredient of the scheduled offence, namely that PC Anderson was acting in the execution of his duty.

You believe on the basis of this research that you can construct an argument to the effect that the prosecution have failed to establish the offence under s 17(2).

Draft a skeleton argument which will form the basis of your submission.

Indictments

24.1 Introduction

There is not a lot of drafting involved in criminal work — basically only skeleton arguments (which were dealt with in **Chapter 23**), grounds of appeal (which are covered in **Chapter 25**) and indictments, which are the subject matter of this chapter.

24.1.1 The drafting of indictments

Most indictments are drafted by the Crown Prosecution Service, but barristers in independent practice do draft some, particularly in complex cases where prosecution counsel may be instructed at an early stage. But every barrister doing criminal work must be competent in the drafting of an indictment, because it is your duty to notice and correct any errors or defects in an indictment. If you are prosecuting a case, and the indictment is defective, the defendant is likely to be acquitted and it will be your fault. If you are defending, and the indictment is defective, it is your duty to prevent your client being convicted on that indictment. If you do not notice the error, he may be wrongly convicted, and it will be your fault. It is arguably a matter of professional negligence to fail to spot a patent defect in an indictment.

24.1.2 The form of indictments

Every count in an indictment follows a standard form. It must contain a statement of the offence, with the relevant statutory section (unless it is a common law offence) and particulars of the offence which must specify who, when, where (if an essential ingredient), did what to whom. The particulars must incorporate the essential ingredients of the offence. If any is missing, the count is bad.

Some terms, however, have a precise meaning and when used import all the elements incorporated within them. Common examples are: 'steal', 'rob', 'murder', 'assault', 'rape', 'attempt' and 'conspire'.

As far as drafting indictments goes, therefore, the count is basically either right or wrong. There is little scope for variation or personal style. If the elements of the offence are included and the standard form followed, it should be impossible to go wrong except through faulty particularisation of an individual element in the offence.

An indictment must always be signed by an officer of the court.

24.1.3 The language of indictments

You will notice that the drafting of indictments is one area in which modern, plain English is not generally used. There are probably two reasons for this:

(a) Indictments must in all cases follow precisely the words of the statute, and most criminal statutes are not drafted in modern English.

(b) Most indictments are drafted according to set formulae, and no one has got around to redrafting those standard forms.

It would actually be quite possible to draft indictments to a much greater extent in plain English, provided statutory terms were retained, and the writer toyed with the idea of doing so in this Manual. But it is probably not a good idea to teach students to draft in a way that is different from what they will meet in practice, and which could therefore cause them problems. So in this chapter alone, old-fashioned language is retained, as it still is in all the criminal courts.

24.1.4 Conventions

Dates in indictments can be in the usual form 'on 12th April 2004', though the longer form 'on the 12th day of April 2004' is still commonly used. Never use 'on or about 12th April 2004'; use 'on a day unknown between' (giving exclusive dates) or 'on a day unknown before' (adding the day *after* the last possible date). So if, for example, the offence was committed either just before or just after midnight on 12 April, the correct form is 'on a day unknown between 11th and 14th April 2004'.

Names are given in full without titles or modes of address (ie not 'Mr' 'Mrs', 'Captain' 'OBE').

Motor vehicles are usually identified by make, model and registration number.

Goods should be identified as precisely as possible; quote model numbers, serial numbers etc where known; but do not include details which cannot be proved. If the indictment specifies that the defendant stole '200 red pencils', the prosecution must prove that there were 200 exactly and that every one of them was red. 'A quantity of pencils' is the safe alternative.

Cheques, cheque cards etc are identified by an appropriate combination of: bank, number of card or cheque, account name, how much the cheque is made out for.

24.1.5 Multiple counts

If there are several counts in an indictment, thought should be given to the order in which to put them. The chief guidelines are:

(a) Put them in the order in which you will want to tell the story when opening the case to the jury. This will usually be chronological order, but not always.

(b) Put the more serious offence before the lesser offence arising out of the same facts.

Where counts in an indictment are alternative to each other, there is nothing on the face of the indictment to indicate this: simply draft the relevant counts.

24.2   What offences should be included in an indictment?

Prosecution counsel is responsible (see *R v Newland* (1988) 87 Cr App R 118) for the indictment being correct. Even if, before delivering the brief, the Crown Prosecution Service (CPS) has drafted the indictment and has had it signed by the appropriate officer of the court, counsel still remains obliged to ensure that it accurately and appropriately reflects the evidence contained in the committal documents. You may therefore have to consider proposing amendments.

In considering whether a count should be included you should bear in mind the CPS Code. An offence should only be charged if there is enough evidence to provide a realistic prospect of conviction.

It is difficult to generalise about the number of counts which should be included. If the defendant has engaged in a series of offences over a period of time, it is enough simply to have specimen charges, picking out a few of the most serious or most typical offences, and the case will be opened accordingly to the jury. While the Crown must elect, at trial, whether to proceed on either conspiracy or substantive counts, it is often useful to have both on the indictment in case the defendant is willing to plead guilty to one but not the other. In any event, a substantive count may not reflect the full criminality of the case. For example, say the police stop two men who are found in possession of recently stolen goods. The police go to their homes and find that there are a number of similar items, which have been received, although it is difficult to say when or in what circumstances. An indictment alleging only the final incident (when they are caught) is not enough, while a conspiracy count (if supported by the evidence as a whole) gives a more accurate picture of what has been going on.

If there is more than one defendant, it is essential to isolate what evidence is admissible against each. This is not always simple, as police will question suspect A about the activities of suspect B, while forgetting to ask suspect B to identify certain documents or other exhibits. One may well be in the position of drafting different counts to reflect the differences in evidence, for example, if one defendant makes admissions while the other does not.

Many offences include, by their nature, lesser offences. For example, a jury which is not sure that a defendant was a trespasser may still convict him of theft rather than of burglary. When deciding whether to include alternative offences on the same indictment, ask yourself two questions:

(a) Is one offence already included in the other? *and*

(b) Will it make it easier for the jury to follow the case if all the alternatives are set out?

The obvious examples are degrees of seriousness in assault cases (Offences Against the Person Act 1861, ss 18 and 20), which generally should all be included to avoid the jury feeling (despite the judge's directions) that it is 'grievous bodily harm or nothing'. Where the prosecution wishes the jury to consider, as an alternative, a purely summary offence (eg, common assault) by virtue of the Criminal Justice Act 1988, s 40, it is not open to a jury to convict on it unless it forms a separate count. The fact that it is contained in a more serious, indictable one is insufficient.

24.3 General form

24.3.1 Two defendants: complementary counts

24.3.1.1 Indictment

<u>IN THE CROWN COURT AT SNARESBROOK</u>   No.

Regina *v* Alexander Crossman and Molly Spinks

who are charged as follows:

COUNT 1

<u>STATEMENT OF OFFENCE</u>

Theft, contrary to section 1 of the Theft Act 1968.

<u>PARTICULARS OF OFFENCE</u>

Alexander Crossman on 24th November 2004 stole a plastic garden gnome, belonging to Supacon Limited.

COUNT 2

<u>STATEMENT OF OFFENCE</u>

Theft, contrary to section 1 of the Theft Act 1968.

<u>PARTICULARS OF OFFENCE</u>

Alexander Crossman on 24th November 2004 stole a wallet and £100 in money, belonging to John Albert Smith.

COUNT 3

<u>STATEMENT OF OFFENCE</u>

Handling stolen goods, contrary to section 22(1) of the Theft Act 1968.

<u>PARTICULARS OF OFFENCE</u>

Molly Spinks on a day unknown between 23rd November and 1st December 2004 dishonestly received stolen goods, namely a plastic garden gnome, belonging to Supacon Limited, knowing or believing the same to have been stolen.

Signature
Officer of the Court

24.3.1.2 Commentary

The heading is simple. The name of the court as given is strictly correct, since there is only one Crown Court in the land. However, you will frequently see also the incorrect 'in the Snaresbrook Crown Court'.

The party prosecuting is named as 'Regina', which may seem old-fashioned, but is still widely used. Also acceptable are 'The Queen', 'The Crown' or simply 'R.'.

There is then always a line stating 'who is/are charged as follows'.

Every count must be numbered (unless the indictment contains only a single count), and this is traditionally done by stating 'COUNT 1' etc against the left-hand margin. Then each count must have a 'Statement of Offence' and 'Particulars of Offence'. These separate parts of the count are identified by headings, capitalised, underlined and centred (though you will come across other styles).

Under the Statement of Offence heading, name the offence (making sure you name it in accordance with the statute that creates it) and identify the statutory section to which it is contrary. Under the Particulars of Offence heading state who, when, did what to whom (add where and how if these are essential ingredients). Make sure that all the necessary ingredients of the offence are included, and further particularised if appropriate. The 'who' *always* comes first and the 'when' *always* comes second. The order of the other ingredients varies according to the needs of precision and clarity.

Note how it is only through the name at the beginning of the particulars of each offence that it becomes apparent which defendant is charged with which offence(s). Here Alexander Crossman faces two counts of theft and Molly Spinks one count of receiving. These counts are all additional to each other — that is, the prosecution will seek a conviction on all three. They are properly joined on the same indictment because the two theft counts, being committed on the same day are all part of the same 'spree', and because the count of receiving relates to the same goods as the first theft count.

24.3.2 Alternative counts

24.3.2.1 Indictment

IN THE CENTRAL CRIMINAL COURT   No.

The Queen *v* Alexander Crossman

who is charged as follows:

COUNT 1

STATEMENT OF OFFENCE

Causing grievous bodily harm with intent, contrary to section 18 of the Offences Against the Person Act 1861.

PARTICULARS OF OFFENCE

Alexander Crossman on 17th September 2004 unlawfully caused grievous bodily harm to Mary Mills, with intent to do her grievous bodily harm.

COUNT 2

STATEMENT OF OFFENCE

Inflicting grievous bodily harm, contrary to section 20 of the Offences Against the Person Act 1861.

PARTICULARS OF OFFENCE

Alexander Crossman on 17th September 2004 unlawfully and maliciously inflicted grievous bodily harm on Mary Mills.

                                                                 Signature
                                                        Officer of the Court

24.3.2.2 Commentary

The Crown Court at the Old Bailey is known as the Central Criminal Court.

These are two alternative counts. The prosecution will seek a conviction on count 1, and if they get it will not expect the judge to ask the jury to reach a verdict on count 2. If however the jury do not convict on count 1, they will expect a verdict on count 2. The lesser charge in count 2 of inflicting grievous bodily harm is actually included within the offence of causing grievous bodily harm with intent charged in count 1, and so the jury *could* return a verdict of guilty under s 20 on an indictment charging only s 18. However, the judge would then have to direct the jury that they could only do this if they first found the defendant not guilty of causing grievous bodily harm with intent. They could not bring in the alternative verdict if they were unable to reach a decision on the greater offence. The addition of the second alternative count makes this possible, because the judge can then relieve the jury from reaching a verdict on count 1 and accept a verdict on count 2. That is why this form of indictment is almost always used when there is a charge under s 18.

But note that there is nothing on the face of the indictment to say that these two counts are alternative to each other. The defendant simply faces two counts. It will be for the prosecution and the judge to explain to the jury that they are alternatives.

24.4   Counts in particular cases

There is no room in this Manual to provide a comprehensive list of sample counts covering all indictable offences. What follows is a selection of common and well-known offences. Many other sample counts can be found in *Archbold's Criminal Pleading and Practice* and *Blackstone's Criminal Practice*.

Not even *Archbold* and *Blackstone* however have precedents for every offence known in law. If you find yourself needing to charge an offence for which there is no precedent, you will have to work the correct form of the indictment out from first principles. Research the law, study the statute and draw up a list of the essential ingredients to be proved. Then find a clear and elegant way to incorporate them into a count, particularising wherever you feel it is appropriate.

24.4.1   Theft

24.4.4.1   Indictment

STATEMENT OF OFFENCE

Theft, contrary to section 1 of the Theft Act 1968.

PARTICULARS OF OFFENCE

Alexander Crossman and Molly Spinks on 25th October 2004 stole a keep left sign, belonging to the London Borough of Brent.

24.4.1.2   Commentary

This is a joint charge against two defendants. This is made clear by naming two defendants at the beginning of the particulars of offence. The word 'steal' is defined by the Theft Act 1968, and so it incorporates all the elements contained within the definition. So when you say that someone 'stole', you are saying they 'dishonestly appropriated property belonging to another with the intention of permanently depriving the other of it'. The property must obviously be identified.

24.4.2   Burglary

24.4.2.1   Section 9(1)(a)

STATEMENT OF OFFENCE

Burglary, contrary to section 9(1)(a) of the Theft Act 1968.

PARTICULARS OF OFFENCE

Alexander Crossman on 25th September 2004 entered a building known as 4 Gray's Inn Place, WC1 as a trespasser with intent to steal therein [*or* with intent to do unlawful damage to the said building by fire] [*or* with intent to inflict grievous bodily harm on John Smith a person therein] [*or* with intent to rape Sarah Crawley, a woman therein].

24.4.2.2 Section 9(1)(b)

STATEMENT OF OFFENCE

Burglary, contrary to section 9(1)(b) of the Theft Act 1968.

PARTICULARS OF OFFENCE

Alexander Crossman on 25th September 2004 having entered a building known as the Police Station, High Street, Neasden as a trespasser, stole therein three notebooks, two helmets, a quantity of documents and a bottle of whisky, belonging to the Metropolitan Police Commissioner [*or* inflicted grievous bodily harm on John Smith, a person therein].

24.4.2.3 Commentary

There are two different forms of burglary, usually known in practice as s 9(1)(a) and 9(1)(b). The statement of offence should state which form is charged. If the prosecution wish to charge both forms in the alternative, they must be in separate counts. The word 'burgle' does not have a statutory definition, so the elements must be set out individually. For s 9(1)(a) burglary that involves (1) entering, (2) a building (or part of a building), (3) as a trespasser, (4) with intent to steal (or inflict grievous bodily harm, do criminal damage or rape), (5) in that building. For s 9(1)(b) burglary that involves (1) having entered, (2) a building (or part of a building), (3) as a trespasser, (4) steals (or inflicts grievous bodily harm). Since under s 9(1)(b) the offence of theft must be completed, the indictment must include all that is necessary for theft as well as burglary.

24.4.3 Robbery

24.4.3.1 Indictment

STATEMENT OF OFFENCE

Robbery, contrary to section 8 of the Theft Act 1968.

PARTICULARS OF OFFENCE

Alexander Crossman on 19th October 2004 robbed Jane Waddle of £52.78 in money.

24.4.3.2 Commentary

Robbery is simple because 'rob' is another word that incorporates all its statutory elements, namely (1) steals, (2) immediately before or at the time, (3) and in order to do so, (4) uses force (or puts someone in fear or seeks to put them in fear of immediate force). 'In money' means in cash.

24.4.4 Going equipped

24.4.4.1 Indictment

STATEMENT OF OFFENCE

Going equipped for theft [*or* burglary] [*or* cheat] contrary to section 25 of the Theft Act 1968.

<u>PARTICULARS OF OFFENCE</u>

Alexander Crossman on 28th August 2004 not being at his place of abode, had with him an article for use in the course of or in connection with theft [*or* burglary] [*or* cheat], namely a stocking [*or* a screwdriver] [*or* a credit card].

24.4.4.2 Commentary

This is one of the comparatively few offences in which the place where the offence is committed is an essential ingredient — the defendant must be (1) 'not at his place of abode'. The other elements are, (2) has with him, (3) an article or articles, (4) for use in the course of or in connection with, (5) theft, burglary or cheat (meaning an offence under s 15). The indictment must specify whether it is theft, burglary or cheat that is alleged. In the example it is intended that the stocking goes with theft, the screwdriver with burglary and the credit card with cheat.

24.4.5   Handling stolen goods

24.4.5.1   First limb: receiving

<u>STATEMENT OF OFFENCE</u>

Handling stolen goods, contrary to section 22 of the Theft Act 1968.

<u>PARTICULARS OF OFFENCE</u>

Alexander Crossman on 26th November 2004 dishonestly received stolen goods, namely a Sony video recorder serial number AB2683 belonging to Peter Alan Jones, knowing or believing the same to have been stolen.

24.4.5.2   Second limb: specific charge

<u>STATEMENT OF OFFENCE</u>

Handling stolen goods, contrary to section 22 of the Theft Act 1968.

<u>PARTICULARS OF OFFENCE</u>

Molly Spinks on a day unknown between 25th and 30th November 2004 dishonestly assisted in the disposal by Alexander Crossman of stolen goods, namely a Sony video recorder serial number AB2683 belonging to Peter Alan Jones, knowing or believing the same to have been stolen.

24.4.5.3   Second limb: general charge

<u>STATEMENT OF OFFENCE</u>

Handling stolen goods, contrary to section 22 of the Theft Act 1968.

<u>PARTICULARS OF OFFENCE</u>

Molly Spinks, on a day unknown between 24th November and 1st December 2004 dishonestly undertook or assisted in the retention, removal, disposal or realisation of stolen goods, namely a plastic garden gnome, belonging to Supacon Limited, by or for the benefit of Alexander Crossman, or dishonestly arranged to do so, knowing or believing the same to have been stolen.

24.4.5.4 Commentary

Handling stolen goods is an offence which can be committed in 17 different ways. However, it has been established that for indictment purposes there are only two limbs of the offence: receiving, and acting by or for the benefit of another in one of the prescribed ways. A count must charge only one of these two limbs. The receiving limb has four ingredients: (1) dishonestly, (2) receives, (3) stolen goods, (4) knowing or believing them to be stolen, and all these ingredients must be included. The second limb has five ingredients: (1) dishonestly, (2) undertakes or assists in or arranges to undertake or assist in the retention removal disposal or realisation, (3) of stolen goods, (4) by or for the benefit of another, (5) knowing or believing the goods to be stolen. The second limb can either be charged specifically, picking out exactly what the defendant is alleged to have done, as in **24.4.5.2**, or it can be charged in general, throwing in everything, as in **24.4.5.3**.

24.4.6   Dishonestly retaining a wrongful credit

24.4.6.1   Indictment

STATEMENT OF OFFENCE

Dishonestly retaining a wrongful credit, contrary to section 24A of the Theft Act 1968.

PARTICULARS OF OFFENCE

Alexander Crossman, on a day unknown between 1st November and 1st December 2004, knowing or believing that a wrongful credit in the sum of £2,568.54 made to an account kept by him at Southern Bank plc was wrongful, dishonestly failed to take such steps as were reasonable in the circumstances to secure that the credit was cancelled.

24.4.6.2   Commentary

This offence was added by the Theft (Amendment) Act 1996. The ingredients are: (1) a wrongful credit has been made to the defendant's account, (2) knows or believes it to be wrongful, (3) dishonestly, (4) fails to take such steps as are reasonable in the circumstances to secure that the credit is cancelled. The offence is doubtless primarily intended to cover the situation where the money was wrongfully credited by mistake, but it also covers the situation where the defendant himself has dishonestly secured a wrongful credit. The indictment cannot distinguish.

24.4.7   Obtaining property by deception

24.4.7.1   Cashing a stolen cheque

STATEMENT OF OFFENCE

Obtaining property by deception, contrary to section 15 of the Theft Act 1968.

PARTICULARS OF OFFENCE

Alexander Crossman on 24th October 2004 dishonestly obtained from the National Westminster Bank plc £50 in money with the intention of permanently depriving the National Westminster Bank plc of the money, by deception, namely by falsely representing to Nigel Worth that National Westminster Bank cheque number 123456 made out in the sum of £50, was a good and valid order for the payment of £50, and that he had authority to present the cheque for payment.

24.4.7.2   Dishonestly bouncing a cheque

STATEMENT OF OFFENCE

Obtaining property by deception, contrary to section 15 of the Theft Act 1968.

PARTICULARS OF OFFENCE

Molly Spinks on 13th October 2004 dishonestly obtained from Supacon Limited a woollen jumper to the value of £65 with the intention of permanently depriving Supacon Limited of the jumper, by deception, namely by falsely representing to one Loretta Higgs that Midland Bank cheque number 123456 made out in the sum of £65 was a good and valid order for the payment of £65 and would be met upon presentation.

24.4.7.3   Commentary

This offence has a large number of ingredients: (1) dishonestly, (2) obtains, (3) property, (4) belonging to another, (5) intention of permanently depriving, (6) by, (7) deception. 'By' and 'deception' are separate elements: the prosecution must prove not only that there was a deception, but also that it was an effective cause of the obtaining. The chief drafting challenge with this offence is to particularise the operative deception(s) correctly. The formula is always 'by falsely representing that'. The name of the person deceived can be included where known, but it is not essential.

This offence is commonly committed through cheque or credit card fraud. Two classic cases of cheque fraud form the basis of the above examples. The representations are implied representations made as a matter of law whenever someone offers a cheque in payment. These are:

(a) that the person is the authorised bearer of the cheque (book) (and maybe cheque guarantee card);

(b) that the person has authority to write that cheque;

(c) that the cheque is a good and valid order for the sum in which it is made out; and

(d) that it will be met on presentation.

You can select from these as appropriate to the facts of the case. Obviously any further express representations made will depend on the facts of the case.

In the case of dishonest use of a stolen credit or debit card, the implied representations are that:

(a) the person is the authorised holder of that card; and

(b) that he is authorised to use that card in payment.

24.4.8   Obtaining a money transfer by deception

24.4.8.1   Indictment

STATEMENT OF OFFENCE

Obtaining a money transfer by deception, contrary to section 15A of the Theft Act 1968.

PARTICULARS OF OFFENCE

Molly Spinks on 13th November 2004 dishonestly obtained for herself a money transfer in the sum of £5,000 by deception, namely by falsely representing to Daniel Briggs that National Westminster Bank cheque number 123456 drawn on the account of Sally Spratt and made out in the sum of £5,000, was a good and valid order for the payment of £5,000, and that she had authority to present the cheque.

24.4.8.2   Commentary

This is another offence added by the Theft (Amendment) Act 1996. The ingredients are straightforward: (1) dishonestly, (2) obtains a money transfer, (3) for himself or another, (4) by (5) deception. It is committed where money is moved from one account to another without the defendant ever getting his hands on the cash. In this case the defendant is alleged to have paid a forged cheque into her account. The false representations are very similar to those in the examples of offences under s 15.

24.4.9 Blackmail

24.4.9.1 Indictment

STATEMENT OF OFFENCE

Blackmail, contrary to section 21 of the Theft Act 1968.

PARTICULARS OF OFFENCE

Alexander Crossman on 11th September 2004 with a view to gain for himself, made an unwarranted demand for £1,000 from Supacon Limited with menaces.

24.4.9.2 Commentary

The elements of blackmail are: (1) with a view to gain for himself or with intent to cause loss to another, (2) makes, (3) unwarranted, (4) demand, (5) with menaces. The indictment simply follows these ingredients. Choose between 'with a view to gain for himself' and 'with intent to cause loss to another'. For reasons that the writer has never been able to understand, it appears not to be necessary to particularise the menaces made.

24.4.10 Obtaining services by deception

24.4.10.1 Indictment

STATEMENT OF OFFENCE

Obtaining services by deception, contrary to section 1 of the Theft Act 1978.

PARTICULARS OF OFFENCE

Alexander Crossman on 1st November 2004 dishonestly obtained from Supacon Limited services, namely the dry-cleaning of an overcoat, by deception, namely by falsely representing to Sally Spratt, an employee of Supacon Limited that it was his intention to pay for the said services.

24.4.10.2 Commentary

Obtaining services by deception has the same ingredients as obtaining property by deception except that what has to be obtained is simply 'services' instead of 'property belonging to another'. If the services are obtained by cheque or credit card fraud, the deception can be particularised exactly as in s 15 offences. However, a common deception in this offence is a false representation that the defendant intended to pay for the services.

24.4.11 Evasion of liability by deception

24.4.11.1 Securing remission of liability

STATEMENT OF OFFENCE

Evasion of liability by deception, contrary to section 2(1)(a) of the Theft Act 1978.

PARTICULARS OF OFFENCE

Alexander Crossman and Molly Spinks on 28th October 2004 dishonestly secured the remission of an existing liability to make a payment, namely rent due to Sally Spratt, by deception, namely by falsely representing to Sally Spratt that they were married to each other, that Molly Spinks was pregnant and that they could not afford to make the payment.

24.4.11.2 Inducing someone to wait for payment

STATEMENT OF OFFENCE

Evasion of liability by deception, contrary to section 2(1)(b) of the Theft Act 1978.

PARTICULARS OF OFFENCE

Molly Spinks on 24th November 2004, with intent to make permanent default on an existing liability to make a payment, namely payment for a plastic Christmas tree sold to her by Supacon Limited, dishonestly induced Supacon Limited to wait for payment, by deception, namely by falsely representing to John Smith, an employee of Supacon Limited, that National Westminster Bank Cheque 123456 made out in the sum of £6.99 was a good and valid order for the payment of £6.99 and that it would be paid upon presentation.

24.4.11.3 Obtaining abatement of liability

STATEMENT OF OFFENCE

Evasion of liability by deception, contrary to section 2(1)(c) of the Theft Act 1978.

PARTICULARS OF OFFENCE

Alexander Crossman on 29th November 2004 dishonestly obtained from Stitch Productions plc abatement of liability to make payment for a theatre ticket, by deception, namely by falsely representing to Olivia Merritt, an employee of Stitch Productions plc that he was a student and that he was the authorised bearer of a student card in the name of Thomas Tucker.

24.4.11.4 Commentary

Evasion of liability by deception is a complex offence which can be committed in three different ways. The statement of offence should make it clear whether the charge is under s 2(1)(a), 2(1)(b) or 2(1)(c). In every case there are three elements in common: (1) dishonesty, (2) by, (3) deception. But then under s 2(1)(a) there are: (4) secure remission of, (5) existing liability to make a payment. Under s 2(1)(b) there are: (4) intent to make permanent default, (5) existing liability to make a payment, (6) induce, (7) someone, (8) to wait for payment. Under s 2(1)(c) there are: (4) obtain abatement, (5) liability to make a payment. The examples illustrate how the indictment might be set out and some circumstances in which each version of the offence might be charged. Deception as always is charged as a false representation, but the operative deception is far from standard in this offence. You need to particularise the deception in accordance with the unique facts of each case.

24.4.12 Making off without payment

24.4.12.1 Indictment

STATEMENT OF OFFENCE

Making off without payment, contrary to section 3 of the Theft Act 1978.

PARTICULARS OF OFFENCE

Molly Spinks on 24th November 2004 knowing that payment on the spot for a meal she had consumed at the Greedy Pig Restaurant was required of her and with intent to avoid payment of the amount due, dishonestly made off without having paid.

24.4.12.2   Commentary

This is a straightforward offence, though it has a large number of elements: (1) knowing, (2) payment on the spot required or expected, (3) intent to avoid payment, (4) dishonestly, (5) makes off, (6) without paying.

24.4.13   Criminal damage

24.4.13.1   Destroying property

STATEMENT OF OFFENCE

Destroying property, contrary to section 1(1) of the Criminal Damage Act 1971.

PARTICULARS OF OFFENCE

Alexander Crossman on 18th July 2004 without lawful excuse destroyed a Ford Granada motor car registration number N876 OLD belonging to John Smith, intending to destroy the car or being reckless as to whether it would be destroyed.

24.4.13.2   Damage with intent to endanger life

STATEMENT OF OFFENCE

Damaging property with intent to endanger life, contrary to section 1(2) of the Criminal Damage Act 1971.

PARTICULARS OF OFFENCE

Molly Spinks on 21st September 2004, without lawful excuse, damaged a caravan belonging to herself, intending to damage the property or being reckless as to whether property would be damaged and intending by the damage to endanger the life of Jack Spratt.

24.4.13.3   Arson

STATEMENT OF OFFENCE

Arson, contrary to section 1(1) and (3) of the Criminal Damage Act 1971.

PARTICULARS OF OFFENCE

Alexander Crossman on 1st September 2004 without lawful excuse damaged by fire a house at 27 Old Street, London SW21 belonging to Sally Spratt, intending to damage the house or being reckless as to whether it would be damaged.

24.4.13.4   Aggravated arson by recklessness

STATEMENT OF OFFENCE

Arson being reckless as to whether life would be endangered, contrary to section 1(2) and (3) of the Criminal Damage Act 1971.

PARTICULARS OF OFFENCE

Alexander Crossman on 1st September 2004 without lawful excuse damaged by fire a house at 27 Old Street, London SW21 belonging to Sally Spratt, intending to damage the house or being reckless as to whether it would be damaged and being reckless as to whether the life of Sally Spratt would thereby be endangered.

24.4.13.5   Commentary

Indictments for criminal damage can be quite tricky. The basic offence is under s 1(1) and the ingredients are: (1) without lawful excuse, (2) destroys *or* damages, (3) property, (4) belonging to another, (5) intent to destroy/damage *or* reckless as to whether it would be destroyed/damaged. Given the alternatives of destroy and damage and of intent and recklessness, we already have four different modes of committing the offence. The indictment must make a choice between destroy and damage, which will affect both the statement of offence and the particulars of offence. However, intent and recklessness may (and indeed should) appear as alternatives in the same count.

There is an aggravated version of the offence in s 1(2). This removes one element of the basic offence: the property does not have to belong to another, it may be the defendant's own property. It also adds an additional element of *mens rea* to the basic offence: *either* intent to endanger life *or* reckless as to whether life would be endangered. In drafting the indictment a choice must be made between these two alternatives: they cannot appear in the same count. If the prosecution wish to charge in the alternative, two counts are necessary. So the statement of offence under s 1(2) must specify (a) destroy or damage, and (b) intent or recklessness, and the particulars of offence must be consistent with this. Note that intent or recklessness with regard to the damage to property should still appear in the alternative in the same count.

If the destruction or damage to property in either the basic or the aggravated form of the offence is by fire, then by s 1(3) the name of the offence becomes 'arson'. So in the statement of offence under s 1(1) or 1(2) the word 'arson' replaces the words 'destroying property' or 'damaging property'. In the particulars of offence the words 'by fire' are added immediately after the word 'destroyed' or 'damaged'. Everything else explained above with regard to the alternatives that may or may not be included within the same count remains the same.

24.4.14   Homicide

24.4.14.1   Murder

STATEMENT OF OFFENCE

Murder.

PARTICULARS OF OFFENCE

Alexander Crossman on 30th September 2004 murdered Sally Spratt.

24.4.14.2   Manslaughter

STATEMENT OF OFFENCE

Manslaughter.

PARTICULARS OF OFFENCE

Molly Spinks on 30th September 2004, unlawfully killed Jack Spratt.

24.4.14.3   Commentary

Murder and manslaughter are easy! They are common law offences, so the statement of offence consists of one word in each case. The particulars of offence are similarly brief. No further explanation is needed.

24.4.15   Wounding or grievous bodily harm with intent

24.4.15.1   Wounding

STATEMENT OF OFFENCE

Wounding with intent, contrary to section 18 of the Offences Against the Person Act 1861.

PARTICULARS OF OFFENCE

Alexander Crossman on 31st August 2004 unlawfully wounded Jack Spratt, with intent to do him grievous bodily harm.

24.4.15.2 Causing grievous bodily harm

STATEMENT OF OFFENCE

Causing grievous bodily harm with intent, contrary to section 18 of the Offences Against the Person Act 1861.

PARTICULARS OF OFFENCE

Alexander Crossman on 31st August 2004 unlawfully caused grievous bodily harm to Jack Spratt, with intent to do him grievous bodily harm.

24.4.15.3 Intent to resist arrest

STATEMENT OF OFFENCE

Wounding with intent, contrary to section 18 of the Offences Against the Person Act 1861.

PARTICULARS OF OFFENCE

Alexander Crossman on 31st August 2004 unlawfully and maliciously wounded Mary Mills with intent to resist the lawful apprehension of him, Alexander Crossman.

24.4.15.4 Commentary

The offence under s 18 of the Offences Against the Person Act 1861 can be committed either by wounding or causing grievous bodily harm with intent, and the statement of offence must specify which. This must then be reflected in the particulars of offence, though the intent must be to cause grievous bodily harm or to resist arrest, not to wound. It has long been held that where the intent is to cause grievous bodily harm the word 'maliciously' which appears in s 18 adds nothing, so do not include it in the indictment. However, where the intent is to resist arrest, the word 'maliciously' should appear, because in that case the offence can be committed where the wounding or grievous bodily harm is reckless as well as intentional.

24.4.16 Unlawful wounding or grievous bodily harm

24.4.16.1 Wounding

STATEMENT OF OFFENCE

Unlawful wounding, contrary to section 20 of the Offences Against the Person Act 1861.

PARTICULARS OF OFFENCE

Alexander Crossman on 31st August 2004 unlawfully and maliciously wounded Jack Spratt.

24.4.16.2 Inflicting grievous bodily harm

STATEMENT OF OFFENCE

Inflicting grievous bodily harm, contrary to section 20 of the Offences Against the Person Act 1861.

<u>PARTICULARS OF OFFENCE</u>

Alexander Crossman on 31st August 2004 unlawfully and maliciously inflicted grievous bodily harm on Jack Spratt.

24.4.16.3 Commentary

The statement offence under s 20 of the 1861 Act is either 'unlawful wounding' or 'inflicting grievous bodily harm'. The choice in the particulars of offence is between 'wounded' or 'inflicted grievous bodily harm', in either case adding both 'unlawfully' and 'maliciously'.

24.4.17 Assault occasioning actual bodily harm

24.4.17.1 Indictment

<u>STATEMENT OF OFFENCE</u>

Assault occasioning actual bodily harm, contrary to section 47 of the Offences Against the Person Act 1861.

<u>PARTICULARS OF OFFENCE</u>

Molly Spinks on 1st September 2004 assaulted Sally Spratt, thereby occasioning her actual bodily harm.

24.4.17.2 Commentary

This is another very simple offence to draft. The word 'assault' is another word which imports all the elements of the offence within it, so all that needs to be alleged is 'assaulted', adding 'thereby occasioning actual bodily harm'.

24.4.18 Carrying offensive weapons

24.4.18.1 Indictment

<u>STATEMENT OF OFFENCE</u>

Carrying an offensive weapon, contrary to section 1 of the Prevention of Crime Act 1953.

<u>PARTICULARS OF OFFENCE</u>

Alexander Crossman on 24th November 2004 without lawful authority or reasonable excuse had with him in a public place namely Oxford Street, London W1 an offensive weapon, namely a bicycle chain.

24.4.18.2 Commentary

This is another offence in which 'where' is an essential ingredient — it can only be committed (1) in a public place. The other elements are: (2) without lawful authority or reasonable excuse, (3) had with him, (4) an offensive weapon.

24.4.19 Rape

24.4.19.1 Indictment

<u>STATEMENT OF OFFENCE</u>

Rape, contrary to section 1 of the Sexual Offences Act 1956.

PARTICULARS OF OFFENCE

Alexander Crossman on 8th August 2004 raped Sally Spratt [*or* had sexual intercourse with Sally Spratt who at the time of the intercourse did not consent to it and Alexander Crossman either knew that she did not consent or was reckless as to whether she consented].

24.4.19.2   Commentary

The ingredients of rape are: (1) has sexual intercourse, (2) no consent, (3) at the time of the intercourse, (4) knowing she did not consent or reckless as to whether she consented. 'Rape' is another word which imports all the ingredients of the offence within it, and so the indictment can be drafted using that word alone. However, it is not uncommonly drafted in the fuller form with the ingredients all set out, so this example shows you how to do both.

The form of an indictment for rape will change when s 1 of the Sexual Offences Act 2003 comes into force.

24.4.20   Indecent assault

24.4.20.1   Indictment

STATEMENT OF OFFENCE

Indecent assault, contrary to section 14 of the Sexual Offences Act 1956.

PARTICULARS OF OFFENCE

Alexander Crossman on 8th August 2004 indecently assaulted Sally Spratt, a woman.

24.4.20.2   Commentary

As stated above, the word 'assault' imports all the elements, so all that is needed is that word with the word 'indecently' added. This offence can only be committed against a woman, so it is essential to state that the victim is a woman.

This offence will be repealed and replaced with the offence of sexual assault when s 3 of the Sexual Offences Act 2003 comes into force.

24.4.21   Dangerous drugs

24.4.21.1   Supply

STATEMENT OF OFFENCE

Supplying a controlled drug, contrary to section 4(1) and (3) of the Misuse of Drugs Act 1971.

PARTICULARS OF OFFENCE

Alexander Crossman on 8th October 2004 supplied a controlled drug namely cocaine to Jack Spratt.

24.4.21.2   Simple possession

STATEMENT OF OFFENCE

Possessing a controlled drug, contrary to section 5(1) and (2) of the Misuse of Drugs Act 1971.

PARTICULARS OF OFFENCE

Alexander Crossman on 10th October 2004 had in his possession 284.65 grammes of cannabis resin.

24.4.21.3 Possession with intent to supply

STATEMENT OF OFFENCE

Possessing a controlled drug with intent to supply, contrary to section 5(3) of the Misuse of Drugs Act 1971.

PARTICULARS OF OFFENCE

Alexander Crossman on 10th October 2004 had in his possession 12.628 kilogrammes of cannabis resin with intent to supply it to another in contravention of section 4(1) of the 1971 Act.

24.4.21.4 Commentary

Offences under the Misuse of Drugs Act 1971 are strict liability offences, so there are not many ingredients. For the offence of supplying a controlled drug, all that is necessary is to state what drug and to whom; for the offence of possessing a controlled drug, all that is needed is to identify the drug. Possession with intent to supply requires merely the drug involved and the intention to supply; it is not necessary to identify anyone in particular to whom the defendant intended to supply the drug. In all drug offences it is usual for the indictment to specify the quantity of the drug involved where known. It will almost always be known in cases of possession, but not necessarily of supply. This is because the quantity is highly relevant to sentencing, and it is useful therefore to have a jury verdict which finds the defendant guilty of possessing or supplying a definite quantity of the drug.

24.4.22 Attempt

24.4.22.1 Specific intent

STATEMENT OF OFFENCE

Attempted burglary, contrary to section 1 of the Criminal Attempts Act 1981.

PARTICULARS OF OFFENCE

Alexander Crossman and Molly Spinks on 26th October 2004 attempted to enter a building known as 32 Acacia Drive, Neasden as trespassers with intent to steal therein.

24.4.22.2 General intent

STATEMENT OF OFFENCE

Attempted theft, contrary to section 1 of the Criminal Attempts Act 1981.

PARTICULARS OF OFFENCE

Alexander Crossman on 3rd September 2004 attempted to steal the contents of a handbag belonging to Sarah Crawley.

24.4.22.3 Impossible attempt

STATEMENT OF OFFENCE

Attempting to handle stolen goods, contrary to section 1 of the Criminal Attempts Act 1981.

PARTICULARS OF OFFENCE

Molly Spinks on a day unknown between 25th September and 3rd October 2004 dishonestly received a Hoover vacuum cleaner believing the same to have been stolen.

24.4.22.4   Commentary

Whatever the full offence, the offence of attempting to commit it is always contrary to s 1 of the Criminal Attempts Act 1981. The statement of offence names the full offence, adding 'attempted' or 'attempting to' in front of it. The particulars of offence in almost all cases will simply be the particulars of the full offence with the words 'attempted to' added at an appropriate point. The example in **24.4.22.1** illustrates this.

The example in **24.4.22.2** is appropriate in two circumstances: either where the full offence was impossible, because the handbag was in fact empty; or where there was only a 'provisional' appropriation — the defendant picked up the handbag and looked inside to see if there was anything worth stealing, decided there was not and replaced it.

The example in **24.4.22.3** deals with a common situation. It is not unusual for a person to be found in possession of goods in highly suspicious circumstances, where there is clear evidence of dishonesty and belief that the goods are stolen, but where the prosecution are unable to prove that the goods are in fact stolen. For example, the defendant buys a brand new vacuum cleaner from a stranger in a pub for £20. In such circumstances the defendant can be charged with attempting to handle stolen goods. The particulars of offence are as for the full offence, but there is no allegation that the goods are stolen, and the defendant is alleged to have believed, but not to have known, that the goods were stolen.

24.4.23   Conspiracy

24.4.23.1   Specific charge

STATEMENT OF OFFENCE

Conspiracy to cause grievous bodily harm with intent, contrary to section 1 of the Criminal Law Act 1977.

PARTICULARS OF OFFENCE

Alexander Crossman on 28th September 2004 conspired with Molly Spinks to cause grievous bodily harm to Jack Spratt with intent to do him grievous bodily harm.

24.4.23.2   Broad charge

STATEMENT OF OFFENCE

Conspiracy to handle stolen goods, contrary to section 1 of the Criminal Law Act 1977.

PARTICULARS OF OFFENCE

Alexander Crossman and Molly Spinks on divers days between 30th June and 1st October 2004 conspired together to receive stolen goods, namely such stolen goods as might be brought into their shop at 16 Antique Lane, Neasden by various persons and offered to them for sale.

24.4.23.3   Commentary

Almost all offences of conspiracy are contrary to s 1 of the Criminal Law Act 1977. The offence can be charged in a limitless number of ways. What must be established is that the person or persons charged agreed with each other or with someone else that a course of conduct should be pursued, which, if it were to reach fruition, would result in the commission of a criminal offence. The statement of offence should allege 'conspiracy to ... (name the full offence)'. If the charge is framed narrowly, because there was a specific agreement to commit one specific criminal offence, then the particulars of offence may well resemble the particulars of the full offence, as in **24.4.23.1**. If however the charge is broad, because it was a conspiracy to commit a series of offences, then particulars of offence may bear little resemblance to those of the full offence, as in **24.4.23.2**. The elements of the full offence never actually need to appear in a conspiracy count, because the prosecution does not have to show that any full offence has actually been committed.

Take care when stating who is alleged to have conspired with whom. A person cannot conspire with himself — it takes at least two to make a conspiracy. So a second person must always be referred to, though not necessarily by name. In **24.4.23.1** the conspiracy is between two named persons, but note that only Alexander Crossman is charged. If both were charged the particulars of offence would say 'Alexander Crossman and Molly Spinks conspired together', as in **24.4.23.2**. Other alternatives are 'conspired with Molly Spinks and others unknown' or 'conspired with a person or persons unknown', but in such a case the prosecution must be able to prove that the unknown persons exist.

Conspiracy is the only offence which does not require a single *actus reus*, but can be committed on an ongoing basis over a period of time. So the date of the offence may not be a single date. In such a case the stock formula is 'on divers days between' (as usual, with exclusive dates).

24.4.24   Aiding and abetting etc

24.4.24.1   Primary and secondary parties

STATEMENT OF OFFENCE

Burglary, contrary to section 9(1)(b) of the Theft Act 1968.

PARTICULARS OF OFFENCE

Alexander Crossman on 23rd November 2004, having entered a building known as 32 Acacia Drive, Neasden as a trespasser, stole therein a silver candlestick belonging to John Smith. Molly Spinks aided and abetted Alexander Crossman by driving him to and from the building.

24.4.24.2   Secondary party only

STATEMENT OF OFFENCE

Burglary, contrary to section 9(1)(a) of the Theft Act 1968.

PARTICULARS OF OFFENCE

Molly Spinks on 23rd November 2004 aided and abetted [*or* counselled and procured] [*or* aided and abetted, counselled and procured] Alexander Crossman to enter a building known as 32 Acacia Drive, Neasden as a trespasser with intent to steal therein.

24.4.24.3   Commentary

Aiders and abettors (and counsellors and procurers) can be and generally should be charged as principals (s 8 of the Accessories and Abettors Act 1861). So the statement of offence will always allege the offence with which the primary party is or would have been charged. However, the particulars of offence should bear some relation to what the abettor actually did. For example, in **24.4.24.1** there is a charge of burglary against Alexander Crossman and Molly Spinks. But Molly Spinks's role was to act as lookout and getaway driver. It would be absurd in this case to allege that 'Alexander Crossman and Molly Spinks entered a building as trespassers', when Molly Spinks never entered the building at all. So Alexander Crossman is charged in the usual way, and there is then a second sentence in which Molly Spinks's acts are specified. Note that they are both in the same count, and that this is therefore a joint charge of burglary.

Sometimes no principal has been charged and only the secondary party is before the court. In such circumstances it is appropriate to begin with 'aided and abetted' and then particularise the offence of the principal, as in **24.4.24.2**.

For reasons that are ancient and probably not very sound the pairings 'aided and abetted' and 'counselled and procured' are never broken.

24.5 Exercise

STATEMENT OF JOHN BONE

I am aged 86. My niece-in-law, Elsie Bone, went to Australia about a year ago and asked me to allow her son, James Bone, to stay with me in my house. Although I do not care much for James, because he plays loud music, which is not to my taste, at the time I consented to his coming to live with me. He moved in sometime in June 2003.

I have a Brooklands Bank Visa credit card which I keep in my wallet. I seldom use it, and in fact remember that the last time I did so was when I bought a ticket over the telephone for Covent Garden last September. I have today been shown a statement from Brooklands Bank Visa which shows that my card has been used to purchase goods at numerous stores in London, so that my credit limit of £1,000 has been exceeded. I can say definitely that I have not bought any of these goods and I gave no one permission to use my Visa card.

I can also say that I have been shown a cheque book containing 5 out of 25 cheques on Brooklands Bank plc. The remaining cheques are personalised J. Bone and the cheques bear my account number 830176. However, I am sure that I did not write any of the 20 cheques which have been apparently used from this book, because I have left this account dormant for a number of years, because I do not like the bank manager, and have put most of my money elsewhere. I gave no one permission to have the cheque book or use any of the cheques.

I have been shown a cheque which comes from the above cheque book; I can tell because its number is in sequence and matches in number the third cheque stub in the book. The cheque is made out to cash and is signed James Bone. It appears from the paid stamp, dated 11th July 2004, on the cheque, and from the endorsement on the back, that £50 was paid on this cheque in cash. Obviously the bank have paid out the money from my account without noticing that the name on the cheque is James and not John.

STATEMENT OF DAWN MITCHELL

I work at the Selfless Super Store Ltd, Tottenham Court Road. On 2nd March 2004, some three weeks ago, I was serving in the gents clothing department and a man approached with a shooting jacket, costing £284. I remember it well because it was mauve in colour and I thought it rather hideous. The man wanted to pay with a Visa card. I did the necessary checks and then validated the voucher which I now produce. It was signed by the man, James Bone; the Visa card was personalised J. Bone and I now see that the signature on the back is in fact J. Bone, but I did not think anything of it at the time. I would not have allowed the man to pay by Visa card had I known that the man was not entitled to use the card.

STATEMENT OF PC JOSEPH BILL

Today, 16th July 2004, I was standing in full uniform at the ticket office at Victoria Station. A man in front of me, who I now know to be James Bone was furtively buying a ticket to Dover. He wanted to pay by cheque and he wrote out a cheque to Kent Trains Ltd and presented a cheque card. At this stage I could not see the name personalised on the cheque, but a moment later I heard the booking clerk say, 'Look, mate; this is a stolen cheque — it's on my list here.' When I heard this I at once arrested the man. I said to him, 'I believe you are in possession of a stolen cheque and cheque card. I arrest you.' I then looked at the cheque and cheque card and saw that they were both in the name of Rowland Dogberry. The accused said, 'It's a fair cop.' He was taken to the police station and among his things I found the Visa card which I now produce, the cheque book on Brooklands Bank with five cheques left in it, for the account number 830176. I said to the accused, 'Why have you got these on you, are they yours?' He replied, 'No, they belong to my uncle. Please do not tell him. He will throw me out.'

Assuming that all missing evidence will be forthcoming, draft an indictment containing such counts as seem appropriate.

Criminal grounds of appeal

25.1 Procedure

25.1.1 The Guide

A clear understanding of the procedure in the Court of Appeal Criminal Division is vital to the proper preparation of grounds of appeal.

The Registrar of Criminal Appeals has published *A Guide to Proceedings in the Court of Appeal Criminal Division* ('the Guide'). The latest version was published in 1997. It should be read by all who might practise in the Court of Appeal Criminal Division. The essential points are set out in *Archbold's Criminal Pleading and Practice*, para 7–163 et seq.

25.1.2 Timetable

The Guide lays down a clear timetable:

(a) Within 14 days of conviction or sentence counsel should send solicitors (i) an advice on appeal and (ii) where so advised, signed grounds of appeal (para 1.4). It must be remembered that in respect of an appeal against conviction, time runs from the date of the *conviction* and not the date of the *sentence* which may be some weeks later.

(b) Solicitors should at once send a copy of the documents received from counsel to the defendant so as to reach him within 21 days of conviction or sentence (para 1.5).

(c) Notice of appeal, accompanied by grounds of appeal, should reach the Crown Court where the proceedings took place within 28 days from conviction or sentence as the case may be (para 1.6).

25.1.3 Counsel's advice

The *Practice Direction (criminal: consolidated)* [2002] 3 All ER 904, para 15.2 requires that a copy of counsel's positive advice about the merits of the appeal should be attached as part of the grounds of appeal. The submission of the advice has two substantial advantages:

(a) It enables the single judge of the Criminal Division, who will first consider whether leave to appeal should be granted, to see the factual and legal basis of the appeal.

(b) It enables the grounds of appeal to be expressed shortly.

The advice on appeal, if it is positive, should therefore be written in such a way as to gain these advantages. An advice which is adverse to the defendant's appeal should never be submitted with the notice and grounds of appeal.

25.1.4   Perfected grounds

The notice and grounds of appeal, together with the advice, are sent by the Crown Court to the Registrar. On receipt of these papers, the Registrar will consider what transcript, if any, is to be obtained, having regard to (but not being bound by) any view expressed by counsel. It is important that the transcript should only be requested if it is essential for the proper conduct of the appeal. Obtaining the transcript invariably causes delay and usually involves public expense. Counsel who seek excessive quantities of transcript are likely to face criticism from the Court.

Where the transcript is obtained the Registrar will in appropriate cases invite counsel to perfect the grounds of appeal in the light of that transcript. He will almost certainly do so where application is made for leave to appeal against conviction.

The invitation to perfect the grounds may not be declined. Where counsel is requested to perfect the grounds, he must do so within the time limit set by the Registrar. The format of perfected grounds is important and is set out in para 4.4 of the Guide:

Perfected grounds should consist of a fresh document which supersedes the original grounds of appeal and contains *inter alia* references by page number and letter to all relevant passages in the transcript. Authorities on which counsel relies should be cited, where possible in the Criminal Appeal Reports. A document mentioned in the grounds should be identified clearly, by exhibit number or otherwise, and if each member of the Court will require a copy an indication to that effect should be given. Similarly if counsel requires an original exhibit he should say so well in advance of any determination or hearing.

If having considered the transcript, counsel is of the opinion that the application should be abandoned, he should set out the reasons in a further advice and send it to instructing solicitors. Counsel should inform the Registrar that this has been done but should not send him a copy of that advice.

Once any perfected grounds have been sent to the Registrar, the papers will be placed before the single judge. They will include (i) counsel's draft or perfected grounds, (ii) counsel's advice (if submitted), and (iii) relevant transcripts.

25.2   Grounds of appeal against conviction

Following the amendment of the Criminal Appeal Act 1968 by the Criminal Appeal Act 1995, there is only one ground of appeal against conviction, namely that the conviction is unsafe. Section 2(1) of the 1968 Act as amended reads:

(1)   Subject to the provisions of this Act, the Court of Appeal—

    (a)   shall allow an appeal against conviction if they think that the conviction is unsafe; and

    (b)   shall dismiss such an appeal in any other case.

There are a great many things that can give rise to an appeal, but no defect or irregularity in the trial, and no error or misdirection by the judge, is enough by itself to result in the conviction being quashed unless the conviction is rendered unsafe. On the other hand, in order to ensure that a defendant has a fair trial, as required by Article 6(1) of the European Convention on Human Rights, if the judge has failed to give a required direction in the summing up, the Court of Appeal must not conclude that the conviction is nevertheless safe unless it is satisfied that no reasonable jury could have come to a different conclusion if they had been properly directed (*R v Francom and others* The Times, 24 October 2000).

Examples of matters that might be relied upon include:

(a) Errors of law by the judge, such as:

    (i)   a wrong ruling on a point of law;

    (ii)   allowing the trial to proceed on a defective indictment;

    (iii) wrongful admission of inadmissible evidence;

    (iv) wrongful exclusion of admissible evidence;

    (v)   an unreasonable exercise of discretion.

(b) Serious procedural defects, such as:

    (i)   an irregularity in relation to the jury;

    (ii)   an irregularity in relation to the verdict;

    (iii) improper behaviour by a witness.

(c) Misdirections by the judge in his summing up, such as:

    (i)   getting the law wrong;

    (ii)   missing out an essential legal ingredient;

    (iii) failing to leave an issue of fact to the jury;

    (iv) failing to give the jury a specific direction required by law;

    (v)   failing to put the defence case properly;

    (vi) failing to leave an alternative verdict to the jury;

    (vii) factual error;

    (viii) improper comment.

(d) Fresh evidence has come to light.

25.3 Grounds of appeal against sentence

Grounds of appeal against sentence are not laid down by statute but are derived from principles and guidelines in Court of Appeal decisions. Six main grounds, not wholly distinct from each other, can be identified:

(a) The sentence was wrong in law; ie it was outside the judge's powers.

(b) The sentence was passed on the wrong factual basis.

(c) Matters were taken into account which should not have been.

(d) Matters were not taken into account which should have been.

(e) The sentence was wrong in principle; ie it was the wrong kind of sentence for the offence.

(f) The sentence was manifestly excessive. Note the word 'manifestly'. It is not a ground of appeal that the sentence was 'a bit tough'.

25.4 Drafting grounds of appeal

25.4.1 The requirements

The Guide emphasises two points in relation to drafting grounds of appeal:

(a) Grounds must be settled with sufficient particularity to enable the Registrar and subsequently the Court of Appeal to identify clearly the matters relied upon. A mere formula such as 'the conviction is unsafe' or 'the sentence is in all the circumstances too severe' will be ineffective as grounds (para 2.2).

(b) Counsel should not settle grounds unless they are reasonable, have some real prospect of success and are such that he is prepared to argue them before the court (para 2.4).

The need for careful preparation of concise grounds of appeal and the time-wasting effect of 'ill-prepared, inaccurate or prolix' grounds were stressed by Lord Bingham CJ in his foreword to the Guide.

Counsel settling grounds should always be aware of the power, both of the full court and of the single judge, when refusing an application for leave to appeal, to direct that part of the time during which a person was in custody after lodging his application should not count towards sentence (Criminal Appeal Act 1968, ss 29 and 31; *Practice Direction (criminal: consolidated)* [2002] 3 All ER 904, para 16.1)). In *R v Wankyln* The Times, 14 November 1984, the Court of Appeal said that the fact that an application for leave to appeal against conviction or sentence is made on the advice of counsel will not prevent an order for loss of time if the case is, in the view of the Court, one without merit at all and one which should never be brought.

Where counsel advises against an appeal, it may be appropriate to remind the defendant that he is not bound to accept the advice and can still pursue an appeal on his own grounds. In such circumstances, the advice should remind the defendant of the deadline for the submission of any grounds and should set out clearly the court's powers to direct loss of time if it finds that the appeal is without any substance.

It is counsel's duty when drafting grounds to see that all the material is fairly and properly put before the court. Sentences from the summing up should not be extracted out of context if within context they cannot properly be the subject of criticism. It is the duty of counsel in drafting and arguing grounds of appeal to act responsibly and not to make sweeping attacks on the summing up of the trial judge unless such attacks can be justified. An allegation of bias against the judge must for example be very precisely particularised if it is to be substantiated. Wide-ranging and imprecise grounds serve only to obscure what may be a good point and add to the burden of the court.

The *Practice Direction (criminal: consolidated)* [2002] 3 All ER 904, para 15.1 says:

Advocates should not settle grounds or support them with written advice unless they consider that they are properly arguable. Grounds should be carefully drafted and properly particularised. Advocates should not assume that the court will entertain any ground of appeal not set out and properly particularised. Should leave to amend the grounds be granted it is most unlikely that further grounds will be entertained.

25.4.2 Advice and grounds

Grounds of appeal must be carefully drafted and properly particularised (see above). But counsel's advice on appeal must always accompany the grounds of appeal. It is almost impossible to write a good advice on appeal that does not explain clearly and fully what exactly each ground of appeal is, and why it amounts to a ground of appeal, and there is therefore potential for very considerable overlap between the grounds of appeal and the advice on appeal.

It is for this reason that the usual practice, followed in this Manual, is to set out the full particulars of the grounds, and the reasons and arguments for them, in the advice, and then to draft the grounds themselves quite briefly, making reference to the relevant paragraphs in the advice. This saves time.

25.4.3 How to draft the advice

You will find it easier to draft the advice before the grounds. Although you are strictly speaking *advising* on appeal, you should treat writing the advice as a piece of drafting rather than a piece of opinion writing. It is on the basis of your advice that the single judge will decide whether to grant leave to appeal, and it will also be the court's first introduction to the case if leave is granted. It therefore needs to be drafted with care and precision. The objective is to show that in all the circumstances of the case the conviction is unsafe and/or the sentence should be reduced or varied.

Begin with a short résumé of the case: the charge(s), the plea(s), the verdict. Then make a short neutral statement of the basic facts, outline the prosecution case and the defence, and give any more factual or evidential details which will be needed to understand the grounds of appeal that follow.

Then deal with each ground of appeal in a logical order. This usually means chronological order. Start with grounds relating to events during the trial and then go on to misdirections in the summing up. Take misdirections in the order in which they appear, unless there is a good reason to vary this, for example, because two grounds are closely linked to each other, or there are several grounds of a similar nature which are best taken together. The use of sub-headings may be an aid to clarity.

For each ground of appeal, there must be a clear explanation of what the ground is, together with the relevant argument. The ground needs to be explained, reasoned and argued, with reference to the transcript (if you have one), the facts, the evidence and the law. This should be done clearly, concisely and persuasively. Try to show not just what is wrong, but why it is wrong and what prejudice has been caused as a result. Relate different grounds to each other where appropriate, and where there is a cumulative effect, make sure this too is dealt with.

Each ground should make reference to specific events, specific passages in the summing up and specific points of evidence. If you have a transcript from which to quote passages, do so. If you are relying on legal authorities, cases or statutes, these should be cited, and mentioned in such a way as to make it clear how each authority is to be used in argument.

In relation to appeals against sentence, 'guideline' cases should always be cited where appropriate. Although the vast majority of decisions on sentencing are no more than examples confined to their own facts, they may be of use as an aid to uniformity of sentence. The usual source for such authorities is the Criminal Appeal Reports (Sentencing).

25.4.4 How to draft the grounds

Assuming the advice on appeal has particularised the grounds fully and effectively, the grounds themselves can be kept very concise. They may amount simply to a list of the points to be raised on appeal, in the same order as they are dealt with in the advice, with references to the transcript and cross-references to the relevant paragraphs in the advice. Of course you can set them out in full if you wish, but you will then be repeating a great deal of your advice, which is not efficient. The first method is recommended, and is illustrated in the example which follows.

25.4.5 Skeleton argument

If leave to appeal is granted, then counsel is required to lodge a skeleton argument. The skeleton may refer to the advice, which should be annexed with an indication of which parts of it are relied upon, and should include any additional arguments to be advanced (*Practice Direction (criminal: consolidated)* [2002] 3 All ER 904, para 17.1).

There is further guidance on skeleton arguments in para 17.5 of the *Practice Direction*:

A skeleton argument should contain a numbered list of the points the advocate intends to argue, grouped under each ground of appeal, and stated in no more than one or two sentences. It should be as succinct as possible, the object being to identify each point, not to argue it or elaborate on it. Each listed point should be followed by full references to the material to which the advocate will refer in support of it, ie the relevant passages in the transcripts, authorities, etc. It should also contain anything the advocate would expect to be taken down by the court during the hearing, such as propositions of law, chronologies, etc. If more convenient, these can be annexed to the skeletons rather than included in it. For points of law, the skeleton should state the point and cite the principal authority or authorities in support with reference to the passages where the principle is enunciated. Chronologies should, if possible, be agreed with the opposing advocate before the hearing.

25.5 Example

25.5.1 Introduction

To give a realistic example is not possible in this Manual. A genuine transcript of a summing up might run to ten or more pages, and in practice would at most only give rise to a handful of grounds of appeal. An artificial example is taken, therefore. This transcript is of an (imaginary!) summing up, which is far shorter than would be realistic and which reveals many more serious errors on the part of the judge than any real judge could possibly make in a single case. The drafts which follow are intended to illustrate techniques, rather than to be realistic.

To be able to identify grounds of appeal from a summing up, you need to be aware of what a summing up should contain. See the ***Criminal Litigation and Sentencing Manual***.

25.5.2 Instructions to counsel

Counsel is asked to draft advice on appeal and grounds of appeal against conviction and sentence in respect of John Hatch. The facts appear from the summing up and the proceedings on sentence.

25.5.3 Summing up of his Honour Judge Spiller

A Members of the jury, let me explain our respective duties. I tell you what the law is and you must accept my decision as being correct: you decide every issue of fact.

B The prosecution have to prove the case and must satisfy you so that you are sure that the defendants are guilty.

C The allegation against the male defendant is that he burgled premises known as 2 The Shire House, Penge, and stole jewellery and silver ornaments to the value of £10,000. The allegation against the female defendant is that she received the jewellery from that burglary.

D What is burglary? A person is guilty of burglary who enters a building as a trespasser with intent to steal therein, and steals therein. Everybody knows what stealing is: it is the appropriation of property belonging to another with intent to deprive that other person of it.

E What is handling? Basically there are two types of handling. First, where the defendant receives stolen goods, and secondly, where the person undertakes or assists in, or arranges to undertake or assist in, the retention, removal, disposal or realisation of stolen goods by or for the benefit of another.

F What the prosecution here allege is that the female defendant received a quantity of jewellery knowing or believing it to be stolen.

G Now the prosecution proceed on the evidence of the admissions made by both these defendants.

H First regarding John Hatch. The owner of The Shire House said that his premises were burgled on 27th May 2004. On 31st May Hatch was seen by the police regarding another matter, unconnected with this, and in interview told the police that this burglary was 'a Hatch job'. He, of course, denied that the admission was true. He told you that he was at the police station because he had been picked up on what he called 'a murder rap' and that the police had told him that if he wanted his denial of murder to be believed he had better own up to the last burglary he had committed.

I Now I ruled that the evidence of the defendant's confession to burglary was plainly admissible, even if the defendant's version of what the police said was true, and it was argued before you, members of the jury, that it was not to be relied upon: that is a matter for you to consider.

J Of course, you heard the evidence of Miss Walker. You remember how she came into the witness-box looking very distraught, and how prosecution counsel asked her about Christmas 2003 and seeing the defendant Hatch, at that time, which she remembered. Then she was asked what he had said to her. She said that she could not remember anything particular. You were, at that point, sent out; and the prosecution applied to treat her as hostile. I acceded to that application and as a result when the proceedings were resumed before you, her original statement was put to her by prosecuting counsel. In that statement, she said how the defendant, Hatch, had said to her over Christmas that he would 'like to do The Shire House at Penge'. It was obviously from this statement that the police suspected Hatch of having committed that burglary. Miss Walker said in her evidence that the statement to the police was untrue, and that it had been forced out of her by threats from the police that if she did not cooperate with them her baby was likely to be taken into care. It is a matter for you to decide whether you believe her on that; but in any event you will bear in mind what she originally told the police.

K   As far as the defendant, Miss Bradshaw, is concerned, she also made an admission. When interviewed by the police she said that Hatch had brought some jewellery round to her on 30th May. He said, 'Here you are, old girl, this is the stuff I promised you'. She told the police that she had sold the jewellery on 31st May, at her stall in Croydon, and could not trace to whom she had sold it. She said that she had 'a pretty good idea it was stolen' because when she was on her stall, a man had looked at it and said that some of it was quite rare, and she knew that Hatch would not honestly have anything which was rare or valuable.

L   As you know, Miss Bradshaw did not give evidence. You heard me warn her of the consequences of not doing so, but still she did not. You are entitled to draw inferences from this failure. It is a matter for you, but you may think that someone who is afraid to tell her side of the story is plainly guilty.

M   The defence in a nutshell is as follows. For Hatch: that he did not do the burglary and that his admission is not to be relied on. For Miss Bradshaw: you cannot draw the inference that she is guilty from what she said.

N   Those are the issues.

O   You must reach unanimous verdicts. If you can't, I'll give you a majority direction later on, but not now. Please retire and consider your verdicts.

[After a retirement of 1 hour 50 minutes the jury returned a verdict of guilty in respect of both defendants.]

25.5.4   The judge's comments when passing sentence

In passing sentence the judge said:

P   You, Hatch, are a professional burglar. You have been burgling for the last 20 years and, I dare say, have done very well out of it. The record shows 15 previous convictions for burglary, the last two years ago.

Q   In the circumstances, and in spite of the views expressed in the pre-sentence report, which I have considered carefully, I am of the opinion that this monstrous offence of burglary is so serious that only a custodial sentence can be justified.

R   I really ought to lock you up and throw the key away, but I shall be lenient. You will go to prison for seven years.

S   I shall also make a compensation order. I simply do not believe what it says in the pre-sentence report, that you have no assets, savings or income. You will pay the owner compensation of, let's say, £10,000.

T   You, Bradshaw, are a different kettle of fish. I think you were tempted and I bear in mind that none of your previous convictions have been for this. Nevertheless handling stolen goods is just as serious as burglary, and I must therefore conclude that only a custodial sentence can be justified. But, in the light of the recommendations in the pre-sentence report, I think this is a suitable case for a suspended sentence of three months' imprisonment. The sentence is suspended for three years: which means that if you commit an offence in the next three years you will be for it.

U   I see that you are a woman of some considerable means, so I shall also impose a fine of £1,000. In default of payment you will go to prison for a further three months.

25.6   Draft advice and grounds

25.6.1   Advice on appeal

REGINA

v

JOHN HATCH

and

AMELIA BRADSHAW

ADVICE ON APPEAL AGAINST
CONVICTION AND SENTENCE
ON BEHALF OF HATCH

---

1.   Introduction

1.1   On [*dates*] these defendants were tried before His Honour Judge Spiller and a jury. Mr Hatch was convicted of a single count of burglary of a dwelling contrary to section 9(1)(b) of the Theft Act 1968. Miss Bradshaw was convicted of a single count of receiving stolen goods, contrary to section 22(1) of the Theft Act 1968, namely the proceeds of that burglary.

1.2   Pre-sentence reports were obtained on each defendant and on [*date*] they appeared before the trial judge for sentence. Mr Hatch was sentenced to seven years' imprisonment and ordered to pay compensation in the sum of £10,000. Miss Bradshaw was sentenced to three months' imprisonment suspended for three years, and fined £1,000 with three months in default.

1.3   I am asked to advise Mr Hatch as to whether there exist any grounds upon which he could properly appeal against his conviction and the sentences imposed.

1.4   For the reasons set out below, I advise that there are properly arguable grounds of appeal against both conviction and sentence. Accordingly, I have drafted Grounds of Appeal and I ask that they be sent to the Crown Court together with a copy of this Advice and the other appeal documents.

2.   The facts

2.1   Hatch

The allegation against Mr Hatch was that he burgled a house in Penge and stole goods to the value of £10,000. It was alleged that he confessed to this burglary in the course of being interviewed about a murder. The defence to the charge was that Mr Hatch was not involved in the burglary, but made a false confession because he was told that his denials of any involvement in the murder would only be believed if he confessed to the burglary. Mr Hatch gave evidence on his own behalf.

2.2   Bradshaw

Miss Bradshaw was alleged to have received the proceeds of the burglary, knowing or believing them to be stolen. The case for the prosecution depended upon an explanation she gave to police which was said to amount to an admission. The case for the defence was that the jury could not be sure that the words bore the interpretation argued for by the prosecution. Miss Bradshaw did not give evidence.

3.   Grounds of appeal against conviction

3.1   *Wrong decisions in the course of the trial:*

3.1.1   Hatch's confession

The learned judge wrongly directed himself in law in relation to Hatch's confession. The defendant contended that he made the confession in consequence of being told by the police that he would be charged with murder, an offence which he denied, unless he confessed to burglary. It was argued on his behalf first that such conduct amounted to oppression (section 76(2)(a) of the Police and Criminal Evidence Act 1984 ('PACE')) and second that these circumstances were likely to render the confession unreliable (section 76(2)(b) of PACE). However, the judge ruled that the confession was admissible even if the allegations were true. This decision amounted to a perverse interpretation of the terms of section 76 of PACE and accordingly it was wrong in law.

3.1.2   Allowing a witness to be treated as hostile

The judge wrongly allowed a prosecution witness, Miss Walker, to be treated as hostile and cross-examined upon a previous statement she had made, under section 3 of the Criminal Procedure Act 1865. She was not adverse to the party calling her, but stated merely that she did not remember anything particular that Hatch had said to her during a conversation which had taken place at Christmas 2003. Miss Walker was unfavourable, but not hostile, to the party calling her and the judge erred in law in permitting her to be treated as hostile.

3.2   *Misdirections in the course of summing up*

3.2.1   Separate consideration of the case of each defendant

The judge failed to direct the jury that they had to consider separately the case against each defendant. This direction was of particular importance in a case where the defendants faced separate charges, the evidence against each defendant was different and where only one defendant chose to give evidence. The judge told the jury only that [paragraph B]:

> The prosecution has to prove the case and must satisfy you so that you are sure that the defendants are guilty.

This direction was barely adequate in relation to the burden and standard of proof and it had the effect of suggesting that the cases of both defendants stood or fell together. A specific example of the prejudice caused to Hatch by this omission is given in paragraph 3.2.2 below.

3.2.2   Bradshaw's alleged admission

Bradshaw was alleged to have told the police that Hatch had brought some jewellery to her on 30th May 2004 and had said: 'Here you are, old girl, this is the stuff I promised you'. Bradshaw did not give evidence and so never adopted the words in the course of the trial. The judge failed to direct the jury that this was capable only of being evidence against her and was not admissible against Hatch. In the absence of the proper direction, there was a very substantial risk that the jury would use this evidence improperly against Hatch.

3.2.3   Ingredients of the offence of burglary

The judge gave the jury the following direction of law in relation to the offence of burglary contrary to section 9(1)(b) of the Theft Act 1968 [paragraph D]:

> A person is guilty of burglary who enters a building as a trespasser with intent to steal therein, and steals therein. Everybody knows what stealing is: it is the appropriation of property belonging to another with intent to deprive that other person of it.

This direction was deficient in the following respects:

(a) it confused the ingredients of burglary contrary to section 9(1)(a) of the Act with those of section 9(1)(b) of the Act;

(b) it failed to direct the jury that dishonesty was an essential ingredient of theft; and

(c) it stated that an intent to deprive was a sufficient ingredient of theft but did not go on to say that the intention must be permanently to deprive.

3.2.4   Evidential value of Hatch's confession

The judge gave the jury the following direction in relation to Hatch's confession [paragraph I]:

> Now I ruled that the evidence of the defendant's confession to burglary was plainly admissible, even if the defendant's version of what the police said was true, and it was argued before you, members of the jury, that it was not to be relied upon: that is a matter for you to consider.

This direction was deficient in the following respects:

(a) The jury should not have been told of the judge's decision of law in relation to the confession's admissibility; his direction confused the issue of whether the confession was admissible with the issue of its evidential value and truth. This tended to lend extra weight to the confession and may have induced the jury to assume that if it was admissible it must also be true.

(b) It failed sufficiently to direct the jury that they had to consider the question of the truth of the confession in the light of the circumstances in which they found it to have been obtained. In *R v McCarthy* (1980) 70 Cr App R 270 the appellant's defence was that he had made a false confession as a result of the inducement. The trial judge ruled that the confession was admissible and the point was taken again in front of the jury. The Court of Appeal held that the jury should have been asked specifically to consider whether or not the statement contained the truth. This principle appears to have been unaffected by the subsequent enactment of PACE.

3.2.5   Miss Walker's evidence

Miss Walker stated in evidence that she did not remember anything in particular said to her by Hatch last Christmas. The prosecution was given leave to treat her as hostile (see paragraph 3.1.2 above). Miss Walker was cross-examined by the prosecution on the contents of her statement in which she had stated that Hatch had told her that he would '... like to do the Shire House at Penge'. Miss Walker did not adopt the contents of this statement. She told the jury that she had only given that version because of threats made to her by the police. The judge correctly reminded the jury of these facts but then went on to say [at the beginning of paragraph J]:

> It is a matter for you to decide whether you believe her on that; but in any event you will bear in mind what she originally told the police.

The correct approach to be adopted where a witness retracts an earlier statement was considered by the House of Lords in *R v Governor of Pentonville Prison, ex p Alves* [1992] 3 WLR 844 at pages 849–850. It approved the rule laid down by the Court of Appeal in *R v Golder* [1960] 1 WLR 1169, that the jury should be directed that the previous statement does not constitute evidence upon which they can act. The direction given here by the trial judge invited the jury to consider the earlier statement and thus allowed them to act upon it. In the light of the highly prejudicial nature of the earlier statement, this amounted to a serious misdirection.

In *Alves* the House of Lords followed the Court of Appeal's decision in *R v Pestano* [1981] Crim LR 397, in which it was held that the credibility of evidence given by a witness inconsistent with a statement previously made by him was a matter for the jury to consider, subject to a proper warning by the judge as to the weight to be attached to the evidence. The trial judge should have given such a direction in the present case, tailored to fit the facts. Such a direction would have reminded the jury that the evidence given by Miss Walker did not implicate Hatch and that there was little, if any, weight capable of being attached to it.

4.   Appeal against sentence

4.1   Seven years' imprisonment

4.1.1   In accordance with s 81 of the Powers of Criminal Courts (Sentencing) Act 2000 ('the Sentencing Act') the judge obtained a pre-sentence report. However, in passing sentence the judge made it clear that the length of sentence was based on Hatch's previous convictions [paragraphs P and Q]. Although by s 151(1) of the Sentencing Act the judge was entitled to take Hatch's previous convictions into account, his comments suggest that he was in effect sentencing Hatch again for past offences. Accordingly, the approach adopted by the judge was wrong in law.

4.1.2   It must be accepted that the judge was entitled to come to the view that a dwelling-house burglary of this nature was so serious that only a custodial sentence could be justified. However, the sentence of seven years' imprisonment was manifestly excessive and therefore wrong in principle.

4.2   £10,000 compensation order

4.2.1   The judge failed to have regard to the defendant's means, as set out in the pre-sentence report. It was clear from the report that Mr Hatch had no capital assets, no savings and no known income. Section 130(11) of the Sentencing Act states that it shall be the duty of the court to have regard to the defendant's means so far as they appear or are known to the court. In *R v Stanley* (1989) 11 Cr App R (S) 446 the Court of Appeal held that it was the duty of the court only to make a compensation order in such an amount as appeared to be within the means of the defendant. On the evidence before the court, there was no possibility of the defendant immediately paying any compensation at all. A lengthy term of imprisonment meant that there was no prospect of such a sum being paid within a reasonable period of time. This compensation order was manifestly excessive and therefore wrong in principle.

JOSEPH BLOGGS

Princeton Chambers
Princeton Street
WC1

5th February 2005

25.6.2 Grounds of appeal against conviction

REGINA

v

JOHN HATCH

and

AMELIA BRADSHAW

PERFECTED GROUNDS OF APPEAL
AGAINST CONVICTION
ON BEHALF OF HATCH

Application is made for leave to appeal upon the ground that the conviction is unsafe for any or all of the following reasons, namely that the learned judge:

1. wrongly directed himself in relation to Hatch's alleged confession, in that he held that even if the Appellant's contentions were or may have been true they were not capable of amounting either to oppression or circumstances likely to render the confession unreliable within the terms of sections 76(2)(a) and 76(2)(b) of the Police and Criminal Evidence Act 1984 [*transcript* paragraphs H and J]; and

> Advice: 3.1.1

2. erred in law in that he allowed a prosecution witness, Miss Walker, to be treated as hostile and cross-examined upon a previous statement she had made, pursuant to section 3 of the Criminal Procedure Act 1865 [*transcript* paragraph J];

> Advice: 3.1.2

3. failed to direct the jury that they had to consider separately the case against each defendant [*transcript* paragraph B];

> Advice: 3.2.1

4. failed to direct the jury that the alleged admission made by Bradshaw was capable of being evidence only against her [*transcript* paragraph K];

> Advice: 3.2.2

5.   wrongly directed the jury in relation to the ingredients of the offence of   Advice:
burglary contrary to section 9(1)(b) of the Theft Act 1968 in that the direction   3.2.3
[*transcript* paragraph D]:

   (1)   confused the ingredients of burglary contrary to section 9(1)(a) of the
         Act with those of section 9(1)(b) of the Act;

   (2)   failed to direct the jury that dishonesty was an essential ingredient of
         theft; and

   (3)   stated that an intent to deprive was a sufficient ingredient of theft but
         did not go on to say that the intention must be permanently to deprive;

6.   wrongly told the jury of his decision to admit the evidence of the Appel-   Advice:
lant's confession, thereby allowing the jury to assume that if it was admissible   3.2.4
it must also be true [*transcript* paragraph I];

7.   failed sufficiently to direct the jury that they had to consider the question   Advice:
of the truth of the confession in the light of the circumstances in which they   3.2.4
found it to have been obtained [*transcript* paragraph I];

8.   wrongly directed the jury that in relation to a prosecution witness, Miss   Advice:
Walker, who was ruled to be hostile a statement made previously by that wit-   3.2.5
ness could be borne in mind when assessing her truthfulness, thus wrongly allowing the jury to act upon that statement, whereas the jury should have been
directed that the previous statement did not constitute evidence upon which
they could act [*transcript* paragraph J]; and

9.   failed to give the jury a proper warning as to the very limited weight that   Advice:
could be attached to the evidence in fact given by Miss Walker [*transcript* para-   3.2.5
graph J].

JOSEPH BLOGGS

25.6.3   Grounds of appeal against sentence

REGINA

v

JOHN HATCH

and

AMELIA BRADSHAW

GROUNDS OF APPEAL AGAINST SENTENCE
ON BEHALF OF HATCH

---

1.   *Application is made for leave to appeal against sentence, pursuant to section 9 of
the Criminal Appeal Act 1968, upon the following grounds:*

1.1   in passing a sentence of seven years' imprisonment the learned judge stated that the length of the sentence was based largely on Hatch's previous convictions rather than the present offence and accordingly the judge's approach was wrong in law;

Advice: 4.1.1

1.2   a sentence of seven years' imprisonment for a single offence of burglary of a dwelling-house was manifestly excessive and therefore wrong in principle; and

Advice: 4.1.2

1.3   a compensation order in the sum of £10,000 was far beyond the means of the offender as they appeared or were known to the court; accordingly it was manifestly excessive and therefore wrong in principle.

Advice: 4.2.1

JOSEPH BLOGGS

25.7 Commentary

25.7.1 Advice on appeal

Although this is an Advice, written primarily for the benefit of the client Mr Hatch, it is also the basis on which you seek to persuade the judge to grant leave to appeal. It is therefore written very much with that purpose in mind, and needs to be drafted with some care.

Heading. This should be as it appeared on the indictment, including the names of both defendants, although this advice is on behalf of Hatch only. The title of the document makes this clear.

Section 1 — Introduction. This is a fairly formal section, which simply sets out what has happened, what you are asked to advise about and your overall advice. Give the date(s) of the trial, the offences charged, the convictions, the date of sentence (particularly important if sentence was not immediately after the verdict), and the sentences passed. If you think there are good grounds of appeal, say so; if you do not, then do not be afraid to say so too.

Section 2 — The facts. This section looks straightforward, but is often harder to draft than it looks. You need to be concise. It is very easy to get carried away and start to set out all the facts and evidence in some detail. On the other hand you need to put the judge in the picture — give him enough information to understand the grounds of appeal on which you are about to advise. So at the very least you should state:

(a)   the nature of the prosecution case, the broad allegation made against the defendant;

(b)   the defence case — what the defence was;

(c)   the evidence against the defendant — how in broad terms the prosecution sought to establish its case; and

(d)   any significant evidence given on behalf of the defence. You probably also need to set out any background evidence or events at trial which will be necessary to enable the judge to understand one or more of the grounds. If it is relevant only to a single ground, it is probably best to deal with it in the context of that ground. But if it relates to several grounds, it may be better to explain it at the outset.

Here, in respect of each defendant, the advice simply covers points (a) to (d) above.

Section 3 — The grounds of appeal against conviction. These should be taken in chronological order. This results in an immediate sub-division into the grounds which arose during the trial itself, and the grounds which arise from the summing up. The former obviously come first, and are best dealt with in the order they arose. In this case we assume that the voir dire on Hatch's confession was held early on, and that evidence of it was then admitted, before Miss Walker was called as a witness. The misdirections in the summing up are taken in the order in which they appear, with one exception: the ground in 3.2.2 is taken out of order, because it is closely related to the ground in 3.2.1, and its impact is heightened by this juxtaposition. Every ground, or group of grounds, is given a sub-heading, which aids clarity and can help you to stick to the point when drafting.

Paragraph 3.1.1. The draft begins by stating what the ground is, and then goes on to give explanation, argument and reasoning, with an outline of the relevant law. Clearly the 'murder rap' needs to be explained, or the judge cannot understand why any application was made to exclude the confession. The arguments put to the judge were essentially the same as those that will be put on appeal, so they are outlined. To succeed on this ground it is not sufficient to show that the judge might have exercised his discretion differently; it must be shown that his decision was wrong in law, so this is the conclusion stated in the last sentence. It is not unlike a skeleton argument.

Paragraph 3.1.2. The approach taken in this paragraph is almost identical to that in 3.1.1. What the judge did wrong is stated at the outset, and then reasons are given as to why it was wrong. Again the conclusion is that the judge was wrong in law.

Paragraph 3.2.1. The judge's error is identified in the first sentence, but the ground then goes on to make a good point ('This direction was of particular importance' etc). If there is a point to be made not just as to why the judge was wrong, but how serious his error was, then make that point! There is then a quotation from the summing up. If a direction given by the judge is to be criticised, then it is important to set out his exact words, not just an approximation of them. This will only be possible when a transcript is available, which will not usually be until after your initial advice on appeal; but when you perfect your grounds, you can 'perfect' your advice as well. When reference is made to the transcript, cite page and paragraph numbers. After the quotation comes the criticism of it: 'it had the effect of suggesting that the cases of both defendants stood or fell together'. If a decision or direction of the judge has had a particular prejudicial effect, always explain as forcefully as you can what that prejudicial effect was. The reference to the direction on burden and standard of proof being barely adequate shows that you have considered whether to make a separate ground of appeal out of this weakness, but have decided against it. Finally, this ground of appeal is linked to the next one.

Paragraph 3.2.2. This ground begins with some background. It is the judge's treatment of a specific piece of evidence that is being complained about, so you need to explain what that piece of evidence was, and the context in which it was given. It is hearsay evidence: the police officer said that Bradshaw said that Hatch said 'Here you are old girl, this is the stuff I promised you'. This is admissible against Bradshaw as a potential admission that she knew the goods were stolen, but it is wholly inadmissible against Hatch. It is important to add that Bradshaw did not give evidence. If she had done so, what she said in the witness box *would* have been admissible against Hatch, and if she then repeated what she is alleged to have said to the police, there would be no ground of appeal. In circumstances where a piece of evidence is admissible against one defendant but not another the judge must give the jury a clear direction and strong warning. This he failed to do, and the prejudicial effect of his failure is clearly stated in the final sentence.

Paragraph 3.2.3. This ground is not of great significance. The judge has erred on the law of burglary in three respects. Hatch was charged with burglary contrary to s 9(1)(b) — that having entered a building, he stole therein. It is not necessary, as the judge suggests, for the prosecution to prove that he entered with intent to steal. So the judge has directed the jury that the prosecution need to prove more than they actually do, which is, if anything, favourable to the defendant. The judge has failed to direct the jury as to the essential ingredients of dishonesty and intention of permanently depriving, but this cannot be said to be prejudicial to Hatch on the facts of the case. His defence was that he was not the burglar. If the jury decided that he was, even if properly directed they were hardly going to conclude that nevertheless he was not dishonest, or did not intend permanently to deprive the owner of the silver and jewellery. The ground is raised, because the judge has erred and this error ought be drawn to the attention of the Court of Appeal, but no attempt is made to argue that any prejudice has been caused.

Paragraph 3.2.4. This ground is quite distinct from that set out in paragraph 3.1.1. Not only has the judge wrongly admitted the confession, but having admitted it, he has misdirected the jury on the effect of it. The paragraph begins by quoting the offending direction by the judge and then goes on to explain what is wrong with it and what harm has been done. There are actually two grounds here. First the judge has confused admissibility with truth, and suggested that the two go hand in hand. Reliability is relevant to admissibility only. The truth of the confession was a crucial matter for the jury to consider, since the words were equivocal: 'It was a Hatch job' does not inevitably mean that Hatch committed it. Secondly, the judge has failed to direct the jury that the circumstances in which the confession was obtained were relevant to the truth of it. They were of course also relevant to admissibility, but that point was not for the jury. Strictly speaking the fact that Hatch was being interviewed about another offence was not something the jury should have heard about, but the defence would have wanted them to do so in this case. Note the way in which the case is cited. It is not just referred to, but its point of principle is set out and adopted as the reasoning and argument in this case.

Paragraph 3.2.5. This paragraph also contains two grounds, and the approach adopted is very similar to that in 3.2.4. However this is an instance where a considerable amount of background needs to be explained in order for the judge to be able to understand the grounds, so the first seven lines explain what Miss Walker's evidence was and what happened at the trial. It is important to say that she did not adopt the content of her statement: had she done so, then its content would have coincided with her evidence and no harm would have been done. The misdirection quoted is short, but the explanation of what is wrong with it takes rather longer. The first point is that the judge allowed the jury to consider the statement as evidence; the second that he failed to direct them properly as to the weight of Miss Walker's evidence. Note again the use of case law in argument: it is not cited neutrally but is used as part of the reasoning. In this instance (in each of the two grounds) the argument takes the point of law first, and then applies it to the facts of this case. Note also that each of the two grounds concludes by pointing out the prejudicial effect of the judge's misdirection.

Other potential grounds. There are one or two other potential grounds of appeal against conviction. The failure to direct adequately on the burden has been mentioned in passing (see 3.2.1 and the commentary on it), but there is arguably a ground that the judge did not really make it clear that the defendant did not have to prove anything. There is also a potential ground in relation to the judge's explanation of his and the jury's functions in paragraph A of the summing-up. It would be usual and desirable for a judge to go on and say that if he expressed an opinion on any question of fact the jury were at liberty to disagree with him. But probably little can be made of this omission, since there is not really any opinion of fact expressed by the judge which might have been taken by the jury as a direction on the law.

Section 4 — The grounds of appeal against sentence. There are two sentences which need to be taken separately. With regard to the term of imprisonment, the real complaint is that it is manifestly excessive, and this is a ground in its own right (4.1.2). But there is also a criticism of the judge's justification for such a long term, which is explained in 4.1.1. With regard to the compensation order the judge seems to have passed a sentence that could not be justified by the evidence before the court: the real complaint is therefore that it was wrong in principle. The reasoning is set out in some detail. Take care when citing cases in relation to appeals against sentence. Only guideline cases, or cases which establish a principle should be relied upon. *R v Stanley* is obviously a case which establishes a principle and can be cited here.

25.7.2 Grounds of appeal against conviction

Note that these are headed 'perfected' grounds. Since they have been drafted by reference to a transcript, it must be assumed that they are the perfected version. The first version would have been headed simply 'grounds'.

This is simply a 'shopping list' of the grounds of appeal against conviction that have already been explained in the advice and which you intend to raise in argument. There is absolutely nothing new in this document. Each ground is stated in simple concise terms, with no explanation, reasoning or argument. There is no need for any more, since the grounds will be accompanied by the advice. The grounds appear in the same order as they are dealt with in the advice.

Note that references are made to the transcript where appropriate, with full citations of page and paragraph numbers. The references to the paragraphs of the advice in the right-hand margin are *not* a requirement, but are undoubtedly helpful, and since your objective is to persuade the judge that leave to appeal should be granted, be helpful.

Grounds drafted by counsel should be signed by counsel.

Once the advice on appeal has been drafted accurately, it is hard to see how you can go wrong in the drafting of the grounds themselves!

25.7.3   Grounds of appeal against sentence

This is a separate document. If the defendant is appealing both against conviction and sentence there are two forms to fill in.

Grounds of appeal against sentence do not normally need perfecting, so this is the original statement of the grounds and no references are made to the transcript.

As above, all that appears is a bare statement of the ground itself, without explanation, reasoning or argument.

25.8   Exercise A

Counsel is asked to draft advice on appeal and grounds of appeal against conviction and sentence in respect of Amelia Bradshaw (see **25.5**).

25.9   Exercise B

Counsel is asked to draft advice on appeal and grounds of appeal against conviction and sentence in respect of Melvyn Brace as appropriate. The facts appear from the summing up and the proceedings on sentence.

Summing up of His Honour Judge Waddington-White

A   Members of the jury, this defendant is charged with theft and assault occasioning actual bodily harm. The prosecution have to make you certain that he is guilty of either or both of these disgraceful offences. Let me tell you what the law is. Please follow my directions as being correct. A person is guilty of theft if he takes somebody else's property with the intention of keeping it, and assault occasioning actual bodily harm is the infliction of deliberate violence on another and thereby hurting him. What the prosecution say happened here was this. The victim, poor John Goode, was walking home rather late at night. He was innocently walking home from a friend's house when, as the prosecution say, he was waylaid by a couple of louts. The man, Robertson, who you may think had the sense to plead guilty and give evidence for the Crown, was standing on the pavement when John came along. As you know John had been given a new wallet for his 16th birthday and he was proudly, though unwisely, carrying it in his hip pocket, and part of it was sticking out.

B   As he walked past, that man, Robertson, pickpocketed that nice boy. It must have been intuition, because he said he didn't feel anything, but he swung round in time to see Robertson with the wallet in his hand. He said, 'Here, give me back my wallet', whereupon Robertson punched him on the nose and made off towards the defendant, Brace. Now Brace was standing, or walking, about 20 yards away and John Goode told you that he thought he saw Robertson hand something that might have been the wallet to Brace as he reached him. John at the time, poor lad, was on the ground with a bleeding nose.

C   Robertson, you remember, came forward and said in his evidence that Brace was keeping look-out for him. He also said that he had made a statement implicating Brace. Asked why he had done so he said, you may think quite frankly, 'I hate him'. You will remember that I sentenced Robertson to six months for the theft and three months for the assault, consecutively, nine months in all, detention. I sentenced him before the trial started, so you may think he had nothing whatever to gain by giving evidence.

D   The other bit of evidence on which the prosecution have advanced their case is that of DC Jones. He says that he saw Brace at the police station. He said that he had had to go up North to investigate a very important case (far more important than this one), and unfortunately Brace had to stay in custody at the police station for about four days before he could be interviewed or produced in court. As soon as he was interviewed he was, of course, released on bail. When he was interviewed DC Jones asked him specifically if he was keeping look-out for Robertson. Brace said, 'I wouldn't do anything for the swine', whereupon DC Jones showed him the statement in which Robertson had told the police that Brace was in fact keeping look-out. When he was shown the statement Brace burst into tears and said, 'First my fingerprints and now this — what can I say?' You may think, members of the jury, that that was tantamount to a confession. It is on those facts that the prosecution say that this man, Brace, is guilty.

E   Now what is the defence? Brace says that at the police station he was told by the police officer that his fingerprints had been found on the wallet. You remember that it was found down the road shortly afterwards, empty of course. In fact you know that his fingerprints were not really on the wallet and the police made that up in order to try and catch him out. They also told his solicitor that Brace's prints were on the wallet, and the solicitor told us that he simply advised the defendant to tell the truth. So, you may think, whatever the rights and wrongs of that little trick, no harm was done.

F   Anyway, what the defendant says is that he had nothing to do with the theft or the assault. It just happened that he was walking along. He said he saw what Robertson did, but had nothing to do with it. He said that after he had punched Goode, Robertson approached him and, as he walked by, gave him a punch in the stomach.

G   In a word he says he was an innocent bystander and he rebuts the prosecution allegation that he was engaged with Robertson aiding and abetting him in these horrid crimes. Well, members of the jury, that's what he says.

H   He also told you that he is of good character, which means he has no previous convictions. You may consider this relevant, both to the question of whether you believe him, and to the question of whether he is the sort of young man that would do this sort of thing. But do not forget that every young criminal has to start somewhere.

I   Consider each one of these counts separately and now retire and consider your verdicts. No majorities: unanimous is what I want, unless of course one or two of you can't agree. Then 10–2 or 11–1.

[The jury retired and after 3 hours and 20 minutes returned a guilty verdict by 10–2 on both counts.]

The Judge's Comments when Passing Sentence

In passing sentence the judge said:

J   Brace, these are shocking offences against a young boy. What you did was not far off a mugging. You have not had the sense to plead guilty as Robertson did and have tried by lying to get this jury to acquit you, and it looks as if you nearly succeeded. If you were not only 19, and if you had previous convictions you would go inside for a very long time; the least sentence I can pass on you is one of three years' detention in a young offender institution.

Part 8 claims

26.1 General

The Civil Procedure Rules 1998 lay down an alternative procedure for claims (that is, alternative to Part 7) in Part 8. Part 8 should be used whenever a rule or Practice Direction requires it, or where the claimant seeks the court's decision on a question which is unlikely to involve a substantial dispute of fact (CPR, r 8.1). PD 8B sets out all the many circumstances in which the Part 8 procedure must be used. PD 8, para 1.4 gives examples of three situations in which Part 8 procedure may be used:

(1) a claim by or against a child or patient which has been settled before the commencement of proceedings and the sole purpose of the claim is to obtain the approval of the court to the settlement;

(2) a claim for provisional damages which has been settled before the commencement of proceedings and the sole purpose of the claim is to obtain a consent judgment;

(3) provided there is unlikely to be a substantial dispute of fact, a claim for a summary order for possession against named or unnamed defendants occupying land or premises without the licence or consent of the person claiming possession.

There is a different claim form, called, not surprisingly, a Part 8 claim form. By CPR, r 8.2, the claim form must state:

(a) that Part 8 applies;

(b) (i) the question which the claimant wants the court to decide; or

   (ii) the remedy which the claimant is seeking and the legal basis for the claim to that remedy;

(c) if the claim is being made under an enactment, what that enactment is;

(d) if the claimant is claiming in a representative capacity, what that capacity is;

(e) if the defendant is sued in a representative capacity, what that capacity is.

There are no statements of case in Part 8 procedure. The claim form contains no particulars of claim. The basis of the claimant's claim will simply be included in the section on the claim form headed 'details of claim', or on an attached document similarly headed. No defence is required. Instead a defendant is merely required to file an acknowledgement of service, on a special Part 8 acknowledgement of service form. In that acknowledgement of service, the defendant may seek an alternative remedy from the court.

A Part 8 claim form either lists the remedies sought, rather like the list of remedies sought at the end of particulars of claim, or poses questions of fact and/or law for the court to answer, or both. It does not contain all the material facts, and tells no story. What the claim is all about will emerge from the written evidence. Written evidence must be filed and served with the Part 8 claim form. This can be in the form of witness statements or affidavits (or even the claim form itself if verified by a statement of truth, but this is most unlikely to be appropriate).

The Part 8 procedure can be used in all divisions of the High Court, and in the county court; however, you will generally only come across them in the context of property law. All the examples in **Chapters 26** and **27** are therefore in this area and in the Chancery Division.

26.2   Drafting the Part 8 claim form

26.2.1   Parties

The claimant(s) will be the person(s) seeking the remedies or asking the questions. This usually means that the claimants are the executors of a will, the administrators of an estate or the trustees of a trust, or one of them. Occasionally the claimant(s) will be one or more of the beneficiaries under a trust or an alleged trust. The defendants will be all other persons who have, may have or claim to have an interest in the outcome of the proceedings, certainly including all (other) beneficiaries, unless a representation order is made (see **27.1.2**). Any trustee who is not a claimant must be a defendant.

26.2.2   The details of the claim

26.2.2.1   Introduction

It is probably appropriate to begin by stating in the first few paragraphs:

(a) Who the claimants are, and the capacity in which they are making the claim.

(b) Who the defendants are, explaining why each of them has been joined as a party and/or what their interest in the matter is.

(c) What the relevant subject matter of the claim is: the trust instrument, the estate or the property in dispute.

(d) Any other fundamental facts necessary for an understanding of the context.

Although these matters are neither a remedy sought, nor a question to be decided by the court, and such information would undoubtedly appear in the written evidence served with the claim, it is going to be very difficult to draft the rest of the claim without these basic facts set out. They always appeared on the equivalent document under the old procedure (an 'originating summons') and it is suggested that this ought to continue.

26.2.2.2   The remedies sought and/or the questions asked

Use numbered paragraphs, each paragraph as far as possible asking a single question or seeking a single remedy. Begin with the words:

'The Claimant seeks the following remedies'; or

'The Claimant seeks the court's decision on the following questions'; or

'The Claimant seeks the court's decision on the following questions and the following remedies'.

The approach to be adopted when asking questions for the decision of the court is dealt with fully in **Chapter 27**.

When remedies are being sought, the details of claim will in some ways resemble the list of remedies in particulars of claim. The remedies required are itemised, identified and if necessary described in some detail. Although the application may be a relatively simple one, there may still be several remedies required: each major remedy may give rise to the need for further consequential remedies. So, as will be seen below, an application for the appointment of new trustees can require seven remedies, and an application under the Trusts of Land and Appointment of Trustees Act 1996, s 14, can contain nine or more remedies.

In the Chancery Division two of these remedies will always be an application for an order as to costs and a claim for further or other remedies.

The background to the questions asked or the remedies sought does not appear in the details of the claim. There is nothing on the face of the claim form which enables the court to see how the question arises, what the answer might be, or why the remedy is required. All this is part of the evidence, and appears in the supporting witness statements. The claim form itself does not contain facts and does not attempt to tell the story. It is intended to inform the defendants what the issues are, what questions need to be decided and what remedies are being sought, but is not intended to provide a complete picture, which will only come when it is read in conjunction with the evidence. For this reason it is fundamentally different in nature to a statement of case.

26.2.2.3 Statutory provisions

Where the application is made under an Act, at the end of the details of claim the relevant section(s) should be set out. It is not necessary to set out every relevant section for minor or incidental remedies, but only for the main or major remedies.

26.3 Appointment of new trustees

26.3.1 Details of claim

IN THE HIGH COURT OF JUSTICE   Claim No 2005 HC 2785
CHANCERY DIVISION

BETWEEN

HENRY WILLIAM THOMPSON   <u>Claimant</u>

and

(1) ALASTAIR MORGAN
(2) MARY JANE SMITH
(3) IAN ALASTAIR SCOTT
(4) JOHN ANTHONY SCOTT
(5) SUSAN ELIZABETH SMITH (a child, by
her litigation friend Angela Scott)   <u>Defendants</u>

DETAILS OF CLAIM

1.   The Claimant, Henry William Thompson, is one of the trustees of a Settlement ('the Settlement') dated 25th June 1978 and made between (1) Graham Scott and (2) Henry William Thompson and Alastair Morgan.

2.   The First Defendant, Alastair Morgan, is the other trustee of the Settlement.

3.   The Second, Third, Fourth and Fifth Defendants (Mary Jane Smith, Ian Alastair Scott, John Anthony Scott and Susan Elizabeth Smith respectively) all claim to be beneficially interested under the trusts of the Settlement.

4.   The whereabouts of the First Defendant are unknown and he cannot be found. The Claimant desires to retire from his trusteeship. Harold McQueen and Kerry Bowman are willing to be appointed as trustees of the Settlement.

5.   The Claimant therefore seeks the following remedies namely:

(1) That Harold McQueen and Kerry Bowman or some other fit and proper persons be appointed trustees of the trusts of the Settlement in place of the First Defendant and the Claimant.

(2) That the freehold and leasehold property specified in the First Schedule below and now vested in the Claimant and the First Defendant may be vested in Harold McQueen and Kerry Bowman or such other persons as may be appointed under paragraph 1 above to be held by them on the trusts of the Settlement.

(3) That the right to transfer the shares and stock specified in the Second Schedule below and now registered in the names of the Claimant and the First Defendant, and the right to receive any dividends or income now due and to accrue in future on those shares and that stock may be vested in Harold McQueen and Kerry Bowman or such other persons as may be appointed under paragraph 1 above to be held by them jointly on the trusts of the Settlement.

(4) That the right to sue for and recover the sum of £532.06 or such other sum as may be standing in the names of the Claimant and the First Defendant in current account no 34562280 under the name 'Trustees of the G. Scott Settlement' at the Penzance Branch of Lloyds Bank plc at East Street, Penzance, Cornwall may be vested in Harold McQueen and Kerry Bowman or such other persons as may be appointed under paragraph 1 above to be held by them jointly on the trusts of the Settlement.

(5) That service of this claim on the First Defendant may be dispensed with.

(6) That provision may be made for the costs of this application.

(7) Further or other remedies.

6.   This claim is made under sections 41, 44, 51 and 59 of the Trustee Act 1925, and is a claim to which Part 8 of the Civil Procedure Rules 1998 applies.

<u>FIRST SCHEDULE</u>

1.   The freehold house and land known as Lochinvar, Acacia Close, Penzance, Cornwall and registered at HM Land Registry under Title Number DN 846701.

2.   The leasehold flat known as Flat 3, Longstead House, Blackbury, near Penzance, Cornwall, held under a lease dated 14th May 1990 and made between Oliver Brook and Graham Scott.

SECOND SCHEDULE

(1) 7,500 £1 ordinary shares in General International Holdings plc.

(2) £15,000 Treasury 10% Stock 2005/2006.

JOSEPH BLOGGS

STATEMENT OF TRUTH

Dated etc.

26.3.2 Commentary

There was a settlement which originally had two trustees. However one has disappeared, and the other wishes to retire. It is therefore not possible for new trustees to be appointed in the usual way under s 36 of the Trustee Act 1925, and so an application must be made to the court for the appointment of new trustees under s 41.

Heading. The claim would normally be made by both trustees, but Alastair Morgan is missing, so he cannot be a claimant. He must however be made a defendant. The remaining defendants are all the other persons interested in the claim, in other words the beneficiaries under the settlement. One is a child, and must have a litigation friend.

Paragraphs 1 to 4. These are neither questions for the court nor remedies sought, but as suggested in 26.2.2.1 it is a good idea to introduce the parties and the subject matter of the claim to give the list of remedies sought at least some context. In paragraph 1 note the use of the enumeration (1) and (2) to differentiate the parties to the settlement. This is a neat way of showing who was the settlor and who were the trustees. Without this, it could appear that Graham Scott and Henry William Thompson were the trustees, and Alastair Morgan the settlor. In paragraph 3 it is stated that the beneficiaries merely 'claim' to be beneficially interested as opposed to 'are' interested. This is because the trust is a discretionary trust, giving no beneficiary an absolute entitlement. Paragraph 4 sets out succinctly the reason for the claim.

Paragraph 5. The remedies sought are all listed in a single paragraph. This is not compulsory. Paragraph 4 could alternatively say 'The claimant seeks the remedies set out in paragraphs 5 to 11'.

Paragraph 5(1). This is the claim for the appointment of new trustees under s 41. The names of the proposed trustees must be put forward, but it is usual to add 'or some other fit and proper persons' in case objection is made to either of them. By way of explanation, the reason why each of the existing trustees needs to be replaced is given.

Paragraph 5(2). Once new trustees have been appointed, the trust property needs to be vested in them. Once the application to the court has been made, this is most easily done by order of the court. The court has power to make a vesting order of land under s 44. The land to be vested is identified in a schedule for convenience because there is more than one piece of land. A single piece of property could be identified in this paragraph without the need for a schedule.

Paragraph 5(3). There is more trust property to be vested. Next come the trust investments in the form of shares and stock, which the court can vest under s 51. The correct formulation is to vest not the shares and stock, but the right to transfer them, and the right to receive dividends both present and future.

Paragraph 5(4). The final piece of trust property to be vested is the balance of the trust's bank account. This is a thing in action, a debt owed by the bank to the trustees, and can also be vested under s 51. The correct formulation is 'the right to sue for and recover' the debt. The figure given is of course the current balance in the account, but 'or such other sum' is added as the figure is likely to change before the claim can be heard.

Paragraph 5(5). The first defendant's whereabouts are unknown, so it will not be possible to serve the claim on him. The court has power under s 59 to dispense with service and give judgment in his absence, provided a diligent search for him has been made.

Paragraph 5(6). A order for costs should as always be expressly claimed in the Chancery Division. It would not be appropriate in this case to order any party to pay the costs, but the court has power under s 60 to order that the costs be paid out of the trust property. 'That provision be made' is a neutral way of asking for this.

Paragraph 6. By CPR, r 8.2, if the claim is made under an enactment, the claim form must state what that enactment is. So ss 41, 44, 51 and 59 of the Trustee Act 1925 are identified. The claim form must also state that Part 8 applies, and this seems an appropriate place to make the necessary statement.

Schedules. Here the property to be vested and referred to in paragraphs 4(2) and 4(3) is listed.

Conclusion. A Part 8 claim form has a statement of truth box on it, so even though there may be hardly any facts to be verified, the claimant or someone on his behalf should sign it.

26.3.3 Applications under Judicial Trustees Act 1896, section 1

For contentious applications for the removal of a trustee, for example, where the trustee is accused of mismanagement or breach of trust, it is not appropriate to apply under Trustee Act 1925, s 41. The choice is between an administration order and a judicial trustee application: the modern practice is to go for the latter.

This is done under Judicial Trustees Act 1896, s 1. The application is made under Part 8 (or if there is another Part 7 claim proceeding, for example, a claim for breach of trust, as an interim application in that claim). The claim form can be drafted just as any other application for the appointment of a trustee (see **26.3**) with the following substitution:

(1) That [the ... Bank plc whose registered office is at [address]] [*or* the Official Solicitor to the Supreme Court of Judicature] may be appointed the sole judicial trustee of the trusts of the Settlement in place of the present trustees, the Defendants Jacob Bottomley and Eunice Vearncombe.

The court has power to make an interim injunction restraining the present trustees from transferring, assigning, charging or otherwise dealing with the trust property until the hearing of the claim for the appointment of the judicial trustee.

26.4 Applications under Trusts of Land and Appointment of Trustees Act 1996, section 14

26.4.1 Details of claim

IN THE HIGH COURT OF JUSTICE   Claim No 2005 HC 1903
CHANCERY DIVISION

BETWEEN

ANNE-MARIE JARVIS   Claimant

and

SEYMOUR TUCKER   Defendant

DETAILS OF CLAIM

1.   The Defendant, Seymour Tucker, is the registered proprietor of the house and land known as 26 Albert Road, Ruislip, Middlesex, and registered at HM Land Registry with title absolute under title number BR 246817 ('the Property').

2.   The Claimant, Anne-Marie Jarvis, claims a beneficial interest in the Property because she has lived there with the Defendant as husband and wife since 1996 and has contributed to the purchase of the Property.

3.   The Claimant therefore seeks the following remedies, namely:

(1) A declaration that the Property is held by the Defendant upon trust for the Claimant and Defendant in equal shares or alternatively in such shares as the Court shall determine.

(2) That the Claimant or some other fit and proper person be appointed as trustee of the Property jointly with the Defendant.

(3) That the Property be vested in the Claimant and the Defendant.

(4) That the Defendant be ordered to sell or concur with the Claimant in selling the Property.

(5) Alternatively, that the Property be sold by order of the Court.

(6) If necessary, that the trusts affecting the Property may be carried into execution by the Court.

(7) All necessary and consequential accounts directions and enquiries.

(8) Further or other remedies.

(9) An order that the costs of this claim be paid by the Defendant.

4.   This claim is made under section 14 of the Trusts of Land and Appointment of Trustees Act 1996, and is a claim to which Part 8 of the Civil Procedure Rules 1998 applies.

JOSEPH BLOGGS

STATEMENT OF TRUTH

Dated etc.

26.4.2 Commentary

This is an application under s 14 of the Trusts of Land and Appointment of Trustees Act 1996 (the replacement for s 30 of the Law of Property Act 1925). By this section, any trustee or person having an interest in land can apply for an order relating to the exercise by the trustees of their functions, or declaring the nature or extent of a beneficial interest.

The situation here is a classic one. An unmarried couple have purchased a house as a home for themselves, but it has been conveyed into the name of one of them only. The non-owner (typically the woman) believes she has a beneficial interest in the house by virtue of her contributions to the purchase price and/or mortgage instalments, giving rise to a resulting and/or constructive trust. The relationship has now broken down, and she wants the house sold so she can realise her share. The court has power under s 14 both to declare her interest and to order a sale.

Paragraphs 1 and 2. Simply identify the parties and the property. State what the interest or claim of each of them is. If the land is registered, give the Land Registry Title number. In paragraph 2 the nature of claim is made clear.

Paragraph 3(1). Before she can get anywhere, the claimant first of all needs the existence of the trust declared. This will only be necessary where the house is in the defendant's sole name. If it is jointly owned, this declaration can be left out. Then she wants the extent of her equitable share declared. She is asking for equal shares as a first choice, but failing that whatever the court decides (probably in proportion to their respective contributions). If you thought she might be entitled to more than a half share, you would put these two options the other way round.

Paragraph 3(2). Once the trust is declared, it becomes an express trust, and it will not be possible to sell the land with only a single trustee. So a second trustee needs to be appointed. Obviously the claimant would like to be that person. Again, this order will be unnecessary if the house is jointly owned, because there will already be two trustees.

Paragraph 3(3). Having appointed the claimant as co-trustee, the next requirement is to vest the house in both trustees.

Paragraph 3(4). This is what the claimant is really after, an order for sale. Assuming the claimant is appointed as a trustee, the order to the defendant to concur in the sale is the relevant one. The order that the defendant sell is only relevant if no second trustee is appointed.

Paragraph 3(5). This is a standard alternative to 3(4). If the defendant is likely to make difficulties the sale may need to be taken out of the parties' hands and taken over by the court. This is an expensive option.

Paragraph 3(6). What this actually means is that after sale by the court the net proceeds of sale should be divided up and the claimant should be paid whatever sum she is entitled to.

Paragraph 3(7). This multiple remedy need not be sought but often is. The court may need to order an inquiry into any sums due to the claimant, or the defendant may be ordered to account for any rents he has received from the property. In any event the court has power to make any directions it thinks fit to a party to do or not to do something. If this is left out, there is still the claim for 'further or other relief' for the claimant to fall back on.

26.4.3 Further remedies

The following further remedies may be appropriate in the circumstances indicated:

(a) If the defendant refuses to co-operate in carrying out the sale, or has disappeared, the court has power under Trustee Act 1925, s 47, to vest the property in the purchaser and under s 50 to appoint someone to convey it. In this case add a claim:

> If and so far as necessary, an order vesting the Property in the purchaser or appointing the Claimant or some other fit and proper person to convey the Property.

(b) If the trust requires someone's consent before the property can be sold, the trustees may seek an order under s 14 for a sale dispensing with that consent, in which case the following claim is appropriate:

> That the Defendants be ordered to sell the Property notwithstanding that the Defendant Mildred Rose refuses to consent to the sale.

(c) The trustees have power under Trusts of Land and Appointment of Trustees Act 1996, s 6, to partition land held on trust where land is absolutely vested in persons of full age in undivided shares. Under s 14 it is therefore possible to order partition where the trustees refuse. The following claim may be appropriate:

> (1) That the Property specified in the schedule below may be partitioned between the Claimant and the Defendant so that the land shown edged red on the attached plan be allocated to the Claimant and the land shown edged green be allocated to the Defendant or in such other manner and with such payment of equality money (if any) as to the Court may seem just.

> (2) If and so far as necessary, an order vesting the parts of the Property thus partitioned in the Claimant and the Defendant respectively.

(d) If the claimant has a beneficial interest in the property, but is not in occupation, she may also claim a sum equivalent to rent from the person (usually the defendant) who is in occupation of her 'part' of the property. In such a case the following claim would be appropriate:

(1) An inquiry as to what sum is due from the Defendant to the Claimant by way of occupation rent for the Property.

(2) An order that the Defendant pay to the Claimant the sum found due by the inquiry.

26.5 Applications under Trustee Act 1925, section 57

26.5.1 Details of claim

IN THE HIGH COURT OF JUSTICE   Claim No 2005 HC 7344
CHANCERY DIVISION

BETWEEN

(1) SPENCER HOLLOWAY
(2) SIOBHAN MAY   Claimants

and

(1) GARRY MALCOLM
(2) HELEN MALCOLM   Defendants

_____

DETAILS OF CLAIM

_____

1.   The Claimants, (1) Spencer Holloway and (2) Siobhan May are the executors and trustees of the Will dated 17th October 1997 ('the Will') of Jeremy Malcolm deceased, probate having been granted to them on 13th May 2002.

2.   The Defendants, (1) Garry Malcolm and (2) Helen Malcolm, are the beneficiaries under the Will.

3.   There are certain investments and transactions which are expedient and which the Claimants, with the consent of the Defendants, wish to carry out, but are unable to because of the absence of any power vested in the Claimants by the Will or by law.

4.   The Claimants seek the following remedies namely:

(1) That the Claimants may be authorised by the Court to invest money now subject to the trusts of the Will in the purchase of the following shares in the following limited companies:

(a)   1,000 £1 fully paid ordinary shares in Mammoth Transport Limited;

(b)   4,000 £1 (50p paid) ordinary shares in Natty Gadgets Limited.

(2) That the Claimants may be authorised by the Court to make a personal unsecured loan of £10,000 out of the trust capital to the Second Defendant to enable her to support herself while undergoing pupillage at the Bar of England and Wales.

(3) That provision may be made for the costs of this application.

(4) Further or other remedies.

5.   This application is made under section 57 of the Trustee Act 1925, and is a claim to which Part 8 of the Civil Procedure Rules 1998 applies.

JOSEPH BLOGGS

STATEMENT OF TRUTH

Dated etc.

26.5.2   Commentary

This is an application under s 57 of the Trustee Act 1925. This section gives the court power to give trustees power to carry out any transaction, including the investment of trust funds, which they would not otherwise have the power to carry out, either because there is no such power in law, or because the trust instrument does not give them the power. The order can be made if it can be shown to be expedient, which means for the benefit of the trust as a whole. The claim is therefore in essence an application for permission, and is drafted as such.

The claimants are the trustees, who are seeking the court's authorisation; the defendants are the beneficiaries under the trust. Paragraphs 1 and 2 state who the parties are. When the trust arises under a will, as here, it is necessary always to state the grant of probate.

Paragraph 3 states the nature of the claim.

The remedies sought are simply orders authorising the desired transactions, so the draft can do no more than state what those transactions are. There is no attempt to state why it would be expedient to carry them out. This would appear in the witness statements that accompany the Part 8 claim.

26.6   Exercise

Instructing solicitors act for Ms Fiona Armitage, the former girlfriend of Richard Naylor. In 1998 Mr Naylor purchased the freehold property known as 36 Pitcairn Road, London N17 for £120,000. It was registered in his name under Title Number GLN 123456. Mr Naylor put up £10,000 of the purchase price, and Ms Armitage £30,000; the balance was obtained by a mortgage from the Accrington Building Society. Ms Armitage contributed substantially to the mortgage payments, but she has kept no record of the extent of her contribution.

The parties lived together until last month, but Mr Naylor found a new girlfriend Zara Pinkerton and ordered Ms Armitage to leave.

Ms Armitage is now living with her mother and would like the property sold so that she can recover her £30,000 or whatever she is entitled to. It is thought that the house is now worth £200,000.

Instructing solicitors have ascertained through correspondence with Mr Naylor that the house is now registered in the joint names of himself and Miss Pinkerton. He does not dispute the contributions she has made, but does dispute that they entitle her to a beneficial interest, and will resist any order for sale.

Counsel is asked to settle an appropriate claim.

Construction claims

27.1 Introduction

27.1.1 What is a construction claim?

A 'construction claim' is a Part 8 claim whose purpose is to ask the court to construe a trust deed, settlement, will or some other document and answer the questions posed by the claimants. A construction claim is almost always brought under CPR, r 64(2)(a), which applies the rules in Section I of Part 64 to claims for the court to determine any question arising in the administration of the estate of a deceased person or in the execution of a trust.

PD 64, para 1 gives examples of the types of claims which may be made under r 64.2(a):

(1) a claim for the determination of any of the following questions—
  (a) any question as to who is included in any class of persons having—
    (i) a claim against the estate of a deceased person;
    (ii) a beneficial interest in the estate of such a person; or
    (iii) a beneficial interest in any property subject to a trust;
  (b) any question as to the rights or interests of any person claiming—
    (i) to be a creditor of the estate of a deceased person;
    (ii) to be entitled under a will or on the intestacy of a deceased person; or
    (iii) to be beneficially entitled under a trust;
(2) a claim for any of the following remedies—
  (a) an order requiring a trustee—
    (i) to provide and, if necessary, verify accounts;
    (ii) to pay into court money which he holds in that capacity; or
    (iii) to do or not to do any particular act;
  (b) an order approving any sale, purchase, compromise or other transaction by a trustee; or
  (c) an order directing any act to be done which the court could order to be done if the estate or trust in question were being administered or executed under the direction of the court.

The question under para 1(1)(a) might be, for example, 'Who are the deceased's friends?'. Under para 1(1)(b) the question might be, for example, 'Who is entitled to the proceeds of sale of the house?'

The remedies made available by para 1(2) are wide-ranging. An order of the kind mentioned in para 1(2)(a) might be more likely to be made in a contentious claim, but can be made in a Part 8 claim. An order of the kind mentioned in para 1(2)(b) was illustrated by the Part 8 claim in **26.5**. Paragraph 1(2)(c) gives the court very wide powers indeed.

The only alternative to a claim under r 64.2(a) is a claim under r 64.2(b) for an order for the administration of the estate of a deceased person, or the execution of a trust, to be carried out under the direction of the court. This is known as an administration order, and is a heavy-handed and expensive solution, which will only be employed as a last resort. PD

64, para 3.1 says that the court will only make an administration order if it considers that the issues between the parties cannot properly be resolved in any other way.

27.1.2   Parties

CPR, r 64.4 deals with who should be parties to a construction claim:

(1)   in a claim to which this Section applies, ...

    (a)   all the trustees must be parties;

    (b)   if the claim is made by trustees, any of them who does not consent to being a claimant must be made a defendant; and

    (c)   the claimant may make parties to the claim any persons with an interest in or claim against the estate, or an interest under the trust, who it is appropriate to make parties having regard to the nature of the order sought.

Essentially the claimants in a construction claim will be the executors or trustees; any trustee who is not a claimant must be made a defendant instead. The defendants will be anyone else who has or may have an interest in the answer to the questions being put. This will normally mean all the beneficiaries, or potential beneficiaries under the will or trust. However not all of them have to be made parties if it is not appropriate. The alternative is to make a representation order.

27.1.3   Representation orders

Where appropriate, a representation order must be sought as a specific remedy. A representation order is an order that someone who is a party to the proceedings should represent the interests of someone else who is not a party to the proceedings. This is done under CPR, r 19.7, which reads as follows:

(1)   This rule applies to claims about—

    (a)   the estate of a deceased person;

    (b)   property subject to a trust; or

    (c)   the meaning of a document, including a statute.

(2)   The court may make an order appointing a person to represent any other person or persons in the claim where the person or persons to be represented—

    (a)   are unborn;

    (b)   cannot be found;

    (c)   cannot easily be ascertained; or

    (d)   are a class of persons who have the same interest in a claim and—

        (i)   one or more members of that class are within sub-paragraphs (a), (b) or (c); or

        (ii)   to appoint a representative would further the overriding objective.

There must be no conflict of interest between the representative and those being represented. The representative's interest should be identical to, or as close as possible to, that of the represented person. A class should usually be represented by someone who is a member of it.

The proceedings described in r 19.7(1) are all ones in which questions might well need to be resolved, so although representation orders are of wider application, they are of particular significance in construction claims.

The four circumstances in which a representation order can be made are set out in r 19.7(2). Persons who are unborn, or whose whereabouts are unknown obviously need to have their interests represented. Persons who cannot easily be ascertained are likely to belong to a class whose members cannot be completely listed. The circumstance 'to appoint a representative would further the overriding objective' is designed to cover the situation where there are a large number of beneficiaries to a trust. It is obviously not in the interests of justice or proportional to the expense to have hundreds, or even thousands of defendants, which would have to happen in some cases if no representation order were made.

27.1.4 The diagram approach

In construction claims, the executors or trustees may be seeking some consequential remedies, but they are primarily asking questions. In order to be able to draft the details of the claim, it is necessary to perform quite a thorough analysis of the facts and the law in order to identify the questions that need (and those that do not need) the decision of the court.

This analysis can quite often and quite helpfully be carried out by means of a diagrammatical approach. It is possible to construct a diagram which shows how the issues arise, what questions need to be put to the court and what the possible answers are. Illustrations of such diagrams appear below in the examples.

The starting point in constructing a diagram is to ask yourself: 'what do the trustees want to know?'. They do not in reality want to know the answer to questions of law like 'is there a valid secret trust?' or 'is the gift of the residue charitable?'. Their position is that they have a duty to distribute the estate or trust property in accordance with the terms of the trust and the law, and yet it is not clear what they should do. The question they want the court to answer is: 'What should we do with the property? How much do we give to whom?' So the starting-point is the total property whose destination is in doubt.

The next step is to ask: who gets first bite? This will usually be clear from the terms of the trust or the sequence of gifts in the will. If it is clear in fact and law whose gift takes priority, and that the gift is valid, there is no problem. But if there is a doubt as to the validity or the extent of the gift, then you must identify questions like: does the donee get this money or not? If not, what happens to it instead? If he does not get it all, who gets the rest? There may be more than one possible answer to these questions, in which case all possibilities should be identified and charted.

Then you must look at each possible answer in turn and ask yourself: if this is the correct answer, does any subsequent question arise? If yes, then it needs to be charted with all its possible answers in the same way as the first question was.

When you finally get to the stage of knowing that if each possible answer is correct, then no further issue arises, you can go back to the main bulk of the property and see who takes second bite, and then go through the whole process again.

When you have finished this chart you will have what is in effect a skeleton plan for the questions in your details of claim. Wherever you have a fork, you have a question to put to the court. For each prong of the fork, you have an optional answer to be included.

From this diagram also you can see who are the potential beneficiaries who need to be included as parties to the claim.

27.1.5 Drafting the questions

Once you know what questions to ask and what the possible answers to each are, drafting them requires no more than precision and clarity of expression.

Questions are always asked indirectly, for example, 'That it may be decided whether ...', not directly, for example, 'Is the trust valid?'.

Questions should not be open ended. They should ask the court to choose between various alternative answers. The possible answers, as well as the questions should therefore be set out. The only exception is where the question can only have two possible answers, yes or no. To cover unforeseen possible answers, some phrase such as 'any other and if so which ...' may be used to give a final option.

Questions may be framed either as questions of fact, or as questions of law, or as a mixture of the two. Draft in whatever way seems simplest and most appropriate. But your question must accurately state the legal or factual issue to be decided.

27.1.6   Three examples

Three examples follow. In each case the instructions to counsel are set out first, because without them it is impossible to see how the draft relates to the facts of the case. There is then an analysis of the facts and the law and a diagram showing how that analysis can be charted. Only then do the details of claim appear.

27.2   Re Rupert Sayer

27.2.1   Instructions to counsel

Instructing Solicitors act for Charles Pelly, the executor and trustee of the will of Rupert Sayer, deceased. Rupert Sayer died, at his home in London, on the 12th December 2004 aged 66. He left a wife, Penelope, and it is probable that three children of the marriage survive, Florence, Paul and Osbert. Some time before 1980 the deceased and his wife separated and since that time, until his death, Rupert Sayer lived with a lady called Millicent Ford as man and wife. There are two children of that relationship, Jean, who was born on 7th July 1984 and Lionel, born on the 8th February 1992.

Rupert Sayer made his will on 9th August 1992. The will was proved by the executor on the 8th February 2005. By clause 1 of the will the testator appointed his nephew, Charles Pelly, to be the executor and trustee. Clause 2 was in these terms:

I bequeath unto my life-long friend, Joseph Nixon, the sum of £100,000 absolutely.

Clause 3 bequeathed all the rest residue and remainder of his property to provide a home of rest for horses and donkeys.

Joseph Nixon has been a friend of Rupert Sayer since boyhood, when they had been together at the Toft House School. Joseph Nixon has informed instructing solicitors that sometime in January of 1993 Rupert Sayer had telephoned to ask him to come and see him. On his arrival, Rupert Sayer had said to Joseph Nixon, 'Look Joe, I have made my Will and if anything happens to me, here is a letter which will tell you what to do'. Joseph Nixon said, 'That's all right, don't worry'. At that point Rupert Sayer handed over to Joseph an envelope which had marked on it 'Not to be opened until after my death, Rupert Sayer'.

This envelope was handed to the executor by Joseph Nixon and has now been opened, and it contained the following letter.

Dear Joe,

I want you to keep £1,000 for yourself, and the balance you shall distribute among such persons as you, Joe, may consider to be my dependants, or to have a moral claim upon me, as you shall in your absolute discretion select, and in such shares and proportions as you shall think fit.

Yours,

Rupert.

The estate of Rupert Sayer consisted of various investments in stocks and shares, and after paying inheritance tax there will be assets to the value of £120,000.

Instructing Solicitors have been informed that Osbert Sayer was last heard of some seven years ago when he left to go to Australia. Florence Sayer is living in the North of England, and Paul has not been heard of for some time. Rupert Sayer had one sister, a Mrs Nellie Pelly, who is the mother of Charles Pelly the Executor. Mrs Pelly is a widow, and is living in considerable poverty, and Rupert Sayer often used to give her sums of money to help her.

27.2.2 Analysis

We begin by identifying the whole of the property about which questions arise. This is Rupert Sayer's estate, worth about £120,000. So we place this at the top of the diagram.

It is apparent from the will that there are two gifts, and subject to the failure of either gift in whole or part, the estate will be divided between these two gifts. So we can immediately put a fork under the estate, dividing it into those two gifts. The gift of £100,000 to Joseph Nixon plainly constitutes first bite, because of the sequence of them and because the second gift is of the residue. So we next consider what happens to this gift.

According to the will the gift is absolute, but it is apparent that the testator has sought to create a secret trust of that sum in the hands of Joseph Nixon. So the first issue is whether there is a validly constituted secret trust.

There are three conditions to be satisfied. First, the secret trustee must have accepted the trust, that is he must have agreed to act as trustee on those terms. Secondly, the terms of the trust must have been communicated to the secret trustee in the lifetime of the testator. Thirdly, the property must be given to the trustee so as to constitute the trust. This last requirement is obviously satisfied and requires no further consideration.

Whether Joseph Nixon has accepted the trust is a question of fact. When he took the envelope, did he know what he was accepting? Is it sufficient for him to accept the envelope, without realising that it contained the terms of the trust? This is a question the court must answer.

The terms of the trust have obviously been communicated, but when? When the envelope was handed over, which would satisfy the requirement of communication in the testator's lifetime, or only when it was opened, which would not? There is some old case law (*obiter*), which suggests that an envelope marked 'not to be opened till after my death' will satisfy the requirement (see *Re Boyes* (1884) 26 Ch D 531 and *Re Keen* [1937] Ch 236) but no binding authority. So this must also be a question for the court.

But the analysis does not stop there. We have identified the legal issues but not the factual ones that need to be answered. The next step is to consider who gets the £100,000:

(a) if there has been acceptance but no communication,

(b) if there has been both acceptance and communication,

(c) if there has been communication but no acceptance, and

(d) if there has been neither acceptance nor communication.

If there has been no acceptance the answer has to be that Joseph Nixon takes the £100,000 absolutely. The will prevails because nothing has happened to impose a trust. If he has accepted the trust, then he has agreed to be a trustee and there must be some form of a trust. If there has also been valid communication, then the requirements of a valid secret trust are prima facie satisfied, and that is how Nixon will hold the money. But if there has been no valid communication, then there must be some form of resulting trust. If the gift under clause 2 of the will is effective, then the £100,000 cannot fall into the residue. It would result back to the estate, it would then be property undisposed of by the will, there would be a partial intestacy and Nixon would hold the money on trust for whoever inherits on intestacy. If however the gift in clause 2 fails, then the money falls into the residue. There is no clear authority on which of these two outcomes is correct, so both must be put forward as alternatives.

We can now therefore draw a fork under the gift of £100,000 showing four possible answers to the question 'what happens to this money?'. The next step is to ask ourselves whether, in the event of each of these four possible answers being the correct one, any further issues arise. If Nixon inherits absolutely, there can be none: that is the end of the matter. If there is a resulting trust for the next-of-kin (who inherit on intestacy), that also gives rise to no further questions. If the money falls into the residue, there are no questions other than those which arise in relation to the residue in any event — so an arrow can be drawn to the residue in the top right-hand corner of the diagram.

But if there is prima facie a valid secret trust, further issues arise — it becomes necessary to look at the terms of the letter itself. There is now another division into first bite and remainder, so another fork appears in the diagram, and the first bite of £1,000 to Joseph Nixon needs to be considered. There is probably not much doubt about this. The letter is clear, the sum is specified and is relatively small and Nixon will probably be allowed to keep it (see *Re Tyler* [1967] 1 WLR 1269), but it would be unwise to so advise him without getting the approval of the court, so the question needs to be put. This gives rise to the question of what happens to it if he is not allowed to keep it. One possibility is that there is a resulting trust back to the estate, and so once again a partial intestacy. Another possibility is that it simply falls into the balance to be distributed in accordance with the terms of the letter. The possibility of a resulting trust for the residue of the will really does not arise. Once the secret trust has been validly constituted, clause 2 of the will has plainly taken effect and the £1,000 is no longer part of the property comprised within the will. So these three alternative answers appear beneath the £1,000 in our diagram.

We now move over to the second bite under the secret trust: the balance to be distributed 'among such persons as you, Joe, may consider to be my dependants, or to have a moral claim on me, as you shall in your absolute discretion select'. The issue here is certainty of objects. This is a discretionary trust, and so the test to be applied is that established in *McPhail v Doulton* [1971] AC 424 — whether the trustee can say with certainty whether any given claimant is or is not a member of the class. This is not a matter of evidential certainty (how easily a claimant can prove he is within the class) but conceptual certainty (whether the trustee would have a good enough idea of what he was looking for that he would recognise a member of the class when he sees one) (*Re Baden (No. 2)* [1973] Ch 9).

There is probably no difficulty about dependants, which was held to be a conceptually certain term in *re Baden (No. 2)*, but what about moral claimants? This seems highly dubious. But then the letter does not say moral claimants, it says 'such persons as you, Joe, may *consider* to have a moral claim on me'. Surely even if a trustee cannot always say whether someone has a moral claim, he can always say whether he considers someone to have a moral claim — for he is appointed to arbitrate. There is *obiter* support for this in *Re Leek* [1967] Ch 1061 (overturned by the Court of Appeal on a different point [1969] Ch 563) where the words 'such persons as my trustee may consider to have a moral claim on me' were held certain. But the problem is the words 'you Joe'. Suppose Nixon were to die and a new trustee were appointed in his place. Would the new trustee be able to say with certainty whether Joseph Nixon considered someone to have a moral claim? Evidently not. So this gift can probably only stand as a valid gift if the words 'you Joe' are construed to mean 'my trustee'. This question must be put to the court, and there are two possible answers: either there is a valid discretionary trust, or the gift fails for uncertainty and there is a resulting trust for the next of kin on a partial intestacy.

We have completed our analysis of what happens to the gift in clause 2 of the will, and move over to the residue. The gift to 'provide a home of rest for horses and donkeys' is plainly a purpose gift, and so will be void unless charitable. Is it charitable? Almost certainly, yes — trusts for looking after animals are widely held to have a sufficient element of general public benefit (see eg *Re Wedgwood* [1913] 1 Ch 113 and *Re Moss* [1949] 1 All ER 495). If by any chance the gift is held not to be charitable, then it fails and there is a partial intestacy on which the next-of-kin will inherit. So these two alternatives can be added to the diagram.

But there is a consequential question which arises also. Does the gift require Mr Pelly to provide a home of rest in the concrete sense, that is to acquire a plot of land, build a home and run it; or only in the abstract sense, that is to use it to ensure that some horses and donkeys are provided with a home of rest, which could be achieved simply by giving the money to an existing institution. If it is the first of these which is correct, then that may simply be impossible with the funds available (£20,000 less the costs of the application to the court). In that case, the court must be asked for an order that the money be applied *cy-près*. So these two further alternatives appear in the diagram in the event of the gift being charitable.

The last step in the analysis is to consider who should be made defendants. We need to look at every final prong of every fork in the diagram, and decide who would argue for that being the correct destination, and then join that person, or at least one member of that class. Joseph Nixon may inherit £100,000 or £1,000 absolutely, so he needs to be joined. Since he has a conflict of interest, he cannot also represent the beneficiaries under the secret trust, so they too need to be joined. Known dependants and or/moral claimants are Penelope, Florence, Paul, Osbert, Millicent, Jean, Lionel and Nellie Pelly. The next-of-kin who will inherit on intestacy in this case is Penelope Sayer alone. Where the deceased leaves spouse and issue, the first £125,000 goes to the spouse. That only leaves the horses and donkeys, who have no one to represent them. But charity in general is always represented by the Attorney-General and so he too needs to be a defendant (see PD 64, para 7).

27.2.3   Diagram

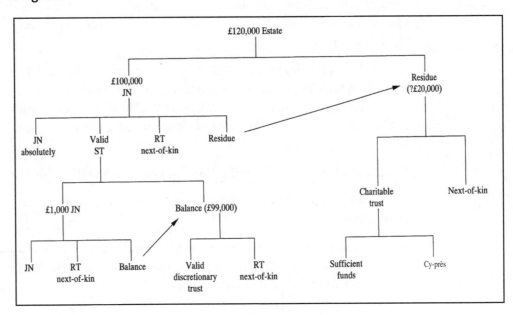

27.2.4 Details of claim

CHANCERY DIVISION

BETWEEN

CHARLES PELLY   Claimant

and

(1) JOSEPH NIXON
(2) PENELOPE SAYER
(3) FLORENCE SAYER
(4) MILLICENT FORD
(5) JEAN FORD
(6) LIONEL FORD (a child, by his litigation
       friend Arthur Magnus)
(7) NELLIE PELLY
(8) HER MAJESTY'S ATTORNEY-GENERAL   Defendants

DETAILS OF CLAIM

---

1.   The Claimant, Charles Pelly, is the executor and trustee of the will dated 9th August 1992 ('the Will') of Rupert Sayer ('the Deceased'), probate having been granted on 8th February 2005.

2.   By clause 2 of the Will the Deceased bequeathed £100,000 absolutely to the First Defendant, Joseph Nixon. By clause 3 of the Will the Deceased bequeathed the residue of his property to provide a home of rest for horses and donkeys.

3.   In January 1993 the deceased gave the First Defendant a letter ('the Letter') marked 'Not to be opened until after my death'. The Letter directed the First Defendant in the following terms:

'I want you to keep £1,000 for yourself, and the balance you shall distribute among such persons as you, Joe, may consider to be my dependants, or to have a moral claim upon me, as you shall in your absolute discretion select, and in such shares and proportions as you shall think fit.'

4.   The Second, Third, Fourth, Fifth, Sixth and Seventh Defendants (Penelope Sayer, Florence Sayer, Millicent Ford, Jean Ford, Lionel Ford and Nellie Pelly respectively) all claim to be interested as beneficiaries under the Letter. The Second Defendant also claims to be beneficially entitled to so much of the estate of the Deceased as is undisposed of by the Will.

5.   The residue of the Deceased's estate contains assets to the value of about £20,000.

6.   The Claimant seeks the decision of the Court on the following questions and the following remedies, namely:

(1) That it may be decided whether on a true construction of the Will and the Letter and in the events which have happened, the First Defendant holds the sum of £100,000 bequeathed to him by Clause 2 of the Will:

   (a)   for his own use absolutely; or

   (b)   upon the trusts declared in the Letter; or

   (c)   upon resulting trust for those entitled to the residuary estate; or

   (d)   upon resulting trust for those entitled on intestacy; or

   (e)   upon any other and if so what trust.

(2) If the answer to question (1) is (b), that it may be decided whether on a true construction of the Letter and in the events which have happened, the First Defendant holds the sum of £100,000:

   (a)   as to the first £1,000 of that sum:

       (i)   for his own use absolutely; or

       (ii)   upon trust for those entitled to the balance of the £100,000; or

       (iii)   upon resulting trust for those entitled on intestacy; or

       (iv)   upon any other and if so what trust.

   (b)   as to the balance of the sum

       (i)   on a discretionary trust to distribute the money among those persons considered by him to be dependent or to have a moral claim upon the Deceased; or

       (ii)   upon resulting trust for those entitled on intestacy; or

       (iii)   upon any other and if so what trust.

(3) That it may be decided whether on a true construction of the Will the residuary estate of Rupert Sayer is held:

   (a)   on a charitable trust to provide a home of rest for horses and donkeys; or

   (b)   upon resulting trust for those entitled on intestacy; or

   (c)   upon any other and if so what trust.

(4) If the answer to question (3) is (a), that the Court may approve a scheme for the application of the funds.

(5) If the answer to question (3) is (a), but it is considered impracticable with the funds available to carry out the charitable purpose, that the Court may approve a scheme to apply the funds *cy-près*.

(6) That the Third Defendant or some other person may be appointed to represent Paul Sayer and Osbert Sayer and all persons who might have an interest under the trusts of the Letter other than Second, Fourth, Fifth, Sixth and Seventh Defendants.

(7) That provision may be made for the costs of this application.

(8) Further or other remedies.

7.   This claim is made under Part 64 of the Civil Procedure Rules 1998 and is a claim to which Part 8 of the Civil Procedure Rules applies.

JOSEPH BLOGGS

STATEMENT OF TRUTH

Dated etc.

27.2.5 Commentary

Heading. There is no correct order in which to list the defendants, but it seems logical to put them in the order in which their interests will come up for consideration if the questions are answered in the order set out. Defendants with the same interest should logically be placed consecutively. So Joseph Nixon comes first, and then the potential beneficiaries under the discretionary trust. Since Lionel Ford is a child, his litigation friend must also be identified. Paul and Osbert Sayer obviously cannot be joined as defendants because their whereabouts are unknown. Instead, representation orders will be needed. The Attorney-General, when a party, by convention always comes last in any event.

Paragraphs 1 to 5. These are the introductory paragraphs (see **26.2.2.1**). The parties need to be introduced in such a way as to establish what is the claim, potential claim or interest of each. It is natural to begin with the claimant (paragraph 1). In introducing him you can take the opportunity to introduce and define the deceased and the will. Remember to state also the grant of probate. It is difficult to introduce the defendants without stating what the disputed gifts in the will and letter are. So the terms of clauses 2 and 3 (paragraph 2) and the letter (paragraph 3) are included. Then the capacity of the defendants can be stated (paragraph 4). Remember that Penelope Sayer claims in two capacities, and this should be made clear.

Setting out the terms of the will and trust not only helps to explain the interests of the parties, but also helps the court to understand the questions which are set out below. This is why they appear more or less in full. If they were long and complicated, however, they could reasonably be condensed, because the court will obviously look at the actual documents and the written evidence in construing the relevant provisions. The introduction is only intended to set the scene, not provide the whole basis for the court's decision.

The value of the residue (paragraph 5) is included because it provides the background to the question of what to do if there is not enough money.

Paragraph 6. This paragraph sets out all the questions to be answered and the remedies sought. There is no rule that it should be a single paragraph sub-divided rather than a series of separate paragraphs, but if you choose the latter format you may find yourself having to repeat the introductory words. It is also helpful to be able to call the questions (1), (2) and (3) rather than 7, 8 and 9. The introductory words 'The Claimant seeks the decision of the Court on the following questions and the following remedies, namely' are virtually standard in every construction claim.

It is not difficult to identify and draft the questions to be decided once you have completed your analysis and drawn up a diagram. The diagram in fact operates as a skeleton plan for your claim. Whenever you have a fork (except a fork which divides property into more than one gift), you have a question to be asked. However many prongs there are to that fork, you have there the answers to be proposed. All you need to do now is convert the diagram into longhand.

Paragraph 6(1). The form in which the question is put is also standard. Always begin with 'that it may be decided whether on a true construction of', go on to identify the document or documents to be construed, and add 'and in the events which have happened' if (but only if) the court must look at matters outside the document as well in order to answer the question. Here the events to be construed are the circumstances surrounding the handing over of the letter. Then pose the question. This can be posed either as a question of fact (as here), or as a question of law, or as a mixture of the two. To ask how the property in question is held is a very common way of putting the question.

Then you must set out all the alternative answers to the question which you have identified in your analysis and diagram. Here (a) is the result if Nixon has not accepted the trust, (b) is the result if he has accepted and the terms have been validly communicated, and (c) and (d) are the alternative results if there has been acceptance but no valid communication. Answer (e) is not essential, but is frequently added just in case there is some other possible answer you have overlooked.

Paragraph 6(2). This question only arises if there is prima facie a valid secret trust, so you begin with the words 'if the answer to question (1) is (b)', then continue with the stock phrases explained above.

The question sub-divides into the questions of the £1,000 and the balance, the answers in each case being those identified in the diagram, with 'any other and if so what trust' added.

Paragraph 6(3). Note that there is no reference to 'and in the events which have happened' in this question. Whether the gift is charitable or not depends on nothing but the terms of the will itself. Otherwise the question and answers are set out according to the same formula as in the previous questions.

Paragraphs 6(4) and (5). If the court decides that the gift is charitable then Charles Pelly wants directions on how to deal with the money. The issue of whether the 'home of rest' is to be understood in a concrete or abstract sense will determine how he spends the residue. He will doubtless propose that he simply gives the money to an existing charity and the court is invited to approve this scheme (paragraph 6(4)). In the event of his being required to provide a home in the bricks and mortar sense, there will almost certainly be insufficient funds, so a *cy-près* application is required. This is also done by inviting the court to approve a scheme (paragraph 6(5)). The scheme would doubtless be identical to that proposed in paragraph 6(4).

Paragraph 6(6). This is a request for a representation order. Paul and Osbert Sayer are obviously potential beneficiaries and must be represented. But there may be other potential beneficiaries who have not been identified and they too must be represented. The obvious person to represent these persons is Florence Sayer, sister of Paul and Osbert and a member of the class. Penelope Sayer would not be appropriate as her chief interest is to argue that as much as possible of the estate is undisposed of by the will.

Paragraphs 6(7), 6(8) and 7. These are also standard and have been explained previously (see 26.3.2).

27.3 Re Charles Elliott

27.3.1 Instructions to counsel

Instructing solicitors act for Mr James Chesterfield the sole executor of the will dated 1 April 1996 of Charles Elliott ('the deceased') who died on 3 July 2004, a bachelor. Mr Chesterfield, who is a retired bank manager, proved the will on 26 August 2004. The will was in the deceased's own handwriting and, after providing for the revocation of previous wills, for the appointment of Mr Chesterfield as executor and for the payment of the deceased's debts etc, went on as follows:

I want my house to be sold and the proceeds of sale to be shared out by Mr Chesterfield amongst my drinking companions as he wishes. He is to have £1,000 for his trouble. One half of all the rest of my money is to go on trust for The Howe School, Dartmouth to create a scholarship for the best student studying Latin and Ancient Greek; the other half is to go to my sister Jane.

The deceased left (a) some £10,000 in cash, out of which all his debts have been paid and which now stands at £7,500, (b) 500 £1 ordinary shares in Dimes & Scott plc, now worth £30,000, (c) £5,000 in the Hightrees Building Society, (d) a small piece of freehold land at 3 Hancock Crescent, London NE3 worth, it is thought, £50,000, and (e) his house at 5 Watson Square, London NE5 which has just been sold for £235,000.

The deceased had a number of drinking companions of whom Mr Joshua Whittell is the oldest (in all senses of the word): Mr Whittell is prepared to represent the class of drinking companions. The Howe School is a registered charitable corporation and may be sued in that name. It used to teach Ancient Greek, but stopped some five years ago. It has no intention of re-introducing Ancient Greek into its curriculum, but it continues to teach both

Latin and the History of Greece and Rome. The deceased's only surviving relatives are his sister Miss Jane Elliott (whom the deceased hardly ever saw) and his nephew Mr Andrew Partington (the only son of the deceased's other sister who predeceased the deceased).

27.3.2   Analysis

The estate in this case divides into three bites, again in the order in which they appear in the will: the house, the £1,000 and the residue ('all the rest of my money').

The proceeds of sale of the house are to go on a discretionary trust to the deceased's drinking companions. We have another problem with certainty of objects. As in the first example, the test will be that laid down in *McPhail v Doulton* [1971] AC 424 — whether the trustee can say with certainty whether any given claimant is or is not a member of the class. There is clearly an issue for the court here. It is likely that even if the term 'drinking companion' is conceptually certain, the trustee will need some guidance from the court as to what the term actually means. If there is no certainty of objects, then the gift is void, and fails, and the money simply falls into the residue of the estate. So there are only two possible answers here: valid or void.

The second gift of £1,000 to Mr Chesterfield looks unquestionable at first sight, but the difficulty is created by the words 'for his trouble'. If the gift for the drinking companions is valid, there is no problem, but if it fails for uncertainty of objects, he will not have the trouble of distribution. Can he still keep his £1,000, or does this gift also fail in those circumstances? This is also a question for the court. It needs to be made clear that the existence of the question is dependent on the answer to the first question.

The problem with the residue is that the deceased has not said 'all the rest of my property', only 'all the rest of my money'. Does all the property he left count as money? Certainly the £7,500 cash must be included, but not necessarily the shares or the money in the building society (which may be in a share account). The piece of freehold land looks dubious, but we would need the authorisation of the court to exclude it from the residue. Finally, if the gift for the drinking companions fails, the proceeds of sale of the house fall into residue. Is this included? Quite possibly not, since at the date of his death the deceased left a house, not its proceeds of sale. So the court must first of all be asked to decide in respect of each piece of residual property whether it does or does not come within the description 'all the rest of my money'. Anything which does not is undisposed of by the will, there is a partial intestacy, and the next-of-kin will inherit.

Once the property to be comprised within the gift is established, then it divides into two equal halves. There is no possible dispute about the half which goes to Jane Elliott, but there is a problem with the gift to the Howe School, which no longer teaches ancient Greek. The first step is to construe the gift. Is it simply a gift *to* the Howe School (to enable it to provide a scholarship)? If so, it is an absolute gift and can take direct effect. Alternatively, is it a gift for a charitable purpose? If so it appears that the purpose cannot be carried out and the gift prima facie fails. But in this latter case, the gift may be saved by the doctrine in *Re Woodhams* [1981] 1 WLR 493: since the gift was not impossible at the date of the will, if the gift can be varied without frustrating the basic intention of the testator, then it can be applied *cy-près*. The obvious scheme here would be to allow the money to be used to provide a scholarship for the best student studying Latin and Ancient History. If that is not possible, then the gift fails altogether and there is a partial intestacy.

All of these questions and answers can be seen charted in the diagram which follows.

The parties to this claim can be identified without much difficulty. Joshua Whittell has already agreed to represent the drinking companions. The Howe School is a registered company and can be joined in its own right. Jane Elliott must be joined: although there is no dispute about her half share, it is in her interest to argue that 'all the rest of my money' comprises as much of the deceased's property as possible and that the gift to the drinking companions fails. The next-of-kin entitled on intestacy are Jane Elliott (again) and Andrew Partington. The Attorney-General must be joined to argue in favour of charity and the saving of the gift for the Howe School.

27.3.3 Diagram

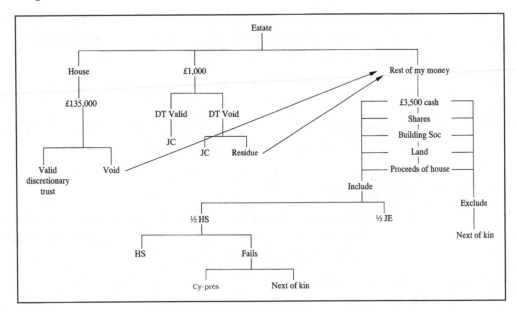

27.3.4 Details of claim

<u>IN THE HIGH COURT OF JUSTICE</u>   Claim No 2005 HC 1668
<u>CHANCERY DIVISION</u>

BETWEEN

JAMES CHESTERFIELD   <u>Claimant</u>

and

(1) JOSHUA WHITTELL
(2) THE HOWE SCHOOL
(3) JANE ELLIOTT
(4) ANDREW PARTINGTON
(5) HER MAJESTY'S ATTORNEY-GENERAL   <u>Defendants</u>

DETAILS OF CLAIM

1.   The Claimant, James Chesterfield is the executor of the will dated 1st April 1996 ('the Will') of Charles Elliott ('the Deceased'), probate having been granted on 29th August 2004.

2.   The Will contained the following provisions:

'I want my house to be sold and the proceeds of sale to be shared out by Mr Chesterfield amongst my drinking companions as he wishes. He is to have £1,000 for his trouble. One half of all the rest of my money is to go on trust for the Howe School, Dartmouth to create a scholarship for the best student studying Latin and Ancient Greek; the other half is to go to my sister Jane.'

3.   The First Defendant, Joshua Whittell, claims to be beneficially interested under the Will as a drinking companion of the Deceased.

4.   The Second Defendant is The Howe School which claims to be entitled to one half of what the Deceased called 'all the rest of my money'. It stopped teaching Ancient Greek in about 2000.

5.   The Third Defendant, Jane Elliott, is the Deceased's sister and claims to be entitled to the other half of what the Deceased called 'all the rest of my money'.

6.   The Third Defendant and the Fourth Defendant, Andrew Partington, each claim to be interested in so much of the estate as is not disposed of by the Will.

7.   The Claimant seeks the decision of the court on the following questions and the following remedies, namely:

(1)   That it may be decided whether on the true construction of the Will and in the events which have happened, the gift to the Claimant of the house ('the House') at 5 Watson Square, London NE5 is:

(a)   valid; or

(b)   void for uncertainty or otherwise.

(2)   If the answer to question (1) is (a), such directions and enquiries as to what persons may properly be considered to be drinking companions of the Deceased as may be necessary.

(3)   If the answer to question (1) is (b), whether the Claimant is nevertheless entitled to the legacy of £1,000 bequeathed to him by the Will.

(4)   That it may be decided whether, on the true construction of the Will and in the events which have happened, the expression 'all the rest of my money' contained in the Will includes any, and if so which, of the following property comprised in the Deceased's estate at the date of his death, namely:

(a)   the Deceased's holding of ordinary shares in Dimes & Scott plc;

(b)   the money standing to the credit of the Deceased's account at the Hightrees Building Society;

(c)   the Deceased's freehold land at 3 Hancock Crescent, London NE3; and

(d)   if the answer to question (1) is (b), the House;

or whether any (and if so which) of the above property is undisposed of by the Will.

(5)   Whether, on the true construction of the Will and in the events which have happened, the gift of one half of 'all the rest of my money' upon trust for the Second Defendant is a valid and effectual gift to the Second Defendant.

(6)   If question (5) is answered in the negative, whether the property comprised in that gift:

(a)   is held for charitable purposes and is applicable *cy-près*; or

(b)   is undisposed of by the Will.

(7)   If the answer to question (6) is (a), such directions with regard to a scheme for the application of the property comprised in that gift as may be necessary.

(8)   An order that the First Defendant do represent all persons claiming to be included in the description 'my drinking companions' as used by the Deceased in the Will.

(9)   That provision may be made for the costs of this application.

(10) Further or other remedies.

8.   This claim is made under Part 64 of the Civil Procedure Rules 1998, and is a claim to which Part 8 of the Civil Procedure Rules applies.

JOSEPH BLOGGS

STATEMENT OF TRUTH

Dated etc.

27.3.5 Commentary

Paragraphs 1 to 6. The introduction. As usual, begin with claimant, the will and the deceased (paragraph 1). The relevant terms of the will are copied out verbatim (paragraph 2). This is because any attempt to paraphrase would probably be less concise. The interest of each defendant is explained in paragraphs 3 to 6 and related to the gifts in the will. Note the addition of the important fact that The Howe School stopped teaching Ancient Greek about five years ago — without this there would be no apparent reason why there should be any issue over this gift. It is also relevant to state what property was left by the deceased, but this is done more conveniently in paragraph 7(4).

Paragraph 7. This is introduced in the usual way and sub-divided in the same way as in the last example.

Paragraph 7(1). The question is introduced using the standard formula discussed in the last example, but the question itself is posed differently. This time it has been drafted as a question of law. There is no particular reason for this, other than that the question if drafted as a question of fact would have been less concise. There are still only two possible answers, and they lead to the same result whether drafted in legal or factual terms.

Paragraph 7(2). This remedy is consequential on question (1). If there is a valid gift for the drinking companions, Mr Chesterfield wants to know who counts as a drinking companion. The court can give directions to this effect. It may also be necessary to hear further evidence, which would be taken on an enquiry (a factual hearing before a Chancery Master).

Paragraph 7(3). This is a straightforward question, though it is conditional on the gift of the house being void. There is no need to ask the court this question if the gift of the house is valid. Since there are only two possible answers, 'yes' or 'no', there is no need to set these out as alternatives.

Paragraph 7(4). Asks about 'all the rest of my money'. Each potential piece of property is listed and the court is invited to say in respect of each whether it is comprised within the residue or undisposed of by the will. The court is not asked whether cash is money — this is too obvious.

Paragraph 7(5). This is another question which can only be answered 'yes' or 'no' and so can be simply drafted.

Paragraph 7(6). This is the subsidiary question which arises only if the gift to The Howe School fails in its original terms. There are only two answers.

Paragraph 7(7). If the court decides that the gift can be applied *cy-près*, a scheme will be necessary to vary the terms of the original gift.

Paragraph 7(8). A representation order is needed for the drinking companions since they cannot all be ascertained.

Paragraphs 7(9), 7(10) and 8. As usual.

27.4 Re Charles Augustus Fortescue

27.4.1 Instructions to counsel

Charles Augustus Fortescue ('the deceased') made a settlement dated 17 July 1981 ('the Cedars settlement'), between himself as settlor of the one part and Henry William Thompson (his solicitor) and Baskerville James Fortescue (his nephew) as trustees of the other part. It recited that The Cedars, Muswell Hill, near Stroding, Derbyshire, had been transferred to the trustees, and it directed them to hold the same on trust for sale and hold the proceeds of sale and the net rents and profits until sale on trust for the settlor during his life, and after his death upon discretionary trusts for the descendants of his brother Francis Anthony Fortescue, to continue until the expiry of 80 years from 17 July 1981.

Despite the execution of the Cedars settlement, the Cedars was never conveyed to the trustees. Mr Thompson, who prepared the documents, remembers that the deceased insisted on executing the Cedars settlement in a hurry shortly before going abroad, despite the fact that The Cedars was not vested in him but in the trustees of his marriage settlement; as a result of the recent death of his wife Fifi he had become absolutely entitled to The Cedars under the trusts of the marriage settlement. Mr Thompson also remembers that the deceased had said to him on some occasion shortly before executing the Cedars settlement that he (the deceased) would hold the property on the trusts of the Cedars settlement until it was transferred to the trustees of that settlement. The trustees of the marriage settlement conveyed The Cedars to the deceased in 1981, and Mr Thompson in about 1984 sent the deceased for execution by him a conveyance of The Cedars to the trustees of the Cedars settlement, but heard no more about it.

From 1987 the deceased became increasingly absorbed in the movement for the preservation of the Stroding and Deepmire Junction Branch Line, which had recently been closed by British Rail, and also the preservation of *St Custard's,* a steam locomotive named after the deceased's old school. He made a new will, executed on 2 February 1995, under which he appointed Henry Thompson and George Stoker his executors and left the whole of his estate as to one half to the St Custard's Trust, and as the other half to the Stroding and Deepmire Junction Railway Society Ltd. The will contains a non-legally-binding expression of a wish that the Railway Society might make use of The Cedars (which overlooks the railway line) for offices, workshops etc.

The deceased died on 9 January 2004, aged 88, and probate to his substantial estate was obtained by Mr Thompson on 18 June 2004 (Mr Stoker having died). The following facts have now come to light:

(a) The conveyance of The Cedars to the trustees of the Cedars settlement has been found unexecuted among the deceased's papers with an undated marginal note in the deceased's handwriting 'Must ask Thompson if it includes the orchard'.

(b) Mr Thompson's probate clerk prepared the 1995 will, at a time when Mr Thompson was away ill. The clerk did not know about the Cedars settlement.

(c) It was the probate clerk's suggestion to add the precatory words concerning The Cedars to the 1995 will. When he suggested it, the deceased said something like 'That's a good idea, but isn't The Cedars tied up in some way by my marriage settlement?' The probate clerk looked up the marriage settlement and assured the Deceased that The Cedars was his absolutely.

(d) St Custard's School has a charitable trust for general educational purposes called the St Custard's Education Trust of which the present trustees are Solomon Grundy and Robson Hoskins. The deceased was a trustee of this trust between 1973 and 1986. From 1987 there was a fund known as the St Custard's Preservation Trust to raise money for preservation of the locomotive, but on the successful completion of the project in 1999 the surplus funds were transferred under a power in the trust deed to the then newly formed Downshire Steam Railway Museum Trust, a company limited by guarantee, with charitable educational purposes.

The deceased's brother Francis had two children, Baskerville James Fortescue, who died in 1990 and had two children, who are both adult (Susan Mary Smith and Elizabeth Patricia Brown), and Augustus Frederick Fortescue, who has one minor child (James Dupree Fortescue). There are as yet no remoter issue of Francis Fortescue.

27.4.2 Analysis

This case looks more complex than the other examples at first sight, but at the end of the day it is relatively straightforward. The property to be considered divides simply into two parcels; The Cedars and the deceased's estate. The destination of The Cedars must obviously be decided first.

The problem with The Cedars is that there is an incompletely constituted trust. The deceased apparently originally intended to settle it on his family under the Cedars settlement, but it was never conveyed to the trustees of that settlement. Prima facie therefore it forms part of the deceased's estate. However there is a possibility that the settlement may be held to have been constituted under the rule in *Re Ralli's Will Trusts* [1964] Ch 288, which is an extension of the rule in *Strong v Bird* (1874) LR 18 Eq 315. The facts here are comparable.

Although the trustees of the settlement were originally Mr Thompson the solicitor and Baskerville James Fortescue, Baskerville James Fortescue has died and Mr Thompson is the sole remaining trustee. Similarly, although the executors of the will were named as Mr Thompson and George Stoker, George Stoker has died and so probate was granted to Mr Thompson alone. He is therefore the sole legal owner of The Cedars, and although the property came to him in his capacity as executor, that may be enough to constitute the settlement trust. It must be shown that the deceased had a continuing intention to constitute the settlement up until his death. Evidence in favour of this is: (a) he said he would hold The Cedars himself as trustee until it was conveyed to him by the trustees of his marriage settlement; (b) the marginal note on the conveyance 'Must ask Thompson if it includes the orchard'; and (c) his query to the probate clerk at the time of making his will. Evidence against is the precatory words in the will, suggesting that by 1995 the deceased believed The Cedars would go to the Railway Society.

The question for the court is simply whether The Cedars is held on the settlement trusts or as part of the estate.

With regard to the estate, issues arise only in respect of the half share given to the St Custard's Trust. The gift to the Railway Society cannot be doubted. The problem is simply, which trust did the deceased have in mind? Obviously the Education Trust and the Preservation Trust have equal claims, but there remains the possibility that the intended beneficiary is neither of these two, but some other as yet undiscovered trust. If the right answer is the Preservation Trust, then the property will go under the trust deed to the Downshire Steam Railway Museum Trust. Alternatively, it may be there is insufficient certainty of objects and the gift will fail. So there are four possible answers to the question.

If the gift prima facie fails, there remains the faint possibility that the funds could be applied *cy-près*. It would be necessary to find that the deceased had a general as opposed to a specific charitable intent. But the possibility should be put to the court — only if the funds cannot be applied *cy-près* does the gift finally fail and pass to the next of kin on a partial intestacy.

The above questions and their possible answers are all charted in the usual way in the following diagram.

There will need to be quite a lot of defendants. In order to ascertain the beneficiaries under the settlement it may help to draw up a family tree. The known living descendants of Francis Anthony Fortescue are Susan Mary Smith, Elizabeth Patricia Brown, Augustus Frederick Fortescue and James Dupree Fortescue. Unborn children will need to be represented by one or more of these. The trustees of the St Custard's Education Trust are Solomon Grundy and Robson Hoskins who will need to be joined, since it is not apparently an incorporated body. The Downshire Steam Railway Museum Trust and the Stroding and Deepmire Junction Railway Society Ltd are incorporated and so can be joined in their own right. The next of kin in the event of a partial intestacy are Susan Mary Smith, Elizabeth Patricia Brown and Augustus Frederick Fortescue. Finally the Attorney-General needs to be joined to represent the general charitable objects that might exist.

27.4.3   Diagram

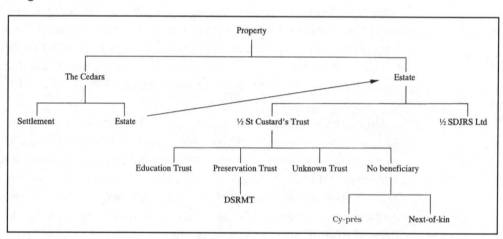

27.4.4 Details of claim

Claim No 2005 HC 6932

CHANCERY DIVISION

BETWEEN

HENRY WILLIAM THOMPSON   <u>Claimant</u>

and

(1) SUSAN MARY SMITH

(2) ELIZABETH PATRICIA BROWN

(3) AUGUSTUS FREDERICK FORTESCUE

(4) JAMES DUPREE FORTESCUE (a child, by his
     litigation friend Jo-Anne Fortescue)

(5) SOLOMON GRUNDY

(6) ROBSON HOSKINS

(7) DOWNSHIRE STEAM RAILWAY MUSEUM TRUST

(8) STRODING AND DEEPMIRE JUNCTION RAILWAY
     SOCIETY LIMITED

(9) HER MAJESTY'S ATTORNEY-GENERAL   <u>Defendants</u>

DETAILS OF CLAIM

1. The Claimant, Henry William Thompson, is the sole executor and trustee of the will dated 2nd February 1995 ('the Will') of Charles Augustus Forescue ('the Deceased'), probate having been granted to him on 16th June 2004, and the sole surviving trustee of a settlement dated 17th July 1981 ('the Settlement') and made between (1) the Deceased and (2) the Claimant and Baskerville James Fortescue.

2. Under the terms of the Settlement the trustees were to hold the Deceased's house and grounds known as The Cedars, Muswell Hill, near Stroding, Derbyshire ('The Cedars') on trust for sale for the Deceased during his life and after his death on discretionary trusts for the descendants of the Deceased's brother Francis Anthony Fortescue. The Deceased never conveyed The Cedars to the trustees of the Settlement.

3. The First, Second, Third and Fourth Defendants (Susan Mary Smith, Elizabeth Patricia Brown, Augustus Frederick Fortescue and James Dupree Fortescue respectively) are the living descendants of Francis Anthony Fortescue and claim to be beneficially interested under the Settlement.

4. By the Will the Deceased gave the whole of his estate as to one half to the St Custard's Trust and as to the other half to the Stroding and Deepmire Junction Railway Society Limited.

5. The Fifth Defendant, Solomon Grundy, and the Sixth Defendant, Robson Hoskins, are the trustees of a charitable trust known as the St Custard's Education Trust and claim to be entitled to one half of the Deceased's estate.

6. The Seventh Defendant, The Downshire Steam Railway Museum Trust, is an incorporated registered charity which is entitled to all the property once held by a trust known as the St Custard's Preservation Trust, and claims to be entitled to the same half of the Deceased's estate.

7.   The Eighth Defendant, the Stroding and Deepmire Junction Railway Society Limited is entitled to the other half of the Deceased's estate.

8.   The First, Second and Third Defendants also claim to be entitled to any part of the Deceased's estate which is undisposed of by the Will.

9.   The Claimant seeks the decision of the Court on the following questions and the following remedies namely:

(1) That it may be decided whether upon the true construction of the Settlement and the Will and in the events which have happened The Cedars is held by the Claimant:

   (a)   as trustee upon the trusts of the Settlement; or

   (b)   as the Deceased's executor as part of the Deceased's estate.

(2) That it may be decided whether upon the true construction of the Will and in the events which have happened the gift of the half share of the Deceased's estate made by the Will to 'the St Custard's Trust':

   (a)   is an effective gift to the Fifth and Sixth Defendants to hold that half share on the charitable trusts of the St Custard's Education Trust; or

   (b)   is an effective gift to the Seventh Defendant; or

   (c)   is an effective gift to any other, and if so which, institution trust or corporation; or

   (d)   is not an effective gift to any specific institution trust or corporation.

(3) If the answer to the question (2) above is (d), that it may be decided whether upon the true construction of the Will and in the events which have happened that half share of the Deceased's estate:

   (a)   is the subject of a valid gift for general charitable purposes and is applicable *cy-près*; or

   (b)   is undisposed of by the Will and devolves under the law relating to intestacy as it applies to the Deceased's estate.

(4) If the answer to the question (3) above is (a), that the Court may direct a scheme for the application of that half share of the Deceased's estate.

(5) That the First Defendant may be appointed to represent all issue of hers who may in future become beneficially interested under the trusts of the Settlement.

(6) That the Second Defendant may be appointed to represent all issue of hers who may in future become beneficially interested under the trusts of the Settlement.

(7) That the Third Defendant may be appointed to represent all issue of his (other than the Fourth Defendant) who may in future become beneficially interested under the trusts of the Settlement.

(8) That provision may be made for the costs of this application.

(9) Further or other remedies.

10.   This claim is made under Part 64 of the Civil Procedure Rules 1998, and is a claim to which Part 8 of the Civil Procedure Rules applies.

JOSEPH BLOGGS

STATEMENT OF TRUTH

Dated etc.

27.4.5 Commentary

Paragraphs 1 to 8. The introduction is rather longer in this case than in the previous examples, because both the Settlement and the Will need to have their terms set out, and there are a large number of beneficiaries to identify, most of whom have slightly different interests. When introducing the settlement it is important to state that The Cedars was never conveyed, or there is no reason why any issue should arise in connection with that property.

Paragraph 9. The questions to be asked and the alternative answers to be put forward should by now be obvious in the light of the analysis and diagram. The drafting of them should also be self-explanatory in the light of the commentary to the previous examples.

Paragraph 9(1). There are only two possible answers to this question. It is very much the events rather than the documents that need to be construed to answer it: the non-conveyance, the fact that the claimant is the sole trustee both of the settlement and the will, the evidence of the deceased's continuing intention.

Paragraph 9(2). Essentially the court must simply be asked to choose between the Education Trust and the Preservation Trust. But an 'any other and if so which' alternative is included in case there is yet another trust that matches the description.

Paragraph 9(3). This question is conditional. If none of the known trusts benefits from the gift, then the court must decide whether there is a general charitable intent. There are only two possible answers and the outcome in either case is clear.

Paragraph 9(4). If the gift is applicable *cy-près*, as usual a scheme must be approved.

Paragraphs 9(5), (6) and (7). Representation orders are needed for the unborn descendants of Francis Anthony Fortescue. It is best for each adult beneficiary under the settlement to represent their own children and remoter issue.

27.5 Exercise A

Your Instructing Solicitors act for Simon and Stephanie Lamb, who are respectively the nephew and niece of the late Selwyn Lamb. He died on 1 October 2004 and by clause 1 of his will dated 1 February 1993 he appointed our clients to be executors and trustees. The rest of the will was in these terms:

2. I give my freehold house at 4 Main Street, Newbury, to my friends Tanya Collins and Fay Denison.

3. I give the rest of my property (a) as to one half to my executors to be distributed by them among my old friends in Newbury (b) as to the other half to the Newbury Home for Distressed Gentlefolk.

The testator was survived by a son, Clive Lamb, who is angry at being excluded from the will and will claim whatever he can under a total or partial intestacy. Probate was granted to our clients on 6 November 2004. The residuary estate will amount to approximately £60,000.

Since the death the following matters have emerged:

(a) Two days after making his will the testator said to Tanya Collins, 'Will you and Fay give anything you get from my estate to the Save the Children Fund?' Tanya said,

'Of course we will', but Fay remained in ignorance of this conversation until after the death of the testator. Tanya lives in Oxford and Fay lives in London.

(b) David Watson claims that he is one of many 'old friends' the testator had in Newbury. Eric Streatfield states that he is the only person who fits this description.

(c) The Newbury Home for Distressed Gentlefolk was a charitable institution. It was closed down in 1996 and its remaining assets were handed over under an order of the court to the charity Help the Aged.

Counsel is asked to draft an appropriate claim, seeking the decision of the court on any questions which may arise.

27.6 Exercise B

Instructing solicitors act for John Rutherford and Robert Greenway, the executors and trustees of the will of Cyril Hookham, who died in an accident on 1 January 2005. Probate was granted to the executors on 6 February 2005 out of the Principal Registry. Cyril Hookham survived his father and died a bachelor with no issue. He is survived by his sister Hilda Hookham. His home-made will, properly signed, witnessed and dated 25 December 2002, reads as follows:

1.   I give my freehold house known as The Kremlin, Washington Avenue, London SE5 to my trustees upon trust for sale for the following equally: my mother; the children of Arnold Lewis who shall attain the age of 21 years; and Peter Parker.

2.   I give Bertha to Robert Greenway absolutely.

3.   I give the residue of my estate to The Actors' Charity.

4.   My trustees shall have power of advancement to any child of Arnold Lewis notwithstanding that he or she has not yet attained 21.

The following problems appear to arise on the will:

(a) Cyril Hookham's mother died in the same accident as the testator. There are no survivors of the accident and there is no evidence to indicate whether Cyril Hookham or his mother died first.

(b) Arnold Lewis has just died. He was married twice. By his first marriage he had two children, Bert (aged 23) and Bill (aged 21). By his second marriage he had one child, Ben (born 1 February 2005).

(c) Bertha was Cyril Hookham's car. Shortly before his death he had scrapped Bertha and bought a new car, Oliver.

(d) There has never been a charity called The Actors' Charity. However, there is a charity called The Charity for Actors and another called The Actors' and Actresses' Charity.

Counsel is asked to settle a claim seeking the answer to all questions which need to be resolved by the court.

Claims for breach of trust and the recovery of trust property

28.1 Introduction

Particulars of claim for breach of trust are in essence no different from any other particulars of claim: they set out the material facts necessary to establish the claimant's entitlement to the remedies sought and do so in such a way as to tell the story. Unlike most common law claims, however, it is difficult to prescribe a formula or pattern for the sequence in which issues should be dealt with.

In some cases, but by no means all, the following pattern may be helpful:

(a) The parties.

(b) The trust.

(c) The trust property.

(d) The dealings with trust property.

(e) The breach of trust.

(f) The loss.

(g) Interest.

(h) The remedies sought.

But this needs to be taken very loosely. A claim for breach of trust basically seeks to recover trust property that has been lost or property due to the trust that has never been received. This may have happened in any number of different ways, and rigid adherence to the above pattern will often produce such a distortion of chronology and/or confusion of issues that neither the story nor the basis of the claim is clear.

A more helpful guideline is therefore probably this: simply tell the story in chronological order, identifying any trust or fiduciary duty as and when it arises, any breach of trust or breach of fiduciary duty as and when it arises, and any liability to account as and when it arises. This story is not fundamentally about people but about property: it is the story of the property that the claimant wishes to recover on behalf of the trust.

The items set out above are, however, essential ingredients in the story and must be incorporated in some way and at some stage:

(a) *The parties.* The claimant(s) will usually be beneficiaries under the trust claiming against the trustees (defendants) or the present trustee claiming against an ex-trustee. It is essential to include facts showing the claimant's entitlement: his capacity and/or his interest under the terms of the trust (the precise details of the claimant's beneficial interest are not material). It is also essential to state the defendant's trusteeship (particularly important when he is not the original trustee) or the relationship giving rise to a fiduciary duty.

(b) *The trust.* It may not be possible to separate this from the parties, in which case don't try, or it may be more convenient to state the trust first and parties second, in which case do so. The full terms of the trust are not material. What is essential is to identify the trust, any relevant beneficial interests, any express powers and duties contained within the trust, if material, or even the absence of an express power, if material. If the trust arose under a will, plead the grant of probate.

(c) *The trust property.* Identify this as precisely as possible. Only identify such property as the claim relates to.

It's probably best to think of ingredients (a), (b) and (c) as 'the preliminaries'. They may appear in any order and wrapped up with each other in any way that seems appropriate. However, they must all be gone through before going further into the story of the property.

(d) *The dealings with trust property.* Tell the story of the property and what the defendant has done with it. Where this is not known, state as much as is known and include a claim for an enquiry and/or an account in the list of remedies sought.

(e) *The breach of trust.* Where the dealing itself was a breach of trust, this can be combined with the previous stage. Where the breach of trust arises through some other default or the manner of the dealing, allege this separately. Any allegation of breach of trust or breach of fiduciary duty must be fully particularised (PD 16, para 8.2).

(f) *The loss.* You should state that the trust has suffered loss or that the trust fund has diminished in value. Identify the loss precisely where you can, but more usually the precise loss can only be identified after enquiries have been held and/or accounts taken.

(g) *Interest.* There is not usually a claim for interest under the Supreme Court Act 1981, s 35A, in breach of trust claims. The claimant is entitled to interest on any sums due under the court's inherent jurisdiction, but if the trust fund is to be restored to its proper value, interest will be part of the sum ordered to be paid and will be mentioned only in the list of remedies sought.

(h) *The list of remedies sought.* May be quite lengthy. The remedies sought may include: declarations, enquiries, accounts, orders for restitution, administration of estate, representation orders, further or other remedies, costs. Each enquiry or account should be treated as a separate remedy.

28.2 Basic breach of trust

28.2.1 Particulars of claim

IN THE HIGH COURT OF JUSTICE   Claim No 2005 HC 5801
CHANCERY DIVISION

BETWEEN

(1) RICHARD TERRELL
(2) MARY TERRELL
(3) PETER TERRELL
(4) SARAH TERRELL (a child, by her litigation friend
Mark Terrell)   Claimants

and

(1) JAMES SCOTT
(2) FRANK GULLIVER   Defendants

PARTICULARS OF CLAIM

1.   By a settlement dated 16th August 1987 ('the Settlement') made between (1) Charles Terrell ('the Settlor') and (2) the First Defendant and David Foley, the Settlor appointed the First Defendant and David Foley to be trustees of the Settlement and vested in them the property set out in the schedule to the Settlement ('the Trust Property'). The trustees were empowered to invest the Trust Property in any manner authorised by law for the investment of trust money.

2.   The Claimants are the beneficiaries under the Settlement.

3.   David Foley died on 20th June 1992 and on 14th August 1992 the First Defendant appointed the Second Defendant to be a trustee of the Settlement in place of David Foley. The Trust Property was duly vested in the Defendants as trustees of the Settlement.

4.   On or about 6th April 1999 the Defendants advanced to Flyaway Tours Limited £50,000 of the Trust Property on a legal mortgage of leasehold premises at 19 Camden Avenue, London NW1 ('the Premises') of which Flyaway Tours Limited was the lessee and where it carried on business as a holiday tour operator.

5.   This investment was made by the Defendants in breach of their duties as trustees.

PARTICULARS OF BREACH OF TRUST

(a) The mortgage was not a suitable investment since the greater part of the value of the leasehold consisted of the goodwill of the business. The Claimants will allege that the value of the lease in April 1999 was £60,000 of which £36,000 was attributable to the goodwill.

(b) Further or alternatively the sum of £50,000 represented more than two-thirds of the value of the lease.

(c) The investment was made without any independent valuation of the Premises.

(d) The investment was made without obtaining and considering proper advice.

6.   In July 2003 Flyaway Tours Limited was compulsorily wound up and the Defendants realised £24,000 from the sale of the lease on behalf of the trust. Because of the Defendants' breach of trust the trust property has therefore been depleted by £26,000.

AND the Claimants claim:

(1) An order that the Defendants pay to the trust fund the sum of £26,000 together with interest on that sum.

(2) Alternatively, the sum of £10,000 together with interest on that sum.

(3) Such other accounts, enquiries or directions as may be necessary.

(4) Further or other remedies.

(5) Costs.

JOSEPH BLOGGS

STATEMENT OF TRUTH

Dated etc.

28.2.2   Commentary

Heading. This being a claim for breach of trust, not surprisingly the claimants are the beneficiaries and the defendants are the trustees. There are only four beneficiaries, so all four are joined as claimants. If there were a large number, then one or two could bring a representative claim under CPR, r 19.6.

Preliminaries. Paragraphs 1 to 3 are what are called the preliminaries in **28.1**. There is no correct order for introducing the parties to the trust, its material terms, the trust property etc, so long as all these essential matters are included before you go on to tell the story of what has happened.

Paragraph 1. Starts with the trust instrument, the settlement, describing it and defining it. The parties to the settlement are introduced using (1) and (2). This is a common and useful technique for differentiating the two sides. Without these numbers inserted, it would not be immediately obvious whether the first defendant belonged with Charles Terrell or with David Foley. The details of the trust property are not material in this case, so it can be identified simply by reference to the schedule to the settlement. The claim is about misinvestment, so the trustees' powers of investment must be stated. 'In any manner authorised by law' in effect means in accordance with Part II of the Trustee Act 2000.

Paragraph 2. Although in common law claims the claimants are almost invariably introduced first, here that would be difficult, since their capacity is entirely linked to the settlement.

Paragraph 3. There has been a change of trustee, so this needs to be stated in order to introduce the second defendant. There can be no claim against him unless he has not only been appointed, but also had the trust property vested in him, so this must also be stated.

Paragraph 4. Now that the preliminaries are out of the way, you can tell the story. The claim relates to a particular investment, so simply say what the trustees did. They invested in a mortgage. If this investment were in itself a breach of trust, you would add the words 'in breach of trust' at this stage. But investment in a mortgage is, subject to the standard investment criteria, a valid trustee investment under the Trustee Act 2000. The breach of trust arises because the criteria were not met, and because of the circumstances of the investment, so the breach of trust allegation is delayed to the next paragraph.

Paragraph 5. The allegation of breach of trust must be expressly stated. The words 'in breach of their duties as trustees' cover both their duty under the terms of the trust, and their duty of care under s 1 of the 2000 Act. The breach must then be particularised. The heading, capitalised, underlined and centred, as in particulars of negligence is very common, though not compulsory. You can instead simply say 'in that ...' and particularise as in breach of contract cases.

Breach (a) is self-explanatory. Goodwill of a business does not provide security for a loan, so the allegation is that they advanced £50,000 of trust capital against security worth only £24,000. This renders the investment unsuitable under the standard investment criteria (see s 4(3) of the 2000 Act).

Breach (b) is explained by s 8 of the Trustee Act 1925. This section protects trustees to some extent if they advance no more than two-thirds of the value of the security by way of mortgage, provided they have a valuer's report and act on the valuer's advice. So even if the true value of the lease was £60,000, they would be not be protected since they have invested more than two thirds of that value. A trustee who forgoes the protection of s 8 is arguably acting in breach of his duty of care.

Breach (c) relates to breach (b), but must also be a breach of the general duty of care.

Breach (d) also relates to breach (b), but is more specifically a breach of s 5 of the 2000 Act.

Paragraph 6. This is the next step in the story, in effect the causation of the loss and the loss itself. The trustees have lost £26,000 of capital through misinvestment. The story is now complete. Note how short and simple it actually is. This is commonly the case in breach of trust claims.

Prayer. Remedy (1): the primary remedy for breach of trust is restitution. The trustees are liable to restore the trust fund to the value it would have had today had there been no breach of trust. So the first remedy sought is the sum required to achieve that result, namely £26,000 plus interest on it to represent the income that proper investment would have raised during the period of the mortgage. Note that the interest is part of the sum due. It is not something added on by the court under its equitable jurisdiction or s 35A of the Supreme Court Act 1981.

Remedy (2) needs some explanation. By s 9 of the Trustee Act 1925 (repealed by the Trustee Act 2000, but still applicable to advances of trust money made before 1 February 2001), if the only breach of trust is that the trustees have advanced more than an authorised amount, then they are liable only to the extent that the investment exceeds the authorised amount. So if here they show that they did get proper advice, and that the value of the lease really was £60,000, then they are only liable to the extent that the investment was more than two-thirds of the value of the lease, ie £10,000. Again, they would be liable to pay interest on that sum.

Remedy (3) is almost always added in breach of trust claims. Once the full facts emerge it may become apparent that the trustees' actions need further investigation. This can be done by ordering them to provide an account of their dealings with trust property, or holding an inquiry into what has been going on; in any event the court may need to give further directions.

Remedies (4) and (5) are included as always in the Chancery Division.

Rounding off. This is a contentious claim under CPR, Part 7, so all the formalities must be complied with (see **Chapter 7**).

28.3 Breach of trust: liability to account: tracing

28.3.1 Particulars of claim

IN THE HIGH COURT OF JUSTICE   Claim No 2005 HC 4982

CHANCERY DIVISION

BETWEEN

(1) CLARA BAGSHOTT

(2) SHERIDAN BAGSHOTT   Claimants

and

BRADLEY ASHE   Defendant

PARTICULARS OF CLAIM

1.   By her will dated 12th January 1987 Maria Bagshott bequeathed her residuary estate to trustees upon trust for sale for Graeme Bagshott for life and after his death for such of the children of herself and Graeme Bagshott as should attain the age of 25.

2.   The Claimants are the children of Maria and Graeme Bagshott and are the sole beneficiaries and absolutely entitled to the residuary estate following the death of Graeme Bagshott on 18th November 2003. The Defendant was at all material times a trustee of the residuary estate and has since June 1999 been the sole surviving trustee.

3.   Maria Bagshott died on 7th February 1989 and probate of her will was granted to her executors on 10th April 1989.

4.   In breach of his duties as a trustee the Defendant has so neglected and mismanaged the investment of the trust fund that the property comprised in the residuary estate which in June 2000 was worth about £120,000 has diminished in value to approximately £50,000 in January 2005.

5.   At all material times the trust property has included a shareholding in Bright Lights Limited and the Defendant was until March 2003 a non-executive director of Bright Lights Limited by virtue of that shareholding. In about May 2002 the Defendant learned that Bright Lights Limited was about to make an offer to the shareholders of Blue Neon Limited to purchase their shares with a view to taking over Blue Neon Limited. The Defendant invested £10,000 of his own money in shares in Blue Neon Limited which in December 2002 he sold for about £23,000.

6.   The Defendant's knowledge of the offer was gained in his capacity as a trustee and he is liable to account to the trust for the profit made on the sale of the shares in Blue Neon Limited.

7.   In April 2002 the Defendant in breach of trust mixed £5,000 of trust money with his own money in an account at the Poole Building Society. In May 2003 the Defendant used the entire contents of that account to purchase a vintage motor car.

AND the Claimants claim:

(1)   An enquiry into whether the trust fund has been properly invested by the Defendant.

(2)   An account of the Defendant's investment and dealing with the trust property, on the footing of wilful default.

(3)   Repayment of the amount found due to the trust by that enquiry and upon taking that account.

(4)   A further account of the profit made on the sale of the shares in Blue Neon Limited.

(5)   An order that the Defendant pay into the trust fund the amount found due on the further account.

(6)   A further enquiry as to what proportion of the money in the account at the Poole Building Society in May 2003 was due to the trust.

(7)   A declaration that the Defendant holds such proportion of the value of the vintage motor car as is found by the further enquiry to represent the trust money upon the trusts of the will.

(8)   Such other accounts, directions and enquiries as may be necessary.

(9)   Further or other remedies.

(10) Costs.

JOSEPH BLOGGS

STATEMENT OF TRUTH

Dated etc.

28.3.2 Commentary

There are three separate claims in one in this example: a straightforward claim for breach of trust by misinvestment (but of a much more general kind that than in the last example), a claim for liability to account under *Boardman v Phipps* [1967] 2 AC 46, and a tracing claim, seeking to follow trust property into a mixed fund. The claimants are the beneficiaries and the defendant is the sole trustee.

Paragraphs 1, 2 and 3. The preliminaries. The essential terms of the trust are set out in paragraph 1. Since the claimants' interest was subject to a life interest for their father, that life interest needs to be stated (paragraph 1), and the father's death needs also to be mentioned (paragraph 2) to show that they are now absolutely entitled. The parties are actually introduced in paragraph 2. The fact that the defendant is the sole surviving trustee is material to the extent that it helps to explain how he was able to deal with the trust property as he did. Where a trust arises under a will, then the grant of probate needs to be stated, as in CPR, Part 8 claims (paragraph 3).

Paragraph 4. The facts relating to the first claim. The situation we have here is not an uncommon one. The claimants have probably been led to believe by their parents that on their father's death they would inherit around £120,000, but the trustee has informed them that their inheritance is only about £50,000. They have no idea how this has happened; they only know that there must have been some breach of trust involved because the trust assets were worth £120,000 in 2000. They are therefore unable to particularise the breach of trust in any way. This does not actually matter. The diminution in value is in itself enough to show that there has prima facie been some breach of trust; exactly what has happened can be determined by means of accounts and enquiries. So paragraph 4 is very short and simple. Do not forget the key words 'in breach of his duties as a trustee'.

Paragraph 5. The facts relating to the second claim. The paragraph simply tells a story. This is a classic *Boardman v Phipps* situation — the trustee has made a personal profit out of knowledge that came to him in his capacity as a trustee. It is important for this reason to state that his directorship of the company was because he was a trustee, not incidental.

Paragraph 6. Once the facts that give rise to the liability to account have been stated, the liability to account must itself be expressly alleged, together with the basis for it (that his knowledge of the offer was gained in his capacity as a trustee).

Paragraph 7. The facts relating to the third claim. At this stage simply state what has happened — the mixing of funds and the use of the mixed fund to purchase an investment. The fact that the claimants wish to trace the trust money to the vintage car is dealt with in the prayer.

Once again, note how short the body of the claim is: the story of the property can be presented factually; there are no complex legal ingredients to work through. The prayer in this case is however rather more complex.

Prayer. Remedies (1), (2) and (3) relate to the first claim. Although what is required is restitution, that cannot be achieved in this case without some factual investigation first. So the first remedy sought is an enquiry, to find out how the trust fund has been invested. Then, the trustee must be ordered to produce an account of all his investments and dealings, so that the trust funds can be followed and identified. An 'account on the footing of wilful default' is a special kind of account: it requires the trustee to account not only for property that the trust has lost, but also for property which, but for the wilful default, the trust would have had. 'Wilful default' in this context means no more than conscious omission on the part of the trustee. Once the enquiry has been held and the account produced, the sum due to the trust can be ascertained and remedy (3) orders it to be paid. This sum would be the sum required to restore the trust fund to the value it would have had but for the breach of trust, so no separate mention of interest is required.

Remedies (4) and (5) relate to the second claim. Under *Boardman v Phipps* the trustee is liable to account for his profit, so that is what remedy (4) requires. An account is required, because that will show what the trust is entitled to receive, namely not only the initial profit of about £23,000, but also any further profits made through investment of that sum. It is called a further account to avoid confusion with that in remedy (2). Once the account has been provided, then remedy (5) requires the defendant to pay the amount due.

Remedies (6) and (7) relate to the third claim. A factual enquiry is first of all required, to ascertain how much money was in the account when the defendant mixed in the trust's £5,000. That will then enable the correct proportion to be established. Then the claimants want a declaration that that proportion of the value of the motor car is held for the trust. This is because the car has doubtless appreciated in value, so the beneficiaries want to recover their share of the enhanced value, not just their £5,000. They could seek an order for sale, but it appears that the car is a good investment and they are happy to leave their money there for now.

The remaining remedies are standard and have been previously explained.

28.4 Constructive trustee: tracing against third party

28.4.1 Particulars of claim

IN THE HIGH COURT OF JUSTICE   Claim No 2005 HC 2006
CHANCERY DIVISION

BETWEEN

(1) MARIE ISAACS
(2) SAMUEL VINCENT

Claimants

and

(1) PHILIP GREEN
(2) SOUTHERN NATIONAL BANK PLC
(3) ANDREW GREEN
(4) THE HOSPITAL FOR SWANS   Defendants

PARTICULARS OF CLAIM

1.   By a settlement dated 31st March 1978 ('the Settlement') made between (1) Augustus Vincent ('the Settlor') and (2) the First Defendant and Victor Paul ('the Trustees') the Settlor vested in the Trustees assets to the value of £400,000 upon trust for, in the events which have happened, the Settlor's 13 grandchildren and great-grandchildren in such shares as the Trustees might in their absolute discretion appoint.

2.   The Claimants are two of the Settlor's grandchildren and beneficiaries under the Settlement and bring this claim on behalf of themselves and all the other beneficiaries. The First Defendant is the sole surviving trustee, Victor Paul having died in June 2000.

3.   The Second Defendant is a bank at whose branch in Hastings, Sussex at all material times the Trustees maintained the trust account and the First Defendant maintained a personal account.

4.   On or about 12th September 2001 the First Defendant issued a cheque drawn on the trust account in favour of the Third Defendant to the value of £65,000 and on the same date paid into his personal account a cheque drawn on the Third Defendant's account to the same value. The Second Defendant cleared the cheque in favour of the Third Defendant without demur.

5.   On or about 19th September 2001 the First Defendant instructed the Second Defendant to issue a banker's draft for £65,000 in favour of Viking Enterprises Limited and to reimburse itself from the funds in his personal account. The Second Defendant did as so instructed.

6.   The First Defendant used the banker's draft to settle his indebtedness to Viking Enterprises Limited.

7.   On or about 3rd July 2002 the First Defendant instructed the Second Defendant to transfer £20,000 from the trust account to his personal account which the Second Defendant did. On 6th July 2002 the First Defendant gave the Third Defendant £10,000 and Fiona Green £10,000 by cheques drawn on his personal account. Fiona Green gave the £10,000 she received to the Fourth Defendant which is a registered charitable institution.

8.   In dealing with the trust money as set out in paragraphs 4, 5, 6 and 7 above the First Defendant was acting in breach of his duty as a trustee.

9.   The Second Defendant knew that the First Defendant was dealing with trust property in breach of trust, and so acted dishonestly.

PARTICULARS OF KNOWLEDGE

The Second Defendant's knowledge is to be inferred from the following facts and matters:

   (a) It knew that the First Defendant was the sole trustee of the Settlement.

   (b) It knew that the trust account was a trust account and that all the funds in that account were held on the trusts of the Settlement.

   (c) It knew that the First Defendant was indebted to Viking Enterprises Limited.

   (d) It knew that none of the beneficiaries under the Settlement was named Andrew Green or Fiona Green.

10.   As a result of the matters set out above the Second Defendant is liable to account as a constructive trustee for the sums of £65,000 and £20,000.

11.   Further or alternatively the Third Defendant knowingly received and dealt with trust property in breach of trust in that he was at all times a knowing and willing partner of the First Defendant in his dealings.

12.   As a result of the matters set out above the Third Defendant is liable to account as a constructive trustee for the sums of £65,000 and £10,000.

AND the Claimants claim:

   (1) As against the First Defendant, replacement of the sum of £65,000 together with interest and the sum of £20,000 together with interest.

(2) Alternatively as against the Second Defendant, repayment of the sum of £65,000 together with interest and the sum of £20,000 together with interest.

(3) Alternatively, as against the Third Defendant, repayment of the sum of £65,000 together with interest and an account of the sum of £10,000 and payment of the amount found due on the account.

(4) Further or alternatively as against the Fourth Defendant an account of the sum of £10,000 and repayment of the amount found due on the account.

(5) All other necessary accounts, directions and enquiries.

(6) Further or other remedies.

(7) Costs.

JOSEPH BLOGGS

STATEMENT OF TRUTH

Dated etc.

28.4.2 Commentary

This is a claim not only against the defaulting trustee, but also against others who may be liable to make good the trust's losses. Two defendants are sued as constructive trustees, on the basis that they have dishonestly received or dealt with trust property in breach of trust, or dishonestly assisted in a breach of trust on the part of the trustee. One of them is simply an innocent volunteer who has unknowingly received trust property and into whose hands the claimants seek to trace that property. The claim is made against these additional defendants presumably because the claimants doubt that the trustee has the assets to satisfy any claim.

Heading. The claimants are beneficiaries suing in a representative capacity on behalf of themselves and all the other beneficiaries. The first defendant is the fraudulent trustee, the second defendant is a bank who is alleged to be a constructive trustee, the third defendant is the first defendant's son and partner in crime, and the fourth defendant is the innocent volunteer.

Paragraph 1. The settlement and the terms of the trust are introduced. Note the useful method adopted to shorten complex trust provisions. The settlement doubtless provided for numerous different contingencies, but the only one that matters is that which in fact arose, so the draft simply states for whom the trust property was held in the events which happened. The first defendant is also introduced as a trustee of the settlement.

Paragraph 2. This introduces the claimants and makes it clear that they are suing in a representative capacity. Since the first defendant has become the sole trustee, this fact is also explained.

Paragraph 3. This introduces the second defendant. The third and fourth defendants are not introduced at the outset — it seems easier to introduce them as and when they come into the story. The fact that both the trust account and the first defendant's personal account were at the same branch is material in that it helps to explain how the fraud was possible.

Paragraphs 4, 5 and 6. The first defendant has been fraudulently embezzling trust funds. There are two dishonest transactions, the first of which is set out in these paragraphs. The story of what he did simply needs to be explained step by step. It involves the second defendant, so includes the actions taken by the bank as well. There is no allegation of dishonesty on the part of either defendant or of knowledge on the part of the bank at this stage. These allegations come later. The aim is simply to describe what happened.

Paragraph 7. This is the second transaction. It also has several steps to it, but they can be more simply explained, so they are all incorporated into a single paragraph. Fiona Green is the first defendant's daughter, and there is no allegation of wrongdoing against her. She simply gave the money she received to charity (the fourth defendant). These facts are sufficient to found the tracing claim against the fourth defendant.

Paragraph 8. This paragraph serves two purposes. It is the last essential ingredient to establish the liability of the first defendant, but it is also an essential ingredient to render the second and third defendants liable as constructive trustees. Note that although the evidence will clearly establish that the first defendant was dishonest and fraudulent, this allegation is not made. There is no need to do so. His liability is fully established simply by showing that he was in breach of trust. The liability of a constructive trustee does not require dishonesty on the part of the primary trustee (as was once thought) — *Royal Brunei Airlines v Tan* [1995] 3 All ER 97.

Paragraph 9. The claim against the first defendant is now complete, but more is required to establish the liability of the second defendant. The bank must have assisted in a breach of trust knowingly and dishonestly (*Royal Brunei Airlines v Tan*). The allegations of knowledge and dishonesty must therefore be expressly made. They must also be particularised. Since the dishonesty flows from the knowledge, it is essentially the particulars of knowledge that must be set out. This is done by means of a headed sub-paragraph, with the heading capitalised, underlined and centred. Stating particulars of knowledge involves saying how or from what the defendant knew — so set out the facts from which the requisite knowledge can be inferred by the court. Actual knowledge is not required — wilful and reckless blindness is also sufficient (*Re Montagu's Settlement Trusts* [1992] 4 All ER 308). In this case it is hard to see from the particulars alleged how the bank cannot have had at least constructive knowledge of the breach of trust.

Paragraph 10. Once the material facts have been stated, it is necessary to allege expressly that the second defendant is liable to account as a constructive trustee, and to what extent (the two sums involved).

Paragraph 11. It is now necessary to go through the same process in relation to the third defendant. But this is more straightforward. He is alleged to be the trustee's partner in crime, so the allegation is simply that he had full knowledge of everything that was going on. This will have to be proved by the evidence, but it is hard to see how the knowledge can be further particularised. The knowledge is not inferred from background facts, but alleged to exist directly. Dishonesty is not required (*BCCI v Akindele* [2000] 4 All ER 221) and so is not alleged.

Paragraph 12. States the necessary allegation of liability to account, as in paragraph 10. In respect of the second transaction, he is not liable to account for the whole of the £20,000 — he only received £10,000, and otherwise played no active part in the transaction.

Prayer. It is important to specify which remedy or remedies are sought against which defendant(s), so each one begins with the words 'as against'. It is also important to recognise that the claimants cannot recover the same sums three or four times over. If the first defendant is ordered to pay in full, then the other defendants cannot also be ordered to pay in full, so remedies (1), (2) and (3) are alternative each other. In each case, what is wanted is full restitution, which will include interest on the missing sums. In the case of the third defendant, what the claimants seek is an account of £10,000 that he has received — he may have invested it and derived further enrichment, for which he is also liable to account. Remedy (4), the tracing claim against the fourth defendant is alternative to (1) and (2), but could be additional to (3), so the words 'further or alternatively' are used. The remedy sought is an account, because it is unknown what the fourth defendant has done with the money, though the likelihood is that most of it has been spent, so that there is little left to trace.

28.5 Trusts of Land and Appointment of Trustees Act 1996, section 14

28.5.1 Particulars of claim

IN THE HIGH COURT OF JUSTICE   Claim No 2005 HC 1387
CHANCERY DIVISION

BETWEEN

ANTHEA EARL   Claimant

and

COLIN DERRINGTON   Defendant

PARTICULARS OF CLAIM

1.   In about December 1993 the Claimant and the Defendant although unmarried started living together as husband and wife in a rented flat at 27 Bourne Street, Nottingham.

2.   The Claimant was then working as a teacher earning about £200 per week net and the Defendant was working as a social worker earning about £150 per week net. Their incomes were pooled and any sums not spent on ordinary living expenses were placed in a joint account with the Victoria Building Society.

3.   On 18th May 1996 the Claimant and the Defendant purchased as a home for themselves a property known as 16 Montague Drive, Nottingham ('the House') for the sum of £80,000, of which £70,000 was advanced by the Victoria Building Society and secured by a mortgage on the House. The balance of the purchase price and all incidental expenses were paid out of their joint account.

4.   The conveyance dated 18th May 1996 of the House was to the Defendant alone. The House was registered in the name of the Defendant at HM Land Registry under Title Number BN 246815.

5.   After the purchase the Claimant and Defendant lived in the House as husband and wife and continued in their respective employments at approximately the same rates of pay as before, but no longer pooled their incomes. A substantial portion of the income of the Claimant was spent on the housekeeping for herself and the Defendant amounting to some £90 per week, so enabling the Defendant to pay the mortgage instalments in respect of the House.

6.   In these circumstances there was a common intention or an implied agreement between the parties that the Defendant should hold the House on trust for himself and the Claimant in proportion to their contributions, or alternatively in equal shares.

7.   In spending her income on the housekeeping as set out above the Claimant was acting to her detriment in reliance on the common intention or implied agreement in the belief that she was increasing her share in the House.

8.   On 19th October 2003 the Claimant left the House leaving the Defendant in sole occupation of it.

9.   Despite requests from the Claimant the Defendant has refused to sell the House.

AND the Claimant claims:

(1) A declaration that the House is held by the Defendant upon trust for the Claimant and the Defendant in proportion to their contributions to its purchase, alternatively in equal shares; alternatively in such shares as the Court may determine.

(2) An order that the Claimant be appointed as trustee of the trust jointly with the Defendant.

(3) An order that the House be vested in the Claimant and the Defendant.

(4) An order that the House be sold by order of the Court.

(5) An order that the trusts affecting the House may be carried into execution by the Court.

(6) All necessary accounts and enquiries.

(7) Further or other remedies.

(8) Costs.

JOSEPH BLOGGS

STATEMENT OF TRUTH

Dated etc.

28.5.2 Commentary

This application arises in the exactly the same context as the CPR, Part 8 claim in **26.4.1**. Such claims can be made under Part 8 where there is no substantial dispute of fact. But not uncommonly in such cases there is a very substantial dispute of fact, and in those circumstances the claim is better made under CPR, Part 7. This example shows what such a claim might look like.

The claimant must show the existence of a resulting trust and/or a constructive trust in her favour. To show a resulting trust, she needs to show that she has made a direct contribution to the purchase price of the house. In this case she will rely on the fact that the deposit was paid out of a joint bank account to which she had made a substantial contribution. The essential ingredients that must be established by the claimant to show the existence of a constructive trust are laid down in *Grant v Edwards* [1986] 2 All ER 426. She must show that there is a common intention or implied agreement between the parties that she should have a share (or, if there is a resulting trust at the outset, an enhanced share) in the house. This common intention must be evidenced by the parties' conduct, in particular the relationship between them and the claimant's direct or indirect contributions to paying off the mortgage. She must then show that she has acted to her detriment on the basis of the common intention, in the belief that she was acquiring a share or an enhanced share in the house. This detriment is usually shown by her making the same financial contributions as evidence of the common intention.

With these ingredients in mind, it is not too difficult to see how the claim is constructed. The material facts are of course set out in chronological order.

Paragraph 1. The fact that the parties lived together as husband and wife is material. Without such a relationship it is very difficult to show the existence of the common intention.

Paragraph 2. The pooling of their savings clearly evidences a common intention. It is also part of the evidence to show that the £10,000 deposit was part paid by the claimant. The figures for their earnings help to show that the claimant has if anything contributed more than half. The shares under a resulting trust will be in strict proportion to their contributions. The shares under a constructive trust will be according to their implied intention, which may be equal, or may be in proportion to their contributions.

Paragraph 3. The purchase of the house is obviously the central ingredient. The fact that it was bought as their home is part of the common intention. Figures for where the money came from are essential to establish shares. The facts necessary to establish any resulting trust are now complete.

Paragraph 4. The conveyance into the defendant's sole name is what creates the claim in the first place. If it had been in joint names, there would have been little doubt about the parties' true intentions. State the title number of registered land.

Paragraph 5. The continuation of the quasi-marital relationship is important, as are the continuing incomes. It does not matter that the claimant did not pay anything directly to the mortgage. If her contributions have relieved the defendant of his other commitments, so making it possible for him to afford the mortgage, then those contributions are worth as much as direct contributions. This is the basis on which paragraph 5 is drafted.

Paragraph 6. The existence of the common intention or implied agreement now needs to be expressly alleged. The existence of a trust inevitably follows if such agreement is established. In this case the claimant's claim is primarily that the shares are in proportion to her contributions, because she will argue that she has actually paid rather more than the defendant, but she claims equal shares in the alternative.

Paragraph 7. States the final essential ingredient for a constructive trust (see above).

Paragraph 8. The claimant seeks an order for sale. This will not be ordered unless it is established that the relationship has come to an end, so she needs to state the fact that she has left.

Paragraph 9. The court would be reluctant to order a sale if there was evidence that the defendant would agree to a sale voluntarily, so his refusal to sell should be stated.

Prayer. For obvious reasons, the prayer is indistinguishable from the remedies listed in the equivalent Part 8 details of claim. These have been explained in **26.4.2**.

One remedy which will be required, though it will be for the defendant to ask for, is an enquiry into how much of the mortgage has been paid off by the defendant alone since the claimant's departure. An adjustment will need to be made in his favour to take account of this.

28.6   Exercise A

By his will dated 4 April 1998 James Ayres appointed William Bagley and Alan Cradock his executors and trustees and after administration costs and various small pecuniary legacies left his estate upon trust for his wife Diana for life with remainder to his two children Edward and Francesca in equal shares. The testator died on 2 January 1999 when Edward was 21 and Francesca 14, and his will was duly proved by the executors on 5 March 1999. The principal assets of the estate (apart from various cash sums which were wholly expended on administration costs and in meeting the legacies) were (a) £100,000 worth of gilt-edged stock and (b) 900 of the 1,000 issued shares in Victoria Kitchens Ltd, a private company specialising in designing and fitting hand-painted kitchens. The other 100 shares were owned by Margaret Ayres and she and James were the directors of the company. In the years prior to James Ayres's death the company had been very successful and in 1999 the 1,000 shares were worth £200,000. The executors were expressly empowered to retain the stock and the shares.

Diana Ayres persuaded Mr Bagley and Mr Cradock to employ a friend of hers, Arthur Hicks, to advise on the investment of the trust fund and to pay him £2,000 per annum for doing so. In 1999 Mr Hicks advised that the gilt-edged stock should be retained for the time being as it was giving the best possible income for Diana. He gave no further advice. Diana died in 2003 when the stock was worth £100,000.

At Diana's request Mr Bagley and Mr Cradock appointed Mr Hicks managing director of Victoria Kitchens in 2000. Mr Hicks paid himself a substantial salary of £40,000 per annum and over the next few years invested most of the company's assets in property developments in the West Midlands.

None produced any return and the company is now practically insolvent. Mr Bagley and Mr Cradock appear to have known nothing about the company's affairs. Mr Hicks turns out to have been Diana's hairdresser and to have had (so far as is known) no knowledge of financial or business matters. He is now bankrupt.

Counsel is asked to settle any appropriate proceedings on behalf of Edward and Francesca.

28.7 Exercise B

By his will dated 1 February 1998 and proved by the executors on 13 May 1998 Arthur Atkinson gave £25,000 to Edward Chapman upon trust for Anne Bolton for life with remainder to such of her children as should attain 21, if more than one in equal shares. Mr Chapman was given full powers of investment as if he were the absolute owner of the trust property. In May 1999 Mr Chapman invested the entire £25,000 by way of a loan to himself at 4% over bank base rate, secured by a first legal mortgage over his own house which was then unencumbered and worth £100,000.

Mr Chapman invested the £25,000 on the stock market and by 2001 his shares were worth £50,000. In January 2002 he decided the stock market was nearing its peak and he therefore sold the shares for £50,000 and bought a property at 21 Park View, Dulwich, London SE21 for £250,000 made up by £50,000 the proceeds of his shares and £200,000 the proceeds of sale of his previous house. Mr Chapman made regular payments of the interest on his loan and has recently repaid the £25,000 capital plus a further £10,000 as, in his words, 'capital growth'. 21 Park View is now worth £450,000.

Counsel is asked to settle any appropriate proceedings on behalf of Mrs Bolton and her two children Caroline and David, aged 21 and 19.

Assessment criteria

29.1 Assessment in drafting skills

29.1.1 The subject matter of assessments

All assessments in drafting will require you to produce completed drafts, and you are likely to be asked to draft more than one document for each assessment. You may be asked to draft any type of document covered during the course, for example:

(a) Details of claim on a claim form.

(b) Any statement of case, including further information.

(c) Request for further information.

(d) Injunction order.

(e) Written evidence.

(f) Indictment.

(g) Grounds of appeal and advice on appeal in a criminal case.

(h) Details of Part 8 claim.

The legal content of any document you are required to draft will not be limited to those areas covered in the examples and exercises on the course, but if the assessment is unseen, you will be given advance notice of the relevant legal areas.

29.1.2 The use of assessment criteria

Whenever you are assessed in drafting skills, you will be given the criteria according to which you will be assessed. You will find similar criteria, called performance criteria, attached to any Practical Training Exercise you are given to do during your training. These criteria can be used for self-assessment, and assessment of your fellow students. They will also be used by your tutor in giving you feedback (formal or informal) on your written work.

It is therefore important that you should familiarise yourself with the standard criteria used, and understand how the criteria are applied. The rest of this chapter sets out and explains the standard criteria used at the Inns of Court School of Law. Other teaching institutions probably use very similar criteria, because they are based on guidelines laid down by the Bar Council. You would be well advised to study the relevant criteria, and then to bear them in mind when practising your drafting.

The more you understand what will be required of you in assessments, the more you will appreciate the skill of drafting, and be able to practise it.

29.2   Criteria for statements of case

The usual criteria applied when you are being assessed on your drafting of particulars of claim (including a Part 20 claim) or a defence (including a defence and counterclaim) are as follows:

In order to complete this exercise satisfactorily you must show your ability to draft a [claim] [defence] which:

(1) LANGUAGE (10%)

Is written in clear grammatical English, correctly spelt and appropriately punctuated.

(2) STRUCTURE (20%)

(i)   Is properly headed and laid out.

(ii) Is neat on the page.

(iii) Deals with the material issues in an appropriate order and in an appropriate number of paragraphs [and in the right part of the statement of case].

(iv) Tells a clear story.

(3) LAW, CONTENT AND EFFECTIVENESS (40%)

(A) LAW AND CONTENT (30%)

(i)   Is based on a sound understanding and application of the relevant law.

(ii) Sets out [the material facts] [any material facts relied on].

(iii) Identifies or helps to identify the material issues.

(iv) Accurately states the client's case [and the remedies sought].

(v)   Omits all immaterial matters.

(B) EFFECTIVENESS (10%)

Serves its purpose in that:

(i)   it sets out a sustainable [claim] [defence]; and

(ii) it goes as far as it reasonably can in helping to achieve the client's objectives.

(4) DRAFTING SKILL (30%)

(i)   Is written in language and in a style appropriate for a statement of case.

(ii) Is precise and unambiguous.

(iii) Is concise.

(iv) Does not rely excessively on precedents or follow inappropriate precedents.

29.2.1   Criterion (1) — language

Is written in clear grammatical English, correctly spelt and appropriately punctuated

This criterion usually carries 10% of the marks. The requirement is simply to produce a draft which is written in clear English, without spelling mistakes, grammatical errors or incorrect punctuation. For example, verbs should be in the correct tense, nouns should have the appropriate article, every sentence should have a main verb and sentences should be separated by a full stop, not a comma. Spell names correctly. Do not miss out words, or use note form.

Your English must be clear in the sense that the words you use must make sense. What you write must be comprehensible, and you should use words so that they have their correct meanings. So, for example, you would be criticised for muddling 'claimant' and 'defendant', for writing 'negligence' when you mean 'negligent', or for using the word 'infer' to mean 'imply'. Your sentences should be properly constructed.

You are not however being assessed on your drafting style or precision of language under this criterion. This comes under criterion 4.

29.2.2   Criterion (2) — structure

As you can see, structure includes formalities and format. This criterion usually carries 20% of the marks.

Criterion (2)(i)

Is properly headed and laid out

Your statement of case should begin will the full heading, stating the correct court, case number (if known — do not invent one), the full names of the parties, the correct description of each party and the title of the pleading. If it is a defence and counterclaim (or a reply and defence to counterclaim) then there should be a sub-heading for each part. The statement of case should then be drafted in consecutively numbered paragraphs and sub-paragraphs, with properly headed particulars where appropriate. Figures should be in numbers not words, and sums should be set out clearly. Each head of loss claimed should be itemised. The prayer should be set out correctly, with each remedy numbered. Your signature (a pseudonym for assessment purposes) should appear in the correct place and the document should be rounded off in the correct way — 'Dated etc' will do. Remind instructing solicitors to include the statement of truth.

Criterion (2)(ii)

Is neat on the page

Format is important. If you are word-processing, you are strongly advised to take the time to ensure that the formatting is neat, and consistent. Take care over line spacing and indents. Do not use very small or very large type. If you are writing by hand, as you will be in an unseen assessment, use space. Do not write into the margins, leave a space between paragraphs and generally ensure that the finished result looks neat. The nature of drafting (careful composition) is such that you should not need to write so fast that your handwriting deteriorates.

Criterion (2)(iii)

Deals with the material issues in an appropriate order and in an appropriate number of paragraphs [and in the right part of the statement of case]

Your paragraph structure is the most important part of criterion (2). Remember that you are supposed to deal with each issue in a separate paragraph, so, except in rare circumstances, separate causes of action should be pleaded in separate paragraphs, and allegations against different defendants should be set out in different paragraphs. If you find that a paragraph is becoming inordinately long, you are probably trying to deal with more than one issue. At the very least it should be broken down into separate subparagraphs, if not main paragraphs. However, ensure that particulars of an allegation appear in the same paragraph as the allegation itself, itemised as appropriate. They should not be in a separate paragraph or paragraphs. Issues should be taken separately and distinctly: do not let them become jumbled up or confused; deal with one issue at a time. When you are dealing with an issue, deal with it all at once. Do not leave some aspects of it to a later paragraph. Finally, make sure you distinguish and separate the body of the pleading from the prayer.

The material facts and issues should be pleaded in an appropriate order. This order is conventional in claims based on well-established causes of action (see **Chapters 7, 9, 11 and 12**). If you are in doubt, remember that chronological order is almost certainly the most appropriate. Follow conventions, such as the convention that express terms are pleaded before implied terms. If you are drafting a defence, then the order of paragraphs is largely dictated by the order in which issues have been dealt with in the particulars of claim. However, as explained in **Chapter 8**, matters which are an essential part of your defence, but which are not mentioned in the claim, should be dealt with at the appropriate stage. As a general rule, make a denial first, then give the reasons for it.

The requirement to deal with issues in the right part of the statement of case applies when you are drafting a two-part pleading (defence and counterclaim, or reply and defence to counterclaim). Take care not to place in the counterclaim matters which are really part of the defence (a serious fault), or to place in the defence matters which strictly belong in the counterclaim (a less serious fault, but still not entirely sound).

Criterion (2)(iv)

Tells a clear story

A good pleading tells a clear story. This is particularly apt for particulars of claim, but it is also true to a lesser extent of defences. The clear story will be achieved if your paragraph structure and sequence of issues is correct and sound. This requirement is largely a description of how good structure can be recognised, but it is a good idea to bear it in mind when drafting, because it can help you to find the best structure. This part of criterion (2) will be omitted if you are asked to draft a reply.

Under criterion (2), you cannot achieve full marks if your draft is incomplete. The structure is judged by reference to what ought to be in your statement of case, not what actually is. If essential content is missing, then it follows that your structure is not appropriate and you probably do not have an appropriate number of paragraphs.

29.2.3   Criterion (3) — law, content and effectiveness

Criterion (3) consists of two criteria grouped together. This is to satisfy the Bar Council's requirement that you cannot pass the assessment overall unless you '(a) demonstrate adequate knowledge and comprehension of the law, and (b) adequately demonstrate the ability to manipulate and utilise such knowledge in the analysis and preparation of the case employed for the assessment'. So criterion (3) is the mandatory criterion on which you must pass, and it usually carries 40% of the marks in total.

29.2.3.1   Criterion (3)(A) — law and content

This part of criterion (3) will usually carry 30% of the marks. It is not possible to separate law and content. It is the law that determines the correct content of your statement of case: you cannot get the content right if you do not understand the law and its requirements.

Criterion (3)(A)(i)

Is based on a sound understanding and application of the relevant law

In drafting a claim, you will demonstrate your understanding of the law by correctly identifying the essential elements of the cause of action and pleading the facts that establish them. In drafting a defence, you will demonstrate your understanding of the law by correctly identifying what it is that can provide the defendant with a legal defence and pleading the facts appropriately. In other words, you will show your ability to satisfy this criterion by satisfying the rest of criterion (3)(A).

Criterion (3)(A)(ii)

Sets out [the material facts] [any material facts relied on]

When you are drafting a claim, you must state all the material facts. As you have learned, the material facts are those facts which, if proved, entitle the claimant to the remedy he seeks, and which, if not proved, will prevent the claimant obtaining his remedy. You have to know the law to be able to identify and plead the material facts, so you can only succeed by accident under this criterion if you do not know the law. The material facts must of course be stated not only in general terms, but by reference to the facts of this particular case, and must be particularised as fully as appropriate.

When you are drafting a defence, you must state any material facts relied on. Remember that CPR, r 16.5 requires you to state any alternative version of the facts pleaded by the claimant, and to give reasons for every denial. There may therefore be a considerable amount of material fact that needs to be pleaded. Also, if relying on a defence which it is for the defendant to establish, you will need to state the material facts necessary to give rise to that defence in law. Again, everything should be properly particularised.

Criterion (3)(A)(iii)

Identifies or helps to identify the material issues

A statement of case works in conjunction with the statement of case produced by the other side. By and large, no statement of case by itself identifies the material issues, but when the particulars of claim and the defence are placed side by side, the material issues should become apparent. So your claim should be drafted in such a way that the defence can respond to it logically, because the material facts are clearly and accurately stated.

When drafting a defence, you must respond to every allegation in the particulars of claim, by admitting it, denying it, or requiring it to be proved. Only if you are thorough and meticulous in this process will you help to identify the issues in the case accurately.

Criterion (3)(A)(iv)

Accurately states the client's case [and the remedies sought]

It should be abundantly clear from your statement of case what cause(s) of action a claimant is relying on, or what the defence is. It should also be clear how the facts relied upon amount to the relevant cause of action or defence. If there are in your instructions facts which clearly support your client's case, and are material facts or relevant particulars, not purely evidence, make sure you have included them in your pleading. Do not omit any material facts, or your client's case has not been properly stated.

Make sure also that you draft in such a way that you establish the cause of action, and justify the granting of the remedies you seek. Use the correct words, eg 'duty of care', 'negligent', 'agreed', 'breach of contract', 'represented', 'express term', 'implied term', 'as a result of', 'loss', 'damage', 'the defendant threatens and intends'.

Plead any material allegations in full. For example, if pleading negligence, make sure you think of all the appropriate particulars of negligence that can be alleged. If the claim is for breach of contract, make sure you include every breach of contract, not just some. If your claim is for breach of statutory duty, identify and plead all the relevant duties, and specify precisely what statutory section or regulation has been breached. If you are pleading more than one cause of action, do not muddle up the requirements of each (for example by pleading particulars of negligence under the heading of breach of statutory duty). If you are making allegations against more than one defendant, make the correct allegations against each defendant. Do not fail to distinguish who is alleged to have done what.

Finally, get your client's case right. Your pleading must be consistent with your instructions. Do not state the facts in a way that is not entirely accurate according to the evidence in front of you. Do not make allegations that cannot be supported by the evidence. If facts are alternative to each other, state them as alternatives. Get dates, places and similar details right. Ensure that any claim for loss is correctly particularised. Do not omit any recoverable head of loss. Get your figures and sums right.

If you are drafting a defence, ensure that you admit what must be admitted, deny what must be denied, and require everything else to be proved. It is a serious fault to respond incorrectly to an allegation in the claim: it can invalidate your defence. When you make a denial, remember to ensure that you have included the reasons for that denial, and include also all other material facts on which the defendant relies.

The requirement to state the remedies accurately will obviously only appear when you are asked to draft a claim. This part of the criterion should remind you of the need to get the prayer and any claim for interest correct, as well as the body of the claim.

Criterion (3)(A)(v)

Omits all immaterial matters

It goes without saying that to get the content of your statement of case right, you must not only include everything that should be included, and set it out in the best possible way, but also avoid including anything which should not be there. You may be criticised for pleading immaterial facts and allegations, or evidence. On a more serious level, you can be criticised for pleading a cause of action that should not be pleaded, together with the material facts that support it. To take the most common example, you will fail to meet this criterion if you plead misrepresentation in a case that should be based on breach of contract.

29.2.3.2   Criterion (3)(B) — effectiveness

This part of criterion (3) requires the assessor to look at your statement of case as a whole and consider how effective it would be. It usually carries 10% of the marks. Overall effectiveness is a very important criterion, but it is not weighted heavily, because almost certainly any significant faults will already have been taken into consideration under criteria (2) and (3)(A). You need to consider whether your draft has served its purpose in two ways.

Criterion (3)(B)(i)

It sets out a sustainable [claim] [defence]

This is essentially a question of whether the statement of case is sound in law. A claim or defence is sustainable if, when supported by the relevant evidence, it would be likely to succeed. So the issue is whether the essential ingredients have been set out, and whether the judge would be able to grant or deny the remedy sought. If the statement of case would be liable to be struck out as disclosing no cause of action or defence, then that is a very significant failure under this criterion. If it could only succeed after amendment to correct your errors and omissions, that is also a serious fault. If it would stand up without too much criticism, that is good.

Criterion (3)(B)(ii)

It goes as far as it reasonably can in helping to achieve the client's objectives

Here the assessor can consider your statement of case on a more advanced level, asking whether it shows tactical awareness and strength. Although tactics have not been heavily emphasised on the Bar Vocational Course, as explained in **Chapter 4** there are tactical decisions that can affect the way you draft a pleading, and it is certainly good to put your case as strongly as it can reasonably be put, so as to encourage settlement. Under this criterion, strength and tactical skill can be rewarded to a modest extent.

29.2.4   Criterion (4) — drafting skill

This criterion relates to your ability to use language in a professional way, and to draft in your own words. It usually carries 30% of the marks.

Criterion (4)(i)

Is written in language and in a style appropriate for a statement of case

Statements of case are formal documents, and the appropriate language has a degree of formality to it. The rules also require statements of case to be concise. But the modern convention is that lawyers should also draft in plain English, so your drafting should be efficient and succinct, while at the same time avoiding archaic, pompous or overly dense language. Also avoid informality, loose sentence structures, repetition and colloquial terms. It is important too that pleadings should be objective and factual rather than emotive and exaggerated, so avoid unnecessary adjectives and prejudicial words. The most important quality of all is clarity. The overall effect should be that your statement of case is clear and easy to read, but has a professional and confident tone.

Criterion (4)(ii)

Is precise and unambiguous

Precision is of the utmost importance. It is the precision of a lawyer's drafting that above all marks it out as a professional piece of work. You should ensure that what you draft says exactly what you want it to say, or what it needs to say, that it states the client's case with complete accuracy, and that it contains no ambiguities. Use definitions where appropriate, but also learn to recognise where they are unnecessary, because no possible ambiguity could arise. If you define a term, stick to it consistently.

Precision also involves proper particularisation. A pleading is not precise if it contains vague or generalised allegations. It is not good enough to state only the broad nature of the allegations you are making; they must be particularised in detail. Being particular means being specific. It is to be hoped that, as you have learned to draft, you have learned to be more and more specific about everything you write.

Criterion 4(iii)

Is concise

Your draft should be concise. This is partly a matter of style: do not put in unnecessary words or phrases and do not ramble aimlessly. But it is more a matter of content. State the facts you are setting out to prove, not the evidence by which you will prove them. This means that, although properly particularised, they are not over-particularised. Do not insert more detail than is necessary to establish the cause of action or the defence. Do not give particulars which belong in the realm of pure evidence.

Criterion (4)(iv)

Does not rely excessively on precedents or follow inappropriate precedents

Your draft should be your own, tailored to the precise circumstances and facts of the case in which you are drafting. Although you may have used a precedent to guide you, it is generally a bad idea to rely on it too heavily. The dangers of this were explained in **Chapter 2**.

If you have followed an inappropriate precedent, you are likely also to have made errors that will mean you have not fulfilled criterion (3). If you are aiming for the very highest standards, you will not allow it to be apparent in your draft that you have used a precedent at all.

Do not deceive yourself that an assessor cannot tell whether you have followed a precedent. It usually stands out a mile. Often a phrase or sentence appears, which is well-written but inappropriate, and too distinctive to have come out of the writer's head. More often, assessors recognise sentences and paragraphs that appear in the answers to exercises you have done during the course, or which are found in this Manual. Even if they do not know where the sentence comes from, they will quickly realise it is from a precedent when they have read the same sentence in several different answers.

29.3 Criteria for a request for further information

The usual criteria applied when you are being assessed on your drafting of a request for further information are as follows:

In order to complete this exercise satisfactorily you must show your ability to draft a request for further information which:

(1) LANGUAGE AND STYLE (15%)
    (i)   Is written in clear grammatical English, correctly spelt and appropriately punctuated.
    (ii) Is written in language and in a style appropriate to a request for further information.

(2) STRUCTURE (10%)
    (i)   Is properly headed and laid out.
    (ii) Is neat on the page.
    (iii) Is structured in an appropriate way.
    (iv) Accurately identifies the subject matter of each request.

(3) LAW, CONTENT AND EFFECTIVENESS (50%)
    (A) LAW AND CONTENT (25%)
        (i)   Is based on a sound understanding and application of the relevant law.
        (ii) Makes requests that can properly be made.
        (iii) Makes worthwhile requests.
        (iv) Does not omit any worthwhile requests.
        (v) Does not make improper or pointless requests.
    (B) EFFECTIVENESS (25%)
    Serves its tactical purpose in that:
        (i)   it is likely to expose weaknesses in the claimant's case; and
        (ii) it goes as far as it reasonably can in helping to achieve the client's objectives.

(4) DRAFTING SKILL (25%)
    (i)   States precisely and unambiguously the information required.
    (ii) Does not rely excessively on precedents or follow inappropriate precedents.

29.3.1   Criterion (1) — language and style

This criterion usually carries 15% of the marks.

Criterion (1)(i)

Is written in clear grammatical English, correctly spelt and appropriately punctuated

For advice how to fulfil this criterion, see **29.2.1** above.

Criterion (1)(ii)

Is written in language and in a style appropriate to a request for further information

For advice on how to fulfil this criterion, see **29.2.4** above, under criterion (4)(i). There is really no need to draft a request for further information in anything other than plain English. The information you are asking for is almost certainly factual, and you will not need to use any precise legal terminology, so be clear and polite. Say 'Please'.

29.3.2   Criterion (2) — structure

(i)   *Is properly headed and laid out*
(ii)   *Is neat on the page*
(iii) *Is structured in an appropriate way*
(iv)   *Accurately identifies the subject matter of each request*

This criterion usually carries 10% of the marks. The structure of a request is largely laid down by PD 18, and is explained in **Chapter 17**. You need to ensure that you follow the correct format. Identify the relevant subject matter of each request, specifying the paragraph number of any document that contains it; quote the sentence, phrase or word that needs clarifying, and then state your request. If the request is in several parts, as good requests often are, use numbered subparagraphs. If you are making several requests, put them in a sensible order. If your request relates to a statement of case, set out your requests in the same order as the relevant issues arise in that statement of case.

For advice on headings, formalities and formatting, see **29.2.2** above.

29.3.3   Criterion (3) — law, content and effectiveness

Criterion (3) consists of two criteria grouped together, to satisfy the Bar Council's requirement with regard to the law (see **29.2.3**). Therefore you must pass on this criterion, which usually carries 50% of the marks in total.

29.3.3.1   Criterion (3)(A) — law and content

This part of criterion (3) will usually carry 25% of the marks. The law is of no more than marginal relevance in a request for further information.

Criterion (3)(A)(i)

Is based on a sound understanding and application of the relevant law

The only 'law' that will really be relevant in this instance is procedural — you must ensure that what you draft complies with CPR, Part 18 and PD 18. If you satisfy the rest of criterion (3)(A), you will have satisfied this part.

Criterion (3)(A)(ii)

Makes requests that can properly be made

Each request you make should be one that seeks information that you can argue your client is entitled to, in accordance with PD 18, para 1.2. It should relate to a matter in dispute between the parties, and should be for information that will further clarify the issues, or lead to a narrowing down of the issues, or the saving of costs, or increase the likelihood of settlement. If you are unsure whether to include a request, ask yourself if you could mount an argument before a judge as to why the information is required.

Criterion (3)(A)(iii)

Makes worthwhile requests

Sometimes there are requests which could in theory be justified, but which will almost certainly advance your client's interests not a jot. In such circumstances the request is not worthwhile, and should not be made. On the other hand, there are sometimes requests which although of doubtful validity in terms of clarifying the issues, are clearly worthwhile for tactical reasons, because merely making the request could help to expose weaknesses in the other side's case and so result in a narrowing of the issues or sooner settlement. For a full discussion of whether and when a request may be justified on tactical grounds, see **17.2.3**.

Criterion (3)(A)(iv)

Does not omit any worthwhile requests

This criterion means that you can be assessed not only on what you have drafted, but also on what you have not. You may be validly criticised for not including a request that would have been both proper and worthwhile, and potentially effective. So always take care to think of all the information you could reasonably ask for.

Criterion (3)(A)(v)

Does not make improper or pointless requests

This is the flip side of the above criteria. It goes without saying that as well as being rewarded for what you have drafted and criticised for what you have omitted, you can also be criticised for including requests that cannot be justified.

29.3.3.2   Criterion (3)(B) — effectiveness

Serves its tactical purpose in that:
(i)   it is likely to expose weaknesses in the claimant's case; and
(ii)   it goes as far as it reasonably can in helping to achieve the client's objectives

This is another important criterion, which also usually carries 25% of the marks. Like the equivalent criterion for drafting statements of case (see **29.2.3.2**), it is about the overall effectiveness of your draft. There is overlap with the other criteria, because if criteria (3) and (4) in particular have not been fulfilled, it is hard to see how you can have fulfilled this one either. Nevertheless, this criterion requires the assessor to take an overview of the likely benefits to your client of what you have drafted.

Tactical awareness is much more important with requests for further information than with statements of case. Although there are circumstances where requests are made purely for the sake of information gathering, in a drafting assessment you are likely to be confronted with a situation where there are real weaknesses in the other side's case and it is your task to expose them. This criterion is a measure of how fully and effectively you have done this.

29.3.4   Criterion (4) — drafting skill

(i)   *States precisely and unambiguously the information required*

(ii)   *Does not rely excessively on precedents or follow inappropriate precedents*

This is an important criterion, which relates to the actual drafting of the requests, rather than the choice of subject matter. It usually carries 25% of the marks. For general advice on precision and unwise reliance on precedents, see **29.2.4** above.

An effective request for further information involves careful formulation of the information asked for. If you do not ask for exactly what you want, you may well receive a great deal of information that you do not want. If you make a request that is too vague or general, you may enable the other side to avoid answering, or avoid giving you the information you believe you are entitled to. Drafting a good request is like cross-examination. Think carefully of the answer you are trying to get, and then ask a question, or a series of questions which are likely to extract that answer. This requires very precise drafting.

29.4   Criteria for an injunction order

The usual criteria applied when you are being assessed on your drafting of an injunction order are as follows:

In order to complete this exercise satisfactorily you must show your ability to draft an order which:

(1) LANGUAGE (10%)

   Is written in clear grammatical English, correctly spelt and appropriately punctuated.

(2) STRUCTURE (10%)

   (i)   Is properly headed and laid out.

   (ii) Is neat on the page.

   (iii) Contains all necessary formalities.

   (iv) Is structured in an appropriate manner.

(3) LAW, CONTENT AND EFFECTIVENESS (50%)

   (A) LAW AND CONTENT (30%)

      (i)   Is based on a sound understanding and application of the relevant law.

      (ii)   Contains all the terms necessary to enable the client to achieve his objectives, so far as is reasonably practicable.

      (iii) Does not contain any terms which are inappropriate because:

         (a) they are too wide;

         (b) they are oppressive;

         (c) they are directed at the wrong respondent(s);

         (d) they do not support a legal right of the applicant; or

         (e) they cannot be supported by the evidence.

   (B) EFFECTIVENESS (20%)

      Is sound overall in that:

      (i)   it is drafted in mandatory and/or prohibitory terms as appropriate;

      (ii)   it is accompanied by any necessary undertakings;

(iii) it is likely to be ordered by the court.

(4) DRAFTING SKILL (30%)

    (i) Is written in language and in a style appropriate for an order.

    (ii) Is concise.

    (iii) Is precise and unambiguous.

    (iv) Enables the respondent to know what he may, must and must not do.

    (v) Is watertight.

    (vi) Does not follow inappropriate precedents or rely excessively on precedents.

29.4.1 Criterion (1) — language

It is written in clear grammatical English, correctly spelt and appropriately punctuated

For advice how to fulfil this criterion, see **29.2.1** above. It usually carries 10% of the marks.

29.4.2 Criterion (2) — structure

(i)   Is properly headed and laid out

(ii) Is neat on the page

(iii) Contains all necessary formalities

(iv) Is structured in an appropriate manner

This criterion is not difficult to fulfil and so usually carries only 10% of the marks. For general advice on headings, formalities and formatting, see **29.2.2** above. For an interim injunction, the correct description of the parties is applicant and respondent. Remember to cover liberty to apply where appropriate.

The formalities and structure of an injunction order are largely laid down by the standard forms that are used. These forms are set out and explained in **Chapter 19** and you should follow the appropriate form precisely. Make sure you do not use the High Court form in a county court claim or vice versa. Some formal parts of the form can be abbreviated for assessment purposes as explained in **Chapter 19**.

The only structural matter of choice remaining to you when drafting an injunction order is the arrangement of the various terms of the order. Take care to separate each individual prohibition or mandatory requirement into a distinctly numbered paragraph or subparagraph. Put these in whatever seems an appropriate order. Maybe the most important or most urgent should come first; maybe there is some kind of chronological order that can be identified; maybe the most sensible arrangement would be to put them in the order in which they will be dealt with in the supporting written evidence. There is no set practice — be sensible.

29.4.3 Criterion (3) — law, content and effectiveness

This is the compulsory double criterion (see **29.2.3** and **29.3.3**), on which you must pass. It usually carries 50% of the marks in total.

29.4.3.1 Criterion (3)(A) — law and content

This part of criterion (3) will usually carry 30% of the marks. The law cannot be separated from the content. You need to know the law to get the content right; if the terms of the order are inappropriate, then you have quite likely got the law wrong.

Criterion (3)(A)(i)

Is based on a sound understanding and application of the relevant law

You cannot draft a sound injunction order without an understanding of the law that lies behind it. An injunction can only be granted to support the applicant's legal rights, so you must know what those rights are before you draft it. Your understanding of the law must pervade everything you draft.

Criterion (3)(A)(ii)

Contains all the terms necessary to enable the client to achieve his objectives, so far as is reasonably practicable

Your injunction is always designed to achieve an objective of your client, and you must ensure that you have covered all the necessary ground. If the order is prohibitory, it is essential that you do not leave anything out, if the effect will be that the defendant can carry on doing some or all of the mischief you wish to prevent. Your order must enforce all, not just some, of the client's threatened legal rights. But of course it cannot go beyond those legal rights, and there will be occasions where the client's objectives cannot lawfully be achieved by an injunction, in which case it should only go as far as it reasonably can. So you need to look at the evidence, think carefully, imagine what the defendant might do or not do to escape the effect of the order, and ensure that as far as possible your order leaves no escape route.

Do not forget the order as to costs.

Criterion (3)(A)(iii)

Does not contain any terms which are inappropriate because:
(a)   *they are too wide:*
(b)   *they are oppressive:*
(c)   *they are directed at the wrong respondent(s);*
(d)   *they do not support a legal right of the applicant; or*
(e)   *they cannot be supported by the evidence*

But on the other hand, your order must not go too far, and contain prohibitions or requirements that are not justified. The criterion itself sets out the main reasons why an order might not be justified, so use subparagraphs (a) to (e) as your guide. A term would be oppressive if it required the respondent to do or try to achieve the impossible. If you have more than one respondent, make sure you have directed the right terms at the right respondent. It does not follow that your client's legal rights are the same against each respondent, or that the evidence shows the same threats coming from each respondent. Take care to get it right.

One of the most common faults is to fail to limit the duration of an order in time, when it can only be justified for a specific period of time (usually because of the terms of a contract). Another very common failing is to seek an order which seeks to prevent something which the client genuinely fears, but which there is no evidence of the defendant ever having threatened to do. Your injunction must be justified on the basis of the evidence available to you.

29.4.3.2   Criterion (3)(B) — effectiveness

Is sound overall

This criterion has some overlap with other criteria, but enables the assessor to take an overview of the effectiveness of what you have drafted. It is important, and usually carries

20% of the marks. However there are some requirements here that do not appear else-where.

Criterion (5)(i)

It is drafted in mandatory and/or prohibitory terms as appropriate

This is not covered by the above criteria. A good order should be mandatory and/or pro-hibitory as appropriate. There is guidance in **19.2.2** as to how to choose. The requirement under this criterion is to make a sound choice. Remember that it may well be appropriate in many cases to include both mandatory and prohibitory terms to achieve the same re-sult.

Criterion (5)(ii)

It is accompanied by any necessary undertakings

Sometimes an applicant is only likely to be granted an injunction if he gives certain under-takings to the court. These undertakings must also be drafted as part of the injunction or-der. There is no need to draft the standard undertaking as to damages, which is included on both the High Court and county court forms, but all other undertakings are up to you. If the application is without notice, there will usually be formal undertakings that need to be given — see **19.1** and **19.3.2**. Other undertakings may be required as a matter of fact in each case. Make sure you include them; their omission can be criticised under this crite-rion.

Criterion (5)(iii)

It is likely to be ordered by the court

This is the part that overlaps with criteria (3) and (4). The test is whether the judge would be likely to grant the injunction you have drafted. If he would not, that is a significant fail-ure under this criterion. If he would need to re-draft it for you, that is also a serious fault.

29.4.4   Criterion (4) — drafting skill

This criterion covers the situation where your order is bad not because of your choice of what to include, or not include, but because of the way you have drafted it. It usually car-ries 30% of the marks.

Criteria (4)(i) and (4)(ii)

(i)   *Is written in language and in a style appropriate for an order*
(ii) *Is concise*

For advice on language and style, see **29.2.4** above, under criterion (4)(i). The modern practice is that injunction orders, more than almost any other legal document, should be drafted in plain English. This is because the standard High Court and county court forms are in plain English, and because of the utmost importance of enabling the respondent to know how to comply with the order. It is not just that a person should find himself in con-tempt of court because he has failed to fulfil an order he does not understand. Conciseness is always a virtue in drafting.

Criteria (4)(iii), (4)(iv) and (4)(v)

(iii) Is precise and unambiguous

(iv) Enables the respondent to know what he may, must and must not do

(v) Is watertight

Precision and unambiguity are explained above in **29.2.4** under criterion (4)(ii). These qualities are of supreme importance when it comes to injunction orders. Paragraphs (iv) and (v) explain why. The respondent needs to be told exactly what he must and must not do, and be able to deduce confidently what he still may do. So you must be absolutely specific in every relevant detail. At the same time, your client's objectives will not be achieved if, through sloppy drafting, you have left the respondent a loophole that he can exploit. You must ensure the order is watertight. Only very precise language can achieve these objectives. To achieve this degree of precision while writing in plain English calls for very considerable drafting skill. It is in this form of drafting that your skill is most tested.

Criterion (4)(vi)

Does not follow inappropriate precedents or rely excessively on precedents

The need to avoid unwise reliance on precedents is explained in **29.2.4**. As you have read in **Chapter 19**, it is in the drafting of injunction orders that reliance on precedents is most dangerous. Almost every order is unique to the facts of the case, and you are most unlikely to achieve the best possible order unless you have drafted it to suit the facts of the case.

29.5 Criteria for a witness statement

The usual criteria applied when you are being assessed on your drafting of a witness statement (or affidavit) in support of an application for an interim injunction are as follows:

In order to complete this exercise satisfactorily you must show your ability to draft a witness statement which:

(1) LANGUAGE

    (i) Is written in clear grammatical English, correctly spelt and appropriately punctuated.

    (ii) Is written in language and in a style appropriate to a witness statement.

(2) STRUCTURE

    (i) Is properly headed and laid out.

    (ii) Is neat on the page.

    (iii) Is of a suitable length.

    (iv) Sets out the evidence it contains in an appropriate order and in an appropriate number of paragraphs.

    (v) Tells a clear story.

(3) LAW, CONTENT AND EFFECTIVENESS

    (A) LAW AND CONTENT

        (i) Contains all necessary formalities.

        (ii) Accurately sets out all the material facts and evidence.

        (iii) Omits any immaterial evidence or anything which is not evidence.

        (iv) Exhibits any necessary documents.

(B) EFFECTIVENESS

    (i)   Presents the evidence fluently, coherently, forcefully and persuasively.

    (ii)   Shows as far as possible why the client should be entitled to the remedy sought.

29.5.1 Criterion (1) — language

(i)   Is written in clear grammatical English, correctly spelt and appropriately punctuated

(ii) Is written in language and in a style appropriate to a witness statement

This criterion usually carries 30% of the marks. Note that this is a greater weight than in other forms of drafting to reflect the particular importance that the quality of your writing has in a witness statement. For advice on paragraph (i) see **29.2.1** above.

The language that is appropriate to a witness statement is as far as possible the witness's own words. The appropriate style is as always plain English, again using the witness's own style as far as possible. But the lawyer drafting a witness statement may have to adjust the witness's language to ensure clarity, moderation and appropriateness to a legal context. There is more guidance on this in **20.4**.

29.5.2 Criterion (2) — structure

This criterion usually carries 20% of the marks.

Criteria 2(i) and 2(ii)

(i)   Is properly headed and laid out

(ii) Is neat on the page

A witness statement should be properly headed with the title of the case and laid out in numbered paragraphs — see **29.2.2** under criterion (2)(i). Advice on formatting for neatness on the page appears in **29.2.2** also.

Criterion (2)(iii)

Is of a suitable length

The suitable length for a witness statement is not an absolute. Its length is obviously dictated to a very considerable extent by the necessary content. However you would be rewarded for achieving conciseness without sacrificing content, but criticised for making your witness statement unnecessarily verbose or unduly short through abbreviation or omission.

Criterion (2)(iv)

Sets out the evidence it contains in an appropriate order and in an appropriate number of paragraphs

There is a lot you can do to improve your witness statement by the way you structure it. As a general rule, a witness is relating events, and the starting point should always be to think of relating those events in chronological order. However, as explained in **20.4.2.2** there are circumstances where you will actually improve the clarity of the evidence by abandoning chronological order, especially if there are numerous issues, so do not tie yourself rigidly to the sequence of events. Thinks what would work best in each case, and adopt that structure.

The paragraphing in a witness statement should follow the normal rules of good prose. Do not allow your paragraphs to get too long, or too short. Do not be afraid to have paragraphs of varying length. Ideally each paragraph deals with one and only one segment of the story, and each paragraph tends to begin with a new thought or step. What is appropriate is what best puts over the evidence that the statement contains.

Criterion (2)(v)

Tells a clear story

A good witness statement is also a good piece of story telling. The qualities required to achieve this are primarily those mentioned in criterion (2)(iv), but also those mentioned below in criterion (3)(B)(i).

29.5.3 Criterion 3 — law, content and effectiveness

This is the compulsory double criterion (see **29.2.3** and **29.3.3**), on which you must pass. It usually carries 50% of the marks in total.

29.5.3.1 Criterion (3)(A) — law and content

This part of criterion (3) will usually carry 30% of the marks. The relevance of the law is that any evidence you present must go to show what in law needs to be proved. So your understanding of the law affects the content. But the law itself does not appear in your witness statement, and so you are not specifically required in this instance to show an understanding of the law in your draft.

Criterion (3)(A)(i)

Contains all necessary formalities

There are formalities required in witness statements, with regard to the information in the top right-hand corner, identifying the witness, indicating the sources of the evidence, introducing the exhibits, etc. These were explained in **Chapter 20**, and should be complied with.

Criterion (3)(A)(ii)

Accurately sets out all the material facts and evidence

Your evidence must be complete. In other words the witness statement should contain everything that the witness can say to show why the remedy should be granted. It is a fault to leave anything out. Particularly important is evidence of material facts, the essential ingredients without which the remedy cannot be granted. If the witness statement is in support of an injunction application, make sure that you justify through evidence every part of the order you have drafted. Evidence that is designed to persuade the judge to exercise his discretion should also be included.

The evidence you give must be accurate. That is to say, it must be strictly in accordance with your client's proof of evidence, or whatever other documents have provided you with your raw material. You must not distort or embellish the facts. This is a matter of professional conduct, not just good drafting. Also as a matter of professional conduct, do not by omission leave your witness only telling part of the truth, or misleading the court. Do not forget to include adverse evidence, where this is required, on an application without notice.

Criterion (3)(A)(iii)

Omits any immaterial evidence or anything which is not evidence

Your witness statement should also not contain anything which ought not to be there. There may often be matters in your instructions which do not belong, and which you should not include. Be aware of what you are trying to show, and which evidence does in fact tend to show that. Do not attempt to show anything irrelevant, or include inadmissible evidence, or matters of prejudice.

Criterion (3)(A)(iv)

Exhibits any necessary documents

This is self-explanatory. Take care not only to exhibit necessary documents, but also not to exhibit unnecessary ones. A judge will not be pleased if he has to wade through irrelevant documents. For assessment purposes, where documents are included in your instructions, it is enough to refer to them. There is no need to photocopy and attach them.

29.5.3.2   Criterion (3)(B) — effectiveness

This is a very important criterion, which usually carries 20% of the marks. As you can see, it is concerned with the overall effect of the witness statement, in terms of content, structure and style.

Criterion (3)(B)(i)

Presents the evidence fluently, coherently, forcefully and persuasively

This can only be achieved by a combination of good drafting style, clarity of thought, logical structure and an awareness of the client's objectives. A good witness statement is a good piece of writing; it is easy to read, easy to follow and easy to digest. There is no confusion, so the reader never gets bored or lost. Every sentence should seem to follow on naturally from what has gone before. To be forceful, it should not understate or overstate any facts and allegations, but be patently clear and objective. To be persuasive, it needs to lead the reader irresistibly to the conclusion that the remedy sought should be granted.

Criterion (3)(B)(ii)

Shows as far as possible why the client should be entitled to the remedy sought

This is the overall effect that you are trying to achieve and overlaps with almost all the above criteria. The assessor will look at your witness statement and decide whether it achieves its objectives. If there is a vital piece of evidence missing, such that the remedy could not be granted, that would be a serious fault.

29.6   Criteria for a criminal appeal

The usual criteria applied when you are being assessed on your drafting of a criminal appeal are as follows:

In order to complete this exercise satisfactorily you must show your ability to:

Draft an Advice on Appeal which:

(1) DRAFTING SKILL (20%)

    (i)   Is written in grammatical English, correctly spelt, appropriately punctuated and neat on the page.

    (ii) Is written in appropriate language and in a suitable style.

    (iii) Is drafted with clarity and precision.

    (iv) Does not rely excessively on precedents or follow inappropriate precedents.

(2) STRUCTURE (10%)
 (i) Sets out the factual background to the appeal concisely and sufficiently.
 (ii) Deals with the grounds of appeal and any other issues in a sensible order and in an appropriate number of paragraphs.

(3) LAW, CONTENT, ANALYSIS AND EFFECTIVENESS (60%)
 (A) LAW AND CONTENT (20%)
 (i) Is based on a sound understanding and application of the relevant law.
 (ii) Puts forward appropriate grounds of appeal.
 (iii) Does not seek to rely on anything which is not a ground of appeal.
 (iv) Does not omit any important grounds of appeal.

 (B) ANALYSIS (30%)
 (i) Explains the legal and factual basis for each ground accurately and completely.
 (ii) Where appropriate explains why something does not provide grounds for an appeal.
 (iii) Makes proper reference to the proceedings at trial, the facts, the evidence and relevant legal sources.

 (C) EFFECTIVENESS (10%)
 Shows as far as possible why the conviction is unsafe and/or why the sentence should be reduced or varied.

Draft Grounds of Appeal which:
(4) GROUNDS (10%)
 (i) Fulfil criteria (1), (2)(ii) and (3)(A) above.
 (ii) Are consistent with and where appropriate refer to the Advice.

As you can see, you will be asked to draft both the advice on appeal and the grounds of appeal. The two are intimately linked, and overlap to a very large extent.

29.6.1 Criterion (1) — drafting skill

(i) Is written in grammatical English, correctly spelt, appropriately punctuated and neat on the page
(ii) Is written in appropriate language and in a suitable style
(iii) Is drafted with clarity and precision
(iv) Does not rely excessively on precedents or follow inappropriate precedents

This is a criterion which pulls together all the required qualities relating to the actual writing and formatting, and usually carries 20% of the marks. These qualities have all been explained earlier in this chapter — see **29.2.1, 29.2.2, 29.2.4**.

The only possible language and style for an advice on appeal is plain English, though you need to recognise that quite often you will be setting out what amounts to a legal argument, so legal terminology is appropriate, and your reasoning needs to make sense more to a judge than to your lay client. It is unlikely that your lay client will be interested in much more than your overall advice as to whether there are grounds for an appeal, rather than the detail of those grounds.

A criminal appeal depends almost entirely on the facts and evidence in the case and how the law relates to them, so it would be rare indeed that you would even think of starting with a precedent. Indeed there are no precedents published except the example in this Manual and answers to practical exercises you may have done on the Bar Vocational

Course. It is most unlikely that these will assist you in the actual drafting of an appeal in anything but the broadest way, and you are not advised to rely on them.

29.6.2 Criterion (2) — structure

The structure of the advice is not difficult, and this criterion usually carries only 10% of the marks. The most difficult part of this one is to set out the factual background concisely and accurately.

Criterion (2)(i)

Sets out the factual background to the appeal concisely and sufficiently

As explained in **Chapter 25**, this factual background needs to make it possible for a judge reading your advice to understand the issues at the trial and the grounds of appeal that you are relying on. He will want to know the charges, the basis of the prosecution case, what the defence was, and what were the fundamental questions for the jury. This requires careful legal and factual analysis. You need to approach the facts with an understanding of the law.

Criterion (2)(ii)

Deals with the grounds of appeal and any other issues in a sensible order and in an appropriate number of paragraphs

By and large the appropriate order for grounds of appeal is the order in which they arose during the trial. Think through the sequence of events at the trial, and work out when each matter arose. Distinguish particularly between irregularities and rulings by the judge during the trial, and misdirections in the summing up. Occasionally, as happens once in the example in **Chapter 25**, it may be logical to take a ground out of order.

By and large, to put each ground of appeal into a separate paragraph is a good starting point, but sometimes it can take several paragraphs to explain a ground of appeal fully. Never put two or more grounds of appeal into a single paragraph. If you have two that are very closely connected, at least put them in separate sub-paragraphs.

29.6.3 Criterion (3) — law, content, analysis and effectiveness

Your correct understanding of the law underpins just about every part of your Advice on Appeal. It is inherent in all three parts of this composite criterion, which therefore carries 60% of the marks in total. This criterion is the one that you must pass to satisfy the Bar Council's requirement (see **29.2.3**).

29.6.3.1 Criterion (3)(A) – law and content

(i)   *Is based on a sound understanding and application of the relevant law*
(ii) *Puts forward appropriate grounds of appeal*
(iii) *Does not seek to rely on anything which is not a ground of appeal*
(iv) *Does not omit any important grounds of appeal*

This is about getting the grounds of appeal right. It usually carries 20% of the marks, but note that criterion (6) largely covers the same area, so there are more like 30% of the marks for including the right grounds of appeal. The question is simply, have you managed to identify what is, and is not, a ground of appeal. Your grounds will be appropriate if they are reasonably arguable. You should not miss any that are there to be found. But you should also not put forward invalid grounds. Obviously your understanding of criminal law, and the law of evidence and procedure, is crucial to your ability to fulfil this criterion.

29.6.3.2   Criterion (3)(B) — analysis

This criterion is fundamental to your advice and usually carries 30% of the marks. The important thing here is to get the law right, and to argue it clearly and accurately. It is your powers of reasoning that are being tested.

Criterion (3)(B)(i)

Explains the legal and factual basis for each ground accurately and completely

This is all about making out the ground, using the law, evidence and any relevant procedure to justify your advice that each ground is in fact a ground of appeal. You are trying to make the case, using sound evidential and legal reasoning. There is a lot of similarity between what you are required to do here, and the drafting of a skeleton argument, or the presentation of an oral argument as an advocate.

Criterion (3)(b)(ii)

Where appropriate explains why something does not provide grounds for an appeal

It will probably not be often that you need to comply with this criterion, but there will be occasions where your instructing solicitors have suggested a possible ground of appeal, or your client has demanded one, or you yourself have considered one, and advised against. Your advice is obviously incomplete unless you explain why it is not an arguable ground of appeal. Again, legal and evidential reasoning are required.

Criterion (3)(B)(iii)

Makes proper reference to the proceedings at trial, the facts, the evidence and relevant legal sources

The need to comply with this requirement was illustrated in **Chapter 25**. At every point of your advice you must make reference to the source of the ground concerned. The source may be the law, the events at trial, what was said in evidence, the direction of the judge, or some combination of these. Identifying these sources stops the ground being generalised. It is like giving particulars in other forms of drafting.

29.6.3.3   Criterion (3)(C) — effectiveness

Shows as far as possible why the convention is unsafe and/or why the sentence should be reduced or varied

This is another criterion that really just invites the assessor to judge the effectiveness of what you have drafted. It overlaps entirely with the above criteria and so usually carries only 10% of the marks. But it allows that assessor to take a view as to whether a judge would be persuaded, on what you have drafted, to give leave to appeal, and to reward or criticise as the case may be.

29.6.4   Criterion (4) — grounds

Draft grounds of appeal which:

(i)   *fulfil criteria (1), (2)(ii) and (3)(A) above*

(ii) *are consistent with and where appropriate refer to the Advice*

This is the only criterion applied to the grounds themselves, and as you can see it is based on the same criteria as those applied to the advice. Because of this repetition, it usually carries only 10% of the marks, and this is largely made up of the extent to which you have correctly identified the grounds — criterion (3)(A). It is most unlikely that the precision and clarity of your writing will be any different when you set out the grounds than when you were writing the advice. You should certainly set the grounds out in exactly the same order as you covered them in the advice.

The only new requirement here is that the grounds should be consistent with and refer to the advice. The need for consistency is self-evident. If there is any contradiction, clearly you will be criticised. The best way to refer to the advice was illustrated in **Chapter 25**.

INDEX

A

Abbreviated particulars of claim 46–8
Account, liability to
  breach of trust claims 391–4
Admissions 70–1
Affidavits
  application for interim injunction 258–62
  assessment criteria 416–19
  examples 258–62
  rules 245–7
Agency
  claim for account 160–2
  particulars of claim 160–2
Aiding and abetting counts
  primary and secondary parties 332
  secondary party only 332–3
Allegations
  bare denials and 77–8
  failing to deal with 71–2
  injury or loss, responding to 79
  paragraph number reference 79
  proof requirement 79
  response not required 79
Alternative counts 317–18
Amendment of statements of case
  amended defence 199–201
  exercise 201
  markings 197
  original defence 198–9
Appeals
  against conviction, grounds 336–7, 347–8, 351–2
  against sentence, grounds 337, 348–9, 352
  assessment criteria
    advice 419, 420–1
    grounds 420–1
  counsel's advice 349–51
    assessment criteria 419, 420–1
    drafting 339
    instructions 340
    sample 343–7
    sent with notice 335
  criminal grounds 335–54
  example 340–3
  exercises 352–4
  grounds 335–54
    against conviction 336–7, 347–8, 351–2
    against sentence 337, 348–9, 352
    assessment criteria 420–1, 422–3
    drafting 338–40
    drafting advice 339
    perfected 336

    requirements 338
  Guide 335
  judge's comments on sentence 342–3, 353–4
  judge's summing up 341–2, 352–3
  procedure 335–6
  skeleton argument 340
  timetable 335
  see also **Judicial review**
Application notice
  Queen's Bench Division 234, 236
Arrest, resisting 327
Arson
  aggravated by recklessness 325–6
  counts 325
Assault
  occasioning actual bodily harm count 328
  particulars of claim 152–3
Assessment
  criteria *see* **Assessment criteria**
  in drafting skills 402
Assessment criteria
  affidavits 416–19
  further information 409–12
  injunction order 412–16
  statements of case 403–9
  use 402
  witness statements 416–19
Atkin's Court Forms
  legal categories in 11–12
  source of precedents 11–12
Attempt, counts
  general 330
  impossible 330–1
  specific 330

B

Bailment
  breach of contract 157–9
  negligence 157–9
  particulars of claim 156–9
  simple 156–7
Blackmail, count 323
Breach of contract claims 42
  background 62
  basic formula 62–5
  breach 64, 67
  contract 63, 67
  example 65–8
  identifying the ingredients 60–1
  ingredients 60–2
  interest claim 65

knowledge of defendant 64, 66
loss and damage 64–5, 67–8
parties 62, 66
performance of contract 64, 67
remedies sought 65
terms 63–4, 67
see also **Contracts**
Breach of statutory duty claim 42, 89–90, 92–7
Breach of trust claims
constructive trustees 394–7
dealings with trust property 387, 388
exercises 400–1
interest 387, 388
liability to account 391–4
loss 387, 388
particulars of claim 389–91
parties 387, 388
remedies sought 387, 388
tracing 391–4
against third party 394–7
trust 387, 388
trust property 387, 388
Trusts of Land and Appointment of Trustees Act 1996 s.14
398–400
Bullen & Leake & Jacob's Precedents of Pleadings 12
Burglary, counts 318–19
Butterworths Civil Court Precedents 12
Butterworths Personal Injury Litigation Service 12

C

Carrying offensive weapon, counts 328
Cause of action 54
Certiorari *see* **Quashing order**
Chancery Division
headings 38
Chancery Guide
denials 78
statements of case 25–6
Cheques
cashing stolen cheque 321
dishonestly bouncing 321–2
Civil trial
skeleton arguments 300–4
Claim forms
content 41–3
rules 41
contract claims 42
details 42–3
injunction before issue 227–30
misrepresentation 42–3
nature of claim 41
Queen's Bench Division 233–4, 235
remedy sought 41
rules, content 41
statement of value 43
tort claims 42
Claim number 35–6
Clinical negligence
particulars of claim 145–8
Commercial Court Guide
denials 78
statements of case 25–6
Consent orders
drawing up 268–9
sample 273–4

Conspiracy, counts
broad charge 331
specific charge 331
Construction claims
analysis 369–71, 376–7, 381–2
details of claim 372–5, 377–9, 383–5
determination without administration 365
diagram approach 367, 371, 376–7, 382
drafting questions 367–8
examples 368–85
exercises 385–6
instructions to counsel 368–9, 375–6, 380–1
meaning 365–6
parties 366
Constructive trustees 394–7
Contents 3–4
Contracts
breach of contract claims 42
background 62
bailment 157–9
basic formula 62–5
breach 64, 67
contract 63, 67
example 65–8
identifying the ingredients 60–1
ingredients 60–2
interest claim 65
knowledge of defendant 64, 66
loss and damage 64–5, 67–8
parties 62, 66
performance of contract 64
remedies sought 65
terms 63–4, 67
claim forms 42
defences 85–7
exclusion clauses 126–8
remoteness 126–8
tender before claim 128–9
interest 44, 45
Part 20 claim 194–6
particulars of claim
agency 160–2
anticipatory breach 107–9
breach of collateral warranty 139–40
breach and negligent misrepresentation 137–8
claim for an account 160–2
damages for wasted expenditure 107–9
debt claim 105–6
failure of consideration 110–11
fraudulent misrepresentation 139–40
injunction 166–7
precedents 160–7
professional negligence 115–18
recovery of money paid 110–11
sale of chattels 163–4
sale of goods, implied terms 111–13
sale of land 164–6
specific performance
sale of chattels 163–4
sale of land 164–6
supply of services, implied terms 113–15
payment of money due 42
precedents for claim
agency 160–2
claim for an account 160–2
injunction 166–7

professional negligence 115–18
sale of chattels 163–4
sale of land 164–6
specific performance
    sale of chattels 163–4
    sale of land 164–6
Contribution
Part 20 claims 188–9
Conversion, particulars of claim 154–6
Counter-schedule 82–3, 84
Counterclaim
defence to 181, 183–6
meaning 169
reply 180–4
set-off 169–70
    exercises 178–9
    partial 174–6
    total 176–8
    without 171–3
title 170
Counts
aiding and abetting
    primary and secondary parties 332
    secondary party only 332–3
alternative 317–18
assault occasioning actual bodily harm 328
attempt
    general 330
    impossible 330–1
    specific 330
blackmail 323
burglary 318–19
carrying offensive weapon 328
complementary, two defendants 316–17
conspiracy
    broad charge 331
    specific charge 331
criminal damage
    arson 325
        aggravated by recklessness 325–6
    damage with intent to endanger life 325
    destroying property 325
dangerous drugs
    possession
        with intent to supply 330
        simple 329–30
    supply 329
dates 314
dishonestly retaining wrongful credit 321
evasion of liability by deception
    inducing someone to wait for payment 324
    obtaining abatement of liability 324
    securing remission of liability 323–4
going equipped 319–20
handling
    general charge 320–1
    receiving 320
    specific charge 320
indecent assault 329
making off without payment 324–5
manslaughter 326
murder 326
names 314
obtaining money transfer by deception 322
obtaining property by deception
    cashing stolen cheque 321

dishonestly bouncing a cheque 321–2
obtaining services by deception 323
order where several 314
rape 328–9
robbery 319
standard form 313
theft 318
wounding with intent
    causing grievous bodily harm 327
    intent to resist arrest 327
    wounding 326–7
wounding, unlawful
    inflicting grievous bodily harm 327–8
    wounding 327
see also **Indictments**
County court
headings 38, 40
interim injunctions
    form N16 injunction 230–1, 233
    form N16A application 238, 239
    form N117 undertaking 232–3
    standard forms 238
Court guides
denials 78
statements of case 25–6
Criminal cases
skeleton arguments 307–10
Criminal damage, counts
arson 325
    aggravated by recklessness 325–6
damage with intent to endanger life 325
destroying property 325

D

Damage *see* **Criminal damage; Loss and damage**
Damages
Part 20 claims 188–9
provisional 267–8, 272–3
special 57–8
Dangerous drugs, counts
possession
    with intent to supply 330
    simple 329–30
supply 329
Debts
late payment 44, 45
particulars of claim 105–6
Deceit 132, 133–4
Deception *see* **Evasion of liability by deception; Obtaining property by deception: Obtaining services by deception**
Defences
admissions 70–1
allegations
    failing to deal with 71–2
    injury or loss, responding to 79
    paragraph number reference 79
    proof requirement 79
    response not required 79
alternative facts 80
analysis of particulars of claim 73–4
contract 85–7
    exclusion clauses 126–8
    remoteness 126–8
    tender before claim 128–9

counter-schedule 82–3, 84
denials 70–1
  bare 76–8
  reason for 71, 78, 83
drafting 75–80
essence of 72–3
exercises 87–8, 129–31
failing to deal with allegations 71–2
misrepresentation
  reasonable belief 141–2
  restitutio in integrum impossible 141–2
Professional Standards Committee guidance 71
proof requirement 70–1, 79
request for further information 210–14
responding to claim 75–80
rules, fundamental rule 70–2
set-off 72, 169–70
  exercises 178–9
  partial 174–6
  total 176–8
  without 171–3
setting out defendant's case 80
structure 73–5
to counterclaim 181, 183–6
tort 81–4
  occupiers' liability 121–3
  trespassers 121–3
  volenti non fit injuria 124–6
Definitions 18
Denials 70–1
  bare 76–8
  Chancery Guide 78
  Commercial Court Guide 78
  Queen's Bench Guide 78
  reasons for 71, 78, 83
Documents
  for interim injunctions 222
  for judicial review application 277–8
Drafting skill
  aims 1
  cause of action 54
  defences *see* **Defences**
  definitions 18
  facts of case 12
  learning by doing 8
  leaving gaps in draft 6–7
  meaning 1
  practice required 8
  relevant law 12
  simplicity 18
  standards 2
Drafts
  content of each paragraph 17–18
  contents 3–4
  number of paragraphs 17–18
  working on 4–6
Drug offences *see* **Dangerous drugs**

E
Employers' liability claim 92–7
Evasion of liability by deception, counts
  inducing someone to wait for payment 324
  obtaining abatement of liability 324
  securing remission of liability 323–4

Evidence
  in statements of case 27–8, 29–31
  written *see* **Written evidence**
Exclusion clauses
  defence 126–8
Exercises
  amendment of statements of case 201
  appeals 352–4
  breach of trust claims 400–1
  construction claims 385–6
  defences 87–8, 129–31
  further information 214, 220–1
  headings 40
  indictments 333–4
  interim injunctions 242–3
  judgments and orders 276
  judicial review 295
  misrepresentation 143–4
  Part 8 claims 364
  Part 20 claims 196
  particulars of claim 68–9, 118–20
  reply to counterclaim 186
  set-off 178–9
  skeleton arguments 310–12
  statements of case 32–4
  written evidence 264

F
Facts
  defence case
    alternative facts 80
    new facts 80
    partly alternative facts 80
  familiarity with 12
  material 28–9
  in statement of case 28–9
Failure of consideration claim 110–11
False imprisonment claim 152–3
Fatal accidents claim 42, 98–101
Further information
  drafting 215–16
  example 216–20
  exercise 214, 220–1
  form of 215
  new procedures 202–3
  old procedures 202
  request for
    about claim 207–10
    assessment criteria 409–12
    decision to request 203–5
    defence 210–14
    disadvantages 205
    drafting 206
    example 207–14
    information 203
    tactical 203–5

G
Gaps in draft 6–7
Going equipped, count 319–20
Goods sold and delivered 46–7
Grammar 18
Grievous bodily harm
  unlawful wounding 327

wounding with intent 327
Grounds for appeal *see* **Appeals**
A Guide to Proceedings in the Court of Appeal Criminal Division 335

H

Handling, counts
general charge 320-1
receiving 320
specific charge 320
Headings
additional parties 40
Chancery Division 38
claim numbers 35-6
county court 38, 40
examples 37-9
exercise 40
Part 20 claim 190
parties
additional 40
names 36
Queen's Bench Division 37, 39
title of proceedings 35
High Court
see also **Chancery Division; Queen's Bench Division**
Homicide
manslaughter count 326
murder count 326

I

Implied terms
sale of goods 111-13
supply of services 113-15
Indecent assault, count 329
Indemnity
Part 20 claims 188-9
Indictments
conventions 314
counts
alternative 317-18
complementary, two defendants 316-17
number of 314
order 314
particular offences *see* **Counts**
standard form 313
dates 314
defendants
number of 314
two 316-17
exercise 333-4
general form 316-18
language 314
lesser offences 315
names 314
offences to be included 315
Injunctions
assessment criteria for order 412-16
County Court 240-2
interim *see* **Interim injunctions**
precedents for claim 166-7
Instructions to counsel
construction claims 368-9, 375-6, 380-1
Interest
breach of trust claims 387, 388

contractual interest 44
late payment of debt 44
particulars of claim 55, 65, 91
period of 45
personal injury or death 44
power to award 44
rates 44-5
rules for claiming 43-5
setting out claim 45
Interim applications
skeleton arguments in support 304-7
Interim injunctions
county court
form N16 230-1, 233
form N16A 238, 239
form N117 232, 233
standard forms 238, 239
documents required 222
duration 222
exercise 242-3
injunction orders 223-4
Queen's Bench Division 234-5, 236
standard forms in County Court 240-2
standard forms in High Court 224-30
with notice hearing 234-5, 236
mandatory orders 224
orders 223-4
see also **individual orders**
plain English 224
procedure 222-3
prohibiting orders 224
Queen's Bench Division
with notice hearing 233-6
without notice application 236-8, 239
standard forms in County Court 240-2
N16 230-1, 233
N16A 238, 239
N117 232, 233
undertakings 232, 233, 240-2
standard forms in High Court
injunction before issue of claim form 227-30
order for injunction 224-30
with notice hearing 234-5
without notice application 236-8, 239
undertakings 232, 233, 240-2
written evidence in support
affidavit 258-62
witness statements 255-8
Interim payment orders 268
Interim procedural application
witness statements 262-4

J

Joint tortfeasor
Part 20 claim to 191-4
Judgments and orders
after trial before judge 270
consent orders 268-9, 273-4
drawing up 265-8
error correction 268
exercise 276
interim payments 268
personal injury claim 271-2
procedural background 265-6
provisional damages 267-8, 272-3

recoverable benefits 268
requirements
  general 266-7
  special 267-8
Tomlin orders 269, 274-5
Judicial review
  claim form
    drafting 278-9
    mandatory order 280-2, 285, 287-9, 293
    N461 277, 278
    N463 277, 279
    quashing order 287-9, 293
  documents required 277-8
  drafting application 278-9
  exercise 295
  mandatory order 277
    claim form 280-2, 285, 287-9, 293
    witness statement in support 282-5, 286, 289-92, 293-4
  permission of court 277
  pre-action protocol 277
  procedure 277-8
  prohibiting order 277, 294
  quashing order 277
    claim form 289-92
    witness statement in support 289-92, 293-4
  see also **Appeals**

L

Late payment of debt
  interest 44, 45
Law
  familiarity with relevant 12
Learning by doing 8
Liability to account
  breach of trust claims 391-4
Loss and damage
  breach of contract claim 64-5
  breach of trust claim 387, 388
  by escaping fire 152, 167-8
  tort, negligence claim 54-5

M

Making off without payment, count 324-5
Mandatory order 277
  claim form 280-2, 285, 287-9, 293
  witness statement in support 282-5, 286, 289-92, 293-4
  see also **Quashing and mandatory order**
Mandatory orders 224
Manslaughter, count 326
Medical reports 55
Misrepresentation 132-44
  breach of collateral warranty 132, 139-40
  breach of contract 132, 137-8
  claim form 42-3
  deceit 132, 133-4
  defence
    reasonable belief 141-2
    restitutio in integrum impossible 141-2
  exercises 143-4
  fraudulent 139-40
  innocent 132
  negligent 132, 135-8
  negligent misstatement 101-4
  particulars of claim 133-40

rescission 135-6
Murder, count 326

N

Names of parties 36
Negligence
  breach of statutory duty 42
  claim forms 42
  clinical 145-8
  fatal accidents 42
  particulars of claim 58-60
    accident description 53
    background 53
    basic formula 52-5
    cause of action 54
    clinical negligence 145-8
    events description 53
    example 56-60
    ingredients 51-2
    interest 55
    loss and damage 54-5
    medical report 55
    parties 53
    remedies sought 55
    special damages 57-8
    statements of case 52
  personal injury 42
  schedule of expense and loss 57-8, 60
Nuisance
  particulars of claim 148-52
Number of claim 35-6

O

Obtaining money transfer by deception
  count 322
Obtaining property by deception, counts
  cashing stolen cheque 321
  dishonestly bouncing a cheque 321-2
Obtaining services by deception, count 323
Occupiers' liability
  defences 121-3
  particulars of claim 89-92
    interest 91
    loss and damage 90, 92
    negligence 90, 91
    special damages 91
  schedule of expense and loss 91
Orders *see* **Judgments and orders** *and individual orders eg*
  Search order

P

Paragraphs
  content of each 17-18
  number 17-18
Part 8 claims 355-64
  exercise 364
  parties 356
  questions asked 356-7
  remedies required 356-7
  representation order 366-7
  statutory provisions 357
  trusts
    appointment of new trustees 357-60

Judicial Trustees Act 1896 s.1 360
    removal of trustees 360
    Trustee Act 1925 s.57 applications 363–4
    Trusts of Land and Appointment of Trustees Act 1996 s.14
        applications
        details of claim 360–3
        further remedies 362–3
Part 20 claims 187–96
    additional claim 191
    additional parties 39–40
    claim in contract 194–6
    contribution 188–9
    damages 188–9
    drafting 189–90
    exercise 196
    headings 38–40
    indemnity 188–9
    issue 187–8
    meaning 187
    proposals for change 191
    to joint tortfeasor 191–4
Particulars of claim
    abbreviated 46–8
    analysis for defence 73–4
    breach of trust 389–91
    contract
        agency 160–2
        bailment 157–9
        breach
            anticipatory 107–9
            background 62
            basic formula 62–5
            breach 64, 67
            contract 63, 67
            example 65–8
            negligent misrepresentation 137–8
        breach of collateral warranty 139–40
        claim for account 160–2
        damages for wasted expenditure 107–9
        debt claim 105–6
        failure of consideration 110–11
        fraudulent misrepresentation 139–40
        identifying the ingredients 60–1
        ingredients 60–2
        injunction 166–7
        interest claim 65
        knowledge of defendant 64, 66
        loss and damage 64–5, 67–8
        parties 62, 66
        performance of contract 64, 67
        precedents 160–7
        professional negligence 115–18
        recovery of money paid 110–11
        remedies sought 65
        sale of chattels 163–4
        sale of goods, implied terms 111–13
        sale of land 164–6
        specific performance
            sale of chattels 163–4
            sale of land 164–6
        supply of services, implied terms 113–15
        terms 63–4, 67
    exercises 68–9, 118–20
    further information 89–120
    ingredients 51
        breach of contract 60–2

    negligence 51–2
    interest 45, 55, 65, 91
    misrepresentation
        breach of collateral warranty and 139–40
        breach of contract 137–8
        fraudulent 139–40
        negligent misrepresentation 132, 134, 135–8
        negligent misstatement 101–4
        rescission 135–6
    responding to 75–80
    telling a story 50
    tort
        assault 152–3
        bailment
            breach of contract 157–9
            negligence 157–9
            simple 156–7
        breach of statutory duty 92–7
        clinical negligence 145–8
        conversion 154–6
        damage 153–4
        damage by escaping fire 152, 167–8
        employers' liability, breach of statutory duty 92–7
        false imprisonment 152–3
        fatal accidents 98–101
        negligence 58–60, 145–8
            accident description 53
            background 53
            basic formula 52–5
            cause of action 54
            clinical 145–8
            events description 53
            example 56–60
            ingredients 51–2
            interest 55
            loss and damage 54–5
            medical report 55
            parties 53
            remedies sought 55
            special damages 57–8
            statements of case 52
        nuisance 148–52
        occupiers' liability 89–92
            interest 91
            loss and damage 90, 92
            negligence 89–90, 91
            special damages 91
        personal injury 49–50
        precedents 148–60
        Rylands v *Fletcher* 150–2
        simple bailment 156–7
        trespass to goods 153–4
        trespass to land 159–60
        wrongful interference with goods 154–6
Parties
    breach of contract 62
    breach of trust claims 387, 388
    construction claims 366
    names 36
    Part 8 claims 356
    in particulars of claim 53, 62
    representation order 366
    tort, negligence claim 53
Personal injury 49–50
    claim form 42
    interest 44, 45

judgment and order 271–2
Planning
  precedents 13–14
  skeleton plan 13–14
Precedents
  advantages 10
  drafting using 14
  drawbacks 10–11
  essential ingredients 13
  facts of case 12
  finding 13
    deciding if appropriate 13
  more than one 13
  reasons for using 9
  skeleton plan 13–14
  sources 11–12
  use 4, 9, 14
Professional negligence 115–18
Professional Standards Committee guidance
  defences 71
Prohibiting order 224, 277, 294
Provisional damages
  judgments and orders 267–8, 272–3
Punctuation 18

Q

Quashing order 277
  claim form 287–9, 293
  witness statement in support 289–92, 293–4
Queen's Bench Division
  headings 37, 39
  interim injunctions
    with notice hearing 233–6
    without notice application 236–8, 239
Queen's Bench Guide
  denials 78
  statements of case 25–6

R

Rape, count 328–9
Receiving, count 320
Recklessness
  arson aggravated by 325–6
Recoverable benefits 268
Remedies sought
  breach of contract claim 65
  breach of trust claims 387, 388
  claim form 41
  Part 8 claims 356–7
  tort, negligence claim 55
Remoteness defence 126–8
Reply 180–4
  example 182
  exercise 186
Representation order 366–7
Requests for further information *see* **Further information**
Rescission
  claim form 42–3
  misrepresentation 135–6
Restitutio in integrum
  impossible 141–2
Robbery
  counts 319
Rylands v *Fletcher* 150–2

S

Sale of chattels
  specific performance claim 163–4
Sale of goods claim 111–13
Sale of land
  specific performance claim 164–6
Schedule of expense and loss
  negligence claim 57–8, 60
  occupiers' liability 91
Set-off 72
  defence 169–70
  exercises 178–9
  partial 174–6
  total 176–8
  without 171–3
Simplicity 18
Skeleton arguments
  appeals 340
  civil trial use 300–4
  content 298–9
  Court of Appeal 300
  criminal cases 307–10
  exercises 310–12
  importance 296
  interim application support 304–7
  length 298
  Practice Directions and Practice Notes 296–7
  structure 298–9
Sources of precedents 11–12
Special damages claim 57–8
Specific performance claim
  sale of chattels 163–4
  sale of land 164–6
Standards 2
Statement of claim
  defence *see* **Defences**
  trusts *see* **Breach of trust claims**
Statement of truth 31
Statement of value 43
Statements of case
  alternative facts 26
  amendment
    amended defence 199–201
    exercise 201
    markings 197
    original defence 198–9
  assessment criteria 403–9
  Chancery Guide 25–6
  Civil Procedure Rules 21
  Commercial Court Guide 25–6
  conciseness 31
  content 3–4
    evidence 27–8, 29–31
    facts 28–9
    general application rules 24
    primary rule 27
  court guides 25–6
  court power to strike out 22–3
  evidence 27–8, 29–31
  exercise 32–4
  facts
    material 28–9
    not evidence 29–31
    not law 29
  function 22
    tactical 23

list of main 21–2
meaning 21
objective 22
overriding objective 22
plain English 6, 15–18, 31
principles behind 22–3
Queen's Bench Guide 25–6
rules
    content, general application rules 24
    format 23
    general application 24–5
    primary 24, 27
statement of truth 31
striking out 22–3
tactical function 23
tort, negligence 52
see also **Claim forms; Particulars of claim**
Striking out
statements of case 22–3
Style 6
vocabulary 6, 15–18, 31, 224
Supply of services claim 113–15
Syntax 18

T

Tender before claim
defence 128–9
Theft, counts 318
Title of proceedings 35
Tomlin **orders** 269, 274–5
Torts
assault 152–3
bailment
    breach of contract 157–9
    negligence 157–9
    simple 156–7
breach of statutory duty 42, 92–7
conversion 154–6
damage 153–4
damage by escaping fire 152, 167–8
defences 81–4
    occupiers' liability 121–3
    trespassers 121–3
    volenti non fit injuria 124–6
false imprisonment 152–3
fatal accidents 42, 98–101
negligence 42
    accident description 53
    background 53
    basic formula 52–5
    cause of action 54
    clinical 145–8
    events description 53
    example 56–60
    ingredients 51–2
    interest 55
    loss and damage 54–5
    medical report 55
    particulars of claim 145–8
    parties 53
    remedies sought 55
    schedule of expense and loss 57–8, 60
    special damages 57–8
    statements of case 52

nuisance
    particulars of claim 150–2
    precedents for claims 148–52
    Rylands v *Fletcher* 150–2
occupiers' liability 89–92
    interest 91
    loss and damage 90, 92
    negligence 89–90, 91
    special damages 91
Part 20 claim to joint tortfeasor 191–4
particulars of claim 51–5, 89–104
    precedents 148–60
personal injury 42, 49–50
precedents for claims 148–60
Rylands v *Fletcher* 150–2
simple bailment 156–7
trespass to goods 153–4
trespass to land 159–60
wrongful interference with goods 154–6
Tracing, breach of trust claims 391–4
against third party 394–7
Trespass to goods claim 153–4
Trespass to land claim 159–60
Trespassers, defences 121–3
Trusts
appointment of new trustees 357–60
breach of trust claims
    constructive trustees 394–7
    dealings with trust property 387, 388
    exercises 400–1
    interest 387, 388
    liability to account 391–4
    loss 387, 388
    particulars of claim 389–91
    parties 387, 388
    remedies sought 387, 388
    tracing 391–4
        against third party 394–7
    trust 387, 388
    trust property 387, 388
        dealings with 387, 388
    Trusts of Land and Appointment of Trustees Act 1996
        s.14 398–400
construction claims
    analysis 381–2
    details of claim 372–5, 377–9, 383–5
    determination without administration 365
    diagram approach 367, 376–7, 382
    drafting questions 367–8
    examples 368–85
    exercises 385–6
    instructions to counsel 368–9, 375–6, 380–1
    meaning 365–6
    parties 366
Judicial Trustees Act 1896 s.1 360
Part 8 claims 357–60
removal of trustees 360
Trustee Act 1925 s.57 applications 363–4
Trusts of Land and Appointment of Trustees Act 1996 s.14
applications
    details of claim 360–3
    further remedies 362–3
breach of trust claims 398–400

U

Undertakings
County Court 232, 233
Unlawful wounding counts
inflicting grievous bodily harm 327–8
wounding 327

V

Vocabulary
archaic 6, 18, 19–20, 224
in indictments 314
modern alternatives 6, 19–20
plain English 6, 15–18, 31, 224
Volenti non fit injuria defence 124–6

W

Weapon
carrying offensive weapon 328
Witness statements
assessment criteria 416–19
Bar Council Guidelines 247–8
examples 251–8
interim injunction application 255–8
interim procedural application 262–4
judicial review support
mandatory order 282–5, 286, 289–92, 293–4
quashing order 289–92, 293–4
rules 245–7
for trial use 251–4
Work done and materials supplied 47–8
Wounding with intent, counts
causing grievous bodily harm 327
intent to resist arrest 327
wounding 326–7

Wounding, unlawful *see* Unlawful wounding counts
Written evidence
affidavits
application for interim injunction 258–62
assessment criteria 416–19
examples 258–62
rules 245–7
application for interim injunction 255–62
Bar Council Guidelines 247–8
barrister involvement 244
choice of form 244–5
drafting 249–51
exercise 264
forms 244
general principles 249–51
rules 245–7
witness statements
assessment criteria 416–19
Bar Council Guidelines 247–8
examples 251–8
interim injunction application 255–8
interim procedural application 262–4
judicial review support
mandatory order 282–5, 286, 289–92, 293–4
quashing order 289–92, 293–4
rules 245–7
for trial use 251–4
Wrongful credit
dishonestly retaining 321
Wrongful interference with goods claim 154–6
With notice hearing
application notice 234, 236
claim form 233–4, 235
draft injunction order 234–5
Without notice application
Queen's Bench Division 236–8, 239